THE POOR OF
EIGHTEENTH-CENTURY FRANCE
1750–1789

THE POOR OF EIGHTEENTH-CENTURY FRANCE
1750-1789

OLWEN H. HUFTON

OXFORD
AT THE CLARENDON PRESS
1974

Oxford University Press, Ely House, London W. 1

GLASGOW NEW YORK TORONTO MELBOURNE WELLINGTON
CAPE TOWN IBADAN NAIROBI DAR ES SALAAM LUSAKA ADDIS ABABA
DELHI BOMBAY CALCUTTA MADRAS KARACHI LAHORE DACCA
KUALA LUMPUR SINGAPORE HONG KONG TOKYO

ISBN 0 19 822519 9

© *Oxford University Press 1974*

*Printed in Great Britain
at the University Press, Oxford
by Vivian Ridler
Printer to the University*

TO THE MEMORY
OF
ALFRED COBBAN

ACKNOWLEDGEMENTS

My gratitude to the late Alfred Cobban can never adequately be expressed. Much of the contents of this work was discussed with him and took initial shape in his seminar in the University of London in 1965–8. Throughout the work I have also built up a mounting debt to Professor Richard Cobb. The study owes much to his continued encouragement and stimulating suggestions. I would wish, in addition, to thank my friends, above all David Higgs who willingly amassed for me material from his work on Toulouse and accompanied us on some of the odysseys this study entailed, and Angus MacKay and Patricia McNulty who, though expert in far-removed fields, often discussed the script with me and put the problems therein into perspective.

Financially the work was made possible by grants from the Universities of Leicester and Reading, from the Centre National de la Recherche Scientifique, from the Twenty Seven Foundation, and above all, in its final stages, from the British Academy.

I should also like to thank the personnel of several departmental archives, predominantly those of Mende, Rodez, Montpellier, Dijon, and Rennes, municipal records and hospital archives to which mention is made in the footnotes. Lastly my gratitude is due to the staff of the Clarendon Press whose meticulous scrutiny of the manuscript saved me from many errors.

OLWEN H. HUFTON

Reading, December 1973

CONTENTS

List of Illustrations   xi

List of Maps   xi

List of Abbreviations   xiii

Introduction   1

PART ONE
THE MEANING OF POVERTY

I.   Who were the poor and why were they there?   11

II.   From Poverty to Indigence   25

III.   An Economy of Makeshifts: (i) Migrations   69

IV.   An Economy of Makeshifts: (ii) The Beggars   107

PART TWO
THE POOR AND SOCIETY

V.   Formal Relief   131

VI.   Government Assistance   177

VII.   Informal Relief   194

PART THREE
THE CRIMES OF THE POOR

VIII.   Begging, Vagrancy, and the Law   219

IX.   Theft   245

X.   Smuggling   285

XI.   Prostitution   306

XII.   Parent and Child   318

POSTSCRIPT   354

APPENDICES

    I. Charitable resources   369

   II. Specimen *hôpital* accounts   382

 III. *Bureaux de charité*   385

 IV. Early arrests of vagrants following the
        legislation of 1764   389

BIBLIOGRAPHY   391

INDEX   405

LIST OF ILLUSTRATIONS

(at end)

EDME BOUCHARDON, *Études prises dans le bas peuple ou Les Cris de Paris*

I. Balais Balais

II. Cotterets

III. Montagnarde

IV. De la belle Fayance

V. Vieux Maçon

VI. Peaux de Lapin

VII. Gagne petit Auvergnat

Illustrations I, IV, VI, VII reproduced by courtesy of the Bibliothèque Nationale, Paris, and II, III, V by courtesy of the Trustees of the British Museum

LIST OF MAPS

I. The Incidence of Seasonal Migration in France in 1810   75

II. Charitable Resources of Departments in 1791   175

III. Main Arenas of Salt Smuggling   288

LIST OF ABBREVIATIONS

A.C.	Archives Communales
A.D.	Archives Départementales
A. Hosp.	Archives Hospitalières
A.M.	Archives Municipales
A.N.	Archives Nationales
B.M.	Bibliothèque Municipale
B.N.	Bibliothèque Nationale
S.R.M.	Société Royale de Médecine

A.E.S.C.	*Annales économies sociétés et civilisations*
A.H.R.F.	*Annales historiques de la Révolution française*
Bull. d'hist. écon. et soc.	*Bulletin d'histoire économique et sociale de la Révolution française*
R.H.	*Revue historique*
R.H.E.S.	*Revue d'histoire économique et sociale*
R.H.M.C.	*Revue d'histoire moderne et contemporaine*

INTRODUCTION

THE idea of this study was conceived some ten years ago in the course of research upon my doctoral thesis, 'Bayeux in the late eighteenth century'. The discovery that about a fifth of that town was dependent on some form of outside relief in order to maintain the most precarious existence gave rise to a whole spate of questions which have beset me ever since: how far was this a typical situation; who were these people; why were they in this predicament; and, perhaps most lastingly, how did people who had ostensibly no means of support manage to survive and procreate in the conditions of the *ancien régime*? If the poor occupied an important part in my study of Bayeux, it was because I was convinced that an understanding of their economy was crucial to an understanding of the whole *ancien régime*: that a fifth of the population could not be lightly cast aside. Local studies published over the past decade, the monumental works of Goubert on Beauvais and the Beauvaisis, Saint-Jacob on Burgundy, Poitrineau on the Massif, Lefebvre on Orleans and the Orleanais, the Chaunu school on seventeenth- and eighteenth-century Normandy—to cite merely a few—allied with older works of Henri Sée and Lefebvre's initial study of the Nord, served to accentuate the ubiquity of the type of problems I had encountered at Bayeux. Moreover, some experience of the records of *hospices* and *bureaux de charité* and of the reports of *curés* and *subdélégués* convinced me that one need not say of the eighteenth century as Pierre Goubert did of the seventeenth:

des plus misérables nous ignorons tout. A Cuigy, comme ailleurs, bien qu'ils fussent sédentaires on les qualifiait parfois de mendiants. On les voit seulement mourir en masse quand les registres reflètent la famine cyclique ou l'épidémie passagère. La détresse rurale se dérobe aux recherches. Seule son existence est attestée, ainsi que le nombre souvent effrayant de ceux qu'elle frappait.[1]

Very evidently, the student of poverty cannot pretend to lend to his work the precision potentially applicable to other sections

---

[1] P. Goubert, *Beauvais et le Beauvaisis de 1600 à 1730* (Paris, 1960), p. 159.

of the community by means of the data afforded by the fiscal documentation of the *ancien régime*. The urban poor and the landless largely escaped taxation. What was there to tax? But if fiscal documentation is set aside, there remains a wealth of material, for the annals of the poor abound in the form of an agonized correspondence between *curés* and bishops, *subdélégués* and *intendants*, and *intendants* and *contrôleurs généraux*. There are the records of *hospices*, *dépôts de mendicité*, and *ateliers de charité*, the almost ubiquitous *enquête* of the *Comité de Mendicité* made in 1790–1 and the more limited, though often more imaginative, surveys of the *Commissions Intermédiaires* of the Provincial Assemblies of 1788. The crimes of the poor are caught in the mass of legal records bequeathed by *prévôtés*, *présidiaux*, and salt courts. Government concern for the evident problems posed by the destitute is reflected in edicts: that of the Church in sermons and tracts: that of those with a social conscience in an abundant pamphlet literature or, less grandiosely, in closely written appendages to wills donating a few *livres* to the local poor to ensure their prayers for the departed.

Much of this material is of course fragmentary, partial, and almost invariably open to the imputation of subjectivity. The reports submitted to the *Comité de Mendicité* were condemned even by the *Comité* itself as grossly exaggerated—a conclusion perhaps too readily arrived at, though evidently there was some overstatement.[1] Of earlier reports it can easily be appreciated that it was always simpler for an overworked parish priest to claim he had 'beaucoup de pauvres' rather than set about the task of counting them, a task which was not so much arduous as invidious, in so far as it demanded that some criterion of wretchedness be determined; and criteria obviously varied according, on the one hand, to the experience of the individual in the area where he was situated and, on the other, to his very personal views of what poverty was. Evidently degrees of deprivation varied immensely from one region to another. In the north estimates of the numbers of poor might well be made by reference to a notion of an adequate bread ration, but such a simple and scientific approach was simply not applicable to vast tracts of the Massif where, to cite only one example for the present, the

---

[1] C. Bloch and A. Tuetey, *Procès-verbaux et rapports du Comité de Mendicité de la Constituante* (Paris, 1911), p. 573.

parish priest of Les Bondons in the diocese of Mende counted as his poor those whose nakedness and debilities permitted them to do little more than huddle together on rotting straw in their wretched dwellings, some of them too weak to stand.[1]

And if assessments, contemporary and historiographical, of poverty were multiple and varied and have left their mark upon the annals of the poor, no less prolific and assorted were approaches to the problem. Social, religious, moral, or political attitudes all came into play in any consideration of the issue. Eighteenth-century France was the uncomfortable arena in which the Catholic philosophy of poor relief came into open conflict with the anti-clericalism and social idealism of the Enlightenment. Whereas in England the principle of voluntary charity organized by the Church disintegrated in the sixteenth century and was formally abandoned in the seventeenth century by the compulsory introduction of the laicized parish rate, in Catholic France both Tridentine principles and their perfect disciple, St. Vincent de Paul, had reinforced traditional Catholic voluntary charity by an immense programme of social reform; and the spiritual efforts of the clergy of France in the second half of the seventeenth century were directed towards arousing in the rich an awareness of their obligations towards their weaker brethren. For was not the alleviation of poverty, and hence the very existence of the poor, the means offered to the rich to achieve eternal salvation? The Enlightenment, on the other hand, saw the prevailing situation as a cogent indictment of a system of poor relief which continued to depend upon the voluntary alms of the faithful. To Montesquieu, to Rousseau, to the innumerable pamphlet-writers of the eighteenth century, to government officials (though most recognized they had no substitute to offer for voluntary charity), and, very importantly, to the members of the *Comité de Mendicité*, concerned in 1790 to endow France with a new poor law, indiscriminate Catholic charity, rather than soundly based, objective, state assistance to the truly poor in the form of work, was alone responsible for the gross inflation in France of the numbers of paupers who were for the most part idlers parasitic on the rest of society. Hence an important part of the documentation on eighteenth-century poverty, and a part which no student

[1] A. D. Lozère G 1834, État des pauvres de la paroisse des Bondons et leurs principaux et plus pressans besoins (1760).

of the problem can afford to ignore, since it comprehends the inquiries of the seventies and the findings of the *Comité de Mendicité* in 1790, is suffused with a rigidly partisan dogmatism; and between the extremes of traditional Catholic philosophy and practice and the hard line of the Enlightenment lie a whole range of intermediate attitudes to ensnare the unwary. As compensation, and serving as partial check, there does exist less speculative material, court records, police files, registers of *hospices* and *bureaux d'aumônes*, lists of abandoned children, to serve as witness to the magnitude of the problems of poverty under the *ancien régime*; but these alone can furnish only part of the story.

Historiographically the eighteenth-century poor have enjoyed one earlier heyday and are presently, in a somewhat different guise, once more edging into the limelight. The first was at the turn of this century when the debate upon state assistance and the growth of socialism focused historical attention upon the institutions associated with Catholic charity and *ancien régime* assistance and in large part revealed their inadequacies. Camille Bloch's *L'Assistance et l'État en France à la veille de la Révolution* (Paris, 1906), though far from being alone, was the most powerful product of this period and has remained to this day the most comprehensive text on institutional relief. Much of the work of Camille Bloch and his contemporaries was of a markedly partisan nature which fed on Enlightenment propaganda. Catholic charity, in this historiographical phase, was either friend or foe (usually foe if one's interest was the *ancien régime*, for Catholic historians chose instead to concentrate upon the plight of France during the Revolution when the institutions of Catholic relief collapsed).[1] Their work was also largely executed without real reference to the social and economic circumstances which produced the poor and

---

[1] A few examples of some of the more objective studies produced during this period are: P. Boissonade, *L'Assemblée Provinciale du Poitou et la question de la mendicité 1787–1790* (Paris, 1904); F. Buchalet, *L'Assistance publique à Toulouse au dix-huitième siècle* (Toulouse, 1904); H. Chôtard, 'La Mendicité en Auvergne au XVIIIe siècle', *Revue d'Auvergne*, xv (1898); J. Coiffier, *L'Assistance publique dans la généralité de Riom au XVIIIe siècle* (Paris, 1905); G. Fleury, *La Mendicité à l'assemblée générale de la généralité de Tours* (Paris, 1904); F. Mourlot, *La Question de la mendicité en Normandie à la fin de l'ancien régime* (Paris, 1903); P. Rambaud, *L'Assistance publique à Poitiers jusqu'à l'an V* (Paris, 1912); X. Renouard, *L'Assistance publique à Lille de 1527 à l'an XVIII* (Paris, 1912); P. Saint-Martin, *La Mendicité à Besançon principalement au XVIIIe siècle* (Besançon, 1910); G. Valran, *Misère et charité en Provence au XVIIIe siècle* (Paris, 1899). The same period produced a plethora of institutional studies, some of which are referred to in the Bibliography.

which have been the preoccupation of succeeding generations of historians. Not surprisingly, the present concern with aspects of the problem of poverty has arisen from the results of their work. A recent generation of quantitative historians has concentrated its efforts upon living standards, the composition of urban proletariats and of the criminal classes, using the massive bulk of legal documentation bequeathed by the old regime or kept by *dépôts de mendicité*. These issues are now the subject of *mémoires de maîtrise* and theses of which many results have been published and are embodied in this work, and still more are announced.[1]

My concern in this study is to answer a number of questions: who were the poor, why were they there, and which areas faced the greatest strain? What was done for them in the way of formal relief and how effectively did Catholic voluntary charity cope with their problems and was there any truth in the allegations of the Enlightenment of the indiscriminate, unreasoned nature of Catholic relief? Equally importantly, though one can perhaps fathom only a very small part of the story, what were the practices and attitudes of the poor themselves and how did they attempt to cope with apparently impossible conditions? I have chosen for the broader issues to give my attention to the whole of France because I became acutely conscious that any smaller geographical unit would be artificial. The poor were easily the most mobile sector of the population in their search for work and attention. An analysis of the destitute of the Mediterranean littoral shows that they were largely drawn from the Rouergue and the Gévaudan; an analysis of those of Bordeaux shows a

[1] An excellent local modern study of poverty in Lyons is J. P. Gutton, *La Société et les pauvres; l'exemple de la généralité de Lyon 1534–1789* (Paris, 1971); students of J. Imbert in Paris seem to be concentrating upon institutional relief, e.g. J. L. Harouel, *Les Ateliers de charité dans la province de Haute-Guyenne* (Paris, 1969), and upon crime, M. Bourquin and E. Hepp, *Aspects de la contrebande au XVIIIᵉ siècle* (Paris, 1969); crime and the *dépôts de mendicité* are currently preoccupying the school of quantitative history in Caen, e.g. B. Boutelet, 'Étude par sondage de la criminalité dans le bailliage du Pont de l'Arche (XVIIᵉ–XVIIIᵉ siècles). De la violence au vol; en marche vers l'escroquerie', *Annales de Normandie*, xii, no. 4 (1962), 235–62, and the highly intelligent study of V. Boucheron, 'La Montée du flot des errants de 1760 à 1789 dans la généralité d'Alençon', *Annales de Normandie*, xxi (1971), 56–86. From the middle of the last century there has been no abatement of studies on local *hospices*. Two of the most recent are Dr Bolotte, *Les Hôpitaux et l'assistance en Bourgogne* (Dijon, 1968), and M. Etchepare, *L'Hôpital de la Charité de Marseille* (Aix, 1962). Such works are to be numbered in hundreds, and selections are found in the Bibliography.

heavy recruitment from the Pyrenees; Orleans served as a pole of attraction to the impoverished Limousin; Lyons to the Forez; the Massif spilled out in all directions; Paris attracted the poor of the north and eastern provinces. Areas themselves without a real indigenous problem of poverty found themselves swamped with immigrants from more wretched areas. For more specific questions—the running of *hôpitaux*, the efficacy of *bureaux de charité*, the extent of child abandonment, the nature of parochial relief—I have drawn heavily on the experience of eight dioceses or *généralités*: Rennes, Rouen, Dijon, Toulouse, Clermont, Rodez, Mende, and Montpellier, partly because of the quality and abundance of the documentation, partly because of the differences in the economy of these regions, and also because there were substantial differences in the application of state measures in *pays d'états* and *pays d'élections*. I would seek to justify my heavy concentration on the Massif on the grounds that no other area so diffused its problems over the rest of the country or attempted to deal with them in such a diverse or interesting manner.

For all the areas I have specifically chosen there exists a comprehensive inquiry conducted in the 1770s either by *intendants*, *subdélégués*, and *curés* or by bishops and *curés* or, in the instance of Rouen, by both. Though most of these inquiries fail to give any real estimate of the numbers deemed in need of assistance, they are particularly valuable on the nature of parish relief and its application. Moreover, parish priests were asked to state in the inquiry not only existing foundations or legacies established for the relief of the poor but those which had lapsed or had been usurped, which in some cases afforded the opportunity for some impassioned writing. In comparison, the lists drawn up by the *Comité de Mendicité*, though apparently more scientific, are more arid. I have drawn on some of them, and particularly their over-all figures, as a general estimate and have tried to include some critical apparatus relating to their compilation. The information in fact collected by the *Comité* is probably of greatest value where it can be checked against the information of 1774 or that collected by the *Commissions Intermédiaires* of the *Assemblées Provinciales* in 1788. Moreover, it is possible to know which parts of the *Comité*'s inquiry are likely to be least accurate. The teeming Massif and many of the poorest areas found the terms of the inquiry too rigid to fit their own problems and simply recoiled before the demand to assess the number of wandering poor. One cannot but feel the intrinsic sound sense behind the district of Rodez's demand of the government for a practical method by which the wandering poor might be counted and of determining whether the wanderers in question were those *in* the area or those *from* the area—a request for information which never received an answer.[1] In the light of such correspondence one can feel little confidence in the statistical information on vagabondage collected by the *Comité de Mendicité* and indeed, one might reasonably question what the districts understood by the term 'vagabond'. In order to obtain any appreciation at all of the mobility of poverty in the town under the *ancien régime* there is little other recourse than the death registers of *hôtels Dieu*, and only in the largest institutions in the most considerable cities were those kept with any regard for detail as to the origins of the wretches who perished therein. Passports were not sought with any degree of consistency; arrests made of suspected vagabonds were sporadic and often highly eclectic; and one has to wait until 1810 for a nation-wide attempt to gauge migrations of labour, and even this was often couched in very general and vague terms.

It is not my intention at this juncture to embark upon a detailed critique of the available documentation, since this can be more properly confined to the footnotes of each chapter; it is sufficient here to stress that it is demanding of close scrutiny. Secondly, I would wish to make explicit from the outset that the approach to a study of poverty must predominantly be a qualitative not a quantitative one. There is no such thing as a graph of human suffering. Poverty was experienced in the home and in one's immediate human relationships. It conditioned the attitude of a man and his wife towards each other and towards their children and their own aged parents. It made their own advancing years something to fear. It meant that ordinary everyday happenings like sickness, an increase in the price of bread, or even a hailstorm which brought the chestnuts down before they ripened, or the birth of a child which temporarily cut the earning capacity of the mother and strained the budget even a fraction further, disrupted the whole pattern of the family economy and entailed recourse to a whole series of ploys and subterfuges often peculiar to a particular family or a particular area. To the social historian

[1] A. D. Aveyron 5 L 236, Assistance publique.

such considerations cannot be marginalia: they are the very heart of the matter and, however fragmentary or impressionistic the findings on such issues might be, they demand attention because without them one can have no real appreciation of the way the poor maintained their tenuous grip on life.

PART ONE

The Meaning of Poverty

I

WHO WERE THE POOR AND WHY WERE THEY THERE?

To describe and roughly to analyse the composition of the poor was a task which parish priests and village officials in the 1770s found far easier to accomplish than that of explaining the occurrence of poverty in the first place.[1]

Les journaliers, les manœuvres, les compagnons de métier et tous ceux dont la profession ne fournit pas beaucoup plus que le vivre et le vêtement sont ceux qui produisent les mendiants. Étant garçons, ils travaillent et lorsque par leur travail ils se sont procurés un bon vêtement et de quoi faire les frais d'une noce, ils se marient. Ils nourrissent un premier enfant, ils ont beaucoup de peine à en nourrir deux et s'il en survient un troisième leur travail n'est plus suffisant à la dépense.[2]

So wrote the curé d'Athis in one of the most expressive replies to the questionnaire sent by his bishop in 1774. Though most of the circular letters dispatched in the early seventies by bishops to their parish priests or by *intendants* to subdelegates and village officials did not specifically ask for an analysis of the poor, but rather for an estimate of their numbers and the means existing for their relief, nevertheless the more intelligent priests and officials felt it incumbent upon themselves to proffer some further comments. Their replies vary immensely in succinctness and, to a lesser extent, in the aspects of the problem on which they chose to linger: 'c'est la cherté excessive des denrées . . . c'est le manque d'emploi des femmes et enfants . . . c'est le défaut d'ouvrage l'hiver quand les travaux des champs cessent . . .'

The letters are far from silent on the problems of the aged, the widowed, and the orphaned—the traditionally deserving poor of

---

[1] The parish inquiries used for this study were mainly: A.D. Ille-et-Vilaine C 1294; A.D. Puy-de-Dôme C 927–38; A.D. Hérault C 5957; A.D. Seine-Maritime G 841–6; A.D. Côte-d'Or C 374–9. Lempereur, *L'État du diocèse de Rodez en 1771* (Rodez, 1906), is the only published set of documents relating to these inquiries.

[2] A.D. Calvados H. Supplément 1308.

any society at any time—but these sectors of the community were not accorded primary importance in this consideration of the poor. Rather was attention focused on the small farmer whose land was insufficient to keep his family, or on the inability of the day labourer to earn enough to support his wife and children, or, put another way, on the lack of work for women and children that would make them self-supporting—in short, upon the total non-viability of the family economy in existing conditions. The impoverished bachelor or spinster is absent from this correspondence: adult, alone, and without the physical debility engendered by sickness or old age, one could evidently manage; but marriage and procreation, as the curé d'Athis pointed out, were the beginning of disaster, a theme to be reflected in the naïve demands of the rural *cahiers* in 1789 for a special tax on bachelors for the sustenance of the children of the poor.[1] The *enquêtes* of the 1770s help in answering the question 'Who were the poor?' by their unanimous insistence upon answering: 'The family of the working man where such an individual cannot earn enough to support every member and where the individual members cannot support themselves.' This answer may need filling out, scrutinizing, and modifying according to regional variation—here the small holder whose land did not provide his family with a living, there the day labourer underemployed except at the peak period of the agricultural year, there the odd-job man unable to stretch his meagre earnings very far—yet it must be the essential point of departure for this study, because it provides the men, women, and children who are its *dramatis personae*.

The second point almost universally made by the *enquête* was that the problem was growing, that there were more poor than ever before. The more analytically inclined amongst the priests and subdelegates laid this squarely at the feet of rising costs. Hence the recurrent theme found, for example, in the observations of the *subdélégué* of Redon to the *intendant* at Rennes:

le prix des journées n'est pas augmenté en proportion de celui des denrées . . . on ne donne à présent que comme l'on donnait il y a 15 ans, 8 et 10 sols par jour à un journalier; à supposer que cet ouvrier soit occupé tous les jours de la semaine, il n'y aura gagné à la fin que 2 livres 8 sols ou 3 livres; il y a 15 ans que le demi de seigle ne valait que 2 livres ou 2 livres 10 sols. Cette mesure locale est actuellement

[1] e.g. E. Anquétil, *Cahier du tiers état de Bayeux* (Bayeux, 1886), pp. 38–9.

vendue depuis 4 livres 10 sols et 5 livres. Comment le journalier peut-il vivre lui et faire vivre une famille qui est souvent nombreuse?[1]

A rhetorical question perhaps, but one which without hesitation elects as prime cause the problem which has been the near concern of much of the recent historiography concerned with French economic and social history in the period: the relationship between prices and wages and the relationship between these and population growth.

Of course a problem of poverty existed long before the late eighteenth century when nothing occurred which, in terms of human suffering, could even approach the plight of the victims of the great famines of earlier periods or the desolation wrought by the pandemics of plague whose impact was felt with such intensity in the closing decades of the seventeenth century. Starvation and the sometimes related systematic annihilation of whole communities by pestilence are seventeenth- and not eighteenth-century characteristics, and one can look in vain in the annals of the eighteenth century for anything which parallels the chilling descriptions of the starving inhabitants of isolated villages in the Massif pouring out *en masse* from their barren hills in the 1660s and 1690s to perish in the hamlets of the plain of Languedoc, too weak to travel any further.[2] Nor does one find the classic manifestations of extreme deprivation as depicted in the Beauvaisis in the 1690s:[3] women rendered infertile by malnutrition, an increase in the numbers of stillbirths, whole family units cut down by quite minor diseases in face of lowered resistance. Such crises took a particularly heavy toll of the old and the young and of the unborn, and therefore altered the whole age-structure of society for generations to come and left in their wake a trail of wrecked households, the widowed, the orphaned, the abandoned. These sharp recurrent crises, the product of cumulative runs of bad harvests in a society where communications were difficult, and the virulent accompaniment of famine, bubonic plague, died mysteriously with the second decade of the eighteenth century. Thereafter there were years of diminished harvest returns and the poorer sectors of the community remained a prey to typhus, typhoid, enteric fevers, and so on; but the

---

[1] A.D. Ille-et-Vilaine, C 1653.
[2] E. Le Roy Ladurie, *Les Paysans de Languedoc* (Paris, 1966), pp. 97–8.
[3] Goubert, *Beauvais*, pp. 45–9.

population of France had embarked upon an upward path, albeit a slow one, whose main characteristic was a declining death-rate, the result of the disappearance of the great crises, *l'aménorrhée de famine*;[1] an upward surge which carried a population of 18–20 million in 1720 to some 27 million by the end of the century, and one which was not achieved without deep-reaching social repercussions. That the French economy was expanding in the eighteenth century needs no elaboration, but it is equally clear that the expansion was not such as to meet the demands made upon it.[2] For either the growth was not sufficiently great or it was not in the direction that mattered from the point of view of those who are the subject of this study, that is, in providing the grain to feed more mouths, and this in spite of the transition to coarse grain crops, millet, maize, buckwheat, and, in limited regions, the introduction of the reluctantly accepted potatoes or rice.

The dying-out of the great local crises characteristic of the seventeenth century may have been in large part attributable to better national distribution of supplies in time of local hardship, grain being more readily dispatched to grievously necessitous regions from those producing a surplus, a tendency which in the long run produced a shift from intensely acute local difficulties to a more generalized, less acute, chronic difficulty.[3] Such an

[1] The phrase is used by E. Le Roy Ladurie in a succinct synopsis of demographic works: 'L'Aménorrhée de famine (XVIIe–XXe siècles)', *A.E.S.C.* xxiv (1969), 1589–1601.

[2] The work of J.-C. Toutain, *Le Produit de l'agriculture française de 1700 à 1958* (Paris, 1961), using random contemporary estimates of production, argued astonishingly high growth-rates in the agrarian sector in excess of population growth, and these have been confusingly embodied in subsequent general histories, e.g. P. Léon, *Économies et sociétés industrielles* (Paris, 1970), p. 272. They have now been effectively demolished by M. Morineau, *Les Faux-Semblants d'un démarrage économique: agriculture et démographie en France au XVIIIe siècle* (Paris, 1971), and 'Y a-t-il une révolution agricole en France au XVIIIe siècle?', *R.H.* 237 (1967), 299–326. M. Morineau's concern is exclusively with grain production; growth in viticulture remains incontestable.

[3] This is the general tendency outlined in C. E. Labrousse, *La Crise de l'économie française à la fin de l'ancien régime et au début de la Révolution* (Paris, 1944), and now embodied in all general social and economic histories of the period, e.g. F. Braudel et C. E. Labrousse (eds.), *Histoire économique et sociale de la France aux XVIIe et XVIIIe siècles* (Paris, 1970), pp. 76–9. M. Morineau, *Les Faux-Semblants*, p. 331, describes 'une paupérisation généralisée de la France. . . . Le terme de paupérisation réclame, d'ailleurs, un maniement prudent. Nous n'avons pas voulu désigner autre chose qu'un rétrécissement du niveau de vie populaire, une détérioration de la condition sociale de beaucoup. Nous ne pensons pas — et les chiffres nous le rappeleraient — que la nation en soit arrivée à une sorte de starvation point.'

approach goes far to explain an apparent contradiction: that it was fully possible for relative emancipation from famine and plague to produce a greater number of poor than ever before. A starving population, generally speaking, cannot reproduce itself; an undernourished one has no difficulty in so doing. In the hierarchy of wretchedness there is a world of difference between the man who is literally starving, even for a short period, and the one who is merely undernourished all the year round. To understand this particular subtlety of the problem of poverty is to understand something of the difference between the situation which characterized the late seventeenth century and that which marked out the eighteenth; for if by the end of the period the number of those fitting into the first category had almost vanished, the other significantly had multiplied. Indeed, the most striking consequence of population movement was the broadening of the base of the social pyramid perhaps more than ever before, a proliferation of people who experienced increasing difficulties in providing themselves with the bare necessities of existence. These people, who might stem from the societies of small holders described by Arthur Young, were men in possession of holdings that had been fractionalized by each generation, men who found that their land was increasingly insufficient for the maintenance of their families and who had to search for some ancillary income or swell the bloated ranks of day labourers.[1] This situation clearly antedated Young's French tour. In parts of Brittany and in the regions of the Massif—the Auvergne, Marche, Limousin, Gévaudan, Pays de Velay, Vivarais, Cévennes, and Rouergue— and those of the Alps, above all Bresse, Bugey, and Dauphiné, or of the Pyrenees and Jura—in short, the *pays de petite culture*, reservoirs of men, sometimes small independent owners of scraps of property, strain was manifest from the 1740s and 1750s.[2] From then on, in these regions, more and more people found themselves unable to live off the proceeds of their land and turned increasingly to a type of economy of makeshifts: an extra job, seasonal migration, turning the children out to beg, involvement in some semi-nefarious practice such as smuggling. These make-

[1] A. Young, *Travels in France during the Years 1787, 1788 and 1789*, ed. C. Maxwell (Cambridge, 1950), p. 278.

[2] A. Poitrineau, *La Vie rurale en Basse Auvergne au XVIIIᵉ siècle* (Paris, 1965), p. 553; M. Chevalier, *La Vie humaine dans les Pyrénées ariégeoises* (Paris, 1956), p. 660; Morineau, *Les Faux-Semblants*, pp. 163–231.

shifts, or an accumulation of innumerable forms of subsidiary income or means whereby the family did not have to support some of its members, were built up gradually as the region became progressively less self-supporting. It took time and experience to learn to live in this way, and there were those for whom the expedients were far from adequate. Some regions, notably the Auvergne, proved remarkably adept at building up an economy of makeshifts; others, above all Brittany, whose problems were somewhat unique, remarkably feeble.

Nor did hardship confine itself to the *pays de petite culture*. The general price-rise which began with the poor harvests of the late sixties and early seventies universalized difficulties. The two closing decades of the *ancien régime* were marked not only by a rise of 65 per cent in the price of grain, set against wage increases of a mere 22 per cent,[1] but also by a deceleration in the rate of population growth attributable to a rising death-rate,[2] by an appreciable expansion in the numbers of destitute, in those of abandoned children, and by a considerable growth in rural criminality. The grain crisis of the late eighteenth century reverberated through the entire French economy. It made particularly acute two other phenomena in the closing years of the *ancien régime*: first, the difficulties experienced in the wine trade of Gascony, Champagne, Alsace, and Franche-Comté, and particularly of Languedoc, where the typical *viticulteur* was a small holder with narrow profit margins who found himself faced with over-abundant wine harvests which slashed the value of the crop on the market at a time when, conversely, grain prices were soaring.[3] Second, steeply rising grain prices intensified industrial depression between 1787 and 1789.

The slump which manifested itself in these years was far from unique in the annals of the *ancien régime*. French industrial performance throughout the eighteenth century was very uneven, and against the robust growth of Lyonnais silk production and

[1] C. E. Labrousse, *Esquisse du mouvement des prix et des revenus en France au XVIIIe siècle* (Paris, 1933).

[2] J. Dupâquier, 'Sur la population française aux XVIIe et XVIIIe siècles', *R.H.* 240 (1968), 59–61, gives as precise a picture as current research allows on regional variations in demographic movement and on the over-all deceleration in growth between 1770 and 1784 (when his statistics end). He suggests that only in Languedoc and the *généralités* of Auch, Pau, and Montauban, in Hainaut, and in Soissons is there any indication of vigorous continued growth throughout this period.

[3] C. E. Labrousse, *La Crise de l'économie française*, pp. 458–89.

the cotton, wool, and linen industries of eastern Normandy, Flanders, and Champagne, and—until the 1760s—the Languedoc woollen industry, must be set the feeble record of the Breton linen industry, of Touraine silk production, and of innumerable local productions of stockings and woollen cloth which peppered the rest of France. Even in the vigorously growing industries, temporary industrial depression was recurrent. At Lyons in 1756, 1766, 1771, 1784, and 1787, slump swept many out of business; and at Amiens, Rouen, Troyes, and in the region of Lille industry experienced sharp turns—though none worse than the crisis of 1787.[1] Such setbacks had serious repercussions upon both town and country, for, with the exception of silk weaving, French industry was predominantly rural industry, with only some of the weaving, dyeing, and finishing processes concentrated in the towns, and if the small holder or labourer was not a part-time weaver or stocking-knitter, his wife almost certainly was a spinner, carder, or lacemaker. Hence both town and country could be caught up in industrial depression. Without doubt the plight of those town workers wholly dependent upon industry was more severe, for overnight a problem of mass destitution could occur in regions which up to that point had known relative freedom from a problem of poverty and which found themselves precipitated into a situation of extreme deprivation, the more terrible because the inhabitants of those regions had not had the time to make the gradual, necessary, part-psychological, part-practical transition to an economy of makeshifts.[2] To learn to

[1] M. Bouloiseau, 'Aspects sociaux de la crise cotonnière dans les campagnes rouennaises en 1788–9', *Actes du 82e congrès des sociétés savantes* (Caen–Rouen, 1956), p. 414; M. Garden, *Lyon et les Lyonnais au XVIIIᵉ siècle* (Paris, 1970), p. 302; P. Wolff (ed.), *Histoire du Languedoc* (Toulouse, 1967), pp. 404–6; P. Deyon, 'Le Mouvement de la production textile à Amiens', *Revue du Nord*, xliv (1962), 201–11; J. Kaplow, *Elbeuf during the Revolutionary Period* (Baltimore, 1964), pp. 39–51.

[2] M. Bouloiseau, *Cahier de doléances du tiers état du bailliage de Rouen* (Paris, 1957), t. 1: *La Ville*, p. liv, and 'Aspects sociaux de la crise cotonnière . . .', pp. 412–13, draws a neat distinction between the plight of those for whom industry was an ancillary income, between the inhabitants of small towns and large villages for whom spinning or weaving constituted a total income, and those of the towns, Rouen, Darnétal, and Elbeuf, concerned with finishing processes which were never fully laid off. The intensity of the crisis fell upon the second group and these were those who tried to make a return to the land.

A similar phenomenon has been noted at Troyes by Stephen H. Johnson of the University of Glasgow, at present concerned with a study of rural industry. There the towns complained in addition that manufacturers laid off rural labour last because it was so much cheaper.

vivre aux expédients was an art acquired only with long practice; and for this reason the inhabitants of the textile bourg of Franque-ville or Gouy near Rouen, who in 1788 had been rendered redundant by the textile slump and were trying to piece together some livelihood by searching for employment as labourers at the harvest, faced a much greater immediate dilemma than did the inhabitants of the poverty-stricken village of Saint-Jean-d'Ollières in the Auvergne, who, having from the 1740s onwards found themselves obliged, at first in handfuls and later in droves, to look for a living outside the village, had set patterns of seasonal employment and makeshifts that had been built up over the years.[1]

In short, the questions 'Who were the poor?' and 'Why were they there?' must be answered by reference to both long-term and short-term considerations: in the first instance to the growing problem of a population pressing on inadequate resources, and in the second to a type of crisis which could occur at any time attendant upon industrial slump and changes in market condi-tions. There were, in addition, the perpetual poor: the old who were past work, the sick who were unable to work, the widow and her children, and the orphaned. Contemporaries knew every nuance of the problem of poverty. They dwelt in an apparently precise, though on first acquaintance baffling, vocabulary: *pauvre, le vrai pauvre, le mauvais pauvre, pauvre valide ou invalide, pauvre honteux, indigent, misérable, nécessiteux, mendiant de profession, mendiant de bonne foi, mendiant volontaire, mendiant sédentaire,* etc. The great blanket term, and that used with least precision by those prone to generalize upon the problem of poverty as a whole, was, of course, *pauvre.* It implied that at best the individual concerned lived at subsistence level, that at worst he fell far below. Such an individual was the day labourer, the wage earner, or the small holder with a holding inadequate for the support of his family, or was the wife or child of such a person. Such an individual, if he was a family man, was crucially dependent even in normal times upon possibilities of employment for his wife and children. His economy was a family economy, dependent upon the earning powers of each individual member for the support of the whole

[1] A.D. Seine-Maritime C 2211, État des paroisses, 1788; A. Poitrineau, 'Aspects de l'émigration temporaire et saisonnière en Auvergne à la fin du XVIIIᵉ siècle et au début du XIXᵉ siècle', *R.H.M.C.* viii (1961), 23–4.

—for nowhere in the conditions of the *ancien régime* could a man expect to earn by the work of his hands more than sufficient to provide himself with food and shelter and possibly support a child.[1] Even so, unless he was employed in certain favoured industries at certain restricted times, in his lifetime such a man could hope for no improvement in his circumstances: he could, in fact, expect deterioration. He was emphatically someone without reserves: someone with nothing to buttress him against disaster. 'Celui qui ne possède ni biens ni mobilier est destiné à tomber dans la misère au moindre accident'[2] was Condorcet's classic definition of the *pauvre*. He, along with many physiocratic writers and indeed the entire *Comité de Mendicité* of the Constituent Assembly, found it easiest to depict the *pauvre* as a wage earner:

La pauvreté est une maladie inhérente à toute grande société; une bonne constitution, une administration sage peuvent diminuer son intensité, mais rien, malheureusement, ne peut la détruire radicalement; tant de causes concourent irrésistiblement à l'entretenir. Car sans parler des calamités qui, rendant des villages, des villes, des cantons, des provinces entières la proie de quelque dévastation passagère, portent l'indigence dans les lieux qu'elles attaquent, la privation de propriété pour une grande classe d'hommes sera toujours, dans quelque constitution que ce soit, un principe nécessaire et permanent de pauvreté.[3]

Their neglect of the small holder perhaps stemmed from the belief that his land lay between him and total destitution; and, interested above all in keeping the numbers of poor down to a minimum, they left on one side the implications of an inadequate holding or the plight of the man forced to part with his land. More imaginative men, like Necker or Turgot, thought otherwise and accorded the *pays de petite culture* first place in any consideration of the problem of poverty and the vulnerability of the *pauvre*.[4]

---

[1] C. Bloch and A. Tuetey, *Procès-verbaux*, p. 77: 'un homme valide peut gagner au delà de ses besoins et faire subsister deux ou trois individus avec lui', but on p. 379, an older and wiser *Comité* admitted that a man paying tax equivalent only to the proceeds of one day's labour (about a fifth of the work force) could not do as much as that.

[2] Condorcet, *Sur les assemblées provinciales* (1788), p. 453.

[3] Bloch and Tuetey, *Procès-verbaux*, p. 315.

[4] A.D. Puy-de-Dôme, C 776, and O. H. Hufton, 'Begging, Vagrancy, Vagabondage and the Law: an Aspect of the Problem of Poverty in Eighteenth-Century France', *European Studies Review*, 2 (1972), 101.

Perhaps, in fact, vulnerability was the main characteristic of the *pauvre*. In contemporary vocabulary such an individual was not necessarily suffering from hunger, cold, pain, or physical deprivation but was one who lived under the constant threat of such. He was part of a continual process and hence the repeated refrain of the *enquêtes* of the seventies: 'celui qui n'était que pauvre est actuellement indigent'.[1] He dwelt on the threshold of a worse state and hence, to contemporaries, shared something with those who had already crossed it and for whom there existed a further range of descriptive terms. The merely *pauvre* became *indigent, nécessiteux, misérable* in times of hardship—hardship due to extraordinary circumstances perhaps, such as bad harvests which pushed up the price of food and reduced grain returns so that the farmer had to become a purchaser, unemployment or illness which prevented a man or his wife from earning, or to everyday events, unemployment, underemployment, increasing old age and feebleness which prevented effective performance of hard physical labour, the arrival of a baby which temporarily curtailed a woman's earning power, or to slight shifts in demands for seasonal employment. To be described as *dans un état d'indigence absolue* was as low as one could sink in the scale of destitution. It meant that one had no food or adequate clothing or proper shelter, that one had parted with the few battered cooking-pots and blankets which often constituted the main assets of a working-class family. This narrow line, that between poverty and destitution, was one which those *nearly* concerned in a practical way with the problem of poverty were constantly at pains to define, and the priests and subdelegates who filled in the questionnaires of the seventies and eighties struggled above all to convey this subtlety.

Des pauvres! Je puis à peine accepter les quatre hauts tenanciers parce que je les vois fort embarrassés pour acquitter les charges énormes de

---

[1] The line between poverty and destitution, between *pauvreté honnête* and *indigence*, was one to which moralists, physiocrats, and administrators alike made constant reference. The first condition was to physiocrats and administrators inevitable (Bloch and Tuetey, *Procès-verbaux*, pp. 315–16) and to moralists like St. Vincent de Paul even virtuous; only the second condition was to be feared, because of the misery and degeneracy it entailed. O. H. Hufton, 'Towards an Understanding of the Poor of Eighteenth-Century France', *French Government and Society 1500–1850*, ed. J. F. Bosher (London, 1973), pp. 145–65, and 'Women in Revolution, 1789–1796', *Past and Present*, No. 53 (1971), p. 95.

leurs possessions. De tous les autres habitants, la moitié est pauvre, et la moitié misérable; pourtant pas de mendiants depuis cinq ou six ans. Curé de Montousse, Comminges[1]

Pas de pauvre qui aille mendier leur pain de porte en porte. Cependant à Lanson, deux ou trois maisons tout au plus qui vivent à leur aise, quoique obligés de travailler continuellement comme des forçats; tous les autres ne font que vivoter. Curé de Lanson, Comminges[2]

Toute la paroisse est pauvre: tout au plus il y a vingt maisons ou familles qui vivent; tout le reste est aux expédients. . . . Les deux tiers de la paroisse auraient besoin d'être soulagée en partie; et il y en a un tiers pour le moins sans ressource. Curé de Laguiolle, Rodez[3]

La moitié tout au moins de la paroisse est composée de pauvres. Ceux-là n'ont d'autre secours pour subsister, eux et leurs familles, que le travail de leurs mains et la santé venant à leur manquer, il leur faut un prompt secours; la plupart même de ceux qui sont dans ce rang ne peuvent avec la santé faire subsister dans ces années leurs nombreuses familles, ce qui fait qu'il y a plus de trente petits enfants qui sont obligés de mendier leur pain dans la paroisse et hors de la paroisse. Ceux d'un certain âge qui ont le même sort peut se réduire à une quinzaine. Curé de Bonneterre, Rodez[4]

The observations of the priests and subdelegates of the seventies leave little doubt as to the magnitude of the problem of poverty; they even make it possible to generalize upon where it was at its most intense and which regions were then relatively prosperous. Those made of the dioceses of Rouen, Dijon, Toulouse, and Montpellier, for example, contrast sharply with those made of Brittany, western Normandy, Poitou, and the Massif—Rodez, Mende, and Clermont. Whereas the second group talked in terms of a problem of poverty embracing up to two-thirds of the population, the first indicated an indigenous problem of the old, very young, and sick, which could in large part be contained. In the diocese of Rouen this could in the early seventies be attributed to the developing textile industry, which afforded work to men, women, and children; while in the dioceses

---

[1] A. Sarramon (ed.), *Les Paroisses du diocèse de Comminges en 1786* (Paris, 1968), p. 219.
[2] Ibid., p. 265.
[3] Lempereur, *L'État du diocèse de Rodez en 1771*, Laguiolle.
[4] Ibid., Bonneterre.

of Dijon and Montpellier the wine trade had brought a degree of ease to the regions as a whole. But the *enquêtes* of the seventies do not take one much further; nor do those of the *Commissions Intermédiaires* of the *Assemblées Provinciales* held in 1788, except that their reports universalize the problem of poverty and illustrate in a peculiarly vivid way the plight of the textile *bourgs* of the north in the textile slump. Even the great and apparently scientific inquiry of the *Comité de Mendicité* in 1790 was not really concerned with counting the poor. The *Comité* was interested in discovering the number of *individus ayant besoin d'assistance* to whom it hoped to accord help. This concept was clearly related to the number of poor, and hence, again, the results of the *Comité de Mendicité*'s questionnaire allow some generalizations to be made about the incidence of poverty within France. But the *pauvre* of the *ancien régime* was not necessarily the *individu ayant besoin d'assistance* of 1791. As a working definition of poverty, the *Comité* offered:

Les véritables pauvres, c'est à dire ceux qui, sans propriété et sans ressources, veulent acquérir leur subsistance par le travail; ceux auxquels l'âge ne permet pas encore ou ne permet plus de travailler; enfin ceux qui sont condamnés à une inaction durable par la nature de leurs infirmités, ou à une inaction momentanée par des maladies passagères. Les mauvais pauvres, c'est à dire ceux qui, connus sous le nom de mendiants de profession et de vagabonds, se refusent à tout travail, troublent l'ordre public, sont un fléau dans la société et appellent sa juste sévérité.[1]

The *Comité* hoped to provide work for the unemployed, hospitalization for the infirm, and a subsidy for the children of wage earners until they were 14 years old. Together these three groups, statistically shown by the *Comité* to be a tenth of the total population, formed the *total des individus ayant besoin d'assistance*—at least in the opinion of the *Comité*. The figures compiled, or rather concocted, by the *Comité* made no allowance for the partially employed or the small landholder or the landowner of insufficient resources. Moreover, until the children of wage earners were in receipt of help, the entire family unit was in difficulties. Parents did not eat while their children starved. In short, the calculations

---

[1] Bloch and Tuetey, *Procès-verbaux*, p. 317.

of the *Comité de Mendicité* were a gross underestimation and cast a highly artificial light on the real problem.[1]

Perhaps the most useful estimate made of the poor was not one made with the poor in mind at all but was the number of those decreed 'passive' citizens for electoral purposes in 1790: those adult males whose tax rating was not equal to the proceeds of two days' labour, or, put another way, those adult males earning less than 17–20 *sols* a day. Around 39 per cent of adult males would seem to have been in this position.[2] The *Comité de Mendicité* estimated at 35 *sols* the cost of giving a basic bread ration to a family of five of whom three were young children, and though this figure was artificial and doubtless varied from region to region, it remains a useful notion.[3] Hence one can say that every passive citizen was a vulnerable citizen—he was a *pauvre* whose fate depended upon the continuation of ideal circumstances. He could manage if he was young, single, employed, and in good bodily health; and, if married, only if his wife was in work—and hence also in good bodily health. Since each married adult male represented a family unit of four to five people, the poor might be considerably more than 30–40 per cent of the population. Of rural society and within the framework of existing area studies, it has been affirmed that according to region, between a half and nine-tenths of families did not have land sufficient for their support and were dependent upon supplementary income from industry, emigration, or the contraction of debt.[4] How many of these could be categorized *indigent*, *misérable*, *nécessiteux* can only

[1] The *Comité*'s questionnaire did in fact ask the districts to add up the number of poor in need of assistance but disregarded the results on the grounds that the districts had a vested interest in swelling the numbers. The global figures of the *Comité* (Bloch and Tuetey, *Procès-verbaux*, p. 573) are not those returned by the districts but are an addition of children, sick, aged, and unemployed. The *Comité* had a vested interest in keeping down the numbers of poor because it had made calculations on modest assumptions and could only expect very limited sums from a financially hard-pressed government. It dared not have as many poor as the results of its *enquête* suggested and had either to bring down the figures by suggesting their unreliability or to admit the futility of its existence.

[2] J. Godechot, *Les Institutions de la France sous la Révolution et l'Empire* (Paris, 1951), p. 74, estimates 4,300,000 'active' citizens and 2,700,000 passive. The *Comité de Mendicité* accepted that a relationship existed between the number of passive citizens and the number of poor (Bloch and Tuetey, *Procès-verbaux*, pp. 48 and 572–3) and that hence 10–11 million people were at least exposed to difficulties.

[3] Cited by C. Bloch, *L'Assistance et l'État en France à la veille de la Révolution*, pp. 4–5.

[4] Braudel and Labrousse (eds.), *Histoire économique et sociale*, p. 147.

be surmised. Urban historians have suggested each for their particular towns in the region of two-thirds or up to 20 per cent of the total town population and there is little to indicate that the plight of the country was any better.[1]

Both *pauvre* and *indigent*, then, together in 1789 formed something above a third (and, speculatively, perhaps as much as a half) of the total population; together they are the concern of this study, for where one merged into the other was, to say the least, obscure. The closer one looks at the conditions of existence of this large proportion of the French population the more difficult it becomes to isolate *pauvre* from *indigent*; for a process of continual recruitment took place from the higher to the lower category: the difference between the two was one of degree.

[1] Figures offered for towns and cities, for example by G. Lefebvre, *Études orléanaises* (Paris, 1962), vol. i, pp. 218–19; O. H. Hufton, *Bayeux in the late Eighteenth Century* (Oxford, 1967), pp. 86–7; Y. Le Moigne, 'Population et subsistances à Strasbourg au XVIIIe siècle', *Contributions à l'histoire démographique de la Révolution française*, iv (Paris, 1962), 33–4; for Vendôme, C. Bloch, *L'Assistance*, p. 6; for Troyes and Rouen and Lyons in the textile crisis of 1787 figures of 40–50 per cent are used. E. Chaudron, *L'Assistance publique à Troyes à la fin de l'ancien régime* (Paris, 1923), p. 10; M. Bouloiseau, *Cahiers de doléances du tiers état du bailliage de Rouen* (Paris, 1957), pp. cxlviii–cl. Garden, *Lyon*, p. 298, etc. For the countryside Lefebvre's estimate for the Nord is of 20 per cent *indigent* (*Les Paysans du Nord* (Bari, 1959), pp. 308–9). H. Sée's for Brittany is of the order of 20–25 per cent, *Les Classes rurales en Bretagne du XVIe au XVIIIe siècles* (Paris, 1906), p. 471. More impressionistic assessments of Rodez based on *L'État du diocèse de Rodez en 1771* suggest a similar figure, and the same assumption underlies M. Accarias, *L'Assistance publique dans le Puy de Dôme sous la Révolution* (Clermont-Ferrand, 1933). Assessments made for some mountain communities in the Pyrenees rise much higher into the realms of 30–40 per cent of the populace. T. Azémar, 'Le XVIIIe siècle à Massat', *Revue de Gascogne* (1883), pp. 322–37 and 335–500, and J. Adher, 'Le Diocèse de Rieux au XVIIIe siècle', *Annales du Midi*, xvii (1905), 490–510 and xxii (1909), 433–73.

II

FROM POVERTY TO INDIGENCE

Il semble que c'est une chose décidée que le pauvre doit
rester pauvre. *Cahier* of Killem (Nord)

FOR the poor the road from poverty to indigence was always an
individual odyssey with very personal refinements. Nevertheless,
generalizations can be made. A man or woman was not necessarily as poor as his or her parents had been, though it was likely
that he or she might be a great deal more so.[1] To be the child
even of the destitute did not, supposing one could physically
survive an ill-nourished infancy, necessarily preclude one from a
viable if fragile existence. Much depended upon one's energies
and opportunities in adolescence. Childhood for those without
prospect of inheriting an adequate holding was brief, and important decisions had to be made in very early adolescence, when
both sexes had to consider not merely their present but their
future condition and were obliged to plan ahead on what were
well-established lines. Between the ages of 12 and 14 and marriage
in one's late twenties much had to be achieved on which one's
future was wholly dependent. Both boy and girl looked, consciously or not, towards marriage which would embody an
important economic partnership; the natural economy of the poor
was a family economy dependent upon the efforts of each individual member and one in which the role of both partners was
equally crucial. To be without the apparent means, in the long
run, to support a family has never been an effective deterrent to
undertaking marriage. There were stronger pressures at work
which need little elaboration: natural instincts, the desire for
companionship, convention enforced by religion, the fear of

---

[1] The odds were on *pauvreté permanente*. This is the purport of Garden, *Lyon*,
pp. 298–309, though the author offers occasional stories of relative success; of
Lefebvre, *Les Paysans du Nord*, p. 69; of Poitrineau, *La Vie rurale en Basse Auvergne*,
pp. 743–6; of P. de Saint-Jacob, *Les Paysans de la Bourgogne du Nord au dernier siècle de
l'ancien régime* (Paris, 1960), pp. 530–1, etc.

being left alone in sickness and poverty. There were other considerations too, pressing particularly hard on a woman. If she had brothers, she had no hope of inheriting even a fraction of land. Female industrial wages were not calculated with an independent existence in mind. They might keep a girl in food, but they would not provide her with much in the way of shelter, or clothing or heating, or even with sufficient candles to allow her to work into the night. Wages were calculated as low as possible, and the lowest cipher on the employment market, least able to defend her economic interests, was the married woman. Her willingness and need to accept work, albeit at the lowest remuneration, determined, with few exceptions, the level of wages of female employ. Hence, if they did not marry and found a separate establishment, working women could anticipate only destitution or, at best, a corner of a brother's or cousin's dwelling, at the mercy of some other woman. The servant girl was employed on the strength of her youth and vigour; only stately homes or philanthropic clergymen could think sympathetically of retaining the ageing woman of diminishing strength. Not to marry certainly entailed a bleak future; marriage was more of a gamble. It could lead to a future equally, if not more, bleak; but, with health and good fortune, a viable existence might be secured.

A country girl began working towards marriage between the ages of 12 and 14 when she assumed employment outside the family unit.[1] For the country girl this almost invariably meant service of some kind: leaving her own home for residence in someone else's. The position might be local, that of the farm *servante*, the girl who cooked, cleaned, washed clothes, fed poultry, milked the cows, and turned out into the fields during the heavy periods of the agricultural year as haymaker and gleaner and filled in any odd hours in the winter with domestic industry. The country, however, did not have the means to provide work for all its daughters and the adolescent girl was obliged to look townwards, thus furnishing urban France with a steady stream of unskilled woman-power. Generally the girl did not have to look very far: the nearest town of 5,000 or more inhabitants was

---

[1] The *Comité de Mendicité* (Bloch and Tuetey, *Procès-verbaux*, pp. 572–3) assumed 14 to be the average age for a girl to leave home for a quasi-independent existence, yet frequently servant girls of 12 and 13 came before the courts, e.g. A.D. Rhône B Maréchaussée 1733, Claudine Lambert; 1770 Marie Grinillade; A.D. Finistère B 843, 851.

usually as far as she would have to travel, for this supply of labour was met with an almost equal demand, that for domestic service. There was no lack of employ for the maid-of-all-work in the towns, provided that the girl was prepared to settle for the lowest kind of labour. The first luxury any family permitted itself was a maidservant, a female drudge, part load-carrier, emptier of privies, carter of heavy washing to and from the local wash-place, a girl ready to work from dawn to dusk in return for her keep and a small sum of money. Moreover, cities and towns with industrial activities absorbed girls who not only performed such menial services but in addition were industrial employees. For some households the profits from the girl's part-time industrial labours, which were retained by the employer, made possible the employment of the *servante* in the first place. Perhaps as many as two-thirds of the 600 servant girls of Bayeux turned to lace-making when their household chores were done and thence worked into the night.[1] The *servante* of Lodève and Clermont, centres of the Languedoc woollen industry, was a girl from the Rouergue or the Gévaudan drawn to the households of weavers and was principally a spinner.[2] The textile industries of the north drew girls from a more restricted radius,[3] but the terms of their employ were much the same, for the cheapest way a master weaver in the woollen, cotton, or, sometimes, linen industries could obtain spun thread over and above that provided by his wife—and it took the efforts of four women working full time to supply one weaver—was to have a girl on his premises to whom he paid about 50 *livres* annually in addition to her keep. The silk industries of Lyons, the south-east (centred upon Nîmes), and, much less significantly, Tours were organized differently; yet even here the *servante chez les ouvriers en soie* was not occupied

[1] A.M. Bayeux F., États de la population, an IV, an VII, and E. Lefebure, *Histoire de la dentelle à Bayeux de 1676 à 1900* (Bayeux, 1913).

[2] For this and ensuing facts on the female personnel of the Languedoc woollen industry I am indebted to Mr. James Thomson currently working upon a doctoral thesis on Clermont-de-Lodève.

[3] A.D. Aube, Hôtel Dieu le Comte Troyes Décès, 1771–5. Out of about 120 female deaths annually, 50 per cent were from Troyes and the diocese of Troyes and the rest from neighbouring dioceses of Langres (22), Sens (4), Châlons (4), and individuals drawn from the Île de France. Four from Franche-Comté were the only long-distance travellers; on the local recruitment of Rouen, E. Le Parquier, *Ouvriers et patrons dans la seconde moitié du XVIIIe siècle* (Rouen, 1933), pp. 33 ff.; on Lille, pertinent remarks are made in A. Lottin, 'Naissances illégitimes et filles mères à Lille au XVIIIe siècle', *R.H.M.C.* xvii (1970), 278–322.

with domestic chores but was a *tordeuse de soie*, a *tireuse de cordes*, or a *dévideuse*. Those of Lyons came from Dauphiné, Savoy, Bugey, or the Forez. Their work was 'si pénible et si rébutant que l'on n'en voit aucune des provinces du Lyonnais et lieux circonvoisins s'y livrer'.[1] But the girls of the villages of Dauphiné, or Bresse, Bugey, and Savoie had no alternative employment and they were girls with a purpose: they came hoping to amass a capital sum and then to return home.

The *servantes*, whether maids of all work or industrial employees or a mixture of both, formed up to 13 per cent of the total population of any town or city (an average perhaps of 8–10 per cent) and 80–90 per cent of them were drawn from the immediately adjacent countryside: in Bordeaux from the Entre-Deux-Mers, in Paris from Norman and Picard girls or those from the Île de France, in Marseilles from the immediate Provençal hinterland, in Bayeux from the Bessin, in Caen from the actual plain of Caen, in Cherbourg from the peninsula of the Manche, in Toulouse from the Lauragais, in Millau from the Causse Noir or Causse Méjean; and one can readily multiply such examples showing that the *servante* on average moved no more than twenty to thirty miles from home.[2] And if the girls of Montpellier, Agde, Béziers, and other cities of the Mediterranean littoral made longer journeys from the barren hills of the Massif, this is to be explained by the continued movement from the hills, where urban life was underdeveloped, to the plain.

Theoretically, *domesticité* offered a large number of attractions to the single girl. First amongst these was that it enabled her to plan her own future. Ten years of a type of bondage, or almost slave-type labour, with only a few hours' leisure each month would, it was hoped, provide her with a dowry. For small as her earnings might be, the girl did not plan to spend them and, unless she was particularly devoted to her impecunious family and prepared to send her money home, she stood a chance of accumu-

---

[1] A.N. F¹² 1441, Comment soulager la fabrique à Lyon. *Mémoire anonyme* cited by M. Garden, *Lyon*, p. 53.

[2] Conclusions based upon A.M. Bordeaux, Hôpital Saint-André, Décès, 1780–6, where 80–90 per cent of girls came from the immediately adjacent countryside; A.M. Marseille GG 652, Sépultures Hôtel Dieu 1780–6; A.M. Bayeux F., États de la population, An IV; A. Hosp. Dijon F³², Décès; A.M. Toulouse, GG 747–9, Les Registres de décès à l'Hôpital Général Saint Joseph de la Grave 1716–90; and O. Paloc, *Recherches démographiques et sociales sur Millau au XVIIIᵉ siècle* (Diplôme d'Études Supérieures, Toulouse, 1958), p. 88.

lating a small hoard; if she persisted, and no untoward events cut her short in her objectives, this, in ten or twelve years, might amount to quite a substantial sum, in the region of 500 *livres*, an endowment which, back in her native village, would render her a very eligible wife or make possible the foundation of an urban marriage partnership.[1]

The obstacles to the full achievement of this goal were legion. Ideally, the adolescent girl went to a family with whom her village had some links. Jobs were found by contacts: cousins succeeded cousins; sisters, sisters; nieces, aunts, and so on. Since the work terminated on marriage, there was a rapid turnover. Bourgeois families in Paris with Norman or Picard antecedents drew girls from those provinces; the wine merchants of Bordeaux brought girls from villages, perhaps those where they had a country residence; the same was true of the Dijon *parlementaires*, and perhaps those of Rennes and Toulouse did the same.[2] Contacts of this kind were of mutual worth: the girl went to a reputable family, and in return the family had a quasi-guarantee of the girl's honesty; she would not go off one night with the family's sheets and cutlery. The law attempted to embody guarantees to safeguard the relationship between master and servant: the servant who stole from his or her employer was doubly culpable; the employer who seduced his servant was subject to peculiar penalties. But this ideal picture is only part of the story. Most servant girls in large cities probably set forth into the virtually unknown, dependent on friends or relatives hearing of a job, or on their own efforts when they arrived. Nor were the bulk of

[1] This represents the most considerable figure I have seen achieved by a servant girl and is found in F. G. Pariset (ed), *Bordeaux au XVIIIᵉ siècle* (Bordeaux, 1968), p. 368 concludes '. . . leur grand souci était de s'établir, venues jeunes, le plus souvent entre 15 et 20 ans, elles amassaient pendant huit ou dix années "leurs pécules", qui arrivaient souvent à atteindre 400 ou 500 livres, et essayaient alors de trouver quelque bon mari pour "s'établir".' Far more modest are the examples offered for Lyons by Garden, *Lyon*, pp. 304–5, where 100 *livres* represents 'un parti avantageux' and at Bayeux, where dowries in excess of 200 *livres* were of the order of 3 per cent. A. Chatelain, 'Migrations et domesticité féminine urbaine en France, XVIIIᵉ–XXᵉ siècles', *R.H.E.S.* xlvii (1969), 511–14, does not commit himself in his cursory study to more than the point that a girl in Brittany could amass little more than 20 *livres* per year but one placed in a wealthy Parisian home stood the chance of five times that amount.

[2] L. Cahen, 'La Population parisienne au milieu du XVIIIᵉ siècle', *Revue de Paris* (Sept. 1919), p. 153, gives interesting instances of the households of the ducs d'Orléans, Conti, Crozat, and the *parlementaires* Aligre.

girls employed by people of social standing. The weavers of the
industrial towns were men of very limited means whose premature death leaving outstanding debts could result in a very
partial remuneration of the sums owing to their employees.[1] The
bankrupt *maître fabricant*, a classic figure in the Languedoc
woollen towns after 1750, had evidently to default on his payments to his spinner *servante*. Even in burgeoning Rouen, bankruptcies were frequent, and each bankruptcy entailed at least
dislocation and at worst a protracted period of unemployment
for spinners above all.[2] Failure of the flax harvests of Britanny
in the 1780s saw girls dismissed from their domestic jobs simply
because without industrial work the family could not afford to
employ them.[3] This was even true of farm *servantes*, but their
security of tenure was infinitely greater than that of the girls in
towns, who came to harsh and highly vulnerable employ. Their
fate was linked to that of the small artisans who employed them;
they were severely hit by any period of *chômage*, when they were
simply shown the door.[4] The nature of the work and the poor
conditions, coupled with inadequate food received in the home
of their employer, ensured an extraordinary death-rate amongst
the *servantes chez les ouvriers en soie* of Lyons; and the history of
their failures to realize the goal of the dowry and the return to the
native village is told in the death registers of the *hôtels Dieu*. In
1756 alone, 108 of them perished; their average age was 21. But
the living were ever ready to step into the shoes of the dead, and
one Savoyard apprentice in turn filled one position of *dévideuse*
with his sister, his aunt, his cousin, and his niece.[5]

The recruits to the industry of Lyons were perhaps peculiarly
weak; elsewhere less catastrophic considerations contrived to
sever the *servante* from her capital sum. The servant girl was
particularly vulnerable. The master who seduced his servant
could easily dismiss her against a small nominal payment for the
upkeep of his bastard if the girl or her family had sufficient resolve

---

[1] Garden, *Lyon*, pp. 303–5, gives many instances of *servantes chez les ouvriers en
soie* whose plans of a dowry were thus disrupted.

[2] P. Dardel, 'Crises et faillites à Rouen et dans la Haute Normandie', *R.H.E.S.*
xxvii (1948–9), 53.

[3] A.D. Ille-et-Vilaine C 1745, Subdélégation de La Guerche, 1785 : '. . . Bien des
fermiers qui avaient des servantes les ont mises dehors par défaut de filasse . . .', etc.

[4] A.D. Ille-et-Vilaine C 1745, La Guerche 1785. A.N. F¹² 1441, Requête des
maîtres fabricants de Lyons, 14 septembre 1785.

[5] A.N. F¹² 1441, Observations d'Antoine-François Brisson.

to take him to court.[1] Moreover, the conditions of the servant girl's employ rendered her little fitted to cope with leisure. She was starved of affection and excitement, and hence a *kermesse* or other religious festival was usually marked nine months later by a crop of unwanted children and dismissed servants. The former will play a further part in this study, the latter will be the most considerable element in the urban *déclarations de grossesse*. Perhaps the most exposed to this hazard were the domestic servants of modest shopkeepers, tradesmen, and *cabaretiers* (the lowest employers of all) and those employed by the keepers of *hôtels* and furnished rooms. These did not remain long in any one employ, and some of the *servantes* who came before the courts had had five, six, or even seven or eight employers before they were 20.

To set against the failures, however, are the success stories. If the rural *servante* confined to the one family in her own village environment stood the best chance of realizing her dowry, success in urban conditions was far from unknown. The *dévideuse* or *tordeuse* of Lyons who married a journeyman silk-worker or even a small master, the two forming a working partnership which eventually permitted the woman to abandon the more distasteful work to a new arrival from the mountains would be one such.[2] The Rouergat spinner-servant of Clermont-de-Lodève who married her master's apprentice and whose capital sum, patiently acquired, was the means of his purchasing a loom and setting up independently, would be another.[3] In the main the servant girl dreamed of returning to her village with her capital sum and there attracting a man whose success as a *valet de ferme* and prospects as a small farmer equalled her own. The importance of the sum that she could offer at this stage was considerable. The average age for marriage for a woman was between the ages of 26 and 28, and this somewhat advanced age for a first marriage is probably to be explained by the amount of time it took in

[1] Where cities kept registers of *déclarations de grossesse* as at Lille, Toulouse, Périgueux, Rennes, Vannes, etc. (see below, pp. 325–6) they are filled with ex-servants, the victims of their employers. Fifty *livres* or less was as much compensation as a girl might get in court.

[2] A.N. F¹² 1441, Observations: 'Un tiers au moins des maîtres ouvriers de la fabrique ne sont mariés qu'à des femmes qui ont pratiqué ces différents travaux, qui occupent quatre à cinq mille personnes, ce qui altère le nombre de celles qui servent à tirer les cordes . . .'

[3] This would presume capital of at least 200 *livres*.

the conditions of the *ancien régime* to amass a capital sum sufficient to embark upon matrimony or the realization that if one had not done so by that age, one's chances of ever doing so were remote.[1]

There is no way of calculating how many succeeded and who failed. Notarial acts embody for the most part the success stories; the girl with nothing to offer is unrecorded. Still, there is enough to indicate that the odds on success were low. Of 100 girls, former lacemaker *servantes* in the Bessin, in the last two decades of the *ancien régime*, just over 50 per cent could only offer a capital sum of between 50 and 100 *livres* as a dowry; only 3 managed more than 200 *livres*.[2] The same story can be told at Millau, at Agde, at Semur-en-Auxois, and at Lyons. The records of the large cities are less significant than those of rural notaries, for the dowry has its greatest justification in rural circles. It could be the means of purchasing an animal or two, the first year's seed, or of buttressing the couple against the initial waves of debt incurred upon leasing a property. At the least, if it only totalled 50 *livres* or so, it procured the household linen, cooking-pots and pans, extra shifts, and pieces of coarse cloth intended to last through marriage. A girl could expect little else to come her way. The death of her parents might, if they had not ended their days in total destitution, bring her a bed, a cupboard, or bundles of old household linen which had survived one couple's lifetime but which would spare hers some wear or, more probably, she would receive those black garments, patched and worn, to which time lent a greenish hue, which one generation of peasant women handed on to the next. These were as much as she might expect in the years to come. The *inventaires après décès* and contracts made when an elderly person renounced all he had to an *hôpital*, in return for care and a bed, would retail a list of items, already inventoried in the dowry but now patched, worn, and relatively useless—'un chétif lit', 'du mauvais linge' tell the story of a marriage.

---

[1] Here I would part company with those quantitative historians such as P. Chaunu in *Histoire de la Normandie*, ed. M. de Bouard (Toulouse, 1970), pp. 344, 356, who attribute the advanced age of first marriage to an instinctive urge to limit the size of one's family and who claim that the property-less could marry for love and physical attraction. Rather does the evidence point to hard-headed economic considerations.

[2] A.D. Calvados C 9263–4, Registres du Contrôle des Actes, Notariat de Bayeux. Examples taken over the period 1784–9.

The country girl needed a dowry in a radically different way from the town girl. The latter did not expect to renounce or shift her employ upon marriage, whereas the country girl assumed different responsibilities: she might continue with work in domestic industry, but she also had jobs on the land, weeding, hoeing, looking after livestock, watering terraces, carrying goods to and from market, and, in areas dependent upon seasonal or temporary migration, assuming responsibility for the entire holding in the absence of her husband—jobs for which there was no monetary remuneration. The town girl's approach was fundamentally different. She did not seek to become a servant; the degree to which she shunned such employ is remarkable. To be a seamstress, a laundress, a stay-maker, a trimmer of hats and bodices might enclose a girl in a dusty, ill-lit, ill-ventilated *atelier* for long hours in pursuit of a pittance permitting of no savings, and such work certainly did not result in a substantial dowry, but the town girl preferred such work to domestic service. She shunned the unhealthiest jobs in the silk and flax industries—hence reinforcing the tendency of the weaver to employ residential labour, drawn from the countryside. Where the urban family formed a small industrial enterprise she might remain within it until marriage; and, apart from linen and utensils, she did not carry capital assets to her partner. Nor did she expect him to have any. Still, the girl who had served an apprenticeship and had a skill to offer, the *couturière*, the milliner, the glove-maker, and so on, though pathetically paid, had the prospects at least of continuing her employ full time. This was her dowry and it did not need a notarial act to lend expression to the fact. In one way or another, in town or country, the girl contributed to her utmost towards her own future.

The contribution of the male partner to the setting-up of a household was obviously no less important and no less prepared. Severance from his family began at the age of 14 for the boy whose family could not offer him any prospects of an adequate inheritance, for he had his way to make in the world. Depending on the region, his actions at that stage were fairly simple. He aspired to become a *valet* or *domestique de ferme*, an individual who occupied an envied position, because not only was he housed and fed and shod but his employer put by for him an annual sum of 50–100 *livres* which twelve years or so later would stand him in good stead when it came to hiring and stocking a farm.[1] His duties as *valet* often combined acting as farm-hand with winter weaving or even, in the Alpine regions, with seasonal migration; but providing his health continued and no ill fortune befell him or his employers, he probably enjoyed as much security of tenure as anyone under the *ancien régime*.[2] Industrial slump could see him a dead weight upon his employer during the winter but, unless it was a protracted depression, the employer was more likely to dispense with the services of the farm *servante* than those of his *valet*.

Not all regions of France gave resident board to even a part of their agricultural labour. In Beauce, Île de France, Lyonnais, and Languedoc, farmers retained very little permanent labour[3] since seasonal workers could be so easily obtained, and even outside these regions the demands for permanent man-power were restricted. The boy in search of a capital sum might then look townwards and seek work as *domestique* or apprentice; and one uses both words in their wide *ancien régime* sense to comprehend, in the first instance, both pure domestic servant and industrial employee who performed domestic chores, and, in the second, the man who was apprenticed to a trade but who was also expected to help about the house. About a third of urban *domesticité* was male, but what proportion of this third was made up of more precisely industrial employees is difficult to assess. Each year about a tenth of all recorded deaths at the *hôtel Dieu* at Lyons were of *domestiques chez les ouvriers en soie*, silk throwsters drawn from the same mountain areas of Bresse and Bugey, the Forez, and the Lyonnais as the female *servantes*.[4] In Languedoc at Lodève, and nearby Clermont, the Rouergat *domestique* was, in effect, apprentice-weaver and odd-job man, and the *domestique* of the textile towns of the north was either weaver, carder, or concerned in some stage of textile production. Not every *domestique* or apprentice thought in terms of remaining in industrial work or of

[1] The lower figure is offered by Poitrineau, *La Vie rurale en Basse Auvergne*, p. 545, the higher by G. Lefebvre, *Les Paysans du Nord*, p. 290, and *Études orléanaises*, vol. i, p. 76.

[2] In Flanders they went so far as to claim they could not be dismissed, G. Lefebvre, *Les Paysans du Nord* (Bari, 1959), p. 305; in Auvergne they were regarded as the most fortunate, Poitrineau, *La Vie rurale en Basse Auvergne*, p. 545; similarly in the Morbihan, T. Le Goff, 'Vannes in the Eighteenth Century' (Ph.D. thesis, London, 1969), pp. 175-6. [3] M. Morineau, *Les Faux-Semblants*, p. 328.

[4] A.M. Lyon 688, samples taken over the period 1776-80.

aspiring to *compagnonnage*; some envisaged instead returning home with their profits and hiring a farm, secure in the knowledge of having enough skill as weaver, carder, or stocking-knitter to be able to turn to this in the dead season.[1] Always, of course, one is talking about the ideal situation, for almost as many obstacles lay in the way of the male *domestique*, industrial worker, apprentice as did in that of the *servante*. Industrial depression, disease and death, the unreliability of employers, all took their toll. The physical environment in which the industrial worker laboured was almost sufficient enemy: conditions in the linen industry were perhaps the worst, but not far behind were silk and cotton. Both flax and cotton weavers worked in damp cellars because the humid atmosphere helped to reduce broken threads. At Voiron in 1788, 'Les boutiques de tisserand, toutes enterrées, presque toujours humides et malsaines, contribuent à la mauvaise santé de presque tous ceux qui font des toiles; après un certain nombre d'années de ce travail, ils deviennent pâles et d'une couleur livide, avec des jambes gorgées ou ulcérées'.[2] Ready parallels to this description exist for Lille, Troyes, and Lyons.[3]

In mountainous regions where seasonal migration was the norm for small holders condemned to work a poor soil during a restricted working year, the boy might seek to place himself in one of the centres receiving seasonal migrants or temporarily establish himself in a distant city where contacts might procure for him some heavy, menial job. As long as youth and physical strength were on his side, the individual who hoped to return to his native village and set up as farmer must struggle to put something aside. It was only while independent from the obligations of a family that he had the opportunity of doing so; and if he failed so to do, there was little point in going home.

For the town-born, sons of artisans, textile workers, and petty shopkeepers, the acquisition of a capital sum had perhaps less purpose, for in the long run it was the trade at their disposal, rather than the ability to hire and stock a piece of land, which mattered. The incentive to leave home and found a separate establishment was less general. Sons followed fathers into trades

---

[1] This explains something of the considerable discrepancy between apprentices and *compagnons*. Perhaps under 60 per cent of apprentices became *compagnons*. H. Sée, *L'Évolution commerciale et industrielle de la France sous l'ancien régime* (Paris, 1925), p. 325.

[2] Cited in Braudel and Labrousse (eds.), *Histoire économique et sociale*, p. 664.

[3] A.D. Aube, C 1151, 1778; Lefebvre, *Les Paysans du Nord*, pp. 301–2.

where guilds accorded them special treatment, demanded lower entry rates and less exigent *chefs d'œuvre*. The mastership (worth on average about 50 *livres*) was the most important capital asset.[1] A capital sum acquired by patient labour might render a young man capable of purchasing his own loom (worth up to 200 *livres*), but lack of this was no real obstacle to setting up in business, for he could hire one—and possession of a loom made him no less vulnerable to industrial slump. For 15 or 20 *livres* many succeeded, before the hard times of the seventies, in setting themselves up in family production. In Mende, most northerly centre of the Languedoc woollen industry, the weaver's economy was thus described in 1732:

l'industrie fait vivre l'artisan; il lui suffit d'avoir en argent une somme de *quinze livres* de faire vivre sa famille; il emploie cet argent en laine, qui est ouvrée dans sa maison par sa femme et ses enfants, en sorte que le maître travaille toujours à facturer des serges et des cadis. Mais le produit de son travail est peu considérable, le meilleur ne gagne que huit sols par jour; la fileuse trois sols.[2]

In Lyons 50 *livres* for rental of premises (a silk loom was large), raw material, and expenses could set a master silk weaver up in business; it cost even less to embark as a cotton weaver at Troyes and Rouen. In other words, the young urban couple could start with very little, a very little which, notwithstanding, took at least the period of apprenticeship to accumulate.

Marriage was the most important turning-point in the life of any individual. At that moment the young couple probably possessed more than they would ever again possess, unless the death of a parent who owned land brought a scrap of property. Hopefully the couple aspired to rent a piece of land; less realistically, they hoped to stock it and with their own physical strength and ingenuity somehow to make out.

There is no simple means of estimating how many did realize their aspirations, though there are many pointers. The couples who, in Arthur Young's phrase, married on the 'idea of an

[1] These prerogatives were rigorously defended by the manufacturers: 'Ce sont des ouvriers nés avec ce talent et qui sont plus au fait à l'âge de dix ans qu'un apprenti étranger ne le serait à vingt.' A.N. F^{12} 1441, Projet de création d'une manufacture succursale. 4e réflexion, les fils et filles de maîtres, 1756. The mastership for testament purposes was valued at 50 *livres* (Garden, *Lyon*, p. 304).

[2] A.D. Lozère C 62.

inheritance'—on what was no more than a cottage garden, those of whom the curé of Mecé wrote in 1790:

C'est que plusieurs se marient sans moyens, sans trouver d'autre refuge qu'une maison ou tout au plus qu'une petite terre dont le produit est incapable de leur faire subsister. Tandis qu'ils n'ont pas d'enfants, libres d'aller à leurs journées, ils vivent. Mais les enfants viennent-ils et la mère, occupée de les soigner, ne peut plus gagner. Le père, surtout dans les années de cherté ne peut pas les nourrir.[1]

—clearly fell short of any required minimum. So did aspirant *métayers* of Sologne, Berry, La Marche, Limousin, Anjou, Burgundy, Bourbonnais, Nivernais, Auvergne, Brittany, Maine, Provence, who lacked the capital fully to stock their land and to provide seed—and this was the dominant form of tenure in the west, the centre, and the south.[2] The most usual peasant farmer, described as *petit propriétaire* of miscellaneous pieces of land and, at one and the same time, *fermier*, *métayer*, *valet*, and *journalier* of several masters—the whole summed up in that part of France lying between the Vexin and the Soissonnais by the term *haricotier*[3] or, in parts of Brittany, by *maisonier*[4]—was not in a position to feed even a small family off the accumulated produce of his land and his agricultural labours. Moreover, between a half and nine-tenths, according to region, of rural families lacked the means to lay hold of sufficient land to support themselves[5] or, because of their lack of capital, could only secure land under forms of tenure which distrained a third to a half of their produce. In other words, the combined efforts of the couple in youth and young adulthood—plus their inheritances—in 50–90 per cent of cases, according to region, fell short of their needs. For such people there was no such thing as self-sufficiency from the land and what mattered was the existence of some ancillary form of income. Progressively throughout the eighteenth century, rural France looked increasingly toward domestic industry as a means of procuring a subsidiary livelihood, and here the earning capacity of both partners, but more especially the woman, was of paramount concern.

[1] A.D. Ille-et-Vilaine L 1002, Mecé.
[2] Braudel and Labrousse (eds.), *Histoire économique et sociale*, pp. 142 ff.
[3] Ibid., p. 139.
[4] H. Sée, *Les Classes rurales en Bretagne du XVIᵉ siècle à la Révolution*, p. 307.
[5] Braudel and Labrousse (eds.), *Histoire économique et sociale*, p. 147.

Dans le rang le plus bas, soit dans les campagnes, soit dans nos villes, les hommes et les femmes sont ensemble occupés à cultiver la terre, à élever les bestiaux, à préparer ou fabriquer les étoffes et des vêtements, à employer leurs forces et leurs talents à secourir et à servir les enfants, les vieillards, les infirmes, les fainéants et les faibles. . . . On ne distingue point parmi eux lequel de l'homme ou de la femme est le maître. Tous les deux le sont . . .[1]

One can reconstruct model family economies according to region and can distinguish four broad types—allowing for plenty of overlapping: a pure agrarian type, which was relatively rare; the mixed agrarian/industrial economy of most of rural France; the purer industrial economies of some towns or cities where the family as a whole was a working unit; and, though much more difficult to classify, the economy of the families of tradesmen or unskilled labourers whose wives might be workers in the garment trades or involved in textile or lace production. Ideally, the rural family as a whole hoped to turn to industry during the dead season or whenever the holding did not occupy its members— and for the woman in the family this could be virtually full time. As spinner in the woollen, cotton, and linen centres, as lacemaker in the Massif, Normandy, and parts of the north-east, as stocking-knitter in Normandy and the Pyrenees, the married woman might hope to earn for her family a sum which rarely exceeded 8 *sous*, which in the poorest areas of the Languedoc woollen industry (the Gévaudan) could fall to under 3 *sous*[2] and which in the lace industry of the Velay—probably the lowest-paid female industry in the whole of France—could fall as low as 2 *sous*, though normally the lacemaker might hope for double that amount.[3] The lace industry offers perhaps the best comments which can be made upon female labour, for its value lay entirely in the handi-work. It was a luxury industry dependent upon the dictates of fashion. It was a female industry right from the spinning of the silk and linen to the finished object. The lacemaker of the Velay was usually a married woman who worked when the holding did

---

[1] Mme de Coicy, *Les Femmes comme il convient de les voir* (Paris, 1785), p. 4.
[2] A.D. Lozère C 62.
[3] A.D. Haute-Loire 501 C 5815, 'Il n'y a point de commerce ni d'autre industrie que celle des femmes et des filles qui travaillent à la dentelle en temps perdu, où elles gagnent un sol ou deux par jour' (1734).

not demand her attention, which, in that bleak mountainous region made yet more infertile by unwise deforestation, soil erosion, harsh winters, and burning summers, was most of the year. The women were desperate for work at any price. The Languedoc woollen industry penetrated no further north than Mende, and the Velay lay away from the silk-spinning regions based on Lyons, Saint-Étienne, and Nîmes. Hence their willingness to work for daily sums of 2 to 5 *sous*. Yet their efforts were essential to the family, and the prospective loss to that family of this pathetic sum, the means to purchase on average two to three pounds of bread in exchange for fifteen to sixteen hours' labour, could cause an *inspecteur des manufactures* to note during a temporary slump: 'cette chute si funeste d'une industrie utile aux campagnes et aux villes et qui n'occupe que les bras les plus faibles . . . menace depuis plusieurs années . . . sa chute serait le malheur d'une population considérable à laquelle un sol ingrat et montagneux . . . ne peut suffire.'[1] The work was subject to considerable market fluctuations, but there were other problems too for the lacemaker. In the Velay she alone often brought money directly into the household and she was usually enmeshed in a web of debt to the lace merchants who advanced money on her labours at highly disadvantageous rates. Indeed, so disproportionate were the relative profits of merchant and lacemaker that churchmen thought laws should be enacted laying down a code of conduct, ensuring that the lacemaker's profits reflected a fair proportion of the selling price.[2] Again, the woollen-stocking industry of the Pyrenees was an exclusively feminine concern financed by travelling merchants.

Il est à observer, qu'à l'exception d'un petit nombre de familles aisées, toutes les femmes et filles de cette partie du département (Cerdagne) ne sont occupées pendant six ou sept mois de l'hiver qu'à tricoter des bas de laine commune. Le marchand fournit la matière première et

---

[1] A.N. F¹² 1430.

[2] The efforts of the bishop of Saint-Flour in this respect were considerable. He wished for legislation so that 'les marchandes seront obligées, au retour du Puy, de dire et déclarer aux ouvrières le prix qu'elles ont reçu de leurs pièces de dentelles et non pas le leur cacher. . . . Les marchandes doivent payer fidèlement les sommes et les prix de leurs dentelles, selon l'argent qu'elles ont touché, ou si elles demandent des denrées, elles doivent les leur vendre au prix courant, et non pas les leur survendre ou les contraindre de prendre les dites denrées au lieu d'argent.' Text published in *Tablettes historiques du Velay* (Le Puy, 1871–2), t. 3, p. 515.

paye la façon des bas, qui coûte, suivant la qualité, de trente à soixante centimes par paire. Ces bas se vendent dans les prix de 40 sols, 50 sols, 3 francs.[1]

A winter's efforts might produce 100 pairs from the full-time worker—a profit perhaps of 50 *livres* to the worker—and to work on this modest scale was attributed the relative prosperity of the Cerdagne in comparison with other Pyrenean regions where primitive communications rendered the establishment of industry impossible.[2]

The lace industry of the Velay and the Cerdagne stocking business are merely two instances of the modest and ill-remunerated female work which was crucial to the existence of the family. One might have lingered upon the pile of spun hemp which represented the most solid capital gain of the Breton small holder's family in the regions of Quintin, Saint-Pol-de-Léon, Morlaix, Landerneau, Rennes, and Vitré or Guérande, Fougères, Locronon, and the Vannetais—areas where the daily sum paid to a male agricultural labourer in the last three decades of the *ancien régime* hung in the region of 4 to 10 *sols* (with bread between $1\frac{1}{2}$ and 2 *sols* per pound).[3] Or one might have chosen the small cotton industry centred upon Saint-Affrique in the Rouergue, which gave, on average, sixty days' work per year at the rate of 7 *sols* to the women of the immediately surrounding villages.[4] With the exception of the enclaves of Auvergne, Périgord, Limousin, Rouergue, and Quercy and the remotest villages of the Gévaudan, Velay, and Vivarais and those of the Alps and the Pyrenees, modest industrial activity of some kind existed everywhere.[5] But outside the main industrial centres of France, concentrated in the north and north-east and upon the Lyons–Saint-Étienne nexus, it did little more than provide either a few weeks' work annually for women and children or, like the lace industry of the Velay, offered unimaginably low rates. Nevertheless, it would be a mistake to write off such activities casually, because they were small scale. The small holder in any region in France could not

[1] A.N. F20 435 Pyrénées-Orientales.
[2] L. Goron, 'Les Migrations saisonnières dans les départements pyrénéens au début du XIXe siècle', *Revue des Pyrénées*, iv (1933), 260.
[3] H. Sée, *Les Classes rurales*, p. 307.
[4] *Journal des voyages en Haute Guyenne de J. F. Henry de Richeprey* (Rodez, 1952), p. 214, Saint-Rome-de-Tarn.
[5] Braudel and Labrousse (eds.), *Histoire économique et sociale*, pp. 236–41.

exist at the most basic level without the industrial efforts of his wife and, perhaps, himself or without finding some alternative source of income to tide him over the idle days, to provide him with a little liquid capital to pay his taxes and meet day-to-day expenses. The pure *journalier* could be yet more dependent, for the odds on securing agricultural work for the entire year were not high.

The edict of 1762 which encouraged the extension of rural weaving and textile production emancipated from guild supervision, may only have given official recognition to a trend already perceptible in the north and the north-east. There, in the region of Rouen, Amiens, and around Lille and Troyes, the balance between industrial and agrarian activity in the towns and villages was radically shifting.[1] From being a *ressource d'appoint*, rural industry became the principal source of revenue and obscured in these regions the basic problem of the small holder with an inadequate holding. This was particularly striking in the *généralité* of Rouen, where ecclesiastics who did not complain of a problem of poverty in the seventies nevertheless expressed concern, and blamed rising agricultural rents upon high industrial wages.

C'est de là qu'est venue l'augmentation des fonds au degré où nous les voyons. Ce commerce qui procurait dans toutes les maisons un travail doux et facile . . . qui les faisait subsister sans peine, a fait la fortune de ceux qui ont été assez avisés pour en tirer parti. Les laboureurs-fermiers ont compté là-dessus dans les engagements qu'ils ont pris avec leurs propriétaires pour leur aider à payer leurs fermages sur le pied de la location actuelle. Pour nous borner à notre paroisse il n'y en a pas un qui puisse y réussir sans ce secours; l'ingratitude du sol provenant de sa qualité qui est universellement pierreuse et à un degré qui n'est pas commun, et de sa situation monticuleuse dont le premier orage enlève toute la superficie, avec nos espérances, nous nécessite plus qu'ailleurs à des frais considérables, soit pour la culture, soit pour les nouveaux engrais qu'il faut substituer à ceux qui se trouvent entraînés, pour y commencer un nouveau fond, frais auxquels nous succomberions absolument sans le produit du coton que nos femmes et nos enfants filent et qui est ce que nous avons de plus assuré.[2]

---

[1] M. Bouloiseau, 'Aspects de la crise cotonnière', p. 406; P. Deyon, 'Le Mouvement de la production textile à Amiens au XVIIIᵉ siècle', *Revue du Nord*, xliv (1962), 201–11; the theme is to be developed in S. H. Johnson's study of Troyes, and I am indebted to him for very generously passing on material on the textile workers.

[2] A.D. Seine-Maritime C 2212, curé of Salmonville-la-Rivière.

The curé was talking of wage rates of 30 *sous* for a weaver, 8 for a spinner, and 4 for a child employed in washing cotton.[1] Around Lille and Troyes and Amiens the same phenomenon of a country-side progressively given over to industrial production was manifest. Here merchants with increasing frequency placed work in the countryside where remuneration was less than in the towns because the worker had in addition some slight income from the land.

If it is difficult to gauge the income of the small holder who was also an industrial worker, still more so is it to generalize upon the income of the rural *journalier*, for often a part of his wage consisted in gleaning rights for his wife and in meals for himself. In Burgundy in 1788 the *États* arrived at a working notion of an annual 100 *livres* (at the same time they suggested that 160 *livres* would sustain a family of two adults and two children);[2] a similar figure was estimated in Seine-et-Oise;[3] in the summer season an agricultural worker in the Auvergne in 1788 could pick up 20 *sous* per day but this in a region where 100 working days to the year was the norm;[4] in Brittany in the eighties the labourer took home up to 10 *sous* for a day's labour and one cannot suppose that his working year stretched beyond 290 days.[5] In towns, very roughly, male spinners, carders, winders, weavers of cheapest cloth, semi-skilled workers in textile printing and iron works might in 1780 aspire to 20 *sous* per day, whilst weavers of dearer cloths, dyers, bleachers, skilled workers in textile printing and iron works, and skilled building workers in the cities might rise to 30 *sous*. A great deal depended on where one was: at Sedan in the east in 1774 almost 40 per cent of textile workers earned under 10 *sous* per day and the rest did not exceed 20 *sous*, whilst in Rouen, Louviers, Elbeuf, Carcassonne, and Lodève, fine cloth workers could get up to 40 *sous*;[6] and before the textile slump

---

[1] A. Lefort, 'Salaires et revenus dans la généralité de Rouen au XVIIIᵉ siècle', *Bull. Soc. d'émulation Seine-Inferieure* (1885–6), p. 219.

[2] P. de Saint-Jacob, *Les Paysans de la Bourgogne*, p. 549, and R. Robin, *La Société française en 1789; Semur-en-Auxois* (Paris, 1970), p. 219.

[3] C. Brunet, *Une Communauté rurale au XVIIIᵉ siècle. Le Plessis-Gassot* (Seine-et-Oise) (Paris, 1964), p. 48.   [4] Poitrineau, *La Vie rurale*, p. 549.

[5] A.D. Ille-et-Vilaine C 1294.

[6] These general rates are given in Braudel and Labrousse (eds.), *Histoire économique et sociale*, pp. 669–70; the high levels for Lyons need modifying against M. Garden, *Lyon*, pp. 304–5, which illustrate the deductions to be made against such a sum.

a compact family economy in Elbeuf of weaver father, spinner mother and daughter could realize a comfortable 50 *sous* per day.[1] Yet shoemakers, tailors, joiners, and masons in small towns, tinsmiths and locksmiths, wheelwrights, and those performing menial services to urban communities might not even hope for a daily 15–20 *sous* or a working year exceeding 290 days.[2] True, these sectors of the community in small towns eked out a precarious livelihood by renting small allotments on the town periphery where vegetables might be grown or a few hens raised.[3] Such a plot was to the urban worker what industry was to the small holder; it permitted him productive employment during periods of enforced idleness. In fact, whether in town or country, the incomes of the poor are composed of too many component elements and imponderables to permit of ready assessment. The possession of a kitchen garden, a few hens or rabbits, miscellaneous rights at stages of the agricultural year could be vital and highly important elements in any individual family's economy. Two factors, however, stand out: the already stressed need for the efforts of each member and the tenuous nature of the entire edifice. What happened if one parent died leaving the other with the support of two or three children? What happened if work dried up for women and children, the plight of the lacemaker confronted with changes in fashion? What happened in sickness, or during debility following childbirth or in old age? What happened in industrial depression when the whole or a part of the family's income was affected, or during an agrarian crisis when the small holder was forced to become a purchaser? Such events were not exceptions to any rule. Everyone in the course of a lifetime could fall sick or grow old and everyone in the last thirty years of the *ancien régime* experienced the effects of bad harvest and mounting prices. The answer to all these questions is that in the event the poor became *indigent*. For even in health and with continued good fortune, the sum of an entire family's efforts might only just sustain the most minimal living standards.

[1] J. Kaplow, *Elbeuf during the Revolutionary Period*, p. 31.

[2] O. H. Hufton, *Bayeux*, p. 81; R. Robin, *Semur*, p. 219; G. Lefebvre, *Les Paysans du Nord*, p. 304, and *Études orléanaises*, vol. ix, pp. 216–19; T. Le Goff, 'Vannes', p. 98, etc.

[3] O. H. Hufton, *Bayeux*, pp. 82–3; R. Robin, *Semur*, p. 219; M. Couturier, *Recherches sur les structures sociales de Châteaudun, 1525–1789* (Paris, 1969), pp. 156–7; J. Kaplow, *Elbeuf*, p. 59.

For the poor the question of how one lived was, above all, a question of how one ate or, more precisely, how much one ate of a restricted range of foodstuffs. Ninety-five per cent and upwards of their diet was cereal, whether this took the form of bread (with the *galette* as a variant) or of some kind of liquid broth or gruel; the predominant constituent elements were rye, barley, oats, buckwheat, maize, or chestnuts; the variations were purely regional. The Breton with his buckwheat *galette* or porridge (*bouillie*) made of the same coarse meal; the Burgundian with bread part-rye, part-oatmeal, supplemented by a *bouillie* of maize in the Bresse and the Saône valley or one of buckwheat in parts of the Morvan—the other parts consuming a rye loaf from which the bran had not been extracted—the Gévaudois again with oat-and-rye bread and his midday barley broth, the peasant farmer of the Périgord with his curious maize loaf or the Auvergnat and Rouergat and Pyrenean of Bellongue restricted for several months of the year to boiled chestnuts do not, with possibly the last group as exception, present a striking range of contrasts.[1] The usual accompaniment was vegetables made into soup: cabbages and turnips, onions, carrots, and greenery from the hedgerows. The soup was sometimes thickened with cereal, old boiled bread, or pearl barley, and sometimes seasoned with a little oil or piece of fat pork in those regions where pigs were kept. If the family had a cow, the milk was used in the preparation of the soup. In fact, milk, an occasional egg, scraping of cheese, a little pork fat, fish on the Breton coast—fresh mackerel in summer, salt cod in winter—and the same salt cod on the Mediterranean littoral were the only protein food the poor ever saw and, fish apart, depended upon the ability of the poor to keep an animal of some kind. Cider or wine, or water in the mountainous regions, accompanied some, if far from all, of the meals. In the Pyrenees, parts of the Rouergue, Forez, and above all the east, Alsace and Lorraine, potatoes had made a feeble and largely unwelcome

---

[1] Regional studies of diet include A. Poitrineau, 'L'Alimentation en Auvergne au XVIIIe siècle', *A.E.S.C.* xvii (1962), 323–31; R. J. Bernard, 'L'Alimentation paysanne en Gévaudan au XVIIIe siècle', *A.E.S.C.* xxiv (1969), 1449–67; P. de Saint-Jacob, *Les Paysans de Bourgogne*, pp. 539–40; M. Chevalier, *Les Pyrénées ariégeoises*, p. 253; E. Le Roy Ladurie, *Les Paysans de Languedoc*, pp. 54–67, etc. Some penetrating comments on the effects of diet on health are given in J. P. Peter, 'Une Enquête de la Société Royale de Médecine 1774–1794. Malades et maladies à la fin du XVIIIe siècle', *A.E.S.C.* xxii (1967), 747, e.g. 'Le pain du Périgord contient deux tiers de maïs, moulu frais qui fermente en farine et donne des aigreurs . . .'.

entry into the diet of the poor[1]—a reluctance understandable if
the form and consistency of the early potato tuber is borne in
mind—whilst in enclaves in Languedoc, Normandy, Dauphiné,
and for a short while parts of the Auvergne, rice appeared as the
cheapest cereal in the urban granaries, only to disappear when, in
the instance of the Auvergne, the water in which the rice was
growing was rightly condemned as a source of fever (malaria).[2]
Innovations in diet were never welcomed; the poor were understandably conservative and reluctant to fall below their meagre
standards, and innovations rarely stood for an improvement in
the quality of the diet. Even when the appetites of the poor were
satisfied, the vitamin and calorie content of their diets was everywhere inadequate.[3] The chestnut eaters of the Auvergne and the
rice villages of Dauphiné perhaps represent the worst levels;
whilst the olive-oil content and the fruit and mixed vegetables of
the diet of Bas Languedoc provided vitamins conspicuously
lacking in the diet of other regions,[4] and in the fifties the diet of
the Languedocian woollen worker (which included both cheese
and salt cod) was probably unsurpassed. This, however, was an
exception, and what is generally clear is that, even if one ate one's
fill, the supply of proteins and vitamins was grossly inadequate and
that rickets, scurvy, and allied deficiency diseases were the normal
lot of families whose stomachs were full and hence were unaware
of hunger pangs. In the Velay and the Vivarais it was possible

---

[1] *L'État du diocèse de Rodez*, Espalion, La Capelle Farcel, Combradet; F. Tomas,
'Problèmes de démographie historique: le Forez au XVIIIᵉ siècle', *Cahiers d'histoire*,
xii (1968), 382–99; M. Morineau, *Les Faux-Semblants*, pp. 165–231, publishes the
Lorraine *enquête* of 1761, which demonstrates the association of a potato diet with
extreme poverty. A.D. Vosges C 391: 'Dans une bonne partie de la province
[Alsace], les pommes de terre fournissent à la subsistance du peuple pendant cinq,
six et même neuf mois de l'année.' At Marlenheim in 1786 the blame for a 'fièvre
putride' was attributed to 'surtout une espèce de pommes de terre blanches et pas
bien mûres', A.M. Strasbourg AA 417/2.

[2] A.D. Puy-de-Dôme, C 1356, Rizières de Thiers, 1741.

[3] This is illustrated with particular vividness by Bernard, 'L'Alimentation en
Gévaudan', pp. 1459–60, and Chevalier, *Les Pyrénées ariégeoises*, p. 671. On general
signs of undernourishment the reports of the Société Royale de Médecine, J. P.
Peter, 'Malades et maladies', p. 748: 'Les filles dans nos pays sont très sujettes aux
pâles couleurs et sont rarement réglées avant l'âge de dix huit, dix neuf et vingt ans.
Elles sont souvent attaquées de fleurs blanches et d'œdèmes aux pieds et aux jambes',
S.R.M. 189, Saint-Maurice-le-Girard, Observations, 1776.

[4] Le Roy Ladurie, *Les Paysans de Languedoc*, p. 67. Diet in this region was observed
to have undergone a marked deterioration in the 1780s. A.D. Hérault C 2226,
Letter from Brûlé, 22 Nov. 1783.

to find entire villages where the inhabitants were crippled or in some way physically distorted;[1] and though Auvergnat and Limousin were rated willing, they were also considered puny workers.[2] These then were the meagre standards which the poor struggled to maintain with progressively less chance of doing so as prices rose, family responsibilities grew, or work potential diminished. Their dilemma can be expressed mathematically. Wage earners in command of the elevated daily wage of 20 *sous*, whether in town or country, at the end of the *ancien régime* needed to spend 88 per cent of their income on providing themselves and their small families with a basic bread ration (with bread at 2 *sous* the pound),[3] and if such mathematical statements are artificial they make it easy to imagine the difficulties of such a person and those who fell below this level. As difficulties grew, anything other than bread was eliminated from the diet and thereafter the bread ration diminished. In the records of the urban *hôpitaux*, institutions designed for the aged, infirm, and orphan children, something of these problems was mirrored. Faced with mounting costs and insufficient revenues, the institutions gradually cut out everything except bread and a small portion of vegetables at midday.[4] But at least here the rations were regular. The same could not be said for the small holder whose grain ran out in the spring, or earlier; who, then, moved on to a series of expedients of roots and vegetables and drew in his belt. The *curés* of the diocese of Rodez described a winter diet of rye and oats increasingly supplemented by chestnuts and vegetables as the bread element gradually dwindled and the lean summer months arrived. If the peasant had the wherewithal to purchase, he might retain the grain element in his diet; otherwise, vegetables and hunger were his lot. To questions seven and eight of the

[1] P. Léon, *Structures économiques et problèmes sociaux du monde rural dans la France du Sud-Est* (Paris, 1966), p. 81.

[2] A.N. F²⁰ 435 Puy-de-Dôme and A.D. Creuse C 360 (1763).

[3] This equation is found in G. Lefebvre, *Études orléanaises*, vol. i, p. 218, and is incorporated into all subsequent socio-economic studies.

[4] Generally, when founded, most *hôpitaux généraux* hoped to give, and many succeeded, one meat meal on the Sabbath and soup in which meat had been cooked (reserving the actual meat for the sick) on weekdays. It is impossible to find an establishment conforming to such high standards at the end of the *ancien régime*. A.D. Calvados C 630, Enquête sur les hôpitaux, O. H. Hufton, *Bayeux*, p. 92; A.D. Côtes du Nord, Hôtel Dieu de Saint-Brieuc A 1752—the year in which all meat was sacrificed; A.D. Corrèze H. Hôpital de Tulle E 78, 79, 80, Situation économique 1750–1773.

inquiry of the seventies, which asked how capable the product of the harvest was of feeding their parishioners all the year round and what happened if it ran out, the answers were slight variants on a single theme.

(vii) Monsieur le curé estime que la récolte faite dans la paroisse n'est pas suffisante car toute la paroisse achète le blé au milieu de l'année et même plusieurs plus tôt, et n'étaient quelques châtaignes et quelque peu de vin, ils seraient la plupart à la mendicité.

(viii) Ils n'ont d'autre ressource que d'emprunter quand ils trouvent ou mourrir de faim. (Testet)

(vii) La récolte d'une année commune peut tout au plus nourrir les paroissiens environ trois mois de l'année.

(viii) Toute la ressource est dans les châtaignes: encore même il n'y en a que peu. (Vialarels)

(vii) Pas suffisant.

(viii) Le vin et les châtaignes étaient autrefois une ressource; mais, depuis le froid excessif de 1766 et la grêle extraordinaire de 1768, elles sont une faible ressource. Ainsi le seul moyen qui leur reste c'est de vendre leurs biens, mendier ou passer ailleurs, de sorte que les vieillards, les femmes et les enfants sont obligés d'endurer la faim. (La Besse)

(vii) La récolte pour nourrir les paroissiens d'une moisson à l'autre n'est suffisante que pour deux tiers de l'année et plus souvent moins.

(viii) Les autres ressources sont les pommes de terre, le jardinage, les aumônes et la souffrance de la faim. (La Capelle Farcel)[1]

This was in normal times; a reduced harvest could see the elimination from the diet of anything of real nutritional value during several months of the year. The mixture of *pain de son* and cabbages during the early seventies was used by poor Breton farmers, victims of excessive damp which had caused the grain to rot while still green.[2] Even worse, the condition of some foodstuffs

---

[1] *L'État du diocèse de Rodez en 1771*, La Besse, La Capelle Farcel.

[2] Between 1769 and 1774 mildewed grain caused by a wet spring and a hot summer appears to have been a recurrent phenomenon in central Brittany and poor farmers were thrown back almost entirely on a vegetable diet: 'plus d'un quart des malheureux va encore être réduit à faire sa principale nourriture de choux bouillis et autres semblables légumes: heureux s'ils n'en manquent point' (A.D. Ille-et-Vilaine C 1404, Subdélégation de Pontivy, where in 1774 there were 2,084 baptisms for 2,364 deaths); 'Les oignons étaient ordinairement une ressource pour cette paroisse dans les années où la récolte des bleds manquait, mais cette année ils ont

during periods of crisis was positively harmful: oats which had mildewed in the damp; grain contaminated by the weevil or *ergoté* (which if it was not a positive killer, and in many cases it was, had possible effects upon the nervous system) could not be disdained, for they were all there was to fill the void in the stomach.[1]

If outright starvation vanished with the seventeenth century, permanent undernourishment was the lot of the poor, and as *pauvre* merged into *indigent* or *nécessiteux*, both the quality and the quantity of food deteriorated. Both *pauvre* and *indigent* knew hunger, but the *indigent* were never free from it.

In comparison with food, housing was not an important priority for the poor and only in the larger cities did rental of a room consume more than 10–20 *livres* annually.[2] The poor family, whether in town or country, dwelt in one room, and degrees of ease were determined more than anything else by the size of the room in proportion to the number of inhabitants. Overcrowding was not a peculiarly urban experience. In the country it was

---

manqué commes les bleds . . .' (A.D. C 1745 Plohinec, Subdélégation de Lorient, 1786); 'Cette année 1770 a été remarquable par la disette et la cherté des grains, qui s'étaient déjà fait sentir les années précédentes. Aussi le peuple s'est vu réduit à retrancher son nécessaire, à ne vivre que de mauvais légumes ou de mauvais grains, ou de grains verts qu'il achetait à bon marché; de là, beaucoup de maladies et par suite des hommes devenus languissants ou qui ont péri par défaut de subsistance' (A.D. Ille-et-Vilaine C 1402).

[1] *Seigle ergoté* was consumed in parts of central Brittany in 1769 and in 1772. 'L'année dernière a été trop pluvieuse; on n'a pas bien pu sécher les blés avant de les ramasser et de les renfermer dans ces grands coffres de bois qui servent de magasin pour cette denrée à tous les habitants de la campagne. Ce bled s'est échauffé, a germé, a pris un goût de moisi; il s'est gâté, il s'est corrompu en grande partie. Les laboureurs ont vendu le meilleur bled, et ont gardé le plus mauvais pour eux dont ils ont fait du pain ou de la farine pour faire de la bouillie' (A.D. Ille-et-Vilaine C 2536). This was the period of virulent epidemics in the province, and how many deaths are to be attributed to *seigle ergoté* is impossible to say. Lysergic acid is contained in the substance. The consumption of *seigle ergoté* in Auvergne in 1772 resulted in what was classified as an 'epidemic' at Saint-Cernin, Drugeac, Saint-Bonnet, Salers, Fontanges, etc.: 'd'abord la tête devient un peu lourde, les membres et tout le corps s'appesantissent; quelquefois les objets paraissent doubles, triples et même sextuples, comme il arriva depuis peu à M. Cabanès, l'aîné, qui voyait six femmes en regardant la sienne' (A.D. Puy-de-Dôme C 1372).

[2] In Rouen a *journalier*'s dwelling cost between 50 and 100 *livres* per year but much subletting occurred, *Histoire de la Normandie*, ed. M. de Bouard (Toulouse, 1970), p. 340; in Lyons, a room could be obtained for 30–100 *livres*, M. Garden, *Lyon*, p. 167; in Nevers, for 30 *livres*, Braudel and Labrousse (eds.), *Histoire économique*, p. 672; in Bayeux, for 10–20 *livres*, A.D. Calvados C 5309, Vingtième de la ville.

common for two or three families to share premises of under twenty square yards. In Auvergnat villages such as Saint-Jean-d'Ollières one-roomed cottages were forced to accommodate twenty or more individuals, and if this is perhaps something of a record, ten to a cottage could be quite common. Sometimes this was the direct result of inheritance where the eldest son, the principal inheritor, was unable to compensate his brothers by providing them with the means to buy or rent separate premises[1] and so was obliged to share his hovel with them—a proximity from which innumerable quarrels could stem. The peasant farmer of Villefranche-de-Rouergue[2] who took a hatchet to his sister-in-law who shared his home, the one of Sarlat who murdered his brother who again dwelt with his family in the same room are merely two instances of this.[3] The poor dwelt huddled together: brothers, sisters, cousins—and perhaps three generations shared the same bed;[4] and only churchmen like the bishop of Rennes found time to worry about incest.[5]

The cottages, in which the poor lived, had solidity only in the regions where stone was readily found, as in the Alps, the Pyrenees, the Gévaudan, or the Auvergne. Elsewhere they were more like shacks, built of rubble and plaster, as in the Nord, the Pays d'Auge, the Périgord, of wood, as in Brie, Berry, or Burgundy, or were earth cabins, as in the miserable Solange and squalid Brittany.[6] The squalor was transmitted down the generations, for the eighteenth-century poor inherited the slums of previous ages. Most of their hovels were thatched. Windows in the country were unglazed and hence infrequent; floors were usually earthen to save the use of wood, and if the initial floors

[1] Goubert, *Beauvais*, pp. 159–60, describes sharing as the norm amongst the rural poor. J. M. Le Quinio, *Élixir du régime féodal autrement dit domaine congéable en Bretagne* (Paris, 1790), p. 61, describes two or three brothers and their wives and children thus sharing as the common practice.

[2] A.D. Aveyron, B. Présidial de Villefranche de Rouergue (unclassified) 1787, Antoine Laguilandie.

[3] A.D. Dordogne, Sénéchaussée de Sarlat B 1737, 1767.

[4] A.D. Ille-et-Vilaine 1 F 2242/2 Fonds Hardouin, L'Hygiène à Dol sous l'ancien régime. A.D. Puy-de-Dôme C 1370, Procès-verbaux de visites.

[5] To have children sharing the bed of adults was a disqualification in the eyes of the bishop for receiving any help from a projected *bureau de charité*. P. Delarue, 'Une Tentative de Monseigneur de Girac pour organiser les bureaux de charité dans le diocèse de Rennes', *Annales de Bretagne*, xxiii (1907), 22.

[6] Lefebvre, *Les Paysans du Nord*, p. 327; Saint-Jacob, *Les Paysans de Bourgogne*, p. 159.

had been wooden the odds on their surviving hard times without being torn up for firewood and sold were slight.[1] The poorest rural houses were single storied; others had an attic in which grain was stored or cellars in which animals or potatoes or other vegetables might be kept. One lived as near as possible to one's livestock—an important consideration, for animal bodies provided heat. In Brittany animals actually shared the family's room; elsewhere they were separated by a slight partition which allowed some animal warmth to penetrate. Firewood was generally expensive or had to be stolen, and what there was of it was needed for cooking purposes. The worst-housed people in France were reputedly the Bretons:

Ces maisons n'ont pas trente pieds de long sur quinze de profondeur; une seule fenêtre de dix-huit pouces de hauteur, leur donne un rayon de lumière; il éclaire un bahu . . . deux coffrets sont établis le long du bahu qui leur sert de table à manger. Des deux côtés d'une vaste cheminée sont placées de grandes armoires sans bâtons, à deux étages, dont la séparation n'est formée que par quelques planches où sont les lits dans lesquels les pères, les mères, les femmes et enfants entrent couchés, car la hauteur de ces étages n'est quelquefois que deux pieds; ils dorment sur la balle d'avoine ou de seigle, sans matelas, sans lits de plumes, sans draps . . .
  Le reste de leurs meubles est composé d'écuelles d'une terre commune, de quelques assiettes d'étain, d'un vaisellier, d'une platine à faire des crêpes, de chaudrons, d'un poêle et de quelques pots à lait. . . . Je n'ai pas parlé du parquet, jamais il n'est carelé, ni boisé, ni pavé; la terre inégale en sert. . . . Imaginez la malpropreté, l'odeur, l'humidité, la boue qui règne dans ces demeures souterraines, l'eau de fumier qui souvent en défend l'entrée, qui presque toujours y pénètre: ajoutez-y la malpropreté, la gâle originelle héréditaire, et des pères et des enfants, la malpropreté d'individus qui ne se baignent, qui ne se lavent jamais . . .[2]

This was not intended as an emotive description: far worse can be found in Dr Bagot's descriptions,[3] and well-travelled Young thought the Breton and Languedoc peasantry were the worst

[1] A.D. Ariège C 233, Letter from the bishop of Pamiers, 24 June 1752, on the Pays de Foix; A.D. Ille-et-Vilaine C 1293, Lorient, 1774.
[2] J. de Cambry, *Voyage dans le Finistère ou état de ce département en 1794 et 1795* (1799), vol. i, pp. 59–60.
[3] A.D. Côtes-du-Nord, ms. 2366. Some of these observations are embodied in H. Sée, 'La Santé publique dans le diocèse de Saint-Brieuc', *Commission des travaux historiques et scientifiques*, viii (1924), 23–35.

housed.[1] Those of the Beauvaisis, Bessin in Normandy, Burgundy, the Pyrenean regions, or the Forez did not, however, rise conspicuously higher, although they perhaps dwelt with less manure. The Breton's proximity to his animals and the pile of dung at the door, to which rotting vegetable stalks were occasionally added, make it easy to understand how typhoid epidemics could prove particularly deadly in this region. In the south the peasantry could live outside in summer, which relieved indoor congestion. Yet of all the rural poor it could be said that overcrowding, lack of ventilation, and unhealthy proximity to livestock (themselves often diseased) were their normal lot.

The adolescent who left his rural home for work as domestic or textile hand in the towns found the physical environment much the same. A master weaver rarely occupied—and that with accommodation for the loom—more than two rooms.[2] A domestic servant could expect to sleep on the kitchen floor, in cupboards or under stairs, or even to share the room of the family of his or her employer.[3] Whole families were crowded into one small foetid room from which light and air in the winter months were rigidly excluded in order to preserve a degree of warmth. In Strasbourg, for example, in certain districts 'le même poêle servait communément à loger deux ou trois familles de manière que 120 pieds carrés de sol étaient quelquefois occupés par dix, douze jusqu'à quinze individus'.[4] This did not distinguish Strasbourg from other cities. In Lyons, where rents were some of the highest in *ancien régime* France, a large room capable of accommodating two silk looms could bring in up to 100 *livres*, small ones perhaps half that amount, and hence families with incomes of 30 *sous* and under per day had little option but to share.[5] The

---

[1] Young, *Travels*, p. 107.

[2] The size of the town would not appear to have been of import, e.g. A.D. Calvados, C 5309, Vingtième de la ville de Bayeux 1782, and Garden, *Lyon*, pp. 166–9.

[3] G. Martin, *Le Tissage du ruban à domicile dans les campagnes du Velay* (Le Puy, 1913), p. 60. A.D. Ille-et-Vilaine 1 F 2242/2 Fonds Hardouin, L'Hygiène à Dol sous l'ancien régime; P. Léon, *Structures économiques et problèmes sociaux . . . dans la France du Sud-Est*, p. 81; Garden, *Lyon*, p. 308.

[4] S.R.M. *Mémoire sur une maladie qui a régné à Schlestatt en l'année 1785 par Lorentz, 1er médecin de l'hôpital de Strasbourg*. S. Dreyer-Roos, *La Population strasbourgeoise sous l'ancien régime* (Strasbourg, 1969), p. 142, on extreme urban overcrowding in the poorest quarters.

[5] Garden, *Lyon*, pp. 166–9, gives 30 square yards (one room) as the living and working space of a family of silk workers.

vingtième lists of small towns—Bayeux, Millau, Semur-en-Auxois, Meulan—tell approximately the same story. For 10 or 12 *livres* per year the families of textile workers, odd-job men, day labourers, and petty tradesmen could find themselves a room in houses shared by others of their kind, the rent payable at Michaelmas or Saint-Jean, the property in the most ramshackle districts where urban authorities would bother least about street-cleaning and policing. Outside the urban slums, as in the country, stood piles of dung and rotting vegetable stalks intended to be used on strips of land rented on the town periphery, or the mouldering heap might be traded for a few *sous*. Manure was always easy to dispose of. Though livestock were forbidden in the streets of Paris and Marseilles, elsewhere, especially in the north, the occasional pig foraged undisturbed; whilst in foetid *garnis* rabbits and hens lived with the occupiers—if the latter could afford such luxuries.

To be poor was to be virtually without worldly goods. A typical *compagnon tisserand* of Troyes in 1776 left his widow a wooden table, five spoons and eight lead forks, six bottles, two dishes and four plates, two beds and four pairs of sheets, and a chest containing wretched clothes. The whole was valued at 140 *livres*.[1] A laundress of Bayeux bequeathed to her relatives, for she was unmarried, a wooden wardrobe, a bed, three old sheets, miscellaneous cloths, an iron and a table, two chairs and a stove in bad condition, two overdresses and aprons and a coat, a knife and fork, a glass bottle, a pair of stockings and a pair of shoes, two handkerchiefs and some hairpins—a legacy valued at 100 *livres*.[2] A *maître fabricant* of Lyons left his widow and child an inheritance of 56 *livres* made up of a table and crockery, bellows and a lamp, two chairs, five spoons and forks, a cupboard, and a bed with sheets. This man was an employer; he employed a *dévideuse* and the widow had debts to acquit to her out of this meagre patrimony.[3] One can readily multiply this sort of example and indeed talk of a 'norm' wherein a bed, a cupboard, a few cooking pots, bed-clothes, shirts and shifts progressively patched and worn constituted the entire assets of a working-class family,

[1] Given by A. Babeau, *Domestiques et artisans d'autrefois* (Paris, 1886), Appendix, pp. 346–7.

[2] Hufton, *Bayeux*, p. 84.

[3] Both Gutton, *La Société et les pauvres*, pp. 37–8, and Garden, *Lyon*, pp. 304–5, report many such cases.

assets which were carefully detailed by the notary along with the *pelle* for the collection of chestnuts, or tools, in the event of an artisan owning his own.[1] The weaving frame of a Languedoc weaver in the 1750s was valued at about 100 *livres*; his other worldly goods rarely exceeded 100 *livres*—the usual bed, table, chest, cooking-pots, and clothes. A lace cushion, marker pins, and lace-bobbins in the lace-making regions might bring in 5–10 *livres*, depending on the number of bobbins. In agrarian communities, the main assets of the poor were animals, varying in species according to region—a cow valued perhaps at about 50 *livres* (a well-fed beast might reach 100 *livres*), a few scraggy sheep at some 15 *livres* apiece, a pig at 20 or 30 *livres* (if it was a sow in reasonable condition), or a few hens.[2] These beasts were not intended for consumption, or at least not for consumption by their owners, apart, perhaps, from some of the cow's milk, the occasional egg, or some of the fat and blood which resulted from the killing of a pig. The butter and cheese, by-products of the cow, the fleece, goat's cheese, and the young of the animals were intended for the market.[3] Fed on common land in spring and summer, sometimes even maintained on weeds that had been gathered at the roadside to make some kind of hay for the winter, often illegally reared on the royal demesne, certainly deprived of salt[4] and sufficient pasture, and, above all, a prey to cattle pest, these scrawny animals were none the less an important element in the economy of the rural poor. To lose a cow through disease or to have to sell it because of debt meant an immediate deterioration in the family diet, by the removal of perhaps the only protein element. It also meant the removal of the only thing worth anything in ready cash which a family possessed. These were powerful reasons, though they were far from the only ones, why animals assumed a sacrosanct character in the eyes of the poor; why, for example, men were prepared to take a whole day off in carrying a chicken to market so as to realize the best possible

[1] There is almost no variation amongst the instances offered by P. de Saint-Jacob, *Les Paysans de Bourgogne*, pp. 627–8, T. Le Goff, 'Vannes', pp. 185–6, C. Geslin, 'Vitré aux XVIIᵉ et XVIIIᵉ siècles' (Diplôme d'Études Supéreures, Rennes, 1962).

[2] Estimates based on haphazard references in wills. The price of livestock was subject to regional variation, and these figures are only intended to convey an approximate idea.

[3] The best expression of this is found in Goubert, *Beauvais*, pp. 160–1.

[4] Frequently salt smugglers claimed that they were so in order to procure the commodity for their livestock. See below, p. 297.

price.[1] In a case of infanticide committed near Sélestat, the culprit, who declared she had killed her child knowing that justice would then put an end to her, was evidently deranged in her deprivation. She demonstrated, however, a fearful logic. At the time of her crime she had in her cottage four hens which, it was pointed out to her, could have been killed and eaten. Yet to do so had not crossed her mind; for after they had been consumed, what then? Her situation would have been what it was at the moment she had killed her child.[2]

Cows, sheep, and pigs were even more than capital assets. They were the only source of manure, the only means of putting anything back into the soil and so of ensuring its continued fertility.[3] The lack of this precious commodity in *ancien régime* France is a common theme. Additional pasture in many areas could only be had at the expense of a bread-crop. Recurrent cattle pest meant the loss of assets which could not readily be replaced. Moreover, debt in time of hardship could mean parting with one's animals. Once a rural family had lost its livestock, it belonged emphatically amongst the ranks of the *indigent*; and the decline in prosperity of communities was often traced by reference to the reduction in numbers of cattle.[4]

The scanty possessions of the poor make readily understandable why most of them lived in a perpetual state of debt—debt necessarily incurred, in the absence of realizable assets, to meet immediately insistent demands. To understand something about debt in eighteenth-century France is to understand something of the nature of poverty, for the road from poverty to indigence usually lay through indebtedness.

In towns, debt could be incurred at any time for two simple purposes, food and rent, and for simple reasons: the inability of the wage to buy enough food, seasonal laying-off of outdoor workers which dried up the money altogether, a textile slump or

---

[1] Young, *Travels*, p. 298.

[2] M. Reisseisen, 'Cas extraordinaire d'infanticide', *Annales de médecine politique de Kopp* (1817), 11e vol.

[3] The people of Ax 'n'élèvent des troupeaux que pour avoir du fient qui sert à l'engrais des terres'; at Saint-Lizier 'le foin qui se ramasse ne suffit pas pour l'entretien de la moitié du bétail qu'il faudrait pour la bonification des terres, et qui, par ce défaut, ne rendent que très peu . . .', Chevalier, *Les Pyrénées*, pp. 267–8, 321. On the general theme, M. Morineau, *Les Faux-Semblants*, pp. 51–2.

[4] A.D. Ille-et-Vilaine C 1748, C 1404, and the Lorraine *enquête* published by Morineau, *Les Faux-Semblants*, pp. 168–231.

an illness in the family which curtailed the earning power of the main earner, and so on. Under such circumstances the poor reacted in a fairly predictable way: if in work, they borrowed against the proceeds of their labour; otherwise, they fell behind in the rent and parted with such meagre possessions as they owned. Low as room rentals undoubtedly were, they none the less placed a real strain on the economy of the urban poor. Often paid quarterly rather than weekly, they demanded the accumulation of a small capital sum. Indebtedness to the landlord was probably the first manifestation of economic strain. One considerable landlord, the hospitals, endowed with quantities of inferior property by elderly people willing to surrender what they possessed in exchange for board and lodging in the *hôpital*, commonly experienced difficulties in getting in their rents, and in any one year up to a tenth of their revenues from this source could be in arrears.[1] Some urban *bureaux de charité* were sometimes prepared to acknowledge that help in paying the rent of a family in difficulties was one of their duties; those of Lyons or Moulins, for example, where funds were fairly substantial and whose registers list innumerable dramas:[2] the *passementier*, 'compagnon chez les autres', father of six of whom three alone were capable of work but unemployed through 'la cessation de leur travail'; the frenzied wife of a sick tailor with two small children, working night and day to deliver her husband's orders but unable to ensure a steady flow; the weaver laid off by slump whose children were already begging their bread—people such as these might put in a petition to the *bureaux* and, provided they had an honest record, a few months' rental might be paid.[3] But such histories evidently relate to the privileged few in privileged towns. The funds of 99 per cent of *bureaux de charité* were not large, and pleas for help in this respect either went unheeded or were never made because of the futility of so doing. The woollen weavers of Vitré near Rennes who asked for a sum of money to pay their rents and to buy bread

---

[1] Certainly this was the fate of the Breton *hospices*, Saint-Brieuc, Morlaix, Quimper, and Rennes, that of Bayeux, and those of Lyons. A.D. Côtes-du-Nord, Hôpital de Saint-Brieuc A 1752, État général des sommes dues à l'hôpital . . . tant d'ancien crédits . . ., 1752, and A.D. Finistère, Hôpital de Morlaix 47 H 246, Revenus certains *1731–68*. Gutton, *La Société et les pauvres*, pp. 67–8.

[2] These are the only two examples found out of over 100 *bureaux de charité*.

[3] Cases from A.M. Moulins 554. (1789–90), Registre des délibérations du bureau de charité établi en la ville de Moulins le 2 décembre 1789.

were subjected to scrutiny by *les Dames de la Charité* who refused
any monetary aid whatsoever as long as the supplicant was the
owner of a bed and cooking-pots.[1] Hence it is often only the
bailiffs' registers that tell the history of the family who fell behind
in the rent and of the moonlight flitters—*ceux qui déménagent à la
cloche de bois.* For example, in Lyons—the best examples are
invariably provided by the city dwellers—Louis Cattin, master
carpenter, had let a third-floor attic room in the rue Luizerne to
Benoît Dupuy, *ouvrier en soie.* The latter had left, three months in
arrears, having stripped the room of such furniture as it contained; a merchant, who had let a room to a street seller in
Sainte-Marie-des-Chaînes when arrears accumulated, put the
bailiff in too late—the room had been cleared.[2] A glazier who
permitted a lavender-seller to fall twelve months in arrears summoned the bailiffs, to find his tenant had sublet and disappeared
with all her effects.[3] The keepers of lodging houses in the capital
and other large cities obviously sustained most losses in this way,
for their tenants could disappear, sometimes taking doors and
floorboards with them, into the impenetrable anonymity of
backstreets. But if this was true of Paris, Lyons, Bordeaux, Strasbourg, or Marseilles, the same could not be said for the small
towns. The woollen weaver of Vitré, the stocking-knitter of
Bayeux, or the ribbon weaver of Saint-Étienne, towns of under
10,000, could not, when the bailiff came to seize whatever
remained to him in the way of personal property, his bed or his
métier, look to the same ready escape into a fresh and unencum-
bered existence. He was known in the town; his credit-worthiness
had vanished; short of leaving the town behind him, there was
little he could do. Probably by the time the bailiff arrived the one
real asset of the textile worker, the *métier*, be it spinning wheel,
weaving frame, whatever, had been pawned. (In which case,
from the landlord's viewpoint, the bailiff's journey had been in
vain.) This pawning of the worker's assets was particularly common during any general crisis in which textile production was
suspended, but even without such a crisis individuals for their
own particular reasons could find themselves forced to part with

---

[1] A.D. Ille-et-Vilaine C 1270, Vitré.
[2] A.D. Rhône B (non classée), Huissier Saint-Maurice, June 1764, cited by
Gutton, *La Société et les pauvres*, p. 67.
[3] A.D. Rhône B, Huissier Tourtier, June 1757.

their *métiers* to raise money. The practice evidently spelt disaster for the family, for it meant that the one means of livelihood had gone. Occasionally *bureaux de charité* gave priority to reproviding workers with equipment they had either pawned or sold.[1] Pawning usually meant realizing a tenth of the value of the equipment, but it could mean substantially less. Hence in Lyons, Claude Gariot and his wife presented their request to the *conseil charitable* for the sum of 15 *livres*: 'ils ont été détruits par la cessation du travail. Leurs métiers et tout leur ménage a resté pour le louage . . . et . . . comme ils n'avaient ni sol ni maille pour s'assister, ils mirent leur rouet en gages chez le nommé Fillion . . . pour six livres'.[2] The same *bureau* accorded Jeanne Barion, a widow, 66 *livres* to buy a *métier à rubans* to be repaid at 3 *livres* per month until the debt had been acquitted.[3] The *bureaux de charité* of Tours, Besançon, and Troyes were all willing to lend money for the redemption of old, or the purchase of new, machinery.[4] They expected, or rather hoped for, repayment of the loan, and such an obligation placed an evident strain on the future finances of the poor. The widow Barion in agreeing to repay at the rate of 3 *livres* per month was parting with the proceeds of four days' labour per month. Less charitable creditors imposed even harsher terms which the textile worker had no alternative but to accept. In short, if he emerged from immediate crisis, recovered from illness, or if prices fell with the new harvest, and so on, he emerged encumbered. He faced the future with debts to discharge: if the next crisis occurred before he had discharged them, then his difficulties were multiplied; one could not legitimately sell or pawn equipment which one did not own. If one did, one's chances of ever borrowing again were not high.

Where the wage earner of the towns also worked a strip of land in the country, he could be in debt at several levels: to the owner of his allotment and to the merchant or manufacturer for whom he worked, to his landlord, and so on.[5] Yet the extent and intricacy of the debt pattern within which he lived in no way

[1] Only urban *bureaux de charité* could even begin to consider such expensive help. See below, pp. 159–63.

[2] A.D. Rhône, 1 G 178, cited by Gutton, *La Société et les pauvres*, p. 68.

[3] A.D. Rhône 1 G 177.

[4] A.D. Indre-et-Loire H 909, Bureau des Aumônes de Tours 1773–4; A.D. Aude C 1151, *Mendicité*, May 1778; P. de Saint-Martin, *La Mendicité à Besançon*, p. 114.

[5] Excellent instances are given by Robin, *Semur*, p. 219.

resembled the complexity of the tangle which enmeshed the small holder.

In the country, debt stalked the small holder and day labourer throughout the agricultural year. The small holder could get into debt for many reasons: when he could not pay his government taxes—the *taille* and *vingtième*—or the seigneurial dues, or the tithes, or, if he did not own his property, when the rent fell due, or if he had to become a purchaser of food.[1] The owner of property could always borrow, using his property as security; he could borrow against the next harvest, hence anticipating his returns.[2] The seasonal migrant could even borrow with the speculative profits of his seasonal work as his surety. Indeed, in the Basse Auvergne the families which seasonal migrants left behind borrowed for their keep throughout as much as six months of every year; when the emigrant returned with the profits of his seasonal labour, he paid his taxes and reimbursed, with interest, what his family had borrowed from the *seigneur* or the *curé* or the local solicitor 'pour des nourritures qu'ils ont faites à leurs femmes et enfants pendant six mois d'absence'.[3] Even the day labourer, hired for the harvest, could anticipate his wages. Often, indeed, he had little option. Emphatically he was a man without reserves; commonly, he could not do without advance payment to feed his family and to meet his obligations.[4]

The period of maximum borrowing in the countryside was the

---

[1] Poitrineau, *La Vie rurale en Basse Auvergne*, pp. 486–9, gives several instances for each of these purposes. A.D. Ille-et-Vilaine C 1293, Machecoul, 1774, C 1747, Quintin, 1786; A.D. Côte-d'Or C 6034, Mirebeau, 1779, where the inhabitants 'ont été obligés de faire des emprunts pour les aider à subsister et à payer les impositions . . .'; Morineau, *Les Faux-Semblants*, pp. 162–231, publishes the Lorraine *enquête*, which makes requent reference to such issues.

[2] M. Couturier, *Recherches sur les structures sociales à Châteaudun*, p. 167, looks at the common plight of the *vigneron* in debt: 'Le revenu tiré de la vigne n'est pas un revenu stable et, sans le crédit des fournisseurs, les vignerons ne pourraient pas vivre. . . . La succession de plusieurs récoltes médiocres conduit à l'accumulation des dettes et à une consolidation ou un règlement. Celui-ci se fait toujours à la même saison, à l'automne, souvent par saisie des fruits sur pied. . . . Ces saisies le [le vigneron] privent souvent de toute ressource pour l'année à venir. . . . Pareille situation est génératrice de nouvelles dettes. Elle évolue normalement vers une cession de la vigne, ou une charge de rente foncière . . .'

[3] A.D. Puy-de-Dôme 4 C 500, Mémoire du comte de Combarel sur la région de Saint-Germain-l'Herm, 1788.

[4] The *recteur* of Josselin in 1786 noted of the *journaliers* of his parish: 'ils demanderaient leur journée pour avoir du pain tout de suite, n'en ayant pas mangé la veille même. Ils en prirent chacun un petit morceau et portèrent le reste à la maison.' A.D. Ille-et-Vilaine C 1386.

early summer—or before, in a year of poor harvests when the grain ran out earlier, whereupon the resourceless small holder had to purchase his food. The period of reckoning was Michaelmas. Once the crops were garnered, the small holder immediately had to put on to the market whatever was needed to meet his obligations. The poor, in short, were condemned to sell their produce at the one period of the year when prices were at their lowest, when there was no shortage of grain in circulation. They were forced to purchase, on the other hand, during the months of scarcity and high prices. Hence the quantities of grain they were obliged to sell to discharge debts were far in excess of amounts actually borrowed and the small holder was never able to profit from rising prices. In autumn of every year the small holder doubtless knew to what extent he would be a borrower over the coming agricultural year. If years of reduced harvest followed in succession, then progressively accumulated debt was likely and the shadow of the bailiff loomed ever nearer.

Debt could in time evidently swamp the small holder, and the amount he owed when subtracted from the proceeds of his harvest could render his situation untenable. At that point, instead of parting with his crop, he entered into arrangements which perpetually encumbered his property. If he was the holder of allodial land he accepted the imposition of a *cens* or *rente* on his property in exchange for a lump sum, or he sold his property to his creditor and received it back against an annual rent, or of course, in the last resort, he parted with it entirely and that often to a creditor able to take the land on very advantageous terms.[1] In Auvergne and Normandy *vente à réméré* or *vente sous condition de rachat* theoretically enabled the debt-stricken peasant to sell with the proviso that if within a specified period (three, five, or seven years) he could repay what he had been paid for the land, then the land might be restored to him.[2] But whilst such stipulations were clearly common, instances of property regained in this way were

---

[1] P. de Saint-Jacob, *Les Paysans de Bourgogne*, pp. 460–1. A.D. Puy-de-Dôme 4 C 33, Pamphlet of 1788, describes children and grandchildren parting with a puny inheritance 'pour retourner aux mêmes ateliers que le grand-père avait conduits. . . . Chaîne perpétuelle . . . facile à prouver par les fréquentes mutations enregistrées dans les contrôles et par le profit qu'en retire la régie . . .'.

[2] Poitrineau, *La Vie rurale en Basse Auvergne*, p. 491; D. Houard, *Dictionnaire analytique historique, étymologique, critique et interprétatif de la coutume de Normandie* (Rouen, 1780), vol. iv.

of the order of 1 per cent. This could lead to the nibbling-away of allodial land, the encumbering of property with *cens* and *rentes*, and the extinction of individual small holders. The peasant could not live without credit and the only form of credit he could command jeopardized his livelihood still more. It is rarely possible to know what was the extent of debt in any community at any time: bailiffs' registers, the account books of attorneys, these tell only a partial story; even the notarial registers, repositories of land transfers, and new impositions of *cens*, are far from comprehensive. A great deal of debt was based on informal agreements. Very often the parish priest was the creditor (one whose power of recovering his money might be slight),[1] and the *cabaretier* allowed credit for drink; these sums go largely unrecorded in a formal sense. The extent of debt would seem to have been at its greatest in the *pays de petite culture*, where the small holder was particularly vulnerable for the obvious reason that such a man had an asset in his land. In the Basse Auvergne in the parish of Saint-Vincent-de-Blanzat, for example, seventy-three out of ninety-nine parishioners had debts in *rentes* which could absorb up to half their incoming harvest.[2] The curés of the diocese of the Comminges defined their poor by reference to the need to contract depth every year. The curé of Anan, a parish of ninety households, estimated about 90 per cent of these to be vulnerable borrowers:

Presque tous les habitants possèdent des fonds, les uns plus, les autres moins; mais la majeure partie n'en possède qu'en petite quantité. ... A l'exception de trois ou quatre familles qui ont du pain à manger, autrement les autres peuvent être mises à la classe des pauvres, car elles sont dans le cas, chaque année, d'être obligées d'emprunter pour gagner le temps de la récolte.[3]

Two kinds of farmer were particularly liable to contract debt: the *métayer*, characteristically a farmer with little or no personal capital, and the small holder, who depended upon the profits of seasonal labour to carry himself and his family through a part of the year. The one, in the event of poor returns, could contract debts to his landlord throughout the term of his lease (five, seven

---

[1] e.g. Sarramon (ed.), *Les Paroisses du diocèse de Comminges*, Melles, p. 409.
[2] B.M. Clermont ms. 625; A.D. Ille-et-Vilaine C 1293, Subdélégation Machecoul, paroisse Saint Philibert 1774.
[3] Sarramon (ed.), *Les Paroisses du diocèse de Comminges*, p. 162.

years) and their repayment was written into the terms of the new lease which became progressively less favourable;[1] the other clearly felt the effects of any shifts in the demand for seasonal employment, and a drying-up of seasonal labour in any one place could have a reverberatory effect throughout the economy of other regions. Thus the crisis in the Languedoc wine industry was acutely felt in the Rouergue, and emigrants who had speculated on their returns came home to debt that they could not repay without encumbering or parting with their property.

Just as it was possible for the town worker to be in debt both to his employer and to the owner of his allotment, so the rural family could contract debts at several levels: to *maître fabricant* in anticipation of his or her labour, to landowner, *seigneur*, and so on. What stands out above everything is that the poor lived continually with debt and in perpetual anticipation of their revenues. Crisis pitch was reached when one could borrow no more and one still had debts to be met. But to reach that point usually took time. Taine's analogy of the peasant as a man walking in a swamp who might at any instant lose his footing and drown suggests an over-hasty process. In difficulty, debts were contracted, property encumbered, animals sold, or a portion of the next harvest was bartered; and so a breathing-space was purchased until the next time difficulty arose. But each time the purchased breathing-space became progressively less. If animals had been parted with, then this took its toll gradually on the manuring of the land and therefore the quality of the next crop: 'avant la cherté, beaucoup de cultivateurs avaient deux bœufs . . . plusieurs vaches ou un troupeau de moutons mais ils ont été obligés de les vendre . . . autrefois, tous les manœuvres avaient un cochon . . . jadis on avait cinq cents moutons dans un petit canton: il reste cinquante à soixante chèvres'.[2] Commonly, too, when land was sacrificed it was pasture-land that went first, for on a diminished holding land

[1] G. Chianéa, *La Condition juridique des terres en Dauphiné* (Paris, 1969), pp. 276–9; Young, *Travels*, p. 297.

[2] A.D. Ille-et-Vilaine C 1404, Subdélégation de Josselin 1774. This is a recurrent theme throughout all the Breton inquiries into poverty in the 1770s and 1780s. 'Sans bestiaux on ne peut faire du fumier, ni travailler la terre, l'agriculture en souffrira considérablement', A.D. Ille-et-Vilaine C 1748; equally pertinent comments are found in the Lorraine *enquête*, parishes of Gérarcourt, Manoncourt, Ville-en-Vermois, Vivier, Loromonzey, Champs, etc. Morineau, *Les Faux-Semblants*, pp. 168, 177, 203, 207. The same issue in the Pyrenees is taken up by M. Chevalier, *Les Pyrénées*, pp. 267–322.

could no longer be spared for pasture.[1] In other words, the process whereby *pauvre* passed to *indigent* was not usually one of speedy strangulation but of gradual oxygen deprivation.

There is a major exception to this rule: the onslaught of disease. Continued physical debility, more than anything else, could push a family over the narrow boundary between poverty and indigence. For if a family in health had to face an endless struggle to make ends meet, the inability to work weighted the stakes so heavily against the family that struggle became progressively meaningless.

Why the poor were particularly prone to disease is evident from the most cursory glance at the inadequacy of their diet and the filth and squalor in which they lived. They were fed on insufficient protein and vitamins, and lived in unventilated rooms to keep warm; they shared their hovels with animals and their droppings; they stored every scrap of rotting vegetable peel, rotting acorns, to use as animal swill, within their homes. Outside the country cottage and the urban slum dwelling stood piles of dung, often leaning against the shack, able to pollute streams and wells. The rural poor never washed; the urban poor rarely did so.[2] They could not afford to change the straw on which they slept very often and they had not the time, inclination, or any alternative covering which would permit them to wash their ragged blankets. Few poor families possessed more than one bed and the entire unit huddled together. One can pick out any regional description of a hovel, its occupants, and the foetid atmosphere in which they lived as typical of the whole country; thus, one for the Gévaudan in the closing years of the *ancien régime*:

Tout couverts de haillons et ayant à peine une couverture de rechange, ils habitent une misérable chaumière entourée de fumiers qui exhalent une odeur insupportable. . . . L'air intérieur de ces réduits obscurs et malsains est à peine renouvelé par l'ouverture d'une ample cheminée d'une porte écrasée et rarement par une petite fenêtre. . . . Souvent un

[1] This was felt particularly hard in regions without, or with insufficient, commons; M. Chevalier, *Les Pyrénées*, pp. 321–2, and A.N. F¹⁰ 503; A.D. Ariège, 13 M 119; Sarramon (ed.), *Les Paroisses du diocèse de Comminges*, p. 280, Soulan. In the rich grain lands of Picardy, Flanders, and the Beauce, there was little or no common grazing; G. Lefebvre, *Études orléanaises*, vol. i, pp. 22–7, and *Les Paysans du Nord*, pp. 289–92, and Braudel and Labrousse (eds.), *Histoire économique*, p. 102.

[2] S.R.M. 184, Poitiers, 1784.

peu de paille couverte d'un lambeau de grosse toile et une couverture de laine leur servent de grabat, sur lequel le vieillard décrépit et l'enfant nouvellement né, la fille et le garçon, le sain et le malade, le mourant et le mort sont souvent confondus.[1]

Under such circumstances the spreading of infection and the general low resistance to it are readily understandable. If the general dying-out of the great protracted grain crises and the virulent accompaniment of bubonic plague had emancipated the poor from pandemics of a disease from which there was virtually no recovery, they remained a prey to lesser diseases, many of them of epidemic nature; typhoid, typhus, smallpox, enteric fevers of all kinds, miliary fever, scarlet fever, and pneumonia were probably the heaviest killers. Indeed, as far as these diseases were concerned, there was possibly no abatement in the eighteenth century.[2] In any locality it was always possible for epidemics to cause an excess of deaths over births in any one year. At Lodève in 1726 and 1751, outbreaks of smallpox pushed up the death-rate by almost 200 per cent; Mende knew three smallpox outbreaks in 1775, 1779, and 1785 which caused deaths to exceed births by 35 per cent. At Pamiers miliary fever in 1782 carried off 600 people.[3] One can multiply such individual examples. In Languedoc, by no means on aggregate a poor province, in any locality there were probably six or seven epidemics in the course of the century;[4] in Alsace, Strasbourg and the large towns would seem to have experienced five between 1745 and 1789;[5] in Normandy and Burgundy between 1751 and 1785 localities would seem to have known four or five.[6] Only in Brittany,

---

[1] Cited by J. P. Peter, 'Malades et maladies', p. 746.

[2] Dupâquier, 'Sur la population française', *R.H.* 240 (1968), 65.

[3] P. Wolff (ed.), *Histoire du Languedoc*, p. 391.

[4] Ibid. The authors of this volume stress concerning population growth: 'le recul est de la mort par carence et non point de la mort par maladie.' R. Dugrand, *Villes et campagnes en Bas Languedoc* (Paris, 1963), p. 433, describes the epidemic diseases that were particularly deadly in the region: smallpox, yellow fever, typhoid (linked to eating fish from polluted rivers), and the malarial outbreaks associated with the *étangs* of the region.

[5] P. Dollinger (ed.), *Histoire de l'Alsace* (Toulouse, 1970), p. 311, and S. Dreyer-Roos, *La Population strasbourgeoise*, p. 218.

[6] M. Bouvet and P. M. Bourdin, *A travers la Normandie des XVIIe et XVIIIe siècles* (Caen, 1965), pp. 292–3; Robin, *Semur*, pp. 115–16, talks of an 'annual return' of epidemics to the area; Lefebvre, *Les Paysans du Nord*, p. 330, suggests that autumn in Flanders was invariably accompanied by typhoid outbreaks. Such examples are easily multiplied: A.D. Puy-de-Dôme C 1355–79, A.D. Côte-d'Or C 69–75.

however, were these sufficient to cause a decline in the population,[1] though generally throughout France disease was certainly the vehicle by which growth was reduced after 1779.[2] The main characteristics of the declining death-rate of the earlier part of the century were in some regions a decline in the rate of infant mortality and a decline in deaths amongst young adults.[3] The picture is far from clear. Moreover, for the most part the medical terminology of the period is rarely easy to decipher: 150 doctors in the last two decades of the *ancien régime* dealt in no less than 128 different forms of fever and half as many forms of dysentery.[4] Some of their vocabulary was probably not mutually intelligible but the doctors had something in common: they were unanimous in attributing much disease to insufficient food and warmth. In the seventies and eighties the government, alarmed by the spread of typhus in certain provinces—Brittany, above all, but also Normandy, Poitou, and the Auvergne—agreed to pay subsidies to doctors and to provide free medicine to those who could not afford it.[5] Most doctors clearly felt that the government was wasting its time unless it was prepared to provide free nourishment as well. Peyrol, surgeon of Pontgibaud, charged with the care of a *fièvre maligne vermineuse*, 'ne trouve pas de meilleur spécifique pour la combattre que la distribution de vivres'.[6] Gaumat, doctor of Clermont, reporting on an outbreak of *fièvre putride*

[1] In the last twenty years of the *ancien régime*, the population of Brittany is estimated to have fallen by 4·5 per cent owing to typhus and enteric conditions which took a heavy toll in central Brittany but left the west coast untouched. J. P. Goubert, 'Le Phénomène épidémique en Bretagne à la fin du XVIIIᵉ siècle (1770–87)', *A.E.S.C.* xxiv (1969), 1562–88, sums up a great deal of earlier work on what are undoubtedly the best documented epidemics of the *ancien régime*. See also A. Dupuy, 'Les Épidémies en Bretagne au XVIIIᵉ siècle', *Annales de Bretagne* (i) (1884), 115–40, and (ii) (1885), 20–49; H. Sée, *Les Classes rurales en Bretagne*, pp. 34–45, and the remarkable *Fonds Hardouin*, A.D. Ille-et-Vilaine I F 2240–8. Some of the work of Paul Hardouin is found in 'L'Épidémie de Plénée-Jugon (1758)', *Mém. soc. hist. et arch. de Bretagne* (1954), pp. 69–80.

[2] Dupâquier, 'Sur la population française . . .', *R.H.* 240 (1968), 59–61.

[3] Ibid., p. 65.

[4] Peter, 'Malades et maladies', pp. 724–6: 'fièvre d' . . . accès, aiguë, automnale, bilieuse, bilieuse inflammatoire, continue, continue aiguë ou continue bilieuse etc., éphémère, exanthématique, intermittente, maligne, putride . . . pourpre, rouge, etc.'

[5] Examples of these essays are found in A.D. Ille-et-Vilaine C 1331–3, A.D. Puy-de-Dôme C 1389–94, A.D. Côte-d'Or C 364. The *pièces annexes* of Bouvet and Bourdin, *A travers la Normandie*, pp. 347–81, contain good medical descriptions of the struggle against epidemic disease in the period.

[6] A.D. Puy-de-Dôme C 1377, Report of the *subdélégation* of Tauves, 1782.

(probably typhoid) in Beaumont, a phenomenon associated also with a late spring, gave as the reasons for the outbreak, in order of importance: insufficient food, unremitting hard labour, insanitary dwellings, filthy mattresses, not enough clean blankets, and an almost total lack of heating.[1] He might have added, as doctors in Brittany invariably did, the practices of the poor with sickness in their midst:

Les gens qui se portent bien ne prennent aucunes précautions pour se garantir de la maladie; ils mangent au même plat, et souvent les restes des aliments dont les malades ont usé; ils boivent dans les mêmes vases, sans les laver; ils couchent avec les malades dans les mêmes lits; ne changent pas la paille de leur lit ainsi souvent qu'elle est gâtée; occupent les lits de ceux qui sont morts de maladie, dès le même jour qu'on a tiré le cadavre, sans prendre aucune précaution pour purifier l'air de ces lits, qui sont fermés de toutes parts comme des coffres.[2]

As long as deaths from epidemic disease were confined to infants and the aged, the community as a whole could emerge unscathed. When an epidemic carried away adults, however, real social dislocation could ensue. The Breton experience of repeated typhus and enteric epidemics between 1758 and 1787 resulted in the kind of social tragedy more readily associated with the seventeenth than the eighteenth century. Land was unsown, agricultural work not finished in time, and family units wrecked by the disappearance of one of the main earners, for the typhus and enteric fever epidemic which struck parts of inland Brittany was one such killer of adults.[3] The Breton experience is largely without

---

[1] A.D. Puy-de-Dôme C 1370, Procès-verbaux de visites. The same message is conveyed by reports on typhus and dysentery outbreaks in Britttany: 'Comme la cause de ces maladies est toujours l'extrême misère à laquelle les habitants sont réduits, ce n'est pas seulement avec des remèdes qu'on pourra se flatter de les guérir; il faudra y joindre des bouillons de viande, etc.' (A.D. Ille-et-Vilaine C 1381); 'Les malades qui ont été attaqués jusqu'ici sont dans la classe des pauvres . . . ce qui prouve qu'elle prend son principe dans la disette et dans les mauvais aliments que les pauvres sont forcés de prendre' (ibid., C 1382).

[2] A.D. Ille-et-Vilaine C 1381; another complained that epidemic grew 'à cause de la mauvaise habitude qu'ont les habitants de nos campagnes de faire coucher les sains avec les malades, de se servir, pour boire et manger les restes des aliments que les malades ont souvent maniés depuis longtemps, portés plusieurs fois à leur bouche et impregnés de leur salive' (ibid., C 1378).

[3] In 1760 at Combourg, Saint-Léger, Meillac, and Vaucouleurs, for example, where some two-thirds of the population were affected: 'Les foins sont dans les prairies (le 11 novembre), les avoines ont été perdues et les seigles ne sont pas encore battus . . . il reste encore plus de la moitié à semer. Nous avons perdu beaucoup de

parallel in the rest of France. Elsewhere there were isolated villages or *bourgs* whose life could be temporarily disrupted, such as Gros Theil in the diocese of Rouen, which was attacked in 1769–71 by an epidemic of miliary fever; the stricken inhabitants, unable to work and needing to buy food, parted with their *métiers*, and therefore the passing of the epidemic did not remove their problems.[1] The disease had similar repercussions in Languedoc, at Villemoustausson in 1767, and at Pamiers in 1782.[2]

One might conjure with a type of map demonstrating the incidence of particular diseases, but one would have to be careful to stress the difficulties arising from the variety and ambiguities of medical terminology. Typhus was clearly at its deadliest in the Breton hinterland; malaria ravaged Dauphiné, the Dombes, the upper reaches of the Loire, and the unhealthy *étangs* along the Mediterranean coast from Narbonne to Marseilles. The incidence of typhoid was perhaps heaviest in these regions and along the valley of the Seine. Both coastal Languedoc and Provence knew outbreaks of yellow fever, probably carried by ships from the Near East.

In an eighteenth-century context, however, epidemic disease for the adult was perhaps less to be feared than the less apparent yet more deadly endemic conditions which were slower to develop and to manifest themselves and which medical science was only beginning to understand. Notwithstanding this ignorance, the reports of the Société Royale de Médecine leave no doubt that tuberculosis was rampant. Flaugères, a doctor of Rodez, noted in June 1784 that the many who reported spitting blood were later prone to heavy sweating.[3] Seasonal labourers, particularly from the Creuse, were held to go to Paris for winter work in a healthy condition and to return weak, racked by coughing, vomiting

chefs de famille et un de nos prêtres.' At Bourseul fever had so weakened even the survivors that 'de là est venue la perte de beaucoup de blés qui ont péri dans les champs. Nous voyons la même chose pour les blés noirs' (A.D. Ille-et-Vilaine C 67, 1760).

[1] A.D. Seine-Maritime G 846: 'Il y eut 700 malades. Certains dans la plus grande détresse mangeaient la paille de leur lit.'

[2] Wolff (ed.), *Histoire du Languedoc*, p. 391.

[3] S.R.M. 148, Report of Flaugères; A. Corvisier, *L'Armée française de la fin du XVIIe siècle au Ministère de Choiseul* (Paris, 1964), vol. ii, p. 665. In 1762 about 9·5 per cent of French soldiers complained of 'crachement de sang' and very probably even at this date the disease was the army's heaviest killer, given that more died from disease than in military combat. Many doctors, however, did not recognize the symptoms, and so one cannot generalize about the incidence of the disease.

blood, and physically debilitated.[1] The *dévideuses de soie*, who descended from the mountains of Bresse, Bugey, and the Forezien hills, also exhibited symptoms compatible with tuberculosis; and the rosy cheeks of the country girl spuriously suggested a health which she did not possess. This disease alone may account for the extraordinary mortality rates found amongst this sector of society.[2] Arthritic joints were the peculiar hazard of the flax worker since he had to work in a damp environment. He was also subject to chest conditions, above all pneumonia, which killed at least 40 per cent of its victims.[3] Other jobs entailed particular health hazards: ruptures and hernias were likeliest to beset the load carrier, the *porte-faix* of the docks, the carriers of sedan chairs, market porters, water carriers, and pedlars. Forge workers were

le plus souvent exposés aux maladies soit par le passage subit du chaud au froid, soit à cause du manque de précautions. En outre des brûlures, des écrasements et des fractures, ils sont exposés aux inflammations des poumons quand ils sont nouveaux et aussi aux rhumatismes quand ils sortent sans être vêtus de chemises de laine.

Glass workers complained of throat disorders, paper workers of respiratory difficulties.[4] There was also *la vue mangée*, the common lot of the cotton- and flax-weaver, who worked in dark cellars, and of the lacemaker. Such a condition led to virtual blindness, whereupon the worker could work no more.

Death or debility, the effects could be the same: the bringing down of the formerly self-sufficient into the ranks of the destitute. Even if the victim recovered, he emerged ensnared in debts incurred during his malady, debts to pay for the food and rent used by his family, perhaps even to call the doctor—though in the country most did not bother. If he or she died, dependants had to try to reconstruct a livelihood and often to acquit debts incurred during the period of sickness. A master weaver of Lyons, potentially capable of earning 40–50 *sols* per day and with

[1] A.N. F²⁰ 434, Creuse.
[2] Garden, *Lyon*, pp. 52 and 53, and J. Rousset, 'Essai de pathologie urbaine. Les causes de morbidité et de mortalité à Lyon aux XVIIᵉ et XVIIIᵉ siècles', *Cahiers d'histoire*, viii (1963), 103.
[3] Peter, 'Malades et maladies', p. 742. Pneumonia could assume epidemic form. It did so in Poitou in June 1784 and again in October 1785; in Burgundy and Normandy in 1784; in the Pyrenees in 1783.
[4] G. Thuillier, *Aspects de l'économie nivernaise au XIXᵉ siècle* (Paris, 1966), p. 67.

capital assets of 600 *livres*, when struck by a fatal malady, left his widow assets which were outweighed by his liabilities to two employees and debts to various suppliers of food and raw materials and to his landlord.[1] Parish priests invariably added as a rider to any comment on the problem of poverty the peculiar plight of the poor when sick and the vulnerability at that juncture even of the self-sufficient:[2]

La plupart sont pauvres et dans leur maladie ils n'ont d'autre secours que celui de la charité.   Crechets, Ilheou, Aveux

La plus grande partie des habitants sont quasi sans fonds. Gens d'eau, de bois, tisserans et peu de commerce. Dès qu'il y a des malades, il faut leur faire la charité.   Ilhet

Il y a au moins 40 familles véritablement pauvres et qui, sans le petit commerce dont j'ai parlé [a woollen industry], seraient au pain quérant. Ainsi quand le dit commerce ne va pas, ces familles sont dans un besoin réel et surtout dans leur maladie.   Mazères-de-Neste

Tous ont des biens. . . . Fort peu sont pauvres, hors le cas de maladie ou de grande disette.   Beyrede

Small wonder that it was at this point that the poor gave up. Doctors were particularly explicit on their lack of will to live once actually smitten with disease; and the problems of the family left behind by the death of one of the main earners will be a recurrent theme in this work.[3]

Debt, disease, deprivation, destitution—the litany which describes the process from poverty to indigence is far from telling the whole story. If, confronted with death, the poor ceased to struggle, the same could not be said of them as long as health remained. They neglected no means whereby they might transform their economy into a viable one, their search for a *ressource d'appoint*. The commonest of these expedients, for the adult, was mobility, based on the expectation, or at least the frail hope, that in some other context a solution existed to their problems.

---

[1] A.D. Rhône B Sénéchaussée, Blaise Chatelu, maître fabricant à Lyon, 3 août 1786.

[2] Sarramon (ed.), *Les Paroisses du diocèse de Comminges*, pp. 113, 252, 254.

[3] S.R.M. 143, no. 6, Mémoire by Lorentz, 1er médecin de l'hôpital de Strasbourg, 1785: 'Je ne vis les plaintes cesser que du moment qu'ils se sentaient malades, parce qu'alors ils espéraient mourir.' A.D. Ille-et-Vilaine C 1365, concerning a typhus outbreak: 'Lorsque le mal attaque quelqu'un, il se résigne à la Providence et les pauvres malheureux ne font quoi que ce soit pour soulager ou guérir.'

III

AN ECONOMY OF MAKESHIFTS

i. *Migrations*

La seule industrie des habitants est de s'expatrier pendant neuf mois de l'année.
(A.D. Puy-de-Dôme C 3150, La Chaise Dieu, 1769)

MOBILITY, the uprooting of oneself from one's native parish in order to move elsewhere in search of a means of livelihood, was a common phenomenon in eighteenth-century France and explains how many families contrived a viable existence.[1] Nor is this intended merely to suggest the simple 'natural' movement by which the town absorbed the excess of the surrounding countryside, an influx which filled the gap left in the town by a mortality rate higher than in the country. The immense contrast in conditions prevailing in different parts of France, the varying demands of widely disparate types of agriculture clearly offered the potentiality for seasonal employment, and, at least theoretically, the demands of one area at the peak period of its agricultural year might be met by labour from another. Poverty certainly put the migrant on the road, but the possibility of a few weeks' work both gave purpose to his journey and determined the direction he took. Hence the emigrant's proceeds, like the remittances

---

[1] The question of mobility under the *ancien régime* is a current preoccupation of French historians, though most of the conclusions are embodied in theses and *communications* which are not readily accessible. A superb synthesis of recent works, without examining details and features of local movements, is found in the introductory essay by J. P. Poussou, 'Les Mouvements migratoires en France et à partir de la France de la fin du XVe siècle au début du XIXe siècle: approches pour une synthèse', *Annales de démographie historique* (1970): *Migrations*, pp. 11–78. M. Poussou's own work in this field—upon the population of Bordeaux, using marriage registers and the death registers of *hôtels Dieu*—e.g. 'Aspects de l'immigration pyrénéenne (Béarn, Bigorre, Comminges, "Ariège") à Bordeaux au milieu et à la fin du XVIIIe siècle', *Bull. société des sciences, lettres et arts de Pau* (1967), is a model of its kind for sensitive and shrewd analysis. These kinds of registers and passports, which were very irregularly taken out, are the historian's only source material for a study of mobility.

crucial to the Irish and southern Italian peasantry today, could buttress a frail regional economy.

Mobility in fact took several forms: the purely seasonal variety in which the migrant left home for a few months of the year; a temporary migration in which the emigrant left for a few years and then returned to his native parish; and finally, permanent displacement, usually of the country dweller in the town. Where one went, for how long, and which members of the family made the move were determined by any number of factors. Something depended upon geography, something upon one's sex, something upon the traditions of one's village, something upon the amount of time at one's disposal and at which time of year the disposable time fell; a great deal depended upon what one was leaving behind—the smallest parcel of land, or the prospect of inheriting such, was sufficient to ensure the return of the migrant. Other considerations might be related to what one was looking for: the type of work, how far one was prepared to travel, the risks one was prepared to take. In addition, something, if not too much, must be allowed for personal whim; not too much, because the basic point of departure for a study of migrations of poor people must be the recognition that the migrant was no Dick Whittington figure lured by a spirit of adventure towards the mythical wealth of some large city. The decision to leave home, even for a short time, was one forced upon the migrant by the impossibility of making a living in his native village and not one taken lightly when the lives of those he left behind might be dependent upon how he made out. Risk-taking was a luxury the migrant could ill afford. Indeed, it is this very conservatism, this persistent clinging to a well-trodden path, which makes it possible to distinguish quite clear patterns of migration and hence to general-ize about the mobility of the eighteenth-century poor.

It should perhaps be stressed from the outset that few of these patterns of movement were new to the eighteenth century. Many existed without extra demographic pressure: there is little remark-able in an interlinked mountain–plain economy. Others, notably the phenomenon of temporary expatriation to parts of Spain, had characterized periods of hardship in France from the late fifteenth century onwards and were merely renewed in this period. The country girl as an urban servant is a figure as old as town life itself. What is new to the eighteenth century is the increasing dependence of communities upon these outward movements and the growth of permanent displacement elsewhere. Moreover, these displacements of people obviously shaped the life of whole villages. They disrupted the pattern of family life in some communities; they had their part to play in determining the breakdown of regular religious worship; they could result in the creation of a problem of poverty in areas without an indigenous problem. In some areas the seasonal migrant was only a few degrees from the vagrant, and the unexpected drying-up of seasonal work could turn him into one. Moreover, patterns of vagrancy conform neatly to patterns of labour migrations. In the cities the immigrant, even if he or she succeeded in finding steady employment, was an uncertain element: the close alliance between urban crime and the uprooted was a fact of which authorities were only too aware, and there are other striking if less dangerous manifestations revealed in the registers of *déclarations de grossesse* or lists of *femmes de mauvaise vie*. In short, perforce, the migrant, male or female, adult or child, seasonal, temporary, or permanent, genuinely in search of work or thinly disguised vagrant, will be a recurrent figure in these pages.

An estimate of 1810,[1] based on very defective information, concluded that seasonal migration was undertaken by some

---

[1] In 1810 the statistics department of the Ministre de l'Intérieur demanded from the prefect of every department a survey of extra-departmental seasonal migration and what this meant in profit to the mother department and a rough approximation of the numbers entering the department for seasonal labour and what they took away. These estimates are found in A.N. F20 434 and 435 and have formed the basis of G. Mauco, *Les Migrations ouvrières en France au début du XIXe siècle* (Paris, 1932), a work which is perhaps somewhat uncritical of the varying worth of different reports and evident lacunae. Their limitations in respect of the Auvergne and the Pyrenees have been examined by P. Arbos, 'Migrations ouvrières en France au début du XIXe siècle', *Revue de géographie alpine*, xx (1932), 61-18, and L. Goron, 'Les Migrations saisonnières dans les départements pyrénéens au début du XIXe siècle', *Revue des Pyrénées*, iv (1933), 230-73. Apart from the general point that the reports allow no appreciation of intra-departmental movement, which was often considerable, or of the international movement into Spain, the main limitation is that the Jura, the Doubs, the Lot, and the Basses Pyrénées, where movement is known from other sources to have been considerable, failed to reply, as did the departments of the Charente, Loir-et-Cher, the Pas-de-Calais, the Seine-Inférieure, the Somme, and the Haute-Vienne, of which the first four are known to have attracted many migrants. In addition, the prefects who did reply founded their estimates on the numbers who applied for passports, and these were generally a mere fraction of the whole, as the prefects themselves admitted. Nevertheless, the reports allow perhaps the best over-all survey and are used as critically as possible in this chapter.

200,000 individuals every year and that the means of livelihood of anything up to a million people was affected. The distribution of migrants was far from evenly spread. On a map of France showing such movements the most useful line of demarcation would be one drawn from Pau to Belfort which would separate two quite distinct areas. The one, a north-westerly sector characterized merely by the short-distance movement, perhaps of country to the nearest town, or even by no movement at all—a cottage-bound France, living and dying within earshot of the same parish bell; the other, to the south-east, a France characterized by its intense mobility, a rootless, restless France where, in sharp contrast to each other, lay regions which condemned their natives to a migrant existence for anything up to nine months of the year and regions which absorbed them and served as poles of attraction to those looking for a living. The great regions of rejection were above all the Massif Central, the Auvergne, the Marche, the Limousin, the Rouergue, the Gévaudan, the Pays de Velay, then the Alps, Dauphiné, Franche-Comté, and the Pyrenees, that is the mountainous regions, each of them a reservoir of men and human suffering. Those of reception were Languedoc, Roussillon, parts of Provence and Aquitaine—in short, the great viticulture region of the Mediterranean and the cities of the Rhône valley, Lyons and Marseilles, and, less significantly, Bordeaux and the Gascon grape harvest. Evidently this was mainly a north-to-south movement and gave rise to the pithy saying 'le français d'oil va en France d'Oc'.[1] But there is an exception to this rule, which is in fact numerically the most considerable movement of all: the movement into Paris and the Île de France. Paris was perhaps not the great wen that eighteenth-century London was; nevertheless, more than any other city—and this included Bordeaux, Marseilles, and Lyons, cities without parallel in Britain—it attracted the poor and the unemployed, the temporary migrant and the permanent expatriate.[2]

[1] E. Le Roy Ladurie, *Les Paysans de Languedoc*, pp. 93, 100. The picture depicted therein is somewhat overdrawn: the cottage-bound France lying to the north of the Pau–Belfort line in fact had its own kind of mobility of a short-distance variety, on which published works are now multiplying, e.g. F. Lebrun, 'Mobilité de la population en Anjou au XVIIIᵉ siècle', *Annales de démographie historique* (1970), pp. 223–7; J. Combes-Monier, 'L'Origine des Versaillais en 1792', ibid., pp. 237–51; A. Chatelain, 'La Brie, terre de passage', *A.E.S.C.* iv (1949), 159–60.

[2] A.N. F²⁰ 435, Seine-et-Marne register some of the heaviest figures for seasonal immigrants: '50 scieurs et charpentiers du Calvados et de l'Orne, 1,380 terrassiers,

The seasonal migrant almost invariably stemmed from the village not the town; he was usually a man of property, a product of the *pays de petite culture*, a wretched small holder whose miserable land was insufficient for the maintenance of his family but which served to tie him to his native village.[1] The purpose of his migrations was to enable him to hold on to his land, and his limited ambition was to be able to feed his family (for the seasonal migrant was typically a married man) and to pay his taxes, or perhaps only to see that his mouth did not consume the food that his holding produced. 'Manger hors de la région', without further gain, was sufficient incentive to make an Auvergnat take to the road for up to nine months of the year.[2] If the migrant was not the head of such a household, then he was the child of such, expecting one day to inherit his patrimony, or was the mother of such a family, whose gleaning rights, or ability to pick fruit, could earn something towards helping the family through the year. The migrant was always poor, a man without reserves, of that every authority was convinced; and nine times out of ten his income from seasonal work was crucial to his existence and that of his family; and a reduced demand for such labour could turn seasonal migrant readily into beggar or permanent expatriate. The migrant in search of seasonal work was also a man in command of very limited skills, and the work he sought fitted very broadly into one of three categories or into an amalgam of the three. Since he himself was a farmer, he sought work in agriculture, as harvester, woodcutter, *défricheur*, *pionnier*, charcoal burner, or *peigneur de chanvre*; he might be a building worker,

maçons et faucheurs de la Haute Vienne, 4,700 scieurs, faucheurs et moissonneurs de l'Aisne, de l'Aube, de la Haute Marne, de la Marne, de la Meuse et de la Côte d'Or; 125 ramoneurs du Cantal, de la Savoie et du Puy-de-Dôme'; and A. Chatelain, 'La Brie, terre de passage', pp. 159–60.

[1] A.N. F[20] 435, Puy-de-Dôme, 'Celle-ci [emigration] est une nécessité car le pays est pauvre et toutes les améliorations possibles de l'agriculture seraient d'une faible ressource pour une population trop pauvre.' M. Dralet, *Descriptions des Pyrénées* (Paris, 1813), vol. ii, p. 188: 'c'est le défaut de moyens d'existence qui les oblige à s'expatrier ainsi. Les terrains en culture produisent à peine assez de grains pour nourrir les habitants des Pyrénées pendant six mois de l'année.'

[2] This is not to say they did not hope for some monetary gain. Priorities are thus outlined by the Prefect of Puy-de-Dôme, A.N. F[20] 435: 'Elle est une source importante de revenus: environ 1,500,000 fr. chaque année. Non seulement elle rapporte les économies des travailleurs, mais pendant six à huit mois, les émigrés nourris à l'extérieur laissent au département des denrées qu'ils y auraient consommées. . . .' In monetary terms the profits of the Massif were the greatest, followed by those of the Alps, Normandy, and the Pyrenees (Mauco, *Les Migrations ouvrières*, pp. 8–9).

tailleur de pierre, terrassier, mason, plasterer, carpenter, thatcher, etc.; he might be some kind of travelling salesman, *colporteur, marchand forain, chaudronnier*—and this type of worker was usually accompanied by child chimney-sweeps. Wherever possible, and if he had any choice in the matter, the migrant looked to a type of agricultural activity to meet his needs, and only when work of this nature could not readily be found, was geographically inconvenient, coincided with the garnering of his own harvest, or did not offer enough to solve the migrant's problems did he turn to other activities. When the migrant looked outside agrarian pursuits to meet his needs, he entered an intermediary stage—he was on the eve of making a permanent breach with his village: his activities might defer that event, but his sons or his grandsons would have to make it. Of the regions described as regions of 'rejection', parts of the Pyrenees, the Alps, and the southern Massif, the Gévaudan, Pays de Velay, Vivarais, Cevennes, and the Rouergue had a classic type of annual exodus in search of seasonal work. Dralet in his *Description des Pyrénées* neatly defined the interlinked mountain–plain economy of the Pyrenees:

. . . les terres y sont successivement semées, savoir: au printemps, de pommes de terre, de maïs, de foin rouge, de petit millet, de blé printanier, appelé tremezou, de haricots et d'une petite quantité de pois et de lentilles; et en automne, de seigle, d'orge, de froment, d'avoine, de fèves et de lin . . .

Il conviendrait d'assigner les époques auxquelles on les ensemence et où l'on fait chaque genre de récoltes; mais ces époques varient suivant les hauteurs et les expositions. Nous nous bornerons à dire que les hivers commençant plus tôt et finissant plus tard dans les montagnes que dans les plaines, les semences du printemps sont plus retardées, et que celles d'automne doivent être plus accélerées à mesure que les terrains s'élevent au-dessus des plaines. Quant aux récoltes, elles se font de huit à quinze jours plus tard dans les vallées que dans les pays plats, et elles sont retardées de plus d'un mois dans les hautes montagnes; c'est ainsi que j'ai vu les orges encore verts à Gavernie à la fin du mois d'août, tandis qu'ils étaient cueillis dans le département du Gers, depuis le commencement de juillet.

Un coup d'œil suffit quelquefois pour observer ces différences. En suivant la route de Lourdes à Pierrefitte, on voit, à l'entrée de la Vallée d'Argelez, une montagne cultivée depuis sa base jusqu'à son extrême sommet, dont l'élévation est très considérable. Vers la fin de juillet, l'épi de froment a acquis une maturité parfaite au bas de

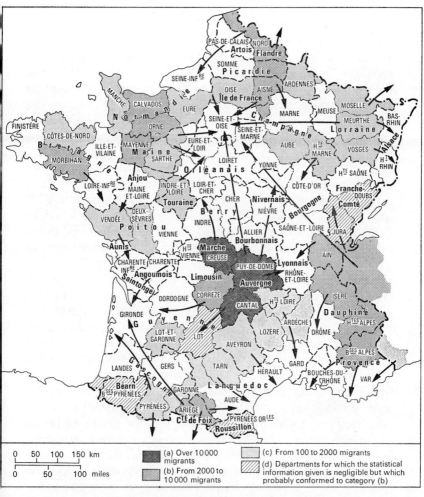

MAP I

The incidence of seasonal migration in France in 1810[1]

cette montagne; un peu plus haut, il commence à se dorer; plus haut
encore, à peine est-il développé. Enfin la récolte est encore verte, et
sa couleur s'affaiblit insensiblement, jusqu'au point où les nuages
dérobent à la vue les pommes de terre qui couronnent cette échelle
de végétation. (Vol. ii, pp. 224–7.)

[1] A.N. F20 434–5.

Migration began from the high mountain villages in spring with the melting of the snow, and the first to leave were those hoping to be taken on for the first hay harvest of the plain. Journeys of up to a week might obtain work lasting up to a fortnight. The migrant lingered on the plain, perhaps unemployed for a couple of weeks and not hesitating to make ends meet by a little begging, until mid June brought the earliest harvests and the haymaker became harvester proper, and by successive jobs, usually on a fortnightly basis and at increasingly high altitudes, he gradually made his way home to his own crops. The hay harvest of the highest mountain villages was usually scanty enough to be gathered by women and children, and the head of the household was usually back by early September for his own grain crops and his potatoes—planted before he left. The harvesting bands of the Pyrenean villages were organized in the villages: the bands, which consisted of about a dozen men of various ages and strength, were engaged as an entity. Remunerative payment was so slight as to be non-existent: at most, the efforts of these months paid the taxes and perhaps would afford a fortnight's sustenance for the family or keep it clothed, but these migrations had two enormous advantages. First, from May to September the adult males of the villages had eaten away from home, and this at the period of maximum pressure, when the old harvest was running out and the new had yet to be garnered. Moreover, on the cereal harvests he had eaten very well, for he made a condition of his employment seven meals per day: two with meat, two with vegetables, and the rest snacks of bread, garlic, and water—or wine if he was very fortunate. For perhaps about a month of the year meat had entered his diet. Though the migrant worked from dawn to dusk, the harvesting period was looked upon as a period of ease when one ate more and better than at any other time of the year. The second advantage was also considerable: the migrant made it a condition of his employment that for one of the harvests for which he was engaged his wife should be given gleaning rights, rights which only women could hold. The group seems to have taken it in turns in successive employments for the wives of some of its members to have these rights. The proceeds accruing were indeed high: a woman could hope to accumulate as much as a hectolitre of grain, and this was grain of a distinctly superior quality to anything grown at home. Profit did not end here because, in addition to this prize to carry home, the gleaner was accorded the right to beg her food in the district while the harvesters proper completed their work in the fields. Hence she too had managed to feed herself independently of the family holding during a difficult period.

The grain harvests over, and the potatoes lifted, some villages reorganized themselves so that the inhabitants looked towards the next harvests that would demand casual labour, that is, the grape and olive harvests. Here the eastern sector of the Pyrenees was particularly favoured because, although Bordeaux and the basin of Aquitaine were not far from the western Pyrenees and certainly offered opportunities to the casual worker, the date of the grape harvest does not seem to have afforded sufficient leeway to the small proprietor of the Hautes- and Basses-Pyrénées to get in his own crops and to arrive there for the harvest. The grape harvests of Roussillon and the plain of Languedoc, however, were of crucial significance to the economy of the eastern Pyrenees, or, more precisely, the departments of the Pyrénées-Orientales, the Aude, and the Ariège. The Mediterranean littoral, the heaviest wine producer of the country, then as now, offered work for three weeks to a month to the seasonal migrant. Time was a very relevant factor. The Pyrenean migrant is not found north of Narbonne, and whole villages in the western Ariège and the Haute-Garonne were unable to participate simply because they would have arrived a few days late. The work was long, remuneration was slight, and the harvesters were not well fed (though they were allowed to eat as many grapes as they pleased), and there was nothing in kind which could be saved and carried home to eke out the family rations throughout the winter. Nevertheless, the work was eagerly sought as an important adjunct to the year's income. Finally, if one was fortunate, one might find work on the olive harvest. This was indeed the privilege of the favoured few. Beginning in early October, work was available throughout the month, but to how many it is difficult to estimate, since preference was accorded to those of the immediate mountain range falling within the department of the Pyrénées-Orientales—only some 300 are stated to originate from without, and the proceeds, particularly valuable, ensured that competition for such work was very high. Again, monetary remuneration was low, but the worker was rewarded at the end of the month with a small cask of olive-oil to take back to his village; and this formed an important part of the winter diet of the mountain family. Whether the olive gatherer of the late autumn became the olive-oil worker of December and January is not clear, but there is a distinct correlation between the figures given for the two processes: several thousands within the department were thus engaged and between 300 and 500 from without. Outside the Pyrénées-Orientales, however, the industry evidently offered little scope to those who needed winter work.

In November the villages would seem to have organized themselves anew for a second batch of departures. In numerical terms the winter movement was much slighter than that of the summer, a reflection of the fact that winter work away from home was only the recourse of those for whom the proceeds of the summer had proved inadequate, and in particular those who had not enjoyed the work of September in the vineyards of the Mediterranean. Predominant amongst these migrants were the *pionniers* or *terrassiers* or *baradiers,* those who cut new terraces or repaired old, knew how to prune vines and clear away dead wood, and who originated in the mountains of the Haute-Garonne, the Ariège, and the Hautes-Pyrénées, and who sought this work on either the Mediterranean littoral or the plain of Aquitaine. The numbers who sought work on the Mediterranean littoral are not recorded, but the movement was regarded as distinctly greater than the movement to Aquitaine, which attracted over 1,000 workers from the Hautes-Pyrénées alone. The *pionniers* returned in March or April for a few weeks' work on their own property before beginning the summer ritual of movement to the plain. Subsidiary winter movements of woodcutters took place from the Ariège into Andorra and the territories of the bishop of Urgel, but these were relatively slight and embraced hundreds rather than thousands of workmen.[1] Not every region of the Pyrenees could achieve an integrated economy of this nature; the particular problems of Castillon and the Comminges will presently be considered as well as the definitive movement out of the Basque country into Bordeaux. Nevertheless, Dralet was insistent

[1] Conclusions based on A.N. F²⁰ 434 and F²⁰ 435, and Goron, 'Migrations dans les départements pyrénéens', pp. 236–8. Goron estimates that Pyrenean migrants perhaps constituted as much as a fifteenth of those of France as a whole. The estimate is perhaps inaccurate since, though he criticizes Mauco's figures in respect of the Pyrenees, he accepts those for the whole of France.

that at least a sixth of all householders sought thus to support their families.[1]

The movement out of the southern Massif to the Mediterranean littoral was essentially of the same type as that out of the Pyrenees, though the numbers involved were probably much greater. The grape harvest of the plain of Languedoc was the weightiest in the country; the bulk of the work fell in summer when a lot of unskilled hands were needed for picking grapes, and there was also some potential for the employment of more skilled hands in March when the vines needed pruning.[2] There was also the important mulberry and silkworm industry. The traditional pruner of the vines was the male Rouergat, who then returned to garner his own crops; the harvester who arrived in September, the same Rouergat but accompanied by his wife and children, or the Gévaudois, who left his wife and children behind to keep an eye on the holding and to pick up the chestnuts as they fell, one by one, to the ground.[3] The women returned within the month to their homes, but the men lingered, the Rouergat in the hope of being retained for the clearing up of the vineyards and the burning of deadwood, after which he made a leisurely journey home, stopping *en route* to offer his services as a mender of dry-stone walls;[4] the Gévaudois remained in Montpellier, Agde, and Béziers as a *porteur des chaises* during the winter months.[5] Usually the migrants had permanent arrangements with the owners of vineyards, and they were certainly allowed to beg undisturbed by the *maréchaussée* until they reached the end of their journey.[6] The

[1] Dralet, *Descriptions des Pyrénées*, vol. ii, p. 188.

[2] A.N. F20 434, 'L'Aveyron fournit annuellement environ 2,000 ouvriers dont: 50 faucheurs en mai–juin vers l'Hérault et le Gard, 1,000 moissonneurs, en juin–juillet vers l'Hérault, le Gard . . . 500 scieurs de long vers l'Hérault, le Gard, les Pyrénées Orientales et l'Espagne en septembre . . .'; F20 435, 'Lozère — Le département fournit 200 moissonneurs et terrassiers de l'arrondissement de Marvejols au Gard et à l'Hérault, 200 travailleurs de l'arrondissement de Mende au Gard et à l'Hérault pour l'industrie du ver à soie, la culture de la vigne et le ramassage des châtaignes. 1,363 travailleurs de l'arrondissement de Florac au Gard, à l'Hérault, à l'Ardèche, au Vaucluse, aux Bouches du Rhône, à la Drôme et au Var pour la fenaison, la moisson et l'industrie du ver à soie.' [3] A.D. Lozère C 62.

[4] H. Affre, *Dictionnaire des institutions, mœurs et coutumes du Rouergue* (Rodez, 1903), article 'Émigration'.

[5] E. Le Roy Ladurie, *Les Paysans de Languedoc*, p. 101, and A. Peloux, 'Étude économique et sociale d'Agde au XVIIIe siècle' (Diplôme d'Études Supérieures, Montpellier, 1965).

[6] A.D. Hérault C 562. The *intendant* of Languedoc insisted in 1767 that the *maréchaussée* continue to permit them so to do.

movement toward the grape harvest was the central one, but there were also subsidiary movements into Bas Languedoc from the mountains in the early summer to work on the precocious grain harvest, while from the Vivarais in the early autumn issued a string of *peigneurs de chanvre* to work on the newly garnered flax crop of the foothills of the Cevennes.[1]

One can repeat the Pyrenean and Languedoc pattern in respect of the mountain dwellers of the Alps who in some cases poured out in the spring with the melting of the snow, directing their steps towards the hay harvest of the Rhône valley or, more probably, left in the autumn, before the snow fell, to serve as *peigneurs de chanvre* on the plain or as terrace cutters and repairers in Provence. A few qualifications are perhaps needed to stress certain regional peculiarities: the Alpine *peigneur de chanvre*, for example, was not so much a small holder as a labourer whose terms of employ insisted that he seek this work during the winter months when he was of no use to his employer.[2] Moreover, the Alps had enclaves whose economy is comparable with that of the Comminges and, even more strikingly, of the Auvergne: in the cities of the north and centre, the Auvergnat and Savoyard were confounded in the popular mind, for they immediately conjured up the idea of a carrier of water or coal, a chimney-sweep (known as a Savoyard irrespective of origin), a navvy or bricklayer's mate, a stonemason (the verb *limousiner* was employed to describe these activities).[3] In Bordeaux and some of the Spanish cities, the Auvergnat, the Béarnais, and the migrant from the Comminges together vied for these fringe trades and only the Béarnais enjoyed any separate recognition.[4]

---

[1] P. Marrès, 'L'immigration en Bas Languedoc sous l'ancien régime', *Congrès d'études occitanes de Montpellier* (1962).

[2] A. Chatelain, 'L'Émigration temporaire des peigneurs du chanvre du Jura méridional avant les transformations des XIXᵉ et XXᵉ siècles', *Les Études rhoda-niennes*, xxi (1946), pp. 166–78. The practice was known as *retenir son peigne*.

[3] Jèze, *État ou tableau de la ville de Paris* (Paris, 1760), p. 335.

[4] Auvergnat movements have perhaps justifiably received more attention than any others: A. Poitrineau, 'Aspects de l'émigration temporaire et saisonnière en Auvergne à la fin du XVIIIᵉ siècle et au début du XIXᵉ siècle', *R.H.M.C.* xix (1961), 2–41; S. Delaspre, 'L'Émigration temporaire en Basse Auvergne au XVIIIᵉ siècle jusqu'à la veille de la Révolution', *Revue d'Auvergne*, lxviii (1954), 2–5; A. Chatelain, 'Un Aspect de la vie rurale au XVIIIᵉ siècle: les migrants temporaires auvergnats', *A.E.S.C.* (1955), 36–7; and the earlier though hardly surpassed M. Juillard, 'Les Émigrants dans les montagnes d'Auvergne au XVIIIᵉ siècle', *Bulletin historique et scientifique d'Auvergne*, xliv (1924), 119–39.

Of these movements of pedlars and odd-job men, that from the Basse Auvergne was the most considerable. Indeed, the estimates of 1810, which calculated the exodus from the Massif Central as furnishing a quarter of all French migrants, rated the Puy-de-Dôme and the Creuse as the most mobile departments of France, each with some 15,000 migrants annually—figures which were said to be based on the numbers of passports issued and which were therefore a chronic understatement of the true extent. The movement from the Basse Auvergne was again a movement from hill to plain, but not the immediate plain, which could not under any circumstances absorb the migrant in search of work. The region felt in a peculiarly profound manner the problem of the small holder: his own land demanded his efforts at the one period of the agricultural year when he could have found employment at home as a day labourer for a relatively high wage and forced him to look outside his holding for work during the protracted dead season which ran from November to April, and though a little work was sometimes forthcoming in the adjacent valleys, where the harvests were more precocious, the region was not, in the main, one of contrasting crops or even of markedly contrasting altitudes. Thus geography made the migrant of the Basse Auvergne look further afield for a period of at least five, more commonly six or seven, and, in some instances, nine or eleven months of the year. The longest absences from home were indicative of increasing difficulties in making a living at or near home. He who spent only a month or two of the year in his native village was almost an expatriate.

The migrant of the Basse Auvergne originated in the hills of the Forez or the Livradois, the plateaux of Couzes and Allagnon, the Monts Dores, the Dômes, and the Cézallier. The particular job he chose and where he chose to practise it would appear to have depended upon the traditions of his village, for whole areas gave themselves over to particular pursuits to which the migrant at least theoretically adhered.[1] Woodcutters, for example, came from the Forez and the Livradois, the *subdélégation* of Lempdes, and the region of the Monts Dores, Combraille, and the plateau of the north-west. They left in September and returned in June and made above all for the ports of the west of France or for

[1] Poitrineau, 'Aspects de l'émigration', p. 2, affords a map showing regional specialities.

the Marne, Burgundy, Champagne, Berry, and the Bourbonnais, the Atlantic coast, and even the Channel ports. Those from Combraille went to Lyons, Saint-Étienne, and the Bourbonnais. Each village made its choice and apparently clung to it. The villagers of Single and Tauves left in groups of three for Bordeaux; those of Saint-Jean-d'Ollières in groups of four to five for the ports of Brittany, and so on. Terrace cutters and repairers were particularly numerous in the region of Vieille Brioude and Saint-Martin-d'Ollières. They left in the late autumn and returned with the spring. Theirs was essentially winter work which had to be done when the vegetation was less dense, and they made for Grenoble and Provence. The terrace cutter travelled alone, for he expected to be taken on singly not as a member of a team; he did not expect a rich employer but a relatively humble one interested in a little extra help when the climate favoured the clearing of marginal land. Hence to travel in a group was a positive disadvantage. Then there were the combers of hemp who came particularly from the plateau of the south-west, the area immediately adjacent to the village of Saint-Jean-d'Ollières. Sometimes, as at Égliseneuve-sur-Billom, the woodcutter also offered to do this work and left his village, ready to turn to hemp combing if he could not find work as a woodcutter. The flax comber made for Berry and the Maine, where a lot of flax was cultivated, and to Orleans, which was particularly promising because of the rope manufacture on the one hand and the repairing of jetties on the other. The Auvergnat flax comber fought shy of travelling east, for there he might come into competition with the comber from the Jura and was less likely to secure employment than the latter who had traditional links with the east.[1]

The masons stemmed from the west of the province and sought work in the cities of the north and east, in Paris, Rouen, Lyons, and Grenoble, and very occasionally they moved westwards to the Atlantic ports. They left in March and returned in December, leaving the work of the fields to other members of the family; they were usually single men. Then there were the child chimney-sweeps drawn from the mountains of Besse, the region of Ardes, and the *pays coupés*, hired out by their parents to *chefs* who paid the parents a fixed sum in advance and then required of the children a certain amount of money from their activities each day.

[1] A.D. Puy-de-Dôme C 101, and Delaspre, 'L'Émigration temporaire', p. 29.

This was a movement beginning in December and ending in spring. Sometimes the *chef* of the chimney-sweeping bands was a pedlar; sometimes the little sweeps themselves were minor pedlars of pins and needles, the product of the steel industry of Thiers, *leur métier une mendicité déguisée*.[1] Peddling under one guise or another was in fact the industry of several Auvergnat villages and the largest number of those seeking passports gave this as their occupation. They peddled anything that could possibly be sold, pins, needles, laces, combs, lace-bobbins, rabbit skins and mole pelts, brooms, patent medicines and concoctions ranging from purgatives and yellow powders to terminate a pregnancy to rat poison, and, if their wares were unwanted, they offered a few basic services as pot repairers, clog menders, menders of rush-bottomed chairs, or used their voluminous smocks for the catching of rats. The Auvergnat had few talents as an entertainer but the bands of pedlars usually took with them a handy portable animal, a marmot or a ferret, which meant they could turn a few *liards* as showmen or rat-catchers.[2] In this respect the Savoyard pedlar was more inventive. The 3,000 Alpine *colporteurs* who left home every October from the age of about 15, supplied Paris, Lyons, and the cities of Normandy and the east not only with haberdashery but with entertainment of one kind or another. They were travelling musicians, organ-grinders, fiddlers, *joueurs de la veille*, conjurers, fortune-tellers, displayers of curiosities, relics, or extraordinary animals, and, if all else failed, story-tellers.[3] The nearest that the Auvergnat ever came to this creative activity was the practice known as *la pique*.[4]

La pique was a hard-luck story of the most spectacular variety, written down and signed by a figure of authority, usually a parish priest, which was then carried by an individual, the *dramatis persona* of the *pique*, throughout the more affluent areas of France and was presented at doors in the hope of raising a little money.

---

[1] Delaspre, p. 32.

[2] A.D. Puy-de-Dôme C 1267, 1784: 'un individu natif de La Chapelle à huit heures de Clermont, mercier, porte-balle autrefois, actuellement ramoneur, rouleur dans la campagne avec un petit garçon . . . il vend des peaux de lapins, il fait voir une marmotte'. See also O. H. Hufton, 'Begging, Vagrancy, Vagabondage and the Law: an Aspect of the Problem of Poverty in Eighteenth-Century France', *European Studies Review*, 2 (1972), 102–3.

[3] A.N. F20 435, Seine, and C. R. Muller and A. Allix, 'Un Type d'émigration alpine. Les Colporteurs de l'Oisans', *Revue de géographie alpine* (1923), pp. 583–634.

[4] A. Achard, 'La Pique', *Revue d'Auvergne* (1916), and A.N. F20 435, Puy-de-Dôme.

Although the practice was never actually declared illegal, authorities were unlikely to give a passport to an individual who left with this purpose alone. Many pedlars carried such a document on their persons to help them out if trade proved slack. *La pique* was in fact a highly developed regional industry. The yarns were said to contain everything—fire above all, cattle pest, theft, and oppressions of every kind. There existed professional *pique* writers (old women were said to be the best), scribes who copied them down, and forgers of signatures. All these received at least a cut from the proceeds of the *pique* carrier.[1] At Tours in January 1771, two carriers of a *pique* from Saint-Jean-d'Ollières were arrested in the possession of a false story about an imaginary fire to which the curé of Saint-Jean-d'Ollières had appended his signature.[2] The latter did not deny the charge. He recognized that without a gilded, if artificial, tale his parishioner would make little from his odysseys and that upon these wanderings depended the livelihood of a family. The closer one looks at the *colporteurs*, whether those of the Massif, the Alps, or the Pyrenees (the latter were specialists in horn combs, woollen stockings, and quack medicines), one thing stands out above all others: they did not expect to make a gainful livelihood from their trays or packs. They lived by their wits and often they were merely more elevated and thinly disguised beggars. Often the Auvergnat pedlars were accompanied by young children, or someone who was crippled or deformed; the latter lent an added pressure to persuade the public to purchase the pedlar's goods, and if trade was slack a begging cripple could usually raise a crust or two. In the name of his numerous family or his crippled son, too weak to make a living, the pedlar beggar made a doubly cogent appeal, and it mattered little that the individuals he presented as specimens were not really his relatives. His pack and its contents, the *pique* letter in his pocket, and the chimney-sweep's brushes which gave him the appearance of usefulness and created an impression

[1] A.N. F²⁰ 435, Puy-de-Dôme: 'Ces émigrants partent sans métier défini, parcourent la France comme mendiants, "incendiés", munis de faux-papiers, porteurs de chapelets, diseurs de bonne aventure, etc. . . . C'est ce qu'ils appellent dans leur argot "aller à la pique". . . . Les profits des piqueurs seraient énormes s'ils n'étaient obligés de les partager avec ceux qui les prennent sur le fait . . .'

[2] A.D. Puy-de-Dôme C 1122, le 7 janvier 1771. Perforce 'la pique soit considérée dans la région comme une industrie parfaitement licite et honorable pour expliquer l'inépuisable complaisance des autorités locales à l'égard des mendiants professionnels'. A.D. Puy-de-Dôme C 1165, le 20 mai 1778.

of industry, which ensured a kind reception and deceived the authorities into conceding him a passport—these were the necessary actor's props which permitted the small holder of the Massif, the Alps, and the Pyrenees to make a living where one would have imagined no living possible.

One can thus reconstruct the life of villages where 'la seule industrie des habitants est de s'expatrier pour quelques mois de l'année'. At Saint-Jean-d'Ollières there were 270 households, making a population of 1,190 adults and 810 children under the age of 14. On 1 October of every year 200 adult males left to cut wood; they returned nine months later for two weeks' work on their own harvest before heading south for three weeks' work on the olive harvest of Provence. Two hundred other men and 100 children under 14 left on 1 November, intending to return at Easter to comb hemp in the Berry; if they could not find work they made for Paris as odd-job workers and beggars because at all costs they must not return until Easter, for there were no resources at home to feed them. After Easter and *la première culture de leurs terres*, this group moved off to Provence to pick mulberry leaves for the silkworms, and this kept them occupied, albeit spasmodically, until the early autumn. Three hundred children left the village annually as sweeps, and the number of pedlars and *pique*-carriers who left defies enumeration. The aged did the sowing of the crops, and even they were expected, if their legs would carry them, to beg during the winter in Lyons and Clermont. Only women and young children spent any time at home, and some of these made for the Limagne in the late summer to exercise gleaning rights.[1] Equally complex were the movements from the canton of Castillon[2] in the Pyrenees, where tinkering and peddling, occasional navvying, and flagrant begging carried the migrant over a circuit far wider than did the circumscribed movement of the rest of the Pyrenees; it stretched as far as Bordeaux in the north and then took him east through Toulouse and the cities of the Aude. Some migrants from the canton are found as far east as Arles and Nîmes and as far south as Madrid. This was an area stretching from the Comminges in the east to Vicdessos in the west and comprehending villages such as

---

[1] A.D. Puy-de-Dôme 4 C 95–100, Passeports. This village enjoyed a particularly low repute in the opinion of the *régisseur* of the *dépôt de mendicité* at Riom.

[2] A.N. F14 Pyrénées-Orientales, Prefectoral report, 1801.

Massat, Castillon, and Aspet and villages like Mas-d'Azil of the
pre-Pyrenean range—in short, the area too far distant to benefit
from either the grape harvest of Aquitaine or that of Roussillon.
Mas-d'Azil produced specialist pedlars who trafficked in combs
of bone and horn fashioned the previous winter by the workers
in a small rural industry that was largely composed of the old
who could not travel far. The village of Saillagouse sent forth
every autumn 150 pedlars with packs of woollen stockings also
made the previous winter by the women who remained at home.
The profits accruing to pedlar and stocking-knitter were slight,
for both were dependent upon the merchant. He supplied the
raw material, purchased the finished product, and sold it to the
pedlar, who, dependent upon credit, never made sufficient to cut
out the merchant and deal with the knitter directly. Aspet, Massat,
and Saint-Gaudens made ends meet by working on the harvest
of the latifundia of Aragon, but more generally by tinkering,
mending pots and tools, in the winter in the Ebro valley.[1] Very
often this was not enough, and every autumn the women and
children packed up and moved out with a view to begging their
living. The proceeds to be made from this activity in the nearest
towns, such as Foix and Tarbes, were unlikely to offer enough
to the begging villages whose hardship was aggravated by the
extreme cold of the mountain winter. Hence each village made
an odyssey for the dead season to a warmer city where the pickings
were likely to be greater. The women and children of Massat
walked to Toulouse, up the valley of the Garonne, to station
themselves on the steps of Saint-Sernin, the cathedral church with
the most important congregation, where they were recognized as
pauvres montagnards deserving of charity.[2] Those of Comminges
chose between Toulouse and Bordeaux.[3]

[1] Dralet, *Descriptions des Pyrénées*, vol. ii, p. 190: 'Parmi les habitants des cantons
d'Aspet et autres de l'arrondissement de Saint Gaudens, il en est qui vont travailler
à la récolte des grains dans les pays de l'Aragon; ils viennent ensuite faire la moisson
dans les vallées où elle est plus tardive. Un bon nombre de ces laborieux montagnards, après avoir ensemencé leurs terres, repartent en Espagne où les uns racom-
modent les utensiles de cuisine et d'autres aiguisent les outils ou exercent d'autres
petites professions que dédaignent les Espagnols.'
[2] D. Higgs, 'Politics and Charity at Toulouse 1750–1850', *French Government and
Society 1500–1850*, pp. 192–3. On the significance of such practices in the mountain
economy, see M. Chevalier, *Les Pyrénées*, p. 671.
[3] J. P. Poussou, 'Aspects de l'immigration pyrénéenne', and J. Rives, 'L'Évolution
démographique de Toulouse', *Bull. d'hist. écon. et soc.* (1968), pp. 137 ff.

From the Couserans–Comminges area also there issued a stream of temporary migrants, those who left their native parish for an indefinite period, to go into Spain. This movement, paralleled by a similar one from enclaves in the Haute Auvergne (the elections of Aurillac, Mauriac, and Saint-Flour), from parts of the Limousin, and from a handful of villages in the Rouergue centring upon Mur-de-Barrèz and one from Béarn, reassumed in the mid eighteenth century important proportions[1]—the province of Andalusia alone harboured 20,000 Frenchmen,[2] and perhaps as many as 8,000 left the Auvergne yearly with a Spanish destination in mind.[3] Moreover, the numbers leaving the Auvergne were markedly inferior to those leaving the Pyrenees.[4] Why did these migrants choose to go to Spain, what sort of work did they seek, what made certain Frenchmen choose to make so long a journey whilst others of the same village made a shorter one to a neighbouring province?

There are no simple answers except about the type of work sought. The movement into Spain is full of mystery, the explanation of which demands a knowledge of both countries. A movement into Spain from France had existed at least from the late Middle Ages; it had been built perhaps upon contacts that had grown up in connection with the pilgrims' route from Rocamadour to Compostella. This movement varied in intensity from

[1] Dralet, *Descriptions des Pyrénées*, vol. ii, p. 190; A. Poitrineau, 'Aspects de l'émigration en Auvergne', pp. 21–3; M. Trillat, 'L'Émigration de la Haute Auvergne du XVIIᵉ au XXᵉ siècle', *Revue de Haute Auvergne*, lxix (1955), 257–94; J. Perrel, 'Introduction à l'étude sur l'émigration corrézienne vers l'Espagne sous l'ancien régime', *Bulletin de la société des sciences et arts de la Corrèze* (1963), pp. 92–101; J. Perrel, 'Aspects de l'émigration bas-limousine en Espagne aux siècles passés', *Actes du 88ᵉ congrès des sociétés savantes* (Clermont-Ferrand, 1963); Lempereur, *État du diocèse de Rodez*, parishes (p. 288) Mur-de-Barrèz, Bromme, (p. 287) Sinhalac, (p. 315) Lieucamp, (p. 584) La Terrisse (district de Saint-Genevère), (p. 587) Vitrac (district de Saint-Geniez).

[2] This estimate, given by Père Labat in 1730, specified: '20,000 français des provinces d'Auvergne, de la Marche, du Limousin et des environs de la Garonne dont le métier était de porter de l'eau dans les maisons, de vendre dans les rues du charbon, de l'huile, du vinaigre, de servir dans les hôtelleries, de labourer les terres et faire les moissons et d'y travailler les vignes.' Text cited by P. Ponsot, 'Des Immigrants français en Andalousie', *Mélanges de la Casa de Velazquez* (Paris, 1969), p. 337.

[3] M. Trillat, 'L'Émigration de la Haute Auvergne', p. 271.

[4] However, no over-all estimate exists of the numbers involved. L. Goron, 'Migrations dans les départements pyrénéens', p. 239. A.D. Haute Garonne C 646–68, reports of the *contrôleur des vingtièmes* 1751–86, indicate the increasing dependence of the Pyrenean regions on these movements into Spain.

period to period. It would appear to have decelerated during the first three decades of the eighteenth century, to have picked up again, and to have been curtailed only during the Revolution.[1] It is easy to explain a sixteenth- or seventeenth-century movement into Spain by reference to the wealth of that country; it is less easy to opt for that reason in the eighteenth century, when contemporaries were agreed that the poverty of the Spanish day labourer was unsurpassed.[2] True, there were areas of vital economic development in eighteenth-century Spain, notably Barcelona and the Catalan coast, which offered on the one hand navvying and building work and on the other terrace-cutting for the expanding wine industry,[3] but Catalonia, curiously enough, did not in the period attract heavy numbers of French. They made above all for Andalusia, and the cities of Cadiz and Seville, and for all the towns of the duchy of Seville, Aragon, and some of the cities of old Castille, notably Valladollid, and for a few in Galicia.[4] Spanish observers tried to explain the success of the French immigrant in psychological terms. The Spanish, they held, were a proud people who would not sink to the lowly, menial, often filthy, labours of the French migrant;[5] for the migrant in Spain sought above all those fringe trades which his opposite number from the Basse Auvergne practised in Paris, the cities of Normandy, and the Rhône valley: they were pedlars, carriers of water and wood, lemonade sellers, vendors of fancy breads, carriers of sedan chairs, and pedlars of haberdashery. They were prepared to sweep streets and empty latrines, and in fact to take on anything which would earn them a little towards the hoard of 300–400 *pesos*—the aim of every migrant who made the long,

[1] J. Nadal and E. Giralt, *La Population catalane de 1553 à 1717* (Paris, 1960), are of the opinion, largely because of the terminal dates they chose, that the movement into Spain from France dried up in the early eighteenth century. Certainly it did so, but only to be resumed as pressure mounted after the 1740s. J. Nadal, *La Población española, siglos XVI a XX* (Barcelona, 1966), pp. 80–8, and P. Ponsot, 'Des Immigrants français', p. 331.

[2] J. Sarrailh, *L'Espagne éclairée de la seconde moitié du XVIIIᵉ siècle* (Paris, 1954), p. 7, is clearly baffled by the phenomenon and cites some contemporary opinions.

[3] Their relative absence is conspicuous, E. Moreu Rey, 'Els immigrants francescos a Barcelona (segles XVI al XVIII)', *Institut d'éstudis catalans*, vol. xx (Barcelona, 1959).

[4] J. Perrel, 'Introduction à une étude sur l'émigration corrézienne', p. 94.

[5] A. Dominguez Ortiz, *La Sociedad española en el siglo XVIII* (Madrid, 1955), pp. 217–18, gives lists of demeaning jobs which tally exactly with those offered by French immigrants listed, pp. 238–9.

once-in-a-lifetime movement into Spain.[1] Broadly speaking, the Auvergnat, the Limousin, and the Rouergat expected to stay from anything from two to nine years—perhaps five would be a working average. The Pyrenean migrant, whose journey was infinitely less, perhaps spent on average two years if he came from Couserans or the Comminges, nine months or so if from Béarn—the *emigración de golondrina*, swallows who came and went with the seasons.[2] The Béarnais in Spain enjoyed his own separate identity as entertainer and quack doctor dealing in mystic incantations in an incomprehensible tongue and with curious specialities —he was a castrator of weakly boys whose parents hoped to provide for them by securing them entry to a cathedral choir. Since his victims often died, his activities were rendered illegal in 1756, but the declaration of illegality did not necessarily bring them to a halt.[3]

Clearly the answer to why the migrant chose Spain lies somewhere in the realms of tradition and hard facts. It was still possible to amass a small capital sum in the way one's ancestors had done in times of stress in the southern ports of Spain, especially if one was prepared to hazard the discomfort and a protracted *séjour* away from home. It took longer to do this than it had done in an earlier period; the French migrant stayed longer in Spain in the eighteenth century than he had done in the seventeenth. The migrant was sometimes a bachelor hoping to earn enough to set himself up in his native village by purchasing an extra piece of land—from then on a few months of every year

[1] There are conflicting views on the precise social standing of the Auvergnats and Limousins who made the trip into Spain. J. Perrel, 'Aspects de l'émigration bas-limousine', and A. Poitrineau, 'Aspects de l'émigration en Auvergne', p. 22, suggest that the poorest peasantry were precluded on the grounds that evidence exists of a company demanding a capital sum and then guaranteeing work to the immigrant. Of this a good description exists in A.N. F20 435, Puy-de-Dôme, but applies to a mere 400 migrants annually. The rest of the 8,000 or so Auvergnat expatriates were clearly lowly people ready to perform menial work. The subject is worth looking at from Spanish sources (as does the work of P. Ponsot). Dominguez Ortiz, op. cit., p. 239, in fact distinguishes two types: the moneyed, finding employ in the American trade, and the very lowly, near-destitute water-carriers and dockers who returned home when 300 or 400 *pesos* had been accumulated, and begged their return journey be pretending to be Santiago pilgrims. P. Ponsot, 'Des immigrants français', p. 335, using instances at Osuña in 1791 from 51 examples, shows that only 5 (3 *commerçants en tissus*, 1 *pourvoyeur de blé à l'armée*, 1 *majordomo*) were men of any means.

[2] Dominguez Ortiz, *La Sociedad española*, p. 242.

[3] Ibid., p. 251.

away from home might suffice. But bachelors were not the most common migrants, the commonest age-group was that between the ages of 30 and 40. (In the Auvergne whole villages paid their taxes in *pesos*, and wives reconciled themselves to a long severance from their husbands.)[1] Moreover, elderly men, conscious of the problems of old age, sometimes tried to accumulate a little nest egg in this manner. Indeed, in the Rouergue the efforts of one such passed into folklore. An old man, so old he could not keep up with his two young companions, was returning from Spain by way of the Garonne valley, a haunt of part-time brigands who preyed on returning immigrants. Having robbed of their earnings the two young men who had gone on ahead, two brigands fell upon the older victim. But he resisted their attack and fought so staunchly that the brigands took to their heels; he had more to lose, for this visit would be his last: better to die in defence of his *pécule* than to return penniless.[2]

The trip to Spain was recognized as a dangerous enterprise. Many never returned, their stay cut short by death in a Spanish hospital. To cross the mountains, to follow the valley of the Garonne, or to cut through Puigcerda (the commonest route), or to take the coastal road through Catalonia or the pass at the opposite side of the Pyrenean range through Saint-Jean-Pied-de-Port over to Roncevalles, and thence to wend a dusty path through the barren sierra of central Spain took a heavy toll on physical health. Polluted water and the unsavoury occupations of the migrants heightened the risk. This perhaps explains why only inhabitants of those parts of the Pyrenees where the hardship was greatest and the potential for seasonal work the least, made this kind of journey. The additional income that could be earned in Spain would ward off the day when the farmer, who was perhaps only a month-a-year farmer, must lose his scrap of land.

How effective were seasonal and temporary migration as a solution to the problems of the poor of the mountain regions? In two instances, the Basse Auvergne and Béarn, the efforts of the migrants made possible the continued existence of those who were left behind, and in the first instance may even have pushed em-

[1] A.D. Puy-de-Dôme C 3073, Lettre à M. Calonne, 15 août 1786.
[2] H. Affre, *Dictionnaire des institutions, mœurs et coutumes du Rouergue*, article 'Émigration'.

ployers into raising the wages of their resident labour.[1] When Young journeyed through these regions, he was struck by the orderliness and the lack of visible signs of distress in areas remarkable for the smallness of the average holding.[2] This lack of visible distress was purchased at the cost of pushing out a large proportion of the labour force. What this force earned in monetary terms perhaps had little significance. Both the prefect of the Puy-de-Dôme and the prefect of the Hautes-Pyrénées insisted that the main value of seasonal work was that it took the worker away from his holding, and so removed the necessity for him to eat out of his own resources, and that any monetary gain was so small as to be superfluous. Of 300 or 400 *terrassiers*, the prefect commented:

Beaucoup dépensent tout le peu qu'ils gagnent avant de rentrer dans le pays. Si l'on suppose favorablement que l'un portant l'autre, ils épargnent dix francs, ce serait une somme de 3 à 4000 francs qu'ils dissémineraient pour prix des travaux de quatre mois, dans leurs nombreuses et misérables familles.[3]

The strength of seasonal movements in these two regions was not sufficient to prevent a permanent exodus into the cities, most especially of young men. Moreover, the interdependence of regions of varying agrarian demands meant that a crisis in the place of seasonal work could have repercussions throughout the economy of other regions. Even so, the small holder cum seasonal migrant, like the investor with a varied portfolio, was able to withstand short-term crises with greater odds on survival than he who was totally dependent upon the resources of his own region or upon industry subject to periodic laying-off; for the whole of his livelihood was never in jeopardy at any one time.[4] Most importantly for the migrant, seasonal labour put off the day when he would have to make a more radical breach with his

[1] Poitrineau, *La Vie rurale en Basse Auvergne*, p. 545, notes surprising increases in this sector.
[2] Young, *Travels*, pp. 295, 299.
[3] A.N. F²⁰ 434, Hautes-Pyrénées.
[4] Emphasis is here on 'short-term crises'. This is perfectly compatible with the observations of M. Couturier, *Châteaudun*, p. 156, that no sector of society was more prone to personal disaster than the seasonal migrant and his family, owing to debts incurred in the absence of the migrant, or simply the failure of the migrant to return.

village; it preserved him for a little while from the radical transition from agricultural worker to urban navvy.

If the movement from country to town was a reluctant step for the poor, it was, notwithstanding, a common one. The rate of urban growth in the eighteenth century was marked: in the case of the ports it was of the order of 80–100 per cent, and if this makes them remarkable, textile cities, provincial capitals, and even insignificant towns could boast growth-rates of the order of 30 per cent.[1] This growth was not self-engendered; indeed, France would have been peculiar in the conditions of the eighteenth century had it been so. The towns grew as a result of a heavy rural influx, an influx which was, it is becoming increasingly apparent, one of the poor, the dispossessed, though, at least until the 1770s, one of the relatively hopeful. No more than the seasonal migrant was the rural immigrant a Dick Whittington figure lured towards the city by the pursuit of mythical gold. Just as seasonal movements were premeditated, so was the decision to move to the city or town. Little was done on impulse. The migrant's path, usually on foot, though the river traffic into Paris, Rouen, Lyons, Orleans, and even Toulouse was also considerable, was subject to certain planning. The immigrant had a clear set of priorities probably depending upon age, sex, and limited ambitions. One distinction based on sex has already been drawn relating to female domestic service. The daughter of a rural family sought out the nearest town and hoped to return home with a dowry. She did not expect to travel far unless relatives had established links with more distant cities, the case of the Rouergat servant girl in Montpellier, Agde, or Béziers, or the Commingeois in Toulouse. Women were still less pioneers of migratory movements in the eighteenth century than their brothers. They arrived with an address in their heads. Patterns of male movement were more complex, but they were no less predictable. Each area had traditional cities towards which it was drawn. North of the Pau–Belfort line—though there are major exceptions to this in Paris, Bordeaux, Orleans, and Strasbourg—urban recruitment was predominantly local, and this whether one

[1] The best general treatment of this theme remains R. P. Mols, *Introduction à la démographie historique des villes d'Europe du XIVe au XVIIIe siècle* (Louvain, 1955), vol. ii, pp. 338–93 and 514–16.

is considering a textile city like Rouen or Troyes or an administrative centre like Caen or Dijon.[1] South of that line, the towns grew by dint of immigrations which conform more or less to lines of seasonal migration. Again, to the north of that division lay towns largely supplied by the dispossessed of the *pays de grande culture*, the landless who, unable to find work all the year round at home, moved out indefinitely into the world of urban life. They had nothing to retain them in their native villages, and if they felt some nostalgia for the place of their birth, the links were of a purely personal nature, lacking the magnetic pull of property. South of the Pau–Belfort line, the bulk of towns and cities were in large part recruited from societies of small holders. He who originated in such societies, the *pays de petite culture*, made the transition to urban life more gradually and perhaps less definitively than did the migrant of *journalier* stock. He dreamed constantly of returning home. When he left his native village he made for those towns or cities of which he or his family or friends had some experience as a seasonal migrant. There are many exceptions, however, to such generalizations. Orleans, Moulins, Bourges, and even Chartres were supplied with manpower not merely by the immediately adjacent rural area, but, since they lay between the teeming Massif and the capital, had also a subsidiary influx from the Auvergne, Marche, and Limousin.[2] The cities that fell in the path of the Savoyard as he made his way towards Paris, such as

[1] The greatest contrasts are obtained by comparing the death registers of the *hôtels Dieu* of the northern with those of the southern cities. At Montpellier (A.M. Montpellier 688) in the Hôpital Saint-Éloi, over a third of the deaths were of immigrants from the Rouergue or the Gévaudan, and under a fifth were native to Montpellier and its diocese. The same generalizations apply to Agde, Béziers, and Lodève (Le Roy Ladurie, *Les Paysans de Languedoc*, p. 96). At Troyes (A.D. Aube 40 H Hôtel Dieu le Comte) over 50 per cent of deaths were from Troyes and its diocese, and the rest were from the neighbouring dioceses of Langres, Sens, Chalons, etc. At Dijon 80 per cent and above of deaths were of immigrants from Dijon and diocese (A. Hospitalières Dijon F³ 4, 1776–80). At Chartres (information based on marriage lists) 94 per cent were of Chartres or the *pays chartrain*, allowing a feeble 5 per cent for outsiders, often from neighbouring dioceses, or the Massif.

[2] G. Lefebvre, *Études orléanaises*, vol. i, p. 151: 'Orléans se fût dépeuplé sans l'immigration rurale . . .'; M. Vovelle, 'Chartres et le pays chartrain. Quelques aspects démographiques', *Contributions à l'histoire démographique de la Révolution française* (Paris, 1962), pp. 129–52; calculations based on marriage lists here suggest about a fifth of unions involving outsiders included one from the Massif. At Moulins, A.M. Moulins 508, Décès, Hôpital de Saint-Gilles, suggest on average a third of annual deaths (av. 73 per year 1764–93) were of Auvergnats. How many were permanent residents of Moulins cannot be surmised.

Strasbourg, Dijon, or Langres, received on a permanent basis handfuls—in the first instance considerably more—of such immigrants annually, and the establishment of an initial handful inevitably ensured that others followed.[1] Bordeaux, Toulouse, and Lyons grew by dint of highly complex movements. Up to 60 per cent of immigrants to Bordeaux were from the adjacent Entre-Deux-Mers, Périgord, and Agenais; but to set against these were long-distance movements out of Béarn and the high Pyrenean regions around Comminges and Couserans, and the Limousin immigrant is conspicuous.[2] Perhaps 40 per cent of Toulousain immigrants were from the diocese of Toulouse, in particular from the area of large farms in the Lauragais, but a subsidiary influx came from Comminges and Couserans.[3] In other words, that region of the Pyrenees already shown to be characterized by peddling, fringe jobs, protracted absences from home, and temporary migration into Spain was, naturally enough, the one forced, when expedients failed, to search out the city. Moreover, this exodus from the mountains was significantly increasing throughout the century, at least up to the eighties, and the Commingeois made a choice between life in a port and that in an administrative capital.[4] Lyons drew not only upon the Lyonnais but also upon Forez, Bresse, Bugey, Dauphiné as a whole, and Savoy—a recruitment[5] only surpassed by the medley which entered Paris. Here in the capital the currents of migration were heaviest from the north, Picardy, Flanders, Normandy, predictably from the Île de France; and there was also a substantial influx of Lorrains and Alsaciens from the east. The Massif supplied its contingent: Auvergnats, Marchois, and Limousins, but rarely anyone from further south because they sought out other

---

[1] Dreyer-Roos, *La Population strasbourgeoise*, pp. 130–3, using marriage registers, suggests 10 per cent of immigrants were Savoyards; at Dijon, somewhat prematurely labelled *le carrefour de la Bourgogne* by G. Bouchard, 'Dijon au XVIIIᵉ siècle. Les Dénombrements d'habitants', *Annales de Bourgogne* (1953), pp. 30–5, in fact only two or three Savoyards died annually at the *hôpital* (A. Hospitalières Dijon F³ 4, 1776–80). However, they are indicated to be resident at the *maison des Savoyards*—suggesting people of passage staying with a small resident community.

[2] Pariset (ed.), *Bordeaux au XVIIIᵉ siècle*, pp. 333–4; 30 per cent were from a radius of up to 40 km.; 30 per cent from a radius up to 150 km.

[3] J. Rives, 'L'Évolution démographique de Toulouse', p. 135.

[4] Ibid., p. 137, and J. Poussou, 'Aspects de l'immigration pyrénéenne (Béarn, Bigorre, Comminges, "Ariège") à Bordeaux au milieu et à la fin du XVIIIᵉ siècle', *Bull. société des sciences, lettres et arts de Pau* (1967), pp. 101–2.

[5] Garden, *Lyon*, p. 51.

cities.[1] There were relatively few who came from the west. The Breton peasant as yet only flocked into his own cities, Nantes, Rennes, and, until 1770, Lorient above all. One further exception must be added to the generalizations made above: the composition of the population of Marseilles. One would expect the peculiarly heavy demands of this rapidly increasing port to command a large sphere of attraction. Yet Marseilles belonged to the Provençaux: the poor who ended their days in the *hôtel Dieu*— except for the isolated Breton or Italian sailor—came at the furthest from the Alps or the Massif, but in over 80 per cent of cases they came from the dioceses of Apt, Valence, Orange, Cisteron, Digne, Saint-Paul-Trois-Châteaux, Die, or Nice.[2] Marseilles was a city associated with pestilence—the memory of 1721 died hard; the long-distance migrant opted instead for Nîmes or Montpellier.

The traditions of one's village and one's age determined above all which particular town or city one sought out and the type of work one hoped for when one got there. The male rural immigrant was less commonly than his female counterpart a pure domestic servant, and the male-servant hierarchy was more closely defined. The coachman and the cook of a noble or wealthy household could make a good living anywhere.[3] In Paris the best cooks were said to be from Carcassonne, the best coachmen and stableboys Normans; and indeed the Norman was everywhere considered to have a way with horses, and his services were generally appreciated.[4] In Lyons cooks came from the Beaujolais

---

[1] A.N. F²⁰ 435, Seine, and R. Cobb, *The Police and the People* (Oxford, 1970), pp. 228–9; J. Kaplow, 'Sur la population flottante de Paris à la fin de l'ancien régime', *A.H.R.F.*, xxxix (1967), 1–14.

[2] A.M. Marseilles GG 652, Sépultures, 1780–6. Annually in the region of 32 per cent of all deaths at the Hôtel Dieu were native-born Marseillais; about 43 per cent were Provençaux; 9–10 per cent from the Alps; 6 per cent from the Lyonnais; a feeble 3 per cent from the Massif; and the rest were isolated instances. M. Vovelle, 'Le Prolétariat flottant à Marseille sous la Révolution française', *Annales de démographie historique* (1968), p. 125, using the *Registre des hôtels et garnis 1791–3*, shows a similar distribution and remarks upon the absence in particular (p. 125) of any considerable influx from the Gard or the Hérault. The Languedocian presumably chose Nîmes or Montpellier.

[3] R. Robin, *Semur*, p. 220, cites the case of Jacques Caillet, *maître de l'hôtel de Mure de la Madeleine*, who had 6,000 *livres* of property on marriage; cf. Pariset (ed.), *Bordeaux*, p. 367, A. Sachet, *Les Rôtisseurs de Lyon* (Lyons, 1920), pp. 70–95.

[4] I am indebted to Professor Richard Cobb for many such details.

and the Lyonnais; in Bordeaux from the Périgord; in Strasbourg from the Île de France.[1] But lackeys and *valets* enjoyed less-elevated status. The Savoyard *valet* is a common figure in Paris, Lyons, and Strasbourg, for he was the cheapest on the market.[2] Elsewhere, the male domestic at the lower level was recruited from the usual zones on which cities drew: the Rouergat in Montpellier, Agde, and Béziers; the Gévaudois at Alais; the immigrant from the Lauragais at Toulouse. The docks of Bordeaux, Marseilles Lorient, Toulon, and Le Havre, and the river traffic of Rouen, Orleans, Bordeaux, Châlons, Lyons, and of the Canal du Midi could evidently draw upon a reservoir of willing *portefaix*, bargemen, dredgers of one kind and another. Otherwise, the young rural immigrant tried to find apprenticeship in a trade as joiner, plasterer, tiler, builder, or else in the garment trades. And in every town or city the immigrant countrymen performed the most menial services, jobs described collectively by the *visiteur du pauvre* of 1804 as those 'qui n'exigent point d'apprentissage difficile ou d'aptitude particulière' and which he reeled off in a two-page litany.[3] Occasionally in the cities that attracted long-distance migrants provincial monopolies were established: the Auvergnat in Paris, Chartres, and Orleans commonly monopolized the position of water- or wood-carrier; the Savoyard that of *portefaix* and *porteur de chaises*; the Limousin perhaps controlled the building trades; the Commingeois controlled the servicing of

---

[1] D. Pétrissans, 'Recherches sur les métiers à Bordeaux 1710–1789: Taverniers — Cabaretiers — Cafetiers — Restaurateurs — Hôteliers — Pâtissiers — Rôtisseurs — Traiteurs' (Bordeaux, Mémoire 1968), pp. 177–9; Dreyer-Roos, *La Population strasbourgeoise*, p. 133.

[2] G. Livet, 'Une Page d'histoire sociale: les Savoyards à Strasbourg au XVIIIe siècle', *Cahiers d'histoire*, iv (1959), 131–45; H. Muheim, 'Une Source exceptionnelle. Le Recensement de la population lyonnaise en 1709. Les Domestiques dans la société', *Actes du 89e Congrès des sociétés savantes* (Paris, 1965), pp. 207–17; and on the particular qualities of the Savoyard *valet* in Paris, A.N. F20 435, Seine.

[3] Gerando, *Le Visiteur du pauvre* (Paris, 1820), pp. 33–5 (*re* information collected in 1804). They were, respectively: marchands ambulants, commissionnaires et portefaix, marchandes de fruits et de légumes, porteurs d'eau, revendeuses, chiffonniers, balayeurs, brocanteurs, décrotteurs, ramoneurs, maçons, manœuvres, terrassiers, menuisiers, serruriers, forgerons, couvreurs, peintres, paveurs, marbriers, vidangeurs, scieurs de pierre, plâtriers, poêliers, fumistes, cordonniers, savetiers, tailleurs, lingères, couturières, blanchisseurs, repasseuses, tricoteuses, fileuses, dévideuses, tisserands, faiseuses de ménage, portiers, cochers, palefreniers, frotteurs, ouvriers en tabac, tourneurs, ouvriers en papiers, relieurs, brocheuses, graveurs, perruquiers, gaziers, gantiers, polisseurs, tapissiers, teinturiers, ciseleurs, doreurs, jardiniers, charretiers, etc.

the Garonne at Toulouse.[1] To a degree, urban well-being was dependent upon the rural influx for the provision of basic services, for urban mortality rates were heavy. It is equally clear, however, that by the second half of the eighteenth century the rural surplus was more than the towns and cities could absorb, and the cramming of petty and peripheral trades meant that most of those who came were chronically underemployed.[2] Strasbourg, Dijon, and Troyes boasted a shoemaker for about every 120 inhabitants;[3] and a substantial proportion of that figure could probably not afford to have their shoes repaired, let alone purchase new ones. The lists of the *bureaux de charité*—whose inadequacies will presently be examined—are perforce filled with the names of those who practised these petty trades; for the inability of the towns and cities to employ effectively all who came did not necessarily arrest growth. Each difficult year, at least well into the eighties, brought its wave of migrants: 'la misère a fait déserter les campagnes: elle a rejeté dans les villes des gens qui les surchargent de leur inutilité'[4] is a comment which has its place in the reports of every *intendant*. Each normal year brought those who had suffered personally or who realized that there was nothing to be gained at home. Nor were all immigrants young and single. Periods of crisis, especially, brought in the older man accompanied by his family.[5] Such a family was in a peculiarly difficult position, for it was a question not merely of finding employment for one member of the family but of supplying each one with some means of livelihood, and under no circumstances could the newly arrived family expect anything of formal relief. Many of the immigrants of crisis had no intention of remaining in the towns for very long. The *intendant* at Rennes and the *subdélégué* of Riom in Auvergne described a winter influx of families

---

[1] R. Cobb, *The Police and the People*, p. 228, and J. Ibanès, 'La Population de la place des Vosges', *Contributions à l'histoire démographique de la Révolution française* (Paris, 1962), p. 85.

[2] Garden, *Lyon*, pp. 239–40; M. L. Larnaudie, 'L'Immigration à Toulouse de 1750 à 1775' (mémoire, Toulouse, 1969); Pariset (ed.), *Bordeaux*, p. 362.

[3] Dreyer-Roos, *La Population strasbourgeoise*, p. 147, and A.D. Côte-d'Or C 3687, Dénombrement des citoyens de la ville de Dijon 1780. At Lyons out of 1,090 'maîtres cordonniers il n'y a pas deux cents qui fassent ou qui soient en état de faire du neuf (parcequ'ils n'ont pas le moyen d'acheter des marchandises, et sont absolument réduits à raccommoder de vieux ouvrages, pour pouvoir subsister avec les aumônes)' (A.M. Lyon HH 180, Communauté des Savetiers).

[4] A.D. Ille-et-Vilaine C 1402, Observations du greffier du présidial de Rennes, 1772.   [5] J. Rives, 'L'Évolution démographique de Toulouse', pp. 135–46.

who were the victims of diminished harvest returns and hoped to cadge their way through the winter.[1] The Mediterranean littoral knew under similar conditions an inpouring of hill dwellers from the Cévennes and the Gévaudan who, in a milder climate and with a little good fortune, hoped to keep themselves alive for a few months before returning to their homes.[2] Yet a proportion of immigrant families clearly came with a permanent stay in mind and hoped in some way to accommodate every member.[3]

The rural immigrant rarely arrived alone in the town or city. Even if he embarked on his own, he invariably joined up with others along the route. Sometimes he joined the flow of seasonal traffic. Certainly he knew where to stay along his route and who would offer him advice. The Rouergat servant girl travelling to Montpellier might accompany her brothers *en route* to work in the vineyards. The two most highly organized migrants were the Auvergnat and the Savoyard. The Savoyard left his native village not only with a passport but with letters of introduction to friends of friends or relatives *en route* to his destination and in the city of his choice. He had a kind of map indicating not only his route but where and with whom he might stay on the way;[4] he knew each city in his path would have a *garni des savoyards* where he could stay for a small consideration and get food.[5] The Auvergnat enjoyed a similar reassurance in that the route from Riom to the capital was studded with Auvergnat doss-houses. He knew which cities would pay him to leave. Moulins had to protect itself against the Auvergnat's demands and to ensure that he did not linger as a beggar. It did so by according him 5 *sous* as he left the city.[6] Limoges had a generous *passade* and might be

---

[1] A.D. Ille-et-Vilaine C 1286; A. Poitrineau, 'Aspects de l'émigration', pp. 23–4.

[2] Le Roy Ladurie, *Les Paysans de Languedoc*, pp. 93–5.

[3] How many families, as opposed to individuals, sought out the cities can never be accurately estimated. Something can be deduced from the presence of immigrant children in *hôtel Dieu* death records. At Bordeaux the marriage registers recording young adult immigrants show a slightly different emphasis of places of origin to those of the death registers at Saint-André, and the comparison indicates that older migrants from Béarn and Comminges were numerically more significant than the young adult from the same area (Poussou, 'Aspects de l'immigration', p. 101). Occasional court cases reveal the presence of entire families.

[4] A.N. F[20] 435, Seine.

[5] They knew too the *hospices* which still accorded the *passade*, e.g. A. Hosp. Langres 1 F 2, Registre des passants, shows the flow of Savoyard seasonal labour and groups of five or six passing through together.

[6] A.M. Moulins, 554, Registre des délibérations du bureau de charité.

worth a detour. Moreover, with few exceptions, the migrant, if he did not have a job to go to, did not arrive friendless in the town or city of his destination. The whole point about patterns of migration was that one followed streams of one's compatriots, some of them one's relatives who would offer one whatever help they could when one arrived. The immigrant's first act on arriving at his destination was to find them.

Usually, even in the largest cities, they were not difficult to find. Each town and city had its streets or entire *quartiers* gradually taken over and ultimately swamped by immigrants and their families and contacts. They were invariably the most derelict, dank, ill-lit, and ill-provided for in the way of water supplies, areas about which public authorities demonstrated the least concern, but where lodgings could be most cheaply found. In Paris the slum dwellings around the Hôtel de Ville and the place Maubert and those of the Montagne Sainte-Geneviève, rue Galande, rue de Bièvre, and rue Saint-Bernard had rooms that were virtual Auvergnat dormitories with fifteen and twenty to a room, sleeping in shifts. The building workers stemming from the Limousin crowded in the place de la Grève.[1] In Bordeaux the parishes of Saint-Seurin and the faubourg Saint-Julien, the rue Long and the rue de Beauvais, the dark vennels fringing upon the old port, were those into which the Commingeois immigrant or the Béarnais, Agenois, or Périgourdin penetrated to search out his compatriots.[2] In Strasbourg the rue du Dôme and the Canal des Faux-Remparts were boundaries within which the *garnis des Savoyards* were distributed amongst other immigrant communities;[3] in Marseilles it was the Grand Carmes which, above all, the poor immigrant sought out and the vieux Marseille, which still resembled that where pestilence had raged.[4] In Toulouse the immigrant from Comminges and Couserans had his *garnis* on the Île de Tounis, and in Saint-Cyprien and Saint-Michel and Saint-Sernin;[5] in Lyons, Foréziens made for the quartier Saint-Paul, Dauphinois huddled in La Guillotière,

[1] A.N. F²⁰ 435, Seine, and G. Rudé, 'La Population ouvrière parisienne de 1789 à 1791', *A.H.R.F.* xxxix (1967), 27.

[2] A. Forrest, 'The Condition of the Poor in Revolutionary Bordeaux', *Past and Present*, lix (1973), 150.

[3] S. Dreyer-Roos, *La Population strasbourgeoise*, p. 139.

[4] M. Vovelle, 'Le Prolétariat flottant à Marseille', p. 131.

[5] J. Rives, 'L'Évolution démographique de Toulouse', p. 143.

Roannais in the Vaise and between Saône et Rhône.[1] In every
city a hotchpotch of humanity sorted itself out into its respective
shambles of lodging houses. Even when the immigrant was from
the immediately adjacent countryside, he still occupied his own
particular *quartier* and lived with his compatriots in the most
crowded of dwellings, sleeping several to a room from which
furniture had long since disappeared. The quartier Martainville
in Rouen harboured the rural influx along with the indigenous
poor population of the city, gradually pushing those who aspired
to a more aesthetic existence out into the suburbs; fashionable,
eighteenth-century Rouen was the quartier hors cauchois stretching
out into the countryside.[2] Some cities, such as Troyes and Périgueux, were virtually cut in two. Troyes had a *quartier bas*, an
area enclosing thirty-six ancient churches and the slums whence
immigrants were drawn; in Périgueux the ascent from river to
cathedral church via the *vieille ville* was totally in the hands of the
poor and the rural influx. Other cities, such as Rennes and
Bourges, had shanty towns on their periphery, but in addition
the centre of the cities here as everywhere else had fallen to the
poor and immigrant.[3] These centres usually included important
churches, cathedrals, and convents, for they were the oldest
sections, medieval slums which were infested with rats and lice
(one reason for the spate of baroque church-building may well
have been to rescue the affluent from the need to walk through
these sections on the way to worship). Yet their location meant
that the immigrant was strategically placed near the ports, docks,
warehouses, and near important arteries to public buildings. If
he had to beg his living, what better place to command than the
approach to the cathedral or the doors to convents? Many of the
keepers of the *garnis* were his compatriots who had made out in
the city; perhaps he could even expect a little credit.

The immigrant would not remain confined to these sections,
but here he would find shelter, help, and advice—crucial if he
arrived without a job to go to—on how to find work. His contacts
in town or city did not end in the *garnis*. He had sisters and
cousins who were urban *servantes*, brothers, uncles, cousins,

---

[1] R. Cobb, *Reactions to the French Revolution* (Oxford, 1972), pp. 43–62.

[2] de Bouard (ed.), *Histoire de la Normandie*, p. 343.

[3] H. Sée, 'Les Classes sociales et la vie économique dans une ville d'ancienne
France (Rennes au XVIIIe siècle)', *La Vie économique et les classes sociales en France
au XVIIIe siècle* (Paris, 1924), pp. 180–205.

friends who were *valets* and *domestiques*, and these lived in the prosperous sectors. If he sought a casual job on the streets or docks as *portefaix*, water-carrier, or errand goer, he needed to know where to go for jobs. The Auvergnat water-carrier of Paris or Lyons maintained provincial monopolies through violence, beating up any outsiders—those who were not Auvergnats— who dared set up in rivalry. No other city immigrant was reckoned so quick to anger, so ready to pick a fight and enforce his rights.[1] The docker was dependent upon being hired—no friendless outsider could expect work in Marseilles. The Savoyard in the cities of northern France, intent upon setting up as errand goer, had only to station himself outside a house staffed by his compatriots who saw to it that their fellow countrymen and no other received orders. Tips of course were shared. *La livrée* had in their patronage a host of minor jobs: they could easily, for example, see to it that when the master of the house required a sedan chair, a compatriot *porteur de chaise* was summoned; that when repairs needed doing to pots and pans, or when furniture or services were called for, chimney-sweeping, joinering, putting tiles on the roof, and so on, someone they knew was to hand; and that when a vacancy occurred in their ranks a compatriot for whose honesty they were prepared to vouch was there to fill it.[2]

Clearly there were limits to such help, and how they could be extended to cope with a crisis year can only be surmised. Yet there are some pointers. In Montpellier and Agde, when the harvests of the Rouergue or the Gévaudan were deficient, or even when the grape-harvest did not demand as much seasonal labour as usual, these cities were flooded by *pauvres montagnards*, beggars who were all of a kind, farmers whose resources had temporarily failed them, and with them came their wives and children. Such people, hoping for enough to tide them over a few difficult months, appealed to their relatives established in wealthy households for simple help, slops, bones, and bits of bread from the master's table.[3] The beggar never used the front door but went round to the servants' quarters, and cook and *valet* determined who received what. This was only one respect, however, in which the beggar sought the support of his compatriots.

---

[1] A.N. F²⁰ 435, Seine, 'Les Auvergnats . . . sont les plus brutaux et plus buveurs'.
[2] Ibid.
[3] Le Roy Ladurie, *Les Paysans de Languedoc*, p. 94.

If the newly arrived immigrant did not fall into a job—and the odds were heavily against this happening immediately he came to town—then begging was his only recourse, and to do this effectively in a city he needed to know the ropes. Urban authorities did not welcome the rural beggar, and most employed *archers* or *chasse gueux* attached to the *hôpitaux* who were paid to drive the alien beggar from the town and even, spasmodically after 1724 and regularly after 1767, to imprison him with the threat of steeper penalties if he persisted in his ways. How effectively the police could hope to do this will presently be examined, but certainly they did make periodic attempts to curb the growth of begging in this way, and when they made such attempts intent upon quick arrests and definite convictions—which secured a bonus—they confined their attention to the immigrant beggar betrayed by his dress, his face, his voice. In some cases the *archers* could be readily corrupted and for a consideration would permit the beggar to continue undisturbed—in the cases of Saint-Brieuc, Tréguier, and Saint-Pol-de-Léon, Riom, Clermont, and Brioude,[1] this was estimated to be the most considerable element in the policeman's income, but knowledge of how to proceed was important. Bribery was not the only weapon against the *archer*. In Montpellier the regular Sunday sport of the Rouergat *valet* was to turn out and beat up any *chasse gueux* reported to have arrested a compatriot.[2] At Brest

les mendiants chassés reviennent continuer leur commerce de nuit et de jour, appuyés qu'ils sont des autres pauvres, dont quelques-uns d'eux ont ôté des mains du chasse gueux ceux qu'il avait arrêtés et l'ont maltraité plusieurs fois en différentes manières, jusqu'à être courus et conduits à l'hôpital par des soldats.[3]

The police force was small; few teams of *archers* numbered more than a dozen, whilst the *valets* were to be numbered in hundreds, and such intimidation could paralyse a police force. In Paris *la livrée* went even further in its protection of the beggar. News that a compatriot or relative of a *valet* or lackey had been arrested by the *archers* would result in the entire household of domestics turning up at court to deny the charge and declare

---

[1] A.D. Ille-et-Vilaine C 1285, responses of Lanion, Saint-Brieuc, Portevoix, Tréguier, Saint-Pol-de-Léon; and A.D. Puy-de-Dôme C 1543.

[2] Le Roy Ladurie, *Les Paysans de Languedoc*, pp. 94–5.

[3] A.D. Ille-et-Vilaine C 1285.

that the man in question was the employee of their master. Or if they actually witnessed an arrest, they amalgamated to beat up the hardy *archer*.[1] Nor did protection for the beggar end here. Street sellers, *revendeurs de fruits et de légumes* served as scouts for beggars and would warn them of approaching authority. The precise place of origin of these *mouches* for the beggars is not always ascertainable, yet something can usually be surmised. Thus Pierre Evreux, for example, a building worker (from the Limousin?), was accused of using his vantage point near the porte de l'église des Feuillants to announce to the beggars in the church porch the arrival of the police 'soit pour leur procurer la liberté de mendier, soit pour faciliter leur retraite et empêcher qu'ils ne soient arrêtés'.[2] An over-zealous policeman seen arresting two beggars from the Limousin at Orleans found himself attacked by a handful of angry women who pinned him down until the beggar had escaped.[3] In Toulouse a group of Commingeois immigrants went so far as to launch an attack on the prison at La Grave in order to liberate their compatriots among whom the men had been taken for begging and the women for soliciting.[4] The beggars in question were not of the habitual ingrained type given over to a love of an idle existence; they were newly arrived and, in default of a job, were forced to occupy themselves in this way.

Indeed, the only element in the *menu peuple* likely to impede the beggar in his supplication to the public was the professional beggar who resented any incursion upon his beat—and even he might well make exceptions for his relatives. The best spots in Marseilles were bequeathed by beggars to their posterity, and posterity in this instance often meant a relative from the Provençal hills.[5]

Clearly, there existed until the last decade of the *ancien régime* a continually accelerating movement from country to town which resulted in the creation in the cities of alien blocks only

[1] For brilliant analyses of the problems of the police and immigrants see J. P. Gutton: 'L'Application de la déclaration royale du 18 juillet 1724: Généralités du Lyonnais et d'Auvergne' (Thèse 3e cycle, Lyons, 1967) and 'Les Mendiants dans la société parisienne au début du XVIIIe siècle', *Cahiers d'histoire*, xiii (1968), 131–41.

[2] A.N. Y 9515 pièce 267.   [3] A.D. Loiret, B. 2118.

[4] N. Castan, 'La Criminalité à la fin de l'ancien régime dans les pays de Languedoc', *Bull. d'hist. écon. et soc.* (1968–9), p. 63.

[5] P. de Dessuslamarre, *La Mendicité en 1789* (Marseilles, 1789), cited by G. Valran, *Misère et charité en Provence au XVIIIe siècle*, vol. ii, p. 39.

partially integrated which monopolized lowly activities, protected the newly arrived, and made the perfect network for the
carrying out of crime. In the continual coming and going of
seasonal migrants and amongst the urban flotsam there was little
of permanence, little that could be readily traced. Men could
disappear overnight without leaving any identification behind or
could vanish into the teeming world of the *garnis* virtually undetected. But how far was the transition from country to town a
solution to the problems of the countryman? At Bordeaux in the
middle decades of the century there were success stories of street
sellers who blossomed into modest *boutiquiers*;[1] in all the textile
cities, at least until the seventies, the apprentice weaver or silk
throwster stood a chance of setting himself up in his mid twenties
with some prospects before him. In all the cities the owners of
garnis, or at least those substantial enough to lease them, were
provincials—success stories of a limited kind. In contrast, the
last decade of the *ancien régime* witnessed in some instances a
deceleration in urban growth as a result of the distinct falling-off
of the movement into the towns from the countryside; and in
the difficult eighties this could not reasonably be argued to be
a result of the improvement of conditions in the country. The
trend, visible in Toulouse, Troyes, Strasbourg, and Bordeaux,
and, more speculatively, at Lille and Rouen, was probably born
of empirical knowledge that city life was no solution to one's
problems. At Toulouse the decline in the annual influx of immigrants from the diocese (more specifically the Lauragais) was of
the order of 13 per cent, that of immigrants from the Pyrenees,
a subsidiary movement, was relatively negligible.[2] At Strasbourg,
whereas in 1784 83 per cent of all *compagnons* in minor trades were
étrangers à la ville, a census of 1789 placed outsiders at 61 per cent.[3]
At Bordeaux a high-water mark in urban immigration had been
passed, and in the late eighties the city was probably losing
citizens—a trend to be continued during the Revolution.[4] At
Troyes and Lille and the textile cities of the north, the textile
slump makes readily understandable a kind of urban exodus of
weavers and their families seeking to build up some kind of

[1] J. Poussou, 'Aspects de l'immigration pyrénéenne', pp. 101–2.
[2] J. Rives, 'L'Évolution démographique de Toulouse', pp. 135–6.
[3] F. Hermann, *Notes historiques, statistiques et littéraires de la ville de Strasbourg*
(1817–19), vol. ii, p. 92.
[4] Forrest, 'The Condition of the Poor in Revolutionary Bordeaux', pp. 150–1.

makeshift existence.[1] The same phenomenon manifested itself at Rouen, where droves of unemployed textile workers tried impotently to be taken on for the harvests in 1788 and 1789, and in Languedoc, where woollen workers *en chômage* tried to find work on a grape harvest whose demands were in any case reduced: 'soit par leur âge, soit par leur constitution [les tisserands] ne peuvent être assujettis à des travaux de cette nature, toujours trop pénible pour des hommes qui n'y sont point faits'.[2]

The crisis years of the late eighties were in fact, like those of the mid nineties, to set up a two-way traffic. They either brought urban workers *en chômage* into the countryside or sent them towards other towns in search of work. Those of Troyes and Lille sought out the canal de Picardie; Rouennais and Cauchois set out in the direction of the digue de Cherbourg or towards Paris. At the same time the hungry of the countryside, the victims of poor harvests, poured into cities in the belief that there the attention of authorities would be focused on their plight. The public works set up in Montmartre served as a magnet for the Île de France, and many had to be turned away.[3] Dismissed farm *servantes* made for their homes, hoping that their parents might feed them. Mountain dwellers of the Causses and the Montagne Noire, feeling the pinch of hunger in the spring, left in search of seasonal work in Bas-Languedoc months earlier than usual, roaming around in search of labour. The Auxois found itself flooded by the hungry of the Morvan—and from the Morvan *il ne vient ni bon vent ni bons gens*. Into the Brie and Valois there teemed Norman, Tourangeau, and people from as far away as Basse-Bourgogne. Anyone who moved was probably exchanging bad for worse, yet everyone who left was convinced that someone, somewhere, was better off. There was a curious exception to this rule. The Auvergnat, with his experience of living off the land of other regions, the *maître ès mendicité* of eighteenth-century France, read the signs aright.[4] He did not make northward towards Paris or Normandy or towards Lyons—for what was the point? What hope did he have as *colporteur* or occasional labourer in such a

---

[1] G. Lefebvre, *La Grande Peur* (Paris, 1932), p. 17.
[2] A.D. Hérault C 2226, Letter from Brûlé, 28 Nov. 1783.
[3] A. Tuetey, *L'Assistance publique à Paris pendant la Révolution* (Paris, 1929), préface.
[4] Poitrineau, 'Aspects de l'émigration', pp. 23–4; Poussou (ed.), 'Les mouvemonts migratoires', p. 69.

market? Instead, he directed his footsteps towards Spain or remained behind to beg in Riom and Clermont. He suffered too, but less than those of more affluent regions, for he had mastered the secrets of survival. The less practised, however, sallied into the unknown, a great reservoir of hungry manpower searching for work and cheap food. The chances of these thousands of men, and behind them even more women and children, remaining on the path of virtue were indeed slender.

IV

AN ECONOMY OF MAKESHIFTS

ii. *The Beggars*

La source de la mendicité dans cette paroisse vient sans contredit de la cherté du blé et des denrées: suite nécessaire du prix excessif des convenants, attendu que les convenanciers pour être en état de payer leur ferme se trouvent obligés de vendre bien cher les blés et autres fruits qu'ils tirent de leurs terres. Les pauvres y perdent doublement, les convenanciers aimant mieux faire tout l'ouvrage par eux-mêmes, tant bien que mal, que de prendre des journaliers dont ils pensent que la nourriture leur coûterait trop.

Les mendiants de cette paroisse sont ou des vieillards ou des infirmes, ou des enfants hors d'état de travailler et même des personnes valides qui ne refuseraient pas le travail, si trois ou quatre sols par jour qu'ils pourraient gagner à la journée, étaient suffisants pour leur entretien et celui de leur famille.

Recteur de Placernon, Saint-Pol-de-Léon
23 décembre 1774 (A.D. Ille-et-Vilaine C 1294).

SEASONAL migration or permanent movement into town or city was clearly very far from providing a total solution to the problems of the poor. Both left untouched the position of the man and woman in full-time work but earning insufficient for the support of a family. What could be the fate, for example, of a Breton *journalier* earning 10 *sous* per day if his wife could at the most bring in only half that amount from her hemp-spinning for a very small part of the year and if there were children to feed? What would be the position of the Orléanais *bonnetier* earning 20 *sous* and his spinner-wife earning under half that amount if there were three children to feed; or the situation of a mason, carpenter, or other building worker bringing in 15 *sous* and married to a lacemaker earning a pittance if they had a family of two or three children? Here one is contemplating the position of people *in work* and perhaps in reasonable health. What happened to the same people if they were laid off work or were unable to work through advancing years or ill health? What did the family do in time of *chômage*? Textile slump rarely meant an immediate total laying-off of labour. First of all it meant a reduction in work and wages. Spinners invariably got into difficulties before weavers did, as their services were most easily dispensed with, and hence the first to be unemployed were women and working children. What did these members of the family do to remedy their need? What happened to family units fractured by the disappearance of the main earner? Clearly those in such situations could not look to work as a source of income. They had little option but to turn to charity. Some members of the family group became beggars.[1]

Even in normal times, without the added pressure of reduced harvests or industrial depression, any parish had a number of begging children, the offspring of those who, though labouring in some instances to their full extent, could not earn enough to support their young. These children were not the product of large and unwieldy families. The average family size in France as a whole was four to five children, but infant mortality rates were high.[2] The odds of surviving infancy for the child fed on a pap of cheap grain and living in a filthy shack were restricted. Lists of *bureaux de charité* indicate that two or three living children were the norm amongst the poor and that, small as such family units might be, they could, nevertheless, very easily run into difficulties.[3]

In any community the commonest beggar was the child; indeed, if any credence is to be lent to the figures of the *Comité de Mendicité*, children comprised between a half and two-thirds of the beggars of any community,[4] and the same message was conveyed by the *enquêtes* of the 1770s.

Il y a dans la paroisse 280 pauvres dont 31 invalides ou vieillards et 122 enfants hors d'état de rien faire. Il y a 77 mendiants parmi lesquels presque tous sont des enfants et de la paroisse.

(Flavin, 808 inhabitants)

---

[1] This chapter is largely based upon the inquiries of the seventies listed above (p. 11, n. 1) and on the returns of the *Comité de Mendicité*. Few of the former dealt in exact figures, but they were highly explicit upon categories of beggars. Equally pertinent are the registers of the *bureaux de charité*.
[2] On this theme see the bibliography of J. Dupâquier, 'Sur la population française', pp. 63–4.   [3] Hufton, *Bayeux*, pp. 288–97; Robin, *Semur*, pp. 221–3.
[4] Bloch and Tuetey, *Procès-verbaux*, p. 573.

Dans le lieu ou les villages il y a 24 familles et ces 24 familles fournissent environ 50 enfants qui demandent leur pain.

(Saint-Laurent-d'Olt, 930 inhabitants)

La plupart même de ceux qui sont dans ce rang [les pauvres] ne peuvent avec la santé faire subsister dans ces années leurs nombreuses familles, ce qui fait qu'il y a plus de 30 petits enfants qui sont obligés de mendier leur pain dans la paroisse. (Bonneterre, 319 inhabitants)[1]

Such statements, made by the curés of the diocese of Rodez, have their exact counterparts in every region of France, and that whether in town or country. Babies, a subdelegate of the Auvergne moaned, have scarcely left the cradle before they are taught how to beg, so as not to be a burden to their families.[2] The smallest toddler—or in fact, in some instances, an even younger child, if he had a brother or sister strong enough to carry him—could be taught to go the rounds of the more prosperous farms in search of food. Often in the Auvergne, as elsewhere, their supplication was largely seasonal. They could get most in the late summer when the harvest had been gathered, and in the early autumn could expect their share of bruised and windfall fruit. This was a kind of patrimony for poor children; they had a right to the wild fruits of the hedgerows, to the wild herbs which grew on anyone's land. They could beg for right of entry to a property to gather sorrel to make *potage d'oseille*, a cheap, palatable, and virtually nutritionless soup. They could beg acorns, dandelion leaves—anything—for animal fodder. On the coast, as well as being active gatherers of shellfish in their own right, they could beg fish heads and sardines and dabs too small to sell. In towns and cities every foodshop, every market stall, had its bevy of small beggars, hungry and deserving, ready to accept the stalest crust, bruised vegetables, rancid butter, or food of which the freshness was clearly questionable. From early infancy, in fact, the children of the poor learnt to cadge a living, learnt about the viability of an economy of makeshifts, learnt the knack of presenting a cogent case and the places and situations under

---

[1] Lempereur, L'*État du diocèse de Rodez*; 99 per cent of the parishes made similar replies.

[2] A.D. Puy-de-Dôme C 1099, M. Mignot, *subdélégué de Thiers* 1768: 'La paroisse de Domaize qui, avec celles de Saint-Jean-des-Ollières, Saint-Dier, la-Chapelle-Agnon et quelques autres fournissent une pépinière de mendiants à inonder le royaume, qui à peine sont sortis de la coquille qu'ils reçoivent des leçons pour n'être pas à charge à leur famille.' This was the area of heaviest seasonal migration in Auvergne.

which they would receive the most sympathy. This apprentice-ship, for it was no less, occurred long before any other formal service as domestic servant, labourer, or textile worker. Should work run out, should they find themselves in later life between jobs or unable to support themselves on the proceeds of their labour, begging was their natural recourse, or at least one in which they as mothers could initiate and indoctrinate their children. The Pyrenean children, who would one day pour into Spain as seasonal migrants or wend their way up the Garonne to Toulouse, spent the summer months cadging beans and crusts at the more substantial farms of the plain. In winter those of Massat accompanied their mothers to Toulouse to beg outside Saint-Sernin. In spring, when the snow melted, the valleys of Massat and Garbet, traversed by merchants *en route* to Spain, became the hunting ground of packs of youngsters demanding alms.[1] A report on the Pays de Foix spoke of 2,000 young people

sans autre savoir faire que de mendier leur pain ou se rendre dans le bien d'autrui comme en se portant presque tous les jours dans les forêts, les autres sur les vignes et les prairies des particuliers pour s'y procurer des fagots de bois, du foin ou des fruits et venir ensuite les vendre sur les places publiques pour s'alimenter de leur produit.[2]

What better training could there be for those whose livelihood would be dependent upon the vicissitudes of seasonal labour?

Less practised perhaps were the children of the textile cities; in normal times from the age of about 8 these could help in some of the less skilful aspects of production, and, in many instances, they turned out on Sundays and saints' days or at fairs and markets to make a supplication. In times of crisis in the textile industry, parents pushed out their children to beg around the parish. Indeed, at Rouen in 1788, when spinners' wages had fallen to an erratic 4 *sous*, even if they could get the work, mothers of families placed more hope in feeding their children by sending them around the more affluent farms to ask for food than in the proceeds of their labour.[3]

The begging children of the Massif and the Alps, little chimney-sweeps and pedlars of pins and needles from Ambert and Thiers,

[1] Chevalier, *Les Pyrénées*, p. 671.
[2] A.N. H 722–3, Mémoire du Sieur Maury, fabricant à Pamiers.
[3] A.D. Seine-Maritime C 2211, État des pauvres par paroisses, 1788, parishes of Guetteville and Betrimont.

made a kind of income for a *colporteur* who engaged them. If they survived their dangerous childhood they would in turn blossom into adult pedlar beggars organizing their own troop of soot-streaked children. Observers of the poor, whether *contrôleurs généraux* or men on the spot like Henrion de Bussy or Richeprey, Necker's emissary in the Rouergue, appreciated that the habit of begging was in 90 per cent of cases acquired in infancy[1] and hence was ineradicable; and they saw nothing contradictory in statements such as, 'Il y a au moins cent individus comme les enfants qui quêtent du pain aux portes par nécessité. Là sont les jeunes fainéants qui méritent d'être corrigés plutôt que les vieillards'.[2] Yet they could not deny the needs of the children in question. Indeed, the work of the *Comité de Mendicité* was to attempt to enshrine the realization in a figure: 1,886,935 children whose parents could not support them.[3]

Along with the children of *journaliers* or small holders, the commonest begging figure in any community was the aged man or woman, those no longer capable of work for physical reasons: diminished strength; defective eyesight—the disappearance of the lacemaker's most considerable asset; knotted, arthritic, and useless joints. Old age, for the poor, began when one reached 50.[4] By then a linen weaver could be expected to have lost his effective eyesight, and workers in cotton or silk were little better placed. Such people could not labour in any industry, could not carry heavy loads, could not walk great distances as seasonal or temporary migrants. Indeed, for the Marchois or Creusois or Rouergat the discovery that his strength was diminishing, or perhaps the hope of amassing a little protection against the years to come, might be the final incentive to undertake an extended period of absence in Spain. The poor never had the opportunity to save; with their strength gone, they had lost their only capital asset.

---

[1] A.D. Puy-de-Dôme C 1310, the contrôleur général, Terray, in a circular of 26 Dec. 1769 particularly drew the attention of administrators of *dépôts de mendicité* 'aux enfants que leurs pères et mères ou ceux qui se les étaient appropriés élevaient dans la fainéantise, et familiarisaient dès l'âge le plus tendre avec la vie mendiante, . . . sans doute . . . une des causes qui ont perpétué le fléau du vagabondage et de la mendicité'. [2] A.D. Ille-et-Vilaine L 1102, Étrelles, 1790.
[3] Bloch and Tuetey, *Procès-verbaux*, p. 573.
[4] G. Lefebvre, *Les Paysans du Nord*, p. 302, and A.D. Somme C 245, Letter of 26 Jan. 1758: 'L'expérience nous apprend que l'ouvrier qui manufacture à la ville ne peut plus supporter le genre de travail dès l'âge de 50 ans . . .'

The aged woman was a more common figure than the aged man: a black bundle of rags with permanent backache and prone to incontinence—the predictable results of an untreated prolapse —and with ulcerated varicose veins.[1] This is not mere rhetoric; such a description is written into every report of the Académie de Médecine. Such a person was a burden to relatives, an unproductive element in a society where everyone had to labour. The *Comité de Mendicité* estimated 804,775, or a quarter of the total number needing assistance in France, to be aged, but this was a very approximate guess.[2] What is more evident is that, along with young children, the aged were in any community permitted to beg respectably. They might, with dignity, beg in the churches, and they had a kind of monopoly of the privilege to sit in the porch or on the steps of churches and make their requests. In parishes in the Auvergne, where begging had been reduced to a fine art, the aged beggar was the only one who caught the eye, for he or she alone remained to beg all the year round, whereas the adult males and most of the children had left on their seasonal odysseys. The more affluent parishes in the *enquêtes* of the seventies might say, 'Outre les vieillards et les enfants nous n'avons pas de mendiants', and even the poorer would accord them primacy: 'Ceux que j'ai dans ma paroisse sont des infirmes ou des vieillards ou . . . ce sont les enfants de pauvres gens à l'entretien desquels le salaire ne suffit pas.'[3] The old could not count on filial piety. The struggling *journalier* or small holder trying to maintain a wife and children treated his parents to short shrift—they were extra mouths to feed and occupiers of valuable space. 'Honour thy father and thy mother' was a recurrent theme in sermons: something of which the poor needed a constant reminder.[4] More concrete evidence of the difficult relationship

---

[1] B.N. Fonds Joly de Fleury 1215, Enquête faite dans soixante dix huit bailliages du ressort du Parlement de Paris sur la pénurie des sages-femmes (1728–9): 'Les femmes ont le malheur de rester affligées de descentes de matrices; malheur qui arrive à plus de la moitié des femmes de la campagne . . .'

[2] Bloch and Tuetey, *Procès-verbaux*, p. 573. Though based on the returns of only forty-one departments, this calculation may have been one of the more accurate and was not one which the *comité* sought to discredit.

[3] A.D. Lot C 822, curé of Saint-Hilaire-de-Montcuq 1775.

[4] A.D. Ille et-Vilaine 5 Fa 108 includes four sermons on this theme. Clearly the issue was capable of provoking much clerical rhetoric. A.D. Ille-de-Vilaine C 4937: 'Leurs enfants mariés . . . chargés de famille regrettent inutilement l'impuissance où ils sont de pourvoir aux besoins de leurs pères. . . . Chacun d'eux se chargerait à ses parens avec empressement si on lui en facilitait les moyens, s'il n'envisageait pas

between parents and children emerges in the *actes d'avancement de succession* in which small holders, no longer physically capable of working the land or trekking to places of seasonal employment, recognized the need to hand over their meagre property to their children, but sought guarantees that meals would in that event be forthcoming, and meals which were something more than left-overs from the children's plates.[1] Such *actes* were common practice in communities of small holders—in the Gévaudan, Auvergne, Brittany, and parts of Normandy. That the same strain between the generations existed in towns can be seen from the registers of entry of the *hospices*, which reveal that the *hospices* were prepared to take in a proportion of the urban old in exchange for such property as they possessed—derelict cottages, old *métiers*, and furniture—property which the children tried to dispute with the institution. In many cases it was probably difficult to choose between the condition of those without relatives and those at the mercy of their children. The curé of Les Bondons (diocese of Mende) thus described his parishioners in his annual report to the prior:

Pradeilhes l'ainé de Lozerette bien pauvre a son père vieux hors d'état d'agir et tout nud: Pradeilhes cadet est très misérable a sa femme infirme et alitée depuis plus d'un an. On avait surtout besoin d'une couverture et de quelque linge pour la servir . . .

Pierre Coudère vieux avait besoin de quelque chose pour s'habiller. Charles Coudère pauvreté commune aurait besoin de quelque linge pour le lit.

Anne Delon vieille avait besoin de quelque chose pour se nourrir.

Baptiste Albanie vieux et bien pauvre avait surtout besoin pour le lit où il n'y a rien qu'un peu de paille.

Courtez vieux bien pauvre a sa femme toute nue.

François Chardonnet pauvre et vieux aurait besoin de quelque chemise.

Antoine Dumas du Crouzet pauvreté commune ayant plusieurs enfants. Il y a la belle mère vieille et négligée par son beaufils et s'il y a quelque chose il faut que ce soit pour elle.[2]

Small wonder the old were sympathetically received by those in a position to help them.

la cruelle nécessité de ne pouvoir leur donner un morceau de pain sans l'enlever à leurs enfans.'

[1] They are the basis of Bernard's article 'L'Alimentation en Gévaudan', and of de Bouard (ed.), *Histoire de Normandie*, p. 361.

[2] A.D. Lozère G 1834, État des pauvres de la paroisse des Bondons et leurs principaux et plus pressans besoins, 1760.

The begging habits of healthy adults were perforce more restricted than those of the young and aged. The mother of the family played a much more important part than the father in the organization of the family begging economy. She it was who taught the children how and where to beg. It was her relationship with the lady at the château, with the parish priest, with pious *bien pensant* families, or with more affluent farmers' wives that determined the reception of the children when they turned up at the back door. Breton society had peculiar qualities in this respect: the area being one with large numbers of nobles of modest wealth, the female members of the noble families took an active interest in poor village children, often acting as their godmothers and serving as references for domestic posts in the towns where they had contacts—even the brigand Marion de Faouët could draw upon the support of her godmother, the dame de Stanghihan, in this way.[1] While the children were young they could count on some help in the way of scraps and milk from the seigneurial kitchen. The same spirit was manifest in that part of Normandy which now forms the Manche; it died in the Bessin but appears to have had some existence in Picardy, in the Lyonnais, where the Vianney family enjoyed particular repute,[2] in Bas-Languedoc, and in the Pyrenees. In the Gévaudan, parts of the Auvergne, the Périgord, the Limousin, and the Beauce, on the other hand, the *noblesse* were proverbially mean, but everywhere it can be said that it was of import to know 'les maisons où on donne facilement la charité' and this was knowledge possessed most effectively by the women of the village. The struggling mother of a family was clearly a virtuous personage, and virtue, as will presently be indicated, was an important criterion for determining who was worthy of charity.

At what point, however, did the mother herself turn beggar? Much depended upon how well the family held together in face of strain. Poverty is an acid: it corrodes and dissolves human relationships. But it was always easier for a father to opt out of his obligations than for a mother to do so—easier for him to return home via the *cabaret* suitably anaesthetized with cheap alcohol to the squalor of home and the hungry family. The

---

[1] A. M. Corre and P. Aubry, *Documents de criminologie rétrospective. Bretagne, XVIIe et XVIIIe siècles* (Lyon-Paris, 1895), p. 249.

[2] Gutton, *La Société et les pauvres*, p. 200.

cabaretier, over-willing to provide a client with drink on credit against the returns of the harvest or some speculative profit on seasonal labour, was already the unsavoury ally of the father of the family, and his enemy, the parish priest, had already taken his stand with the womenfolk. The conflict is implicit in the Rouergue *enquête* of the 1770s; it existed in the Auvergne, the Comminges, in Lorraine—it penetrates the ecclesiastical *cahiers* of the *bailliage* of Auxerre; it is found above all in Brittany, where drunkenness was a major social problem and where priests expostulated in vain against inebriated, underemployed men with family responsibilities swilling down cheap cider 'afin d'empêcher le bien de Dieu de se perdre' while their wives hammered at the door begging bread for their children.[1] As the relationship between husband and wife deteriorated, so the mother of the family turned progressively to charity and became more insistent in her demands.

The broken home was a common phenomenon, and in almost 100 per cent of cases the one who severed his ties, cleared off altogether and either turned temporary migration into permanent disappearance or merely failed to come home, was the father of the family. Any married woman whose husband joined the army was as good as abandoned. In the main, wives did not accompany their men, and military pay was not calculated with the support of anyone but the soldier in mind.[2] Auvergnat priests equated the enlistment of the married with the pressures of poverty and the anxiety of the male to be quit of his obligations.[3]

The abandoned mother and the widow could be in roughly the same position. The odds on widowhood for a woman who survived the birth of two or three children were high. Since the norm was for a couple to work together, the disappearance of one partner could totally jeopardize the family economy. Hence Jeanne Michon of Lyons, former *dévideuse* who brought to her master silk-weaver husband a dowry of 300 *livres*, was left with 'un vieux bois de lit garni d'un couette, une couverte Catalogne, un drap, le tour de lit de cadis vert, un chevet de plume, le tout usé qui peut valoir en tout douze livres'.[4] If the widow was left

---

[1] A.D. Ille-et-Vilaine C 1294, Landerneau 1775; C 1745, Josselin, 1784; L 1137 Medréac, 1790; Lempereur, *L'État du diocèse de Rodez*, parishes Coubisou, Calmont et Naves, etc.; Saint-Jacob, *Les Paysans de la Bourgogne*, pp. 546–7.

[2] A.D. Puy-de-Dôme C 879.

[3] Ibid., letter of curé of Bort, 1740.

[4] Charité Lyon, F 34, dossier Jeanne Michon.

with a young family, her plight could be pitiable in the extreme. The widow Tetrelle, washerwoman, trying to cope with three small children; innumerable lacemakers whose 2–6 *sous* per day were the only regular source for families of two and three children; the widow Masson, struggling as a street fruit-seller to support five children all under the age of 10, when her shoemaker husband died leaving her only with the usual bed and cooking-pots and not even a *métier* which might raise a few *livres*—these cases, from Bayeux, are far from isolated; they came in for the few *sous* of an annual hand-out made by the *bureau de charité* (70 out of 310 households helped were those of widows with an average of three children; a further 52 with an average of two children were households where the father had abandoned his responsibilities).[1] One can multiply such examples from the records of any *bureau de charité*.[2] When the curé of Les Bondons (diocese of Mende) made his annual report to the prior of how he had spent a donation made by the latter, he described the families of seven widows all without shirts to their backs, clogs to their feet, or bed covers, and that in a rocky, barren, mountainous region covered in snow for three months of the year.[3] In the neighbouring diocese of Le Puy, at Emblavès 17 widows, 12 of them lacemakers, had dependent upon them 49 people. There were also 3 single women with 11 dependants and 5 households of orphans totalling in all 9 children. Together these formed the bulk of the *pauvres misérables*. In the 25 households thus enumerated, at least one person was in full-time work, and there were none committed to a perpetual begging existence. There were a further 32 households of 93 people who were given over to cadging a livelihood: 21 of these were headed by widows (62 people), 4 by widowers, and the rest were young orphan children. Most of these 32 households included at least one infirm or insane member: 'Jeanne . . . veuve de Jean Maurin, mendiante, a deux fils dont l'un est aveugle et une fille aussi mendiante. . . . Françoise Bonnet, fille orpheline, mendiante, son frère innocent, et deux

---

[1] A.D. Calvados C 955, Registre du bureau de charité de Bayeux, 26 janvier 1785; Hufton, *Bayeux*, pp. 288–97.

[2] This generalization holds good for all the *bureaux de charité* of Languedoc, Brittany, Burgundy, Normandy, etc., see below, pp. 159–67, and Robin, *Semur*, pp. 221–3. Twenty-one out of fifty-nine family units assisted were headed by a widow. Cf. also M. Couturier, *Châteaudun*, p. 85; here widows were the largest single grouping of destitute.   [3] A.D. Lozère G 1834.

petites sœurs mendiantes . . .'[1] Small wonder the widow and her brood were common beggars. What other resource had they?

The old, the young, the widowed, the abandoned mother and her brood fit emphatically into the category of deserving poor, *vrais pauvres, mendiants de bonne foi, mendiants par nécessité, mendiants en permanence*, those whom society at any time and in any place has deemed deserving of pity. But the vocabulary of poverty comprehended more than the above. Who were the *mauvais pauvres* and the beggars who were described by further complexities, *pauvre passant mendiant, mendiant sédentaire vagabond, mendiant vagabond, errant, errant vagabond, errant incorrigible, vagabond, vagabond brigand*? The traditionally deserving poor were only one aspect, and a fairly minor one, of the problem of begging. Far more considerable was the question of the adult male and the point at which he joined the ranks of the beggars. The curé of Athis in his remarkable analysis of the recruitment of the begging population of Normandy described a continual process in which the bachelor labourer with a little to spare developed into a hard-pressed father unable to support his brood of two or three children.[2] At such a time, demoralized by his struggles, he did not hesitate to take up the beggar's staff and take to the open road—the more readily if his father had done it before him. At this point, such people became *mendiants volontaires*, a role they had chosen, and if they abandoned their homes altogether for a life of vagrancy, they were officially classed as *errants*. As such, the odds were heavy that they would fall into a life of crime and would become *vagabonds*.

The good priest scurried a little hastily over the initial stages of the process: long before begging became a way of life for the *journalier*, and often while he was in full employ, his children would have tried to make themselves self-sufficient by begging; before he became a full-time beggar, the *journalier* or small holder would become a part-time one. The decision to leave the parish and seek a livelihood in a town might be a genuine search for work—though the odds on finding it were not high and he was therefore likely to turn beggar. Any number of factors might throw the adult male into the ranks of the beggars. Even as full-time worker, inadequately remunerated, he might find himself

---

[1] A.D. Haute-Loire 501 C 5815. See also Appendix III.
[2] A.D. Calvados H, Suppl. 1308, cited above, p. 11.

with hand outstretched on Sundays, saints' days or, in Brittany, *pardons*. Master weavers and hatters in Orleans turned out to beg on Sundays surrounded by their families, as evidence that they needed bread even on days when they could not earn.[1] Master silk weavers in Lyons did the same. *Propriétaires-mendiants* of the *généralité* of Tours used fairs and saints' days to enter the city and, with hand outstretched, tried to beg a few coins, and part-time efforts of this kind can be found everywhere.[2]

Some jobs, more particularly in some regions than in others, presumed a degree of *errance*—probably accompanied by begging. Such jobs were not the preserve of the married man. In the Beauce, Brie, Languedoc, parts of the Auvergne and the Lyonnais, Quercy, and parts of Gascony, employers in the main only took on farm *valets* or *domestiques* during the peak periods of the agricultural year; for the rest of the year they had to move around in search of work. In September *servantes, vachères, valets de labours, petits bergers* found themselves dismissed until the following spring.[3] In Velay the girls might return to their parents' home and make lace; but for the men, apart from living off the scanty proceeds of the summer's labour, there was nothing to do in the area, and so they might make for Nîmes and the cities of the Rhône valley in the hope of finding a little casual work, but with small chance of success. The Beauceron *valet*, having earned good wages in summer for a few short weeks, looked to Orleans or Paris, via the farms of Normandy or the Île de France where he begged a living, knowing that his hopes of finding winter work were restricted.

Moreover, to be a *valet* or a *servante de ferme* was clearly the aspiration of far too many in the countryside, and the quest for such work frequently met with failure. Nor was a domestic situation on a stable basis invariably easy to come by in the towns. *Venu ici pour servir de domestique* is often the accompaniment of those accused of *mendicité* before the courts; while the

---

[1] Lefebvre, *Études orléanaises*, vol. i, p. 218.

[2] e.g. at Godewaesvelde and Boeschèpe, 'le petit peuple, jusqu'aux fermiers de deux vaches même, est dans cette habitude . . . de courir mendier trois lieues à la ronde, ce qui a donné l'exemple aux fainéants des autres paroisses' (Lefebvre, *Les Paysans du Nord*, p. 313); Lempereur, *L'État du diocèse de Rodez*, Coupiguet, Gillorgues, Saint-Julien de Rodelle, La Bessenoit, etc.; A.D. Ille-et-Vilaine, C 1294, Saint-Pol-de-Léon, Ploërmel, Nantes, etc.

[3] P. Léon, *Structures économiques et problèmes sociaux du monde rural dans la France du Sud-Est* (Paris, 1966), p. 81.

rapid turnover in domestic servants is revealed by people coming
before the courts who had had eight or even ten situations while
still in their teens, and this applied to both men and women. It
was in no way remarkable for a farmer's wife near Quimper to
find her barn shared by a dozen girls between jobs. A young
Savoyarde, aged 15, had left her home at the age of 12 to seek
work at Bourg-en-Bresse, but found only temporary work. She
moved to Grenoble, begging on the way, and, finding little
satisfaction there, embarked on a search which led her—no mean
trip on foot—to Fontainebleau. Work dried up, and despairing
of the resources of Fontainebleau she sought work at Villefranche in the Lyonnais. Much of this girl's adolescence had
clearly been spent begging her bread, yet she was considered by
the courts neither *mendiante* nor *vagabonde* because her search for
work was reckoned serious and the nature of her employ was
deemed liable to frequent disruptions.[1] In a case at Gray in
Franche-Comté, a 16-year-old had seen service at Vesoul, Besançon, and Dole.[2] Army recruiting agents even worked upon young
domestiques between jobs, promising them shoes and regular
meals, which seemed an attractive proposition to the footsore
temporarily begging their bread.[3] Allied to this might be the
sporadic begging of a limited type—bed and, it was hoped, a
crust—practised by the seasonal migrant *en route* to his seasonal
employ. Such a man was regarded at the farms he passed on the
way to his work as a *pauvre passant*, a term that meant simply a
man or woman passing through (and not lingering) *en route* to a
specific destination. The government acknowledged the need for
people of certain regions, which it listed in a circular of 1766, to
seek work elsewhere during certain periods of the year.[4] It sought
to control this movement by insisting that such persons carried
a passport, though it was confident that the seasonal migrant
with a limited amount of time at his disposal was usually *en route*
to a specific job, often by previous arrangement, and likely on his
journey only to beg (in which case he became a *pauvre passant
mendiant*) and to seek shelter at farms which he knew and where
he was known or went at the recommendation of a friend, and

[1] Gutton, *La Société et les pauvres*, p. 144.
[2] A.D. Haute-Saône B 2335, Antoine Guerry.
[3] A.D. Cher, Maréchaussée B 2490, Case of Renvoyé *domestique*.
[4] A.D. Puy-de-Dôme C 776.

where sometimes on the return journey he performed minor jobs to reimburse any hospitality. Hence the Rouergat travelled with a trowel sticking out of his bag, and at least made the gesture of offering to repair stone walls on the farm where he begged his bread and a night's lodging (he was held to be a more scrupulous guest in this respect than the Gévaudois); in the same way the Savoyard's talents as entertainer, the *joueur de veille*, the fortune-teller, the retailer of stories, were a kind of payment for hospitality received.[1] The Auvergnat on his way north or east was prepared to use his ferret for rat-catching or permit his little team to sweep the chimneys against food and lodging. But for much of the time he was, without doubt, a beggar and an *errant*.

A subtle line distinguished *errance* from *vagabondage* in the minds of *ancien régime* legislators, and it was a distinction which had a kind of reality. In the economy of certain regions a degree of mobility, a degree of *errance*, was implicit. The economy of Languedoc could not exist without the continual flux of man-power from hill to plain, and though the type of seasonal labourer so far described was most commonly a small holder in his native Gévaudan or Rouergue, there was clearly scope for the casual labourer, the *'rouleur'*, to snatch a few weeks' employ here and there, begging in between times and existing without a fixed abode. The great grain regions of the Beauce and the Île de France, though a pale reflection of the Languedocian scene, threw up opportunities for intensive and well-remunerated labour during the summer season, while winter work on the Loire and refuge in the cities during the dead season again made possible a kind of itinerant existence not entirely lacking in purpose. Even so-called 'cottage-bound' Brittany knew *lakât war ar beoz* or *mond el leo*, to take to an endless road, and hence to push along by an accumulation of small jobs and expedients, now here, now there.[2]

That the *colporteur* was in fact a thinly disguised wandering beggar has already had some mention. Clearly the situation was a kind of half-way stage between respectable profession and unconditional vagrancy, a phasing out of an individual from his social responsibilities. The *marchand quincaillier*, unable to pay

---

[1] H. Affre, *Dictionnaire des institutions, mœurs et coutumes de Rouergue*, article 'Émigration', and O. Hufton, 'Begging, Vagrancy, Vagabondage, and the Law', p. 101.

[2] N. Quellien, *L'Argot des nomades* (Paris, 1886), p. 46.

rental on his premises, the *mercier*, shoemaker, tailor, *limonadier*, *marchand d'eau de vie*—anyone, in short, dependent upon an element of trade could hit the open road, ostensibly 'de colporter des marchandises de villages en villages', and never be seen again by wife, children, or landlord—to whom rent was invariably due.[1] Such a type might originate anywhere in France, though probably the peddling communities of the Massif, the Alps, the Pyrenees, and Jura produced more per head of the population than other areas.[2] The government recognized *colportage* as a definite job; the distribution of much industrial produce, particularly ribbons and lace, could not have existed without it, yet no word covered a broader spectrum and the mass of *colporteurs* were *errants* and beggars of dubious worth. Equally necessary in some instances and of dubious repute in others were sailors who worked on inland waterways—most particularly the Loire, though in a subsidiary sense on the Seine, the Saône, and the Allier. The traffic on the Loire was seasonal and one way.[3] The laden vessels could reach Orleans from Nantes but the sailor had to make his way back on foot, for on the return journey the flat-bottomed boats which had carried timber and sugar had to be horse-drawn and required only limited manpower or, in the case of timber, they were entirely dismantled. Hence the river valleys of the Loire, the Saône, and the Allier were periodically traversed by men *sans domicile fixe* who slept on boats upstream and in barns on the return journey and for whom *errance* and accompanying *mendicité* were crucial parts of their livelihood, activities to which they turned especially when paid work ran out or if they suffered some diminution of physical strength.

Industrial slump could see the adult male attempting begging on a more protracted basis. During the periodic crises of Lyonnais silk production, weavers *en chômage* had little alternative other than begging on the streets or packing a few possessions

---

[1] Some excellent examples of this from Lyons are provided by J. Gutton, *La Société et les pauvres*, p. 137.

[2] A.D. Puy-de-Dôme C 920, letter of the Chevalier of Manoux 9 July 1770, contains a peculiarly telling indictment of these itinerants who opted out of their obligations 'laissant mourir leurs femmes et enfants chez eux'.

[3] F. Billaçois, 'La Batellerie de la Loire au XVIIIᵉ siècle', *R.H.M.C.* xi (1964), 163–90, and R. Dion, 'Orléans et l'ancienne navigation de la Loire', *Annales de géographie*, xlvii (1938), 128–54. A.D. Seine-Maritime G 841, the parish priest of Authieux describes the needs of the families of *bateliers* on the Seine 'surtout pendant l'hiver où les travaux de nos bateliers se trouvent suspendus'.

on their backs and making for the Beaujolais to do occasional work on the vines or striking southwards down the Rhône valley, begging an existence when work failed to materialize. The textile slump of 1787 at Rouen and Troyes saw *urban* worker turned *rural* beggar. The decline of the Compagnie des Indes in the 1760s caused a movement out of Lorient into the surrounding countryside of workers on the docks, porters, and sailors who could find no work in the town and who could expect little from urban charity.[1] These are a few examples which could be readily multiplied in the closing decades of the *ancien régime*. A second root cause for protracted begging might be the failure to find the work one was anticipating: the case, for example, of the seasonal migrant who might even have borrowed against the proceeds of his seasonal labour and found after his walk that the work he was expecting had dried up owing to harvest failure or other disaster, or of the newly arrived urban immigrant faced with the problem of finding work in a highly competitive labour market. Above all, however, the particular economic problems of the last twenty years of the *ancien régime* inflated the numbers of those who turned to begging as a part of their livelihood. This might be a sudden experience, the case of the small holder and his family who were the victims of unusually low harvest yields, or the gradual realization that the total sum of the family's labour was inadequate. Families were used to coping with crisis. Nine times out of ten, by a mixture of debt and deprivation the family survived, but there was always the blow which led to final destitution and perhaps to the disintegration of the family unit. The decisive factor in its disintegration was usually the dis- appearance of the father, leaving his family behind. Sometimes the departure was due to purely personal reasons—the result of the death of the female partner when the man in question found himself with children on his hands and only his earnings. In such a case his children became *enfants trouvés* but of known parentage, and the hospital registers take account of the factor. On 8 March 1764 a mason of Bayeux abandoned his three children with the message that since his wife had died he had parted with all his possessions and now must leave his children; a few months later a draper left another three behind him and debts amounting to over 100 *livres*, incurred since the death of his wife.[2] At Clermont

---

[1] A.D. Ille-et-Vilaine C 1294, Lorient.   [2] A.D. Calvados H, Suppl. 561 B 1.

a third of those abandoned in 1737 were of known parentage, and of those 105, 20 were the children of widowers; at Lyons out of 20 children of known parentage abandoned in 1779, 4 were the children of widows and 8 of widowers.[1] The same story can be repeated at Rennes, Bourges, Strasbourg, and wherever the hospital administrations saw fit to keep detailed records. The professions of the fathers look remarkably uniform: at Lyons in 1772, out of 31 children of known parentage, 21 belonged to silk workers, 2 to *affaneurs*, 3 to building workers; in 1778 out of 46, 17 were offspring of *ouvriers en soie*, 4 *affaneurs*, 2 building workers, 3 shoemakers, 3 tailors, and the rest a hotchpotch of petty trades.[2] In Auvergne the *colporteur* is a recurrent figure.[3] In Bourges and Rennes petty traders, servants, shoemakers, and navvies figure most frequently. At Strasbourg the *rapeur de tabac* clearly experienced difficulty in holding his family together.

Sometimes the decisive factor in making the decision to give up and opt out was the result of a difficult year or accumulated difficult years. In the words of the curé of Athis, 'ils se découragent', they wearied of the strain of keeping a family on means barely adequate for one person, and, having done so, they gathered their few remaining garments into a bundle and hit the open road, never to be seen again by their families. The divorce lists of the Year II confirm just this factor: in Metz, for example, 268 working women sought divorce, the most usual grounds, separation, the duration of the separation commonly being nine or five years, corresponding to the extreme hardship years of 1785 and 1789.[4] The story is the same at Toulouse where working women pleading abandonment constituted a significant category of those seeking divorce.[5] The results of the inquiries conducted by the bishops into the state of their dioceses are no less explicit. 'I am overwhelmed', wrote the curé of Bort, near Clermont, 'with women who come to me not only beseeching bread but accusing their husbands of threatening them that if they do not let the youngest children perish they will leave them and that alone they can manage but that even

[1] A.D. Puy-de-Dôme C 1323.

[2] Gutton, *La Société et les pauvres*, p. 136.

[3] A.D. Puy-de-Dôme C 1326, letter of M. Bournet at Issoire 2 Sept. 1740 on twenty children of known parentage abandoned at the *hôpital*.

[4] J. L. Hôte, 'Le Divorce à Metz sous la Révolution et l'Empire', *Annales de l'Est*, 5th ser., iii (1952), 175–83.

[5] M. Cruppi, *Le Divorce pendant la Révolution* (Paris, 1909), pp. 150–61.

working all day they cannot feed their families.'[1] In making the decision to leave, the man concerned had no hope of indulging in an idealized bachelor existence, of having a full stomach and money in his pockets as a result of his labours as he had had in his youth. He had aged and was not the most desirable employee in an overcrowded labour market; he had left his native parish and was not dealing with employers he knew. Moreover, he had been the victim of an irreversible process of brutalization; in making his decision to leave he had sunk almost as low as he could sink. He might intend to make a living by working—and for this reason was known by the vague generic term of *errant*—but the odds were against his finding work on a regular basis and so he was likely to turn into an *errant—mendiant—vagabond*. Initially when a man left his native village he made in the direction of those places of which he had some experience as a seasonal migrant, in the hope of picking up a little work. Hence currents of *errance* correspond precisely with those of seasonal mobility: the Auvergnat struck north or eastwards; the Commingeois went to Bordeaux or Toulouse; the Rouergat or Gévaudois turned his steps towards the Mediterranean coast. Languedoc, with its potential for seasonal work and its mild climate which made sleeping rough much easier, was particularly attractive.[2] The *errant* was unlikely to remain a lone wanderer for very long. Psychologically he felt the need for company and there were also strong practical reasons for companionship. He was not a welcome visitor at the farms where he begged his bread. The farmer's wife could not know if he was a petty thief after her poultry or washing, or the precursor of a group of bandits intent upon pillage, and would try to turn him away. Hence, in order to make sure that his demands were met, threats and intimidation were often essential and they were more effective when made by a group of men than by an individual. The moment, however, that the *errant* had recourse to threats or joined a group, he became to the populace and the law a *vagabond*—and *vagabondage* in a group was an offence which incurred a spell in the galleys.

The *vagabond* group, most often composed of from two to a

---

[1] A.D. Puy-de-Dôme C 897.

[2] R. Liris, 'Mendicité et vagabondage en Basse Auvergne à la fin du XVIIIe siècle', *Revue d'Auvergne*, lxxix (1965), 65–78; Rives, 'L'Évolution démographique de Toulouse', pp. 135–7; Le Roy Ladurie, *Les Paysans de Languedoc*, p. 96.

dozen, usually had a favoured focal point and a set itinerary. Forest regions adjacent to towns, like the hill country behind La Chaise-Dieu or Saint-Seine-l'Abbaye near Dijon or the forest of Crépon near Caen, were *rendez-vous* to which vagrants retired with their pickings. Monasteries giving weekly hand-outs that formed the basis of some kind of existence could be a pole of attraction to the down-and-out. At Fécamp, where a bread distribution worth 15,000 *livres* annually caused as many as 1,000 vagrants to muster, both monks and local farmers dwelt in constant fear of violence and pillaging.[1] The same was true of the parishes surrounding the Trappist monastery of Bonnecombe in the Rouergue and of those around Fontevrault—wherever, in short, 500–600 people could count on a daily or weekly bread ration and could for the rest of the time poach or beg from local farms or walk into the nearest town on market day or holidays. Unsurpassed in this respect was the present tourist *route des abbayes* of the Seine valley which was then trodden by another type of traveller whose starred places of call, according to days of distribution, were Saint Wandrille, Jumièges (where an absentee abbot ensured the pickings were mean), Bec, and Saint Martin-de-Boscherville.[2]

Legal records suggest that amongst the wandering poor, men outnumbered women by at least six to one. Though this figure may be some way from the truth, given that the male vagrant was more to be feared and hence more often reported, women had perhaps less incentive to turn to vagrancy as a remedy for their ills. But—and this is an important exception—in the Beauce–Burgundian belt professional vagabondage merged into brigandage in the great bands of the 1760s to 1790s, and two whole generations came into being who had never known any other way of life, and women had their own special and highly important role to play.

An entire family on the move would appear, on the highly limited information offered by the law courts, to have been rare, perhaps because families took care never to be caught together, perhaps because mobility meant that someone, somewhere, would be left behind—the wandering child that the *hôpital général* knew so well, jettisoned at some juncture by his parents as they passed on. Administrators were insistent on the existence of a problem

[1] A.D. Seine-Maritime C 996.   [2] Ibid. G 841–6.

they called *l'errance des jeunes*, but this referred rather to the
itinerant begging practices of groups of youngsters forced to
cadge a living but not necessarily rejected by their parents, than
to the family on the move.[1] When the family as a whole did take
to the roads, it was likely to be in the direction of a town or city
where it would hope to construct some makeshift existence in
which the begging practices of the children would be a significant
element.

One cannot pretend effectively to count those who were
mendiants or *errants* or *vagabonds* in eighteenth-century France
chiefly because of the difficulty of distinguishing between those
committed wholly or partially to these pursuits. Something
approaching a third of the population had been, or would be,
forced at one time or another—the lucky ones only in childhood
or old age—to make an appeal to charity. Whether or not they
would do so at other junctures depended upon the continuance
of favourable circumstances, good health, employment, and so
on. The odds on missing out altogether on some catastrophe,
such as loss of work, debt, illness, and the types of disaster already
outlined, were obviously not high. In Brittany the *intendant*, de
Molleville, estimated that a quarter of the entire province begged
its living.[2] Inquiries held in 1788 in the Auvergne concluded that
a tenth of the population were 'mendiants qui ne quittent pas
leurs paroisses et qui mendient en permanence'.[3] No estimate was
made of those who moved out to do their begging elsewhere. In
Flanders, Velay, Gévaudan, Rouergue, and Quercy similar
calculations were made but always with the careful proviso that
they left out the wanderers who traversed the area, the *vagabonds*
who descended in packs upon the innocent farmer.[4] In Bas-
Languedoc the number of resident beggars was modest—perhaps
under a twentieth of the total population—yet no region, unless
it was the Beauce, was more beset by groups of *rouleurs*, *errants*,
vagabonds—the line of demarcation is imprecise. In short, the

---

[1] Gutton, *La Société et les pauvres*, p. 123.

[2] A.D. Ille-et-Vilaine C 1294 and H. Sée, *Les Classes rurales*, pp. 470-2. It is
important to distinguish between the crisis years, 1766-8, 1772-6, 1784, 1785,
1789 and less acute phases. Notwithstanding, the magnitude of the problem is clear.

[3] A.D. Puy-de-Dôme C, Commission Intermédiaire, 1788.

[4] Lefebvre considered in *La Grande Peur*, p. 15, a tenth to be a reasonable assumption of the numbers who begged their living on a full-time basis at the end of the
ancien régime. This would seem the most reasonable assumption.

balance between domiciled and itinerant poor clearly varied from region to region. The provinces which threw up the largest numbers of beggars and vagrants were not necessarily those condemned to support them.

The wandering poor are most difficult of all to count. About a quarter of a million seasonal workers every year ran the risk of finding that they were unwanted in their place of seasonal employ and were therefore potential *errants*. The *Comité de Mendicité* estimated the numbers on the roads committed to a full-time vagrant existence as about a twentieth of the total poor of France, but this was a notional idea, for there was no mechanism available for counting the numbers on the roads.[1] It is, however, generally evident that the numbers committed to a begging and itinerant existence were growing throughout France, at least from the 1740s, and, moreover, they were to be rapidly inflated in the seventies and eighties in the ambience of diminished grain harvests and textile slumps. This growth would evidently present numbers of problems of administrators who hoped to curb and alleviate, to repress the manifestations of poverty, on the one hand, and afford meagre help, on the other; problems for the rest of society who had to live with the existence of the poor; and, most of all, problems for the poor themselves, for the growth in the numbers looking for work and help meant increased competition for available resources. In the country, vagrancy was a particular expression of the problem of poverty. For the towns an influx of the down-and-out was no less menacing if the means effectively to employ or to help them did not exist.

How could government and society cope: was it possible in any way to alleviate the problem of begging and its varied manifestations, and if not, what were the attitudes of those able to make the proudest boast of the *ancien régime*, 'il y a toujours du pain à la maison', when confronted with the destitute?

[1] Bloch and Tuetey, *Procès-verbaux*, p. 571.

PART TWO

The Poor and Society

V

FORMAL RELIEF

> Entre les serviteurs de Dieu, les uns s'adonnent à servir
> les malades, les autres à secourir les pauvres, les autres à
> procurer l'avancement de la doctrine chrétienne entre
> les petits enfants, les autres à ramasser les âmes perdues
> et égarées. En quoi ils imitent les brodeurs, qui, sur
> divers fonds, couchent en belle variété les soies, l'or et
> l'argent, pour en faire toutes sortes de fleurs.
>
> Saint François de Sales, Introduction à la vie dévote,
part III, chapter I.

> Je dis que ces dames sont généralement haïes et détestées
> des pauvres . . . si ces dames voyent chez un ouvrier
> chargé de famille quelques écuelles, quelques plats
> d'étain, un chétif lit, quelque petit meuble de peu de
> valeur, elles lui refusent le secours de la charité en lui
> disant, mon ami, vous avez encore quelque chose,
> vendez-le pour vous subvenir et quand vous n'aurez
> plus rien, que vous serez réduit à l'état de Job, on vous
> donnera des secours.
>
> A.D. Ille-et-Vilaine C 1270, Marmite des pauvres de Vitré.

THE history of European poor relief is at least as old as European
Christianity and is one of change from a religiously based, voluntary charity, as expounded by the evangelists, to the complete
assumption by the state of responsibility for the neediest members
of society. The relief of the poor in medieval society had been
the concern of seigneur, Church, and, with increasing frequency
as society grew more complex, the alms of pious lay folk from
the monarch downwards, directed by spiritual counsellors from
archbishop to lowly parish priest. In the Christian ethic, holy
charity clearly enjoyed pre-eminence amongst virtues.

As long as communities remained small, perhaps Christian charity had some adequacy during the medieval period,
though it could not be expected to cope with disasters such as
famine and plague. Certainly it had become inadequate by the
sixteenth century when it was confronted with a population

pressure that forced upon governments and theologians a fundamental reappraisal of the situation. The debate upon the nature
and extent of relief was long and troubled. In Protestant countries where the new national churches were state directed, the
state assumed functions that had been hitherto the preserve of
voluntary charity. The state might well still use the vocabulary of
Christian charity and pronounce the blessedness of almsgiving,
but if alms alone would not contain the armies of paupers then
it had to shoulder the responsibility and take action; hence, to
cite only one example, the steady evolution in England by the
mid seventeenth century of the obligatory parish rate. In strong
contrast, Catholic France took a different line. There a growing
tendency towards secularization in the sixteenth century was
arrested in the seventeenth by the hand of the Catholic Counter-
Reformation which sought to reinfuse society with a conscious-
ness of its obligations. The pauper was, after all, in Christian
doctrine, the linchpin in the salvation of the rich: for only by
charity, the giving of their substance to the poor and weak, could
the wealthy elicit divine mercy. Essentially for the Tridentine
Councils the question was something far more fundamental than
the mere consideration of what was materially good for the
pauper in this world: what was at stake was the fate of the rest
of society, and particularly that of the rich, in the next. The
Councils were prepared to admit the failure of the Church to
cope with the problem of poverty in changing circumstances. At
the same time, they insisted that the bishop assume control over
diocesan charity and they reiterated the obligations of ecclesiastical institutions and of society itself, in the traditions of the
medieval schoolmen. Their appeals met with considerable
response. The system of relief, if it may so be called, which is
largely on trial in eighteenth-century France is still that based
upon private donations, voluntary almsgiving, and the institutions erected in the spirit of the Counter-Reformation to deal
with the problem of poverty.

Very broadly speaking, institutionalized Christian charity
existed at at least four levels. First, there was the ritualized almsgiving sustained out of the revenues of any bishopric, chapter, or
ancient religious house for the maintenance of the poor and which
might easily be restricted to special donations and bread distributions during Lent, the ceremonial washing of the feet of twelve

beggars and the gift to them of pieces of silver on Palm Sunday or Maundy Thursday—acts intended as much for the good of the souls of the religious as for the benefit of the beggars. Secondly, and often of equally ancient derivation, were the village *fonds*: gifts of property or *rentes* on which the income belonged in perpetuity to the parish poor. Thirdly, as long as attention is confined to formal relief, the most consequential organ of public assistance was the *hôpital général*, brain-child of St. Vincent de Paul, and for long the main hope of impecunious governments. Lastly, the *bureaux de charité* or *bureaux d'aumônes*, or *marmites* or *bouillons des pauvres*—the style is relatively irrelevant—were pools of voluntary alms, village collections, small legacies, and so on which were to be administered, sometimes in the form of soup and bread (hence the *bouillons* and *marmites* incorporated into the name of the institution), to the deserving poor of the parish by some individual or group capable of judging the needs of the recipient and the validity of his claims. These were the Catholic equivalent of Luther's 'common chest' but, unlike the concept of the common chest, they did not grow into an obligatory tax. These four broad categories of formal assistance leave a number of local practices unaccounted for—for example, the unique Flemish custom of auctioning off the truly helpless pauper to whomsoever would feed him or her for the least possible expense (to be met out of a kind of parish rate). Nor do they comprehend the attempts by some large cities—Lyons, Bordeaux, Troyes—to apply, spasmodically, some parochial rate, for such essays were generally so rare and so short-lived that their impact was highly restricted. Together then, ecclesiastical hand-outs, village *fonds*, *hôpitaux généraux*, and *bureaux de charité* represent what there was to be had in the way of formal relief, and each demands separate consideration.[1]

i. *Ecclesiastical hand-outs*

Though the most venerable of the resources intended to assuage the sufferings of the poor, the sums reserved for ritualized almsgiving by monastic houses, secular chapters, and bishops were over all the most negligible and were dependent upon the

---

[1] This chapter is largely based on the *enquêtes* of the 1770s; the results of these for the dioceses of Clermont, Mende, Montpellier, Rennes, and Rouen are reproduced in Appendix I.

strength and wealth of ecclesiastical foundations within a particular region and upon traditional methods of distribution. Such foundations were at their most extensive in the north and east, and here an area such as the diocese of Rouen, where the Church enjoyed considerable wealth amongst both the secular and the regular clergy, might have as many as six religious houses offering substantial help, sometimes merely on an annual, more often on a weekly, basis, and a handful more making token gestures. At Bec, for example,

le chapitre des aumônes monte annuellement à 6000 livres environ, non compris la soupe que l'on distribue trois fois la semaine, le vin, le cidre, la viande, le bouillon, la médecine, les onguents, qui sont distribués non seulement aux pauvres de nos paroisses, mais encore à ceux qui viennent demander lorsqu'ils sont attaqués des maladies; l'on donne aussi de la toile pour ensevelir les morts et des bières pour les mettre en terre.[1]

Much of the 6,000 *livres* went in twice-weekly *passades* to fifty callers, but at least to the surrounding villages Bec did offer some assistance. At Fécamp an annual 15,000 *livres* was spent upon daily bread distributions of half a pound per person. Saint-Wandrille and Saint-Martin de Boscherville made similar though less generous contributions. Jumièges, formerly generous, had passed into the less scrupulous hands of an absentee abbot. The abbey of Cival gave some 200 *livres* at Lent; Tréport 1,200 *livres* at other festivals; whilst the parish of Chaussy clearly leaned upon the three-times-weekly soup distribution made by the Bernardines of Villarceaux.[2] The diocese of Rouen was not typical. The great Cistercian and Cluniac houses of Burgundy did not behave with quite the same generosity as Bec and Fécamp. In the district of Dijon the most generous establishments, the abbaye Saint-Pierre, the Prieuré des Chanoines réguliers de Saint Jean l'Évangéliste scattered throughout four or five parishes (usually those in which the *seigneurie* was held by the establishment) sums varying from 300 to 500 *livres*.[3] In Brittany, where monasteries were few and revenues slight, the diocese of Rennes could only count upon 'le prieur de Saint-Nicholas de Montfort et de Saint-Pierre de Breteil [qui] doit donner par chacun an tant aux pauvres passants

---

[1] A.D. Seine-Maritime C 995, Bec 1774.   [2] Ibid.
[3] A.D. Côte-d'Or L 1200, Œuvres de bienfaisance et fondations charitables, 1790.

qu'aux pauvres des susdites paroisses vingt mines de bled seigle pour leur être distribuées par les chapelains dudit prieuré commis pour cet effet'.[1]

The diocese of Vannes boasted three small donations, mainly for *pauvres passants*;[2] that of Saint-Brieuc one of 400 *livres* for *pauvres malades*, another of 16 *livres*, and a more substantial (though unspecific) donation from the Abbaye de Beauport, whose generosity varied according to the rigour of the times;[3] that of Saint-Malo seven small donations restricted either to *pauvres passants* or specific parishes or to be allotted at the discretion of the institution in question.[4] The diocese of Nantes also had seven monasteries prepared to give something, of which the following is typical:

L'abbé et religieux du couvent de Villeneuve sont tenus d'employer et distribuer en aumônes chacune semaine tant pour l'aumône accoutumée estre faite le lundi et le jeudi que celle qui a été accoutumé être faite chaque jour deux septiers de bled seigle mesure de Nantes. Plus sont tenus de donner à dîner le jeudi absolu à quinze pauvres et une pièce d'argent à chacun après l'office de Mandatum qui se fait pour lesdits pauvres. Plus après le décès de chacun religieux deladite abbaye de donner et distribuer à un pauvre pendant trente jours la portion de pain, vin et pitance qui eut été distribuée audit religieux s'il eut été vivant.[5]

The bishoprics of Léon, Dol, and Tréguier had no such foundations, and Quimper claimed all was at the discretion of the monks. In the diocese of Clermont monastic generosity totalled an annual 3 *septiers* of wheat and 4 of beans, distributed every Good Friday to the parish of Montaigut-le-Blanc-sur-Champeix.[6] Such handouts in the diocese of Mende reached the exalted sums of 70 *livres*

[1] A.D. Ille-et-Vilaine C 1285, Dépouillement des aumônes que chaque prieuré ou monastère des évêchés de la province de Bretagne sont obligés de distribuer aux pauvres, 1724, Évêché de Rennes.

[2] Ibid., Évêché de Vannes.

[3] Ibid., Évêché de Saint-Brieuc: 'L'abbaye de Beauport doit 150 livres pour la pension d'un frère oblat ou un soldat estropié. Plus ladite abbaye est obligée aux aumônes ordinaires et extraordinaires par chaque semaine depuis Noël jusqu'à la Madeleine, sans y comprendre celles qui se font journellement. Lesquelles aumônes se peuvent régler selon la nécessité des temps.'

[4] Ibid., Évêché de Saint-Malo. The abbeys of Beaulieu, Saint-Jacques, Combourg, Mont Saint Michel, Taupont, Saint-Jean-des-Prez, Bodieu, and Locmaria.

[5] Ibid., Évêché de Nantes.

[6] A.D. Puy-de-Dôme C 930, *Assistance publique*, Montaigut-le-Blanc-sur-Champeix, 1775.

for the village of Saint-Jean-la-Fouillouze, given by the prior, and 4 *septiers* of rye to Quézac from the chapter of regular canons, 44 *septiers* of corn at Monastier from the priory, which also gave something to Chirac, and 6 *septiers* of corn to Salelles.[1] At Rodez, the entire resources of the diocese were concentrated in the extraordinarily large donation, made in bread, valued at 6,656 *livres* and handed out to *passants* by the Trappists at Bonnecombe.[2] Such examples are sufficient to indicate the very sporadic nature of monastic generosity. Moreover, religious houses often refused to be bound to continue traditional donations, and the amalgam of two houses could mean the disappearance of customary gifts. In Languedoc where few houses accorded anything, the parish of Saint-Geniès in the diocese of Montpellier grumbled

qu'autrefois les dames abbesses qui étaient seigneuresses et prieuresses fournissaient à tous les besoins, mais depuis la desertion des abbesses il y a environ 40 ans le prieuré à été réuni à Sainte-Marie qui donne peu aux pauvres quoi que le prieuré soit considérable et la seigneurie est à M. de Castries qui ne donne rien.[3]

Monastic charity was the object of severe criticism from Enlightenment thinkers, largely for its lack of discrimination, but other reasons could be found. Mercier on the almsgiving of the Chartreuse, Saint-Lazare, and the Célestins in Paris delivered an impassioned invective.

L'évangile l'a dit: Mangez votre pain avec les pauvres. Les moines étaient autrefois les pauvres; mais, devenus riches, ils font à leur tour des charités. Or, voici comment ils mangent leur pain avec les pauvres. Un tas de gueux s'assemblent le matin à la porte du couvent. Ils sont déguenillés. Le moine ouvre: il ne les fait pas entrer chez lui, mais il jette dans chaque écuelle un peu de potage, et ces malheureux se chamaillent à qui obtiendra une plus grande portion de cette soupe. Est-ce là manger son pain avec les pauvres selon l'instruction de l'Évangile?[4]

From 1778 the *parlements* sanctioned a number of *arrêts* aimed at the abolition of arbitrary distributions of all kinds which fell into the hands of the wrong type of poor and their conversion into a regular scheme for the assistance of the deserving poor. They had little success, however, with most of the monasteries. Some

---

[1] A.D. Hérault C 562, Assistance publique, diocèse de Mende, 1775.
[2] A.D. Aveyron 5 L 236, Assistance publique.
[3] A.D. Hérault C 5957, Assistance publique, diocèse de Montpellier, 1774.
[4] L. S. Mercier, *Tableau de Paris* (Hamburg, 1781), chapter cccxxiii.

houses resented any dictation as to the disposal of their revenues, which they claimed were in any case at their discretion, whilst larger foundations such as Bec, Fécamp, Fontevrault, and Bonne-combe were only too anxious to convert their hand-outs to a different purpose but feared riots from the recipients if they attempted so to do.[1] For the few, admittedly the very few, monastic charity had its contribution to make towards an economy of expedients.

Monastic charity had clearly changed less than the more flexible donations customarily made to the poor by bishops and chapters who, when opportunity occurred to convert such tolls upon their income into regular donations to *hôpitaux* and *bureaux de charité*, did so.[2] Where the donations in question were attached to some village of which the *seigneurie* fell with the prebend of the canonry or the estates of the bishop, they might retain their original form of a few *livres* distributed annually in money or kind to a number (sometimes a specific thirteen) at Easter or Michaelmas and might more readily be associated with village *fonds* than monastic hand-outs, but most commonly such resources had been deflected to the use of the *hôpitaux*.

ii. *Village* fonds

Of greater general significance, though the term is relative, to the villages were the small legacies, gifts of property or *rentes*

---

[1] Bloch, *L'Assistance et l'État*, p. 343, gives instances of such *arrêts*. A.D. Seine-Maritime C 996, Fécamp: 'Les religieux emploieraient volontiers cette dépense à un établissement plus utile; mais ils ont toujours craint le soulèvement de la populace . . .' *Souvenirs d'un nonagénaire*, vol. ii, p. 238 (ed. Célestin Port, 1880), describes riots at Fontevrault.

[2] Bishops would seem to have set aside anything up to a tenth of their revenues annually for formal charitable purposes, including the maintaining of village school-masters, the Lenten distributions, and their regular donations to *hôpitaux* or *bureaux de charité*. This does not include abnormal donations made to the *hôpitaux* or during a time of acute distress. Bibliothèque du Chapitre de Bayeux, 210, État des revenus de l'évêché de Bayeux en 1763; A.D. Lozère G 2287, État du revenu et des charges de l'évêché de Mende; A. Rebillon, *La Situation économique du clergé à la veille de la Révolution* (Rennes, 1913), pp. 18–19 (a very small contribution of 664 *livres* out of revenues of 42,940 *livres* but offset by discretionary charities at Rennes); C. Robert, *Urbain de Hercé, dernier évêque et comte de Dol* (Paris, 1900), p. 112; A.D. Aveyron G 324. In the south where the revenues of bishoprics were very small (under 10,000 *livres*) this meant that relatively little could be accorded on a permanent basis. See below, pp. 153, 164. In the most impecunious Breton dioceses such as Saint-Brieuc, all donations to whatever source were sporadic and no regular sum was set aside.

made by individuals, clerics, *seigneurs*, *bien pensant* families of one
kind or another, on which the income was used for the parish
poor under the conditions laid down by the donor—usually as
a death-bed direction. The intentions of the benefactor had to
be rigorously respected. If his bequest was intended for the sick,
the instruction of children, the financing of a midwife, or the
apprenticeship of poor boys, or as a Maundy Thursday bread
distribution to thirteen selected paupers known for their piety,
theoretically it could not be distrained for the assistance of anyone else, though in individual cases, after 1778, several *arrêts* were
aimed at using these funds for the specific purposes of establishing
bureaux de charité.[1] How extensive were such bequests? In the
diocese of Clermont only one exceeded 100 *livres* annually[2] in any
village, at Mende eight rose above this figure.[3] Similarly in the
diocese of Montpellier, only two parishes—Lunel-Viel (230 *livres*
annually) and Saint-Drézery (two bequests respectively of 130
livres for the parish poor and 45 *livres* for the *pauvres honteux*)—
could claim bequests of more than 100 *livres*.[4] At Rodez the story
was virtually the same. At Dijon, three villages of the *subdélégation*
had donations ranging between 100 and 110 *livres*; in that of
Avallon five villages rose to the exalted heights of 200 *livres*, 140
livres, 100 *livres*, 500 *livres*, and 22 bushels of wheat respectively;
in that of Bourg-en-Bresse fifteen villages had *fonds* totalling
1,284 *livres* fairly evenly divided—but another ten did not reach
40 *livres*.[5] In the diocese of Rouen (1,388 parishes) only twenty-
four parishes rose above the 100-*livres* level.[6] Curiously enough,
it was in Brittany that the parish *fonds* would seem to have
been most extensive: in the diocese of Rennes (211 parishes)
twenty-five claimed *fonds* exceeding 100 *livres*.

[1] See below, pp. 167–72, and Bloch, *L'Assistance et l'État*, p. 343.

[2] A.D. Puy-de-Dôme C 905, Aumône en faveur des pauvres de Sauvagnat. This
was in dispute. In 1702 'le sieur Sisternes de Lorme (prêtre) avait fait don aux
pauvres de la dite paroisse de deux legs: l'un de 3,260 livres dont la rente devait
être employée à faire chaque année une distribution de grains; l'autre de 3000
livres, dont la rente annuelle de 150 livres serait consacrée à doter deux filles pauvres
de la paroisse; par transaction en date du 16 novembre 1750 les héritiers du sieur
Delorme se reconnurent débiteurs des arrérages du legs de 3000 livres, s'élevant à
2000 livres et s'engagèrent à payer cette somme en 4 annuités de 500 livres'.

[3] A.D. Hérault C 562, Diocèse de Mende, 1775. See Appendix I.

[4] Ibid., C 5957.

[5] A.D. Côte-d'Or C 378, État général de tous les établissements, fondations,
revenus et charités dans la généralité de Dijon 1693–1788.

[6] See Appendix I.

The village, however, which had any *fonds* at all was very much in the minority. Over 60 per cent in every diocese, and in the Massif well over 90 per cent, were without any such resources at all, and the typical *fonds* destined for the poor were more likely to hang in the region of 50 *livres* than to reach more exalted levels. Such a sum might, in a few cases, temporarily give assistance in sickness, or during the harsh winter might afford a little relief to a handful of families, but what, over all, could such meagre resources contribute to the alleviation of poverty?

iii. L'hôpital général

As far as *ancien régime* charity was concerned, the institution with the greatest substance and which was for long the main hope of legislators concerned to eradicate the more offensive manifestations of poverty and begging was the *hôpital général*. In this establishment, churchmen hoped, the principle of voluntary charity, the donations of the wealthy, would be given concrete form and so offer asylum to the suffering. Successive French governments hoped for something more. They hoped, without having to dip significantly into state coffers, to achieve in the *hôpital général* an institution which would clear the streets of beggars. They indulged at intervals, 1685, 1724, in a kind of fantasy that the *hôpitaux* could be turned into establishments in which the deserving poor, the aged, the crippled, and orphan children might be given help but where, in addition, the undeserving idlers who refused to work might be inculcated with habits of industry and punished if they did not mend their ways. For governments, the *hôpitaux* embodied *un projet du grand renfermement des pauvres*—a concept which was very far from the original design of St. Vincent de Paul.

For St. Vincent the idea at the root of the *hôpital général* was the provision of shelter, food, and suitable employment for the aged, the crippled, and the orphaned. One needs to return to the earliest foundation in Paris to see more clearly what was intended and to understand certain aspects of the *hôpitaux* at the end of the *ancien régime*.

A pamphlet of 1655 drawn up by the directors of the Paris experiment states that the idea was derived from the *fonds charitables* of the Fronde which had been funds set up in some towns and large villages, consisting of money and superfluous goods, clothes, furniture, and utensils which could be given to help the needy. By extension, communal effort could produce buildings and the requisite beds and needful clothing, so that permanent shelter under a type of workhouse regime might be secured for the crowds of destitute folk who infested the streets and churches, homeless, demoralized, and a glaring indictment of the failure of existing Christian charity.[1]

The essence of the *hôpital général* to St. Vincent was its voluntary nature. There was to be no coercion to make the rich contribute; there was to be no attempt to force the poor to enter. But the one must be aware of its obligations and the other would see in the institution an asylum from the miseries of its current existence.

After St. Vincent had assumed control of the Hôpital du Saint Nom de Jesus in 1644, the elaboration of the details for the running of the institution slowly evolved. The *hôpital* was committed into the hands of Louise de Marillac, and by 1653 she had devised what she considered the ideal plan. Twenty poor folk of each sex were to be chosen at first. These were to be lodged in the two separate wings, though the chapel and refectory were to be used in common. The domestic staff was to be drawn from an order formed by St. Louise, the Sisters of Charity. Louise de Marillac placed great emphasis on the need to choose the first internees with great care; more particularly, there should be some men and women capable of teaching the others trades or crafts which would help to defray expenses: a silk weaver, cobblers, button-makers, lacemakers, glovemakers, seamstresses, and pin-makers; such people were an investment for the future since they could transmit their skills.

She was insistent too that the first members should belong to the 'decent poor' and that measures should be taken to inculcate

[1] The bibliography of works concerning St. Vincent de Paul and the early *hôpitaux* is immense. P. Coste, *Le Grand Saint du Grand Siècle: Monsieur Vincent* (Paris, 1933) and *Saint Vincent de Paul. Correspondance* (Paris, 1930) remain the best. M. Simard, *Saint Vincent de Paul et ses œuvres* (Paris, 1894), is very wide ranging; the more recent A. Dupoux, 'Sur les pas de Monsieur Vincent', *Revue de l'assistance publique* (1958), concentrates upon the practical aspects of the saint's work. It is to be regretted that E. Archer's 'The Assistance of the Poor in Paris and the North Eastern French Provinces 1614–1660' (Ph.D. thesis, London, 1935) was never published, since it is based upon the archives of the Sisters of Charity which do not appear to have been exploited since. The following paragraphs are based upon her work.

a Christian and orderly tone. The quasi-monastic atmosphere of
the place is shown in the 'Order of the Day'. The old people rose
at 5.0 in summer, 6.0 in winter. Morning prayers were said in
common, and on Sundays and on weekdays in Lent a reading
from the Gospel followed. They then took up their work until
it was time to hear mass, which was said at 6.30 in summer, 7.30
in winter. After breakfast (a piece of bread) they worked during
the morning and could chat together, provided they spoke
quietly and avoided quarrelling. They worked in silence, however, from 10.10 to 10.30, while a passage from some edifying
book was read aloud to them. They dined at 11.30, and the after-
noon was passed in the same manner as the morning. Supper was
served at 5.30 in winter, 6.0 in summer, and the short interval
between that meal and night prayers (7.0 in winter, 8.0 in summer)
was again occupied by work. Set time for relaxation is not mentioned; probably on working days, the conversation which they
enjoyed while they sat at their crafts was deemed adequate recrea-
tion. On Sundays and feast days, however, they were permitted to
divert themselves in the garden after dinner and again after
Vespers, the men in their own enclosure, the women in theirs.

All the internees were really poor, but most of them were not
too infirm to perform light work. However, a few who could not
learn a trade were employed in the house and outside it, the
'intention of the donor not being to erect a factory, but to furnish
a decent existence to a small number of respectable poor'. Louise
de Marillac herself kept the accounts. From the very beginning,
expenses exceeded the estimate which had been made (by 585
livres in the first year). The sum total of the workers' earnings in
one year was not large—only 51 *livres*. The old people had the
right to a quarter of their earnings, but, as the price of their
ration of wine was deducted, these diminished in proportion,
indeed, in the case of the hearty drinkers, a negative result was
obtained and they owed money to the house.

The employment of these forty people on this very modest
scale attracted widespread attention from town councils who
desperately needed to find some means of alleviating distress
and from the government which could not but be conscious of
the problem. Placed in context, government encouragement of the
foundation of such institutions is seen to have coincided with the
intense economic crisis, protracted famines, and endemic plague

characteristic of the second half of the seventeenth century—
crises which left in their wake a trail of wrecked households and
social dislocation. But even without that stimulus it is easy to
perceive the attraction of the *hôpital* to a government whose
financial situation was far from secure. Here was a potential means
of clearing the streets of the weak, the aged, and the orphaned
and at the same time of the unemployed poor who could be set
to work, and all this without dipping into government revenue
or imposing a new tax on society: the Christian Church would
be the inspiration, the rich—not least those wealthy tax-evading
clerics—would be the financiers. Moreover, the dirty, lice-ridden,
hungry poor would also be subjected to work under a monastic
discipline embodying order, sobriety, cleanliness, prayer, honesty;
in short, the Christian virtues with which the poor were so rarely
endowed would be *forced* upon them. 'Forced' is chosen deliberately, because here the government intended to depart from the
ideals of St. Vincent. To him, as has been pointed out, the essence
of the *hôpital général* was its voluntary nature. The poor would
come, without coercion, because they would see in the institution
an asylum from their wretchedness, a place provided by an all-
merciful God to succour them; and the rich would freely donate
towards its maintenance because they would be aware that this
was their Christian duty. For the government it seemed an
attractively easy means of interning the poor—in short *un grand
projet du renfermement des pauvres.*

The project was essentially one for the future, nevertheless the
government drew encouragement from the conscious imitation
of the Paris experiment by the bishops of Toulouse, Poitiers,
and Clermont in their diocesan centres, and the royal edict of
1662 tried to oblige all towns to do the same:

Ordonnons et voulons qu'en toutes les villes de notre royaume où il
n'y a point encore d'hôpital général établi, il soit incessamment procédé
à l'etablissement d'un hôpital et aux règlements concernant mendiants
invalides, natifs des lieux ou qui y auront demeuré pendant un an, comme
aussi les enfants orphelins ou nés de parents mendiants. Tous lesquels
pauvres y seront instruits à la piété et religion chrétienne, et aux
métiers dont ils pourront se rendre capables, sans qu'il leur soit permis de
vaguer ni, sous quelque prétexte que ce soit, d'aller de ville en ville.[1]

---

[1] Isambert, *Recueil général des anciennes lois françaises depuis l'an 420 jusqu'à la Révolution de 1789* (Paris, 1822–8), t. xviii, p. 18.

The points to note in this edict are, first, that the government at this juncture thought of the *hôpitaux* as designed to cope with two types of poor, the *invalides*, sick, aged, crippled, and then orphaned children: these were deserving poor in the narrowest sense of the word. Secondly, the *hôpitaux* are regarded as urban institutions—there is absolutely no mention of the countryside—and, moreover, to be eligible for help a residence qualification of one year in the town where the *hôpital* was situated was necessary. Finally, the government possessed no real coercive powers to enforce this edict: no penalties were threatened to towns which did not obey the royal injunctions. Imperious as this piece of legislation sounds, the actual work of foundation was still in the hands of individual initiative.

The first two points are the most important. The institutions were destined for a very special sector of the urban community, and hence even had one been established in every single town in France, it would in no wise have made possible the grandiose aim of interning the poor of an overwhelmingly rural population.

The decree was carried through the towns and villages of the kingdom, largely by a group of Jesuits, PP. Chaurand, Dunod, and Guévarre, who crossed France from Brittany to Provence and from Languedoc to Flanders invested with special powers as carriers of the royal instructions.[1] The enterprise was seen as a highly important mission; the Jesuits preached sermons on the issue in cathedrals and churches, and the results on the whole were impressive. Precisely how many *hôpitaux généraux* existed in France at the end of the seventeenth century is not known. An official source stating 156 is a gross underestimate, just as the estimate of 2,185 made by the *Comité de Mendicité* in 1790 was a fanciful conjecture arrived at by bestowing the qualification *hôpital* on curious foundations of no more than a room in a house occasionally visited by a Sister of Charity.[2] What can be said is that by the mid eighteenth century all cities, all diocesan centres, and all towns of more than 5,000 inhabitants had such a foundation, though some of them were only capable of receiving a score or so of internees.

---

[1] C. Joret, *Le Père Guévarre et les bureaux de charité au XVIIe siècle* (Toulouse, 1889), p. 8. In fact this work is as much concerned with the establishment of *hôpitaux*.

[2] Bloch and Tuetey, *Procès-verbaux*, pp. 568–9, shows information existed to confirm 1,438 *hôpitaux* and *hôtels Dieu*.

It is possible to generalize about the founding fathers of these institutions, though the matter is closely allied to one of pure finance—who would put up the money to cover the costs of the buildings and installing the nuns to run them, as well as providing for the upkeep of the internees? Setting this aside for the moment, one can say that the guiding hand and often the financial figure behind those *hôpitaux* in diocesan centres was usually the bishop; indeed, had the bishop in question not done this by 1676, he would have received a reproving letter from the King. Occasionally, if the bishop proved recalcitrant, a cathedral canon or, in other important towns where clerical influence was not as extensive, town councils would undertake the task, and, where town council and ecclesiastics were slow to act, governors of provinces or *intendants*. Lastly, but more rarely, the initiative could be taken by pious lay folk. Any combination of these diverse elements might of course take place, and any one figure or institution claiming credit as founder did not necessarily supply all the money; he or it might merely come forward with the idea of where to get the money from, or even do as little as form a committee for suitable action and discussion as to where and how funds might be raised. The initial obstacle was, of course, the buildings; where these had to be started from scratch, sometimes five or ten years might elapse before any internees could be received; the most zealous founders did not always start with sufficient funds to carry the enterprise to completion, and in some cases ambitious local projects, like medieval cathedrals, were never finished.

Where possible the point of departure was an older foundation: medieval France had its share of *maladreries* and *léproseries* to cope with pilgrims and lepers, institutions whose funds and, more rarely, buildings (they usually consisted of no more than a cottage) could serve a new purpose. Secondly, in those towns where they existed, *hôtels Dieu*, hospitals in the real sense, intended to house the sick might be extended to form an *hôpital général*, and hence radical economies might be achieved in buildings such as kitchens and offices, which could be shared, and in personnel.[1]

---

[1] Because of this, in some instances *hôpital général* and *hôtel Dieu* became indistinguishable, if not in name, at least in purpose. In the large towns *hôtels Dieu* retained a separate identity and were concerned with the sick or, more precisely, dying sick and with the reception of *enfants trouvés*. As such they are considered in Chapter XII.

Once a town could show it had a plan under way, it could demand *lettres patentes* for its *hôpital général*. These were of immense importance because they were the guarantee of some funds to aid in the running of the institution. *Lettres patentes* accorded the *hôpital* the right to absorb any legacies left, no matter how long ago, to the poor of the area and to receive gifts and legacies intended for the poor in the future. Then the *hôpitaux* were granted certain extraordinary privileges of a very wide variety. Finally, *lettres patentes* accorded the institution the profits on any industrial activities carried out within its walls.

Utterly typical of an early act of foundation is that recording the establishment of the *hôpital général* of Morlaix in 1686:

que les maisons et issues de l'ancien hôtel Dieu de notre ville de Morlaix . . . où étaient autrefois les pauvres malades, soient et demeurent affectées, unies et jointes audit hôpital général, soit pour en faire l'établissement ou pour servir à la subsistance d'icelui . . .

Voulons que tous dons et legs faits par contrats, testaments et autres dispositions, les adjudications d'aumônes faites dans ladite ville et fauxbourgs en termes généraux aux pauvres sans n'avoir point été faites soient appliquées audit hôpital général . . .

Avons accordé audit hôpital seul le droit de faire débit de viande pendant le carême . . .

Voulons que toutes aumônes de fondation auxquelles sont tenues les églises de ladite ville et fauxbourgs qui sont d'ancienne fondation soient doresnavent appliquées audit hôpital général.

Nous accordons audit hôpital, le quart des aumônes qui sont accoutumées d'être ordonnées par nos juges lors des marchés, baux et adjudications d'héritages, navires, marchandises qui seront faites dans l'étendue du ressort de notre dite ville de Morlaix . . . le quart des amendes, aumônes et restitution de police et toutes les confiscations qui seront prononcées par nos juges. . . . Permettons audits directeurs de recevoir tous dons, legs et gratifications permises par la coutume de la province . . . par quelqu'autre acte que ce soit . . . acquérir, échanger ou aliéner, ordonner et disposer des biens et domaines dudit hôpital ainsi qu'ils jugeront pour le plus grand bien et avantage d'icelui. . . . Leur donnons droit et pouvoir de faire fabriquer toutes sortes de manufactures et de les vendre au profit des dits pauvres sans être sujet à visite ni à aucuns droits imposés ou à imposer . . .[1]

[1] A.D. Finistère 47 H 26, Droits de l'hôpital de Morlaix, 1790. This was an older foundation converted into an *hôpital général* in 1678.

Fines, taxes on goods seized for illegally entering the port, exemption from death duties paid on inheritance of property, the income from alms, certain notarial rights, the privilege of selling meat during Lent, to which were later added monopolies on the making of coffins and exemptions from taxes on alcoholic drinks, were broadly speaking, apart from the maritime rights, generally accorded by the monarchy to the *hôpitaux*. Some had other minor gifts as well.

Clermont had the right to collect on all seats placed in the market-place on market day and the right to the wax from candle droppings in the churches.[1] In every town a fixed number of poor were chosen from the institution for service at large funerals. In Mende, and there are many parallels elsewhere, children from the *hôpital* were used as the twelve poor at the Maundy Thursday foot-washing ceremony and received a fee from the bishop which went to the institution.[2] In Bayeux and Vitré the *hôpital* had the right to send paupers into the streets at mealtimes with a bell and a pot to urge those enjoying a hearty meal to spare the leftovers to enrich the poor-house soup.[3] The *hospices* in the Gévaudan had the right to the head and feet of every animal killed in the slaughter-houses.[4] Most of the Breton *hospices* had the income from the Papegault, an ancient fair.[5] Mourning clothes had to be purchased from the *hospices*, as had coffins and, occasionally, funeral banners. Other *hospices* had the monopoly of selling drugs and liniments.[6] Troyes, Marseilles, and Montpellier periodically had the right to march the entire group of paupers round the city in their uniform in order to illustrate the extent of the needs of the institution and at the same time to organize a massive *quête*.[7] Periodic lotteries, with government permission, were held.

These extraordinary privileges are certainly revealing about current attitudes towards the poor, if no more: the constant association, for example, of the deserving poor with death and

---

[1] A.D. Puy-de-Dôme, Archives hospitalières Clermont-Ferrand, hôpital général, III A 6.

[2] A.D. Lozère L 321, Hôpital de Mende, 1790, Revenus.

[3] A.D. Ille-et-Vilaine C 1270.

[4] A.D. Lozère H 441, Hôpital de Marvejols; L 321, Hôpital de Mende, Hôpital de Langogne.

[5] This was particularly true in the diocese of Rennes.

[6] More commonly, however, this was a privilege of the *hôtel Dieu*.

[7] E. Chaudron, *L'Assistance publique à Troyes*, p. 54; P. Béral, *Histoire de l'hôpital de la Charité de Montpellier* (Montpellier, 1899), p. 8.

death ceremonies, coffins, mourning, candle-bearing, and with following the hearse, chanting prayers and incantations to make easier the path of the deceased to heaven where the poor were apparently more highly esteemed than the rich. How efficacious these privileges were as a source of revenue will presently be discussed.

Evidently certain sectors of the community might feel they bore an unfair brunt of the cost of the *hôpitaux*: butchers in particular; joiners, blacksmiths, and court officials could reasonably claim that the exactions to which they were subjected did not amount to voluntary charity.[1] The exactions could, however, be justified, at least in part, on grounds of antiquity, as rights previously held by various pious *confréries*. Indeed, one cannot examine the sources of income of the *hôpitaux* without being struck by the devious lengths to which the government had recourse while evading an obligatory tax.

Great stress was laid by both the government and the founding fathers themselves on the potential income to be made from industry, a stress which stemmed from current economic thought rather than from empirical evidence. The whole plan in fact was couched in terms of the future: buildings which would be constructed, gifts which would be given, bequests which would be made, industry from which profits would ultimately come.

The composition of the board of administration of these institutions was largely dependent upon who had been responsible for the foundation. Where the initial impetus had been given by a cleric, the chairmanship and preponderant voice in the administration was usually assumed by ecclesiastics, and where the lay element, town councillors and *intendants*, had led the way the roles were reversed. In all diocesan centres in the early days the bishop headed the administration: by the end of the *ancien régime* this assiduity had somewhat slackened—perhaps because

---

[1] The amount of litigation which arose between these communities was enormous. A.D. Côtes-du-Nord, Hôpital Saint-Brieuc H.A., 10 février 1787, Contest over *viande de carême*; A.D. Finistère 47 H 30, Hôpital de Morlaix, 1789, *viande de carême* realized a mere 9 *livres* for the *hôpital* because an exemption clause allowed sailors to kill cattle for their own use on board ship, and a treaty was struck between butchers and sailors to the detriment of the *hôpital*. A.D. Lozère H 730, 1743, Procès entre l'hôpital et les bouchers de la ville de Mende lesquels par ordonnance de la cour du bailliage du Gévaudan, sont condamnés à payer aux pauvres de l'hôpital toutes les têtes et pieds de bœufs et vaches qui se tuent dans la ville de Mende, etc.

the running of the institution had become so much more routine. In the town-run institutions the lay element was predominant amongst the administration, yet care was taken to have the local parish priests present because these were invaluable sources of information on the claims of those seeking entry and because they knew more about the collection of alms than anyone else and because, most importantly, they were present at the last, ready to urge the repentant sinner to make an appropriate gift in money or land to the succouring of the needy. Conversely, where the ecclesiastical element was in control, it needed the lay element, sometimes in order to borrow money, certainly to undertake the investment of bequests, and lastly, though perhaps this was not apparent from the beginning, because the ownership of property entailed litigation as did the possession of even quite minor privileges. Most of the *hospices* by the mid eighteenth century were heavily involved in these respects and needed, above all, an able lawyer.

The actual work of running the institutions, catering for the wants of the needy and seeing that they conformed to the monastic discipline imposed upon them, was given into the hands of a whole spate of new female religious orders. These assumed office at the invitation of the administration, which in fact hired as many as it could afford to support. The Sisters of Charity have already been mentioned, but they were perhaps only the most striking element in a women's religious movement of unparalleled intensity, with highly practical ends. Similar orders were legion: the Sisters of Providence ran them numerically a close second; in Brittany the Sisters of Saint Thomas de Villeneuve, the Filles de la Sagesse, the Paulines of Tréguier; in central France the Sœurs Chrétiennes de Nevers, the Sœurs Hospitalières de Saint Alexis de Limoges, and the Sœurs Hospitalières de Saint Joseph du Puy—to name merely three.[1] Occasionally, either

---

[1] Apart from the Sisters of Charity, who command a large bibliography in their own right, each of these orders has its hagiographer, e.g. A. Couanier de Launay, *Histoire des religieuses hospitalières de Saint Joseph du Puy* (Paris, 1890); E. C. de Beaucamp, *Nos Vieilles Écoles normandes* (Le Havre, 1896), on the origin of the Sisters of Providence; L. Aubineau, 'Histoire des petites sœurs des pauvres', *Journal de Rennes* (24–31 janvier 1852); A. Caurier, 'Les Origines des religieuses de Saint Thomas de Villeneuve', *Semaine religieuse de Rennes* (1890), pp. 588–90, etc. Though highly emotional and unscientific, some of this literature conveys the depth of zeal of some of these women. An excerpt from Caurier (p. 589) cites a letter of the Reverend Mother when assuming control of the *hôpital général* of Lamballe in 1684:

where demand for nuns on a regular basis outran supply or where the town councils wanted to keep a very tight rein, the work was left to a handful of celibate women held together not by a corporate vow but by an individual promise of a lifetime's devotion to the poor. Indeed, it is very tempting to assume that only those administrators who were prepared to concede a great deal in the actual decision of how the house should be run had recourse to the Sisters of Charity, a formidable group of women capable of decisive action and stopping at nothing to achieve their ends. In face of financial difficulties at Rouen, they shaved the heads of the entire institution to sell for wigs; at Bayeux the privilege of not paying *aides* on wine entering the town gave them the opportunity to undersell in the public market any wine merchant in the town—a length to which the privilege had never been intended to be stretched.[1] Their medical ignorance may well have caused them to do more harm than good—though the reputation of the Sisters of Providence was lowest in this respect —but they did not lose sight of the ideals of their foundress. On the other hand, after the early days their numbers underwent a marked decline, and by the 1720s the mother house in Paris was refusing to take on new commitments, claiming difficulty in maintaining existing obligations.[2]

To survey the history of any *hôpital* in France between its foundation and 1789 is not to be conscious of any profound change. The way in which the old and the orphaned were tended, the monastic discipline, the occasional bits of industrial activity which rarely brought much profit to the house look basically as they had done in the lifetime of St. Louise. More significantly, few *hôpitaux* had conspicuously expanded the numbers in their care.

'lorsque j'entrai dans l'hôpital je fus fort étonnée de ne voir personne. J'appelai à plusieurs reprises, nul ne me répondait; enfin, avec un long effort, une tête se souleva à demi du milieu d'un tas de fumier et dit d'une voix mourante: au nom de Dieu assistez-nous. Je découvris alors que ce quelque chose qui gémissait et rampait dans une paille infecte, c'étaient les enfants de l'hospice.'

[1] Hufton, *Bayeux*, pp. 90–1; F. Hué, *Histoire de l'hospice général de Rouen, 1602–1840* (Rouen, 1903), p. 61.

[2] A.D. Lozère H 944, Letter of Mme Sébastienne Mazurier, Fille de la Charité de Paris, to M. Bonnet, relating to a request from the *hôpital* of Mende for four Sisters of Charity: 'il est impossible de les fournir vu la rareté des sujets car de soixante qu'il y en avait autrefois dans notre séminaire, il n'y en a pas vingt présentement' (8 mai 1729).

One of the largest institutions, that of the *hôpital général* of Rouen (population 87,000), catered to the needs of some 2,005 in 1777 divided into the following categories:[1]

Côté des hommes	Côté des femmes*	
	180	Alités par maladie et caducité.
	114	Femmes scorbutiques et ulcérées.
86	230	Aveugles, paralytiques, épileptiques, galeux, vénériens.
5	150	Petits garçons 1 à 15 ans en langueur ou scrophuleux.
	234	Petites filles dans le même état.
	40	Malades d'esprit à la chaîne.
166	199	Hommes, femmes, garçons, filles employées dans l'infirmerie, cuisines, buanderie, cordonnerie, etc.
129		Vieillards employés au calfat, gagnant 6 à 9 deniers par jour.
	52	Filles de police employées à coudre et à filer.
	15	Filles de 7 à 14 ans, dites demi-libertines employées comme dessus.
156	72	Petits garçons et filles de 7 à 14 ans employés dans la filature du coton.
	54	Filles de 18 à 20 ans, pour carder, dévider et montrer aux enfants.
30	48	Pensionnaires par fondation ou par cause de démence.
22	32	Hospitalières, officiers de la maison et maîtres d'écoles.
594	1,411	

* This is a geographical distinction referring to two wings of a building.

The establishment at Rouen is impressive for its comparative scope and organization. (The entire Basse-Auvergne had institutionalized relief for only 800 people.) Few houses undertook the incarceration of *filles publiques*, however mild their offences, and few could hope to manage any small industrial adventure so successfully. Some of the *pensionnaires* had their board paid. The

[1] A.N. H¹ 1322, Hôpital général de Rouen, 1777, État des pensionnaires dans l'hôpital général.

old and faithful retainer in a noble or wealthy household might reasonably expect his employer to do him this favour, and the *hôpitaux*, in need of funds, were prepared, at a price, to rid families of the mildly mentally defective—presumably such cases as the mongoloid, who died young, and those suffering from congenital diseases or epilepsy. An institution such as the *hôpital général* at Mende (Sainte-Catherine) catered to a mere 152, of whom 95 fitted into the category of old or infirm, 29 were children, and the rest religious and employees concerned in the running of the house.[1] (Mende had a population of over 5,000.) Another diocesan centre, Saint-Brieuc (population over 8,000), had room and funds for 124, of whom 68 were infirm, either aged or ill, 5 were feeble but could help the others, 38 were children, and 13 could be described as *'valides'*—social undesirables for whose board the *hôpital* was paid by the municipality.[2] One can multiply to infinity such examples without demonstrating much more than that, in a city of about 50,000, there were usually about 1,500 hospital beds, and that, *pro rata*, one of 5,000, if poorly endowed, might have under 150 beds, if well endowed might rise a little higher. The types of people, however, who were thus catered for by the institutions did not vary. They were town dwellers, aged, infirm, or orphaned. The first two reserved their places at the *hôpitaux* for years in advance. 'J'ai une place à l'hôpital' was a boast and was also taken in the courts as an attestation of good conduct. Nuns were often accused of favouritism in regard to those whom they chose to admit; assertions usually justified by reference to cases where old women with a little property—if not necessarily sufficient on which to live— had, against the surrender in perpetuity of that property, been taken into the establishment for the rest of their lives, or instances of servants admitted to places against the payment of a pension to the institution by their former employers.[3] Why did the

---

[1] A.D. Lozère L 321, Hôpital de Mende, 1790.

[2] A.D. Côtes-du-Nord H., Hôpital de Saint-Brieuc A., État de l'hôpital, 1733.

[3] Ibid. Saint-Brieuc offers some neat examples: 'Mme la comtesse de Beaucourt désirerait qu'on voulût bien admettre à l'hôpital en qualité de pensionnaire un ancien cocher et offre pour sa pension une somme de 200 livres par an (le 19 mai 1786). . . . M. l'Abbé Soubens chanoine de la cathédrale offre 96 livres, une fois payée pour toujours, pour recevoir au nombre des pauvres de l'hôpital la nommée Anne Amice fille aveugle . . . ayant un vêtement et linge honnêtes qu'elle porterait à l'hôpital (le 18 septembre 1786)'—this last offer was only accepted because of the past (and anticipated future) generosity of the canon to the *hôpital*.

hôpitaux remain so small and so inflexible? The question relates directly to finance, for it was on this thorny issue that the concept of the *hôpitaux* as a panacea for the suffering poor as a whole was to become ensnared. The first priority in the setting up of an *hôpital* was buildings, which meant living quarters for the internees—separating the sexes—and for the personnel—to every nun her cell—an infirmary for the sick and a chapel for religious observance. Funds were then needed for the upkeep of every individual concerned, and for doctor (slight), almoner, and chaplain (even less), and for the accountant.[1] If industrial enterprise was envisaged, raw materials and equipment had to be purchased. How much all this might cost is perforce conjectural, but a rough guide might be that at the beginning of the century the cost of providing for the wants of an adult internee was about 120–50 *livres* and that this rose by the end of the *ancien régime* to a figure in the region of 180–200 *livres* (an inflationary trend itself likely to have an impact on an institution with a fixed income). By 1789 an institution catering for some 200 adults (an orphan child cost appreciably less) needed revenues of 40,000 *livres*; more specifically, it could not expand its numbers without a sum guaranteeing an income of 200 *livres* for each new individual taken (which implied a bequest in the region of 4,000 *livres*), and this without consideration of the extra space needed to accommodate him.[2]

The initial fervour on the part of municipal authorities, clerics, and philanthropic families was in many ways impressive, the 'extraordinary' donations of the monarchy endowed the institutions with a minor range of privileges, but dependence for the future was clearly upon bequests or forthcoming subventions. Bequests were relatively frequent in the 1680s and 1690s but they declined into a trickle as early enthusiasm on the part of the philanthropic public waned, a waning due at least in part to a

---

[1] A doctor or surgeon generally received an honorarium of 50 *livres*, a chaplain merely his meals, the accountant anything up to 200 *livres*.

[2] These figures include heating, clothing, and maintenance costs. Inflation meant that some *hôpitaux* in the closing decades of the *ancien régime* actually reduced their numbers, e.g. Tulle, Laval, Dôle; at Poitiers it was suggested 'aucun indigent ne sera reçu qu'après le décès ou le départ de deux pauvres renfermés afin de réduire à 300 la population de l'hôpital' (P. Rambaud, *L'Assistance publique à Poitiers*, p. 542). Attempts were made to effect this suggestion, which was reinforced by strong government insistence.

questioning of the efficacy of the *hôpitaux* as a means of relieving the problem of poverty.[1]

The deceleration in donations coincided with the feverish speculations attendant upon Law's schemes, and many *hôpitaux* became involved by investing the income on property and financial donations in this direction. Few escaped unscathed, but whereas in Brittany, Burgundy, Normandy, and Languedoc the *hôpitaux* lost a few hundred *livres*, the *hôpitaux* of Provence, which had attempted to expand their resources to cope with families shattered by pestilence, faced bankruptcy and had to be bailed out by the bishops and the monarchy.[2] Other financial hazards stemmed from the lack of control of the *hôpitaux* over their funds. Property left to the *hôpitaux* could not be alienated and the intentions of the donor had to be rigorously respected. To raise ready money to cope with a difficult period, one of the few resources open to the *hôpitaux* was the *rente viagère* and this could involve real disaster.

The *rente viagère* was an annuity payable to an individual in his lifetime against the payment of an immediate lump sum. The institution gained ready money for insistent purposes but encumbered itself during the lifetime of its creditor. The hôpital La Grave at Toulouse was merely one institution which found its obligations towards its *rentiers* rapidly forcing it into bankruptcy and was only saved by a royal edict sanctioning the alienation of property.[3]

---

[1] All the *hôpitaux* in the diocesan centres, Clermont, Dijon, Mende, Montpellier, Bayeux, Rennes, Rouen, were main beneficiaries under the testaments of their bishops in the period 1680–1740. A.D. Puy-de-Dôme H.D., Clermont-Ferrand 1 B 85, 1 B 98; A.D. Lozère H 495, Testament de Mgr de Piencourt, 1704. This is a classic instance; the text ran: 'Si je suivais les mouvements de ma tendresse naturelle, je ferais mes parents mes héritiers; mais je suis persuadé que cette dernière action de ma vie serait ma condamnation devant Dieu: que ce bien même qui est le patrimoine des pauvres ferait *périr le leur,* je leur donne donc à chacun 10 livres pour la validité du testament. Je déclare donc l'hôpital de la ville de Mende mon héritier universel de tous les effets de ma succession [204,949 livres] . . . on distribuera 2000 livres aux pauvres des paroisses où sont situés les biens de l'évêché . . .' A.D. Gers, Archives Hospitalières Condom. Donations, shows three successive legacies (1697, 1716, and 1757) of 10,000 *livres,* 36,000 *livres,* and 12,000 *livres* from the bishops. But the association between bishop and *hôpitaux* of the diocesan centres (which totalled after all, only 139) slackened, and other charitable purposes claimed priorities, *bureaux de charité,* etc. *Hôpitaux* which were not in diocesan centres did not get this help.

[2] A.N. H¹ 1311 and M. Etchepare, *L'Hôpital de la Charité de Marseille* (Aix, 1962).

[3] Bloch and Tuetey, *Procès-verbaux,* p. 100.

When examined closely, the finances of the *hôpitaux* look like so many delicate balancing acts. Equilibrium existed in normal years, normal in this instance meaning years unmarked by rapid inflation or catastrophe, such as building subsidence or epidemic. The houses which contrived the best performance held their assets in property or careful investment in *rentes sur le clergé de France* (offering a mere 2 per cent return but the safest of all) or *rentes sur les États de Languedoc* or *sur l'Hôtel de Ville de Paris* or *sur les Cinq Grosses Fermes*, etc., which were little more adventurous.[1] There might in any year be a deficit which, it was hoped, would be filled by a donation from the government, bishop or chapter, Provincial Estates, a local lottery or a special *quête*.[2] By the end of the *ancien régime* a deficit was the norm. Moreover, any balance which was made to exist was achieved by rigid economies, a point which needs stressing because Enlightenment propaganda and the *Comité de Mendicité* were convinced that extravagance and financial malversation were what lay at the roots of the economic problems of the *hôpitaux*. Staffing was cut to a minimum. At Rodez 472 poor, of whom 50 were dangerous lunatics and 160 bedridden by paralysis or old age, were tended by four nuns—and it is hardly surprising that a further 122 able-bodied but frail and elderly poor should find themselves tending the sick, cleaning and scrubbing, and tending the orphaned children.[3] Four Sœurs de Saint Joseph du Puy assisted by one gardener managed the *hôpital* of Mende,[4] while Rouen was, by comparison, abundantly staffed because fifty-four people were employed in the tending of 2,000.[5] Nor can one point to any cleric who grew fat upon the revenues of the *hôpitaux*. Most only employed a priest to come to the aid of the dying, to see that the

[1] See Appendix II for specimen budgets.

[2] Out of eighty-five *hôpitaux* enumerated by Bloch, *L'Assistance et l'État*, pp. 282–4, thirty-six showed a deficit in 1764. In diocesan centres the bishop's help was first sought, e.g. in Provence, A.N. H¹ 1311, Hôpitaux d'Aix, et Marseille, A.D. Côtes-du-Nord, Hôpital Saint-Brieuc, Donations, Dons de Henri-Nicolas Thessault du Bragnon, évêque de Saint-Brieuc 1745–64 (totalled 25,190 *livres*); at Quimper the bishop occasionally handed out 500 *livres*, M. Faty, 'Les Hôpitaux de Quimper avant la Révolution de 1789', *Bull. soc. arch. Finistère*, x (1883). In the *pays d'États* some appeal was made to the *États* in Burgundy (A.D. Côte-d'Or C 3687), a few hundred *livres* were usually available; in Brittany, Rennes alone received attention. Otherwise, appeal had to be directly to the government.

[3] Lempereur, *L'État du diocèse de Rodez*, Rodez.

[4] A.N. H¹ 1322, Hôpital général de Rouen, 1777.

[5] A.D. Lozère H 461.

children knew their catechism, and to say an extra mass on Sundays, and this priest received as his payment little more than a good meal on the days he attended the *hôpital*. Next to nothing was spent on medical care. Such money as there was went towards the purchase of a basic coarse bread ration, on vegetables, on milk for the children, and sometimes on wine for one meal of the day. Beyond this, all that the nuns could do in face of an inflationary situation was to keep their numbers down. By the end of the *ancien régime*, only abandoned children between the ages of 7 and 14 could be entirely sure of a place in an *hôpital général*. The mentally sick, the blind, and the paralytic native to the town in question could usually expect to get one, but only a small proportion of the old could have any such ambitions.

This restricted achievement was far from fulfilling the early hope placed in the *hôpitaux* by the government. Between the launching of the *hôpitaux* and the edict of 1724, which represented the official government line on poor relief and the extirpation of begging until the 1760s, there were no official inquiries or statistics compiled to inform the governments of the number and size of the *hôpitaux* throughout the country. But one must assume that in government circles they were presumed to exist substantially in every town; the government believed that with a little monetary assistance they could be convincingly extended to become not merely an asylum for *all* the unfortunate but workhouses in which *anyone* taken in the act of begging or loitering on the streets with such an intent could be incarcerated and provided with work. Without such an assumption it is impossible to understand how any government could enact such a piece of legislation. The terms of the edict were fully explicit. The poor were divided into *valides* and *invalides*, and for the latter, who had no means of supporting themselves, there was the immediate enjoinder to present themselves (or be conducted thence by the *archers* or *maréchaussée*) at the nearest *hôpital* 'où ils seront reçus gratuitement et employés au profit des hôpitaux à des ouvrages proportionnés à leur âge et à leur force'. For the able-bodied, instructions were more complicated. They were instructed to find work within fourteen days. Should they fail to do so, they were to present themselves at the *hôpital*, which would provide them with work against their board and lodging and a small and unspecified *gratification*. They would be released from *hôpital* work if they

could show they had alternative work to go to or if they volun-
teered to join the army. Failure to present themselves would lead
to incarceration in an *hôpital* 'prison' for a period of time ranging
from two to six months, branding with the letter 'M', and correc-
tive punitive training based on hard work and a diet of bread and
water.[1] The type of work the government envisaged was the
digging of roads and the levelling of disused and dangerous
buildings. Moreover, the government did not see the *hôpitaux*
undertaking all this without some financial aid, accordingly they
promised this on the basis of an estimate of the cost of feeding
and clothing each able-bodied beggar.

It is relatively easy to explain why legislation was enacted in
the 1720s: the social dislocation caused by pestilence in Provence,
the bad harvests of the early twenties, the problems surrounding
the collapse of Law's schemes, the male unemployment associated
with the disbanding of armies after a protracted war, and—a
point emphasized by earlier historians of this legislation—the fact
that the government had recently reformed (or thought it had)
the *maréchaussée*, a force which specifically concerned itself with
beggars and vagrants in the countryside. A reformed police force,
it could be argued, was the first instrument in bringing the lusty
beggar to justice.[2]

The capabilities of the police force will be examined presently;
the issue here is how far were the *hôpitaux* capable of responding
to this legislation?

The answer is, in no way. Up to this juncture *hôpitaux* had been
intended for the weak; under this persuasion donations had been
made, buildings had been carefully purchased, young women had
idealistically undertaken religious vows and training. No *hôpital*
had a prison or personnel capable of superintending vast numbers
of able-bodied adults. The government offered to pay for the
upkeep of the new internees but it left the vital problems of
accommodation, type of work, and personnel to the *intendants*,
municipalities, and, in the last analysis, to the *hôpitaux* themselves.

In Paris, Lyons, Toulouse, the Auvergne, and, above all,
Provence, administrators laboured to convert the larger *hôpitaux*

---

[1] Isambert, *Recueil des lois*, t. xxi, pp. 271–3.

[2] C. Paultre, *De la répression de la mendicité et du vagabondage en France sous l'ancien
régime* (Paris, 1906), pp. 326–7. This author also urges the marked inspiration of a
mémoire sent to the government by the Abbé Saint-Pierre entitled 'Projet pour
renfermer les mendiants', *Ouvrages de Politique*, t. iv, p. 56.

into workhouses but without any real semblance of lasting success. The *intendant* of Auvergne, who was one of the few *intendants* to take the edict seriously, attributed the failure of the edict to lack of buildings, lack of money, foresight, and planning.[1] Before the edict could even begin to come into effect, he argued, special premises would have to be purchased or constructed and a special personnel hired and trained. Towns like Bayeux or Saint-Brieuc whose *hôpitaux* had the means to look after under 200 greeted the edict with derision. It would demand, the town of Bayeux pointed out to the *intendant*, the arrest of 1,800 people in the town alone.[2] Perhaps in deference to the royal edict, the municipality explained that they had, on receipt of the edict, persuaded the *hôpital* to take into custody a handful of *femmes de mauvaise vie, mais non mendiantes*. Saint-Brieuc and all the other Breton towns which answered the *intendant*'s letters concerning the edict denied having either *archers* capable of arresting offending beggars, a place to put them, people to look after them and maintain discipline or any means whatsoever of putting the edict into effect.[3]

The lack of response to the edict at least informed the government of the limitations of the *hôpitaux*, and the related correspondence put official circles in command of knowledge of the incidence and effective strength of these institutions throughout France. Though the government's defeat was never officially recognized and though the government did not cease in a half-hearted way in the 1730s and 1740s to urge the *hôpitaux* to greater action, its disillusionment with their effectiveness in relation to the problem of poverty as a whole was total. This did not mean that the government ceased to afford them some financial aid in face of impending bankruptcy. Indeed, the government was perhaps their first source of help in emergency and some 1,800,000 *livres* of government money were in the last decade of the *ancien*

[1] The struggle to make this edict work in the Auvergne is found in A.D. Puy-de-Dôme C 1046–81. By 1734 the attempt had been abandoned, C 1082 and J. P. Gutton, 'L'Application de la déclaration royale du 18 juillet 1724: généralités du Lyonnais et d'Auvergne' (Thèse 3e cycle, Lyons, 1967).

[2] A.D. Calvados C 626, *Hôpitaux de Bayeux*, and Hufton, *Bayeux*, p. 99.

[3] A.D. Ille-et-Vilaine C 1285, Saint-Brieuc, Dec. 1724: 'Personne bonne à capturer les mendiants si ce n'étaient peut-être les sergents royaux et les justices seigneuriales et subalternes des lieux; mais quoi que la pluspart de ces gens soient souvent aussi gueux que ceux à la capture desquels on les voudrait assujettir je ne sais s'il serait possible d'en venir à bout tant cet emploi est regardé en haine.'

régime to be used to this end.[1] Government legislation in 1749 did, however, play its part in freezing hospital revenues. In 1749 an edict was passed limiting the amount of land which could in the future pass into *mortmain* (and hence be exempt from taxation). In this hospital property was included and hence new revenues from land rendered uncertain.[2] Moreover, if the government's loss of faith in the *hôpitaux* was never openly expressed, nevertheless, in drawing attention to their feebleness and general inefficacy, implicitly the government did contribute powerfully to what was at best a growing feeling of indifference and at worst overt hostility to these institutions. Potential benefactors were deterred. There were no new creations. Monetary bequests also virtually dried up, and it is from the 1730s that there can be traced a mounting wave of criticism. The *parlements* had little inclination to respect the memory and ideals of the intrepid anti-Jansenist, St. Vincent, and criticism of the *hôpitaux* became embodied in anti-government propaganda.[3] The government found itself in an undesirable position, unable to abolish the *hôpitaux* since they catered to the needs of at least two sectors of the deserving poor, the orphaned, aged, and debilitated, and enjoyed property rights which could not be infringed, and simultaneously obliged to subvent them—albeit at a very low level of generosity. In 1775 Turgot tried to curtail their powers of borrowing without sufficient backing, and successive governments tried to persuade the *hôpitaux* to sell property to rid themselves of debt. Here, though there are exceptions, the *hôpitaux* refused on the grounds that it would be a direct contravention of the pious intentions of the donors. The suggestion made to the *hôpital général* of Rouen in 1763 met with the rejoinder:

Cette idée n'est-elle pas combattue et par la nature même de ces biens dont la plus considérable partie serait seulement vendue le denier vingt, et parcequ'ils ont été donnés ou acquis à des charges les uns de messes, offices, services et prières, les autres de l'entretien d'écoles publiques et dans l'intérieur de l'hôpital, une portion pour doter de pauvres filles, une autre assez considérable pour servir spécialement à retirer dans l'hôpital les filles et femmes débauchées, une autre portion

[1] See below, p. 193.
[2] Bloch, *L'Assistance et l'État*, pp. 305–6.
[3] Simard, *Saint Vincent de Paul*, in his final chapter embarks on a consideration of this theme.

pour recevoir et entretenir des pauvres sur présentations et nomina-
tions, d'autres pour être toujours en la possession de l'hôpital et servir
à la subsistance des pauvres, sans qu'il soit permis de les aliéner, et
parce qu'ils sont enfin le gage et l'objet de toutes les charges, dettes et
rentes de l'hôpital qui excèdent de beaucoup les revenus des biens
fonds.[1]

In spite, however, of the fight put up by the *hôpitaux* to cling
to their property in face of mounting debt, progressively inroads
were made into the principle of the immutability of bequests and
foundations: a bankrupt or potentially bankrupt *hôpital* like La
Grave at Toulouse or the *hôtel Dieu* in Paris was summarily
ordered by the government to alienate property to meet its
creditors. Finally, in 1780 came the edict which, if it largely
remained a dead letter, was in effect the precursor of the revolutionary 'hard line' towards the *hôpitaux*. The work of Necker, it
stipulated that the work of the *hôpitaux* should be reduced to
correspond to their revenues; that in case of debts their property
should be sold to acquit the debts and the rest assumed by the
state against a guaranteed income whose management would be
supervised by the government.[2] The *hôpitaux* were pushed more
and more on to the defensive.

The *Comité de Mendicité* inherited these attitudes towards the
hôpitaux along with inflated notions about vast endowments,
mismanaged by a group of pious amateurs, and was condemned
to square them with the evidence it rapidly accumulated on scant
revenues stretched to their utmost. The truth was that they were
frail, impecunious, and incapable of meeting the demands made
upon them, least of all a demand which no seventeenth-century
institution anywhere could have realized, that of locking up the
pauper and thus emancipating society from the more offensive
manifestations of poverty.

iv. Bureaux de charité

The reforming zeal of the late seventeenth century did not, at
least theoretically, leave the larger villages totally untouched in
the provision of formal relief. The concept of the *bureau de charité*
or *bureau d'aumônes* was exactly what its name suggests, that is of

---

[1] Cited Bloch, *L'Assistance*, p. 308.
[2] Isambert, *Recueil des lois*, t. xxvi, p. 257.

a pool of alms, the voluntary alms of the faithful, administered to the deserving poor of the parish by some individual or group capable of judging the needs of the recipient and hence the validity of his claims. Its essence was voluntary, but not indiscriminate, almsgiving. The *bureau de charité* theoretically promised some form of outdoor relief for the poor, and relief which might be extended not only to the aged and the orphaned but to the deserving poor of a somewhat wider category, namely the struggling family. Both Catholic philanthropists and the French government pinned great hopes on the extension of *bureaux de charité*, since initially they promised to be the most flexible charitable institution of the *ancien régime*. Obviously buildings— and a consequent large initial capital outlay—did not come into question, nor, necessarily, a full-time personnel, and the way in which funds were distributed could be changed to cope with varying needs from month to month or year to year as different situations arose. Particular local situations might serve as stimuli to greater effort. This was indeed what Louis XIV's government and all succeeding ones came to hope. Long after the *hôpitaux* had fallen into discredit, the idea of the *bureau de charité* remained alive, regarded in official circles as the most suitable way of helping the families of the labouring poor, and it is no accident that the periods of office of de l'Averdy, Turgot, and, latterly, Necker, all saw renewed attempts on the part of the government to inspire the setting up of such projects. 'Inspire' is used deliberately: the government did not intend in any way to finance them, that was the concern of Christian charity.

It should be borne in mind at the beginning that of all the charitable institutions of the *ancien régime*, the *bureaux de charité* are the most difficult to trace because so many were run on an informal basis, on the product of *quêtes*, irregular amounts, rather than on a fixed income in *rentes* or property. Moreover, the bulk of them did not have a continuous existence. This was particularly true of those established in villages where there was no solid regular income from *rentes* and property, in contrast to the larger towns where such an income existed. In such cases the impetus for the *bureau de charité* came from the presence of some philanthropic individual, or group of individuals, and the efforts these were prepared to expend to help the poor vanished with their death, perhaps subsequently to revive through the efforts of another individual or perhaps not. There are few genuine rules which one can apply to the institutions as a whole. What one can do is to look at where they were established, the sort of existence they enjoyed, the funds at their disposal, and how they chose to apply those funds.

The guiding hand of St. Vincent is much less apparent than is the work of the Jesuits in the foundation of *bureaux de charité*. True, the saint had envisaged the setting up of soup kitchens, *le bouillon* or *la marmite des pauvres* run at a practical level by the Dames de la Charité, wealthy ladies with backgrounds similar to that of St. Louise herself who would muster the necessary resources and provide the requisite facilities. Indeed, there exists a kind of blue print which bears greater witness to the ideal of the gentle Christian society held by St. Vincent de Paul than anything else. Whilst one Sister of Charity should attend to indigent families who should come to her for their assistance, another should be peripatetic, carrying food to those confined to their beds at home.

Elle apprêtera le diner, le portera aux malades, en les abordant les saluera gaiement et charitablement, accommodera la tablette sur le lit, mettra une serviette dessus, une gondole et une cuillère et du pain, fera laver les mains aux malades et dira la Benedicite, trempera le potage dans une écuelle, puis conviera le malade, Jésus et sa sainte Mère, le tout avec amour comme si elle avait affaire à son fils ou plutôt à Dieu, qui impute fait à lui-même le bien qu'elle fait aux pauvres. Elle lui dira quelque petit mot de Notre Seigneur, en ce sentiment tachera de le réjouir s'il est fort désolé, lui coupera parfois sa viande, lui versera à boire et l'ayant ainsi mis en train de manger, s'il a quelqu'un auprès de lui, le laissera et en ira trouver un autre pour traiter en la même sorte, se ressouvenant toujours de commencer par celui qui a quelqu'un avec lui et de finir par ceux qui sont seuls, afin de pouvoir être auprès d'eux plus longtemps.[1]

But the cosy charitable atmosphere herein envisaged was little likely of realization, on the one hand because the Sisters of Charity were too hard worked and on the other hand because the philanthropic zeal of the Dames de la Charité did not, with important exceptions, outlast the seventeenth century. Indeed, St. Vincent himself soon despaired of the Dames as too removed

[1] P. Coste, *Les Filles de la Charité* (Paris, 1933), pp. 13–14.

from the truly poor to understand their problem fully. Here and there, however, some institutions were created on the lines envisaged by St. Vincent and remained to bear witness to the early activities of the Dames de la Charité and pious male *confréries* even if the work involved in the running of them often passed into other hands.[1] In the diocese of Rennes only the diocesan centre itself and the neighbouring town of Vitré had such an institution. The first had reserved the property of the expelled Jesuits, and so by the end of the *ancien régime* had a substantial income of 24,000 *livres* per year, permitting the running of a soup kitchen to provide 800 paupers with a meal a day and a bread ration towards a second meal and some aid to the sick of the town who could not be received into the *hôpital*.[2] Such funds contrast sharply with other *bouillons* or *marmites*. The only such institution in the diocese of Rodez (needless to state, at Rodez itself) had gifts and legacies totalling 72 *livres*, which were largely used in providing food for the sick;[3] at Mende also the only institution was in the diocesan centre, and its revenues hovered in the region of 2,000 *livres*.[4] In the diocese of Rouen, outside Rouen itself Gournay, Eu, and Le Havre had *bouillons*.[5] In 1774 that of Eu merely helped the sick with meals; that of Gournay had become an outright annual monetary grant of about 2 *livres* per head to 250 poor; while La Miséricorde of Le Havre was one of the few such institutions to afford real help. It was endowed with a mere 1,575 *livres*, but in crisis years the wives of *négociants* and noble women succeeded in raising 12,000 *livres* to

---

[1] A *confrérie* was a group of people united with a single aim, and those which are our concern existed with the purpose of alleviating a sector of the socially unfortunate (sick, aged, etc.). Very occasionally (two instances in the *généralité* of Lyons, one in Burgundy, none in the dioceses of Rouen, Mende, Montpellier, Rodez, Clermont) these dated back to the Middle Ages, otherwise they were the product of seventeenth-century effort. Usually one emerged in the diocesan centre and in all towns of 5,000 or more, but unless fairly substantially endowed, had no permanence.

[2] P. Hardouin, 'La Marmite des pauvres et la fondation des Sœurs de la Charité à Rennes', *Bull. mém. soc. arch. et hist. Ille-et-Vilaine*, lxx (1956), 41–77.

[3] A.D. Aveyron 5 L 236, Assistance publique, 13 septembre 1790.

[4] A.D. Lozère H 989–91. The purpose of this institution was: 'assister les pauvres de la ville de Mende et ceux du Chastel Nouvel, succursale de la paroisse de Mende, qui sont détenus dans leur lit pour cause de maladie, vieillesse, infirmités, honteux et autres, ne pouvant gagner leur vie ou mendier, ni être admis à l'hospice, à cause de leurs infirmités passagères, ou de leurs épouses et enfants.' At any one time in the closing years of the *ancien régime*, 100 people might be in receipt of help.

[5] A.D. Seine-Maritime G 846, Gournay; C 995, Eu, Le-Havre-de-Grâce.

run a soup kitchen which could cater to 400 or so poor daily.[1] Even so, one is dealing in extremely small figures. Another handful of towns in each diocese had *marmites* which came and went with the rigour of the times or the enthusiasm of the bene-factors, but which were incapable of doing anything substantial. In diocesan centres informal *marmites* sprang up during crisis periods, usually as a result of the efforts of a philanthropic bishop or higher cleric supported by contributions from other people. One such sprang up in 1777 in Rodez when the bishop undertook to feed 200 of the 1,200 poor who had been drawn to his attention by the municipality; another at Dijon in 1770.[2] The criteria for help, beyond dire need, were evidence of regular religious wor-ship and good conduct.

Much more widespread than *bouillons des pauvres* were the simple *bureaux de charité* or *aumônes générales* which the Jesuit fathers Chaurand, Guévarre, and Dunod so actively advocated on their great charitable odyssey through France. They thought in quite straightforward terms: first, a pool of alms—no need to wait for property—to be used for food and perhaps work material for indigent craftsmen, and secondly, help of a more rudimentary nature even than this, a depot of discarded clothing (especially shoes), of material which could be used for blankets, and even of old furniture which would be of potential use to the family that had been forced to sell all that it possessed in order to procure the food to feed it. They saw no reason why every town and village should not be endowed with such a *bureau*, nor did they think that it needed the administration of either Dames or Sœurs de la Charité—merely a little local initiative, whatever the source.[3] From the efforts of these Jesuits stemmed the first outcrop of *bureaux de charité*: in the diocese of Rennes, those of La Guerche, Bruz, and, possibly, Balazé; in the diocese of Mende, those of Florac, Chirac, and Villefort; in that of Rodez a mere four emerged; the dioceses of Clermont and Limoges were untouched by their work. Following the pattern of these early establishments were the *bureaux de charité* set up at Bain, Châtillon-en-Vendelais, Fercé, Louvigné-de-Bais, and Tresbœuf (diocese of Rennes),

[1] Ibid. C 995. In normal years the Dames de Charité helped the *pauvres honteux* and the sick.
[2] *Journal de . . . Richeprey*, p. 93; Bolotte, *Les Hôpitaux et l'assistance en Bourgogne*, p. 330.
[3] Joret, *Le Père Guévarre*, pp. 8–30.

Saint-Étienne-Vallée-Française (diocese of Mende), and the twelve small *bureaux de charité* set up by Pradel, bishop of Montpellier in 1689. Pradel was a great advocate of the important clerics setting an example for lesser mortals to observe and emulate.

Pradel, bishop of Montpellier, chose to scatter a little money very widely in the hope that when he had, nominally, at least, created a *bureau de charité*, others would be encouraged to contribute to the institution. Thus, the twelve *bureaux* in the diocese of Montpellier that were attributed to Pradel in 1689 were founded by the bishop on the unimpressive sums of from 25 to 200 *livres*, which bear greater resemblance to the small *rentes* and *fondations* characteristic of traditional village charity than to the initial outlay required to found a new institution designed to eradicate the problem of poverty. In spite of early hopes, the efforts of the 1680s and 1690s were, however, extended relatively little during the first half of the eighteenth century. Only Rennes, Montpellier, and Mende of the dioceses analysed saw any extension whatsoever of the *bureaux de charité* to villages and small towns, and in each instance merely to a handful on any permanent basis. At Rennes the most successful could only bestow small bread distributions annually on a score or so of poor and give parcels of cast-off, virtually worn-out, clothes which, when the best had been cut out of them, might cover a ragged child.[1]

One village of the diocese, Hennebont, had a *bureau de charité* which apparently came and went:

Ce bureau n'a de solidité que la bonne volonté de ceux qui en sont membres, et de ceux qui voudront les remplacer. Il peut se détruire d'un moment à un autre, comme il a été établi il n'a d'autres revenus que les habitants veulent bien lui confier, à l'exception de 95 livres de rente qu'on perçoit autre fois aux pauvres honteux, et que ce bureau perçoit aujourd'hui.[2]

The resources of the diocese of Montpellier were somewhat greater—at least at first glance—in so far as by 1770 the diocese boasted twenty-five *bureaux de charité*. On the other hand, of these, three had no fixed annual revenues, eight had under 50 *livres*, a further ten had between 50 and 200, two under 300, and

[1] See Appendix I.
[2] A.D. Ille-et-Vilaine C 1293, Bureaux de charité d'Hennebont, 1774.

apart from Montpellier, only one, Lunel, a town of some 6,000 inhabitants, had one with a regular income of 1,500 *livres*. None was able to accord help to any one individual totalling more than an annual 2 *livres*.[1]

Again the diocese of Mende provides a telling example of just how restricted the help afforded by the *bureaux* was. In Mende itself, 100 poor received one meal twice per week while there were at least 1,000 destitute; Florac confined efforts to a distribution of a piece of bread on Sundays to the poor who had attended mass and an annual distribution of 3 *sols* per head to about forty paupers. Villefort could aim at no more than occasional help to the sick and the costs of the lawsuits incurred in seeing that the comte de Morangis fulfilled his responsibilities as *seigneur* towards the *enfants trouvés* of the town. At Chirac funds permitted a yearly grain distribution—worth about a *livre* per head—to some 112 people. Here there were no *bureaux* outside the towns.[2]

The full list of *aumônes générales* for Burgundy, where village *bureaux* were non-existent, comprehended Dijon (revenues of 3,900 *livres* per year), Mâcon (1,000 *livres* at most), Autun (1,500 pounds of bread distributed per week in the winter season), Auxerre (unspecified funds which in crisis years could for short periods permit the expenditure of 800 *livres* per month on grain), Beaune, Bourg, Tournus, and Chalon-sur-Saône.[3] Of the last group only the revenues of Beaune had any substance. The legacy made in 1714, plus the product of an annual *quête*, seems to have realized a sum of about 7,000 *livres*.

La distribution se fait en argent, par mois, aux pauvres dont on fait un rôle chaque année; en pain, chaque semaine aux pauvres qui sont portés sur un autre rôle, et en grains et argent, par mois, aux pauvres malades et aux artisans chargés d'enfants. Les charges ordinaires vont à 1200 livres environ, elles consistent en messes à faire acquitter, en une certaine quantité de droguet pour habiller les pauvres, en sommes à donner pour faire apprendre des métiers, en pensions pour séminaire à des pauvres ecclésiastiques de la ville . . .[4]

[1] A.D. Hérault C 5957.
[2] A.D. Lozère H 445, Livre de délibérations du bureau de charité de la ville de Florac; E 1000 and 1049, Bureau de charité de Villefort; J 760 Fonds Volpelier, Bureau de charité de Chirac. See Appendix III.
[3] A.D. Côte-d'Or C 378, État général de tous les établissements, fondations, revenus et charités dans la généralité de Dijon 1693–1788.
[4] Ibid., Subdélégation de Beaune, diocèse d'Autun.

In fact, the early hope of the Catholic reformers that a *bureau de charité* would be set up in each parish met with scant and disappointing response. In the context of the seventeenth or eighteenth century it is impossible to pick out a town or village which did not need a *bureau de charité*. On the other hand, the creation of one depended upon the existence of individuals affluent enough and generous enough to make donations. The affluent were conspicuously lacking in the *pays de petite culture*. This becomes particularly apparent when one considers the incidence of the *bureaux de charité*, which was lowest in the teeming Massif where the likelihood of finding an affluent sector of the community to set up and endow such establishments was extremely remote. Even where the *seigneur* was a personage of reasonably philanthropic disposition—or indeed where he was, for example, an ecclesiastic—alone he might well, without immense personal sacrifice, be incapable of offering any real help to the indigent village of which he was *seigneur*. Hence the dioceses of Clermont and Limoges never knew a *bureau de charité* outside the diocesan centre, nor did that of Le Puy outside Espalion. One seeks such institutions almost in vain in the Comminges or the Alpine regions.

Even where they did exist, however, what could they do to touch the over-all problem of poverty? The paucity of funds not only restricted the numbers of poor who might be helped but also determined the types of poor to whom assistance might be accorded. How, under these circumstances, could the poor who were to receive help, be chosen?

The answer is valid everywhere: they were chosen according to a strict residence qualification and on an attestation by the *curé* of good conduct. The residence qualification was nowhere less than three years, and at Rennes was up to seven. 'Dans l'impuissance', wrote the administrators of the *bureau de charité* of Brive, 'de secourir tous les pauvres, il sera juste de préférer les habitants naturels';[1] good conduct was judged according to regular presence at mass, yearly confession, occasionally, as at Mende and Vitré, a test in the catechism, and in addition, above all, not to have been caught begging in the streets. Some *bureaux* went further and applied a test involving a thorough inspection of the property

---

[1] A.D. Corrèze H., Brive G 1, Bureau de charité.

of the pauper and expected him to have parted with bed and cooking-pots before asking for help.[1]

Apart from the residence qualification, physical debility and widowhood, when the widow in question had children to support, were the main claims upon such scant funds as existed. These victims of distress might expect in their malady a few *livres*, or a few pounds of bread, or, in the case of the widow and her brood, a few *livres'* annual hand-out. On the evidence of the extent of these institutions in the 1770s, there is little to justify the government's continuing faith in the *bureaux de charité* as the main source of relief for the deserving poor. Yet the 1760s were to see a government, confronted with increasing numbers of destitute, seeking to reinfuse bishops, nobles, municipal authorities—anyone with any kind of authority or funds at their disposal —with the incentive to try again to found *bureaux de charité*, and if possible take them a stage further and make of them training centres where the poor might be taught manufacturing skills.[2]

This line followed hard upon the edict of 1762 encouraging the growth of rural industry emancipated from guild control and was an expression of a somewhat changing attitude towards remedies for the problem of poverty: the hope that in rural industrialization lay the salvation of the many. The government may have been inspired by experiments made in Normandy in the early 1760s; certainly it hoped that new *bureaux de charité*, in some cases topically renamed *manufactures des pauvres* or *écoles de filature*, would offer a new chance to the women and children of poor families. Then, with the deserving poor thus provided for, a more unreservedly punitive line could be taken against the ingrained vagrant.

The exhortations of the government met with some response. The duc de Rochefoucauld Liancourt made his reputation as a philanthropist as a result of his efforts to establish an *école professionelle d'arts et métiers*, a manufacture of playing-cards, a cotton-

---

[1] A.D. Ille-et-Vilaine C 1270, Marmite des pauvres de Vitré; A.D. Indre-et-Loire H 909, Bureau des aumônes de Tours. At Troyes, 'Les assistés devaient "pratiquer" et s'approcher au moins une fois l'an, de la table de communion; en 1730 . . . le bureau décida que les pauvres secourus par "l'aumône" feraient leur confession pascale et remettraient aux directeurs leur billet de confession sous peine d'être rayés de rôles de distribution' (E. Chaudron, *L'Assistance*, p. 54).

[2] Thereafter *bureaux de charité* became the focal point of philanthropic activity, especially on the part of the higher clergy.

spinning school, a tileworks, and a brickworks. The marquis d'Hervilly set up a small establishment for the production of cloth near the château of Lanchelles, the Duchess of Choiseul Gouffier a cotton-spinning school at Heilly, the Prince of Condé a muslin works at Condé, and Voltaire a clock works at Ferney. At Mondidier, Madame de Romanet started a spinning school, and similarly *bien pensant* titled ladies followed her example at Roye and Doullens. At Orleans an industrialist opened a *bon-neterie* production for 800 workmen. In Cahors the bishop headed the list of experimenters with a *manufacture*, and the bishop of Auxerre drew up a project outlining a silk works for the poor of the diocese. But what did all this amount to? Four or five lace and cotton schools emerged in Normandy: of these the cotton-spinning schools at Rouen and Bayeux had the greatest permanence. The *manufacture des pauvres* created at Bayeux—the model, Turgot considered, on which all such projects should be based—had a typical history of successive, characteristic difficulties.

Two canons of the cathedral of Bayeux had spent between them in the 1750s 50,000 *livres*, an important sum, on the extension of a lace school and the setting up of a cotton-spinning school. The lace school was an unqualified success, and the enterprise encouraged the canons to undertake the ambitious project of the industrialization of Bayeux. The founding of a school to teach cotton-spinning to the children of impoverished families, using the funds of a *bureau de charité* and the capital provided by the Abbé Hugon, was intended as the beginning of a much larger project. Tragedy struck before the idea advanced to any significant extent. The children employed produced work of inferior quality and even the little money that was paid to them to encourage them to work caused an expenditure the *bureau* could not afford. The philanthropic Abbé Hugon contributed 10,000 *livres* out of his own money to keep the enterprise going and indeed was so hopeful of ultimate success that he was in process of building a school to train woollen workers when he died. His place was taken by another canon of the cathedral, de Loucelles, who applied himself to the project with equal enthusiasm. Indeed, such was his anxiety to succeed that he travelled throughout Normandy learning about the manufacture of cloth so that he should know what faults to look for. Fear of being tricked by unscrupulous middlemen led him to undertake, personally, all purchase of raw material. This led him to fairs, markets, farms, and to rub shoulders with merchants and manufacturers.[1]

The thought of such a man, obviously motivated by genuine philanthropy, is impressive until one remembers the recession currently taking place within French industry. Bayeux even without the *manufacture des pauvres* already produced far more cloth than it could sell. Failure to find a market for the goods it produced was attributed initially to the poor quality of the work, and this prompted the struggling *manufacture des pauvres* to cut down on the number of children it employed. With adult labour and a preferential tariff in respect of the *octroi*, it managed to sell the cloth at the Foire de Guibray. Here it met the opposition of local manufacturers, who already had trouble in selling their goods, and by the mid seventies the *manufacture des pauvres* had closed its doors.

The Rouen experience was roughly analogous. An experiment undertaken in the early seventies simply foundered when confronted with the mounting economic crisis of the 1780s.[2] The history of similar manufactures was the same. If the *lanifice* (woollen manufacture) of Mende at least staggered into the closing years of the *ancien régime*, it only did so in a purely nominal sense.[3]

Elsewhere, in the cities the government's exhortations in the late sixties did resurrect occasional lapsed *bureaux de charité* or, alternatively, reinfused some of them with a little more energy to the extent that bishops and parish priests attempted to secure pledged donations on a regular basis, and accounts of these were kept and carefully audited by the old *bureaux*.

The *bureaux* in diocesan centres or those in the capital of the *généralité* generally reformulated the principles according to which donations would be made. The *bureau* of Besançon declared it would no longer spend its funds on a small bread distribution after Sunday mass to a handful of families, as it had done since 1712, but would 'donner du travail à ceux qui en réclameraient;

---

[1] Hufton, *Bayeux*, pp. 104–5. This passage is based upon the earlier version.

[2] C. Lion, 'Notes sur les travaux publiques et la filature de coton établis à Rouen dans les paroisses Saint Maclou, Saint Vivien, Saint Nicaise en 1768–9', *Bull. soc. d'émulation* (1932).

[3] R. Tinthoin, 'Le Lanifice de l'hôpital de Mende au début du XVIIIe siècle', *Lou Païs*, 20 août 1961.

fournir des matières premières et des outils aux ouvriers qui étaient en état de travailler'.[1] The transition was not to be effected with enhanced funds, and perhaps it was announced in the expectation of drawing the attention of philanthropists who thought assistance should be based on work. By 1780 the *bureau* had reverted to giving help in the form of bread. Similarly at Moulins, a project to confine the funds of the *bureau de charité* to a bread donation to the sick, road work for adult males, and to providing the raw wool for spinning for adult women had reverted by 1789 to an outright bread distribution in every case. At Tours a declaration made in 1773 that raw materials would henceforth be the backbone of charitable effort simply collapsed since the funds of the *bureau*, even with a donation from the bishop, only amounted to some 1,200 *livres*:

En assistant ces chefs de famille, on leur procure les moyens de se soutenir dans leurs professions, d'élever leurs enfants; on prévient le découragement qui les précipite dans la misère et la fainéantise, on conserve des hommes précieux à l'État qui en perpétuant la société, transmettent leur arts et leurs talents à la postérité.[2]

But while this was evidently true, 1,200 *livres* was little able to help 3,000 indigent.

In other dioceses and *généralités*, the early seventies saw a feeble response to the government's hopes. In Burgundy one *bureau* emerged at Bourg-et-Nolay which, even with a small subsidy from the États de Bourgogne, could only provide shoes for barefooted children and a small subsidy for the sick.[3]

In the diocese of Mende a solitary *bureau d'aumônes* emerged from the efforts of the sixties and seventies, that of Saint-Étienne-Vallée-Française which bore no resemblance whatever to what the government had envisaged. Founded with an initial capital of 600 *livres* donated by a local philanthropist, Jacques Dupas de la Pastèle, the institution enjoyed a total income of 1,207 *livres* 15 *sous* 6 *deniers* between 1775 and 1780. It attempted to subsidize the widowed and the families of the sick to the extent of some 2 or 3 *livres* per month, but entire years elapsed when it was without the means to accord even such scant assistance.[4]

---

[1] P. de Saint-Martin, *La Mendicité à Besançon*, pp. 113–14.
[2] A.D. Indre-et-Loire H 909, Bureaux de charité, 1773.
[3] A.D. Côte-d'Or C 378, Subdélégation de Beaune, diocèse d'Autun.
[4] A.D. Lozère GG 12, Bureau de charité Saint-Étienne-Vallée-Française.

At Rennes the bishop took seriously what he regarded as a reminder from the government of his pastoral duties and as a way of helping to eradicate the evident vices of the poor, namely, dishonesty, drunkenness, indifference to their children, and incest:

Toutes les charités des fidèles, versées dans un dépôt commun, en seront tirées avec connaissance; elles seront appliquées aux indigents et aux plus dignes; elles seront réparties avec prudence, selon les circonstances et la nécessité; l'oisiveté n'aura plus d'excuse. Par là on empêchera le mendiant d'aller de maison en maison grossir l'histoire de ses misères, multiplier ses mensonges, et porter fréquemment dans les cabarets le produit des aumônes. Les enfants . . . ne verront plus d'exemples qui conduisent à l'oisiveté, au libertinage, et souvent au crime. . . . Le recteur aura soin de faire tous les ans un état exact des pauvres et autres nécessiteux de la paroisse, de la cause et du genre de leurs enfants. Il n'y inscrira que ceux qui sont nés, ou véritablement établis dans la paroisse *cum anima manendi*. Ceux qui ne seraient pas d'une bonne vie, ou qui auraient manqué de respect aux commissaires, de même que les pères et mères qui ne sépareront pas de lit leurs enfants, dès l'âge de six à sept ans, lorsqu'ils sont de différents sexes, ou qui les mettront à coucher avec eux, seront très sévèrement réprimandés et rayés du catalogue de charité, jusqu'à ce qu'ils aient réparé leur faute et changé de conduite.[1]

But even accompanied by propaganda of this nature, nothing emerged, although his evident concern may have influenced a friend and neighbouring cleric, Urbain de Hercé, bishop of Dol, who in 1767 endowed a *bouillon des pauvres* in the diocesan centre with a capital sum of 20,000 *livres*, the interest on which was to provide two Filles de la Sagesse with sufficient to distribute a soup ration to as many poor of the town as possible. His testament also accorded two parishes, Pleudihen and Épiniac, with *rentes* of 120 *livres* and 40 *livres* respectively with which the *recteurs* could attempt the foundation, if no more, of *bureaux d'aumônes*.[2] Other Breton bishops—those of Tréguier, Saint-Pol-de-Léon, Saint-Brieuc, Quimper, and Vannes—were not so active, or perhaps so rich. Only Saint-Brieuc had a *bureau d'aumônes* enjoying an annual income of 450 *livres* (to be distributed among well over 2,000 poor), and this was a seventeenth-century foundation.[3]

---

[1] P. Delarue, 'Une Tentative de Monseigneur de Girac pour organiser les bureaux de charité dans le diocèse de Rennes', *Annales de Bretagne*, xxiii (1907), 22.

[2] C. Robert, *Urbain de Hercé, dernier évêque et comte de Dol*, pp. 111–13.

[3] A.D. Ille-et-Vilaine C 1292, Saint-Pol-de-Léon, etc., 1786.

The Quercy in fact responded more than anywhere else to the appeal for new *bureaux* in the seventies, perhaps because their *intendant* and provincial assemblies were competing with each other to prove their efficiency. In Caussade, Montauban, Martel, Lauzerte, Villebourbon—five towns—a *bureau de charité* temporarily emerged. The first raised in one year 5,931 *livres* to buy rice; the second did not record its receipts but professed itself unable to provide for 1,500 families and asked the *intendant* for a subsidy. At Martel the work of the *bureau* remained a dead letter, since funds were not forthcoming; at Lauzerte the *intendant* agreed to a 'loan' of 10,000 *livres* of which 6,000 was to be spent on grain and the rest on work projects; while at Villebourbon success was claimed for the relief of the immediate parish poor but complaints were made that without similar establishments in the rural parishes little of lasting effect could be done. The rural case was most succinctly expressed by the curé of Saint-Christophe (Molières): 'Voici toutes les difficultés qui peuvent s'opposer à la bonne œuvre d'un bureau de charité. La première est que j'ai dans ma paroisse beaucoup plus de personnes dans le cas de réclamer les secours du bureau de charité que de lui en fournir.'[1]

Indeed, the *pays de petite culture* again rejected the feasibility of a *bureau de charité*. In the *généralité* of Clermont the *intendant* circulated in 1777 an urgent letter from Necker pressing for the introduction of *bureaux d'aumônes* into the Auvergne as a means of cutting down the numbers of homeless beggars upon the roads. The form in which the *bureaux* were urged is utterly typical:

ces bureaux auraient pour objet de procurer des charités et des secours et de les employer utilement; ils indiqueraient des travaux, fourniraient des matières et des outils à ceux qui sont en état de travailler, procureraient des remèdes, des soins et des aisances aux malades, ne feraient que des prêts à ceux qui n'ont que les besoins momentanés . . .[2]

The answers, however, were again exactly what might have been expected. Only the cities of Clermont and Riom thought the proposition in any way feasible. The *subdélégué* of Aurillac stated quite openly that the idea was totally incapable of realization in his area: 'parce que la misère y est trop grande et générale,

---

[1] A.D. Lot C 287. E. Sol, 'Les Bureaux de charité en Quercy à la fin de l'ancien régime', *Annales du Midi*, lx (1948), 260–84.
[2] A.D. Puy-de-Dôme C 1162.

les subsides trop forts, la pluspart recevraient au lieu de donner s'ils osaient demander . . . beaucoup de gens ont quitté le païs et passé en Espagne . . .'[1] He suggested the formation of *ateliers de charité* with government aid. At Besse the *subdélégué* M. Godival claimed that twenty years ago such an experiment had been tried and had met with total failure; charity, he declared, was out of the question, even those who could perhaps afford a few shillings, who were few, would not contribute lest the appearance of even scant affluence send their taxes soaring. At Brioude an experiment made in 1745 to establish an *école de dentelle* had collapsed because, in order to find funds for it, every possible source had been exhausted and the bulk of the poor had been left helpless, and this had brought the institution into disrepute and cut off any further funds. Montaigut and Lezoux returned equally pessimistic answers.[2] Clearly the *bureaux de charité*, revamped or otherwise, could not support the burden of the eighteenth-century poor.

The Sum of Formal Relief

For antiquarians and Catholic historians it has always been possible to be impressed by the range of institutions, produced by the efforts of the pious, which characterized formal relief before the Revolution: institutions to care for the orphaned and aged, the wayward girl, the epileptic, or to distribute soup or blankets to the sick or the paupers of the parish, or to teach the children of the poor their catechism.[3] One can isolate any town of 5,000 or more and expect to find any amalgam of the institutions outlined above. After 1724 governments periodically made counts of these institutions and resources, and the *Comité de Mendicité* was to do the same. There existed, for example, at Bourbon Lancy: 'un hôpital des eaux minérales pour les pauvres malades' with an income of 4,039 *livres* and capable of tending thirty disabled poor; 'une confrérie de la charité', founded in 1663 (a kind of *marmite*) and run on an annual *quête* held by the worthy ladies of the parish; 'une communauté des Dames de Saint Ursule', which was prepared to 'donner tous les lundis le pain à tous les pauvres qui se présentent et à un seul le pain et la soupe tous les

---

[1] Ibid.   [2] Ibid.
[3] Bolotte, *Les Hôpitaux et l'assistance*, pp. 335–6; T. J. Schmitt, *L'Assistance dans l'archidiaconé d'Autun aux XVIIe et XVIIIe siècles* (Autun, 1952), pp. 291–2, etc.

jours de la semaine'.[1] At Autun there were: an *hôpital général* with
revenues of 17,345 *livres*, capable of looking after 24 old people,
60 orphans, and 33 dying sick; *un bouillon des pauvres*, with a
revenue of 2,150 *livres*, to give sustenance to the sick; an *aumône
générale* with an income of 1,060 *livres* and 500 bushels of rye to
help the poor who had been proven taxpayers in the area during
the past seven years; and 'une fondation pour marier les sages
filles de la ville d'Autun' and whose revenues were sufficient to
give three girls 500 *livres* as dowries every three years; a *fondation*
(1671) of 300 *livres* per year for teaching a trade to six children;
a *confrérie des pénitents noirs* to help prisoners, which had revenues
of 100 *livres* per year; and an *aumône* (which the poor could not
claim by right but had by custom) of 18 *cordes de bois* to provide
firewood for the sick poor and women in childbed. Paray-le-
Monial had an *hôpital général* with twenty beds and an *aumône
en pain* of 1,200 bushels of rye 'réduit en pain et distribution faite
trois fois par semaine pendant les trois premières semaines de
l'avent et toutes celles du carême'—the domiciled poor might
eat while others fasted. At Anzy-le-Duc there was 'une charité
de 90 livres pour les réparations de l'église at à défaut le soulage-
ment des pauvres'.[2] In the large cities, Rouen, Lyons, Marseilles,
Toulouse, Rennes, the list is longer and proliferation greater,
perhaps to include *manufactures des pauvres* and a *maison des filles
repenties* (passing under various names, La Charité de Lyons, La
Tour des Toussaints de Rennes, etc.). A piecemeal enumeration
of the resources of any diocese is usually long, and the only
immediately striking generalization that can be made from such a
tally is the contrast between resources available to the towns and
the village *fonds*. Yet this contrast should not cloud the main
issue, the total inadequacy of formal relief anywhere. In 1790 the
Comité de Mendicité drew up a set of tables indicating the extent of
relief in each *département*. The calculations were made on the
basis of the combined funds of *hôpitaux généraux*, *hôtels Dieu*,
bureaux de charité, and like institutions, and the *fonds libres* and
formal ecclesiastical hand-outs. The *Comité* was far from satisfied
with the returns it received and, where districts did not reply, it
used the results of earlier inquiries made in the 1760s and 1770s,

---

[1] A.D. Côte-d'Or C 378, Subdélégation de Bourbon Lancy.
[2] Ibid., Subdélégation d'Autun and Paray-le-Monial. These examples are expressly
taken from a single diocese.

MAP II

Charitable Resources of Departments in 1791

and even did some multiplying, to arrive at what it considered a
convincing figure.[1] Globally the sums were made to look impressive, but if each department's total resources are related to
population density (see Map II) and if those in need of some

[1] The *Comité* drew heavily upon the sixteen-volume de l'Averdy *enquête* of 1764
(A.N. M 672). Some guesswork was needful as many districts (probably over 50
per cent) were dilatory in making returns.

assistance—albeit perhaps only for part of the year or for certain stages in their existence—are recognized to be in any department between 10 per cent and 20 per cent of the whole, then the real extent of the resources available for formal relief becomes evident. In the wealthiest (from the point of view of charitable funds) departments (the Seine-Inférieure, Flandre, Marne, Côte-d'Or, Bouches-du-Rhône, and Loiret) they stood in the region of a *livre* per head of the population or 5–10 *livres* for each pauper per year; in average departments they ranged from 4 to 8 *sols* per head of the population or 1–4 *livres* per head of destitute per year. Worse than this, in a belt running from the Basses-Pyrénées, through Gascony—the Landes, Gironde, Lot-et-Garonne, and Lot—up through the Dordogne, Charente, and the Corrèze to the Creuse and the Puy-de-Dôme and bounded by the Indre and the Cher, the total resources divided by the number of destitute would not have been sufficient in any one year to buy a single pound of bread for each hungry person.[1]

To indulge in such arithmetic might constitute an artificial approach to the subject since no one sought thus to divide the funds of formal relief. Yet to assess it in this way offers some perspective and makes clear why the poor had to look outside institutional relief. For the privileged few—and the history of the *ancien régime* is a history of privilege—who found asylum in an *hôpital*, for those whose problems were reduced by an annual bundle of clothes from the Sisters of Charity, for the 800 fortunate possessors of meal tickets at Rennes, or for those living adjacent to the abbey of Bonnecombe or Fécamp, formal institutionalized charity had some meaning. For the mass of rural poor, however, for the immigrant communities in the cities, for those without a sponsor to ensure they spent their declining years in an *hôpital*, formal institutional relief was not a factor in their struggle for survival.

---

[1] These calculations are based upon the tables found in Bloch and Tuetey, *Procès-verbaux*, pp. 568–9, and M. Reinhard, *Étude de la population pendant la Révolution et l'Empire* (Paris, 1961), pp. 48–9.

VI

GOVERNMENT ASSISTANCE

i. *Grants of Relief*

THE government, though disillusioned by the relative inefficacy of the *hôpitaux* in the 1720s and 1730s, did not feel moved to make any immediate alternative provision for the poor. This is not to suggest that the poor were totally ignored but attention was not focused upon them in normal years. *Abnormal* circumstances, on the other hand, a bad harvest, an epidemic, meteorological disaster—flooding was invariably the best plea—were likely to win for the area in question some special favour. This might, according to the problem and the year in question, and depending especially upon the financial position of the government, take one of a number of forms. First, and the most likely, the government might accord a reduction in taxes for the individual area in question; secondly, an actual monetary grant might under exceptional circumstances be granted, or a quantity of food might be dispatched or, in the event of epidemic, from the 1770s, free medical supplies might be rushed to the area.

How effective and how far reaching were the measures taken to alleviate local disasters and how prompt was government response? The Auvergne provides some instructive examples, the more so because it fell within a *pays d'élection* where monetary matters were exclusively the affair of royal government without the intermediation of *États* which might make special provisions and then proceed to haggle with the central control.[1] In 1740 the Auvergne experienced chronic and widespread harvest failure with classic results. The towns Clermont (*c.* 25,000 inhabitants),

---

[1] In the *pays d'États* it is virtually impossible to extricate from the evidence the actual source of funds. The monarchy's usual method of relief was to agree to the non-sending of certain elements of taxation, usually the *taille* and the *moins imposé* part of the *taille* in particular. This might then be the money in question or it might be drawn from other funds over which the *États* had direct control. Certainly in the *pays d'États* monetary help, or help in kind, was usually through the medium of the *États*, though Brittany would appear at least in part to be an exception to this rule.

Riom (*c.* 12,000 inhabitants), Thiers, Aurillac (*c.* 10,000 inhabitants each), and to a lesser extent Issoire and Brioude and Saint-Flour (*c.* 5,000 inhabitants) underwent an immediate winter influx of hungry country folk; ugly scenes occurred in the markets. The *intendant* at Riom found himself besieged by municipal officials fearful for public order and his office full of priests and *syndics* lingering on the plight of their villages. He was authorized to use for the relief of the poor of Clermont and Riom (10,000 people?) 8,000 *livres* to be taken from the *octrois* levied to repay for the sale of municipal offices in 1733.[1] The *intendant* and the bishop of Clermont agreed that the best way to spend a sum which would last a month at the most was to give it to the nuns who ran the *hôpital général*, on the understanding that they would not use it for the internees but to erect a soup kitchen. Food was only to be distributed to the known, domiciled, deserving poor. Brioude, Saint-Flour, and Aurillac then asked for 10,000 *livres* (probably hoping to receive 5,000) for immediate needs. They were accorded 3,000—also out of the *octrois*—and informed that no more would be forthcoming 'à cause du trop grand nombre de villes dans d'autres provinces qui se trouvent dans le même cas'.[2] The next plea came from Thiers, the last to be considered, perhaps because the administrators of the *hôpital* had persuaded the municipal officials, and had gained the hearty support of the *intendant*, to levy a tax on the more substantial citizens—with negligible results. The *intendant* had hoped this would be efficacious in helping 2,000 beggars. He now asked the central government for help for Thiers and a little more for Saint-Flour and Aurillac whose *hôpitaux* in the crisis had run into difficulties. The *intendant* took the hardest line he could with the government: 'les hôpitaux de cette province sont d'autant plus dignes de ces grâces, qu'il se fait annuellement en Auvergne deux impositions d'environ 52,000 livres, l'une des trois deniers pour livre en sus de la taille et l'autre pour la moitié des gages des offices municipaux réservés aux hôpitaux par l'édit de juillet 1724.'[3] This wave of correspondence produced 4,000 *livres* with the firm declaration from the *contrôleur général* that the Auvergne had now had all it was going to get and that this sum must be used to help the poor of the crisis and to defray any increased costs incurred by the

---

[1] The history of this crisis is found in A.D. Puy-de-Dôme C 898–904.
[2] Ibid. C 899.   [3] Ibid. C 900.

hôpitaux. Now followed the contest for funds which every *intendant* knew so well. Aurillac (10,000 people) was allocated 700 *livres*. Immediately, the administrators of the *hôpital* claimed the whole, on the grounds that any distribution made to the poor on the streets would only bring the rural poor flooding into Aurillac for the hand-out and that in any event the sum was so small that it could have no impact on the over-all situation but would save the *hôpital* severe embarrassment. The *intendant* said the *hôpital* could have 500 *livres* and the rest if it would guarantee to make provision for clearing the streets of beggars.[1] Whilst this correspondence was going on, the poor received no aid. Then there was the struggle of large and small, town versus village and large village versus small village. Invariably the larger won, the towns always on the plea that the artisan and his family were totally resourceless, whereas one could never truly divine the state of the countryman. Were the country people not, the curé of Brioude asked, in possession of *quelques raves*?[2] The crisis of 1740 had raised for the entire Auvergne 17,000 *livres*, and of this the rural poor had officially received nothing. This sum *in toto* would not have provided a day's nourishment if divided by the total number of hungry. Crisis did not end for the Auvergne in 1740–1. It had entailed the consumption of grain needed for the sowing, and the payment of debts incurred by the rural hungry only sorted themselves out in the autumn of 1741, when once more the province was seen to be in difficulty. The experience of 1741–2 showed further struggles for the funds the government was prepared to accord. This time they were in kind: 3,850 *livres* of rice for the entire *élection* of Aurillac were promised (a couple of meals for each of the city's 3,000-odd beggars, or a struggle between city and town, town and village?).[3] The *intendant* found himself under immediate attack from Chavagnac, *seigneur* of Blesle 'dont les habitants n'ont rien à mettre sous la dent . . . ne vous attendez pas qu'on puisse payer la taille, on tirerait plustôt de l'huile d'un mur que de l'argent de ce pays-ci'. The *intendant* replied that when the rice arrived Blesle would get something. Chavagnac followed up his request by saying that, as he now understood it, the *intendant* was obliged 'de donner la soupe à 900 pauves de la terre de Blesle, et cela sans exagération

[1] Ibid. C 901.   [2] Ibid., Letter of curé of Brioude.
[3] Ibid. C 904.

ni par vanité'.[1] If the *seigneur* chose thus to interpret the *intendant*'s words the intendancy could do little about it. 3,850 *livres* of rice divided amongst the 900 poor of Blesle would feed them at most for a week. No *ancien régime* administrator could scatter *largesse* so thickly. The donation must be divided, sent to this town, this *hôpital*, this village, in order to keep hopes raised and the *intendant*'s office free from suppliants. Government relief under such circumstances had psychological rather than practical effects: the promise that 'something was coming', that next week food was on the way, was a contribution to the surmounting of crisis. Any *intendant* in any *pays d'élection* could count himself fortunate if only called upon to perform such juggling acts once or twice during his tenure of office. In the *pays d'États* attitudes were not dissimilar to those taken by the government. In times of extraordinary hardship a village might expect a marked reduction in its tax contribution, and under peculiar circumstances, where there was a special object to fulfil, pecuniary assistance of a token kind might be made. The failure of the olive-oil crop in 1766 provoked attention because not only was the harvest reduced but some of the trees appeared permanently damaged by blight, and the États de Provence were prepared to subsidize their replacement.[2] Flooding and hailstorms might again merit a token response—depending upon the size of the disaster. In normal years the États de Languedoc and those of Provence and Burgundy confined their activities to subsidies to the *hôpitaux*.[3] The États de Bretagne were not even generally prepared to go so far. In the last twenty years of the *ancien régime* only the *hôpital général* at Rennes could expect any regular meagre subsidy—it totalled on average 600 *livres*. In 1772 and 1785 grants from the *taille* were made to the province by the monarchy. In the second instance they were to provoke what are perhaps the most tragic series of begging letters from priests and subdelegates that have survived.[4]

---

[1] A.D. Puy-de Dôme C 904.

[2] T. Sheppard, *Lourmarin in the Eighteenth Century* (Baltimore, 1972), p. 113.

[3] It is possible to get some idea of the extent of help given in Burgundy. Help to the *hôpitaux* rose from an annual donation totalling up to 500 *livres* in the 1740s to between 2,000 and 3,000 in the 1780s. This was taken from the *taille* and sanctioned by the monarchy. Less regular were sums intended to cope with local hardship. The city of Dijon received 60,000 *livres* in 1770; the province about 30,000 *livres*' worth of rice in 1771–2 (A.D. Côte-d'Or C 3687), but no other such extraordinary grant seems to have been made until 1785.

[4] A.D. Ille-et-Vilaine C 1745–6, Secours destinés aux pauvres, 1785–6. The

200,000 *livres* had to be divided up. It was technically the most generous grant ever made to a single province. The contest was acute. Typhus-ridden villages sent in grisly reminders of the victims of disease; others described the effects of harvest failure—the reason why the grant was accorded in the first place—families who had consumed grain needed for sowing and had nothing left, those with a problem of unemployment, each couched a letter to the *intendant* and hoped to receive its cut. The money was divided: in the *subdélégation* of Nantes 1,957 people, made up of the old, the infirm, and needy children, received 2 *livres* each (perhaps a week's supply of bread); in that of La Guerche 2,360 people received 1,428 *livres* between them; the *subdélégation* of Plélan sought to help 2,210 people with 1,500 *livres*. In the last instance they were families who had been living on boiled cabbages for two months. The *recteur* of Guer did not know how to begin dividing 240 *livres* amongst 5,000 people. Many of the parish priests had made promises to their parishioners of the help that was coming. Its failure to arrive made a deep impression. The resentment lingers in the *cahiers* of 1789: where were the evil people who had distrained the government grant from its rightful purpose?

These occasional hand-outs represented by the second half of the century only one aspect of government assistance. By the sixties government attitudes towards the alleviation of distress were changing to what was, at least in theory, a radically different line towards the alleviation of poverty. Others have explained this in terms of a growth of humanitarianism or attributed it to the impact of physiocratic influence upon government, but what probably impelled official action more than anything else was a real and visible growth in the destitute and partially employed as manifested in the numbers upon the roads, the increasing number of abandoned children, and the swelling volume of administrative correspondence concerned with rural under-employment and hardship. The theories as to how to treat these problems obviously drew upon economic and social philosophy currently in vogue. Briefly, these might be described as threefold: adopt a hard line towards the *hôpitaux* as extravagant and useless;

cahiers of Trédaniel, Meillac, and Hénon complained they received nothing; others complained that the little they had had they had subsequently been forced to purchase dearly, Janzé, La Baussaine, Gurguen. H. Sée, *Cahiers de doléances de la sénéchaussée de Rennes* (Rennes, 1912).

make an attack on the idle work-shy poor and teach them the habits of industry; concentrate upon helping the small holder and the agricultural labourer, who should be the main concern of governments as the mainstay of the state. The last should be helped by encouraging rural industry, which could be left to itself to develop helped along by a well-intentioned government and right-minded people—in short, the *manufacture des pauvres* described above; and secondly, the government should grapple with the small holders' main fear—unemployment during the dead season. To cope with this the government evolved the concept of the *atelier de charité*.

ii. L'atelier de charité

The *atelier de charité* is perhaps the easiest and most obvious of essays in poor relief to describe, since essentially it consisted of putting the poor to work on state-financed enterprises, a common procedure elsewhere in eighteenth-century Europe and one whose roots in France would seem to lie, at least theoretically, in the fifteenth century.[1] As a form of relief it has been depicted as a dramatic breach with the past but it was so only in two respects: first, a sum of money for such use was guaranteed by the state and hence the system did not have to wait upon private subscription, as in the case of the earlier *bureaux d'aumônes*, and, secondly, the poor who came to work in these establishments were given a wage in return for a day's labour rather than alms on a charitable basis. The *atelier de charité* has been represented as the total rejection by the state of the principle of voluntary charity, but this is certainly to overstate the situation. The state expected private subscription to supplement state donations; in granting monetary privileges to the *hôpitaux* it had already allowed the principle of voluntary donations to be eroded. In a free-lance way the cities,

---

[1] The bibliography on *ateliers de charité* is very small. J. L. Harouel, *Les Ateliers de charité dans la province de Haute-Guyenne*, is the only extensive one in print. H. Hemmer, 'Les Ateliers de charité à la veille et au début de la Révolution', *Mém. soc. sci. nat. arch. de la Creuse*, xxxi (1935), 405–17, is very cursory. More can be found on the issue as regards Troyes in E. Chaudron, *L'Assistance publique à Troyes*, p. 46, and in general upon the theme see A. Lesort, *La Question de la corvée sous Louis XVI après la chute de Turgot* (Paris, 1902); A. Tuetey, *L'Administration des ateliers de charité 1789–90. Rapport de J. B. Edme Plaisant* (Paris, 1906). It is to be regretted that M. Cros, 'Les Ateliers de charité dans la généralité de Limoges de 1770 à 1783' (Diplôme d'Études Supérieures, Poitiers, 1963), has not been published.

by means of municipal funds, had occasionally used public works in times of rising costs and unemployment to help the poor, so that the idea of public, if not state, help was far from new. What was new was the generalization of the project and the fact that it was intended not for the towns but the countryside. The form of the *ateliers* of the 1770s was essentially Turgot's conception of relief, the result of experiments carried out whilst he was *intendant* of Limoges and yet more clearly defined during Necker's tenure of the controller-generalship. If some parts of rural France knew any institutionalized relief at all, it was as a result of the practice of the *ateliers de charité*; that the extent of that relief was restricted was because the government did not have sufficient funds at its disposal, and that the country, at least in some provinces, such as Champagne, progressively lost out even in respect of *ateliers de charité* to the towns, was very far from being Turgot's intention.

The blue print for *ateliers de charité* was in fact dispatched to every *intendant*. It outlined a three-tiered system in which the rough navvying involved in road-building and terracing was undertaken by women, children, and grown men too unskilled to do anything else, each performing according to his or her physical ability; the more sophisticated work, such as paving the same road, would be confined to the adult male—possibly under professional supervision; and separate from this scheme would be schools for textile working, particularly spinning, in which women and children could learn to be self-supporting. Payment would be according to need: an adult male cost more to feed than a woman, a woman than a child. Moreover, an adult male with a wife currently tending a young baby, or the head of a family of very young children, had the greatest need of all, since he had others dependent upon his efforts, and he needed to be paid accordingly. In other words, payment needed to be scaled. The organization of the *atelier* would be on a parochial basis, and the *curé* was of pivotal importance because he knew the needs of each individual family and could divide up his poor into work brigades, seeing that children were not separated from their parents and so on. The *atelier de charité* would be created where need was greatest and was not to be permanent. Ideally, and where the ground was not frozen hard, it would be most common during the winter months when the agricultural labourer needed employment and would finish in the spring when work in the fields began again.[1] Or, and this was the case in the *généralité* of Limoges, the *ateliers* would open in those months when there was no local work or potentiality for seasonal migration. In this instance it would fill a gap in the agricultural labourer's year and would help out the subsistence farmer during the dead season.[2] There was no question at all of *ateliers* existing for the irrevocably unemployed, and initially the offering of wages with family allowances was not considered liable to lure away those in other employment. The *atelier* was to offer needful ancillary income: it was a sympathetic and highly imaginative recognition that the problem of poverty was a family problem and that something had to be done to help women and children in order to keep the family on the right side of the line between poverty and destitution. In restricted areas of the *généralité* of Limoges, where it was tried out on an experimental basis, it was highly successful and convinced Turgot that this was the answer, at least in *pays de petite culture*, to the problem of poverty.

Perhaps at the outset a number of factors need stressing. The part of the scheme that envisaged the creation of industrial schools was destined to early failure. There are indeed instances of attempts to industrialize the country by the importation of English and Irish—the tireless Mademoiselle O'Flanegan—usually via the royal manufacture at Sens, to teach the use of the jenny.[3] This part failed for obvious reasons: artificial efforts of this nature, even in eighteenth-century England and Holland, could never produce consistently good or competitively priced work, and in France the experiment was tried against the background of an industrial recession. Hence the *ateliers de charité* must above all be considered in the light of the public road-works and building schemes. The second factor to be recognized is that the creation of this scheme did not mean the existence of unlimited funds or the unqualified acceptance by the government of any potential project in any area with a high problem of poverty. The *ateliers* were to be financed from an annual grant made by the monarchy from *le moins imposé*, part of the *fonds*

[1] A copy of this appears in most departmental archives in *pays d'élections*, e.g. A.D. Calvados C 3416, Instruction pour l'établissement et la régie des ateliers de charité, 1775.

[2] Cros, 'Les Ateliers de charité dans la généralité de Limoges', pp. 8–10.

[3] She was, however, at least at Bayeux, Avranches, Troyes, and the villages of Champagne and in Touraine, financed by local philanthropic effort.

extraordinaires of the *taille* and chosen for this purpose by the government because levied on the poorer peasantry, *brassiers*, *manœuvriers*, *haricotiers*, those with a fragment of land which might or might not be adequate for the support of a family.[1] Hence the relatively poor of the country were by the cumulative effect of a light imposition to support the really poor of the country, and the fact that they were to do so meant to Necker that the *ateliers* must be totally rural-based: it was unfair to use rural taxation to support the poor of the towns. (He seems, in fact, to have seen *le moins imposé* as a kind of parish rate.) Both Turgot and Necker had a very near appreciation of the problems of the *pays de petite culture* and the precarious nature of the livelihood of the small proprietor whom the state had a special interest in buttressing,[2] perhaps because in physiocratic doctrine no element in society was of more crucial significance than the agricultural worker, but perhaps, more realistically, because the bulk of those who turned themselves into beggars, dangerous or otherwise, originated in this section of society. Apart from a government-accorded grant from *le moins imposé* (which ranged from *c.* 60,000 *livres* to 100,000 *livres* per *généralité* annually), in some *généralités* (Caen, Rouen, Montluçon) the commuted *corvée* was used, at least partially, to help out the poor.[3] In any event, the funds at the disposal of

[1] Harouel, *Les Ateliers de charité*, p. 14.

[2] Necker spelt out this belief explicitly to the *intendant* of Basse Auvergne whom he clearly felt had not sufficiently demonstrated commitment to the *ateliers de charité* scheme (see below, pp. 191–2): 'Les regards et les soins des administrateurs doivent donc se porter essentiellement sur les pays de petite culture et sur ceux dont l'ingratitude du sol rend toujours incertaine l'espérance de la production; si les misères quelconques affligent un pays riche et abondant, le mal est promptement réparé, et les fermiers aisés ont toujours soin dans leurs calculs d'y faire entrer les pertes que peut leur occasionner l'intempérie des saisons; dans les pays de petite culture, au contraire, la concurrence y est plus grande, la nécessité de cultiver pour vivre met les propriétaires dans le cas de faire la loi aux cultivateurs et d'exiger des prix plus chers; alors une grêle, une gelée met des milliers d'hommes à la mendicité; je vous exhorte donc, Monsieur, non seulement de ne point oublier cette observation importante dans la répartition des impositions, mais encore de réserver la diminution de taille, les décharges de capitation, les ateliers de charité, les distributions de ris et remèdes préférablement pour les cantons qui sont d'autant plus intéressants qu'ils sont plus malheureux et que cependant ils fournissent une culture plus utile et une population plus abondante.' A.D. Puy-de-Dôme C 1162, Necker to the *intendant* at Riom, 10 Dec. 1777.

[3] This was not universally the case, for although Turgot's edict transferring the old tax in kind to a money payment was eventually registered, it did not in every province pass into law—though it did so, for example, in the *resort* of the *parlements* of Paris, Rouen, and Nancy—the area of jurisdiction of the *parlement* of Bordeaux

intendants and provincial assemblies for the purpose of the *ateliers* were not large and priorities had to be very carefully defined. Moreover, much depended upon whose concern the running or financing of the *ateliers* was. Not surprisingly the *pays d'États* were in some instances independent of the scheme, for their control over their finances was considerable. Hence *ateliers de charité* were unknown in Brittany, almost unknown in Provence and Languedoc, and relatively undeveloped in Burgundy. Flanders had more extensive schemes corresponding more closely with the experience of the *pays d'élections*.[1] No province had greater need of *ateliers* than Brittany, yet successive *intendants* could not push the *États* into monetary grants in this direction. The striking contrast between the reception of the idea in the *pays d'États* and the *pays d'élection* means that, in considering the experiment at all, one must recognize that at least 50 per cent of French territory had never even heard of it. Then there were areas where geography made its application impossible. To construct roads over snow-bound mountains in winter is scarcely possible. Hence the inhabitants of the Alps, the Pyrenees, Jura, and even Cevennes, however much they might have needed an ancillary income, could not find relief from this source.

Contrast between areas in which the experiment of the *ateliers* was seriously undertaken does not end here. It was undertaken against a background of administrative change, even—at risk of overstressing—of conflict, for it coincided with attempts in some of the *pays d'élections* to shift the *intendant*'s control over finance to the provincial assemblies. The outcome of this experiment varied from province to province.[2] Necker favoured giving as much authority as possible to the provincial assemblies, but his successor, Clugny, swung away from this tendency. As a rough

---

being the most noteworthy area of rejection. Technically, to use the *corvée* for the purpose of financing *ateliers de charité* was unjustifiable since the *atelier de charité* was designed to be concerned with the minor road, the *chemin vicinal*, and not the *grande route* which was the concern of the *corvée*. An *intendant* or provincial assembly really bent upon assistance, however, could usually find some means of diverting money from this source, and in the case of the provincial assembly of Lower Normandy did not hesitate to push up the *corvée* tax with the poor in mind (Hufton, *Bayeux*, p. 107).

[1] Lefebvre, *Les Paysans du Nord*, p. 309.

[2] Harouel's work is largely concerned with this conflict. It is, above all, an administrative study rather than one conducted with regard to the problem of poverty as a whole.

rule, to which all kinds of exception can be made, the *intendants* controlled the experiment of the *ateliers* up to 1779; the provincial assemblies thereafter in the provinces of Berry, Haute-Guyenne, Dauphiné, and Bourbonnais. Elsewhere the application of *intendants* varied and clearly some were more efficient in launching the experiment than others. Where the *intendant* had neither the time nor the inclination to bother himself, the scheme could become waterlogged. After 1799 the conduct of the *ateliers* in the provinces which had provincial assemblies was dependent upon how easily the relationship between *intendant* and provincial assembly resolved itself, for strife could lead to uncertainty in the disposal of funds. The provincial assemblies of Haute-Guyenne and Berry in the main were soon in control.

From the outset it was anticipated that local donations would supply a significant proportion of the funds: that *seigneurs* would seize the opportunity of a royal subsidy to advance the rest in order to make improvements upon their *châteaux*, or would be glad to contribute towards the construction of a road connecting their estate with a main artery. Turgot expressly laid down this principle, even though his experiments in the Limousin had not attracted much local help:

Il semble que tous les propriétaires aisés pourraient exercer une charité très utile et qui ne leur serait aucunement onéreuse en prenant ce temps de calamité pour entreprendre dans leurs biens tous les travaux d'amélioration, ou même d'embellissement dont ils sont susceptibles. S'ils se chargent d'occuper ainsi une partie des pauvres compris dans les États; ils diminueraient d'autant le fardeau dont les bureaux de charité sont chargés.[1]

Necker tried to establish norms for both state aid and private subsidies, but he finally admitted that they must vary from area to area. In a letter to Bertier, *intendant* of Paris, in 1778 he pointed out that only substantial donations from *seigneurs* were justification for using the poor in the *seigneur*'s interest and that the *intendant* should see to it that the *seigneur* gave at least a third and preferably a half of the required expenditure.[2] In fact a private donation of a

[1] Cited by M. Lecoq, *L'Assistance par le travail en France* (Paris, 1906), p. 86. This is a useful passage demonstrating that the *ateliers* were conceived of as *charity* and the new system was to complement and help out the old, not in any way to render it redundant.

[2] A.N. H² 2105, Necker to Bertier, July 1778.

third seemed to Necker the ideal balance in areas where such prosperous personages could be found,[1] but their existence, he was soon forced to concede, was far from being universal. The *intendant* of Montluçon, in reply to parish priests requesting the immediate introduction of *ateliers* in their stricken parishes, drew their attention to Necker's recommendation:

Il a été arrêté que la préférence pour les fonds de charité sera accordée à ceux qui s'engageront à contribuer à la dépense pour une plus forte somme de manière que celui qui offrira de contribuer pour moitié à la dépense sera préféré à celui qui n'offre que le tiers et celui qui offrira le tiers à celui qui n'offrira que le quart.[2]

But the *pays de petite culture* which interested the *contrôleurs généraux* so nearly were not necessarily productive of prosperous nobles or clerics. Neither the *intendant* of Montluçon nor the *intendant* of Clermont nor the provincial assembly of Guyenne was able to report the donation of substantial sums by property-conscious *seigneurs*, and an alternative form of subsidy had to be evolved whereby whole communities, by making available tools, carts, horses or oxen, even materials for road surfacing or wood for repairing bridges, could be considered to have made a contribution replacing that of a *seigneur*. Once this principle had been conceded, there existed innumerable *rivalités du clocher* between more substantial parishes interested in link roads (*chemins vicinaux*), and difficult choices had to be made. In all this, however, the parishes without such resources could easily be overlooked. From this principle of seigneurial donation or communal participation in kind certain features of the experiment emerge. First, that the *ateliers* were not necessarily located where they were most needed, but, in the case of provinces with a prosperous nobility, in those areas where the noble or cleric in question was prepared to make a donation; where communities replaced the seigneurial donation, the poor of the area were dependent upon the more prosperous of the area making materials and implements available. They were under no compulsion to do so. Hence the fact of being poor and needing work in an *atelier* did not mean that one could

[1] A.D. Indre-et-Loire C 323, 1785, Liste des ateliers à établir tant pour l'emploi des 100,000 livres de fonds de charité accordées par le roi en 1785 que pour celui des contributions particulières, s'élevant à 38,255 livres 10 sous. A similar balance was achieved in Champagne, Chaudron, *L'Assistance publique à Troyes*, p. 46.
[2] A.D. Creuse C 335.

necessarily expect work. Moreover, the reliance on local added to national funds obviously meant that the work undertaken was often of a very restricted use—often exclusively the use of the *seigneur*. The *assemblée provinciale* of Champagne in 1788 was particularly explicit on this issue:

Le riche propriétaire essaya bientôt de faire tourner un établissement si pur et si sacré à son intérêt personnel. La contribution volontaire lui servit de prétexte pour attirer tout à lui. On pava les cours et abords des châteaux, on fit réparer les châteaux, curer et faire des fossés, des murs de cimetières et des croix de mission, travaux dirigés et payés par des maîtres d'hôtel, des garde-chasses, des cuisiniers ou des frotteurs.[1]

In the *généralité* of Tours, contributors to the *ateliers* read like an extract from the *armorial de France* and the eighteenth-century work project made its own individual contribution to terracing and linking up the great *châteaux de la Loire*[2] whilst more vital communications, such as the road between Mayenne and Falaise on which essential repair work was needed and with which the village of Lassay sought a link, went untouched.[3]

There was also a limit to the amount of work of this nature which important nobles and ecclesiastics wanted doing, and hence private subsidies receded visibly over the years. Moreover, nobles

[1] A.D. Marne C 2871, Essai sur l'emploi et la manutention des fonds de charité. Generally provincial assemblies were anxious to find scandals in the running of the *ateliers* while under the control of the *intendant*. Only one out of six of the scandals investigated at Montauban contained a shred of truth. Harouel, *Les Ateliers de charité*, p. 88. On the other hand, at least two of those investigated at Troyes revealed flagrant abuses of the spirit of the *ateliers*.

[2] In 1785 contributors of a total of 38,255 *livres* were Pocquet de Livonnière, le marquis de Charnace, la vicomtesse de Rouge, M. de Contades, le marquis de la Roche du Maine, le comte d'Argenteuil, le comte de la Motte Barace, le marquis d'Usse, Achard de la Haie, le baron de Blou (A.D. Indre-et-Loire C 324). In ensuing years le comte de la Galissonière, le marquis de Clermont Gallerande, le comte de Broc (C 325), Gaultier seigneur de Congrier, Tripier de l'Aubrière, le comte de Croismare (C 326), Hauterive seigneur d'Argentré, le comte de La Fallière, la duchesse de Beauvilliers, le marquis de la Ferronays, le marquis d'Autichamp, le marquis de Montclerc, le duc de Charost, le marquis de Charteloger (C 327) were the most important contributors.

[3] A.D. Indre-et-Loire C 326, Requête des habitants de Lassay relative au rétablissement du chemin de Mayenne à Falaise qui est impraticable les deux tiers de l'année. Similarly a road linking the bishop of Bayeux's palace at Sommervieu with Bayeux was authorized because of the bishop's donation, whilst another linking the mines of Littry with Bayeux was rejected, A.D. Calvados C 7655. Hufton, *Bayeux*, p. 108.

were not the promptest of payers. In 1787 an *ingénieur* of Troyes
wrote on the subject of a road going from Montsuzain to the
grande route from Troyes to Arcis, 'Le chemin est ouvert dans
l'avenue du château; on a fait un déblai pour donner au château
la vue de la grande route . . . il paraîtra toujours n'avoir d'autre
but que de faire un chemin au seigneur.'[1] The *seigneur* in question
had contributed a mere eighth of the total cost although he had
promised the regulation third. Those who worked in the *ateliers*
were dependent upon daily payment, and failure on the part of
the *seigneurs* to pay resulted in some ugly scenes.[2] Necker was
insistent that *intendants* should, if possible, get payment in advance
from *seigneurs* on whose property or in whose interest *ateliers* were
to be established, but the *seigneurs* could easily claim that they had
no guarantee that work would be effectively concluded and that
their interests were not being safeguarded.[3] The brigades were
often reported as drunken, violent, disorderly, and irregular
in their approach to work, and *seigneurs* were quick to stress these
aspects and to withhold payment. *Entrepreneurs* to whom *intendants*
and provincial assemblies committed the organization of the
work, the supply of raw materials, and the payment of workers
were occasionally dilatory in the last instance, usually because of
delays in the arrival of funds from the *généralité*, or because costs
had overrun estimates. Employees could demand their wages in
vain: workers in the *atelier* at Bayeux in 1788 had had nothing in
their stomachs for several days except blood from the slaughter
house made into soup with a few herbs.[4] Confronted with such
information, it is easy to paint a gloomy over-all picture; yet to
do so without qualification would be far from telling the whole
story because it is possible to find areas where the *ateliers* worked
efficiently and made a small but important contribution towards
helping the poor, and of such areas a few tentative generalizations
can be made.

Clearly the experiment had a limited success in Haute-Guyenne
and Lower Normandy. After an unhappy start in which the

---

[1] This was a scandal which appears to have had some truth behind it. A.D. Aube
C 1142, C 2327, C 2330. *In toto* the *seigneur* contributed 250 *livres* towards a project
costing 2,050.
[2] A.D. Calvados C 3088; A.D. Côte-d'Or C 3687.
[3] A.N. H² 2105.
[4] A.D. Calvados C 3088, Letter from Maillard to Lefebvre, *ingénieur en chef*,
Bayeux, 2 May 1789.

intendant deflected the funds intended for the *ateliers* to make good the effects of flooding in Montauban, the Haute-Guyenne had over the first seven years thirty-three *ateliers* costing the government 385,000 *livres* from *le moins imposé* and 170,000 from *contributions volontaires*, perhaps a record in point of private donations, and of these sums 60 per cent was paid directly to the poor in the form of wages. For a full day's labour an adult male received 12 *sols*. Wages did not rise in the eighties, but the provincial assembly of Haute-Guyenne, which assumed control in 1779, contrived a rapid extension of the scheme. Between 1779 and 1789 the area knew 622 *ateliers* and spent on them on average 100,000 *livres* per year of which again about 60 per cent went directly in wages to the workers.[1] What this meant in real terms was that in any one year about 5,000 people were helped with the proceeds of a single month's labour during the most difficult period of the agricultural year.[2]

Generally the *ateliers de charité* worked best and most coherently in the *pays de petite culture*. There were several reasons for this, of which the most important was that there they served their intended purpose of providing a stopgap in the agricultural year and the type of work undertaken was generally useful, extending beyond the usage of the local *seigneur* and hence not dependent upon his subsidy which might or might not be forthcoming.

There are, however, major exceptions to this rule. In Auvergne the system of the *ateliers* never really got started because the *intendant* in the 1770s clearly did not know where to begin. The first 75,000 *livres* destined for public works had, the *intendant* pointed out, to reach 500,000 people. With almost total disregard of the villages, the sum went directly to the towns, where puplic-works projects were opened for the levelling of ancient foundations and the filling-in of tracts of stagnant water for which adults received 4 *sols* per day and children 1 *sol*.[3] The *intendant*'s action is understandable. He could not envisage such a slender sum doing anything for the problem of poverty in the countryside

---

[1] Harouel, *Les Ateliers de charité*, pp. 75 ff. The high number of *ateliers* is somewhat deceptive: the title could grace an enterprise lasting a couple of weeks and employing a mere score of men.

[2] This is supposing the average wage to be, as it was in Haute-Guyenne, 12 *sols* per day. It might have meant fewer were helped for longer as it is impossible to calculate the average duration of any one *atelier*.

[3] A.D. Puy-de-Dôme C 924.

nor could he get anything out of the local *noblesse*, notoriously
mean but also notoriously impecunious.

Apart from the Auvergne, however, in the *pays de petite culture*
the claims of the cities were kept subservient, perhaps because in
the main the *pays de petite culture* did not have sizeable cities with a
depressed industrial population to make more cogent claims upon
the government's funds. Although the government urged upon
provincial authorities the necessity of confining the *ateliers* to the
rural parishes, the industrial crisis which left thousands of workers
resourceless caused provincial assemblies and *intendants* in some
instances to reverse the government's decision. By the late 1780s
the provincial assemblies of Champagne, Basse and Haute Normandie, and Touraine were using from a third to three-quarters
of the funds conceded by the government for the urban poor
who posed a threat to public order or for textile villages faced
with permanent unemployment. The instance of the *généralité* of
Troyes is particularly revealing. Between 1771 and 1781 the
ateliers were used during the winter months largely for the unemployed agricultural workers; in 1782 the situation abruptly
changed, and by raising loans intended to meet the requisite third
demanded by the government, the municipal authority of Troyes
pressed claims upon the *intendant* and subsequently the provincial
assembly. The work project was the demolition of the city's
ramparts—perhaps the commonest type of urban work project.
What was striking was the large number of women who turned
up to carry out this work for which they were little fitted since it
consisted of carrying heavy stones, but as unemployed spinners
they had little alternative. The municipal authority recognized
that it could not employ all who came, even though in the course
of two months it doubled those it admitted to work. 'Le nombre
des pauvres s'accroît aux ateliers de charité: de 700 à 800, il est
porté à 1100 et 1200 de sorte qu'au lieu de 1800 livres que nous
dépensions par semaine, il n'y en a point actuellement qui soit
au dessous de 2400 livres.'[1] Two months later the mayor talked
of 1,400 employees in the *ateliers*, the bulk of them women and
children.

In the *généralité* of Rouen, help for textile workers hit by
chômage progressively ousted the agricultural labourer from the

---

[1] Chaudron, *L'Assistance publique à Troyes*, pp. 44–5. The town in all paid 6,000
livres out of a total cost of 26,000.

ateliers de charité.[1] It was at Rouen, Darnetal, and Elbeuf that *ateliers* were concentrated. In Lower Normandy, Caen, Bayeux, Avranches, and Mortain each put in important urban claims to the limited funds the monarchy was prepared to dispense.[2] Though the needs of the towns were evidently pressing, equally evidently the *ateliers de charité* provided no lasting solution to the problem of permanent unemployment or under-employment. Divorced from the context of the gap in the agricultural year, they were a feeble palliative to a chronic malady.

Moreover, perhaps the most lasting appreciation of how slight was the over-all impact of the *ateliers* upon the problem of poverty is found in the debates of the *Comité de Mendicité*. Although the *ateliers* were at their most extensive during the hard winter of 1789, at that moment they gave temporary work to 31,000 men, women, and children.[3] Clearly an experiment of such limited extent could have little over-all impact on the problem of poverty.

What was the total sum of government assistance to the poor in the 1780s, a time when government expenditure in this direction had reached its peak? Necker's statistics in the *compte rendu* were shown to be largely accurate by the *Comité de Mendicité* and are worth reproducing:[4]

	livres
Mendicité (i.e. expenditure on *maréchaussée* and *dépôts de mendicité*)	1,200,000
Moins imposé (*indemnités pour sinistres, pour ateliers de charité*)	3,000,000
Dons, aumônes, secours aux hôpitaux	1,800,000
Objets épars et casuels	80,000
Enfants trouvés des provinces	12 à 15,000,000

Setting aside the *enfants trouvés* as demanding separate treatment and expenditure on the *dépôts* as restricted to a very special section of the poor, what this meagre figure would have meant if divided amongst the total needy was under a *livre* per head per year.

[1] A.D. Seine-Maritime C 882–7 illustrates some of the shifting priorities of authorities confronted with textile crisis.
[2] A.D. Calvados C 3421, Ateliers de charité.
[3] Bloch and Tuetey, *Procès-verbaux*, p. 278.
[4] Cited by Bloch, *L'Assistance*, p. 315.

VII

INFORMAL RELIEF

Passons à la charité. Voyons à quoi cette vertu nous oblige. D'abord qu'est-ce que c'est que la charité? La charité est une vertu surnaturelle, qu'on appelle théologale, qui nous porte à aimer Dieu pour lui-même et notre prochain pour Dieu.

Sermon of a parish priest of Rennes
(A.D. Ille-et-Vilaine 5 Fa 108).

Les laboureurs préfèrent donner aux étrangers par la crainte d'éprouver quelqu'accident fâcheux par le refus d'aumône passagère.

A.D. Seine-Maritime G 841, Parish of Bornambuc.

THE frail institutions, *hôpitaux*, *bureaux de charité*, or their Enlightenment equivalent, the *ateliers de charité*, clearly did not mark the beginning and end of help given to the poor. Every school of commentators from Catholic philanthropists to the anti-clerical Enlightenment was adamant that the mainstay of the poor was not these tottering institutions but informal charity. Indeed, the writers of the Enlightenment, whether mere pamphleteers or more considerable intellects, such as Montesquieu and Rousseau, and the entire *Comité de Mendicité*, which was soaked in Enlightenment ideas, were prepared to consider informal relief as so extensive that it alone might be assumed responsible for the existence of so many beggars, parasites upon society. The blame for their existence could only be attributed to Catholic social policy which had failed in the most important respect, that is, in drawing and making effective a real demarcation between the deserving and undeserving poor. The points put forward by the director of the *dépôt de mendicité* at Riom illustrate such an attitude:

Partout on parle du pauvre . . . partout on vante et on exalte les soins ou secours immenses que lui distribuent en secret les âmes les plus renommeés en charité. Ces soins, ces attentions si exaltées me paraissent l'écueil et l'abus de la charité . . . l'entretien de la paresse, de l'hypocrisie et du vice . . .[1]

[1] A.D. Puy-de-Dôme C 1204, Observations de Henrion de Bussy.

Informal relief clearly had a bad press but it existed, and one must, as far as possible, question its extent or its limitations, its priorities, the relationship between donor and recipient: the allegation that it was both indiscriminate and excessive. Catholic social philosophy evidently gave the pauper a privileged position in its theoretical social scheme, but to what extent was theory a reality? Evidently society was not without attitudes towards the poor: the vocabulary of poverty comprehended *le pauvre, le vrai pauvre, le mauvais pauvre, le mendiant de bonne foi, le mendiant volontaire*. These were value judgements, what do they reveal?

To answer these questions is obviously to become enmeshed in economic and psychological complications. The act of giving is automatically conditioned by how much one is able to give and how much one is prepared to give as well as by predilections of one sort or another. One can take a kind of model situation by starting with the poor family, resident in a particular rural parish, whose difficulties were due to the inadequacy of the family economy to provide for its members, difficulties which were known and appreciated by the curé, by the neighbours, and by the wealthier inhabitants of the parish (who might have been put in the picture by the priest or have a genuine and near interest). If a *bureau de charité* did not exist, or even if it did, such a family might make a supplication to other parishioners, according to a very set pattern.

Begging took place, in fact, by previous arrangement, even by appointment in the manner described by a curé of the diocese of Tours in 1774. Each morning the women and children who attended mass and were known to be poor received after communion a slice of bread; then later in the morning, by arrangement with the curé, the children were divided up, and in groups of two or three called at specific houses and were given a bowl of milk. Finally, after the midday repast, the mothers of the children called at the same houses and were given a crust dipped in stew or gravy, or the scrapings of the main meal of the day.[1] In this way the poor family was at least buttressed against the main pangs of hunger until the evening, and the family budget could be expended on that meal. The aged were similarly divided up: each comfortable household helped out a regular caller by scraps of food. The visit was expected and provided against, and at an

[1] A.D. Indre-et-Loire C 304.

arranged hour the pauper presented himself and his chipped bowl and was admitted to the kitchen. This was, of course, the ideal pattern, the way in which St. Vincent de Paul envisaged that the poor family should be helped, because it made the giving of charity available to a broad spectrum—the widow's mite. Provided one's stew-pot contained a few scrapings and one's milk jug held sufficient to fill the bowl of a ragged child, one could offer simple help. Moreover, the sort of people to whom help was offered were the verifiably deserving—women, children, aged. Certainly, occasional parishes appear in the *enquêtes* of the 1770s and 1780s where voluntary relief of this nature could fairly efficiently cope with the major problems of poverty. At Huglo-ville-en-Caux in the diocese of Rouen, the parish officials confidently reported:

La paroisse quoi qu'étendue s'est trouvée jusqu'à présent dans l'heureuse position d'être parvenue à satisfaire suffisamment sans doute aux besoins de ses pauvres puisqu'aucun de ses domiciliés ne s'échappe en mendiant au dehors de la paroisse mais les secours de tous les habitants concourent à la subsistance des pauvres et il est peu facile de déterminer suivant vos désirs à combien peuvent monter les aumônes volontaires des habitants. Ici on accorde à l'indigent du pain, là de la boisson, là du bled, chez d'autres du bois, chez quelques uns des hardes. Le concours de ses efforts est déterminé par les besoins de l'indigent et la position d'icelui à qui il s'addresse. Or comment de tous les moyens faire une décapitulation qui puisse servir à donner une base juste des aumônes volontaires du Sieur Curé et des habitants? Nous n'osons l'entreprendre dans la crainte de vous tromper en nous trompant nous-mêmes.[1]

Such a model situation, however, clearly depended upon a number of factors. Most important was the existence of some kind of balance within the parish of the numbers of rich or comfortably placed and the numbers of poor; somewhat less so was the willingness of those in command of excess wealth to donate —a parish which had a wealthy parish priest and a poor *seigneur* was likely to do better from the point of view of *largesse* than one where the reverse was true.[2] Something depended upon the

---

[1] A.D. Seine-Maritime C 2211, Hugloville-en-Caux, 1774.

[2] The contribution of the nobility to the poor clearly depended upon the economic standing of the noble in question. Where affluent and distinguished noble houses held a *seigneurie*, something might be expected. A.D. Seine-Maritime G 841–6, the following fifteen parishes claimed help from the *seigneur*: at Bosc Edeline, the

organizing powers of the parochial clergy: the parish priest prepared to exert pressure upon parishioners he felt had something to spare or upon an absentee *seigneur* was the best ally the needy could have. There was also a marked difference between the problems of normal and abnormal times: food shortage, epidemic, industrial slump could all disturb the balance between affluent and needy in any locality, and areas which in normal times could cater to the needs of their own socially unfortunate could find themselves unable to cope under new pressures. Lastly, there was the problem of preventing the destitute of other areas from making demands which might divert local generosity from the known deserving poor of the locality to the unknown, perhaps undeserving, vagrants. In the last decades of the *ancien régime* these last considerations were clearly assuming new proportions and posing problems for regions in which in normal times local generosity might suffice for the sustenance of the parish poor.

Broadly speaking, even without the pressures of bad harvests and attendant disasters, informal relief was at its weakest in the Massif, the dioceses of Clermont, Saint-Flour, Mende, Le Puy, Rodez, Tulle, Vabres, and in the mountain communities of the Alps and the Pyrenees or the hill country of the Jura, the Morvan, the scrub and heath of inland Brittany, and the miserable Solange. Here the problem was one of numbers, too many poor and too few affluent, so that the demands of the one outran the means of the other. What can you expect, the parish priest of Les Bondons asked his bishop at Mende, of a community of poor shepherds who sleep on rotting straw and whose children are unshod and where the entire village, clinging to a hillside rendered barren by deforestation, presented such a miserable aspect that the *seigneur*

seigneurs give 24 pounds of bread weekly; at Bourg-Théroulde, 'le marquis de Londe abandonne aux pauvres le produit de son droit sur la boucherie de carême'; at Clerres, the duc de Charost gives 100 *livres* per year; at Cordelleville, Criquetot-sur-Onville, Écotigny, Mussegros, Rouvray, Sommery, Gonfreville-l'Orcher Grostheil, Heugleville, Neuville-Ferrier, Raffetot, Serqueux, the curés stressed the *bienfaisance* of the *seigneur*. They represent a small percentage of the total number of parishes (1,388), but contrast favourably with the record at Clermont where only three parishes, Collanges, Égliseneuve-sur-Billom (*seigneur* the bishop), and Vodable, received any aid at all from the *seigneur*. In Brittany (dioceses of Saint-Malo and Saint-Brieuc) 75 per cent of the nobility were pronounced unable or unwilling to give alms (A.D. Ille-et-Vilaine C 1292, Saint-Brieuc, Saint-Malo). The individual contributions of *parlementaire* nobles in Languedoc may have been considerable but were insufficient to stem an influx of distress into Toulouse from the Lauragais.

had long since pulled out?[1] From Clermont the same kind of weary reiteration pervades the replies to the *enquêtes* of the seventies conducted by the bishop of Clermont. At Collanges 'tous les habitants sont sans pain; la dame de lieu toute charitable qu'elle est, ne peut suffire à soulager tant de misères';[2] at Saint-Gervais-sous-Meymont (700 communicants) 'il n'y a pas six maisons en état de faire l'aumône. MM de la Chaise Dieu, prieurs et décimateurs, sont trop éloignés pour entendre les cris et gémissements des malheureux';[3] at Peschadoires 'les deux tiers des habitants sont métayers, l'autre tiers journaliers et pauvres . . . il y a grande misère . . . la cure rapporte 1000 livres sur lesquelles il faut payer un vicaire'.[4] Yet more explicit were the parish priests of the diocese of Rodez; in village after village, when replying to the questionnaire of 1771, they added as an unsolicited adjunct to the number of those in need of help a comment on the mere handful of houses in any parish capable of offering any kind of assistance. At Vors, a parish of 375 people, the priest claimed: 'Il n'y a plus de six maisons où il y ait du pain; les autres sont misérables et manquent du nécessaire.'[5] At Caplongue little help could be given, 'n'y ayant dans la paroisse que des paysans dont très peu sont en état de donner des soulagements'.[6] The curé of Durenque, a parish of 600 inhabitants, stated 'Si on en excepte une douzaine de maisons, tout le reste peut être mis au nombre des pauvres, qui languissent dans la misère.'[7] At La Capelle Farcel, a parish of 330 inhabitants, the priest stated:

Il n'y a que quatre maisons dans la paroisse qui n'ayent besoin dans un temps ou dans un autre, ce qui peut faire cinquante habitants qui n'ont pas besoin, et autres 280 sont, toutes les années, dans le besoin d'être soulagés, scavoir 230 en partie et les autre cinquante sans aucune espèce de secours.[8]

At Coubisou, a parish of 630 people, the priest replied to the question 'How many of your parishioners are indigent?':

Il est plus aisé de dire combien il y a des riches; le fermier de Monsieur le Prieur et un cabaretier. Il y a environ dix maisons aisées qui par leur

---

[1] A.D. Lozère G 1834, État des pauvres de la paroisse des Bondons et leurs principaux et plus pressans besoins, 1760.

[2] A.D. Puy-de-Dôme C 928, Collanges, 1775.

[3] Ibid. C 932, Saint-Gervais-sous-Meymont.   [4] Ibid. C 931, Peschadoires.

[5] Lempereur, *L'État du diocèse de Rodez en 1771*; 75 per cent of parishes replied in this fashion.   [6] A.D. Puy-de-Dôme C 931, Caplongue.

[7] Ibid. Durenque.   [8] Ibid. La-Capelle Farcel.

scrupuleuse économie peuvent vivre; trente incapables de rien faire: environ 200 en état de travailler, mais ce travail est insuffisant pour l'entretien de leur famille.[1]

The priest of Coubisou, who was *à portion congrue*, depicted the problems of a village in which those who were usually the main supporters of the parish poor, priest, *seigneur*, and substantial farmer, were either unable or, in the case of the second, unwilling to give. The parochial clergy often were (and invariably believed themselves to be) the linchpin of local relief, and where they themselves were poor and unable to accord assistance they were deeply resentful and highly critical of those they considered able to help if they failed to do so: 'Le patrimoine de l'église et par conséquent des pauvres se trouvent entre les mains d'opulents cœnobites sans titre réel, sans juridiction, sans sollicitude' (curé of Doré);[2] 'Les dîmes appartiennent au chapitre d'Ennezat, à M. des Martres, seigneur d'Ennezat, à Madame de la Tourrette, à M. d'Haumières; ils n'envoient aucunes charités' (Saint-Ignat);[3] 'Les RRPP Minimes du prieuré de Chaumont, curés primitifs de la paroisse, comme ils n'en tirent aucun revenu, en rebutent les pauvres: le sieur abbé du Moutier de Thiers reçoit les dîmes mais n'exerce aucune charité' (Teyssonière);[4] 'Le curé pour se nourrir, lui, son père et sa mère, est obligé de tenir les écoles' (Bousselargues);[5] 'Le sieur curé peut se dire le premier de ses pauvres' (Brousse).[6]

The resources of the parish priest clearly depended upon his own income, from both private means and his benefice, supplemented by the *tronc des pauvres* in the church. Where he was *à portion congrue*, as was the case in most of the *pays de petite culture*, he could do little to help. The average income of the parish priest has been estimated at 1,000 *livres* per year; from this a deduction of at least a half must be made for his own upkeep, that of a servant, and often a minimal preservation of the presbytery as well. Even supposing, and probably in 80–90 per cent of cases this is not supposition, the priest in question was prepared to put the whole of the rest of his income at the disposal of the poor,

[1] Ibid. Coubisou.
[2] A.D. Puy-de-Dôme C 929, Doré, 1775.
[3] Ibid. C 932, Saint-Ignat.
[4] Ibid. C 933, Teysonnière.
[5] Ibid. C 927, Bousselargues.
[6] Ibid. Brousse.

the question of its efficacy must still depend upon how many sought help from this source.[1]

Significantly easier in normal times was the position in areas of greater agrarian and industrial wealth such as the dioceses of Rouen, Dijon, and Montpellier, where voluntary charity of the gravy-and-bread variety was easy enough to come by for the deserving poor of the village whose wants were verifiable. The parish priests in reply to the questionnaires of the seventies rarely expressed doubts as to the adequacy of informal charity to sustain the aged, the children, and the temporarily incapacitated. 'Rien que les aumônes; elles suffisent à leurs besoins' (Folleterre),[2] 'Aucun fonds, pas d'autre ressource que la charité des fidèles' (Biville-la-Rivière)[3] are the type of remark that accompany descriptions of the parochial poor as confined to the widow, the orphan, and the feeble old person. In such parishes some balance existed between those who would give and those who would receive: at Gamache (diocese of Rouen) the priest and three families of *laboureurs* found it fully within their means to sustain a dozen or so village poor;[4] at Pitres (diocese of Rouen) the parish

---

[1] The curés' struggle emerges very clearly from the *enquêtes* of the 1770s. Some curés, and the phenomenon is particularly apparent in the archdiocese of Tours (A.D. Loir-et-Cher H 909–10) and the diocese of Clermont, were more than willing to sacrifice the principle of Christian voluntary charity for an obligatory tax, though others thought it should be levied by the parish priest. In the dioceses of Rennes, Saint-Brieuc, and Saint-Malo the parochial clergy were reported generous in the inquiries of 1785–6 as far as in them lay (A.D. Ille-et-Vilaine C 1746). From Péaule near Vannes the *recteur* addressed to the *intendant* a type of missive which characterizes this correspondence:

On m'a dit que votre grandeur avait déjà fait distribuer des secours dans plusieurs autres paroisses et Péaule n'en a reçu aucun; j'ai 2000 communiants sur lesquels je suis seul décimateur. Je n'ai levé de dixme que neuf tonneaux de seigle et de froment que 1¼ tonneaux depuis la récolte. J'ai essayé de secourir les malheureux, j'ai déjà distribué cinq fois deux tonneaux et chaque distribution de deux tonneaux n'a produit dans chaque ménage que 14 ou 15 livres de pain de sorte que malgré les secours que les moins pauvres donnent à leur porte la mendicité s'accroit d'un manière effrayante . . .

The inability of the clergy to help as one might expect is a recurrent theme in the *cahiers*:

le curé, réduit à une portion trop médiocre pour administrer une paroisse aussi considérable en habitants, malgré la meilleure volonté qu'il puisse avoir, ne peut se répandre en aumônes sans se priver du nécessaire et s'exposer à en manquer dans le cas qu'il devint infirme . . .

(*Cahiers de doléances du Tiers État du bailliage de Gisors* (Paris, 1971), Forest-la-Folie, p. 206.)   [2] A.D. Seine-Maritime G 842, Folleterre, 1774.
[3] Ibid. G 841, Biville-la-Rivière.   [4] Ibid. G 846, Gamache.

priest claimed that the needy posed no problem at all, since the alms of the faithful were well able to succour them.[1]

Yet this idyllic picture was not to remain undisturbed. Even in the *enquêtes* of the more prosperous areas in the seventies, there are pointers to the inadequacy of voluntary relief to cope with an extensive problem however temporary: the textile *bourg* of Gros Theil, near Rouen, struck by an epidemic of miliary fever could not muster sufficient to assuage the hunger of the families of the sick, and the combined efforts of priest and *seigneur* realized little, for in Gros Theil, as elsewhere in the area, the adequacy of voluntary charity depended upon relatively full employment.[2] Any drop in the numbers in work radically inflated demand for relief while reducing the numbers of those able to share what they had. 'Leur trop grande nombre tarit la source des charités.'[3] Indeed, in the closing decades of the *ancien régime*, what might be called a crisis of voluntary charity was generally experienced. It arose from an inflation in the numbers demanding help and a simultaneous reduction in the numbers able to give it, for unemployment curtailed the ability of some to give and, even more generally, the rise in the price of bread made the giving of charity in kind more costly than ever before and hence eliminated many potential donors. Moreover, an increase in the number of wandering poor saw the rapid development of a contest for relief between locals and outsiders. There can be little doubt that villagers believed that whatever they had to give should go to their own parish poor rather than to a crowd of unverifiable outsiders; but what if they feared the outsider and his potentiality for evil and knew that no civil authority would protect them?

Les laboureurs préfèrent donner aux étrangers par la crainte d'éprouver quelqu'accident fâcheux par le refus d'aumône passagère (Bornambuc, diocese of Rouen).[4]

Les étrangers enlèvent aux véritables pauvres des endroits où ils se présentent, les charités qu'ils auraient lieu d'attendre de leurs concitoyens (Riom).[5]

---

[1] Ibid. G 843, Pitres.

[2] Ibid. G 846, Gros Theil: 'Il y eut 700 malades. Certains dans la plus grande détresse, mangeaient la paille de leur lit.'

[3] A.D. Ille-et-Vilaine C 1402, Observations of the *greffier du présidial de Rennes*, 1772.　　　　　　　　　　　　　[4] A.D. Seine-Maritime G 841, Bornambuc.

[5] A.D. Puy-de-Dôme C 1162.

Une multitude de vagabonds du Gévaudan et des environs de Rodez viennent exercer annuellement une sorte de contribution sur l'hospitalité publique. Ils ajoutent les menaces aux prières, on les redoute et on en est quelquefois volé . . . (Millau).[1]

Wherever one turns, the lament is essentially the same. In those areas where there was something to be had, voluntary charity was ceasing to exist; it had become a forced levy. The minute it did so, it was no longer holy charity, for in Christian doctrine the spontaneous generosity of the donor was what mattered: to give under compulsion was no virtue. Moreover, indiscriminate almsgiving had always been decried by moralists: no man conscious of the hereafter could believe there was a reward in heaven for subsidizing a potential robber or murderer.

The wandering poor, in fact, had always been treated differently from the known domiciled beggar. Whereas the latter might expect help in kind and a place by the fire whilst he ate, the former could not, even in the most generous of households, expect such favoured treatment.[2] There were farmers even in the poorest areas who were always prepared to offer the basic gift of overnight shelter in a barn; most offered a blanket or some other form of covering, but not all offered bread, which was, after all, a fairly expensive commodity, without demanding in return payment of a few *liards* or, more commonly, some work. The known migrant offering to repay his board and lodging by work or entertainment was probably welcome enough, but otherwise some remuneration was expected by the farmer of limited means. This is not to say that hospitality was totally denied to the unknown *errant*. Such a person spent his day in trying to cadge bits of bread and, failing that, *liards*; the farmstead he chose to spend the night in was merely his last port of call. He came with a *besace* which was not usually totally bereft of bits of bread or a few *liards*, the result of begging around or performing a few menial jobs. Thus Marie-Madeleine Podevin near Alençon claimed that she usually paid 6 *liards* for bread for herself and her daughter 'quand on lui trempe la soupe'.[3] Some Normandy farmers (who may always have been particularly mean) actually profited from a kind of

---

[1] *Journal des voyages en Haute Guyenne*, p. 192.

[2] This spirit is even caught in the work of the brothers Le Nain, emphasizing the difference between the beggar in the doorway and the one before the fire.

[3] A.D. Calvados 9 B, Maréchaussée, 7 juin 1786.

overnight fee. François Rousseau at Saint-Michel-de-Sommaire (Orne) hurt his leg and was forced to ask a farmer for a month's shelter and was charged 50 *sous*. He left his leather belt and promised to pay when he next passed.[1] A month's lodgings to any single *errant* clearly passed beyonds the bounds of what any farmer considered it reasonable to give.

Where religious houses accorded a daily bread hand-out, the nearby farms could find themselves readily swamped with nightly callers, a fact which roused deep resentment because there were limits to the numbers any farmer expected at any one time to receive. Two, three, at most four, vagrants were accepted to sleep together in a barn. Perhaps more were turned away. The vagrant had an interest in arriving early: once night had fallen he had no hope of reception, and he usually presented himself at about five o'clock, alone. If he was not then accepted he had time to make an alternative supplication. The lone beggar and vagrant clearly stood a better chance of a good reception. Hence, even if links were formed, and the *errant*, like anyone else, has need of companionship, they were not demonstrated to the host farmer. Thus Thomas Élie and Jean Malherbe of the pays d'Auge, newly become *errants*, met two other *errants* near Almenesches and sought their advice about the best farms to sleep in. After that, the four were always together, in the sense that every morning they decided upon a farm, separated, and met up there in the evening, always taking care to arrive alone.[2]

In the poorest regions, the Massif, the Morvan, the area around Langres, there was a kind of traffic between farmer and *errant* for the contents of the *croûtons* in his *besace*. *Pain de mendicité* was after all bread. One successful beggar at Montpellier became a landowner on the sacks of it sent back and sold in his native Cévenol village to the woollen workers;[3] and if a success story of this kind is rare, there are others more common that are equally revealing

---

[1] A.D. Orne B, Maréchaussée, interrog., 10 novembre 1784, cited by V. Boucheron, 'La Montée du flot des errants dans la généralité d'Alençon au XVIIIe siècle', p. 82.

[2] A.D. Orne B, Maréchaussée, 20 juin 1776, cited Boucheron, p. 80.

[3] The story is told by Le Roy Ladurie, *Les Paysans de Languedoc*, p. 96. P. Rascol, *Les Paysans de l'Albigeois à la fin de l'ancien régime* (Aurillac, 1961), p. 167, has occasional success stories amongst his *mendiants propriétaires*. A single instance of relative wealth emerges from the 1,000-odd dossiers at Clermont (A.D. Puy-de-Dôme C 1117), that of Perceval who had taken from his person 34 *livres*, clothes, and tailor's tools. He may well have stolen them.

about beggars who fed pigs on the profits of their *besaces*, pigs kept by farmers on their land with other pigs but supplied with food by the beggars themselves. At Langres, at Rodez, at Mende, examples of beggars selling bread to farmers, in some instances against a night's lodgings, are recurrent;[1] bread which, however old, mildewed, and dirty, could be used to thicken soup—and the farmer's soup at that. In the diocese of Saint-Brieuc there was a traffic between small farmer and *errant* for manure which the latter theoretically picked up from animal droppings on the high road or in the woods, but probably most often stole. The purchaser did not ask too many questions. A night's shelter cost him little.[2] Such exchange reveals the very fine line of demarcation in these regions between host and beggar. The former was only degrees removed from the latter and at any moment might find himself demoted. A night's lodgings cost him nothing and he may possibly have hoped to profit from the visit.

Traditionally then, the humble farmer was clearly prepared to receive the wandering poor and accord them a limited amount of help which in no way overtaxed his resources; his real generosity, if he was in command of a surplus, was directed towards the known parochial poor. In the course of any one day such a farmer, or more likely his wife, might give a little food to village children who called, a *liard* or so to a passing stranger, and make the barn available to the vagrants or poor travellers who called in the evening. Unfortunately, however, times were changing. The difficult harvests which characterized the seventies and eighties or the industrial slump of the eighties reduced the potential for generosity: 'dans ma paroisse les pauvres n'ont point de secours. Il y a quelque porte où on leur donne quelques liards et encore peu, on donne rarement du pain, chacun n'en ayant pas trop pour soi.'[3] Moreover, a growing feeling of mistrust was entering the relationship between host and vagrant, a

---

[1] A.D. Haute-Marne B, Maréchaussée de Langres, 25 octobre 1769. Not only did the accused Thomas Bourgeois in this instance sell bread to farmers but 'il nourrissait un cochon des morceaux de pain qu'il rapportait des villages où il mendiait'. A.D. Eure-et-Loire J 584, para. 81: one Baraillon, a small farmer accused of complicity with the *bande d'Orgères*, claimed as his only contact: 'dans le temps que le pain était cher, j'en ai acheté de deux ou trois mendiants'.

[2] M. Habasque, *Notions historiques sur le littoral des Côtes du Nord* (Saint-Brieuc, 1832), t. 1, p. 96. On the vegetable thieves of La Roche-Derrien who behaved in similar fashion, see Quellien, *L'Argot des nomades*, pp. 6–14.

[3] A.D. Ille-et-Vilaine C 1294, Mouazé, 1774.

feeling which prompted the host to attempt to curtail his hospitality and, as he did so, forced the suppliant to back his demands with threats if they were not accepted. This feeling doubtless had its origin in the growth of the numbers of destitute and their age. Numbers of men in the same village might possibly be a band of thieves, whereas individuals might be relatively harmless. Young men were more to be feared than old or decrepit ones. The economic crisis which characterized the closing decades of the *ancien régime* certainly put large numbers of people on the roads, and, once groups of vagrants formed, the temptation to back up demands with threats was always there. Moreover, once a farmer or his wife had been a victim of threats he was unlikely ever again to feel the same about the bundle of rags which presented itself on his doorstep, and hence in future he would give only under duress. Petty theft was the commonest deterrent to repeated hospitality: 'Elle volait le linge partout où on lui donnait à coucher'; 'voleur de linge dans les fermes où il couchait.'[1] Jean Huet allowed two men, a woman, and two small children to spend the night in an outhouse; the next morning four shirts and other linen were missing.[2] Eggs and chickens disappeared; cows were milked in the fields; horses lost their tails; *valets de ferme*, who often slept in lofts, woke to find their shoes had gone. All this had its repercussions. Farmers tried outright rejection. Thus one Launay, requesting a night's lodgings from the miller of Sainte-Colombe (Orne), found himself faced with the rejoinder 'Je ne donne pas l'aumône à tout le monde et surtout pas à un étranger inconnu'; at the next farm he was told 'C'est seulement au moulin que l'on donne à coucher'.[3]

Doubtless here someone had a grudge against the miller. He was in fact the person most likely in Normandy and Brittany to find himself confronted with a mass of threatening vagrants and least able to defend himself or call on villagers to come to his aid, for he had few, if any, allies.[4] Where possible, if dubious of the appearance of the suppliant, some resistance was put up by dogs and farm-hands. Even in Brittany, which was perhaps most tolerant of the *errant*, hospitality was not automatic. One farmer's

---

[1] A.D. Haute-Marne B, Maréchaussée de Langres, 4 juin 1774; A.D. Lozère 21B6, 1774, etc.   [2] A.D. Calvados 9 B, Maréchaussée, 17 fevrier 1787.
[3] A.D. Orne B, Maréchaussée, 19 mai 1775, cited Boucheron, p. 82.
[4] A.D. Finistère B 814, 818, 824, 834, 883 show how favoured a victim he was of Marion de Faouët.

wife near Quimper stated quite adamantly in a case of infanticide that her barn was only available to women travelling in search of work, and of the four who gave evidence against the girl who had murdered her newborn baby in the night, three had an actual job to which they were travelling.[1] Others tried to secure themselves by locking the vagrants in. In entire villages in the Lyonnais only one or two farms were prepared to receive *vagabonds*; at Dardilly, Darnet 'retire tous les pauvres', at Champlitte near Langres, one Pinget alone would seem, and he perhaps under duress, to have offered shelter.[2] In the Beauce, where from the 1760s group vagrancy was a way of life, the simple suppliant at a farm received short shrift. Gates were barred early; dogs were invariably kept. A little bread might be thrown over the wall and the vagrant told to be on his way.[3] All this led to begging with menaces, menaces which could take many forms. Marie Flechère of the Lyonnais 'se faisait donner l'aumône par force, menaçant de la morsure d'un serpent qu'elle portait avec elle'.[4] Here were threats to join huge bands and wreak vengeance: 'si vous ne voulez pas me donner l'aumône, je me mettrai de la bande de Cartouche';[5] there were threats to poison streams and ponds or threats against animals: 'sur ton refus, tu t'en repentiras tant pour toi que pour tes vaches';[6] or threats to kidnap children. Most common and most fearful of all was the threat of fire: 'Cette ferme mériterait bien d'être brûlée, on me refuse la charité partout', and as if to carry out the threat several of the wandering beggars of the Lyonnais would produce a little tinderwood from their rags.[7]

Well-intentioned or frightened farmers who offered something found themselves confronted with a kind of barter situation: the farmer offered a little bread; the vagabond demanded more bread and milk; he settled for bread and cider or bread and cherry juice. In the Beauce the vagabond added salt pork to the list, and probably got it, for in this most peculiar of regions the vagabond

---

[1] A.D. Finistère B 2210.   [2] Gutton, *La Société et les pauvres*, p. 200.

[3] A.D. Loiret B 2141, Louis Phélypeaux, 1783.

[4] A.D. Loire B 846, dossier M. Flechère, cited Gutton, p. 201.

[5] A.D. Rhône B, Maréchaussée, 1744, dossier P. Corbas. One might compare: 'Va, nom de dieu de garce, j'y logerai malgré toi ou ta tête de chien en sautera plutôt, si ce n'est pas cette année ce sera une autre, si ce n'est pas par moi, ce sera par d'autres aussi bien que tes garces de servantes . . .' (A.D. Eure-et-Loire J 584, para. 89, evidence of Charlotte Joussay.)

[6] A.D. Orne B, Maréchaussée, 30 juin 1780, cited Boucheron, p. 82.

[7] See below, pp. 267–8.

was in control.[1] In the *généralité* of Alençon a degree of literacy permitted one devious vagrant (doubtless the product of some charity school) to indulge in the anonymous threatening letter 'de remettre au pied de la borne des Trois Croix la somme de cent livres avec trois jours pour tout délai, sous peine d'être brûlé, de perdre meubles et moutons', or one directed at an entire community 'de remettre 400 livres au pied de la croix du Calvaire en moins d'une demi-heure sous peine d'essuyer un affreux désastre dans tous les fermes'.[2] He was caught by the *maréchaussée*, but the practice of sending threatening letters thereafter had some vogue in Normandy. It was in Flanders that the threat of fire by letter was most highly developed, to the extent that local *cahiers* in 1789 demanded the regular indemnity of victims who had failed to pay up and where the *métier* of *sommeur* reached its apogee.[3] In Brittany failure to give could result in the levelling of hedges with the vagabonds carrying off the firewood to sell in the streets of Lorient and Nantes.[4] In the Rouergue, farms were confronted with packs of seven and eight against whom the farmer, his wife, and a couple of *valets de ferme* had absolutely no defences: if they went off with the chickens to sell in the market at Rodez or Villefranche, what could one do?[5] The need to use threats to get anything obviously multiplied the incentives to band together, and the band of threatening vagrants was what the farmer feared most.

One cannot overemphasize that often by preference the menacing vagabond sought out, not the wealthy and heavily guarded farms, with dogs and stout *valets de ferme*, but the relatively vulnerable. The *propriétaires mendiants* of the *généralité* of Tours, the small farmers of Brittany, Normandy, Languedoc, and the Rouergue were not necessarily immune to the threats of the vagrant: not necessarily able to cope with men whose economic standing was not far different from their own.

Confronted with the potential violence of the vagrant, it is easy to understand why farmers dwelt in fear of the unfamiliar wandering poor and why reluctantly they ceded to their demands.

[1] A.D. Loiret B 2150, Boudinet.
[2] A.D. Orne C 572, cited Boucheron, p. 83.
[3] Lefebvre, *Les Paysans du Nord*, pp. 314–15.
[4] A.D. Ille-et-Vilaine C 1293, Lorient, 1774. Pleumeur, Caudan, Quéven were the parishes which suffered most because of their proximity to Lorient.
[5] Richeprey, *Journal des voyages en Haute Guyenne*, p. 192.

But they gave out of fear rather than any misguided Catholic generosity. The message of the *cahiers* as far as the wandering poor are concerned is loud and clear: send them back to their place of origin; give us more effective police in the countryside; 'la mendicité semblable à une lime sourde nous mine peu à peu et nous détruit totalement'. 'Nous ne nous couchons pas sans crainte; les pauvres de nuit nous ont bien tourmentés, sans ceux de jour dont le nombre est considérable.'[1]

The Great Fear was in large part a rural revolt against the unknown itinerant, the cutter-down of trees and hedges and crops in the fields, the stealer of eggs and chickens, the incendiary of barns, the assassin of the innocent. Where, and one would wish to have directed this question at the *Comité de Mendicité*, in the vocabulary of 1789 can a description of the pauper be found as *un membre souffrant de Jésus-Christ*?

The situation in the French countryside was only partially reflected in the towns. The efficacy of the vagrant's threats depended upon the farmer's isolation in a lonely farmstead—a situation less readily produced in the towns. The affluent town-dweller was, provided he kept out of the shanty towns and ghettos of the large cities, relatively immune to violence; on the other hand, he was exposed in public places, at fairs, markets, churches, to the supplications of the immigrant beggar and to those of the working population of the towns in time of industrial crisis, seasonal laying-off, Sundays and holidays, or when the price of bread made a mockery of the low wages of the working man and his family. How did he react to the demands of the beggar? What was the relationship between donor and recipient? Was this relationship changing with the evident increase in those making demands upon charity?

Theoretically there was little superficial reason why the towns should be any less charitable at an informal level than the countryside. The Scriptures supported the beggar in his claims upon the charity of the faithful, conscious of a final reckoning in which only pious acts would preserve them from eternal damnation. But such reasoning was clouded by other considerations. Predominant amongst these was suspicion of the genuineness of the

[1] G. Lefebvre, *La Grande Peur*, pp. 18–19, extracts from the *cahier* of Villambale and the observations of a *cultivateur* of Aumale.

designs of the seemingly unfortunate—the eternal problem of separating the deserving from the undeserving poor; secondly, for the charity-conscious in the towns there did exist the outlet of donations to *hôpital* or *bureau de charité*, and if faith in the one had diminished, the concept of the *bureau* remained green, or there was the *pauvre honteux*, a type of poor person who existed in the country but to nothing like the same extent as in the towns. Lastly, of course, economic crisis had its particular manifestations in an urban environment: the number of those able to give fell as the numbers needing help grew, and those with real means at their disposal, fearful for public order and conscious of the visible manifestations of suffering, were more likely to form a temporary association to open a soup kitchen for the domiciled poor of the towns than to dispense *liards* more freely and indiscriminately to unknown outsiders.[1] The last thing any townsman wished to see was any considerable influx of the rural poor. For the wealthy they represented a threat to public order and a rise in the crime rate; for the urban poor they threatened to distrain a part of the charitable resources or government hand-outs, scanty as these might be, which belonged by right to them. Corrupt and impotent as the municipal *archers* might be, urban society still felt a need for them.

Le laboureur n'abandonne son clocher, et ne vient mendier dans les villes que lorsqu'il y est forcé par le besoin le plus impérieux. Il devient souvent de mendiant de bonne foi, un fripon, un assassin. La société qu'il fréquente le corrompt par degré et le conduit enfin aux plus grands crimes.[2]

The initial need of the individual in question was recognized; it was his ensuing corruption when once he took to a begging life that was to be feared. He became, if he was to enjoy any success as a beggar at all, a 'professional', someone who was able

---

[1] As at Elbeuf, Darnetal, Le Havre, in the textile crisis of the 1780s.

[2] A.D. Ille-et-Vilaine C 4937, Observations sur les moyens de détruire la mendicité, 1782. (A *mémoire* addressed to the Commission Intermédiaire de département, 1783.) The reports of the commissions are some of the most penetrating appreciations of *ancien régime* poverty. That of Orleans: 'La position d'une grande ville, placée au centre des plus grandes communications, y attire continuellement une infinité d'êtres oisifs, parasites incommodes ou de mercenaires réduits pour leur subsistance au travail de leurs bras et dont la moindre maladie dévoue à la misère la plus affreuse la famille entière dont ils sont les soutiens. . . . Par cette raison, nos rues, nos places, nos temples même sont peuplés, couverts de mendiants.'

to present a special 'case', spurious or other, to a society so used
to the spectacle of the outstretched hand that it could without
a twinge of conscience walk past it, in order to demonstrate a
particular claim to generosity. His 'case' might be founded on
genuine need, or depend merely upon the exasperation or fear
of the victim as he struggled to get past a persistent suppliant.
In any city (the opportunities were conspicuously greater in the
cities than in small towns) one stands a good chance of catching
glimpses of minor *cours des miracles*. At Rennes the remarkable
Tronjolly, *procureur du roi au présidial de Rennes*, fervent ally of the
deserving poor, put pressure upon the *États* for legislation aimed
at preventing the commercialization of sores and scabs displayed
around streets and markets by unscrupulous beggars:

Pour peu qu'on ait été attentif à l'impression que font sur les sens la
vue de certaines plaies, on ne peut pareillement ignorer le danger qui
peut en résulter pour la plupart des citoyens, et particulièrement pour
les femmes enceintes. Quelques mendiants feignent souvent de tomber
d'un mal; d'autres, au lieu de mettre des bandages sur leurs plaies
affectent de les découvrir; les mauvais pauvres savent se faire naître
des plaies en faisant usage de certaines spécifiques afin d'exciter la
commisération, et pour servir de prétexte à leur fainéantise. Il en est
même qui vendant aussitôt les vêtements qu'on leur donne, affectent
de paraître dans un état de nudité qui fait rougir.[1]

Tronjolly picked out an apparently old man with a fake hump
and club foot, another who had succeeded in blacking out one
eye—with terrible dramatic effect—to give the impression of
blindness, another who could convey all the symptoms of epilepsy
—all of whom claimed as their begging pitch the very steps of the
États. The concocted sores were intended to persuade the passer-
by, fearful of smallpox or syphilis, to toss a coin in order to avoid
contamination by the scab-encrusted hands which clutched at his
garments.

In Clermont, where the local *cour des miracles* has to be recon-
structed from the cases before the *prévôtés* and the embittered
invectives against the deviousness of the Auvergnat beggar of the
governor of the local *dépôt de mendicité*, sores were convincingly
and cheaply created from egg yolk—one egg would garnish a
regiment, and it did not need to be fresh—and a little dried blood.

[1] Tronjolly, *Règlement de la police générale de la cour*, 22 *septembre 1787*.

Full effect could be obtained from working the yolk into a minor scratch, as did Guillaume Delair, to make a realistic encrustation.[1] Thus embellished, and clutching rosary, crucifix, or mouldering *scapulaire*—lest society forget its obligations to the poor and diseased—the beggar might sally forth, sharing his ill-gotten gains with spies who warned him if the *archers* were near.[2] Public vomiting and the spitting of noxious—or seemingly noxious—substances were other ploys designed to secure the revulsion of the public and a suitable pay-off to keep one's distance.

In Montpellier in 1764 eighty *professionnels du pavis* were enumerated: some were without one or both legs, two had St. Vitus's dance, four were blind, five had club feet, one had no hands, two had so little flesh they were veritable walking skeletons, a dozen had leprous-looking scabs, six were demented and given to public ravings.[3] The physical manifestations of suffering doubtless were in many cases real enough, but there were charlatans amongst them. Ninety-five per cent or so came from the Rouergue, Gévaudan, Vivarais, or Dauphiné. Few were native to Montpellier. The Abbé Favre, a village priest of the diocese of Montpellier, himself a Rouergat, took to creative literature and in 1750 traced a kind of family history of beggars of the Languedocian capital. A penniless Rouergat *rouleur*, Truquette, marries a bastard scarcely remarkable for her sex appeal and the pair throw a feast of stuffed fox and crows, frogs, and a few turnips. Such married life as the couple has rapidly becomes a sparring match, marked by his violence and her bad temper, against a background of total penury, brief periods of employment, and long periods of begging. The family rapidly acquires the sobriquet *meurt-de-faim*, and of this union there was one surviving son Jean, who, when of age, marries another beggar, part-prostitute —when she can get the work, for she is *vilain magasin de rogne et de teigne*. Fortunately for Jean, who emerges as the hero of the tale, she falls ill and dies in the *Hôtel Dieu* whereupon, during an unusual spell of employ for the grape harvest, he has the sense to pursue and seduce his employer's daughter. A hasty marriage follows and Jean leaves the begging life for greater comfort. The account has a picaresque quality and there is more than a vein of satire, yet this disease-ridden, skeletal, dishonest, violent crew

---

[1] A.D. Puy-de-Dôme C 1079, Guillaume Delair.   [2] Ibid. C 1203.
[3] A. Hôp. génl. Montpellier G 16 and 17.

were intended to be archetypal, never missing a trick in the struggle for survival, exploiting every contact to the full.[1] Abbé Favre's audience had seen and smelt such people, avoided their hands which clutched at their garments, sidestepped their spittle, watched them being beaten sometimes by an *archer*, and applauded as their flea-infested bundles were burned. In Languedoc such effects spelt pestilence. In Dessuslamarre's famous description of Marseilles appears an account of 4,000 professional beggars who were reckoned to extort from an unwilling populace over a million *livres* every year.

La rue, les porches des églises leur appartiennent: ils y campent, s'y querellent, s'y battent et surtout battent les gens: le 24 janvier 1786 à quatre heures de l'après midi, au pied des fonts baptismaux de l'église St. Férréol, ils insultent le vicaire, M. Fabre, revêtu des vêtements sacerdôtaux, le brutalisent au point qu'il meurt des suites de ses blessures. L'auteur du meurtre, emprisonné, purge sa peine, se venge sur le vicaire M. Auberty, son successeur, avec les mêmes menaces que contre M. Fabre; la veille et le soir des grandes fêtes, journées plus lucratives que les dimanches ordinaires, les postes devaient être vraisemblablement plus disputés et emportés de haute lutte entre les professionnels du pavis.[2]

M. Fabre had perhaps attempted to close the church to the beggars; few churchmen would have dared so to do. The professional beggar had his favourite prey. He knew how to select a victim, for preference a pregnant woman or wealthy woman foolish enough to walk in the street, and to follow her relentlessly until bought off. Dessuslamarre spoke of a woman of Marseilles who refused a beggar giving birth some time after to a son whose features were wizened and whose shape was deformed like that of the man to whom she had refused alms.[3] With legends such as

[1] A. Favre, 'Jean l'an pré (1750)', *Milhous Moncels* (Nîmes, 1928).

[2] P. de Dessuslamarre, *La Mendicité en 1789*. In the *Souvenirs de Lenoir, intendant* of police of Paris in the 1760s, reproduced in M. Peuchet, *Mémoires tirés des archives de la police*, vol. iii (Paris, 1899), pp. 80–100, many such descriptions occur. He describes a *rendez-vous chez* Drouet *cabaretier* in the rue Saint-Jacques: 'Je reconnus là des gourgandines qui se tiennent à la porte des églises, parées, bichonnées, décrassées pour ce jour-là, et que dans tout autre temps, on ne toucherait certainement pas avec des pincettes. . . . Le trait caractéristique de la plupart de ces physionomies était un regard perçant et moqueur. Quelques aveugles furent amenées par leurs soi-disant filles, squelettes liés au sort de ces braves gens pour l'intérêt de leur commerce, et sur lesquelles un carabin prendrait des leçons d'ostéologie sans avoir besoin de les faire écorcher . . .'

[3] Dessuslamarre, *La Mendicité*, p. 5.

these to draw on, what pregnant woman could risk refusing a suppliant? *Le regard perçant, le regard moqueur* of the beggar could be sufficient to engender fear.

The female beggar, however old and ugly, used other ploys, choosing in preference the wealthy cleric, the magistrate, or some aged respectable citizen and following him hurling abuses mixed with obscenities and aspersions on his honour if he should be foolish enough to try to brush her aside.[1] The most favoured ploy, however, found everywhere, was to muster a band of children suitably endowed with qualities demanding compassion, extreme youth, deformity, physical malady, by borrowing them or hiring them and using them to demonstrate one's need to help one's family.[2]

The children were of course able beggars in their own right. A child still unable to walk could be propped up on the steps of a church with a little begging bowl while his sister or brother made use of the exit from mass to draw attention to his needs. The children developed real expertise in the tricks of the begging trade, making full use of physical deformities, whether real or fake, and embroidering fanciful tales to demonstrate their needs to an incredulous public. Their strength lay in their persistence, in their readiness to accept rebuffs and blows and still make demands. They knew each bread-shop, each market stall, and would wait until a customer had made his purchases and then importune him for a fraction of them.[3] In the cathedral churches and massive *collégiales* of large cities, where the congregation was large and often important and where circulation was easy, small children were active during offices. Darting out from behind columns with hand outstretched to confront the worshipper while he was actually on his knees in prayer, the simple word *caritas* was all that was needed. Effectively, they put the worshipper in a difficult position by intervening at the moment of his closest communication with his God, the friend of the weak and oppressed. By this means the children might hope to distrain a coin which might else have been put in the *tronc des pauvres*. This was

[1] A.C. Rodez, Ville et Bourg FF 1; A.D. Puy-de-Dôme C 1203.

[2] Ibid. At Riom there are hundreds of women 'qui comptent sur la compassion qu'inspirent leur faiblesse et leur talent à demander surtout si elles peuvent avoir plusieurs enfants! Aussi en volent-elles, en achètent-elles, s'en prêtent-elles.' On the same theme A.C. Rodez, Ville et Bourg FF2.

[3] B.N. Fonds français 8130, Projets et Mémoires, p. 5.

not the only business for them to accomplish in church: next to horses' tails and fruit, the easiest things to steal were prayer-books, and pickpocketing was perhaps at its most remunerative when people were dressed in their Sunday best.

What was abundantly clear to society as a whole was that trickery, petty crime, and intimidation were employed by the pauper to wrest funds from the hesitant donor. Moreover, it was easier for society to stress the deception involved rather than the dire poverty which made the deception needful. Charity was perhaps blessed, but the same could not be said of extortion, and the menacing, filthy, violent figure perhaps with a weapon concealed in his rags and with obscenities constantly upon his lips was difficult to reconcile with the concept of poverty as extolled by the evangelists. The comfortably-off citizen was prepared to put coins into the *tronc des pauvres* after mass or confession and to remember to include in his testament sufficient to ensure that his hearse was accompanied by twelve virtuous paupers, hand-picked by the parish priest and paid for their efforts as incantors of prayers for the deceased. What he was not prepared for was personal daily confrontation by unknown, unverifiable supplicants with perhaps criminal tendencies. If his conscience troubled him, he could always buy peace of mind by bestowing *largesse* upon a type of poor person who commanded universal respect, the *pauvre honteux*, the man or woman who had once known better times but who had been the victim of disaster, illness, or bank-ruptcy. At Marseilles, a *pauvre honteux* was commonly someone obliged to sell his ship through failure in commercial specula-tion.[1] Such people had friends to whom they could immediately turn, though they did so reluctantly, seeking to hide their penury. One of the few to whom they confessed their state (such people were invariably pious) was the parish priest who would see to it that if any help was to be had, they would be the first to receive it. Moreover, he would do so without betraying their confidence —parish lists of the poor never mentioned the *pauvre honteux* by name. This type of pauper has slipped easily into literature. Sterne in his *Sentimental Journey* identifies him as a man who never openly asks for anything but who might be betrayed by his emaciated looks and his proud mien.[2] Restif in *La Paysanne*

---

[1] G. Valran, *Misère et charité en Provence au XVIIIᵉ siècle*, p. 51.
[2] L. Sterne, *Sentimental Journey* (Signet edition, 1964), pp. 44–6.

pervertie draws upon popular appreciation of the subtle distinction between *pauvre honteux* and the rest when Ursula, the wealthy prostitute keeping up her social reputation, is urged:

Soyez généreuse, ayez quelques familles pauvres, auxquelles vous ferez du bien, et qui en diront de vous. Choisissez-les bien . . . ce seront des gens un peu relevés au-dessus du commun, obérés par des malheurs, des faillites, et obligés de garder dans le monde un certain décor. Ces gens là, qui verront la bonne bourgeoisie, ne diront pas qu'ils sont vos obligés, mais ils exalteront votre bienfaisance, ils en parleront la larme à l'œil, et feront aller votre réputation partout. Pour leur donner des sujets à citer vous aurez aussi deux ou trois pauvres manœuvres, bien chargés d'enfants, à qui vous donnerez le nécessaire, que vous leur porterez de temps en temps vous-même mise avec modestie, et presque en grisette, mais ayant de belles dentelles, . . . et tout ce qui peut annoncer une grande dame qui se cache.[1]

The *pauvres honteux* were a privileged élite amongst the poor. They were those who had not fallen below a certain standard; they had a regular roof over their head, clean clothes, and moral values acceptable to the rest of society. As long as they could maintain the delicate balance between poverty and destitution they had little to fear. In any case they were the newly poor who had once known an easier way of life; they had not been accustomed since birth to an unremitting struggle against hunger nor had they had a lifetime in which to acquire the vices and dishonesty necessary to make one's way in the world of the totally destitute.

The priorities of urban charity clearly made force or some kind of intimidation increasingly necessary for anyone whose only recourse was to beg in the towns, and many observers felt that the cities were in fact subject to a forced levy in favour of the unemployed outsider. Yet in a town or city the potential for a successful begging existence was too narrow for the mere amateur, and hence the practical solution of turning instead, even on the part of the poor town-dweller, to harassing the isolated farmer in the rural areas. For whereas the town-dweller had some defences, the isolated farmer had none.

If informal charity continued to be the means whereby the poor of eighteenth-century France received some slight subsidy,

[1] Restif de la Bretonne, *Le Paysan et la paysanne pervertie*, adapted M. Talmeyr (Paris, 1888), pp. 144–5.

this should not in any sense be depicted as the voluntary charity so close to the heart of St. Vincent and his acolytes. Catholic informal charity existed, to be sure, and whilst it can be shown to be grossly inadequate, in fairness it cannot be labelled indiscriminate—even if one might question its priorities. There were those who could, like the *pauvre honteux*, expect to receive something without demanding and those who might constantly demand without being sure of receiving anything. However informal provisions for according relief might be, there were *vrais pauvres* and *mauvais pauvres*—and the unverifiable poor were lumped with the latter—and only the claims of the first were regarded as legitimate, while the demands of the second were granted *at best* under duress. When forced to give, the donor felt abused; he had a cause for grievance: he expected protection against such assaults on his generosity. Moreover, in the countryside begging was too often coupled with theft, violation of property rights, and menaces of fire. It thus became not a moral concern but a question of law and order, a matter not for the clergy and the devout but for government and the police. The beggar needed to be considered not as *un membre souffrant de Jésus-Christ* but as *le fléau de la société*. How capable was *ancien régime* government of affording protection?

PART THREE

The Crimes of the Poor

VIII

BEGGING, VAGRANCY, AND THE LAW

> Délivrez-nous des incursions d'un tas de gens qui,
> moyennant une balle qu'ils charrient partout, se font
> escorter par un tas d'enfants qui sont, ainsi que leur
> mère, à chaque instant à nos portes et pénètrent jusque
> dans nos maisons . . . outre que nos campagnes se trou-
> vent assez souvent pillées et violées par ces gens là.
>
> Letter of the curé of Villemoyenne, 1788
> (A.D. Aube C 2342).

THE *hôpitaux*, *bureaux de charité*, *ateliers*, and private donations
represent only one approach to the problem of poverty, the
palliative, the attempt to assuage and to understand the problems
of the needy. But there was, perforce, because the combined
efforts of government, institutions, and society at large were
unable to offer effective help and stem the problem at source, a
second approach, the punitive. Society needed protection against
the more violent and, indeed, criminal beggar, whose existence
was a menace to public order; it needed guarantees against those
whose demands, however morally justified, were backed up by
illegal acts. It also hoped for *largesse* to be reserved for the truly
deserving poor. Government in some way must provide for these
requirements by legislation designed at least to counteract, at
most to deter, the more heinous acts associated with begging and
vagrancy.

The response of *hôpitaux* and police to the edict of 1724 finally
conveyed to a reluctant government a few basic points. First,
that the *hôpitaux* were inflexible institutions unable to cope with
any but the most privileged of the urban poor. Secondly, that to
protect rural France there must be a police force capable of
bringing offenders to justice, a judicial structure able to deal
efficiently with offenders, effective punishments of a truly deterrent nature, and some institution to serve as house of correction
to the ingrained idler or the vicious vagrant. The police needed
looking into. Could existing courts stand the pressure of business
that would fall upon them if all beggars and vagrants were brought

to justice? Delay at this level would cost money. A solution must
be found to the question of institutional punishment; some
substitute for *hôpitaux* and galleys, which could only use the male
able-bodied. Reform must take into account past experience and,
above all, the government must cease to look to the *hôpitaux*. In
this respect the efforts of the government in the 1760s mark a
fundamental breach with the past. Without full employment and
with the increasing inadequacy of the daily wage in the face of
mounting costs and the scanty resources of assistance, any efforts
in the direction of deterrent justice were perhaps doomed from
the outset. Moreover, the problems of the sixties were only a
pale shadow of those of the eighties for which past experience
was of little relevance. Even so, *ancien régime* governments, beset
with financial problems and social questions they only dimly
understood or wanted to understand, did not choose to linger on
the theoretical efficacy of punitive treatment without constructive
means to combat poverty at source. What follows is an attempt
to judge how far punitive measures could be put into effect and
how likely they were to enjoy any success.

In the bringing to justice of beggars and vagrants a great deal
obviously depended upon the police, perhaps the most neglected
element of *ancien régime* society and one which awaits its historian.[1]
In the meantime, however, a number of characteristics stand out:
above all, the difference between the policing of town and country. The former was perhaps rudimentary; the latter was non-
existent. In the towns policing was weak or strong depending
upon how much the towns were prepared to spend upon it.
Paris and the larger cities clearly had the greatest sums at their
disposal, but even here it must be questioned how effective was
the policing of the streets. The police proper did not regard
beggars and vagrants as their concern unless they troubled public
order, for their business was rather with the policing of markets,
refuse-tipping, and street-cleaning. The actual apprehension of

---

[1] Many of the premises of the *ancien régime* police were doubtless those of their
revolutionary counterparts analysed in R. Cobb, *The Police and the People*; the
bibliography in M. Le Clère, *Histoire de la police* (Paris, 1947), illustrates how little
has been written on this important subject. The best over-all institutional study,
without reference to the actual functioning of the *maréchaussée*, is G. Larrieu,
Histoire de la gendarmerie (Paris, 1933), and a good local study is J. Plique, *Histoire
de la maréchaussée du Gévaudan* (Privat, 1912). A doctoral thesis on the *maréchaussée*
of Provence is announced. A more general study drawing upon national and local
archives is in process, the work of Iain Cameron at Reading.

beggars and vagrants in large towns was left either to *chasse gueux* or *archers-gardes des hôpitaux*, who were sometimes paid entirely by the municipality, sometimes partially paid out of the funds of the *hôpitaux*. Corruptible and readily corrupted, frequently beaten up by beggars or their compatriots, and miserably paid, the *chasse gueux* or *archers* were indeed a broken reed for anyone concerned with the extirpation of urban begging. But at least the *archers* were there and had to arrest the token few to keep their jobs as municipal employees. The same could not be said of the rural *maréchaussée*. Even after the reforms of the sixties, the police force of provincial France added up to 3,882 individuals in all, of whom 468 were higher administrative officials; these 3,882 individuals were then divided up into thirty-four *compagnies* and distributed throughout the *généralités*. The *compagnies* were divided into brigades of four members, which were stationed in a town and expected to patrol a given area. It would seem that each town of more than 5,000 inhabitants had a police force of four who had to ride out and patrol the surrounding rural area. The whole of the Brie, for example, with its centre at Meaux (a town of 6,500) had a total police force of four.[1] Chartres, a city of 13,000 and centre of the Beauce, terrorized by the great Hulin band of the 1760s and again by the *bande d'Orgères*, was the headquarters of six policemen. Similarly in the Lyonnais, another centre of brigand bands, twenty-eight men tried to patrol an area equal to the present department of the Rhône.[2] Périgord was relatively well policed with forty policemen,[3] while theoretically best of all was Brittany with fifty-six *brigades*—over 250 men for one of the most heavily populated provinces in the country (almost 2 million people).[4] Faced with these pathetic numbers, one might reasonably question why they were not increased by a government interested in deterrent justice, and one can only guess at an answer: reluctance to spend more money. More positively, one can draw obvious inferences from such numbers. The likelihood of being arrested in a village, unless one hung around too long and so allowed parish *syndic* or interested villagers time to ride into the town

[1] Marion, *Dictionnaire des institutions de la France aux XVIIe et XVIIIe siècles* (Paris, 1923), pp. 362–3.
[2] H. Hours, 'Émeutes et émotions populaires dans les campagnes du Lyonnais au XVIIIe siècle', *Cahiers d'histoire*, ix (1964), 150.
[3] *Inventaire des archives départementales de la Dordogne* (Périgueux, 1899), Série B, p. x.
[4] A. M. Corre and P. Aubry, *Documents de criminologie rétrospective*, p. 10.

and summon the *brigade* or unless the *maréchaussée* happened to ride through an area on a particular day, was remote. The *sub-délégué* of Mauriac in the Basse-Auvergne summed this up perfectly: 'Cette brigade est bonne à faire capturer un homme qu'on lui remet entre les mains.'[1] Clearly this was no protection for the isolated farm confronted with packs of vagrants. A group of villagers of Saint-Igny-des-Vers in the Lyonnais refused to assist the *maréchaussée* in the arrest of one band of vagrant-thieves, declaring: 'Vous n'êtes pas toujours ici et si nous prêtions main forte pour les arrêter, ils nous le rendront chez nous.'[2] Other villagers were not prepared to waste time in summoning the *maréchaussée* when the offending vagrants might have passed on, and even if they passed on leaving behind a trail of minor thefts, of eggs, milk, washing from the hedgerows, villagers clearly did not regard summoning the *maréchaussée* as an effective way of gaining redress. If a known vagrant-thief was captured and brought to trial and if he was not known to be one of a powerful pack, villagers might come forward and report minor atrocities committed up to five years before.[3] And if vagrancy accompanied by theft or begging using threats of force were rarely reported, vagrancy and begging alone never were. The *maréchaussée* could not count on the support of the local populace in bringing offenders to justice simply because, in turn, the local populace had no faith in the *maréchaussée*. The numerical weakness of the *maréchaussée* had other implications. A brigade of four was hardly likely to confront any assembly of vagrants, and priests and *sub-délégués* claimed that the *cavaliers* avoided anyone likely to put up resistance. To cope with major emergencies, such as the arrest of particularly large and dangerous *bandes*, either the brigades had to amalgamate or the army had to be called in. Without the army, neither Charles Hulin dit le Blond nor Mandrin the smuggler could have been brought to justice; and before the army was brought in or brigades amalgamated a highly dangerous state had been reached.

A further consideration was that members of the *maréchaussée* were chronically underpaid. A *cavalier*, after the reforms of 1769,

[1] A.D. Puy-de-Dôme C 1543.

[2] A.D. Rhône B, Maréchaussée, 1776, dossier P. Chamot. The nearest brigade was stationed 10 miles away. Gutton, *La Société et les pauvres*, p. 203.

[3] Phenomenon noted by Corre and Aubry, p. 223. The accused could then be presented as a *mendiant d'habitude*.

could count on an annual 270 *livres* or 15 *sous* per day. This poverty clearly laid them open to bribery, and the corruption of the police manifests itself at many junctures. The *intendant* of Basse-Auvergne, who felt unmitigated contempt for the entire police force of his *généralité*, described one member of the force who coupled policing with running a *cabaret* which known crooks and *vagabonds* frequented without concern, another who was a murderer, and one who, for a small sum, would permit anything to happen under his eyes.[1] Such corruption had several effects. The first was that magistrates were suspicious of the unsupported evidence of the police; and the able female beggar could readily counteract charges brought by the police with allegations against the policeman's intentions. More seriously, the poverty of the police meant that the incentive to work efficiently was extremely small. Many regarded policing as a sideline or as an unremunerative office to be coupled with another job.

The government was not thinking in terms of increasing the number of policemen but of improving their efficiency when in 1767 it offered a reward for every beggar arrested. The result was a spate of arrests with which neither the judicial framework nor the new houses of correction could cope, and the *intendants* on the spot hastily withdrew the promised award. The *maréchaussée*, they realized, were not going forth into the countryside to search out those who really offended society. The thief and threatening vagrant in isolated villages were being allowed to proceed undisturbed whilst the harmless beggar on the high road, most particularly those labourers who cadged their supper and a night's lodging *en route* to and returning from their seasonal jobs, were apprehended as quick and easy arrests likely to secure a good bonus for the *cavalier*.[2] When rewards ceased, the numbers arrested fell dramatically as the police lost incentive. Hence the numbers of vagrants brought before the *prévôtés* do not necessarily reveal very much about the intensity of vagrancy in any particular area; they suggest fluctuations in its incidence, which tell more about the efforts of the police than anything else. Usually the graph of

---

[1] A.D. Puy-de-Dôme C 1529. In fact, running a *cabaret* would seem to have been the commonest way of supplementing income.

[2] The *intendants* claimed they had little control over the *maréchaussée* and were often infuriated by random arrests (A.D. Hérault C 562). This struggle was clearly at its most intense in Languedoc (C. Paultre, *De la répression de la mendicité et du vagabondage en France sous l'ancien régime*, pp. 498–9).

arrests in a given area made between 1767 and 1789 conforms to a certain pattern. The legislation of 1767 was marked by an immediate heavy crop of arrests which then fell when the *intendants* refused to pay for each one. Then in 1774, when arrest with conviction was promised a bonus, figures rose again, only to decline during the Turgot period when the *dépôts de mendicité* were closed.[1] Thereafter they settled on a fairly even level until the closing years of the *ancien régime*. But whereas these generalizations hold good for areas where policing was relatively good, such as Normandy, Guyenne, the Auvergne, the Île de France, and the east, elsewhere, particularly in difficult mountainous country, the legislation made little difference. At Mende, Vesoul, Rodez, Langres, and Périgueux, for example, the numbers arrested for begging and vagrancy show little movement throughout the last fifty years of the *ancien régime* and this in areas where beggars and vagrants proliferated.[2]

The measures of the sixties were also directed towards speeding up the mechanics of judicial procedure in order to deal with the expected increase in business. Before 1767 beggars and vagrants arrested by the *maréchaussée* had to stand trial before a *prévôté* court which had special jurisdiction over these sectors of society and over deserters. After that date, those arrested on a charge of begging alone were brought before a magistrate established within the *maréchaussée* and the verdict was subject to the confirmation of the *intendant*. Cases of vagrancy and related offences continued to be the preserve of the *prévôtés*. If the charge was the specific one of vagrancy the authority of the *prévôtés* stretched even into towns which otherwise had their own special justice in the form of *présidiaux* or, in some instances, *bailliages*; but in practice it was always difficult in a town to sustain a charge of vagrancy, since the urban begging flotsam who lodged in the crowded *garnis* were always ready to provide a dubious address or 'claim' a vagrant, if one of their number came before the

[1] The history of this legislation is found in both C. Bloch, *L'Assistance et l'État*, and Paultre, *De la répression*, pp. 381–404.

[2] The numbers of arrests for the whole of France from 1764 to 1777 are given in B.N. Fonds Joly de Fleury 1309, fol. 186. The studies of P. Crépillon, 'Un Gibier des prévôts. Mendiants et vagabonds au XVIIIᵉ siècle entre la Vire et la Dives, 1720–89', *Annales de Normandie*, xvii (1967), 223–52, and V. Boucheron, 'La Montée du flot des errants de 1760 à 1789 dans la généralité d'Alençon', *Annales de Normandie*, xxi (1971), 55–86, offer statistically what one would expect.

courts. The *prévôtés* had jurisdiction not only over vagrants but over the crimes committed by such people within the area of their jurisdiction. Appeal was to the *présidiaux*, but it was not expected on the grounds of begging and vagrancy alone, and in fact never seems to have occurred. In those cities which had *parlements*, all justice, even if it dealt with the relatively insignificant crimes of beggars, had to be concentrated in that institution and was the specific business of La Tournelle. The Châtelet of Paris had similar powers.

There was scope for dispute, such as characterized other judicial issues, over the competence and limits of jurisdiction of various courts; but since the crimes of the beggar were, from the point of view of everyone except the policeman who apprehended him, non-profit-making, a legal structure sustained by *épices* and fines did not trouble itself. Far more serious from the point of view of the government was the fact that many *prévôtés* had ceased to exist.[1] Since their business was dependent upon the efforts of the *maréchaussée*, some had fallen into disuse long before 1767, and attempts (frequently unsuccessful) had to be made to resurrect them or infuse them with a little more energy. Secondly, there was the tricky problem of discovering whether the individual concerned had a record. Liaison between *prévôté* and *prévôté*, let alone between these and other courts, was non-existent. A man had only to pass from one jurisdiction to another to escape his past.[2]

The government in 1724 had hoped to establish records of repeated offenders by circulating to the *maréchaussée* lists of beggars registered by the *hôpitaux* throughout France. But, except for two or three major cities, Paris, Lyons, Rouen, the scheme met with no response, and even these cities did not keep it up.[3] If and when beggars and vagrants were brought before the courts between 1724 and 1767, judges contented themselves with branding (M for *mendiant*, V for *vagabond*), public flogging, spells

---

[1] This clearly happened, for example, in the cases of the *prévôtés* of Mende and Bourges (A.D. Cher C 747).

[2] A good instance of this is given in Crépillon, 'Un Gibier des prévôts', p. 114.

[3] J. P. Gutton, 'L'Exécution de la déclaration royale du 18 juillet 1724 concernant la mendicité (Généralités de Lyon et d'Auvergne)' (Thèse de doctorat de 3ᵉ cycle, Lyon, 1967) and 'Les Mendiants dans la société parisienne au début du XVIIIᵉ siècle', *Cahiers d'histoire*, xiii (1968), 131–41, discuss the limited efficacy of this legislation. See above, pp. 156–7.

in the galleys if able-bodied men were in question, and, above all, banishment from the province. Hence the only record the *maré-chaussée* might expect to find—and here the new legislation made no new departure—was the purely physical one of scars on the body. Had the person in question been branded? Was there a patch of skin on the shoulder lighter and of a different texture from the rest? Sometimes the most indecipherable mark was used as proof of a record:

lui avons trouvé sur l'épaule droite, partie moyenne et externe, à un poulce de l'angle de l'omoplate, une oréole de la largeur d'un écu de trois livres, d'une couleur moins noire que toute la peau dans la ditte oréole; du côté de l'angle moyen nous y avons remarqué 2 petites cicatrices d'environ deux lignes de longueur et d'une demi-ligne de largeur et distantes de près d'une ligne scavoir la première plus courte et supérieure du côté de l'angle externe de l'omoplate, posée oblique-ment, la seconde plus longue et posée presque perpendiculairement ou latéralement droite à la première, et c'est notre rapport, etc. . . .[1]

There were other physical signs: did the individual concerned drag one leg?—a limp, in the eyes of the law, was the sure sign of the ex-*forçat*. Thirdly, did his back bear any scars from a flogging? It was unlikely that a public flogging would show up a few years afterwards, but the protracted flogging incurred during a spell in the galleys might well leave its mark.

Legislators in the sixties were also aware of the need to define their terms of reference. The de l'Averdy commission in 1764 redefined the word '*vagabond*' to take account of the frequent periods of unemployment which characterized the existence of the day labourer or small land-holder. The edict, the result of the work of the commission, ran: 'Seront réputés vagabonds . . . ceux qui depuis six mois révolus n'auront exercé ni profession ni métier, et qui n'ayant aucun état ni aucun bien pour subsister, ne pourront être avoués ou faire certifier de leurs bonne vie et mœurs par personnes dignes de foi.'[2] The punishments were made harsher. Able-bodied vagrants between the ages of 16 and 70 were punished for a first offence by being sent to the galleys for three years, nine years for the second offence, and the galleys in perpetuity for a third. The sick, the old, women and children were to be incarcerated in the *hôpitaux* for corresponding periods.

---

[1] A.D. Finistère B 818 and B 834.   [2] Isambert, *Recueil des Lois*, t. iv, p. 404.

The beggar was to be treated differently. Attempts to implement the edict of 1724 had foundered on the incapacity of the *hôpitaux*; de l'Averdy's commission advised the setting-up of two or three *dépôts* in each *généralité* in which anyone caught in the act of begging could be interned, without real trial, for a period of up to eighteen months. The advice was accepted and from then on the *dépôts de mendicité* became the cornerstone of the suppression of begging and vagrancy. Though not originally intended for the vagrant, in fact those interned in the *dépôts* were, technically at least, in this category, for the simple beggar was unlikely to be drawn to the attention of the *maréchaussée* by a society tolerant of the familiar deserving suppliant. Furthermore, magistrates had never handed out sentences in the galleys if there was any ready alternative either because they felt the practice repellent or inefficacious in the eradication of vagrancy or because most of the human specimens on whom they were asked to pass judgement were clearly physically incapable of manning a galley oar. The result of de l'Averdy's edict, then, was that magistrates sought to use the *dépôts* for the vagrant. Moreover, though it was possible to draw some distinction between beggar and vagrant in theory, in practice this was very difficult to accomplish, because after de l'Averdy's edict the word *vagabond* acquired a much broader meaning and both police and judges applied their own criterion. Broadly speaking, proof of *mendicité* was everywhere established according to two very simple principles. First, the *mendiant* could be arrested on the spot in process of soliciting or receiving alms. In this case he was convicted out of his own mouth. So rare were instances of this that the point is almost academic. Secondly, he could be denounced by those whom he had importuned for alms, particularly had he done so in a threatening or in any way violent manner. Or a suspicious-looking character could be picked up—this was commonest—by the *maréchaussée* on its rounds. When the *maréchaussée* had then made an arrest, he was searched and his guilt could be established in one or both of two ways. First, if his *besace* or beggar's bag contained several bits of bread: 'trouvé porteur d'un sac de pain de mendicité'; 'chargé d'un havresac garni de pain coupé en morceaux'; 'trouvé porteur d'un sac contenant de huit à dix livres de morceaux de pain'; 'porteur d'un sac de vingt livres de morceaux de pain'; 'une vingtaine de morceaux de pain de différentes façons'.[1] *Pain de mendicité* or *pain de différentes façons* were essentially the same thing, small pieces of bread of differing kinds and age cut at random from a farmer's loaf or kept by him in a basket near the door (since it was too stale for the farmer's family to eat) ready to give to the begging caller. For the police, possession of such bread incriminated the owner beyond all doubt, as he could not claim he had purchased it when it was not all of the same age and in court he would be thrown back upon the untenable defence of claiming he had bought it from a beggar. Almost as incriminating was the possession of large numbers of *liards* since these virtually valueless coins were almost entirely reserved for almsgiving. De l'Averdy's edict was designed to make the punishment of anyone even suspected of begging and/or vagrancy easy. Whereas, for example, before 1767 the *mendiant* was distinguished from the *vagabond* if he had a fixed abode, after 1767 this ceased and from then on, at least theoretically, one could be domiciled and still classified as a *vagabond* if found wandering and looking suspicious a mile from home. By the same law one did not even need to beg to be arrested; a doubtful appearance, and particularly the garb of another region, physical deformities, and the lack of apparent resources were sufficient to justify police action, and the *procès-verbaux* of the late sixties show such principles at work: 'mal habillés mais fort robustes'; 'avec un air menaçant et apparence de vagabond'; 'porteur d'une figure à faire peur'.[2] Mistrust, the police were urged by Le Noir, *lieutenant de police de Paris*, the ragged and those who have evidently come from afar.[3]

Magistrates adjusted cautiously to the changes of 1767 and continued to make their own distinction between beggar and vagrant, seldom using the word *vagabond* without further qualification, for example, *vagabond-mendiant-sédentaire* as opposed to *errant-vagabond*. In court they sought as conclusive evidence of vagrancy proof that the individual in question had had no work during the past six months. The accused could be asked to produce two kinds of documentation, the passport and the *aveu*. The passport was issued initially in one's native village and stated a purpose and a destination. Such documentation was, however,

---

[1] These are recurrent phrases used in the records of any *maréchaussée*.

[2] A.D. Calvados 9 B 65 *bis* no. 299.

[3] Some of Le Noir's correspondence to this effect is published in A. Garnier, 'Histoire de la maréchaussée de Langres de 1720 à 1789', *Mém. soc. pour l'histoire de droit bourguignon* (1952), pp. 239–40.

easily lost or could expire, or the holder could claim his seasonal employ had dried up and he had been forced to move elsewhere. Under such circumstances he was supposed to get another passport from the local authorities, and here endless abuses could creep in. Most large cities had an infamous *cabaretier* or someone who ran a doss-house who was prepared to vouch for the shadiest character seeking a passport from the local authorities, and even the authorities when confronted with someone allegedly about to *leave* the area did not ask too much.[1] Moreover, many seasonal migrants, particularly those pouring south into Languedoc, did not equip themselves with these documents. Hence, possession of a passport was not conclusive evidence of innocence, and lack of one did not prove guilt. Nor was the *aveu* of much greater assistance to the magistrate. This was an attestation of good character issued by one's parish priest or municipal officials or the *maréchaussée* in one's native area. Priests, however, in particular were known to give these indiscriminately, often judging their parishioners' odysseys as vital to the existence of their families.[2] Faced with such considerations, magistrates rejected documentation in favour of hard evidence of legal occupation within the previous six months; but even here difficulties could arise, for example, in the case of François Levalet, a native of Saint-Agnan who was tried in 1759 in the *présidial* of Gray. Levalet, a gardener, was accused of turning up at the local priory and declaring himself a former servant of the bishop, Cavaillon, *en route* to a new job; he was given supper and a night's shelter. Next day, he learnt in the *cabaret* of a family whose son was absent and presented himself at their house with the son's greetings, and was given another day's hospitality. Had he been able to keep his hands off the maidservant and hold his wine better, all might have been well, but the girl repulsed his advances and denounced him as a trickster, and he found himself on trial. Levalet, who had no less than three passports on him, stuck rigidly to his story that he had only been without work for a mere five months; he explained that his type of labour was perforce always casual and that he could remember neither the names nor the places where he had

---

[1] Doublet, *traiteur* of Chartres, was held to have vouched for anyone in the *bande d'Orgères* (A.D. Eure-et-Loir J 584, para. xxvi).

[2] Those of the Auvergne were allegedly totally indiscriminate. A.D. Puy-de-Dôme C 1197.

given his services. He could not produce an *aveu*. On the other hand, he was not dressed in rags and had a little money on him, which was not in *liards*, and what he said about the nature of the job was true. Levalet was whipped and banished from the province—a light punishment.[1]

In other words, the line between poor occasional worker and beggar or vagrant could be difficult to establish in spite of the nice demarcations envisaged by government legislation. Judges were well aware of the problems, as were the *intendants*, who were particularly irritated by the arrests of policemen intent upon a quick reward. Certainly, after 1767, the beggar and vagrant are recurrent figures in the annals of most *prévôté* courts. How capable would the new *dépôts de mendicité* be of coping with them? The answer lies in the institution itself.

The *dépôt de mendicité* is perhaps rendered most readily understandable if from the outset it is appreciated that it was meant to be, like the English Bridewell or the Dutch *Tuchthuis*, a house of correction, not for the ingrained idler or *vagabond* whom the government felt merited service in the galleys, but for those newly embarked upon a primrose path, who might be deterred by a short sentence and made to see the error of their ways by a spell of regular labour. An ordered, working life for disordered human beings: such was the aim of the de l'Averdy commission. In this respect, partly at least because magistrates found it impossible to apply the categorization the government laid down in 1764, but also for many other reasons, it was an unqualified failure, as were indeed the English Bridewell and the Dutch *Tuchthuis*. Moreover, the whole experiment was conducted in an aura of hostility— from *philosophes* and physiocrats, from the Church for it ran counter to the time-honoured prescriptive right of Christian charity to succour the weak, from provincial estates because it made inroads into their budgets, and from the *Commissions Intermédiaires* of 1788. Added to this, society expected the *dépôts* to protect it in some way from the criminal beggar. The *dépôt* was regarded by the public at large as something far more important in coping with the vagrancy problem than the de l'Averdy commission had ever intended.

The scheme in fact only got off the ground in 1767 (1764 in the Auvergne, where the problems were such that the *intendant* did

[1] A.D. Haute-Saône B 2630.

not feel safe in delaying). Immediately, it ran up against practical problems: the difficulty of finding sufficient and adequate buildings, of appointing personnel, of coping with problems, such as disease, of which the government had little conception, the whole thorny question of finance—the *dépôts'* expenses were to be met out of the *fonds de l'intendance*, except in the *pays d'États*. Equally important was the question of liaison with the *maréchaussée* on the one hand, and with the curés on the other, the one pivotal in arresting the right people regularly, the other the main determinant in who was *domicilié* or *non domicilié* and who could command an *aveu*.

Practical questions of this nature beset the establishments in the first five years or so of their existence. By about 1767 most *généralités* had either three or four *dépôts* holding between 100 and 200 offenders.[1] The *pays d'États* refused to make a major contribution towards their upkeep, and, in Brittany and Hainaut especially, the intense opposition explains why the institution was peculiarly weak in these provinces.[2] Nor did the installation of the institution enjoy an easy passage in Languedoc where the archbishop of Toulouse was a vociferous critic of the whole idea and even more of the potential financial burden.[3] The buildings chosen were usually the most ramshackle collection of disused edifices, old castles or fortifications, corners of *hospices* regarded as too insalubrious for the sick, old convents, converted barracks, prisons which had fallen into disuse for unspecified reasons, crumbling stately homes which the owners could not sell.[4] With inadequate or polluted water supplies and in many cases without windows or adequate ventilation, and, nine times out of ten in the early days, without an infirmary, it took no time at all for these institutions to establish themselves as breeding grounds of

[1] B.N. Fonds français 8129, fol. 333, État de tous les dépôts destinés et servant au renfermement des mendiants, vagabonds et gens sans aveu dans toutes les provinces du royaume, 1767.

[2] A.D. Ille-et-Vilaine C 4937, Commission Intermédiaire, 1788, embodies the brunt of the controversy between the Breton estates and the central government.

[3] A.N. H¹ 892, États de Languedoc, and B.N. Fonds français 8129, fol. 339. The archbishop put forward one of the most humane manifestos on behalf of the beggar on record: 'la mendicité n'est pas un délit quand l'état n'est pas en mesure de remplir le devoir d'assistance qui lui incombe vis à vis des pauvres.'

[4] At Vannes and Rennes old châteaux were used from which escape was simple; at Dijon, unused buildings belonging to the abbey of Clairvaux, at Chalons an old barracks; etc.

disease. Within months an attempt to maintain a *dépôt* in Clermont in 1767 in a disused corner of the *hôpital général* had resulted in an epidemic which not only decimated the *vagabonds* but killed the administrators, so that all the internees had to be sent home.[1] In the same year the older establishment at Riom underwent an unspecified epidemic which was blamed on polluted water and bad bread. De l'Averdy sought to prevent such experiences by insisting that each internee be allowed a space of two square yards and that each building have a bath where entrants could be deloused and their rags burned before they entered the actual house of correction.[2] But regulations about space presupposed an inelastic problem of poverty and facilities which the limited funds the government was prepared to put at the disposal of the *dépôt* simply could not buy. Hence the history of the *dépôts* is peppered with sporadic outbreaks of epidemics—usually the dreaded jail fever of which record is found in all the *dépôts* of Languedoc, Rodez, Bourges, Tours, Rennes, and so on. The administrators of the *dépôt* at Tours thus described the physical condition of the internees:

Ils deviennent jaunes, bouffis, avec une disposition prochaine à l'hidropisie, les nouveaux arrivés en sont si subitement saisis qu'ils perdent l'appétit, ils dorment peu, ne mangent point. Les yeux deviennent inquiets et égarés, le pouls se déprime, la voix s'éteint et ils tombent dans un dévoyement qui termine leur existence.[3]

Of the 71,760 *mendiants* and *vagabonds* on record as having been arrested by the *maréchaussée* up to 1773, 13,899 died in the *dépôts* in the course of their short sentence.[4] The highest recorded mortality rate was at Vannes where it reached 28 per cent during fifty-one months.[5] Clearly something could be attributed to the condition in which the *vagabonds* arrived; and, indeed, their

[1] A.D. Puy-de-Dôme C 1191, Letter of Bertier, 8 Aug. 1786.

[2] Ibid. C 1089, Mendicité.

[3] A.D. Indre-et-Loire C 304, Dépôt de Mendicité, 1781.

[4] B.N. Fonds Joly de Fleury 1309, fol. 186. Between 1768 and 1772, 21,339 perished out of 111,836 interned (the second figure may include the same people twice, as no distinction was made in the figures for recivists).

[5] E. Guéguen, 'La Mendicité au pays de Vannes dès la deuxième moitié du XVIIIᵉ siècle', *Bull. soc. polymatique du Morbihan* (1970), p. 117. The *intendant* at Rennes (where mortality rates were of the order of 22·8 per cent) was disturbed by the rates (A.D. Ille-et-Vilaine C 1297 and C 1310).

general physical condition had its part to play in determining the
efficacy of the *dépôts* as houses of correction where the poor might
be inculcated with the habits of industry. As a *mémoire* of the
États de Languedoc pointed out:

Les maladies avec lesquelles un grand nombre de mendiants arrivent
au dépôt, scorbut, gâle, maladies vénériennes, cette sorte de peste
infecte les dépôts. Plusieurs Hôtels Dieu ne reçoivent pas ces maladies;
dans l'état actuel on ne donne à ceux qui en sont atteints que des
palliatifs; et il en résulte qu'ils languissent et qu'ils périssent. Si on
veut employer les mendiants au travail il faut les guérir; la nature
souffrante se refuse à la fatigue, et on ne peut rien exiger de celui dont
une longue maladie consume les forces.[1]

The number of those capable of work was in fact highly
restricted; it usually stood in the region of 50 per cent, though
there are wide variations. Moreover, in some *dépôts* there simply
was no room for *ateliers*. By 1785 the *dépôt* at Bourges had 3,388
internees, all of whom were totally unoccupied.

In 1773 the task of providing work and supplies for the *dépôts*
was in most places put into the hands of a single company (Manie,
Rimberge et Compagnie, succeeded in 1776 in some cases by
Jacques Dangers et Compagnie). In part this was for reasons of
economy: the companies agreed to feed and clothe the internees
against 6 *sols* per day per person; but also it was designed to
ensure some uniformity. That the *dépôt* at Vannes should have had
a mortality rate of almost a third can perhaps in large part be
explained by a daily bread ration of under a pound: the internees
were dying of virtual starvation.[2] The companies undertook to
provide two pounds of bread and either two ounces of rice or
four ounces of vegetables to each internee per day; clothes and
straw for mattresses were also to be supplied, and raw materials
for working. The company hoped to profit from the handiwork
of the internees, a hope in which it was to be severely disillusioned,
and within months economies were being made which could not
but be detrimental to the well-being of the internees. Paramount
amongst these were economies in soap and clothing materials,
economies in the costs of an infirmary and the employment of a
doctor. Soap was not provided for personal washing purposes

---

[1] B.N. Fonds français 8130, Mémoire des États de Languedoc, 1772.
[2] A.D. Ille-et-Vilaine C 1310.

nor for all laundry. The wet nappies of babies who accompanied their mothers into the *dépôts* or who were born there were simply dried and put back. As for the adults: 'On leur laisse depuis cinq à six mois le même habit de laine qui se remplit de vermine et désole les pauvres gens . . . l'entrepreneur prétend que l'étoffe en est trop faible pour résister à ces lavages. . . . C'est son affaire d'en fournir une meilleure . . .'[1] This was at Rennes, but the same basic criticism is found at Caen, Rouen, Rodez, and in the *dépôts* of Provence and Languedoc, and in Auvergne before the de Bussy administration. In some cases the economies were to be attributed, not to the company responsible merely for supplying the institutions, but to the *régisseur* or *concierge* and corrupt officials who superintended what was done with the food and clothing supplied by the companies. These officials often sought to make a living out of goods intended for the *vagabonds*. Corruption on all fronts was at the root of criticism of the administration of the *dépôts*, particularly that voiced by ecclesiastics. Hence six *recteurs* of Rennes presented their cases in the 1780s to the *États*:

Le vice est dans l'établissement en lui-même, dans ses formes, dans les traités qui abandonnent à un entrepreneur intéressé la distribution de la subsistance des détenus, n'ayant le plus souvent à le surveiller que des yeux qu'il peut facilement corrompre. . . . C'est cet entrepreneur, le Sieur Cabane, entré sans fortune dans cette maison, qui commande en chef toutes les dépenses, c'est lui qui règle la quantité, l'espèce, le nombre de tout ce qui est fourni aux détenus. . . . On se plaint de retranchement dans les subsistances; on se plaint de fraudes dans l'appréciation du modique salaire reservé aux détenus; on se plaint que l'entrée de la maison soit rendue à ceux qui viennent les secourir en leur vendant les denrées supplémentaires à l'insuffisance de la nourriture de la maison; on se plaint que les malades soient entassés dans les mêmes lits et sans rechange. La maison de force renferme présentement . . . environ 600 détenus; sur ce nombre, dans l'espace de onze mois et demi, il en est mort 137 et cette maison dans les principes de sa constitution paraît destinée aux vagabonds et mendiants valides . . .[2]

The attack was taken up by the bishop at the *États*, reinforced by a genuine rising of distress in the *dépôt* at Rennes, which resulted

---

[1] A.D. Ille-et-Vilaine C 3796, Plainte de six recteurs de Rennes, 1786, and F. Mourlot, *La Question de la mendicité en Normandie à la fin de l'ancien régime*, p. 9.

[2] A.D. Ille-et-Vilaine C 3796.

in loss of life.[1] Less effectively the bishop of Bayeux outlined the filth and deficiencies of the *maison de force* of the *généralité* of Caen, Beaulieu, to the *intendant*, Fontette, only to receive the curt rejoinder that Monseigneur should not expect the institution to resemble in cleanliness an *hôtel Dieu*.[2] The bishops of Provence succeeded in closing two *dépôts* at Aix and Digne and in blocking the establishment of one at Marseilles on the pretext that they were breeding-grounds of disease.[3] The bishop of Rodez, Champion de Cicé, descended in full pontifical robes on the *maison de force* at Castelgaillard accompanied by a doctor and one of his *grands vicaires* and proceeded to denounce the establishment to Necker on the grounds of the drunkenness and corruption of the *concierge*, the inadequate supplies of the company, the failure to keep the internees clean, the failure to remove the dead immediately so that sick and dead shared the same bed, the lack of work, and, finally, the pervasive atmosphere of despair found in the institution.[4]

Of the *dépôts* of the *pays d'élections*, those of Bourges and Tours and of Rodez certainly represent the worst of those studied; those of Riom and Soissons the best; those of Caen, Alençon, and Rouen were probably about average. Riom, under the philanthropist—a philanthropist who was generous with time and energy rather than with funds—Henrion de Bussy, was regarded as the model *dépôt*, and de Bussy was under continual pressure to move on and, in particular, to reorganize the *dépôt* of Grenoble, regarded by the government as being in great need of attention.[5] It is worth looking at the *dépôt* of Riom and its inherent deficiencies and limitations because in this way one can assess the *dépôts* in their most favourable light. In 1785 when de Bussy arrived, the *dépôt* of Riom was remarkable for its restricted quarters. Cramped in a corner of the *hôpital général*, in a building of which the rental was 250 *livres*, the institution was running at a considerable loss because the company had pulled out, leaving the enterprise to an honest local curé who saw to it that the

---

[1] A.D. Ille-et-Vilaine C 4937, Commission Intermédiaire. Maison de force établie à Rennes. Mémoire pour en demander la suppression.
[2] A.D. Calvados H, Suppl. 1308 11 G 5.
[3] C. Paultre, *De la répression de la mendicité*, p. 482.
[4] A.D. Aveyron C 324, Letter from Mgr de Cicé to Necker, 13 Aug. 1780.
[5] The *dépôts* of the Auvergne are abundantly documented; see A.D. Puy-de-Dôme C 1044–1221, yet the source has been little used.

internees received a proper daily ration of $2\frac{1}{2}$ pounds of maslin bread and two daily rations of vegetables and that they changed their linen twice a week. The infirmary was so small as to be useless; the internees had no bed-clothes but slept on straw that was renewed at intervals; moreover, there was little or no work for them. The size of the establishment did not mean that the *maréchaussée* curtailed the numbers of arrests but that the sentences given had to be of short duration. In other words, the composition of the establishment was constantly changing; the average sentence lay between three and six months, and the deterrent nature of a sentence of this length was questionable. Indeed, de Bussy argued that, far from being a deterrent, it was a positive incentive to get oneself arrested:

Une réclusion de trois à six mois n'est rien pour ces gens là, à présent ils sont tous instruits de la règle, ils ne la craignent pas. Loin d'en être effrayés, ils s'y livrent souvent avec plaisir, c'est un moment de repos de leur vie, qui, toute attrayante qu'elle est pour eux, ne laisse pas que d'avoir des fatigues. Voyant un terme fixe et court à leur détention ils calculent d'une part que c'est le tems nécessaire pour se délivrer de leur vermine, se guérir de leurs maux et ulcères, pour se rafraîchir le sang, renouveller leurs forces et s'engraisser.[1]

As for women, and Henrion de Bussy was a woman-hater of the first degree, he claimed that when the side effects of a licentious existence became apparent, that was the time to get arrested for a three-month cure: 'la vermine, la gale, une grossesse, une maladie vénérienne, une dissolution de société, une diffamation, un discrédit dans leur quartier, et un banissement leur présentent alors un dépôt comme un secours nécessaire'.[2] In other words, not only was there a rapid turnover in vagrants far from deterred by their stay but also a continual influx of noxious disease. De Bussy arrived in the middle of an epidemic of dysentery and he was alarmed at the rapidity with which such an affliction could spread. He needed, urgently, a better pharmacy, improved water supplies, since he was convinced that the water at the disposal of

[1] A.D. Puy-de-Dôme C 1195.
[2] Ibid. One can profitably compare the case of Marie-Jeanne Prioult, '23 ans, native d'Alençon, ayant une maladie vénérienne et n'ayant pas le moyen de se faire traiter, elle est venue mendier en cette ville (Caen) pour se faire arrêter et mettre au dépôt, vu qu'on ne guérit point de ces sortes de maladies au dépôt d'Alençon'. A.D. Calvados 9 B 63. 200.

the *dépôt* was polluted, and, most important, extended buildings. The next years were to see an endless struggle with the *contrôleur général* to achieve all these things. He wanted, above all, to get sentences extended so that real correctional training could take place. The children who were taken in should learn both the habits of industry and the virtues of a regular life. They should also have some religious instruction—particularly the catechism. The present system of keeping them only for a few weeks and then boarding them out with families little better than those from which they originated was futile. Under no circumstances should the young be taken from their mothers. Three months was insufficient to persuade a vagrant prostitute to mend her ways. The ingrained vagrant needed the deterrent of a long period of correctional incarceration with cuts in diet and solitary confinement for insolence.

The net result of four years' campaigning was an improved pharmacy, a number of sheets and primitive bunks, and an improved water supply. An irritated *contrôleur général* refused to allow de Bussy to extend sentences, or indeed to keep anyone in the *dépôt* beyond the normal short period, or to introduce innovations into the treatment of children. The *dépôt* of Riom, he stated, must conform to the practices carried out in the rest of the *dépôts* of France.[1] At the root of the hostility to de Bussy's proposals was the reluctance to spend more money on larger buildings. De Bussy knew this to be true and tried to supply the government with new ideas—stop paying the *maréchaussée* a bonus for each beggar arrested and use the proceeds to improve the *dépôts*.[2] By 1788 he had despaired. His indictment of the whole system of the *dépôts*, based on experience at Riom, summarized above, was printed and read out to the *Commission Intermédiaire* of the provincial assembly.[3] He might have included his register, which showed that many of those arrested—over 50 per cent in fact— were making an appearance in the *dépôt* for the third, fourth, or fifth time.[4] Few areas produced so many vagrants as the Auvergne, or vagrants so devious, yet many of the features outlined at Riom have their parallel elsewhere. The enforced shortness of sentence owing to the inadequacy of the buildings is found everywhere, in both *pays d'élections* and *pays d'États*, and the total futility of life

---

[1] A.D. Puy-de-Dôme C 1202.   [2] Ibid.
[3] Ibid. C 1204.   [4] Ibid. C 1216.

in the *dépôts* is repeatedly manifest. Dangerous associations were formed, the nucleus of bands of thieves; disease was contracted, particularly syphilis. If life in the *dépôt* was a deterrent (and there is no evidence that it was), it was so because the odds on succumbing to epidemic were so high.

One final point remains to be examined: did the *dépôts* contain the right people; did they protect society against the sort of vagrants it feared? Who were the internees of the *dépôts*?

Terray in a letter of 1772 sought to divide them into three categories:

Les pauvres âgés ou infirmes et les mendiants de profession qui doivent être retenus jusqu'à ce que des parents ou amis les réclament et signent pour eux une soumission de ne plus mendier.

Les mendiants valides qui savent un métier; il ne faut les garder qu'un temps suffisant pour leur servir de correction et les relâcher, sans même exiger de soumission, dès qu'ils manifestent de repentir.

Les détenus que le défaut d'ouvrage ou la cherté des denrées a amenés au dépôt; on peut les mettre en liberté pour profiter des travaux qu'amènera la récolte . . .[1]

Then there were two special categories: the insane whose families refused to care for them, and prostitutes if they were *vagabondes* (i.e. taken soliciting or begging one and a half miles from home) or if contaminated with venereal disease and interned at the request and at the expense of the army. The *vénériennes* were a special problem for all *dépôts*, not only because of the disease they spread, but because their condition, if advanced, and it usually was, was incurable. Hence they could not be released without danger. The *intendant* at Montpellier described three *vénériennes*: one was in the final stages of disintegration, and two were physically still capable of work but incapable of finding it, for who would employ them?[2] To release these three could only entail disaster.

The 1,047 individuals who passed through the *dépôt* of Riom between 1769 and 1789 have been analysed as 25 per cent rural *iournaliers*, 18 per cent urban *ouvriers*, 8 per cent *laboureurs*, 4 per

[1] The text of this edict is found in A.N. T 978 and A.D. Puy-de-Dôme C 1132.
[2] A.D. Hérault C 562.

cent *vignerons*, and 3 per cent *laboureurs*, up to 20 per cent *colporteurs*;[1] at Soissons in 1786, 256 out of 854 held in the *dépôt* were 'ouvriers réduits à la mendicité par le chômage' (tailors, wigmakers, weavers, and, above all, shoemakers), and 294 'ouvriers des campagnes qui deviennent mendiants aussitôt que les travaux des champs cessent de les occuper', the rest were insane, *filles publiques vénériennes*, and aged perpetual beggars.[1] At Alençon, out of a restricted number of known occupation, 29·5 per cent fitted into the category of rural *journaliers*, 25·3 per cent into that of *ouvriers* (tailors, hatters, wigmakers, bakers, millers, shoemakers), followed by out-of-work textile workers (17·8 per cent), then pedlars and tinkers (11·9 per cent), servants (6·9 per cent), masons (5·6 per cent), and former soldiers (not deserters) (3·2 per cent).[2]

At Vannes about 40 per cent of 524 internees were agricultural workers, seasonally unemployed, 10 per cent *marchands ambulants* or *mercelots*, as they were known in Brittany, 15 per cent unemployed textile workers, and the rest women, children, and aged.[3] Approximately the same 'mix' could be found at Rennes. In fact these instances are sufficient to indicate the narrowness of difference. At any one time a *dépôt* could usually be shown to contain between 30 and 40 per cent rural *journaliers* seasonally laid off, up to 30 per cent *ouvriers réduits par le chômage*, 10 per cent itinerant traders, and the rest an indeterminate hotchpotch of unclassified trades, derelict prostitutes, aged and children, and insane of the wilder variety.[4] Evidently, in offering an occupation, the accused were stressing the more positive side of their existence and many had not practised the occupation they chose to give for months, some even for years.

The origin of the internees reflects something of the varying regional incidence of seasonal migrations. In Vannes and Rennes

---

[1] R. Liris, 'Mendicité et vagabondage en Basse Auvergne à la fin du XVIIIe siècle', *Revue d'Auvergne*, lxxix (1965), 70.

[2] M. Montlinot, *État actuel du dépôt de Soissons* (Paris, 1789), pp. 10–15.

[3] Boucheron, 'La Montée du flot des errants', p. 66.

[4] Guéguen, 'La Mendicité', pp. 126–9.

[5] This is very approximate. At Caen in 1777, of the 240 internees 40 were prostitutes, 35 insane, 22 children (usually of imprisoned women), 6 were put there at the request of relatives for stealing, and 2 were old and blind. The remaining 135 were former *ouvriers* or *journaliers* (A.D. Calvados C 611, Dépôt de Beaulieu). Only 50 per cent of the total number of internees were physically capable of light cotton-spinning (A.D. Calvados C 678, Dépôt de Beaulieu).

between 92 and 95 per cent of those arrested were Bretons—
'la province la plus casanière de la France'. They were inland
Bretons from Faouët, Guéméné, Pontivy, Locminé, Bannalec and
Cahaix, Loudéac, Quintin, La Guerche; the prosperous coastline
threw up few beggars, with the exception of Lorient, which felt
the collapse of the Compagnie des Indes.[1] In Normandy, at least
in the *dépôts* at Caen and at Rouen, three-quarters would seem to
have been of the region, but at Alençon the proportion was considerably smaller, somewhere around 50 per cent coming from
the region and the rest mostly drawn from the north, seasonal
workers either going to, or returning from, the harvest of the
Beauce.[2] The *dépôts* of Moulins and Bourges strongly reflected
the northward movement of Auvergnats towards Paris;[3] that of
Lyons the Forézien, Bresse–Bugey influx.[4] The *dépôt* at Montpellier might have borne witness to the mobility of seasonal
labour from the Rouergue and the Gévaudan, had not the *intendant* refused to accept such internees.[5] Certainly La Grave at
Toulouse, part *hôpital général*, part *maison de force*, had its contingent
from the Comminges and this was largely composed of women
who had left the mountains for the winter to beg in the warmer
city and turned prostitute.[6]

By law, after arrest and conviction, beggars had to be trans-
ferred to the *dépôt* nearest their parish of origin. Over half of those
sent back to Riom were seasonal labourers making their way
north who had been caught begging a livelihood at Moulins,
Bourges, Orleans, and Saint-Denis, a further third making their
way east were taken to the *dépôts* of Lyons and Chalons.[7] The
link between seasonal migration and part-time begging is writ

[1] Guéguen, 'La Mendicité', p. 121, and A.D. Ille-et-Vilaine C 1308.

[2] The *dépôts* of Normandy have received extensive coverage, Boucheron, 'La
Montée du flot des errants'; Mourlot, *La Question de la mendicité en Normandie*; and
M. Deschamps, 'Le Dépôt de mendicité de Rouen, 1768–1820' (Diplôme d'Études
Supérieures, Caen, 1965) and *Résumé Bull. soc. fr. d'hist. des hôpitaux*, xix (1968),
24–5.

[3] Liris, 'Mendicité et vagabondage', pp. 65–78.

[4] Gutton, *La Société et les pauvres*, pp. 462–5.

[5] A.D. Hérault C 574, Registre contenant les noms des mendiants arrêtés et
conduits dans les trois dépôts établis dans la province de Languedoc, 1768. Under
a sixth of internees at Montpellier were Rouergats or Gévaudois, more were
Cévenols or Provençaux.

[6] Ibid. and A.D. Hérault C 563, Hôpital général de Saint Joseph de la Grave à
Toulouse. États.

[7] Liris, 'Mendicité et vagabondage', pp. 65–78.

large in the registers of Riom. The Serre brothers of Mazoires had worked 'à remonter les bâteaux sur la Loire', but the river had become ice-bound and they were forced to beg their way back home; Antoine Julliard, 56 years old, native of Murols, 'avait coutume d'aller tous les hivers à Paris, pour y porter de l'eau et du bois';[1] Antoine Buisson, 13 years, chimney-sweep, 'abandonné par le maître à qui on l'avait loué';[2] Saint-Jean, 25 years, *décrotteur de souliers*, making his way to Paris.[3] There was evidence, too, of occasional returns to the family by those who had made a longer severance with their native village. Pierre-Antoine Benoît, *garçon meunier*, 44 years old, native of Riom, who had lived in Paris for four years, faubourg Saint-Antoine, 'chez le nommé Giroux, marchand de moulins à café', had begged his way home to see his wife;[4] Jean Burand, aged 23, having spent five years away from home, peddling and making rosary beads.[5]

The threat of the *dépôt de mendicité* was certainly no disincentive to the seasonal migrants who left the Auvergne according to their own patterns and begged their way north or east, nor did it stop the aged or homeless children from trying their hand. For what alternative had they? The boy of 12, of Scaer in Brittany, for example, whose father had died and whose mother had struggled alone to support him 'par son travail et par une vache qu'elle avait. Elle est morte de misère.'[6] Homeless, he was taken in 1770 at Quimperlé and died ten months later in the *dépôt* at Vannes; or two brothers of Ploemeur, near Lorient, whose parents were in prison for helping thieves: aged respectively 12 and 14, they had worked as rope-makers at Lorient until the collapse of the Compagnie des Indes, when they found themselves forced 'de chercher l'aumône pour se nourrir, eux et leur petite sœur âgée de cinq ans'.[7] There were those taken by the *maréchaussée* in the act of begging who were too young to reply to questions: Gervaise and Anne Séranges, aged 2 and 6 respectively, or Jean Masson, 6 years old, put out to beg by his aunt.[8] Marie, Michelle, and Antoine Bertrand were more lucid, 'leur mère ne peut pas les nourrir'. François, Anne, Julien, and Marie Gaby, aged 6–12, the children of school teachers at Riom, were found with

---

[1] A.D. Puy-de-Dôme C 1235, Antoine Julliard.
[2] Ibid. C 1253, Antoine Buisson.   [3] Ibid. C 1265, Saint-Jean.
[4] Ibid. C 1240, Pierre-Antoine Benoît.   [5] Ibid. 1232, Jean Burand.
[6] Guéguen, 'La Mendicité', p. 124.   [7] Ibid., p. 125.
[8] A.D. Puy-de-Dôme C 1227, Séranges; Masson.

outstretched hands in the market-place.[1] Children of a year are
found in the registers of arrests at Riom. More frequently they
accompanied out-of-work parents in the move from country to
town. In 1779, out of 127 'vagabonds' arrested in the streets of
Riom and Clermont, twenty-seven were *ouvriers réduits par le
chômage* who had left the country for the town in search of work.[2]
Their wives and children followed, and entire family units
could be picked up—though to get a whole family at one fell
swoop was rare. Parents rarely begged together: one adult in
charge of a brood of children was more deserving of pity than
were two.

Nor can one see much hope of an alternative source of existence
for the old in cases such as that of Nicolas Miniard, 72 years old
and of limited strength, native of Jumeaux and *portefaix* of the
parish of Saint-Pierre-de-Clermont, or François Vigier, 70 years
old, former cook to the canons of Vieille-Brioude.[3] One can
multiply such examples. Each of the seventy-five old men and
women held at Vannes offered a case-history that reads like a
martyrology: senility, debility, loneliness, suffering. Where were
the relatives who were supposed to claim them? Where were the
hôpitaux designed to succour the old? Where was shelter for the
deformed? (Illness or an accident incurred at work put many on
the roads, and the *procès-verbaux* notes an individual, 'ayant eu la
jambe gauche cassée, devenu estropié du bras droit et de la jambe
gauche, ses yeux ne lui permettant plus de travailler.')[4] The
answer to these questions would seem to be that they were non-
existent and that what the *dépôts* were doing for the weak and
infirm was providing an uncomfortable substitute for the *hôpitaux*
which were too small and inadequate to cope. Certainly these
were not elements society had any reason to fear. From the point
of view of the public, more pertinent is a consideration of how
many of those held in the *dépôts* at any one time were social undesirables, had begged to the tune of threats, had stolen, had been
in some way violent and so had shown themselves to constitute
a real danger to society. The answer would seem to be never
more than half and usually less than a third. Hence of the 6,650

[1] A. D. Puy-de-Dôme C 1236, Gaby.
[2] Liris, 'Mendicité et vagabondage', p. 70.
[3] A.D. Puy-de-Dôme C 1228, Miniard; Vigier.
[4] Boucheron, 'La Montée du flot des errants', p. 67.

men, women, and children in the *dépôts* in 1789, probably about
2,500 were beggars or vagrants of this type, a derisory figure.[1]
For society at large equally important is the question, did the
dépôts stem the rising tide of vagrant bands intimidating the
countryside?

That these bands were on the increase throughout the 1770s
and 1780s needs no arguing—bands of a dozen, such as ravaged
the environs of Plouay, Lorient, and Hennebont in Brittany in
1775, 1779, 1785, 1786, and 1787; bands of fifty, like that of
Gautier in the Loire valley; bands of 100, like that of François
Bridat near Langres; bands of 200, like that of Hulin in the
Beauce, or the curious, amorphous, and violent *bande de Forez*.
Individual members of these doubtless passed into the *dépôts*—
and out again—and the recurrent question: *étiez-vous associé avec
quelque autre mendiant* certainly showed the preoccupation of judges
with groups of intimidating vagrants. About a quarter of the
Hulin *bande* had at one time or another passed a spell in the *dépôt*.
Clearly, then, the *dépôts* were little, if any, deterrent. The random
swoops of the *maréchaussée*, the higher probability of being picked
up in the town than in the country, the impotence of the farmer
when confronted with a group of vagrants served only, as Turgot,
the États de Bretagne, and the bishop of Rodez—to cite merely
three instances—proclaimed, to push the vagrant more deeply
into the countryside, to multiply the incentives to band together
so as to lessen the likelihood of resistance from the country
people. Though Turgot's attempts at closing the *dépôts* in 1776
met with popular opposition from a society which believed any
institution better than none, their reopening had little long-term
effect. A few months after their reopening the *intendant* of Brittany
wrote to Necker:

La publicité de cette loi a eu en apparence, dans le premier moment
tout l'effet qu'on devait en attendre; la plus grande partie des mendiants des villes ont disparu; quelques uns ont profité des travaux de
la campagne pour y chercher de l'emploi, les autres (et c'est le plus
grand nombre) se sont retirés dans les campagnes pour y mettre les
paysans à contribution et y continuer avec insolence leur profession
de mendiant. La maréchaussée a arrêté en partie les incursions de ces
vagabonds en les faisant arrêter et conduire au dépôt de Rennes; mais

---

[1] Bloch and Tuetey, *Procès-verbaux*, p. 523.

ce moyen est devenu bientôt impraticable par l'impossibilité où on s'est trouvé de recevoir un plus grand nombre de mendiants dans cette maison.[1]

Yet another *grand projet du renfermement des pauvres* had met with unqualified failure.

[1] A.D. Ille-et-Vilaine C 1294, Letter of 8 Aug. 1777.

IX

THEFT

Les journaliers qui sont les deux tiers du pays . . . sont
réduits faute d'ouvrage à la plus désolante misère. . . .
Le besoin extrême ou le vol sont les deux alternatives
nécessairement inévitables d'un pays dont le grand
nombre d'indigent ne peut vivre que par son travail, son
seul bien.
Subdélégué of Corlay, 1772 (A.D. Ille-et-Vilaine C 1720).

'— Interrogé . . . d'où provient un drap dont il a été
trouvé saisi en sortant de l'Hostel Dieu,
— A dit qu'il allait voir un de ses camarades malades, . . .
qu'il a été en effet trouvé saisi emportant un morceau de
linge qu'il avait trouvé dans les commodités qu'il ne prit
pas pour un drap et qu'il crut pouvoir se l'approprier
sans aucune consequénce . . .'
Interrogatoire de Jean Malechecq (A.N. Y 10464).

THE acts of begging and vagrancy clearly placed the practitioner
on the wrong side of the law even if the chances of apprehension
were restricted. It was unlikely, however, that the crimes of the
poor would be confined to these simple acts, and the purport of
preceding sections has been to stress that in a popular sense
begging and vagrancy only became offensive when coupled with
theft and menaces of fire. Poverty, in spite of the evangelists, is
usually a corrupting process. Certainly it is rarely conducive to
honest living, and to live in the midst of those possessed of something posed a temptation for the obviously deprived. One might
reasonably expect a period of hardship for the poor such as
marked the second decade of the eighteenth century to be one
of mounting crime, at least in respect of minor theft. The results
of attempts to quantify eighteenth-century crime confirm this
expectation.[1] Thieves and bandits were evidently on the increase,

[1] A plea for criminality under the *ancien régime* as a quantitative study is found in
F. Billaçois, 'Pour une enquête sur la criminalité dans la France d'ancien régime',
A.E.S.C. xxii (1967), 340–9. Published studies dealing with Normandy include
B. Boutelet, 'Étude par sondage de la criminalité dans le bailliage du Pont de l'Arche',
Annales de Normandie, xii (1962), 235–63, and J. C. Gégot, 'Étude par sondage de la

as the registers of lawcourts from *prévôtés* to *parlements* uniformly attest, and theft of one kind or another—*vol, vol avec effraction, vol avec attroupement, vol avec porte d'armes, vol en grand chemin, vol domestique, vol d'église,* often subtle distinctions but carefully classified by *ancien régime* legislators—tops the bill in any enumeration of crimes committed. Up to 80 or 90 per cent of the business of *prévôtés, présidiaux, bailliages* and *sénéchaussées,* and the *parlements* fell into this category,[1] and this without consideration of thefts and property offences brought before the seigneurial courts and the special offences which were the preserve of the *eaux et forêts.*[2] Poaching, transgressing against the property rights of the *seigneur,* and, above all, stealing firewood, acorns for animal fodder, or

criminalité dans le bailliage de Falaise (XVIIe–XVIIIe siècles)', *Annales de Normandie,* xvi (1966), 103–64, and, isolating special cases, P. Crépillon, 'Un Gibier des prévôts. Mendiants et vagabonds au XVIIIe siècle entre la Vire et la Dives', *Annales de Normandie,* xvii (1967), 223–52. Unfortunately much of the preoccupation of the above work is testing the *violence au vol* syndrome of Lucien Fèvre, and there is little attempt to classify the crimes committed beyond the simple crude categorization of theft. Work on criminality in Languedoc is well under way and heralded in a brilliant *aperçu*: N. Castan, 'La Criminalité à la fin de l'ancien régime dans les pays de Languedoc', *Bull. d'hist. écon. et soc.* (1969), pp. 59–68. Already the subject is a favoured one for minor theses, and a good instance is A. Rignac, 'La Criminalité à Toulouse à la fin de l'ancien régime' (Diplôme d'Études Supérieures, Toulouse, 1962). Some interim results and a bibliography of theses in progress have now appeared in A. Abbiateci and F. Billaçois, *Crimes et criminalité en France 17e–18e siècles* (Paris, 1972), comprehending matter ranging further than the crimes of the poor.

¹ 99·2 per cent of Parisian crime fell into this category: P. Petrovitch, 'Recherches sur la criminalité à Paris dans la seconde moitié du XVIIIe siècle', in Abbiateci and Billaçois, *Crimes et criminalité,* p. 209. Otherwise the generalization is based upon the works listed above (p. 245, n. 1), and A.D. Lozère 21B5–21B11 (Prévôté de Mende); A.D. Haute-Marne, Maréchaussée de Langres (unclassified); A.D. Finistère B 830–900; A.D. Aveyron B, Présidial de Villefranche de Rouergue, 1780–9; A.D. Haute-Saône B, Présidial de Gray, 1770–89; A.D. Dordogne B 1624–42, Sénéchaussée-présidial de Sarlat, B 1695–99, Prévôté de Sarlat, B 1142–3, Maréchaussée de Périgueux.

The *inventaire* of the destroyed archives of the Loiret is also a mine of information, and though it merely offers summaries of cases, they often embody the crux of the issue. One of the main problems confronting the would-be historian of criminality is that many departmental series B remain unclassified; others are fragmentary and the series as a whole abounds in incomplete documentation. One of the best old studies (albeit astatistical) is that of two retired lawyers: A. M. Corre and P. Aubry, *Documents de criminologie rétrospective, Bretagne, XVIIe et XVIIIe siècles* (Paris, 1895).

² Seigneurial justice awaits more historians, but see A. Combier, *Les Justices seigneuriales du bailliage de Vermandois sous l'ancien régime* (Paris, 1897), P. Lemercier, *Les Justices seigneuriales de la région parisienne de 1580 à 1789* (Paris, 1933). On forest offences, H. Hours, 'Émeutes et émotions populaires dans les campagnes du Lyonnais au XVIIIe siècle', *Cahiers d'histoire* (1964).

allowing one's scraggy beasts to pasture themselves at the expense of the royal demesne were probably the commonest crimes—to such an extent that in a popular sense they were scarcely considered crimes at all, though punishable by severe fines. The almost equally common theft of manure was regarded more seriously. In Brittany whole villages in the vicinity of Tréguier gave themselves up to such pursuits either for their own usage or for that of neighbouring villages,[1] whilst smuggling, robbing the revenue—an abstraction which few in eighteenth-century France could say a good word for—was so integral a part of the economy of the poor that it requires separate treatment. We are here concerned with theft in its narrowest sense: a crime committed against another individual.

Crime of course was not the monopoly of the poor, but the crimes of the poor were those most likely to come before the courts, and that even in a society where crime was under-recorded and the chances of actually being caught and brought to justice for one's misdemeanours remote.

This was because legislators assumed that the poor were the most crime-prone sector of society, liable at any time to attack the property of the more affluent, and shaped the judicial structure to cope with this assumption. The mechanism for the apprehension and punishment of the *poor* criminal, though a primitive combination of a derisory police force dependent upon informers and confessions and a confusing tangle of jurisdictions, at least had some reality. In the *maréchaussée* and *prévôté* courts, beggars, vagrants, and poor thieves commanded a monopoly of attention.[2] To be brought before such a court was almost proof that one belonged amongst the down-and-out, amongst those whose word could not be trusted without the testimony of parish priest or syndic. In a rare case a bourgeois woman was caught pickpocketing at a fair, held by two women who saw her in the act, and reported to the police. Brought before the jurisdiction at Bégard, she was sentenced to a public flogging and restitution. She appealed to the *présidial* at Rennes, which rescinded the sentence, on the grounds that one could not thus treat a woman of some social standing, and substituted a fine.[3] This sort of treat-

---

1 Quellien, *L'Argot des nomades*, p. 7.
2 G. Larrieu, *Histoire de la gendarmerie*, pp. 135–73.
3 A.D. Côtes-du-Nord B 151.

ment was by definition reserved for the poor and was intended
both to punish the wrongdoer and to deter other poor people
who might be thus inclined. A bourgeois lady, however errant,
was not the concern of the *prévôtés*. Justice was not designed to
deal with the wealthy and sophisticated embezzler, murderer,
thief, or trickster who stood a good chance of evading justice
unless brought to court by an interested party. The justice of the
bailliage or *sénéchaussée* is about compensation; that of the *prévôtés*
about punishment.[1] *Prévôtal* justice is the brutal justice of the
harsh example: the justice of an unpoliced society which made
its assumptions and acted accordingly. People who came before
such courts could not expect any leniency, no matter how extenuating their personal circumstances might be. Most did not bother
to put up any defence beyond outright denial, and appeal was
almost unknown. Much of what follows reflects the workings
of the *prévôtés* or *maréchaussées*, though their coverage was not
universal. The domiciled offending poor of the towns might fall
under the justice of the *bailliage* or, in the cities with *parlements*,
be the concern of the Tournelle or the Châtelet. It could make an
enormous difference, for the *bailliages* had no power to inflict the
death penalty, whilst the *prévôtés* had the power. Indeed, it is a
mark of what administrators thought about the poor that they
permitted the severest penalty to be inflicted by the least important, the lowliest court of first instance. Moreover, it ensured that
for the homeless and jobless there was nothing but the most
harsh, the most summary, justice.

Though the letter of the law varied from province to province
and some *coutumes* treated some kinds of theft differently from
others, everywhere a number of broad categories of theft were
employed. First, *vol simple*, a large categorization comprehending
all theft without additional offences. The penalty varied according
to the value of the goods and according to the circumstances.
It could entail for goods valued at less than 10 *livres* a simple
flogging, but above that sum it could, at the discretion of the judge,
entail the death penalty though, unless it was a repeated offence,
it almost never did. Theoretically the *coutume de Bretagne* authorized the death penalty for those who stole oxen needed for plough-
ing the fields, since the implications of such a crime could threaten

---

[1] P. Chaunu compares 'la criminalité accidentelle des bailliages et la société en
marge des cas prévôtaux', Foreword to Gégot, 'Étude par sondage', p. 106.

the livelihood of several people, but by the end of the eighteenth
century the steepest punishment inflicted for such a felony was
life in the galleys; it was the same in Normandy and Anjou, where
the *coutume* offered death to the horse thief.[1]

Vol avec effraction, breaking and entry, was potentially a more
serious offence than *vol simple*; it was regarded as even more
serious if it occurred at night, and most serious of all if the
burglars sought in addition to disguise themselves or use violence.
Theft accompanied by any kind of disguise, even a primitive
mask, added to the penalty because it widened the burglar's
chance of escaping undetected and hence, in the event of apprehension, had to be given an extra punishment. *Vol avec effraction*
accompanied by violence could entail death by hanging preceded
by breaking on the wheel. *Vol avec effraction* at night could incur
in addition *la question*, torture immediately before the application
of the death penalty to reveal one's accomplices. Torture in the
late eighteenth century was only applied to those already condemned to death—needful, for few survived the stretching,
burning, or drowning, varying according to the provincial
coutume.

Armed robbery in which no one had actually suffered physical
injury was punishable by a fine of 500 *livres* in the first instance
and incarceration for six months; the second time the offender
was fined 1,000 *livres* and sent to the galleys for two years.[2] This
was of course a very academic type of punishment: the thieves
of the *prévôté* courts would probably not have been there had they
had such sums at their disposal in the first place and hence the
punishment for armed robbery tended to be, at the discretion of
the judge, a number of years in the galleys, or, if any violence at
all had been used, the death penalty. The arms in question were
rarely firearms, unless the offender happened to be a deserter;
clubs and axes were the commonest weapons, and if the offenders
did by chance have firearms at their disposal, the odds on their
being able to use them efficiently were remote. The *prévôté* at

---

[1] Corre and Aubry, *Documents de criminologie*, p. 136; D. Houard, *Dictionnaire
analytique . . . de la coutume de Normandie* (1782), t. iv, *Vol*. The *coutume d'Anjou*
treated the theft of a horse in the same way and accorded the death penalty to the
horse thief on the grounds that the horse was a noble animal and without it the
chevalier could not fight. This aspect of the *coutume d'Anjou* passed into English
law.

[2] Larrieu, *Histoire de la gendarmerie*, pp. 172-3.

Mende dealt with at least two would-be robbers who shot themselves instead of their victims.[1]

Vol en grand chemin incurred the death penalty; the highwayman
was condemned to *expirer vif sur la roue*, and the full penalty was
exacted at the least suspicion of violence, and often without such
suspicion. *Vol domestique* was a tricky issue. The servant had considerable advantages in performing a theft from his master's
dwelling. He knew where the keys were kept and the likely place
for the concealment of valuables. He could gauge the resources
of the household. He could act when the family slept. But more
than this, a master needed to be able to trust his servant and the
thieving domestic violated a contract. The employer needed
guarantees against such a violation and the law sought to give
them by awarding the thieving servant death on the gibbet.
Moreover, the word 'servant' was given a broad application; it
extended to the porter one employed to carry one's parcels and
who absconded taking them with him; it extended to the laundress
who collected the soiled linen from one's residence and either
never returned it or profited from the visit. It automatically embraced all one's employees, journeymen, apprentices, *valets de
ferme*, seamstresses who turned up to perform work in one's
house and who used the opportunity to rob their employer. It
comprehended employees in the hotel where one was staying.[2]
Vol domestique of the most trivial nature could entail the death
penalty unless the culprit was under 15 and the theft of an extremely minor nature, in which case the judge might show
clemency and content himself with a public flogging and branding,
so that if a repeated theft occurred the offender could go straight
to the gibbet.[3] The employer could make matters easier for the
offending servant by taking the affair into the *bailliage* court—in
which case he sought only restitution and costs.[4] Or, if very
clement, presumably he simply dismissed the servant. *Prévôtal*

---

[1] A.D. Lozère 21B10, Alègre Rouverand, 21B11, Pierre Nogaret.

[2] A.D. Finistère, Fonds des régaires de Léon (cited Corre and Aubry, pp. 124–6)
offers the case of two hôtel cooks thus accused; at Périgueux, A.D. Dordogne
B 649 1773, B 694 1778, a *portefaix* and *couturière* were in question.

[3] A.D. Finistère B 843, 845, 848, 851 are instances of *vol domestique* terminating
in the death sentence. Even in the case of children this could occur, Y. Bougert,
'Délinquance juvénile et responsabilité pénale du mineur au XVIIIe siècle', in
Crimes et criminalité, p. 79.

[4] A.D. Dordogne B 698, B 731, etc.

justice merely offered punishment and a social guarantee that the crime would not be repeated by the offender in question.

Vol d'église was of course, technically, sacrilege. The profane merited death by fire. It was in dealing with this particular crime, however, that the greatest provincial discrepancies occurred. In Languedoc the *prévôté* of Mende claimed the full penalty against two brothers who stole an altar cloth in 1787; a similar instance occurred at Montpellier in 1789.[1] In Brittany the thieves of *troncs* and church silver could expect a minimum of twelve years in the galleys;[2] the *prévôté* of Langres and the *présidial* of Gray (*coutume de Bourgogne*) imposed two to five years in the galleys. Where parish priests brought cases against their parishioners for stealing church property in Normandy and Périgord—to the *bailliage* or *sénéchaussée*—they gained restitution and a fine.[3]

For any kind of crime the individual judge and the individual court varied in the sentences they sought to impose. At Mende the theft of a horse under analogous circumstances entailed sentences varying from five to nine years in the galleys, and that for a first offence;[4] similarly, the theft of four handkerchiefs fetched in the same court on one occasion a penalty of three years in the galleys, on two others, hanging—nor were the circumstances offered in the first instance peculiarly extenuating.[5] Repeated crime, however, which usually meant a second *known* offence, almost automatically entailed the death penalty anywhere, no matter how trivial the value of the goods in question. Hence whether one turns to Breton courts or those of Burgundy, Périgord, Berry, the Rouergue, or Languedoc, the sentences are essentially the same, and Guillaume Pariou (aged 16), *faiseur de filets de pêche* of Poulan, tried at Landerneau on the following charges

d'avoir le dimanche 4 mars 1731 entré par la fenêtre chez le nommé Vincent Philipot, du village de Keryven, paroisse de Plouneventer, et d'y avoir enlevé et volé une pièce de Berlinge et d'y avoir le trois

---

[1] A.D. Lozère 21B11, the case of the three Arnals.

[2] A.D. Finistère B 814, 840.

[3] In the cases cited by J. Gégot, 'Étude par sondage', p. 116: one *pilleur des troncs d'églises* was merely banished from the jurisdiction of the *bailliage* of Falaise and received a fine of 100 *sols*; another who stole a church bench had to replace it and pay a fine of 60 *sols* and the costs of the suit.

[4] A.D. Lozère 21B5, Estvenon, 1773; 21B6, Pergorier, 1774; 21B8, Dumas, 1779.

[5] A.D. Lozère 21B5, J. Antoine, 1773, Mercier, 1773; 21B8, Robert.

du même mois, volé une paire de bas de soie chez Vincent Paramount
de la ville de Landerneau

and sentenced to hanging and 'la question extraordinaire et
ordinaire pour avoir révélation de ses complices et receleurs',
would have fared no differently in any other *prévôté* court.[1]
Previous records of course were not easy to establish unless the
offender carried with him the purely physical one of a brand
mark on his shoulder: G.A.L. marked the *galérien*—death for
him the next time he came before a *prévôté*; V the vagabond; M the
man who had begged with insolence—he too if now proved guilty
of theft of any considerable nature could expect short shrift. The
maréchaussée clearly made a point of inquiring in the vicinity about
an apprehended offender, and people anxious to be rid of someone
generally feared or regarded as a nuisance would come forward
and report crimes of up to fifteen years ago in the hope of being
quit of him once and for all (hence 'que le dit Faugin est reconnu
dans le pays pour un voleur d'habitude' or 'il fait métier et
profession d'attendre sur les grands chemins et chemins de
traverse les passants pour les attaquer et les voler').[2] If this proved
unsuccessful, the overlapping of jurisdictions made the establishment of a record almost impossible.

Broadly speaking, the law and the judges who applied it
followed a few simple principles. The rudimentary nature of
policing meant that the number of offenders who came before the
courts was an infinitesimal proportion of those who committed
crime; they must be severely punished to deter other would-be
offenders. The *easier* the crime they had committed, the steeper
the penalty. Theft of corn and timber *exposés à la foi publique* on
wharves or in warehouses, animals grazing in fields beyond the
surveillance of shepherd or cowman, merchandise laid on stalls
or in carts at fairs, luggage left in carriages awaiting the owner,
and any attack on the isolated traveller—such were the crimes
liable to incur the longest spells in the galleys or, if violence had
been used, the death penalty; for here the need for severe deterrent justice was greatest. The existence of the galleys made it
easier to give a heavy punishment to men rather than women;
in fact, between a spell in a *dépôt de mendicité* and death by hanging,

[1] A.D. Finistère B 847; A.D. Lozère 21B8, Robert, 21B6, A. Blanc.
[2] A.D. Côtes-du-Nord B 912, B 1121, Dinan.

there was almost no penalty that could be inflicted upon a woman. Moreover, the death penalty had to be the straight one of hanging; one could not break a woman on the wheel for the public to gaze upon, nor could one torture her. Added to this, one could not take the life of a pregnant woman.[1] Judges usually dealt with women with relative leniency. They awarded them the death penalty for the same reason as men on most occasions—though the Jeanne Arnal who filched the altar cloth with her husband and brother-in-law at Mende got a mere three years in the *dépôt de mendicité* at Montpellier, while they perished by fire[2]—but otherwise, for even quite large thefts they escaped with a short spell in the *dépôts*, and the general principle of death for repeated thefts occasionally breaks down in respect of a woman. Marguerite Mazel (*veuve Oliver, maître d'école de la ville de Marvejols*), *errante, vagabonde*, stole 3 *sols* from a cobbler and 10 from one Planchon of Barjac; she was sent for three years to a *dépôt*. It can only have been her sex that saved her.[3]

The last generalization which can be made about the working of *ancien régime* justice was that it feared, more than anything else, collective crime—*vol avec attroupement*. This began with four people and the penalty, whether or not violence occurred, was usually death.[4] A group of people was of course more dangerous than a single individual; their potential for violence was greater and their chances of succeeding in their enterprises much more likely. But there was perhaps more than this: a group of four might be the beginning of a bigger band, the sort of band which plagued vast tracts of eighteenth-century France and which could become so considerable that the *maréchaussée*—those pathetic four-man brigades—was powerless to confront it. *Vol avec attroupement* is demanding of separate and lengthy consideration.

The largest single number of thefts which came before the courts fell into the category of *vol avec effraction*, followed by *vol simple*, which was usually, in the case of *prévôtal* justice, accompanied by the additional charge of *vagabondage*. *Vol d'église* was a recurrent theme, though the apprehension of the criminal was

[1] This is the point of offering the plea of pregnancy which some judges received —understandably—with scepticism; it does not bear witness to a 'pre-Malthusian' society as suggested by J. Gégot, 'Étude par sondage', p. 126.

[2] A.D. Lozère 21B11.

[3] Ibid.

[4] Larrieu, *Histoire de la gendarmerie*, p. 135.

often difficult and the offence varied in its manifestation before
the courts. *Vol en grand chemin* was relatively rare as an individual
crime unless the terrain was particularly favourable; the exits
from Mende, whether towards Le Puy, Marvejols, or the south,
were tailor-made for the highwayman, and the lone operator
attacking a single traveller stood some chance of success, so that
nine out of fifty-eight offenders tried in the *prévôté* at Mende
in the last twenty years of the *ancien régime* evidently thought the
risk worth while; so too in the Pays de Velay; a handful of
offenders were caught every year in the tricky terrain near
Guémené, where the road to Nantes and Lorient took a few doubtful turns, and in the wooded country running to the south-east of
Bar-sur-Seine to the plateau of Langres—anywhere, in fact, where
nature increased the odds on success. Usually highway robbery
fell into the serious category of *vol avec attroupement*. *Vol domestique*
was above all an urban crime, and in the cities, Bordeaux, Toulouse, and Lyons, the thieving servant perhaps tops the bill in
types of criminals (though not necessarily for *vol domestique*).[1]
Only about 1 per cent of individual criminals were armed in any
way at all, and where the offender was armed he was usually
intent upon highway robbery. Otherwise, weapons, however
primitive, were usually a mark of *vol avec attroupement*, of the
crimes of the deserter, or of the repeated offender.

Broadly speaking, of those who came up before the *prévôtés*,
about a third fell into the category of *journaliers, manouvriers,
travailleurs de terre, métayers* (or in Brittany, where the term did
not mean very much, *laboureurs*); a third were people who were
unable to offer any sort of profession at all; and the rest were a
mixture of pedlars (whether they called themselves *marchands
forains, mercelots, trafiquands, revendeurs*, or *colporteurs*, they are never
absent), deserters (less numerous but also never absent), cobblers
(rarely absent), and small tradesmen, masons and thatchers, locksmiths and joiners, weavers and spinners. In city courts, the
accused were servants, whether male or female, *portefaix* and
allied occupations, building workers, *compagnons* and apprentices
in the garment trades, laundresses, seamstresses, *brodeuses, reven-*

---

[1] Paris forms an exception to this trend. There the building worker accounted
for 20 per cent of all criminals, followed by workers in the garment trades or
involved in the second-hand clothes trade (Petrovitch, 'Recherches sur la criminalité
à Paris', p. 246).

deuses, tireuses de cordes (at Lyons), and prostitutes (usually ex-servants).[1]

One cannot pretend that the *procès-verbaux* offer detailed information about the economic circumstances of the offender, for these courts were not interested in extenuating circumstances (unless the offender was a widow with a relatively clean slate). A certain amount can be inferred from descriptions, such as 'couchant tantôt d'un côté tantôt de l'autre, n'ayant point de domicile et . . . faisant des commissions pour les aubergistes des breteaux de la Part-Dieu',[2] or Joseph Berger, aged 27, but newly arrived nine days ago in Paris, who had stolen food 'dit qu'il est sans gîte, dormant sur les bancs au hasard de ses pérégrinations dans la ville',[3] or (the case of an unemployed *fabricant de bas*) 'dit qu'il est marié et que la misère lui avait fait faire le vol';[4] or from the reiterated claim that the burden of debt had pushed the offender into theft; or from the plea of hunger, for example, Étienne Castel, a weaver of Severettes (near Mende) accused of stealing bread from one Malabouche on the road to Severettes (and hence technically a *vol en grand chemin*). 'A répondu qu'il est vrai que l'hiver dernier ayant rencontré sur le chemin de Seve-rettes à Ribanès le nommé Malabouche du Crouzet, étant pressé par la faim il lui ôta 18 livres de pain bis qu'il portait avec deux livres d'étain et bientôt après il lui fit rendre l'étain.'[5] Such offerings and such pleading, however, are rare, and any inferences made can only be based on profession, place of origin, and the nature of the crime. One feature stands out above all others, however: that delinquency was linked to the pattern of mobility. In an urban context this meant that the newly arrived immigrant or the rural servant employed in the town was most likely to fall into temptation, and so crime patterns tallied with the pattern of

---

[1] For example, out of 55 criminals at Mende 20 were *travailleurs de terre*, 20 *sans profession*, 4 *colporteurs*, 3 *tisserands*, 2 prostitute-spinners, and 1 deserter, *tourneur, serrurier, trafiquand, cordonnier, maçon*. At Langres, out of 45 up for theft, 15 were *travailleurs de terre*, 10 *sans profession*, 8 *colporteurs*, 3 weavers, 5 deserters, 1 *cordonnier, charpentier, maçon, maître de forge*. A similar 'mix' is offered by J. C. Gégot, 'Étude par sondage', pp. 132–3, etc.

[2] Gutton, 'La Société et les pauvres', p. 108.

[3] A.N. Y 10356(117). Between a seventh and a ninth of Parisian criminals would appear to have been without abode; Petrovitch, 'Recherches sur la criminalité à Paris', p. 243.

[4] A.D. Lozère 21B5, Prévôté de Mende, Jacques Roussel, 1773.

[5] Ibid., Étienne Castel.

urban recruitment. The criminal of Toulouse was likely to stem from the Lauragais, the area of large farms to the south-east of that city which threw up quantities of unemployed *journaliers*, or from the Comminges, the most poverty-stricken area of the Pyrenees, whose occupants gradually made an uncomfortable choice or gamble between life in Toulouse and life in Bordeaux (and the trip to Toulouse up the Garonne valley was easier).[1] In Montpellier the criminal might originate in the Rouergue, the Gévaudan, the Vivarais;[2] Bordelais criminality was Béarnais, Basque, or Commingeois in origin or it reflected the servant influx from Entre-Deux-Mers.[3] In Lyons the worst criminals were likely to originate in the Forez, the milder ones in Bresse or Bugey.[4] The crimes of the capital inevitably reflected the strong influx from the Île de France and of Picards, Normands, Beaucerons, or their near neighbours from the Gâtinais, or the criminals were Champenois, Alsaciens, Lorrains, a few from Burgundy and Franche-Comté and Savoy, and a certain number of Auvergnats.[5] In northern and western cities the clientele of the courts might reflect less lengthy journeys of ten or twenty miles, but still they were those whose ties with their native villages had been partially severed.[6]

The urban immigrant entered an uncertain world—a world of casual odd-job men and women increasingly in and out of work by the very nature of their labour. In one sense the urban world could be an unfamiliar world in that it entailed a radical change of environment, though very often the immigrant came to a city of which he had already some temporary experience. But the immigrant did not arrive friendless. He did not even arrive alone.

---

[1] Castan, 'La Criminalité à la fin de l'ancien régime', pp. 62–3.

[2] C. Barrière-Flavy, *La Chronique criminelle du Languedoc au XVIIe siècle* (Paris, 1926).

[3] A cursory survey of the excellent *inventaire* of A.D. Gironde sous-série 12 B leaves little doubt as to this.

[4] Lyonnais crime is perhaps the best studied of all: C. Bussod, 'La Criminalité à Lyon entre 1750 et 1789' (Mémoire, Lyons, 1966). Gutton, *La Société et les pauvres*, pp. 97–111, and R. Cobb, *Reactions to the French Revolution*, pp. 44–62.

[5] Petrovitch, 'Recherches sur la criminalité à Paris', pp. 238–9, shows a mere 33 per cent of Parisian crime committed by native-born Parisians, about 16 per cent by immigrants from the Île de France, about 7 per cent each by Normans, Lorrains, Burgundians, and Picards, and 3–6 per cent each by Bérrichons, Comtois, Auvergnats, etc.

[6] This seems the overwhelming conclusion of the school of quantitative history of Caen.

The concept of the fresh young country girl stepping off the stage-coach alone to be pounced upon by the urban vice-trade and whisked off to a brothel belongs amongst Restif or Mercier's flights of masculine fancy. Migrants, whether male or female, arrived in handfuls; they either stemmed from the same village or they met up in barns along the route; they arrived dusty on foot, by barge (the river traffic into Paris, Lyons, and Rouen should never be forgotten), at best they arrived by donkey—which doubtless belonged to some more organized *colporteur* who charged for his services. The whole point about patterns of mobility is that one followed streams of one's compatriots, one was welcomed—or at any rate sheltered—by one's compatriots, who thus cushioned the transition between town and country. Stress has already been laid upon many points in order to reinforce this principle. The urban immigrant dwelt in ghettos of his own people: his relatives, male or female, were 'in service' in the more prosperous houses; the sort of fringe work he found took him into the streets and often ensured that, as load carrier, odd-job man, navvy of one kind or another, he had time on his hands and an empty stomach. One need not be surprised that the urban floating population turned to theft and with it the servants and lackeys, street vendors, and performers of menial trades, for the existence of both was inextricably interknit by ties of kinship, fraternity based upon parish or region, and by a kind of obligation—the in-work helping the out-of-work. The urban immigrant dwelt in a world of collusion.

Pickpocketing was largely an urban monopoly, for it was a characteristic of crowded streets or the gatherings in fairs and markets. It was the speciality of women—often street vendors or children trained in the act: thefts of purses and watches,[1] above all pocket handkerchiefs, or, if the offence occurred in church, of prayer-books as well. The pious girl at her orisons, whether in Langres or the capital, stood a good chance of emerging from the most fashionable church stripped of gloves, mass book, handkerchiefs, and ribbons. The decaying relics still stored in the crypt of Saint-Sernin of Toulouse provided a subsidiary income for the begging children from the mountains of Massat and the Comminges. While their mothers begged at the entrance to the cathedral with the thinner and weaker of the little *montagnards*

---

[1] On juvenile crime see Bongert, 'Délinquance juvénile', pp. 49–90.

(those whose appearance was most likely to arouse pity), the deft fingers of their little brothers or sisters were at work in the basement, pickpocketing those who lingered before the *autels privilégiés*—a few of many on the crime-strewn route between Rocamadour and Compostella. The servant girl pushed into *vol domestique* by brothers, cousins, lovers, *domestiques* themselves, or employed in casual trades, is a recurrent figure at Bordeaux;[1] the servant, male or female, who slipped up from the kitchen to answer the doorbell, let in thieves while his master was out, told the cook (or so he said, but on whose side was the cook?) that there was no one at the door, and thus sat in the kitchen confirming his own alibi while the thieves stripped the house, has an oft-played role in urban crime.[2] Accumulated case histories reveal some links. In 1788 an ex-*métayer* and his wife from Verdun-sur-Garonne, chased from their holding by debts they were unable to pay, took refuge at Toulouse: the head of the household was a load carrier; his wife took in washing and sold firewood; the eldest child worked on barges on the Garonne; one daughter was a servant at Toulouse; the youngest children were unemployed but filled in time as pickpockets; and the mother, amongst her other activities, sold the proceeds of their crime.[3] Or two women caught pickpocketing in Lyons, immigrants of the Bresse, one *portefaix*, one *ci-devant ouvrier en soie*, had struck up an association to maintain a precarious livelihood. The ghetto of Saint-Irénée at Lyons was almost as impenetrable for the police as Saint-Cyprien at Toulouse—one raid on a house produced evidence against five thieves, one a *dévideuse en soie*, a couple of pedlar drapers, a *portefaix*, and a *vendeur d'allumettes*—three were interrelated, the *dévideuse* bound by the tie of affection.[4]

In cities the two commonest victims were the keeper of a *garni*, who clearly could not leave about any saleable property whatsoever, and the employer of any casual labour or domestic servant.[5]

The links 'servant', 'casual worker', 'thieves' lack an important element: the receivers and distributors of stolen goods, and here

---

[1] Pariset (ed.), *Bordeaux au XVIIIᵉ siècle*, p. 368.
[2] R. Anchel, *Crimes et châtiments au XVIIIᵉ siècle* (Paris, 1933), p. 31, recounts many such tales.
[3] Castan, 'La Criminalité à la fin de l'ancien régime', p. 62.
[4] Gutton, *La Société et les pauvres*, p. 109.
[5] Petrovitch, 'Recherches sur la criminalité à Paris', p. 255.

the urban immigrant had an ally—the *colporteur* (not infrequently a compatriot) and the *revendeuse*, who might be a compatriot too and who was the linchpin of the second-hand clothes trade.

Over half of all thefts were thefts of clothing or materials and a certain amount of ancillary metal-ware, shoebuckles or belt buckles, buttons, brooches, and trimmings. When a robber entered a house or a merchant's premises, he could not be sure of finding ready cash but he could be sure of finding, in the case of the merchant, bales of new cloth and, in the case of private individuals, chests of sheets, blankets, towels and table linen, and clothes. Before the advent of cheap cotton goods, these commodities were regarded as an investment for life. Moreover, household linen and clothes were not purchased *new* by a considerable section of the community. The modest farmer's family, that of the artisan, and certainly that of the *journalier* purchased second or even third or fourth hand via the *revendeuse*, the second-hand clothes dealer whose talents consisted in knowing exactly what to do with the goods, even of dubious provenance, that came her way. She knew how to alter and unpick. She had a clientele which communicated its wants to her and which she satisfied when the goods came her way. She had a circuit rather than a shop: goods did not linger long in her possession.

Yet clearly not all goods came within her province; there were some that the pedlar was more fitted to dispose of—in fact there was little of a portable nature that a pedlar was not prepared to sell: one was caught selling gold medallions and cherubs taken from a chalice in a *vol d'église*.[1] Bargains in watches and buckles and, above all, handkerchiefs (the pickpocket is always left with a surfeit of these), pots and pans mysteriously missing from kitchens—all these and much besides filled the *pécule* of the pedlar.

In the annals of the crimes of the poor one returns time and again to these two figures. The *colporteur*, the stranger to the town with contacts amongst the more dubious sectors of society, how the law loathed him and how hard (but ineffectively) it tried to erect legislation to control him. Here was a man who went hither and thither, snapping up trifles and objects of more considerable worth, and able to offer them for sale, openly or surreptitiously depending on the circumstances, with knowledge of the most shady *cabarets* and *guingettes* frequented by the poor and criminal, sleeping

[1] A.D. Côtes-du-Nord B 1010, Régaire de Saint-Brieuc.

in *garnis* with his crime-prone compatriots, or, when he left the
towns, with disreputable *vagabonds*. A *colporteur* summoned before a
prévôté court could not be labelled a *vagabond*, for the very nature
of his activities took him miles from home and hence he could
appeal to be tried at home, but if the charge was possession of
stolen goods, contraband, and counterfeit money, then he could
also be considered a *vagabond*, tried on the spot, and given a
doubly harsh punishment.[1] The *colporteur* in possession of stolen
goods could never protest his innocence—'ce métier de mercelot
qui est pour l'ordinaire un état de fripons et de *voleurs*', said the
juge-prévôt of Vannes when confronted with one in the dock;[2]
and others concerned with the elimination of crime, like Henrion
de Bussy at Riom or Le Noir in Paris, would have liked to have
seen peddling of any kind declared illegal, but to do so would
have disrupted the economy of whole regions. The *maréchaussée*,
appraised of a theft, automatically searched every pedlar within
its limited purview and if it could prefer any charge at all did so
—at worst it had to content itself with charges of organizing
gambling if the pedlar's pack only contained a deck of cards or
dice. Above all, the police strove to keep an eye on these people
—though in vain—and at the same time, in the cities, sought to
introduce some regulation of the second-hand clothes trade.

During Le Noir's tenure of office in Paris a degree of control
by the police over the rag trade was attempted. In 1767 an edict
from the Châtelet pronounced: 'Tous marchands vendans par
poids et mesures et tous autres faisant profession de quelque
trafic de marchandises, arts ou métiers, soit en boutiques ouvertes,
magasins, chambres, ateliers ou autrement, ou exerçans professions qui intéressent le commerce ou qui concernent la nourriture,
logis, vêtement et santé des habitants . . .'[3] must register at the
Châtelet within three months. Those whose attention was drawn
to the edict and who subsequently registered belonged to a far
narrower category: of the 1,263 women who registered, 823 sold
old clothes, 78 rags, 33 old metal-ware, 207 were unqualified
revendeuses, and 76 kept furnished rooms, and the others failed to
give a clear definition of their business; of the 486 men, 240 sold
old clothes, 33 old metal-ware, 19 *médicaments pour les yeux*, and

---

[1] Gutton, *La Société et les pauvres*, p. 199; A.D. Lozère 21B10, Joseph Charbon-
nier, 1783.   [2] Guéguen, 'La Mendicité au pays de Vannes', p. 179.
[3] A.N. AD I 976.

163 kept furnished rooms. Only a half of those thus employed had been born in Paris; the rest were of immigrant origin and, corresponding with the general pattern of Paris immigration, 63 were from the Île de France, 55 from the Brie, Gâtinais, and Beauce, 28 from the Orléanais, 61 from the dioceses of Sens and Auxerre, 130 from Artois, Picardy, and Flanders, 134 from Normandy, 107 from Champagne, 99 Alsatians, 86 Lorrains, 45 Burgundians, and the rest, in groups of 20 or so, Auvergnats, Savoyards, etc.[1]

The police hoped by this means to know where and when to swoop and to limit what was doubtless the shadiest traffic of the capital by seizing stolen goods from a restricted number of individuals and then placing pressure upon them to reveal their sources. Once a *revendeuse* had been marked as a *receleuse*, a receiver of stolen goods, then the police would not stop harassing her.[2] It was a brave attempt, though its efficacy in the capital remains to be proven; Le Noir hoped other cities would emulate it, but in places where the police were weak, they simply did not have the means for such regulation at their disposal.

In a rural or small-town context the close-knit criminal fraternities of the cities are not found outside the organized bands. Nevertheless, there is a common element, for the crime-prone of considerable sectors of eighteenth-century France were the uprooted, the mobile. The Pau–Belfort line has some relevance to the situation. South of that line the patterns of criminality reflect the cross currents of long-distance seasonal migratory movements such as characterized above all Languedoc, that important third of France which embraced almost every type of agriculture and every type of physical feature. Here movements of hill dwellers, shepherds, and chestnut growers who descended to the plain to work on the grape and olive harvests or as terrace cutters, gatherers of mulberry leaves, repairers of irrigation canals and dry stone walls comprehended the widest spectrum. There was no other province which received so many diverse elements; none where 'rouler' was such a way of life. Before

---

[1] J. Kaplow, 'Sur la population flottante de Paris à la fin de l'ancien régime', *A.H.R.F.* (1967), p. 6.

[2] Petrovitch, 'Recherches sur la criminalité à Paris', p. 194, states the *revendeuse* to be the most frequent of informers. She had, however, little option but to feed the police a certain amount of information if she wished to continue her traffic undisturbed.

the courts, where naturally they chose to stress the more positive aspects of their existence, such people declared themselves shepherds on the Causse, grape harvesters on the plain, road diggers and canal dredgers, and, inevitably, *colporteurs*. 'Gens sans aveu, sans terre ni travail'—thus the *maréchaussée* of Toulouse, region of Mazères, described the criminals of the district. Moreover, in Languedoc the criminal element was invariably inflated by deserters profiting from the casual nature of employment and the constant toing and froing of dusty travellers. The case histories of those brought before the Tournelle at Toulouse reflect the movement between uncertain and unsteady occupation, the army and seasonal labour. A thief of 26 from Le Puy thus outlined his career: at 13 he had left home to be placed as a servant and served six months at a priory where the living was reputedly hard, two years as *valet* to an officer in a town in the Rhône valley, eighteen months at the monastery of Chaise-Dieu near Le Puy, and a short and unspecified spell at Saint-Agrève. Then he joined up with the régiment d'Auvergne but deserted at Lille a few months later and went back to the Vivarais, where he admitted that *rouler* was his way of life and, inevitably, work had run out and he found himself cadging or thieving a living.[1]

The deserter brought before the *prévôté* of Mende was no less explicit on this point. Joseph Vidal, a tailor by trade from the Velay, had found the obligations of wife and child simply too much and enlisted with the régiment de Bourgogne. He served in Alsace for a couple of years but then deserted and, doubtless remembering the hills of home—but not wanting to get too close to his family—opted for a life as part grape-harvester on the plain of Languedoc and part highwayman on the difficult artery between Mende and Alais.[2] The cases at Mende reflect odysseys of incredible length: Jean-Baptiste Roussel had started life as a *tourneur* in Grenoble, had heard of the possibilities of work in Orleans, had failed to find it, and had moved on to Clermont on his route south to Montpellier where everyone knew work abounded. Outside Mende he was stopped and held to have robbed the man with whom he had spent the night in the barn. He did not have the money on him and his accusers were of little worth in the eyes of the law (a servant looking for work and a

---

[1] Castan, 'La Criminalité à la fin de l'ancien régime', p. 61.
[2] A.D. Lozère 21B5, Prévôté de Mende, Joseph Vidal, 1774.

man of Le Puy making for the grape harvest), so he was released.[1]
A week later the case of Pierre Pégorier, a horse thief still in his
teens, came up. He was caught at Marvejols and was said to be a
vagrant. He denied this. He said he was a Rouergat and in his
native village had been an apprentice locksmith but, having heard
of a relative who had done well as a servant in Paris, he had made
for the capital, duly found employ, and was returning to Rodez
via Marvejols to bring his younger brother to a job he had found
for him in Paris. No one questioned the validity of his story, but
he was still condemned to nine years in the galleys as *vagabond*
and horse thief.[2] In 1775 at Chanac, four or five miles from
Mende, a *journalier* by the name of Tarif from a village near Saint-
Flour claimed to be *en route* to the capital but, unable to gain even
a crust by begging from the lean farmsteads in that region, he
entered an *auberge*, ordered and consumed a large meal for which
he could not pay. He threatened the *aubergiste* with a pistol—
which backfired—and with a mutilated arm he was held for the
maréchaussée and duly condemned to his five years in the galleys.
In fact of the eighteen cases between 1774 and 1777, only two
did not reveal some itinerant job or some intended if unlikely job,
and the last case of the year was almost classic. Joseph Grimal,
aged 18, *marchand colporteur* of Saint-Martin-de-Brug in Rouergue,
'il y a neuf mois qu'il a quitté ladite lieu de sa naissance et que
depuis ce temps là il a roulé dans le Gévaudan et dans la Rouergue
faisant son petit trafic de mercerie et par intervalle mendiant son
pain'.[3] Two years later a widow, Marie Daverst, aged 39, came
up for shop breaking; originally of Lyons, she said 'qu'elle
habitait dans différents endroits des côtes du Rhône, à Nîmes et
à Montpellier'. Her two sons, of whom the elder was 16, accompanied her. All claimed to be pedlars (of what?); none had
passports.[4] The other pedlars who came up before the *prévôté* at
Mende stemmed from the Gévaudan, from the Rouergue, and
from Béziers on the Mediterranean littoral: they had either robbed
those who slept with them in barns or, in the instance of the one
from Béziers, had stolen money from men at fairs. One had a
previous record as a smuggler and had a V branded on his
shoulder.
In contrast to these travelling criminals registered at Mende,

[1] Ibid. 21B6, J. B. Roussel, 1774.   [2] Ibid. 21B7, Tarif, 1775.
[3] Ibid. 21B8, Joseph Grimal, 1777.   [4] Ibid., Marie Daverst, 1780.

the Breton, Norman, and Burgundian courts have a more local recruitment; indeed, one can state categorically that 99 per cent of Breton justice was concerned with Bretons—allowing 1 per cent for the occasional non-Breton (and either Norman or Auvergnat) pedlar who passed through and was arrested on suspicion of being in possession of stolen goods or as a *voleur d'église*. The Auvergnat pedlar down on his luck was very likely to attempt the robbery of a convenient church poor-box—often using the 'glue' method. The trick was to insert a glued stick into the *tronc d'église* in the hope that the offerings of the pious for the sick, the poor, or the upkeep of the church would adhere to it. This was a favoured method—one did not have to wrench the box from the wall—though the pickings must have been slender. It was the sort of trick which might purchase an evening's bread; certainly it would not do more.[1] Such an outsider, however, was the exception. North of the Pau–Belfort line, with exceptions made for the heavy harvest demands of the Beauce, the Île de France, and the regions of viticulture, the clientele of the courts reflects a largely local recruitment. Everywhere the servant between jobs, the *journalier* waiting for, or *en route* to, employment, and the pedlar—people of marginal occupations with uncertain remuneration—were likely to find themselves on trial for petty theft. Those who came before the *bailliages* were often those of whose repeated petty thefts a community had tired whilst those who came before the *prévôtés* were often occasional thieves caught and handed over to the police.

The commonest things to steal in the country were everyday commodities, probably designed for immediate personal use: food, corn, honeycomb, cheeses, fruit, flitches of bacon from more affluent farms, clothing (here shirts and shoes headed the list), blankets, handkerchiefs, and, a long way behind, small sums of money. The theft of livestock at fairs was common, but in the countryside a hen-house was as likely to be raided for the eggs as for the hens. Thieves of this nature were fairly easily satisfied. The limited nature of thefts may reflect the availability of the goods stolen and the fact that those from whom the goods were stolen were not people of considerable means. More likely, however, it reflects urgent and immediate needs. No one was more likely to be robbed at a fair than the merchant who offered shoes

[1] A.D. Finistère B 638.

for sale—the ploy was to try on the shoes, get someone to divert the merchant, and to walk off wearing them. Fairs were the best days for thieves of all kinds, *le rendez-vous des filous*—Guibray, Beaucaire, Pezenas, the fairs of Champagne or the Bordelais— the location is unimportant, for all of them put on the roads streams of travelling merchants with bales of new cloth, pedlars with packs of new goods (and those with illicit bargains), people with money to make purchases. These commodities were carried by horses and donkeys, themselves valuable prey. The fairs also served for the sale of animals; livestock were left tethered whilst their owner bartered a deal, cheeses and fancy breads were left in carts. Hence if the fairs brought merchants from a wide radius, that from which the thieves and sharpsters were drawn was no less broad. Highway robbers, dishonest pedlars, pickpockets, and confidence tricksters all found victims on these days. Fairs were run a close second in Brittany by *pardons* and holy days. These were occasions when people dressed up, opened their coffers and took out gold rings and crucifixes, silver buckles, the best linen, and lace *coiffes*. These were days when they put money in their pockets, when they drank more and when their vigilance dimi- nished, and when they were easy meat for those intent on robbery or cheating a man of what was rightfully his in *cabaret* or *guingette*. These were the days when the *maréchaussée* turned out in full strength and secured custom for the *prévôtés*.

For the thief on the move, mass time was a convenient time for larceny—better even than night time—for Sunday mornings saw the more prosperous citizens and their entire households leaving their property unguarded for up to an hour. The parish with more than one mass was a rarity. Moreover, the exit from mass was the time when the parish syndic assembled the community to draw its attention to new legislation and matters of communal interest. This was the time to break in undisturbed and be far away before the household's return. The accustomed thief could assess the movements of a community so that he knew when and where to strike. But the habitual thief rarely acted alone: breaking and entry by one person was rarely a lucrative business; the thief needed accomplices—fellow thieves to plan, assist, carry off the loot, and if necessary use violence. The small-time operators who constituted the bulk of *prévôtal* justice were not those who filled the countryside with fear; that fear was reserved for group banditry, the robber band, the *nec plus ultra* of eighteenth-century criminality, *vol avec attroupement*.

Vol avec attroupement: Les bandes

The phenomenon of the band of thieves did not originate in the closing decades of the eighteenth century: the 1740s and 1750s had seen bands forming in Brittany, the Beauce, Forez, the Bordelais, and above all, they always, thanks to the permanent attraction of smuggling and the obviously repellent nature of life in the army, existed in the Vivarais. These bands, however, had been of an ephemeral nature. Formed during years of intense hardship, they lasted for a short while—two or three years at most—and then disintegrated. What the closing decades of the *ancien régime* saw was the multiplication of group banditry and the birth of groups which enjoyed a continuous existence for ten, twenty, or more years and, even when the *maréchaussée* believed them annihilated, left behind isolated members, the nuclei of newer, more practised, criminal brigand groups. The absolute numbers of bands will never emerge even from the most minute study of the registers of *prévôtés* and *maréchaussées*. This was not an aspect of his existence that a thief would touch upon if brought before the courts, even though judges tried to wrest a confession of group membership ('Êtes-vous attroupés avec autres vagabonds?') simply because it entailed the severest penalties. The *maréchaussée*, if fortunate, might apprehend individual members of a group; it might have its suspicions about group membership but, unless it could wrap on to the thief in question the charge of theft with murder or multiple theft under the conditions which merited the death penalty, and secure conviction—in which case it could proceed to the *question* to find out his accomplices—the odds on finding the kind of evidence that might lead to the arrest of a band were not high. The charge of *vol avec attroupement* began with four people, and a robber band never acted as a whole for the actual robbery. When one talks of bands of brigands, one is discussing association rather than the form of a robbery. All this and more besides weighted the stakes against the *maréchaussée*; the bringing to justice of a large band, like that of Charles Hulin in the Beauce, had to be a very slow and careful business indeed, a ritual in which the clumsy techniques of *ancien régime* justice and its police force were fully exposed.

Yet if evidence is fragmented, it is extensive enough to make a number of generalizations: to contrast the packs of *rouleurs* fallen on difficult times that were typical of the Languedocian scene, bands of seven or eight, often of young people between the ages of 15 and 28, who made a living by menacing the farmsteads of prosperous Languedoc with fire and by thefts of corn and livestock, occasionally eked out by a little smuggling, with the family or parish bands of cottage-bound Brittany. There is enough to pick out the happiest hunting grounds of group banditry. The most conspicuous of these was the area of *grande culture*, the Beauce, the Brie, Champagne running into Burgundy, areas characterized by a large number of almost pure *journaliers*, men who might stand a chance of work in the summer season, but little else, who certainly could not maintain an existence in informal parochial relief alone, and who, instead of making for the towns and seeking to compete with that rural surplus who sought to make a living by marginal trades in the towns, opted to stay behind, *vagabonder dans la région*—and this was possible only in a region where there was some wealth in the countryside to be exploited, that is in the *pays de grande culture*, areas of large, isolated farms and straggling villages. From the 1760s there was a belt running from La Ferté-Bernard (Sarthe) in the west to Langres in the east, taking in the Orléanais and having a hearth-land in the Beauce, the Île de France, with a main centre in the Soissonnais, through Champagne (where it was claimed that there were more *vagabonds* per head of the population than anywhere else), and petering out somewhere in the northern reaches of Burgundy, not the Burgundy of the vineyards but that of the grain-growing regions around Châtillon-sur-Seine.[1]

The second major banditry region was the Forez, which was in itself one of the poorest regions of eighteenth-century France: a region of potato-eaters and shabby farmsteads which at first

---

[1] This was the territory of the *bande Hulin* whose activities ranged from one end to the other. Lesser *bandes* like that of François Bridat confined their activities to more circumscribed territories—notably the plateau of Langres. The *bande d'Orgères* centred its activities upon the area bounded by Chartres in the east, by Pithiviers and Dourdan in the north, and by Arthenay in the south. R. Cobb, *Reactions to the French Revolution*, p. 180. Earlier, the *bandes* of Breton Le Mignon, Gautier, and Tavernier had had a similar field of operations, A.D. Loiret B 2125–7.

sight would seem to offer little to the thief. Yet it was a region constantly traversed by merchants, merchants of Lyons and Saint-Étienne, for it was the seat of *le tissage du ruban à domicile*. There was always likely to be someone with wages or raw silk on the roads or with the finished product in packs upon the backs of horses and donkeys. Moreover, the region fringed the affluent Beaujolais; it commanded the northern arteries to Lyons. From a strategic viewpoint, it was a thief's paradise.

These regions could not claim a monopoly of robber groups, but here they were at their most extensive. The *bande Hulin* probably comprehended 300 or more and it succeeded bands of from sixty to a hundred; the *bande de Forez* boasted at least a hundred and spanned three generations. Elsewhere the *bande* rarely exceeded a dozen, and there were regions in the north and in the east of France where they were restricted to small groups of deserters. Poverty was not a good recruiting agent: the French army suffered from almost constant defections, and all over the country small bands formed of men who dared not show themselves too openly in their native villages lest they be apprehended. Such men knew how to use firearms (a capacity which marked them out from other would-be robbers) and usually took their arms with them when they defected. What sort of a band they formed or joined probably depended on what there was to hand: in the areas of large associations they were likely to become affiliated members; in Languedoc and the Rhône valley they were indistinguishable from other *rouleurs* with whom they joined up; elsewhere they were prone to form autonomous groupings such as the *bande Bridat*, active in the plateau of Langres and responsible for recurrent highway robberies in the region.[1]

Equally ubiquitous were bands of children. These were an urban as well as a rural phenomenon. At Toulouse children slept under benches in the markets and near the churches, in the door-ways of public buildings, and in carriages stationed for the night in the courtyards of hostelries; they amalgamated in groups of three and four for the purposes of petty theft and disposed of their loot to the *colporteurs* who traversed the Île de Tounis, Saint-Cyprien, and Saint-Aubin.[2] In Paris the 1740s saw the emergence

---

[1] A.D. Seine-et-Marne B, Maréchaussée, Bande Bridat.

[2] N. Castan, 'La Criminalité dans les pays de Languedoc', p. 63, and Rignac, 'La Criminalité à Toulouse'.

of the *bande de Raffia*, boys between the ages of 11 and 18 who stole chickens and rabbits in the suburbs and sold them in the capital and specialized in the theft of watches—one of their members knew how to cut noiselessly through the grills that covered watchmakers' windows. They also stripped drunks of their possessions. Band after band of these *enfants de la gance*, as they were known, ravaged the capital.[1] At Lyons in 1751 a band of about thirty young thieves operated in La Guillotière. Some of them shared furnished rooms, one slept in an oven of the brickworks at Vaise. Their ages ranged from 11 to 25. They were 'porte-faix sur la quai du Rhône, manœuvres dans les voitures de bois descendant sur le Rhône'. Of the two 11-year-olds, one 'a été placé chez un satinaire', the other 'a cherché à porter des paquets pour gagner sa vie'.[2] A group of five children was captured between Vannes and Rennes, stealing food on the way. They were all orphans; some could not even remember their parents.[3] Often, of course, the children were organized by an adult. A *journalier* of Tracy, aged 27, a *milicien* who had not joined his regiment after the expiry of his leave of absence, headed a band of children (aged 10, 11, 13, 13, 14, 14, 15, 16, 18) along the coast from Isigny to La Délivrande, using his knowledge of the region and particularly the experience he had gained in the past as an employee at various farms to put the talents of his juveniles to the best advantage.[4]

The *maréchaussée* of Lyons brought to justice in 1769 a *vagabond* who had 'dans la campagne plusieurs jeunes mendiants sous ses ordres qui mettaient les paysans à contribution et venaient ensuite lui rapporter le produit des aumônes qu'ils avaient reçues ou de rapines qu'ils avaient faites'.[5] They received for their exertions 10 to 12 *sols* per month—a sum on a par with that earned by a group at Toulouse, whose average age was 11 and of whom the youngest was 6 and who worked as pickpockets for a group of adults.[6]

The *bande*, whether large or small, composed of children, adolescents, or young adults—and the age-structure of the *bande* never ranged further—existed everywhere for one major reason:

[1] R. Anchel, *Crimes et châtiments*, pp. 23–5.
[2] Gutton, *La Société et les pauvres*, p. 108.
[3] Guéguen, 'La Mendicité au pays de Vannes', p. 125.
[4] P. Crépillon, 'Un Gibier des prévôts', p. 236.
[5] Gutton, *La Société et les pauvres*, p. 203.
[6] Rignac, 'La Criminalité à Toulouse', gives many such instances.

to commit theft with greater efficiency. In the case of the great bands, their *raison d'être* was to terrorize their victims so that they dared not report individual members to the police lest the rest of the band carry out reprisals. Communities had little faith in the efficacy of the *maréchaussée*: 'Vous n'êtes pas toujours ici' accompanied an outright refusal to give evidence against a known member of the *bande de Forez*.[1] The great bands of the Beauce–Burgundian belt and the Forez had other reasons for their existence as well: both re-created in a rural environment some of the advantages enjoyed by the urban criminal in that within the rural communities they had informers—blacksmiths, *salpêtriers, maîtres de poste*—time-honoured suppliers of information on where there was something of value, and the necessary distributors—the inevitable *colporteurs* and *revendeuses*—of stolen goods. There were those members of the *bande* who knew how to melt down precious metals; there were those who did no more than find out where a suitable raid might be made and surveyed the premises—women's work *par excellence*. The great *bandes* never acted as one but in small autonomous groupings. Most of the members of the *bande Hulin* had probably never seen their supposed leader; he only acted with the most daring and esteemed members, but what he succeeded in doing in the Beauce, and what the *bande de Forez* also partially engineered in the Forez, was the erection of an elaborate protection racket. If one wished to thieve or be a vagrant in the region one had to join the *bande*; outsiders were labelled *mouches* and 'c'étaient des gens à assomer quelqu'un à qui ils auraient voulu mal'. These bands, as Julien Grignan was to say of the *bande d'Orgères* (which succeeded the *bande Hulin* in the Beauce), ruled the region.[2] There was too the value of companionship. Neither Hulin's *bande* nor that of the Forez lived a communal existence as did the *bande d'Orgères* during the summer months, but they met together in special taverns and *rendez-vous*; they shared food, drinks, and sometimes their women. Belonging to a group meant complicity, excitement, and companionship. The beggar picked up by the police on the way into the Forez who said he was going there because he had heard of the meeting

---

[1] Gutton, *La Société et les pauvres*, p. 203. 'Les gens volés n'osent se plaindre dans la crainte de devenir de plus en plus victimes du ressentiment des vagabonds' stated the *procureur du roi* in the affair Dumont Lelièvre in 1785–7 at Falaise (J. Gégot, 'Étude par sondage', p. 132).   [2] A.D. Eure-et-Loir J 586, Grignan.

of large groups of *vagabonds* 'pour se divertir avec leurs concubines' perhaps had a somewhat over-coloured picture,[1] but there was, notwithstanding, a real feeling of corporateness. The initiates shared a common language. The *argot* of the *vagabonds* of the Soissonnais was jotted down by the Abbé Montlinot; examples of that of the *bande de Forez* emerge at the trials (*suage*, the term for torturing a peasant to make him reveal the hiding-place of his fortune; *aller manger des fèves*, to spend a period in the galleys). Montlinot has left on record the curious ceremonies reputed to take place when a man and woman formed *une union libre* within the band: he took a stick while she solemnly shattered a pot to pieces, a practice held to solemnize the event.[2] Clearly they were a little state within a state.

The sort of people who belonged to any band, large or small, were no different from the type of criminals who came before the courts for individual crimes. Eighty-five per cent of those who gave an occupation were agricultural workers (or had been so), the rest small artisans, navvies, pedlars, with a crucial 1 per cent of shady *cabaretiers*. Bands usually reflected the peculiar agrarian situation of their province and in addition, if it is not too vague a concept, the psychology of the region. The diffuse nature of the Languedocian bands has been touched upon as a reflection of the varied aspects of the economy of that province; those of Brittany are no less revealing. The *bande* of Marion de Faouët, though larger than most (it perhaps comprehended twenty or thirty members), might be offered as typical of the bands which ravaged parts of Brittany in the second half of the eighteenth century.[3] It was founded on a type of family unit of which the link was Hélène Kerneau who made a living out of peddling haberdashery at fairs and the children of her two marriages. The first, to Philicien Tromel, *journalier et petit fermier*, produced Marion herself, Corentin, Marguerite, and Louise; the second, to Jean le Bihan *sénéchal* (on her marriage record Hélène is qualified

---

[1] Gutton, *La Société et les pauvres*, p. 204.

[2] M. Montlinot, *État actuel du dépôt de Soissons précédé d'un essai sur la mendicité*, pp. 22–3.

[3] The history of this remarkable woman is found in A.D. Finistère B 814, 818, 824, 834, 883, Marie Tromel dite Marion de Faouët, and the literature relating to her is prolific. Some analysis of her career appears in Corre and Aubry, *Documents de criminologie*, pp. 248–57, and J. Lorédan, *La Grande Misère et les voleurs au XVIIIᵉ siècle. Marion de Faouët et ses associés 1740–70* (Paris, 1910).

as *mendiante*), produced Jeanne le Bihan and Joseph, the latter, with Marion, perhaps the most active member of the band and the one who lasted longest into the 1770s. Corentin also had his own band, active while Marion was in prison and after her death. All of his three children who survived infancy joined his band; of the two boys Joseph (*tambour de ville*) was to be hanged with his father and Guillaume at the age of 15 was condemned to ten years in the galleys *pour avoir quêté avec insolence* and for suspicion of group membership. Hélène's other daughters brought lovers or husbands into the band. One, that of Jeanne le Bihan, a certain Pierre le Loudéac, was a shoemaker who was to have a distinguished career as a highway robber; the others were married to poor small farmers. Marion's career began as a servant girl in Lorient, but a sudden dismissal at the age of 21 saw her out of work and back in Faouët with her mother; the age of 22 saw her with an unwanted pregnancy and forced to make a living as a pedlar at fairs (*vendeuse de cribles et de petite mercerie*) in the way her mother did. By the time she was 25 her family group was organized. The basis of her initial business was the links she had formed at fairs with various pedlars, and for a year she contented herself with minor highway robbery aimed at travelling merchants. During this time, the entire family never ceased to be domiciled at Faouët—in a cottage barely twelve feet square. Business extended: highway robberies in the region of Nantes multiplied—what a boon were these ports to the robbers of Brittany—and when business was slack Marion's band lived on credit with the farms about, credit which, by all reports, she repaid scrupulously when trade looked up. If it failed to do so, she extended the range of her activities to *vol avec effraction* on large and distant farms. For a good ten years Marion clearly enjoyed, and other members of her band with her, the complicity of large elements of the local community, a complicity which other Breton bands enjoyed to such an extent that it might be labelled active support. This was because the main brunt of their attack fell on the travelling merchant, a man of the distant town not of their own parish. Where the *bande* existed at the parochial level it did not attack its own members but outsiders. If it went in for assaults on farms, they were those of other parishes.

These bands composed of tightly knit family groups or extended kin were extremely hard to crack. The parishes of Languengar, near Lesneven, known by the euphemism of Terre des Saints, and La Roche Derrien, near Tréguier, were hamlets where everyone was implicated or knew something but no one gave anything away.[1] Various members of Marion's band were captured, condemned, and put to the *question*, but it revealed nothing: the blood tie was too strong.[2]

Parishes never acted as a single unit; the group of five was the commonest unit for a highway robbery, but many more were behind the scenes or acted as the sullen providers of alibis should the occasion demand. The entire village benefited from the handouts. Faouët *en entier* profited from Marion's *largesse*, the kind of generosity of which the habitually poor but sporadically affluent are capable—free drinking in the *cabaret*. In 1786 the *maréchaussée* of Quimper caught a beggar from a village known to be the repair of one of these bands. He was induced (by a fee or more likely a pardon for some offence) to give information which led to the apprehension of the band—at least in part—but after their incarceration and pending their trial the informer had his tongue ripped out, either by members of the band who had escaped or by angry villagers. He was thus unable to give evidence at their trial since he could neither read nor write.[3] At these trials two worlds were in confrontation: a French-speaking urban merchant accusing a sullen Breton-speaking set of men and women and trying to pick out which had battered him to unconsciousness with the *pen baz* (a kind of club both men and women carried on these occasions). Highway robbery was usually accompanied by incredible brutality; the victim was fortunate if he lived. Marion de Faouët was present at no less than six murders resulting from battery. The technique was to deliver a number of hard blows to the head of the victim from behind and then strip him of anything of value. Brittany was free from vagrants or seasonal migrants from other provinces. Breton murdered Breton, disposed of the loot to Bretons, took refuge with Bretons or returned to his own filthy Breton shack; the world of Breton *métayer*, *servant*, *journalier*, *colporteur* mingled in the most incestuously criminal of French provinces.

[1] On the traditional malpractices of these villages into the nineteenth century, see Quellien, *L'Argot des nomades*, pp. 6–12.

[2] Lorédan, *La Grande Misère*, p. 236.

[3] A.D. Finistère B 1318, Contre une bande de vagabonds accusés de différents vols et d'avoir coupé la langue à un mendiant (1786–9).

In comparison with the tight-knit Breton scene, family, clan, parish, the bands of other regions are less readily defined. Even with bands of up to a hundred members, family groups or family ties were not lacking, as the four Baiotats, the two Martinets, the La Rue brothers of the *bande Hulin* and the type of kin-group formed by the Dimier nexus of the *bande de Forez* bear witness.[1] François Verne had by Manon dite Dimier ou La Pucelle, two sons, Antoine Verne dit le Basque de Thirange, Vantard, or Dimier, and Jean-Baptiste known as Le Vantard. There was also a cousin, Antoine Larderet dit Fiolant. Moreover, the family ties, where they existed, were clearly the most important. The Baiotats and the Martinets, linked by wives and concubines (Cécile Baiotat, sister of the Baiotat brothers, was the concubine of Charles La Rue and her common accomplice was Marie Françoise, legal wife of Nicolas Baiotat), acted out their crimes together. The two families Paca and Ponchon of the *bande de Forez*, who specialized in the theft of holy vessels from churches, always acted within the family unit.[2] But the family group within the large bands was the exception not the norm. How bands originated is difficult to say. Hulin was a deserter—so was one of his predecessors in the region, Pierre Brieu dit Fleur d'Épine. Clearly a couple of armed deserters could get a *bande* under way—as Bridat did in Langres. Once a nucleus had formed, the organization could quickly spread. In the trial records of some of the members of the *bande de Forez* lie indications of how links were formed. Some met each other while sleeping in barns; others whose activities had been confined to begging joined up with members of the *bande* to beg more effectively 'avec menaces' and gradually became aware of other practices of the *bande*. One had met up with La Bourbonne who had offered to show him 'les maisons où l'on donne facilement la charité'.[3] La Bourbonne only put him in the picture casually, telling him to be careful for these were violent people, ready to suspect the outsider. Some of the groups within the band formed

---

[1] A.D. Loiret B 2135, 2163, La Rue brothers; B 2158, Martinet; B 2138, Nicolas and Pierre J. B. Baiotat; B 2135, Cécile Baiotat; B 2131, Simon and Louis Rouge; on relationships within the *bande de Forez* Gutton, *La Société et les pauvres*, pp. 207–11, includes a good map.

[2] A *bande* of eighteen people operating in the Rouen area in 1795–6 included four brothers, a brother-in-law, a son-in-law, a wife, and a mistress (Cobb, *Reactions to the French Revolution*, p. 257).

[3] Gutton, *La Société et les pauvres*, p. 209.

around women—Montlinot, who was a woman-hater, was of the opinion that this was the commonest way for a group to form and that these groups then merged into a *bande*.[1] This is hard to reconcile with the record of Hulin's band where, numerically, women accounted for under a third of those who came up for trial and only one group within the *bande* was directed by a woman, Anne Chaumette dite Nanette d'Arceville, whose accusation ran:

nous l'avons déclarée dûment atteinte et convaincue d'avoir de tout temps mené une vie errante et vagabonde; d'avoir vécu en concubinage avec plusieurs voleurs qu'elle engageait à commettre des vols; d'avoir assisté à leurs complots de vol et profité de l'argent et des effets en provenant, etc.[2]

It is easy to see how a woman could assume a preponderant role in a group within a band by a purely sexual hold. A tramp, vagrant, outlaw has little to offer a woman; even a prostitute works for a fee which he cannot regularly provide, and to be attached to a woman presumably entailed its rewards.

Some associations were perhaps formed in a *dépôt de mendicité*. The *dépôts* of Moulins and Bourges figure prominently in the records of the *bande Hulin*. What, in short, the evidence adds up to is that small groups preceded the *bande* but that once in existence, a *bande* attracted both individuals and other groups.

The members of the *bandes* had not made a permanent severance with the land. They were, for the most part, declared *sans domicile fixe* but, for example, those in the Beauce worked on the harvest during the summer months when wages were more lucrative than banditry and settled for a life of crime in the winter and the spring. Perhaps their period of employ was a sounding board for crimes. Some of the members of the *bande de Forez* were small holders with periodic commitments to their land; others were prepared to put in work on the grape harvest of the Mâconnais. Both the Beauce and the Forez were continually washed by tidal waves of pedlars pouring out of the Massif on their way to Orleans and Paris or eastwards towards Lyons, Grenoble, and the cities of the Rhône valley, ready to pick up

[1] Montlinot, *Essai sur la mendicité*. C. Bloch, taking his cue from Montlinot, made the same observation, *L'Assistance et l'État*, p. 34.
[2] A.D. Loiret B 2147.

goods and put them at the disposition of the city underworld. Hulin made occasional trips to the capital in furtherance of his business. The *colporteurs* were the link between rural and urban crime. They were also the only considerable grouping of outsiders, for the recruitment of the bands of the Beauce–Burgundian belt was not wide: Beaucerons, Berrichons, Normands, Angevins, Tourangeaux, Poitevins. One of the attractions of group crime in this region was that one might stay near home. The Breton *bande* could depend on the complicity of the parish because of blood relationships and because of the victim it chose—the outsider. The *bande Hulin* could also depend on a degree of support from an element in the local populace. In no region of France were there fewer peasant proprietors; nowhere were farms larger; nowhere was the proportion of landless or near landless to the rest of the population greater:

La Beauce est connue par la fertilité de son sol et la beauté de ses grains, principalement de ses froments. Néanmoins c'est un pays pauvre parce que les terres à blé ne sont pas assez divisées, ce sont les fermiers et les seigneurs seuls qui sont riches, le paysan n'a rien, pas même un enclos autour de son habitation pour y mettre paître une vache, aussi vit-il misérablement au milieu d'un pays fertile . . .[1]

The poor peasantry was a recruiting ground for thieves; it was also an important support for them. Such people had no love of the wealthy farmers for whom they worked in the summer season. They were prepared to watch, tolerate, even perhaps enjoy the raids made upon them and to rejoice in their having to maintain nightly a score or so of threatening vagrants. Lefebvre was puzzled by the immunity of the region from the Great Fear of 1789. Here, surely, he thought, the movement against the *seigneur* should have been considerable.[2] It is tempting to speculate that the region was too accustomed to brigands to give in to a movement set in train by fear of them and that brigands were regarded, not as the friends of the rich, but as those of the poor. Moreover, had not the Beauceron *journalier* watched the *seigneurs* and their *fermiers* struggle impotently against successive bands? Was there need for further revenge? Could it not be left to the *bande d'Orgères* to terrorize them as effectively as the *bande Hulin* had done in the seventies? *Valets de ferme*, whose presence one might

---

[1] A.N. F¹² 562.   [2] G. Lefebvre, *Études orléanaises*, vol. i, p. 27.

have expected, were mysteriously missing when farms were robbed; watchdogs died conveniently, mysteriously poisoned days in advance of attack; doors were left open to receive intruders. These were crime patterns suggestive of co-operation from the inside.

The *bande de Forez* did not operate with quite the same general complicity: its strength lay in the nature of the terrain—wooded hills—and in its success in terrorizing the local populace with the threat of fire if it refused to harbour its members or summoned the *maréchaussée*. These were threats which it occasionally put into effect at Montrottier, Saint-Clément-des-Places, Saint-Romain-de-Popey, etc., by the destruction of a barn containing a household's corn, or a valued beast, or even a couple of haystacks.[1] Fire was the key to terrorizing a rural populace, but it was not needed in the Beauce, for there bandit and *journalier* were one at heart.

Of the crimes (totalling over 300) committed by the *bande Hulin* between 1767 and 1780,[2] the bulk, perhaps 70 per cent, fall into the category of petty theft, theft of shoes, linen left to dry on hedges, cloth, food and drink, small sums of money, basic jewellery—gold crosses, rings—and a number of *vols d'église* of indeterminate value; the other 30 per cent soared into the higher reaches of thefts to the value of 100 *livres* or more. Three crimes of the *bande Hulin* were to be valued at several thousand *livres*. The attack on the *messageries royales de Moulins* which fetched 26,400 *livres* put there the night before by the *Directeur des Aides* saw their capacities stretched to the full. It was the work of five men, an informer (doubtless a *maître de poste*), and preparatory plans which involved the poisoning of a dog.[3] Someone in the *bande d'Hulin* dealt in poisons and drugs: the trials were to reveal three poisonings of animals and an elaborate plot 'de voler un voyageur à qui ils avaient administré un narcotique dans du tabac'.[4]

One cannot draw a line to delimit the large from the small operators. Usually each thief had a combination of large and small thefts to his name. The first wave of the *bande Hulin* brought to trial included Jean Vivet, dit Petit Jean.[5] He stood accused of

---

[1] Gutton, *La Société et les pauvres*, p. 211.
[2] Individual members of the *bande* had longer records. Mostly the trials concern felonies committed after 1775.
[3] A.D. Loiret B 2133.
[4] Ibid. B 2141, René Fromentin, René Plet.
[5] Ibid. B 2131, Vivet.

an abortive raid on a farm at Baccons and a successful one on that of two sisters at Moque Souris, parish of Nozay. There, with four others, he had beaten the two women unconscious and had stolen two gold crosses, linen, and an unspecified but 'grosse' sum of money. On 30 September 1781 he, with four others, broke into the parish church of La Trinité near Chateaufort and stole the altar cloths. On 8/9 October 1781 he robbed Pierre Berger *vigneron* at Dadonville; on 10 October he committed a highway robbery on a servant carrying out an errand and knocked the man unconscious. On 11/12 October he broke (in the company of others) into a farm at Sécheresse, parish of Montigny, by forcing the door; he beat up the occupants and stole linen and 260 *livres*. A few days later at Marolle he stole food and also robbed a shoemaker of a pair of shoes. Vivet never rose to the heights of Meynadié or Hulin himself, but his chequered record was typical of many of the members of the *bande Hulin*. A thread of violence ran through the *bande*. Clearly some members were more prone to take life than others. The record for the *bande* was held by Pierre Baiotat who had five murders to his name, one committed in course of a robbery which brought in a mere 5 *livres*, another which only realized 26 *livres*.[1]

The role of women within the *bande* was threefold: as scouts, decoys, and distributors of stolen property. As scouts they were unsurpassed. Posing as an 'abandoned mother', preferably with a child in her arms, a woman could turn up at any farm and stand a reasonable chance of being given a crust and the right to spend the night in the barn and hence the opportunity to survey the premises, to assess the likely wealth of the inhabitants, whether there were dogs, the easiest way to gain access, what the strength of possible resistance to intimidation might be, the location of storehouses and cupboards—and all this before involving the gang in a worthless enterprise. In this way Marie Jeanne Bonnichon dite Monte en chambre had secured the necessary information for the thefts committed at Vignory in Brie, at Corbeil, and at La Clotée.[2] Anne Rosalie Janson had similar charges to her name. Indeed, the terms of her conviction summarize the customary roles of women within the *bande*:

---

[1] A.D. Loiret B2 138. He seems to have had a predilection for strangling his victims in their beds.

[2] Ibid. B 2139. Sometimes the children were the scouts.

errante, mendiante et vagabonde, concubine de plusieurs voleurs, assista au vol avec effraction commis en juin 1776, par Charles Noel Larue, Louis Grillon, dit Paquet d'Échalottes, Jean Limousin, son concubin, et plusieurs autres, chez la dame Bance à Amphonville paroisse de Gatelles, près Chartres. Elle assista au complot fait par le même Limousin pour voler un habitant de Marchenoir. Elle dit même qu'elle tiendrait son couteau à la main pour égorger ceux qui résiste-raient. Elle alla trouver, dans l'hiver de 1780, son amant d'alors, Delair, André Forestier, dit le Petit Boucher, et un autre, à la ferme de Limon, paroisse de Voilan, près Versailles, pour les engager à s'embusquer sur le grand chemin d'Arpajon voler une veuve de Palaiseau. Elle eut connaissance du vol et de l'assassinat commis, dans la nuit du 28 au 29 septembre 1781, chez Pierre Marchand, laboureur à Prinvau, et donna, sous la halle de Beaune en Gâtinais, trois livres à Delair, pour les frais de son voyage. Elle prépara l'affaire en mendiant chez ledit Marchand, visitant les issues de la maison. Elle eut connaissance du vol avec effraction commis, dans la nuit du 26/27 novembre 1781 par Delair et six autres ... chez Henri Blondeau, vigneron à Fleury en Bière. Elle reçut une jupe provenant du vol de Janville en 1775 ...[1]

The *maréchaussée*'s dossier on Anne Rosalie was clearly defective. There are too many gaps in her activities. What is clear, however, is that she carried orders, perhaps from Hulin, to her various lovers and associates. Delair was evidently of an unreliable nature: he had to be provided with 3 *livres* to make possible the journey to Prinvau (Hulin or someone obviously felt that without this sum he might delay proceedings by some independent theft). Examples of women sporting the spoils of theft are common. They also dressed up their children. They were young women and conscious of themselves, attractive enough to have an obvious use as decoys. La Brêche, whose real identity was never discovered, lured a merchant Cuisinier into a trap which cost him his life. La Fesse was accused of having drawn into a trap a 'marchand de chevaux pour jouir d'elle sur une meule de foin'—he was merely robbed.[2] Monte en chambre's talents in this respect were evidently extensive. The crimes of the *bande* were often well planned; always, in the case of the larger enterprises. The small *ad hoc* thefts, however, were mismanaged as often as not. The members of the *bande* drank too much, talked too much (the indiscreet utterances of the tavern gave much away), they readily became

---

[1] Ibid. B 2134. [2] Ibid. B 2132.

violent, and they ran unthinking risks. Perhaps it was over-confidence which allowed a woman to bedeck herself in the proceeds of a crime committed nearby; perhaps it was a not too studied consideration of what the future might bring. Ages were rarely given at trials, yet these would appear to have been young adults, both agile and energetic. The children who accompanied them were often babies in arms. At least a quarter of the men had spent periods in a *dépôt*—a comment upon its efficacy as a deterrent.

How could a *bande* of this nature be brought to justice? The *maréchaussée* could amass a certain amount of evidence from major victims, but in addition it had to combat a degree of hostility from the local populace, its own numerical weakness, various smokescreens thrown up by the *bande* itself, and the lack of reliable informers—at least four spies were murdered by the *bande Hulin*. Its success in bringing men and women before the courts was due first of all to a concentration of brigades and the military upon the Beauce in the autumn of 1781 (and hence a shifting of crime to the Soissonnais—the hard times of one *bande* were the heyday of another) and the rounding up of anyone who happened to be in various taverns when the swoop was made. Which taverns were worth raiding might have emerged from informers, or from the trial of Jacques Cussy dit le Limousin, caught in process of a theft at Melun, condemned, and tortured. The *coup* was to catch Hulin, and how this was done is unrecorded. Then from this criminal hotchpotch, some doubtless innocent, some guilty, the *maréchaussée* had to decide *whom* to bring to trial. This was a crucial decision: at the outset of the trials, beyond a certain amount given away by the five broken on the wheel at Melun, the police knew very little and deciding who had done what, or even who was who, was no easy task. It was consciously complicated by the habit of members of a large *bande* of assuming a pseudonym.

The police obviously relied heavily on informers to bring the bands to justice. The need to thwart the informer, who relied very much on tales told in taverns and the indiscreet utterances of the robber drunk on the proceeds of his crime, and the fact that, once brought to justice, they would be tortured to reveal the names of their accomplices meant that the members of the band attempted a dual existence and adopted pseudonyms to conceal their real identities from their associates. The pseudonym was of great importance for the security of the individual concerned. If his associates knew only the assumed name then they would be unable to incriminate him either to the police in the course of being tortured or by any careless utterance dropped in the tavern. In the event of capture, the *vagabond* gave his real name and the officials of justice had to try to discover the pseudonym in order to marshal the evidence. On the other hand, when the individual was subjected to the *question*, he could refer only to pseudonyms and the value of the results was much diminished by knowing only that the Grand Nez had robbed the curé of —— or that the assassin of a certain individual was le petit Vermandois. Most pseudonyms were regional (le Limousin, l'Auvergnat, Langevin, Tourangeau, Versailles, Berrichon), others embodied certain physical traits which were sometimes added to a regional designation (Grand Nez, Sans Dents, Jambe Croché, Le Blond, le Borgne du Mans, Petit Normand, etc.). A child took the pseudonym of his father, whilst the names assumed by women referred either to flowers, La Rose, La Fleur, or to sex (one can have little doubt as to the activities of Monte en chambre or La Fesse), or they simply called themselves Femme whatever the pseudonym was of the man to whom they were attached as wife or concubine: Marguerite Grand Nez did not necessarily have a large nose but either the man she slept with had or, if he was a second generation *vagabond*, his father had or he or his father had a remarkably small nose. To add to the confusion many robbers had multiple pseudonyms or discarded one which they considered risky. The pseudonym was intended to confuse.[1]

It could easily succeed in doing so. If some of the intricacies of piecing together the *bande Hulin* have been lost, excellent instances of such difficulties are found in the bringing to justice of the *bande de Forez* where the Verne–Dimier–Vantard clan baffled police inquiries. Antoine Verne was known both as Dimier (his mother's name) and as Vantard; his brother, Jean-Baptiste, was known as Vantard (his father's name). For a simple informer to unravel such complexities to the police was almost

---

[1] A.D. Loiret B 2158. The Martinet brothers had in common the pseudonym Blanc. Étienne was known as Blanc le tondu and Claude as Blanc le grêlé, but the latter also passed as Barat and François Alix. Two members of the *bande Hulin* took the name Le Blond, Hulin himself and Louis Phélypeaux (A.D. Loiret B 2141).

impossible, and it was not until enough evidence had been amassed against one member for him to be brought to trial and tortured that any clarity at all emerged as to who had committed what. Even then, it is doubtful if the entire record was set right, and the police contented themselves with sufficient evidence—if what is revealed under torture may be thus described—to hang the bunch.

The techniques employed in unravelling the records of the component elements of Hulin's band were long and tortuous. In all, the trials extended over three years, and much of the evidence was accumulated as the trials proceeded. The first step was to bring before the *prévôt* at Orleans on 7–8 October 1782, two groups, totalling in all fourteen people, against whom sufficient evidence was already at the disposal of the *maréchaussée* to secure the death penalty for twelve of them and *la question* in addition for seven of these. The *maréchaussée* did not have, by any means, a complete dossier of the offences committed by the men it brought to trial first. It did not know the names of the accomplices of the felons—the phrase *avec un ou deux quidams* is a recurrent one in the *procès-verbaux*—but the police did have sufficient to prove the involvement of more than three people in some of the crimes, so that the charge could be *vol avec attroupement*. This alone would ensure that the convicted would be tortured and hence would supply the police with information to proceed further. Evidence against the first fourteen tried was probably supplied by the confessions of one Jacques Cussy dit le Limousin, tried and condemned at Melun some months previously. The seven men convicted on 7 October were immediately tortured. They were presumably asked to give evidence against Hulin, whose trial began on 8 October. Hulin was convicted, condemned to be broken on the wheel and hanged, and tortured. His confessions were doubtless crucial. The material supplied by Hulin and the seven provided the police with sufficient evidence to incriminate a second batch of men and women, and this was carefully sifted by them over the next five months. The next trials took place in March 1783. During the interval many incarcerated thieves may have lost their nerve and turned king's evidence. Details were filled in. The bulk of evidence grew as each successive wave of convicted men implicated their associates, until one robber towards the end of the trials was charged with eighty-eight thefts. This man, François Boussard (*manœuvre*) dit la Joie, admitted in July 1784 to robberies ranging from a few dozen handkerchiefs to 773 *livres*, with a norm nestling in the range of 100 *livres*.[1] He had twenty *vols d'église*, the least profitable but clearly the easiest of his enterprises, to account for.

It is useful to compare the methods used by the *maréchaussée* of the Lyonnais to implicate the *bande de Forez* in the 1750s. On the basis of the confessions of a thief awaiting trial a handful of men were proven guilty and subjected to the *question*—in the Lyonnais the particularly brutal one of stretching by ropes and burning the palms of the hands and soles of the feet—it was not important if the tortured man died. Then, with some information against Marie Dupuis, the *maréchaussée* intimidated her into turning informer, and thus a part of the *bande* was brought to justice.[2]

Without torture the puny police force of the *ancien régime* would have got nowhere. As it was, it did not root out group banditry, it temporarily drove it elsewhere; it annihilated the leaders of one generation, scattered the rest for the time being, but left the issue essentially unchanged. The mother of Monte en chambre had perished in the aftermath of the *bande* of Dourdan, her daughter with the *bande Hulin*; her granddaughter would be counted with the *bande d'Orgères*. The great-niece of Marion de Faouët would have her day as a beggar, *vagabonde*, and thief in the region of Faouët and Guémené, and the *enfants de la gance* defied annihilation. In the agrarian conditions of the eighteenth and early nineteenth centuries, the *bande* was clearly ineradicable.

[1] A.D. Loiret B 2147. His earliest crimes were committed in 1767.
[2] Gutton, *La Société et les pauvres*, p. 208.

X

SMUGGLING

Leur industrie et commerce de passer des paquets en
Espagne au péril de leur vie et d'aller abattre les sapins
sur le haut des montagnes pour pouvoir subsister avec
leurs familles.
> Curé de Sailhan (Comminges), 290 inhabitants.

IN the history of the economy of the poor smuggling commands
a more important place amongst the makeshifts of certain regions
than any other single factor.[1] The centres of smuggling which
offered scope to the small-time operator not only kept the native
poor within the region, however desolate that region might be,
but the existence of the potential for smuggling served as a
magnet to the down-and-out of other regions. No study of the
poor would be complete without some consideration of the petty
smuggler, though he is, on occasion, even more elusive than the
petty thief, for his aim was to stay anonymous and circumstances
on the whole conspired to preserve his anonymity.

When Charles Lamb in the nineteenth century spoke with
warmth of the smuggler, an honest personage who robbed only
the revenue—an institution he had never greatly cared about—he
voiced what was doubtless at the time a popular sentiment. The
smuggler, docking his vessel in some picturesque Cornish cove,
loading his pack-horse in the mist and proceeding over the hills

---

[1] For the incidence of the levy of the *gabelle* and tobacco taxes see M. Marion,
Dictionnaire, pp. 249–50, and G. T. Matthews, *The Royal General Farms in Eighteenth-
Century France* (New York, 1958), pp. 82, 118–19. There is no good comprehensive
history of smuggling in eighteenth-century France. M. H. Bourquin and E. Hepp,
Aspects de la contrebande au XVIIIᵉ siècle (Paris, 1969), is concerned with existing
knowledge of tobacco smuggling and comprehends a bibliography which does not
move into the realm of local studies. Clearly the smuggler aimed at a degree of
anonymity which precludes any idea of an accurate quantitative study, yet there is
sufficient, as is shown by P. Cochois, *Étude historique et critique de l'impôt sur le sel en
France* (Paris, 1902), old, impressionistic as it may be, to find out a great deal. A full
study would include an examination of the *entrepreneurs* and the organizers of the
trafficking as well as the heavy implication of actual employees of the *ferme* itself
and would far exceed the scope of this short *aperçu* concerned only with smuggling
in so far as it impinges upon the economy of the poor.

with his brandy, tobacco, and silks, while a conniving populace heard the hoof-beats and whinnies of the ponies but remained silent in their beds, was a romantic figure and contemporaries did not linger long on the violence which often accompanied his practices. If this was true in nineteenth-century England, a country where smuggling was relatively undeveloped and where smugglers looked mere amateurs in comparison with their European counterparts, how much more was it so in eighteenth-century France where the commonest smuggler dealt in the most basic commodity, salt; where the authority which was defied was not the government, unpopular enough by any reckoning, but a set of unscrupulous government contractors, leasers of the monopoly from the government, known profiteers from the needs of the innocent and impoverished. Moreover, in France, the numbers involved in smuggling were not to be counted in handfuls or even hundreds but in thousands, perhaps even as many as a million, numbers which neither government nor government contractors could hope effectively to curtail—much as the latter might struggle so to do. Smuggling was a national industry in which men, women, children, civilians, military, even the employees of the *ferme* (the government contractors who held the monopoly) were actively involved, and the economy of at least three provinces received an important support from the potentialities that smuggling salt alone afforded. The traffic in salt was based on the anachronisms in the administration of the *gabelle*; the *gabelle* was levied lightly or not at all in Brittany and Flanders (the areas *par excellence* of free salt), Béarn, Navarre, and Hainaut, and relatively lightly in Poitou, Guyenne, Limousin, and the Marche, while elsewhere the levy was heavy. In the areas of *grande gabelle*, salt sold at 62 *livres* the *quintal*, in the *pays exempts* it fetched some 5 *livres*. The attractions of the traffic between the areas of light and heavy levy were therefore enormous.[1] Any child could smuggle a couple of pounds of the substance and clear a profit of 14 *sols* (equal to the daily wage of an agricultural labourer).[2] A man could multiply these profits. Nor was salt the only commodity lending itself to illicit distribution, for there was also the state tobacco monopoly to be evaded, while the

[1] Marion, *Dictionnaire*, pp. 249–50.
[2] G. F. Le Trosne, *De l'administration provinciale et de la réforme de l'impôt* (Paris, 1788), vol. i, pp. 3–10.

proximity of the Swiss frontier made possible a nice, though strenuous, traffic in cambric, Swiss lawn, and printed cotton. The *ferme* employed 23,000 men to combat salt smuggling alone and was forced for larger jobs to call in the army—help by no means always loyal to the interest of the *ferme*. The folk heroes of eighteenth-century France were not Jack Straw- or Dick Turpin-like figures but Mandrin and Cartouche, who operated within the capital and were transformed by popular imagination helped on by *livres de colportage* (small books usually published in Troyes and peddled throughout the country) into figures resembling at one and the same time Robin Hood, Casanova, and St. Vincent de Paul, even, in the case of Mandrin, with a touch of Prynne added.[1] For after his death, with a good forty murders to his name, the violent, unscrupulous, daring young deserter without a principle in his head beyond self-profit was to be endowed by posterity with a political testament proclaiming the principles of 1789, the iniquities of indirect taxation, the follies of government; his was the 'cause' of the people. The government dared not hang Cartouche publicly, even though he had a score of murders to his name (employees, inevitably, of the *ferme*, about whom no one cared), because this might have provoked an insurrection in the capital: hence he was quietly strangled in his prison cell.[2] Cartouche and Mandrin were two big figures; they practised openly on a large scale what others did more or less surreptitiously on a small scale, and envy was at the root of the idolatry of these two unworthy figures. The contempt they demonstrated for the letter of the law gave them added lustre. Yet very clearly the law dealt with them in a peculiar manner. When Mandrin was arrested he was hiding in the house of one of the chief magistrates of the Parlement of Grenoble. The magistrate in question knew he was both a smuggler and a murderer and yet was prepared to harbour him. The *parlementaires* saw in the famous smuggler what the political pamphleteers recognized when they endowed him with a political testament: that what could be represented as his stand against the *ferme* could be extended to be a struggle against absolute monarchy financially ensnared in the hands of the

---

[1] J. Egret, *Le Parlement de Dauphiné et les affaires publiques dans la seconde moitié du XVIIIe siècle* (Paris, 1942), pp. 219–32, and Bourquin and Hepp, *Aspects de la contrebande*, p. 79; on the popularity of Mandrin in the Lyonnais and Forez, L. Galle (ed.), *Les Cahiers de Monsieur Séguin* (Lyons, 1901), pp. 24–9.

[2] Bourquin and Hepp, *Aspects de la Contrebande*, p. 81.

fermiers généraux; and the *parlements* keenly appreciated the capital they could make out of this in their own struggle with the monarchy. Mandrin, they appreciated, had popular support; their sponsoring of his cause—though they could not in the final analysis eradicate his murders and so save him from the gallows —could only enhance the popular image of the *parlementaires*. Taking their tone from these high courts, lesser justices dealt leniently, and as spasmodically as they could decently manage while remaining on the right side of the law, with the minor smuggling offender. True, Necker, that arch-compiler of the dubious statistic, who had also an axe to grind with monarchy and the financiers of the *ferme* and who was ever conscious of his popular image, contrived to suggest that 2,300 men, 1,800 women, and 6,600 children annually came before the courts for an offence which in any decent society would go unheeded,[1] but even if these figures bear some semblance of truth, which is questionable, they reflect but a minute fraction of those who gained a livelihood by dealing in illicit salt and tobacco. Le Trosne, another critic of the financial mismanagement of Louis XVI's government (there was no more popular subject in the 1780s), cited 146 pieces of legislation designed to punish the offender and concluded with the following scale in relation to salt and tobacco. Smuggling without arms, the goods carried upon one's person, was to be punished in the first instance by a fine of 200 *livres*, the second by six years in the galleys. Smuggling without arms, on horseback, was to be punished in the first instance by a fine of 300 *livres*, the second by a fine and six years in the galleys. Smuggling in an armed band to be punished the first time by a fine of 500 *livres* and nine years in the galleys, the second time by the galleys in perpetuity. Young and vigorous men might substitute for the galleys enrolment in the army. Women and girls caught smuggling goods on their persons to be punished in the first instance by a fine of 100 *livres*, the second by one of 300 *livres* and a public whipping, the third time by banishment from the province. Children under the age of 14 caught smuggling were assumed to be the responsibility of their parents

[1] Necker, *Traité de l'administration des finances* (Paris, 1784). The costs of imprisonment for the *ferme* were enormous. At the beginning of the eighteenth century the guards and the imprisoned together took 1,719,785 *livres* from the total profits: J. Pasquier, *L'Impôt des gabelles en France aux XVIIᵉ et XVIIIᵉ siècles* (Paris, 1905), p. 109.

and punishment was to be borne by the parents, who were to be
fined on a scale ranging from 50 to 200 *livres*.[1]

But how far could this legislation be put into effect? Put another
way, how effective could a struggle be of 23,000 employees of

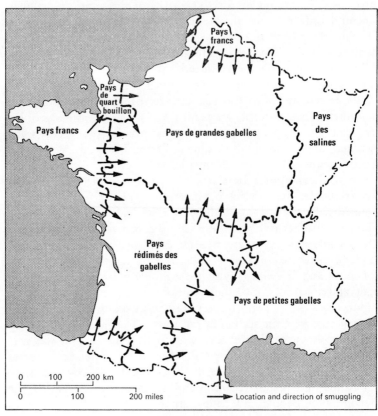

MAP III

Main arenas of salt smuggling

the *ferme*—some of dubious loyalty—against a populace of 25
million who if they were not smugglers were willing recipients
of illicit salt and tobacco? Fortunately for the *ferme* their efforts
could be concentrated upon the borders of those provinces which
paid a light levy or none at all and those paying a high one. To
attempt to control the traffic between Brittany and Anjou, for

[1] Le Trosne, *De l'administration provinciale*, vol. i.

example, 1,500 men were employed in the region of Laval alone.[1] At Laval itself, the *ferme* had its own court and could pass sentence; but it did not have its own prisons and therefore could not be arbiter of the fate of those its court condemned. Where the *ferme* did not have a court, offenders caught by the employees of the *ferme* were tried by the *bailliage*, and here the local civil judges were in control.

In Brittany and the Maine the villagers of the boundary area found in salt smuggling an important subsidy to a precarious livelihood. In an ordinance of 1680 on the *gabelle* Louis XIV had inserted the proviso that in recognizing Brittany's exemption from the tax he could demand in return the prohibition on the sale of salt in any towns or villages less than two miles from the provincial boundary except for those of Dol, Fougères, Vitré, La Guerche, Châteaubriant, Ancenis, and Clisson, all of which rapidly became smuggling centres. In these towns salt could be sold in the market on market-day only.[2] The Parlement of Brittany in an *arrêt* of 1684 sanctioned an edict stipulating that the inhabitants of villages less than two miles from the boundary might purchase only sufficient for their needs for six months at a time and a record should be kept of this by the *fermier des gabelles de France*. Attempts at evasion would be punished by arrest and a fine.[3]

The penalties imposed were steep but ineffective, since they could only be applied if the smugglers were caught and their knowledge of the territory coupled with an almost general complicity rendered capture unlikely. How many individuals were involved in Brittany is impossible to know; in order to understand the attraction of smuggling it is perhaps sufficient to say that an adult male could in a single trip between Brittany and the Maine carry enough to realize 20 *livres*—equivalent to a month's wages. Far more numerous than the actual load carriers were the villagers who, against a suitable remuneration, procured the salt from the market to pass on to the smugglers. Whole villages on the provincial frontier lived by this, and the *intendant* thus described one such village: 'Chaque cabane de cette peuplade corrompue est une mine de sel inépuisable. La seule paroisse du

---

[1] Lefizelier, *La Gabelle dans le Maine et l'Anjou* (Laval, 1869), p. 23.
[2] J. Gautier, 'La Contrebande du sel de Bretagne', *Mém. Soc. hist. arch. Bret.* (1957), p. 107.   [3] A.N. H[1] 426.

Pertre a fourni pour sa part aux faux sauniers plus de 300 minots de sel en l'espace d'un mois.'[1] Small wonder Pertre did not complain of paupers amongst its 2,200 inhabitants, in spite of the poverty of its soil and apparent scanty resources. Indeed, the *recteur* of Gennes declared that the attraction of salt was such that his village was constantly inundated with strangers from Anjou.[2] Ogée's description of this area talks of *landes peu fertiles*—heath covered with gorse and scrubby bushes. The undergrowth was sometimes several feet high and to know one's way through it was knowledge carefully passed on from father to son. The *faux sauniers* went barefoot, wrapped in goatskins, and carrying long sticks (*fertes*) for use against an *archer de la gabelle* rash enough to accost them, and often they were accompanied by dogs. Legislation against bands of salt smugglers became increasingly severe; indeed, by 1733 bands of three or more were punishable by the death penalty, though the sentence was not applied.[3] In 1723 a prison for female salt smugglers was founded at Saint-Maure in Touraine, but was obliged to close three years later because it could not hold all who were arrested even though those caught represented, as the *ferme générale* knew only too well, a minute percentage of the total. Villagers connived at smuggling by oversalting butter to be sold in Mayenne and by baking loaves of salt in a thin crust of dough to disguise them. The salt merchants were in league with the smugglers not the *ferme*; at Vitré they paid villagers to feign disputes in the market so as to distract the *gabelle* officials in the hope that they would not notice the large quantities of salt purchased by known smugglers; and at Ancenis the carters of salt stopped the carts a mile from the town and did a brisk trade with the smugglers before entering the official market.[4] The villagers engaged in minor personal dealings each as he could afford, whilst the *ferme* declaimed in vain against 'ce funeste métier qu'ils préfèrent à tout autre et qui devient la cause de l'abandon de l'agriculture et la source de toutes sortes

---

[1] This was about 6,000 *livres*' worth on the black market. A.D. Ille-et-Vilaine C 3475.

[2] A.D. Ille-et-Vilaine G 496[F], Fabrique de Gennes, 1777: 'Autre raison de la population dans cette paroisse, c'est son voisinage de l'Anjou. En cette dernière province, le laboureur est extrêmement gêné tant par le sel que la taille et autres impositions, il n'ignore point que cette gêne est moins excessive chez nous. Aussi trouve-t-il jour à se placer au nombre de nos colons, aussitôt il déserte sa province pour venir habiter la nôtre.'   [3] A.N. H7 426.

[4] A.N. G7 1227.

de crimes'.[1] At a session of *Parlement* held on 22 April 1776 the *procureur du roi* demanded new punitive measures to be taken against smugglers:

le nombre des fraudeurs et les attroupements de gens armés est fort multiplié depuis dix ans. Les prisons regorgent d'hommes, de femmes et même d'enfants arrêtés pour faux saunage. Les parents pauvres, au lieu d'accoutumer leurs enfants au travail, les envoyent chercher un petit minot de sel. . . . Devenus grands ils persévèrent dans le même métier.[2]

The question of child salt smugglers is an important one. Salt smuggling was an obvious way of making children self-supporting in the border villages, and in a small way their competence was unsurpassed. In any salt court the numbers brought up for trial in any one year always contained far more children than any other section of the community. The profit on a pound of salt was 7 *sous* and the frailest waif was capable of carrying at least that amount in a bag suspended from his waist or his neck, or, if a little girl, in one of those small carts used to collect food for rabbits appropriately camouflaged with the right sort of greenery. In the salt court of Laval alone, in 1773 over 12,000 children of both sides of the frontier were arrested, and that figure included only those caught with 15 pounds and more.[3] And how cogently they could plead their case. Any 6-year-old was capable in court of a heart-rending story designed to soften the judge: he had no shoes, no shirt, a sick mother, a drunken, feckless father—tales perhaps true or perhaps taught him by his mother. Eight-year-old Jean Gué of Vitré explained how his father, stricken with fever and unable to earn his bread, lay helpless in bed while his wife wept at her inability to feed her baby daughter; hence he, Jean, had sought his *minot*. Hélène Miniac and her sisters, ranging from 8 to 12 years, informed the judge at Laval that their parents had left them to fend for themselves, and what could they do?[4]

Some families were adept at the use of a dog. The trick was for a family in the Maine to make an arrangement with another

[1] A.D. Ille-et-Vilaine C 3475.

[2] Cited by Gautier, 'La Contrebande du sel', pp. 150–1.

[3] Callery, *La Fraude des gabelles sous l'ancien régime (1730–1786)*, article extrait de la France judiciaire, 1882, and A.N. AD IX 426 on similar instances for Touraine.

[4] A remarkable collection of such stories appears in C. Geslin, 'Vitré aux XVIIe et XVIIIe siècles' (Diplôme d'Études Supérieures, Rennes, 1962).

over the Breton frontier and to leave with the Breton family a dog, which was tethered, starved, and finally released by the Breton family bearing a parcel of salt around its neck. It headed homewards in all possible haste and a *commis* afraid of being savaged or bitten made no attempt to stop it. Repeated legislation directed against the owners of canine *faux sauniers* was of no avail and the *ferme* sought to retaliate by training dogs of its own with the purpose of tearing the limbs of smugglers.[1]

While Brittany provisioned Anjou, Maine, and Normandy with salt, Flanders provisioned Picardy. Here formal attempts had been made to restrict the amount of salt at the disposal of any household by allowing the purchase of only two months' supply at a time and by limiting the number of distribution centres near the frontier with Picardy.[2] But such efforts were in vain, and Artois and Picardy swarmed with salt smugglers of two basic types: on the one hand, the long-distance smuggler, dealing *en gros*, bands of 200 and 300, in which soldiers often predominated—indeed, one commander, the colonel de Pontis, reckoned that his regiment cost the king nothing to maintain.[3] On the other hand, there was the family organization wherein villagers on one side of the line made informal arrangements with villagers on the other side; they relied on the usual camouflaging loaves or small bags hidden on the person, subterfuges employed not because severe penalties were expected if one were caught but to avoid having one's salt confiscated.[4]

Less lucrative, though no less crucial to the economy of the area, was the salt smuggling which took place between a part of the Basse Auvergne and the Bourbonnais and between the Basse Auvergne and the Forez. At its most remunerative in the first instance, the practice was at its most developed in the subdelegation of Montaigut, where the curé of Dourdat considered it likely that each of his parishioners probably took part, and the curé of Saint-Didier himself was suspected of organizing an entire village

[1] Lefizelier, *La Gabelle*, p. 24.

[2] G. Lefebvre, *Les Paysans du Nord*, p. 192.

[3] 'En 1718 en Champagne et en Picardie, il s'était formé une association de 5000 faux sauniers; on dut envoyer contre eux le gouverneur d'Amiens; mais les soldats eux-mêmes se livraient au faux saunage par bande de deux à trois cents, et pillaient le sel déposé dans les magasins du Boulonnais et de la Picardie' (Cochois, *Étude historique*, p. 85).

[4] Cochois, op. cit., p. 89.

for smuggling purposes.[1] It is significant that the area of the Auvergne immediately adjacent to the Bourbonnais was almost unique in the Auvergne in that it produced no seasonal migrants,[2] and this not because it was more fertile or less teeming in surplus manpower than elsewhere, but because the labourer or peasant farmer here had an important and regular source of income in illicit salt. He did not even need to run any risks. The salt was purchased in the open market with every appearance of legality, in small quantities, by the most innocent-looking, even impoverished purchasers, particularly humble housewives. If the salt merchant raised any queries, he was silenced at the rate of 5 *sous* per *sac* and *pro rata*—a modest sum. The salt was taken home and hidden until the *faux sauniers* of the region let it be known where a *rendez-vous* would take place for the collection of the salt. The *faux sauniers* were said to visit every group of parishes every month; they used for collection purposes a handy barn or the premises of a complacent tavern keeper. For every *sac* he turned over, the peasant could expect a profit of 20 *sous*—15 if he had been forced to tip the merchant. Three or four *sacs* thus amassed monthly made a net profit that compared favourably with a week's labouring wages for all but the summer season. Moreover, to get this sum had entailed no absence from work and no risks, because he had not even crossed into the *pays de grande gabelle* and hazarded being caught disposing of the goods.[3]

Technically, because he dealt in salt outside the *ferme*, the Auvergnat peasant was a *faux saunier*, but there was a real difference both of level and of risk involved between his small-time activities and those of the *faux saunier* who, having amassed enough to make a trip worth while—he was said to wait until he could be sure of a comfortable profit of 100 *livres* on the goods he carried—made the journey into the Bourbonnais, *pays de grande gabelle*. Though such an individual was evidently recruited from the same milieu, smuggling was his main activity and he

[1] A.D. Puy-de-Dôme C 1542, Plainte du curé de Dourdat, 1758; C 4872, 1729, Le Curé de St. Didier est soupçonné d'être faux saunier. Poitrineau, *La Vie rurale en Basse Auvergne*, p. 370, gives more precise smuggling locations.

[2] Delaspre, 'L'Émigration temporaire en Basse Auvergne', p. 8, cites this region as constituting an important exception to the rules of seasonal and temporary migration within the region.

[3] The organization of the illicit salt rings in Auvergne is outlined in A. Boislisle, *Correspondance des contrôleurs généraux des finances avec les intendants de provinces* (Paris, 1874), t. ii, n. 668.

needed to be physically fit; the full-time *faux saunier* was usually a young man. In the north-west of the *généralité* of Riom many of them lived a communal life in the Bois des Collettes, hidden and provided with the salt they smuggled by the local populace, and periodically their numbers were inflated by numerous soldiers on leave, anxious to supplement their army pay and able to lend both horses and arms.[1] If the occasional *faux saunier* was brought to justice, he was pardoned but forced into the militia. Indeed, the military as a whole received a substantial influx from *faux sauniers* who had been brought to justice and given the alternative of military life to a fine and the galleys.[2] Small wonder that whole regiments often gave themselves up to salt smuggling. The life of a *faux saunier* had its attractions. A large-scale expedition was usually followed by four or five days' eating and drinking. The Auvergne also knew incursions of bands of professional *faux sauniers* from the Lyonnais, usually via the Forez, bands of eighty or ninety with pack-horses, ready to purchase from the peasant who had hoarded a little and to pass on.[3] Against the *bandes* the *ferme* was powerless. In the Auvergne, as indeed within Brittany, the attitudes of civil authorities towards smuggling salt on this scale were liberal in the extreme. Some clerics plainly saw smuggling as a way of bringing ease to households apparently living in poor conditions and were even prepared to help organize the trade; at least one, the curé of Saint-Didier, was suspected of making a monthly trip over the provincial boundary laden with the salt collected in the market by his parishioners.[4] The curé of Gennes was not opposed to lending his younger parishioners the wherewithal to buy a pound of salt to carry over into the Maine; and one can only guess at the attitudes towards smuggling of the parish priest of Elne whose church was searched by an official of the *ferme*:

---

[1] Poitrineau, *La Vie rurale en Basse Auvergne*, p. 370.

[2] Marion, *Dictionnaire*, p. 249. 'Tout le monde y compris les troupes (d'ailleurs souvent recrutées d'hommes condamnés aux galères pour faux saunage) y compris même quelque fois les commis des fermes, étant faux saunier de fait ou d'inclination . . .' (see also Cochois, *Étude historique*, pp. 84–5; Pasquier, *L'Impôt*, p. 113).

[3] M. Juillard, 'Le Brigandage en Haute Auvergne au XVIIIᵉ siècle', *Revue Haute Auvergne* (1936), p. 467 (this author worked a great deal on traditions and folklore): 'après avoir écoulé paisiblement leurs marchandises, les bandes se réunissaient au grand complet chez un nommé Mathias Estienne, aubergiste à Condat et là, au nombre de 15 à 20 compagnons on se livrait à une bombance formidable qui ne durait pas moins de quatre à cinq jours.' [4] A.D. Puy-de-Dôme C 4872.

ce jour là à midi, on commença la recherche du sel prohibé dans ladite église, et on la continua jusqu'à 5 heures du soir, à la réserve du temps de vêpres, et on ramassa, durant ce petit espace de temps, plus de 60 minots de sel provenus desdits étangs, parmi lesquels on trouva même quelques paquets de sel d'Espagne. Tous ces sels étaient cachés dans des armoires et des coffres, et une bonne partie dans des sacs qui étaient derrière les autels de ladite église. On en trouva dans la sacristie et dans le chœur une très grosse quantité. Il fut de plus trouvé dans la même église plus de cent livres de poudre de contrebande et deux livres de tabac aussi de contrebande. On trouva aussi dans une église qui est à la ville basse environ 30 minots de sel des dits étangs cachés pareillement derrière les autels et dans la tribune de la même église.[1]

If the *ferme* prevailed and the smuggler was brought before the courts, the odds were that the children would be released with a warning to the parents, the men if they had acted in a group sent into the army or for a spell in the galleys, and the women would be released as well on the grounds of 'pregnancy'. One of the loopholes in the law related to the pregnant women. The worst that could happen to a woman in this condition when caught dealing in illicit salt was that the salt she carried was confiscated; her condition prevented her incarceration. The result was not only that any woman visibly pregnant became a small-time smuggler (it was, after all, peculiarly easy at that time to conceal the stuff on one's person) but that women on the right side of fifty—some, if the *ferme* is to be believed, substantially older— made the plea of pregnancy and escaped without punishment, and nothing the *ferme* could do could get the law altered.[2] Adult males in a band using arms were the most likely to be punished. Apart from these, the only type of person against whom the full penalty would be exacted was the employee of the *ferme* who had stolen salt by giving underweight to the populace and who had sought to peddle what he had falsely withheld. The *commis des fermes* was universally detested: edged out of the *cabaret* and peculiarly liable to be murdered if he found out too much. He had the humiliating experience of seeing those whom he sent before the courts dismissed and he took his revenge on the civil populace in the worst possible way. Instead of concentrating upon capture of the smuggler, he turned his attention to the

---

[1] Boislisle, *Correspondance*, t. iii, n. 351.
[2] Callery, *La Fraude des gabelles*, p. 398; Cochois, *Étude*, pp. 76–7.

purchasers of illicit salt, and descended upon the peaceful family to examine the contents of its salt pot or searched its dwelling with scant regard for property and not hesitating to use physical violence. Occasionally the *commis des fermes* took the law into their own hands, and isolated parish registers, like that of Montaigut-en-Combrailles which reported in 1761 the death of two unknown men 'murdered by the brigade of the *ferme d'Échassières*',[1] bear witness to their brutality.

Such violence was not the monopoly of the major smuggling regions. Quercy belonged to the *pays rédimés*, its neighbour, the Rouergue, to the *pays de petite gabelle*, a difference which gave rise to a commerce, particularly a winter one, in illicit salt, picked up by Rouergats, *gens sans aveu*, *travailleurs de terre* (probably returning from seasonal work with a little ready money in their pockets), and dumped in the Rouergue. In 1785 a number of quite bloody confrontations took place between these bands and the employees of the *ferme*.[2] Similarly in the Gévaudan (*pays de petite gabelle*), which procured from Poitou.[3] Anywhere in fact where a region of fairly expensive salt could procure from a cheaper one, scope as risk-runners existed for the poor.

If salt smuggling had its main centres, so had the smuggling of tobacco. They were in the main threefold: the first, the north, Artois, Flanders, Cambrésis, Hainaut; the second, Alsace, Burgundy, Franche-Comté, the territories of Gex and Bayonne and the Comtat, which gave rise to the smuggling rackets of Champagne and even more so to those of the Vivarais and Dauphiné where the Rhône was the main artery; the third was that centred upon Roussillon.[4] The first two sprang from an anachronism in the levy of the tobacco tax which exempted these provinces; the third from the peculiar proximity of Spain.

---

[1] A.D. Puy-de-Dôme C 1574, Assassinat d'un garde des gabelles de Montaigut, 1762. A.C. Montaigut-en-Combrailles, 25 Oct. 1761. The Bois des Collettes was part of the commune of Échassières.

[2] A.D. Lot C 1390, Report of 1785.

[3] A.D. Lozère J 259, Mémoire contenant l'avis de M. Debernage de Saint-Maurice, intendant en Languedoc sur la demande faite au conseil par le syndic du Gévaudan en diminution du prix de sel.

[4] Matthews, *Royal General Farms*, pp. 118–19, and Bourquin and Hepp, *Aspects de la contrebande*, pp. 41–2. E. Gandolf, *Le Tabac sous l'ancienne monarchie* (Vesoul, 1914), pp. 3–19; A.N. G¹ (ferme générale) dossier 38, Mémoire sur le faux saunage et la contrebande du tabac en Espagne (1769); M. Four, *Le Tabac, privilège comtois au XVIIIᵉ siècle* (Besançon, 1947).

Roussillon was a seat of passage whence Italian tobacco was distributed throughout the cities of Spanish Catalonia, but the distributors, if not the entrepreneurs, were French. These were the main theatres of tobacco smuggling but there were lesser ones almost everywhere. There was a neat minor Breton traffic in Italian tobacco which was brought in Spanish vessels to the small ports of Vannes and Lorient, and doubtless subsidiary vessels dumped loads in the convenient creeks of the Breton littoral. There was the *artisanal* approach of individuals in parts of the Massif, where the humblest family, if it could procure the seeds, found it worth its while to have as few as half a dozen tobacco plants in its garden. Léonard Lelarge, a poor share cropper of Auge (near Guéret in the Creuse), had eighty large tobacco plants in his garden, edging out vegetables perhaps, but ensuring a good profit;[1] whilst Jofre, a shoemaker of the nearby village of Granges, had a dozen such plants and nothing else on his small patch of land[2]—had he had more land he would doubtless have grown more. The tavern was the centre of distribution, and the innkeeper expected a small cut in return for quietly passing on a packet to the wealthier customer.[3] Evidence of small-scale operators such as these is superabundant, and occasionally the officials of the *ferme* made their swoop and brought the small offender to justice. In the Haute Auvergne the church was again the favourite *entrepôt*, for example, at Chavaniac where the *vicaire* of the parish supplied his wealthy parishioners with tobacco grown or supplied by the poorer,[4] or at Vernols where the curé was held responsible for a massive hoard found in the sacristy— but the ecclesiastic in question refused to reveal his source.[5] For the few small providers of illicit tobacco brough to justice many more escaped undetected. The abbé Colson, parish priest of Mitting in Lorraine and deputy to the Estates General, left on record, in his memoirs, a justification for his activities as a tobacco and salt smuggler: his parishioners and their salt-starved cattle needed the money and salt he could thus acquire, and he considered it his duty to provide them with it.[6]

In terms of sheer numbers involved, the most considerable

---

[1] A.D. Creuse C 196.   [2] Ibid.

[3] Hemmer, 'La Contrebande du tabac au XVIIIᵉ siècle', *Mém. société scientifique historique, archéologique de la Creuse*, xxxi, 401–4.

[4] A.D. Cantal C 7563.   [5] Ibid. C 1628.

[6] A. Fournié, *Les Faux Sauniers en Lorraine* (Saint-Die, 1900), p. 22.

tobacco-smuggling area in France was Roussillon and yet, ironically, it was the one which concerned the *ferme* least, for the bulk
of the tobacco was intended for the Spanish market and, though
Roussillon was also the centre of reception of tobacco going into
Languedoc, it was far from being Languedoc's main source of
supply.[1] The tobacco, grown in Piedmont and Lombardy, was
brought to the small ports of French Catalonia, Cébère, Port Bou,
and Banyuls, by small Spanish vessels which, under the Spanish
flag, were free from the right of search of the officials of the *ferme*.
The Spanish tax on tobacco was if anything higher than the
French (on the Spanish market legal tobacco sold from 40 *reales*
the line, contraband for 8 *reales*). The entrepreneurs of the traffic
were Spanish merchants or merchants who set themselves up in
Banyuls, but the employees were almost 100 per cent French, and
hence the trade drew into France considerable amounts of coveted
Spanish money. The work force was complex: local fishermen
found an important increment to their livelihood by stacking the
tobacco in useful caves from which it was picked up by armed
smuggling bands. These were of two kinds: there was an element
of deserters, but more commonly they were *montagnards* of the
Cerdagne who did not need to have belonged to the military to
have arms at their disposal, for it was the privilege of all Roussillon that anyone might carry arms.[2] The route was either by
Perthuis, through the mountains to Custoja, or through Ceret,
Arles-sur-Tech, and over into Spain via Puigcerda, which became
an important centre of monetary exchange. Each of the villages
of passage became a recruiting ground (it was also important
work for the Spanish Catalan peasantry): 'Ils font des recrues,
comme les troupes . . . ceux qu'ils engagent comme domestiques
reçoivent sept réaux et demi de vellon par jour, plus la nourriture
. . .'[3] The size of the bands far surpassed anything known anywhere else in France. One, in the region of Banyuls, comprehended 700 men out of a potential force of 2,000. The *ferme*, even
had it been interested in suppressing this traffic, could not confront such numbers: 'On ne peut pas faire un pas en Roussillon
sans rencontrer des bandes de contrebandiers armés, dont la

---

[1] This traffic is brilliantly depicted in M. Defourneaux, 'La Contrebande du
tabac en Roussillon dans la seconde moitié du XVIIIe siècle', *Annales du Midi*
(1970), pp. 171–9.   [2] Ibid., p. 173.
[3] Affaires Étrangères, Correspondance Politique, Espagne, t. 570, fol. 332.

moindre est de 50 hommes et qui se suivent à peu de distance l'une de l'autre pour se secourir mutuellement.'[1] Moreover, the *contrebandiers du débarquement* were ready to come to the aid of the *contrebandiers de terre*. The employees of the *ferme* pleaded for permanent military support, but in 1782 even the military received a defeat from the smugglers: the conflict was between fifty-five smugglers and a brigade of the *ferme* assisted by twenty-two soldiers. A soldier was killed and several were wounded, while the smugglers evaporated into two villages.[2] The complicity of the local populations on either side of the frontier was total. Doubtless any potential informer was deterred by the obvious strength of the smugglers, but, more importantly, the economy of the region hinged upon the trafficking: 400,000 *livres* in solid Spanish money every year percolated into the region. In addition, the smugglers were fed whilst on the job by the entrepreneur.[3] Small wonder the governor of the province declared that any attempt on the part of the monarchy to confiscate the peasants' weapons would end in a provincial rebellion, or that Arthur Young found such evident prosperity as he crossed into Roussillon from Catalonia—a prosperity which, ironically, he attributed to 'good' government.[4]

The *ferme* could not afford to take as casually the heavy contraband traffic that grew up based on the privileged position of Franche-Comté, Burgundy, pays de Gex, and the Comtat Venaissin, because here it was distrained of its greatest profits. In areas where the *ferme* held the monopoly, the price of tobacco was 58 *sous* the pound; in the exempt territories 12 *sous*. Contraband tobacco could be expected to sell at 30 *sous* the *livre*—half the price of the product of the *ferme*.[5] Allied to this traffic was that in Swiss goods of which tobacco was only a part. Geneva, city of Calvin and Rousseau, was the Hong Kong of eighteenth-century Europe, a city of corruption and speculation and an international centre in which anything could be acquired. Lawn, cambric, muslin—known to the smugglers as *marchandises fines*—were goods

---

[1] Ibid., fol. 437, 23 June 1773.
[2] A.D. Pyrénées Orientales C 1034. This is merely one of many such stories.
[3] A conservative estimate in comparison with that offered by a Toulousain merchant who believed 60,000 *piastres* left Puigcerda every week (Defourneaux, 'La Contrebande du tabac', p. 175).
[4] A. Young, *Travels*, p. 38.
[5] Bourquin and Hepp, *Aspects de la contrebande*, pp. 43–4.

for which there was a ready market in France, and the entrepreneurs of the business were respectable merchants of Nîmes
and Lyons. Not that the merchants took any risks. Fontanieu,
intendant of Dauphiné, thus described the traffic:

La Contrebande des marchandises fines se fait ordinairement par
Genève, mais le temps où elle est la plus vive est celui de la foire de
Beaucaire. Le reste de l'année, elle dépend des demandes des marchands
de Lyon ... la troupe la plus célèbre pour ce commerce illicite est celle
que l'on appelle la bande d'Orange, parce qu'elle est composée de gens
de ce canton ou du Comtat. ... Cette bande ne fait communément que
deux voyages par an; elle est composée presque toute de déserteurs
armés ... elle est au moins de 80. ... Les chefs de cette troupe font leur
commerce de deux manières; ou en achetant les marchandises prohibées
et les débitant pour leur propre compte ou en les assurant à raison de
tant pour cent du prix depuis Genève jusques au lieu de leur destination ...

La contrebande du tabac ne se fait pas avec tant de précautions,
parce que la marchandise ne serait pas en état de supporter les frais.[1]

The bands were divided into *chefs*, *valets*, or *domestiques*, and
thirdly *journaliers*. The *chefs* were the entrepreneurs who were in
command of sufficient capital to purchase merchandise in bulk,
the horses for carrying the goods, and the arms to defend them,
and it was the *chefs* who hired the *valets*. The *valets* were full-time
accomplices, while the *journalier* usually engaged for a particular
job for which he was paid a fixed sum, dependent upon the degree
of risk, the physical hardship involved, and the likely profit of
the entrepreneur. The entrepreneur did not necessarily count on
a quick sale, and in order to command the highest prices was
occasionally prepared to peddle his goods over a wide area—
this was certainly true of Mandrin's band in the 1750s, which,
though based on Dauphiné, disposed of the goods in the Velay,
Bresse, and even as far west as Rodez.[2] The deserters formed
a hard core among the *valets*; their use is obvious: they were
trained to handle weapons and did not hesitate to use them in
face of imminent capture. The deserters sought in smuggling a

[1] E. Esmonin, 'Contrebande et contrebandiers en Dauphiné au XVIIIe siècle;
Un mémoire sur la contrebande en Dauphiné en 1730', *Cahiers d'histoire*, ii (1964),
201.
[3] Funck Brentano, *Mandrin, capitaine général des contrebandiers de France* (Paris,
1908), p. 44.

full-time occupation and so were used not only for the importation of the goods into France but also for their subsequent disposal. Lastly, the bands contained *journaliers*—farm labourers and those male inhabitants of the area who were young enough and sufficiently strong to carry packs on their backs in mountainous country where horses and mules could not go and who did not seek in smuggling a full-time occupation. They were of use because of their familiarity with the terrain and were called upon when the occasion demanded.[1]

But the direct participants represent only a fraction of those involved in smuggling. The police force was small and relied perforce on informants, whose silence had evidently to be bought by the *chefs*. The usual method, when needing to stay overnight in a village or to conduct transctions there, was to send a couple of men ahead, as much as twenty-four hours in advance, to make arrangements and to see that *largesse* was suitably distributed and that any likely member of the *maréchaussée* was lured away. Employers, for a bribe, complied in the temporary absence of *valets de ferme*, and more elderly men who could no longer make the trip were given a tip to ensure their loyalty.

The two provinces most actively involved in contraband were Dauphiné and Vivarais, situated on opposite banks of the Rhône and using that artery to reach the cities of the valley. Clearly, apart from the entrepreneurs, those who ran the risks were deserters, armed and violent men; and the two regions certainly served as poles of attraction to those fleeing their military commitments, those whom poverty had driven into the army but for whom army life had little appeal. For the deserter in the region contraband was part of the life of the *rouleur*: the most lucrative if the most risky part. But the deserters were not the only element who undertook the actual searching out of the tobacco and brought it into the Vivarais for distribution in the Velay. The young of entire villages in both Vivarais and Dauphiné gave themselves up to such pursuits. Saint-Étienne-de-Saint-Geoirs, birthplace of Mandrin, Saint-Genix-d'Aoste, les Échelles, Le Pont-de-Beauvoisir mark themselves out as villages of Dauphiné and Savoy[2] in which every male inhabitant was implicated and the employee of the *ferme* was on very dubious and dangerous ground. Saint-Martin-de-Valamas, Saint-Agrève, and surrounding

[1] Ibid., p. 203. [2] Funck Brentano, *Mandrin*, pp. 44–5.

hamlets, Colombier-le-Jeune, Mezonnac, Annonay, Mariac, Sainte-Eulalie-Vanosc, Saint-Félicien, Saint-Jean-Roure, Gillioc in the Vivarais are but a few where bands were organized on a parochial basis and brothers and sons acted together.[1] These villages had one thing in common: they were situated in three valleys, the Cance, the Doux, and Erieux, whence penetration into the Forez and the Velay from the Rhône was relatively simple. Who the entrepreneurs were is of less relevance to this study than is the hinterland of distributors who assumed control from the smuggling bands once the latter had moved the tobacco into the Velay, the Forez, and Bas Languedoc. The bands traded directly with *cabaretiers*; Piaron *cabaretier* at Saint-Agrève, Le Pin *cabaretier* at Dunières, Gitrol *cabaretier* at Monistrol-en-Velay, Désormes *cabaretier* at Saint-Didier-en-Velay—a pivotal *dépôt* because it commanded the route into the Forez—emerge as favoured *étapes*.[2] Some of them also accepted Swiss cambric, though most of this made its way into Lyons. From the *cabaretier* who may have dealt with other clients, contraband traffic passed —perhaps inevitably—into the hands of the *colporteurs*. These dealt in ounces of tobacco and small quantities of materials. A Dauphinois, François Rocher, caught in the Lyonnais sold rosaries, prayer-books, and contraband tobacco;[3] a Beaujolais *colporteur* dealt in *mousselines*—he refused to give detailed information about their source except that they came in from Switzerland and a Savoyard ferried them over the Rhône. At Lyons 'il couche pour deux sols par nuit chez un gargottier'. In his twenties, this young man had left home at the age of nine because his mother could not afford to feed him.[4] There clearly existed a level at which *vagabond*, *mendiant*, *contrebandier*, and *colporteur* merged into single individual. Thus Jacques Duchamp, *laboureur mendiant* of Saintonge, dabbled in a little contraband tobacco distribution in the Beaujolais and the Forez, but he was also *moissonneur et faucheur dans les saisons*. His concubine was a beggar, and his companion Denis Chalumeau, also caught carrying contraband tobacco, came from Chalon-sur-Saône and he ranged the Beaujolais. His mother was a washerwoman at Villefranche, his brother a servant

[1] A.D. Hérault C 1697, Signalements de contrebandiers en Vivarais.
[2] Ibid.
[3] A.D. Rhône, B, Maréchaussée, 1772, dossier F. Rocher, case cited by Gutton, *La Société et les pauvres*, p. 199.
[4] A.D. Rhône, B, Maréchaussée, 1761, dossier F. Poyet.

in the Dombes.[1] Nor was small-scale dealing in contraband goods a male monopoly. The widow of a *travailleur de terre* in the Beaujolais declared she lived by gleaning, begging (she was on trial for petty theft), and carrying contraband goods.[2] The Lyonnais received goods from the Forez, which in turn drew upon the Vivarais, and tobacco from Burgundy (via Mâcon and the Beaujolais); small wonder smuggling played an important part in the economy of poor *vagabonds* and itinerant *colporteurs*, and in fact of anyone prepared to run the risks amongst the domiciled poor.

Behind many, lies the concealed hand of the entrepreneur. Mandrin in the 1750s went into business with a capital of 100,000 *livres*—his entire patrimony. Merchants, *cabaretiers*, and, curiously, religious houses were all prepared to put money into smuggling, even if they were not prepared to run many risks. In 1717 the Récollets of Bourg-Saint-Andéol (near Nîmes) were brought before the courts and a few months later those of Sommières; in 1716 the Carmelites of Nîmes were found in possession of large stores and in 1717 those of Perpignan. Then the Capuchins of Alais and a daughter house at Agde were searched and found to be hoarding considerable quantities of tobacco. The same order was fined for being in possession of large stores at Pont-Saint-Esprit. Everyone knew that the Couvent de la Trinité in the city of Montpellier could be relied upon to supply the needs of anyone dissatisfied with the price set by the *ferme*.[3] One can only guess at the degree of involvement of the Dames de la Miséricorde of Montpellier, a *confrérie* which in 1728 took an active interest in a lawsuit involving one Antoine Garnier (was he one of their agents?) caught carrying illicit tobacco and condemned to five years in the galleys. In a letter to the *intendant* and subsequently in one to the monarchy asking for pardon of the accused, they pointed out that the young man had a wife and four children dependent on him for support and offered to pay any fines. Could not the birth of the dauphin be sufficient reason for the monarch to show clemency? The end of the story is not recorded, but the interest of these worthy ladies is noteworthy.[4]

The *ferme* regarded the Rhône valley as the place where it must concentrate its attack upon smuggling, and after the setting up

---

[1] Ibid. 1759, Duchamp, Chalumeau.   [2] Ibid. 1731, Marie Vaulieu.
[3] R. Labrély, *La Contrebande du tabac en Languedoc au XVIIIe siècle* (Bourg-Saint-Andéol, 1911), p. 10.   [4] A.D. Hérault C 1696, Signalements de contrebandiers.

of the Commission de Valence (1733) twenty years of fairly active repression ensued which reached a culmination with the defeat of Mandrin. In a sense, and for a restricted period of time, the *ferme* would seem after 1759 to have curtailed the activities of the large operator, entrepreneur, and full-time employee.[1]

From the 1760s the smuggling of tobacco lost a great deal of its tone and fell more decisively into the hands of those who were more positively *vagabonds*, brigands, and people whose livelihood was bound up with the perpetration of crime. These formed bands looking very much like the marauding bands of *rouleurs* who characterized the Languedocian scene, except that in the Vivarais and the Dauphiné smuggling was a constituent element of their economy and they were usually composed of fifteen to twenty members. The bishop of Le Puy thus described this transition to the *intendant* of Languedoc:

Vous êtes instruit, monsieur, des excès où se porte depuis quelque temps dans le pays d'alentour une troupe de quatorze à quinze bandits dont quelques uns ont été contrebandiers, et qui est aujourd'hui composée de voleurs. Elle ne se borne plus aux recettes des fermiers généraux, elle a pénétré dans plusieurs maisons isolées où elle a rançonné des paysans, des curés, des gentilshommes, des religieux tels que les Chartreux de Bonnefoy. Toutes les petites villes du voisinage, à commencer par celle où je suis maintenant, font réparer leurs portes qu'elles tiennent fermées la nuit et montent des gardes bourgeoises la nuit et le jour pour se mettre à l'abri d'une surprise et d'un coup de main.[2]

At Annonay a *bande* of 'soi-disant contrebandiers' (but in fact minor if vicious thieves) centred upon, and took refuge in, the wood of Devesset and throughout the sixties kept the *maréchaussée* of Privas, Tournon, and Annonay (twelve men in all) fully occupied. They raided larger farms, carried off poultry, clothing, money; murdered, burnt, and, when the *maréchaussée* levelled the wood in an attempt to extirpate them, fled into the Ardèche.[3] Finally five were apprehended, but the rest remained at liberty. The Vivarais, in fact, with its streams of seasonal migrants returning with the proceeds of their work, offered immense

---

[1] J. Regné, *La Contrebande en Vivarais au XVIIIᵉ siècle (1728–9)* (Paris, 1914), p. 41, was of the opinion that the main characteristic of smuggling after 1754 was its fragmentation into small, group banditry. This is also implied in *Histoire de Provence*, ed. E. Baratier (Toulouse, 1969), p. 374. [2] A.D. Hérault C 2625.

[3] A.D. Ardèche C 1079.

potential to the highway robber, and any accumulated money could be rapidly increased by a trip into the Comtat to purchase tobacco to be peddled elsewhere. In short, the bands of the Vivarais of the 1760s–1780s had something in common with the group banditry of the Beauce and the Forez: they were as much the concern of the *maréchaussée* as of the *ferme* and they had their origin in the peculiar social structure and traditions of the area. The withdrawal of the great entrepreneur from the scene left the smuggling villages without a steadily paid and organized traffic in tobacco but they had no option, no alternative source of income, and so continued in whatever small way they could, using contraband as merely one of a number of expedients that permitted some kind of dubious livelihood. In this way they troubled the working of the *ferme* less, but they troubled elements of the civil populace considerably more. Attacks on entire hamlets were common in the winter months.[1] The smuggler who had once been a friend had degenerated into a bandit.

[1] A.D. Hérault C 1993.

XI

PROSTITUTION

> au bas de la rue des Martyrs s'attroupent nombre de
> femmes et de filles prostituées, lesquelles entrent dans
> les cabarets et se font donner forcément du vin . . . et
> font ce qu'elles peuvent pour attirer à débauche les
> passants.
>
> (B.N. Fonds Français 8130, Projets et Mémoires.)

THE history of prostitution in the eighteenth century is even
more difficult to unroll than that of smuggling, where at least the
ferme générale had an interest in drawing the attention of the
monarchy to the problem from time to time. No one had the same
interest in prostitution. The crime did not fall within the purview
of the *prévôtés*, and the *maréchaussée* were not interested in the *fille
publique* unless, disease-ridden, she was a problem for the army.
Even then, the arrest of a prostitute did not bring with it the prize
money that accompanied the arrest of a beggar. The crime was
predominantly an urban one and the urban police had more to
do than to keep an eye on the vice trade. Occasionally the prostitute, living in the most run-down quarters, might be prevailed
upon to turn informant, in which case it might well pay the
police to keep her under surveillance. But this did not mean
arrest unless she made the transition from prostitute to thief.
Prisons did not abound in eighteenth-century France and were
certainly not used for prostitutes. Moreover, the *dépôts de mendicité*
were interested only in the *vénérienne*. Civil attitudes in fact made
it easy for the prostitute to continue to ply her trade undisturbed.
The *intendant* of Clermont wrote to the curé of Ambert, who felt
that civil authorities should deal more harshly with the problem
and who had offered the *maréchaussée* sufficient information to clean
up the streets of the town: 'La tranquillité publique ne souffre
aucun préjudice de ces sortes de commerce, et vous ne pouvez y
apporter d'autres remèdes que de l'exhorter à changer de conduite.'[1] The interest of ecclesiastical society was rarely so marked.

---

[1] A.D. Puy-de-Dôme C 1314, Letter of the *intendant* to the curé of Ambert, 1756.

Ecclesiastics might make unsuccessful attempts to offload a village girl of easy virtue into the *dépôts* by proclaiming her a habitual beggar,[1] but the village priests dealt only with individuals. They knew their parishioners. The same could not be said for the city clerics who rarely penetrated the urban slums and were not in command of sufficient knowledge of the milieu from which prostitutes were recruited.

Evidence on prostitution is clearly limited, and only when the prostitute had committed some other crime—resorted to violence, murder, or, most likely, theft—or could be accused of using her female favours to lure a man into a trap for robbery was legal action taken. Nor did the fact that she was a prostitute necessarily make sentence heavier. The fact was reported accidentally, usually in course of recounting the circumstances of the crime and not further to discredit the girl. *Bailliage* justice, as has been said before, was about compensation and hence prostitution was not the focal point at issue. In the *bailliage* of Falaise in the entire course of the seventeenth and eighteenth centuries only three prostitutes came before the courts, and that for theft; in that of Pont-de-l'Arche none at all; in the *prévôté* at Langres 10 out of 140 women were so described but their crime was robbery or they were *vénérienne* camp-followers; in the *prévôté* of Mende, 3 out of 58 accused were prostitutes and thieves; at Villefranche-de-Rouergue and in the *présidial* at Gray the crime is unrecorded in the court annals, and such negative examples can be multiplied. The *maréchaussée* at Lyons dealt with a score or so, in as many years, of those who had troubled public order.[2] The Breton *prévôtés* threw up a mere handful, and that in a province where women's favours were rated as easily obtainable.[3] Lack of court evidence does not mean that the practice was uncommon or that the authorities were ignorant of its existence. At Bordeaux 140 *filles de joie* appear on the capitation lists;[4] the prefect of Toulouse in 1806 was capable of a social analysis of the city's prostitutes which would have delighted the modern sociologist. He picked out the full-time professional outsiders who had come from other

---

[1] Ibid. C 1315, Femmes de mauvaise vie, 1768, and C 1201, Letter of M. de la Millière, 10 Feb. 1788.

[2] Gutton, *La Société et les pauvres*, pp. 103–5.

[3] A.D. Côtes-du-Nord G 65, Archdeacon's reports on the diocese of Tréguier, 1734–6.

[4] *Bordeaux au XVIIIᵉ siècle*, ed. Pariset, p. 366.

towns in search of better pickings and the local girls full-time and part-time:

beaucoup de filles d'artisan, de petites couturières, de femmes de chambre et de servantes quittent leur état pour se mettre en chambre et vivre dans la débauche. D'autres qui ne quittent ni leur état ni la maison paternelle et qu'on appelle Grizettes, se rendent furtivement dans des maisons où elles s'abandonnent à la lubricité des hommes pour des présents de l'argent. Elles suppléent ainsi à la médiocrité du salaire qu'elles reçoivent de la marchande de modes, de la couturière, des tailleurs, etc.: étant logées et nourries chez leurs parents elles employent tout ce qu'elles reçoivent à la belle tenue qu'elles montrent dans les promenades et autres lieux publics.[1]

He said there were hundreds of them, but that they were harmless, harmless that is, until they contracted syphilis and sought to infect the army. At that stage, and without trial, in the conditions of the *ancien régime* the prostitute was unceremoniously incarcerated in a *dépôt de mendicité*. The length of time she remained there was indeterminate; the only sure release was death. The *intendants* who were responsible for the running of the *dépôts* did not welcome prostitutes since they ensured the rapid spreading of the disease through the institution; on the other hand, they admitted that to release them would further endanger society: better hazard the lives of vagrants than those of the military.[2] Moreover, the prostitutes were financed by the army, anxious to contain the contagion as far as possible. The registers of the *dépôts de mendicité* are one of the few, scanty, incomplete sources for the history of prostitution; they show the prostitute in the final stages, disease-ridden, covered in sores, often losing her sight and, in some cases, her sanity. Occasionally, as at Vannes, one can trace something of their mobility: from the diocese of Rennes to Lorient, where the sailors and the Compagnie des Indes ensured good business until the bankruptcy of the latter caused a slump in the vice trade and a flight of the *filles de joie* to the interior.[3] But such details are rarely given. In the registers of the *dépôt* the prostitute's name,

[1] A.D. Haute-Garonne M 27. I am indebted to Dr. David Higgs for this reference.

[2] A.D. Hérault C 562 and A.D. Puy-de-Dôme C 1315, Letter of 10 Sept. 1768. The army paid for their incarceration to the tune of 5 *sous* a day and the government paid for treatment by *les boîtes du sieur Keyser*.

[3] Guéguen, 'La Mendicité au pays de Vannes', pp. 122–3.

age, place of origin, and physical condition are usually all that remains of her history, and those who would find out about the *femmes de mauvaise vie* are condemned to deal in tantalizing snatches of information, travellers' tales, analyses of misogynists such as Henrion de Bussy or the abbé Montlinot, or the masculine distortions and half-truths designed for literary effect of Restif. At best, though they are very occasional, there are the registers of institutions designed for *filles repenties*. These institutions were few and far between. They were the result either of philanthropic effort in the late Middle Ages or of a second wave of such towards the end of the seventeenth century. Most provincial centres had one, as in the Rouergue, Quercy, the Pays de Velay, Burgundy. Brittany was well endowed: at Rennes La Tour des Toussaints, intended also for the mad and potentially vicious, took in some eighteen *filles débauchées* in the 1780s; Vannes had a similar institution in the Petit Couvent, which took in about a dozen girls; while Nantes and Quimper had small foundations which might cater for a handful. Provence boasted three such institutions at Aix and one at Marseilles. Lyons, Bordeaux, Strasbourg had sufficient institutional resources to intern about sixty *filles publiques*;[1] while the resources of the capital pivoted upon the Maison Sainte-Pélagie which sheltered about forty girls whose parents could not pay for their keep.[2] At Toulouse the *filles publiques* deemed receptive to correctional training were accorded a corner of the workhouse at La Grave.[3]

The scale of these institutions is typical, as is their concentration in diocesan centres. They were intended to rescue the young, and one can be more precise: they were designed to help back to the path of virtue those who had but momentarily strayed and whose families were concerned enough to draw them to the attention of the mother superior—in the north often a sister of Saint-Thomas de Villeneuve. Sainte-Pélagie in Paris, Sainte-Marcelle in Aix and the Bon Pasteur in Dijon were quite exclusive. Other sought a somewhat broader recruitment. The purpose of La Pureté at Aix was expressly 'de recueillir les pauvres jeunes

---

[1] Lempereur, *L'État du diocèse de Rodez*, Rodez; Bolotte, *Les Hôpitaux et l'assistance en Bourgogne*, p. 325; A.D. Ille-et-Vilaine 1 F 2246, Fonds Hardouin, La Tour des Toussaints (*manuscrit*); Valran, *Misère et charité en Provence*, pp. 259–61; Gutton, *La Société et les pauvres*, p. 105, etc.

[2] Bloch and Tuetey, *Procès-verbaux*, pp. 614–15.

[3] A.D. Hérault C 562.

filles lesquelles par nécessité de leurs parents ou leur mauvaise
conduite perdent malheuresement leur honneur et leur innocence'.[1] It took girls between the ages of 8 and 16; at 16 they
were placed in service. The house at Rodez had a higher age-
range.[2] It was prepared to consider girls up to the age of 20.
None of these houses was prepared to countenance a girl already
infected with venereal disease. The eighteenth century had already
begun experimenting with mercury as a cure for syphilis, but as
yet much had to be learnt, and perhaps as many lost their sanity
through mercury poisoning as in the course of tertiary-degree
syphilis. In other words, once a girl became diseased, the good
sisters saw little in her future, *repentie* or not. Many religious
foundations refused to treat the disease in any case, as going
beyond the limits of their obligations.[3] To picture these institutions as places making any real impact upon the problem of
prostitution would be totally false. Exception to most rules
should be made for the Compagnie du Saint Sacrement at Lyons
which understood the problem but had so few resources at its
disposal that it could hardly make a start. Most were not concerned with the problem of prostitution as a whole but with
preserving the young, the domiciled young, from falling into bad
ways. There was no question of taking in anyone who needed
correctional training; the nuns took as many as could be provided
for, and no more. Some provision was made at the Refuge in
Aix for the repentant prostitute who was still clean to spend the
rest of her days in penitential vestment and prayers, but such
women were not at the root of the problem of prostitution.

The word 'prostitute', as the prefect of Toulouse pointed out,
comprehends a broad spectrum: the girl who is wholly maintained
in her own establishment by one man and who might be quite
lavishly maintained at that (success stories of this kind are
restricted to the very few in a few provincial cities). Here Bordeaux with its mercantile opportunities was clearly in a class of
its own. More importantly, it comprehends the street walker, full
or part-time, who might or might not be a home-based *grizette*,
the woman in the bawdy house sharing her income with *concierge*

---

[1] Valran, *Misère et charité*, p. 260.
[2] A.M. Rodez, Bourg et Cité FF1-2, Enquêtes des procès contre les femmes de
mauvaise vie.
[3] The *vénérienne* was never taken into a *hôtel Dieu* for this reason.

and ponce, the waitress in the *cabaret* willing to oblige the customers for a consideration, the camp-follower (the girl who catered
to the needs of the military was likely to end up a prostitute).
The military were poorly paid, so anyone who sought to make an
income from them had to oblige large numbers, and the payment
of a regular rental was clearly difficult. Such women are caught
in the pictures of de Wouwermann, grey, dirty, huddling around
camp-fires, they were the habitual accompaniment of any regiment.[1] At the end of the line were the *vénériennes*, many no longer
able to ply their trade and left to rot in a *dépôt*. One can make a
few more generalizations which fill out the picture a little. The
first is that the prostitute stemmed from the poor and that city
prostitution tallies with the pattern of urban recruitment. The
prostitutes of Paris were Alsatians and Lorrainers, from the Île
de France, Burgundy, and the Bourbonnais;[2] of Lyons from the
Bresse, Bugey, Forez;[3] of Toulouse from the Comminges, the
Rouergue, the Lauragais;[4] of Bordeaux from Béarn, Comminges, Entre-Deux-Mers; of Montpellier from the Gévaudan,
Velay, Rouergue, and Cevennes; of Marseilles from Valence,
Orange, and the Provençal hinterland; those of Strasbourg,
Dijon, Lille, and Troyes were more locally recruited. The eighteenth-century image of the country girl losing her virtue in the
big city is a slightly distorting concept. The girl most likely to
end up on the streets was the servant girl, run second by the
seamstress, worker in the garment and textile trades—the *dévideuse* or *tireuse de cordes* at Lyons, the spinner at Lille and Troyes
and in the textile cities of the north.[5] Admittedly these girls were
rural in origin, but the nature of their jobs rather than any other
consideration was what started them on the streets. The servant
between jobs or unable to find employ and the textile worker
confronted with a slump were clear recruits for the vice trade, for

[1] There is a good example in the Fitzwilliam Museum, Cambridge, and there are
several in Dulwich College.

[2] R. Cobb, *The Police and the People*, p. 236. A detailed study of Parisian prostitution
is promised from M. Benabon, 'Libertinage, prostitution et police des mœurs dans
le Paris du XVIIIᵉ siècle'.

[3] Gutton, *La Société et les pauvres*, p. 104, and C. Lucas, 'La Police et la pègre
lyonnaise', *A.H.R.F.* xxxix (1967).

[4] Their nicknames often included their place of origin: Castan, *La Criminalité
dans les pays de Languedoc*, p. 63.

[5] A conclusion based upon professional qualification of the women in the *dépôts*
of Languedoc, Brittany, Auvergne, and Normandy, and on the works cited above.

they had nothing else to turn to. At the Place Bellecour in Lyons late on the night of 6 July 1770, six girls were arrested for troubling public order—they were involved in a brawl. One described herself as 'ci-devant domestique chez un cabaretier rue St Jean', another 'fait des bas, coud pour les fabricants et file la laine', another described herself as 'ci-devant domestique chez un gargotier', the fourth 'brodeuse', the fifth 'ci-devant domestique chez un aubergiste, maintenant dévideuse de soie', and the sixth 'a travaillé chez les tireurs d'or' but was currently a *coiffeuse*. Clearly four of these were *grizettes*, but two were ex-servants now totally unemployed.[1]

At Montpellier three peculiarly pathetic cases of servants too feeble to work who had turned to the vice trade only to end up *vénériennes* were described by the *intendant*: 'Il en est une de ces trois appelée Elizabeth Dangles qui est dans un état si triste pouvant à peine marcher . . . il est certain que n'ayant aucune resource elles pourront communiquer leur mal à bien de personnes.'[2] Marie Renard of Recoules near Rodez had followed her brother into employ at Lodève, where, seduced by her employer and with an unwanted pregnancy on her hands, she took the obvious step of paying some woman all she had to support her child and making for the coast. Catherine Jacob of Le Puy was a more classic *coureuse* formerly employed as *servante* by at least six religious houses, a carpenter, and finally a *cabaretier*. She was 19 and *vénérienne*. Others clearly operated from home, like Anne Maliche, or had left Béziers, Agde, or Pézenas for the larger city.[3] The servant girl was, of course, the one most likely to find herself with an unwanted pregnancy, seduced by her employer, or his son, or simply because such a girl was usually totally unable to cope with leisure. A day off, a religious festival, saw her an easy prey for the military or for the apprentice or fellow servant who was assiduous in his pursuits—these are the message of the urban *déclarations de grossesse*.[4] Once pregnant, dismissed, and virtually alone in the world, the girl faced a bleak future. But even without an unwanted pregnancy, the temptation to supplement a slender

[1] Gutton, *La Société et les pauvres*, p. 104.
[2] A.D. Hérault C 141, États des filles et femmes de mauvaise vie arrêtées pour discipline militaire . . ., 1787; ibid. L 2972, Listes de filles de mauvaise vie détenues depuis 1788.
[3] Ibid.
[4] See below, pp. 320–1.

income or to provide oneself with better clothes was considerable. The Compagnie du Saint Sacrement considered three
reasons for prostitution in Lyons. First, that the opportunity was
afforded by a clientele who came on business and who were constantly passing through; that the military in permanent garrison
were an entrenched source of corruption; but that above all the
practice was constantly fed by 'la cessation des manufactures qui
donne lieu à une infinité de jeunes filles de s'abandonner malheureusement pour trouver la plupart du temps dans leurs crimes
un secours pour la subsistance de leur famille'.[1]

The suggestion of general family dependence upon the activities of a young prostitute is also found at Toulouse, where the
commonest street walker was the girl from the Comminges. The
incarceration of several of these girls as *vénériennes* in the *dépôts*
led to an attack on the building by their families whose livelihoods
depended upon their activities.[2] The servant girl might start out
on her dubious career as a *grizette*, merely supplementing her
wage from her job, but the odds would seem heavily weighted
on her becoming a full-time prostitute, the more so if the military
were her main customers. The ex-servant camp-follower trailing
from garrison town to garrison town is the most recurrent type
of full-time prostitute in the records. All those who came before
the court at Langres for theft fitted into this category and were
always taken at Bourbonne-les-Bains, seat of a military hospital
where some 500 soldiers were permanently in receipt of treatment
or convalescing from wounds, and in either case with time on
their hands. Some girls had a particular taste for one regiment:
the Jeanne-Marie who had followed the régiment de Provence
from Lyons to Langres had made a trip impressive by its length.
But the working lives of such girls were short. Once involved
with the *dragons*, the *dépôt* was not far distant. When a full-time
fille de joie of the military came before the courts, the magistrates
did not linger long over her background.[3]

There was a level of society that was clearly reconciled to the
idea of its children ending up on the streets—necessity is a hard
master. The prefect of Toulouse declared that the *grizettes* operated
from home: some actually used their parents' homes as a basis

[1] A.M. Lyon GG 149, cited by Gutton, *La Société et les pauvres*, p. 102.
[2] Rives, 'L'Évolution démographique de Toulouse', p. 127.
[3] Instances taken from A.D. Haute-Marne B, Maréchaussée de Langres.

of operation and their parents evacuated the premises whilst the act was committed. Indeed, the fallen girls put with the Dames de l'Union in Rodez almost invariably had parental connivance if not positive encouragement; hence Anne Mazars, aged 40, *couturière* married to a *manœuvre*, accused of having 'favorisé les prostitutions de sa fille' (also a *couturière*) had procured for the girl, bartered her favours, and, even more cunningly, had received advance sums from men in anticipation of her daughter's services, and on one occasion had stolen the man's clothing as he slept and even made off with his shoes. Mazars could only plead poverty in her defence and claimed that her husband had in any case tricked her into marriage by saying he had property, whereas really he was resourceless, and that the girl's profits had bought shoes for them both—the daughter, Antoinette, also had, however, a lace *coiffe* valued at 8 *sous* and an apron valued at 4 *sous*—luxuries which the judges deemed beyond the resources of a decent working girl.[1]

More pathetic was perhaps the case of the Vidal sisters, taken a little too late, for they had contracted syphilis. Jeanne and Marguerite were the two eldest daughters of a blind mason; they were seamstresses like their mother and there were other children. When work did not come in the Vidal girls took to the streets, and brought their customers home whilst the mother and the other children hung about outside, and the father, being blind, sat in his corner. As *vénériennes*, there was no hope for them at the *repenties* and they were sent to a *dépôt de mendicité*.[2]

At Mende a case of petty theft, linen left to dry, involved two girls, Marguerite Planchon and Catherine Jolicoeur aged 20 and 19 respectively, both spinners. Both had been abandoned in childhood. Catherine Jolicoeur stated espressly 'que c'est depuis l'âge de quatre ans qu'elle se vit forcée par la misère de mendier son pain' when her parents had left her; there is no mention of a period spent in an institution for *enfants trouvés*. Both stemmed from Marvejols and had spent time both there and in Mende, and when work earned them insufficient 'ont eu le malheur, faute d'avoir de quoi vivre de se livrer à la débauche'.[3] Their garments were wretched; they were without shoes. There were too many

---

[1] A.M. Rodez Bourg et Cité FF 2, Anne Mazars.
[2] Ibid., Jeanne and Marguerite Vidal.
[3] A.D. Lozère 21B5, Prévôté de Mende, 1775, Planchon and Jolicoeur.

at the same activity for it to be fully profitable. At Rodez a young girl counted herself indeed fortunate if she could earn 12 *sous* from an evening's activities; to earn 6 was to do tolerably well; 3 *sous* might be all that could be expected from the military; and if trade was really slack a girl would be content with bread, a little Rocquefort, a glass or two of red wine, and a few sugared almonds for the little girls who procured for her.[1] The *grizettes*, declared the prefect of Toulouse, plied their trade primarily to buy clothes, cambric aprons, shoes with buckles, lace for trimming, which their wages as seamstresses or servants would not buy. Adornments such as these helped to further their business. Similarly, when being considered as potential material for the *repenties*, the girls' wardrobe was scrutinized.[2] But others were out to provide themselves with necessities, not luxuries, and there is a little evidence to suggest on occasion rivalry between the two groups. At least one girl at Rodez, Antoinette Vialaret, declared that jealousy from women no better than she was over her new shoes had caused them to report her to the *repenties*.[3]

Some evidence of the less salubrious bawdy houses emerges from the registers of the *repenties* at Rodez: that of the Huqs who catered to the needs of the military on the one hand and students on the other and sheltered whole teams of young girls who operated in the open air in the bois de Madame l'Abbesse. Two of the Huq girls, Marianne Noë, *fille charpentier*, taken for seducing students, three at a time, and Marie Chaussy, who obliged schoolboys, found their way to the *repenties*.[4] Then there was the Artisse house, also in Rodez, over which presided Madame Jeanne, wife of François Artisse, *brassier*, the repair of travelling merchants during fairs. Several of Artisse's girls were pregnant and she claimed that they were working at various jobs to save a little to support their children, while she merely afforded them cheap shelter. Artisse, however, was a reputed abortionist—though nothing could be proven. *Dragons, marchands, comédiens, un individu habillé en ecclésiastique* pass through the pages of her file as reputed clientele.[5] One of the cases for theft appearing before the *bailliage* of Falaise treats, albeit less graphically, of a similar establishment

[1] A.M. Rodez Bourg et Cité FF 2, Marie Baulez. Antoinette Mazars tried to bargain for 20 *sous* but brought a good customer down to 12. She was 16 and pretty.
[2] Ibid.   [3] Ibid., Antoinette Vialaret.
[4] Ibid., Noë and Chaussy.   [5] Ibid., Artisse.

in the small town run by the Vasseurs: he was a *maître de danse*, but the *maison de passe* side of the business was clearly run by his wife. Information on this came to light when Marie Lefebvre, ex-servant girl, was tried for stealing handkerchiefs. By the age of 19 she had had four jobs: first as a servant to a merchant tanner, then as a spinner *chez* Bellenger, then a seamstress employed by the Logis du Sacq, and finally servant again for Jouenne *cafetier*. She had met a young man at the Vasseurs', where he rented a room for her for several months, after which she had had other clients; 'son malheur a commencé quand elle a dit à la femme Vasseur qu'elle avait la gale', at which point Madame clearly wished to be rid of the girl, whilst her obvious infection meant that employment as a servant became difficult to find and potentialities for prostitution were reduced. Interestingly enough, Madame Vasseur was the main witness for securing the girl's imprisonment for theft. Neither the facts about her house nor her reputation were called into account as being in any way relevant to the case.[1] The police records of Lyons allow glimpses not only of brothels but of ponces at work: the unsavoury Léonard Renaud, for example, who lived in the rue Tupin and styled himself a *compagnon maçon*, whilst in fact he made a comfortable income by money-lending, running a *maison de passe*, and employing a number of prostitutes; or Dugrand, *aubergiste*, who ran an establishment of doubtful repute in Saint-Irénée.[2] Cities, then as at a later date, clearly had their red-light districts: the rue Sainte-Melaine in Rennes, the rue Long in Bordeaux, the entire Île de Tounis in Toulouse; and favoured spots for plying the prostitute's trade: the Peyrou in Montpellier, the Place Bellecour in Lyons; examples which are easily multiplied. Occasionally, grim reports signal a traffic in children. There were girls in the *dépôt* at Riom who by the age of 12 were already *coureuses* in Languedoc and *vénériennes* long before they menstruated.[3] There were young prostitutes of 16 and 17 in the *dépôts* of Vannes, Rennes, and Caen who had been at their trade for several years. There were girls of 7 styled *demi libertines* in the *hôpital* at Rouen.

What the scanty evidence on this most tolerated of crimes adds

---

[1] Gégot, 'Étude par sondage', p. 157.

[2] Gutton, *La Société et les pauvres*, p. 105.

[3] A.D. Puy-de-Dôme C 1195, Report of Henrion de Bussy, 1787. The Compagnie du Saint Sacrement at Lyons was concerned about 'des femmes qui enlèvent des petites filles pour les prostituer plus tard', cited by Gutton, p. 105.

up to is a widespread practice in which the daughters of the poor predominated. Occasionally curés reported exceptionally difficult times, such as widespread harvest failure and inflated grain prices, when married women offered themselves. The curé of Bort near Clermont spoke in the 1740s of such a crisis: when questioned, husbands were insistent that their wives did it to get food for their children, but the women were adamant that they had been pushed into this line of action by their husbands.[1] A parallel situation existed in Brittany in the 1780s when, in the aftermath of epidemic, shattered family units sought out the towns and tried to piece together some kind of livelihood.[2] Such grim reminders reinforce the close link between poverty and prostitution. Unlike Restif's well-fed, well-dressed Ursula whose early adventures in metropolitan vice were in pursuit of excitement, these women started and finished hungry and in rags. There is sufficient in the tallies of the *dépôts* to make clear that prostitution in the economy of the poor was a one-way ticket.

[1] A.D. Puy-de-Dôme C 897.
[2] A.D. Ille-et-Vilaine C 1745, Subdélégation de Josselin, 1784.

XII

PARENT AND CHILD

Pater et mater meus derelinquerunt me Deus autem
assumpsit me.

(Notice above the door of the foundling
hospital of Rennes.)

THE crimes of the poor as detailed above are lacking in at least
one important constituent, those committed by parent against
child. Amongst offences, whether criminal or moral, some recognition must be made of infanticide, child abandonment, or the
neglect which might in the end amount to the same, and, amongst
offenders, of the women who gave birth to these children. Whether
left to face certain death with an ill-paid, uncaring wet-nurse
while his mother carried on with a job crucial to her own existence
and perhaps that of her other children, whether jettisoned on a
doorstep, church porch, or in the basket of the local *hôpital*, or
strangled and stuffed down a drain, the unwanted child figures
large amongst the victims of the problems of poverty. He does
so most particularly in the annals of the *enfants trouvés*, for by the
1770s the sheer weight of numbers of children left to charity had
forced itself upon administrators, from the *contrôleur général* downwards, as they threatened to swamp the entire resources of the
hôpitaux. Every year in the closing decade of the *ancien régime*,
something in the region of 40,000 children were left, anonymous,
to the care of society, and the problem was escalating and forcing
administrators to query their likely provenance, to redress standard
assumptions about the motives for abandoning children, and confronting them with evidence they did not always find it easy to
stomach.[1]

---

[1] To arrive at any over-all estimate of the numbers of *enfants trouvés* is difficult.
The *Comité de Mendicité* accepted 40,000 (Bloch and Tuetey, *Procès-verbaux*, p. 549),
an estimate which perhaps errs on the side of generosity. In Paris *c.* 8,000 children
were abandoned each year in the 1780s (ibid.); in Lyons *c.* 2,000 (E. Fayard, *Histoire*

The *enfant trouvé* was, by definition, anonymous, and of his origins much will always remain a mystery.[1] It is easy to conjure with two types of children who might find themselves, irrespective of the season, left to charity. First they might be illegitimate and, given the more rigorous surveillance of middle-class and richer girls, the children of the poor, and secondly they might be the legitimate offspring of a family too impoverished to support them. That they were the product of poverty is not speculation: puny, lice-ridden, diseased, stinking of urine, and bundled in dirty rags, such infants were hardly the product of illicit unions amongst the more affluent sectors of society.[2]

Although his parentage was unknown, the *enfant trouvé* until the last two decades of the eighteenth century was automatically assumed to be illegitimate, the unhappy victim of the evil conduct of his parents. Explicitly or implicitly this assumption pervades even the writings of Saint Vincent de Paul and was accepted unquestioningly by society from its middle-class echelons upwards. When in the seventies the *hôpitaux* were asked to comment on the likely origins of the *enfants trouvés* they replied almost with one voice: 'La distinction entre les bâtards exposés et les légitimes abandonnés n'a point lieu, parce que quand ces derniers sont abandonnés, ils sont réputés bâtards.'[3]

Those *hôpitaux* which were obliged in some way to care for the *enfant trouvé* usually kept a register in which three types of children were enumerated: *illégitimes*, or those of known illegitimate parentage whose father or mother had made a financial settlement with the institution; *légitimes*, or orphans admitted usually after

---

administrative de l'œuvre des enfants trouvés avandonnés et orphelins de Lyon (Lyons, 1859), p. 417); Bordeaux, *c.* 600 (A. Rebsomen, 'Le Registre de réception des enfants trouvés des enfants de Bordeaux', *Revue historique de Bordeaux* (1926)); Marseilles, *c.* 500, Aix, *c.* 300 (A.N. H^1 1322); Rouen and Le Havre together, *c.* 400 (A.D. Seine-Maritime C 1001); towns of the Auvergne together, *c.* 800 (A.D. Puy-de-Dôme C 1340); Rennes, Vannes, Quimper, and Nantes together, *c.* 1,000 (A.D. Ille-et-Vilaine C 1286); Bourges, *c.* 300 (A.D. Cher, Hôtel Dieu. Registre d'entrée des enfants trouvés); Dijon, *c.* 300 (A.D. Côte-d'Or L 1102). Such instances give an idea of the range of the problem. Towns of 8,000–10,000 such as Bayeux, Rodez, Mende, Saint-Malo, etc., produced 50–70 abandoned children every year.

[1] For this reason some historians of poverty, e.g. Gutton, *La Société et les pauvres*, have refused to treat the issue.

[2] Many of the *registres de réception*, as at Bourges, Bordeaux, Montpellier, and Bayeux, actually include a physical description of the rags worn by the children as well as the exact location where they were picked up.

[3] A.D. Ille-et-Vilaine C 1270, Hôpital de Port Louis, 1777.

some financial negotiation with existing relatives; and *enfants trouvés*, the unknown, the most numerous, and the most socially problematic. Yet by the mid seventies, the central government, whose dossiers on the subject were growing daily, was unable to enjoy such an easy confidence. Gradually its approach to the enigma posed by the abandoned child became that of the social historian: was there any evidence available which might, in the terminology of the eighteenth century, decide whether he was *un produit de la honte ou de la misère*?

i. *The Illegitimate Child*

The extent and incidence of illegitimacy in *ancien régime* France conform to an almost uniform pattern. In rural society the illegitimate represented from 1 to 2 per cent of all births. The figures, however, rise steadily in towns of under 10,000 to about 4 per cent, and in cities reached staggering proportions of 12 per cent, 17 per cent—even perhaps in the capital over 20 per cent.[1] The simple town–country contrast, however, is a somewhat deceptive one. Pregnant country girls had innumerable reasons for seeking out the towns: they might thus escape the attentions of family and village and so afford themselves the possibility of a fresh start; the towns had more facilities for coping with an un-wanted baby, and in some instances had institutions where the child could be abandoned; and, if all else failed, they always had baby farms where a mother in search of employment could leave her baby against a minimal payment for minimal care. The illegitimacy rates in the towns were therefore likely to be inflated. Equally relevantly, those most likely to conceive an illegitimate child were from the lowest notches on the social scale: servant girls above all, also textile workers and casual labourers who were recruited from the countryside and who, it might be argued, though pregnant as a result of activities in the town, were really country girls.[2]

---

[1] *L'Histoire sociale. Sources et méthodes*, Colloque de l'École Normale Supérieure de Saint-Cloud, 15–16 mai 1965 (Paris, 1967), p. 225. Illegitimacy rates are at their lowest in the south.

[2] This is the message of the *registres de déclarations de grossesse* kept in all towns. Those of Lille have formed the basis of A. Lottin, 'Naissances illégitimes et filles mères à Lille au XVIIIᵉ siècle', *Revue d'hist. mod. et cont.*, avril–juin 1970. Those consulted for this chapter were of Rennes and Vannes, thanks to Dr. T. Le Goff, of Toulouse, Montpellier, and Périgueux.

Illegitimacy rates in the cities were rising steadily throughout the century: in Lille they jumped from 4·5 per cent of all live births in 1740 to 12·5 per cent in 1785; in Strasbourg from 6 to 15 per cent; and in Lyons the pattern is similar.[1] The explanations for this have usually embraced the decline of moral standards as one moves away from the restrictive Jansenist ethic of the seventeenth century.[2] But perhaps this is too academic an approach and more can be understood if concentration is placed instead on the increasing uprootedness of urban populations, born of the growing need in the countryside to find work elsewhere; a need which brought the unmarried, the lonely, the penniless into the cities and exposed them to temptation. However, this is to embark with a premature conclusion. Much of the information which remains on the unmarried mother and her child can be better understood if it is accompanied by an appreciation of her status and the law.

The legislation on the subject reflected a dual concern, part moral, part material, and started from the basic premise that the problem of the illegitimate child needed controlling. Laxity of this nature has always secured the disapprobation of Christian society and the bastard child has served to complicate every law of property ever devised. The double concern of Henri II's law (1556) was, first, to prevent a secret confinement which might make infanticide easy, a crime with sacrilegious implications, and, secondly, to find out the father with the hope of making him marry the mother if possible, and, if not, at least support the child.

To these ends the law obliged the pregnant unmarried girl or widow to declare her pregnancy to a magistrate who must question her on how long she had been pregnant, who had made her so, and where the event occurred. The magistrate had to be summoned when the girl was in labour and the three questions had to be put to her afresh. The idea behind this was that at the climax of her pain, the girl was most likely to denounce the real author of her agony. Failure to comply incurred grave penalties. Any woman against whom it could be proven that she had 'celé, couvert et occulté tant sa grossesse que son enfantement, sans

---

[1] Lottin, p. 290; Dreyer-Roos, *La Population strasbourgeoise*, pp. 186–7, etc.

[2] This is P. Deyon's explanation of the phenomenon at Amiens, P. Deyon, *Amiens, capitale provinciale* (Paris, 1967), p. 11.

avoir pris de l'un et de l'autre témoignage suffisant, serait réputée avoir homicidé son enfant et, pour réparation, punie de mort'.[1] The parish priest had, as part of his duties, to read out this law every three months before mass so that no one should be ignorant of the penalty. Indeed, the priest was regarded as crucial in the enforcement of this edict, and he was reminded of his obligations in this respect at every archdeacon's visitation.

The curés discharged the obligation, at least in some rural parishes, very conscientiously. One Auvergnat curé prided himself on the quality of his female spies, dotted about the congregation, who made a point of surveying the stomachs of the unmarried and reported any suspicious signs—vigilance which can only have served as an additional incentive to flee to the anonymity of the city.[2] In the rare instances where cases of infanticide came before the courts, the curé was usually instrumental in bringing the girl to justice, thanks to the information of a devoted parishioner.[3] More than this, in spite of the elaborate provision made in the legislation of Henry II, it was to the curé in rural areas, the *sage-femme* in the towns, that the task of finding out the father usually fell. The curé's interest was a purely moral one: if the pair were both single, they could be pushed into marriage; if the man was married, then his sin was double, and curés did not hesitate to pass on the information to the appropriate authorities.

The Ordinance of Henri II sought to find out the father with a view to making him pay for the child's support. It was followed in 1586 by the Ordinance of Moulins, which sought to make provision for abandoned and destitute illegitimate children whose parents could not provide for them by making them the financial responsibility of the *seigneur* or, in towns, of the *seigneur haut*

---

[1] Bloch and Tuetey, *Procès-verbaux*, p. 346, and Isambert, *Recueil*, t. xiii, p. 471. This paragraph was incorporated *in toto* into provincial *coutumes*, e.g. Potier de la Germondaye, *Introduction au gouvernement des paroisses suivant la jurisprudence du parlement de Bretagne* (Rennes, 1776), p. 334 (Houard, *Dictionnaire analytique . . . de la coutume de Normandie . . .*, Filles mères).

[2] A parish priest of Dinan adopted similar tactics. 'Les personnes du sexe se mettent aux églises dans un lieu séparé des hommes, aucune d'elles n'échappe aux regards curieux des connaissances. Comme elles sont toutes par intérêt d'une attention extrême aux personnes suspectes; lorsque le doute se change en certitude, elles avertissent ceux qui en sont chargés qui prennent les précautions ordinaires pour que la personne déclare sa grossesse et le père de l'enfant.' A.D. Ille-et-Vilaine, Fonds Hardouin, L'enquête de 1740. L'éducation des enfants assistés.

[3] This is certainly the Breton experience, where the case cited by Corre and Aubry, *Documents*, p. 267, is typical.

justicier (usually the monarch). Thus, to know where the event occurred was as important as knowing who the father was. The implementation of this ordinance was extremely erratic, and the monarchy only tardily accepted any very summary responsibility for the foundlings, let alone children of known though illegitimate parentage, in the 1770s. The fate of the illegitimate child of an impoverished mother and that of the abandoned child of unknown parentage were confused in the minds of legislators simply because it was assumed that the latter were recruited from the former. Where the monarch was *seigneur haut justicier*, the subvention of the poor illegitimate child was unlikely unless the mother abandoned it. *Seigneurs* paid up only with great reluctance and frequently not at all.[1] Certainly the child had to be deserted by its parents before a *seigneur* saw fit to make even the most nominal payment.

In the *pays d'États* the application of the Ordinance of Moulins was either non-existent or changed to meet provincial custom, and some provinces emerged with more comprehensive arrangements than those that were more directly under monarchical control. In Flanders, joined to the French crown in the late seventeenth century, the parish was responsible for its own abandoned children and theoretically for illegitimate children whom the parents were unable to support.[2] In Brittany the *générale des habitants* had a similar obligation.[3] Where the parish had this near financial concern, then it was likely to take a more active interest in the paternity of any illegitimate offspring, lest the father should offload his financial responsibilities on to the parish.[4] These were then the provinces *par excellence* of the paternity suits undertaken by the parish, the *générale des habitants* against the father, or alleged father, who if he wanted to escape payment to the parish for the support of the child had to prove his innocence, and innocence under such circumstances was almost

[1] A. Poitrineau, 'Aspect de la crise des justices seigneuriales', *Rev. hist. de droit français et étranger*, xxxix (1961), 564; M. Mortier, 'La Normandie et les enfants abandonnés', *Cahiers Léopold Delisle* (1967), pp. 147–70.

[2] Lottin, 'Naissances illégitimes', pp. 280–1.

[3] Potier de la Germondaye, *Introduction au gouvernement des paroisses*, p. 332, 'Des enfants exposés'.

[4] A comprehensive bibliography on the tricky question of respective responsibility for the upkeep of the bastard is found in N. Arnaud Duc, 'L'Entretien des enfants abandonnés en Provence sous l'ancien régime', *Rev. hist. de droit français et étranger*, xlvii (1969), 53.

impossible to prove once a girl in the throes of labour had made a denunciation. Indeed, Breton magistrates were prepared to accept anything up to five names when a girl was a little hazy as to who was the real father of the child and to demand a sum from them all, on the grounds that if they indulged in lax practices and enjoyed loose company, they must be prepared to pay for the consequences.[1] Resourceless women in Brittany and Flanders and Languedoc were not reticent in naming the author of their trouble or even several authors—perhaps because they knew that the authorities would see to it that the child's father would be held to a payment, however small, which would rid them of supporting the infant.[2] Their readiness in this respect is most striking when the mothers were servant girls made pregnant as a result of the master's activities. Here the openness of Breton and Flemish girls contrasts sharply with, for instance, the tight-lipped Normans who protected their masters, and presumably their jobs, for they had nothing to gain from denunciation.[3]

It is possible to construct the prototype of the unmarried mother. Aged between 20 and 30, engaged either as a servant, an employee in the textile trade (*dentellière*, *fileuse*, *tricoteuse*), a *couturière*, or as a casual labourer (a member of the great crowd of *blanchisseuses* and street traders), she was emphatically a woman on her own, in so far as she lived away from her family and several miles from her native village. She had been born in the country, but her misfortune was likely to have occurred in town. In short, she belonged to that large contingent of country girls who sought employment in the town. She lived in a cellar or an attic, sometimes even in a cupboard. She was unlikely to make

[1] P. Hardouin, 'Une Pratique criminelle en Bretagne au XVIIIe siècle: l'envoi clandestin des enfants abandonnés à Paris', *Nouvelle Revue de Bretagne* (1949), pp. 13–14.

[2] The payment in question was usually of 30–50 *livres* which coincided with the sum demanded from an *hôpital* or *hôtel Dieu* for the reception of such a child. The low figure presumably represents some gamble on the life expectancy of such a child.

[3] P. Chaunu thus touches upon the situation in Normandy: 'Le curé de Port en Bessin se plaint d'avoir été mal reçu par la patronne d'une servante en difficulté. La mauvaise humeur de la maîtresse s'explique par les soupçons très précis qu'elle a à l'encontre de son mari! En d'autres circonstances, le curé se plaint du mutisme des interrogées en face de la question rituelle "Quel est le père?" et de la réponse presque aussi rituelle dans le bocage quand il s'agit du maître: "Je ne sais." Et le curé ajoute: "Mais moi, je le sais."' (*L'Histoire sociale. Sources et méthodes*, Colloque de l'École Normale Supérieure de Saint-Cloud, 15–16 mai 1965, Paris, 1967, p. 236.)

the same mistake twice and she was definitely not a prostitute. If a servant girl, she was often the victim of rape by her employer.[1]

There is no prototype of the unmarried father, though certain groups predominate: the employer of the servant girl or the *fils de famille* of the house where she was working; the textile worker who supplied the spinner with raw material—entrepreneur is too elevated a designation; the lodging-house keeper—it probably did not do to fall behind with the rent. The fellow servant is also a common figure, particularly prone to have *décampé dans le temps de la grossesse* or to have the qualification *présentement expaïsé* after his name. The soldier is well represented—though any girl who slept with a *dragon* deserved all she got, and significantly, where the military was involved, the girl was rarely able to give the father's name. Imminent paternity evidently gained many recruits for the army; hence 'l'enfant provient des œuvres de Séraphin Joseph Longay, fils d'Antoine maître calendrier . . . ce garçon étant actuellement dragon au régiment royal' or 'l'enfant provient des œuvres de Baudouin Lemaire, bourgeteur, après soldat au régiment de Meuse'—a cause of enrolment doubtless good for a ribald joke in the barracks and an excellent apprenticeship for a leisure-time activity almost *de rigueur* amongst the military.[2] In Strasbourg students were often cited,[3] whilst in cities attracting long-distance migrants a girl's worst enemy was the boy from her native village. The sheer physical proximity in which provincial migrants lived, huddled together in *garnis* glorified with names designating the provenance of the lodgers—Hôtel des Auvergnats, des Limousins, des Marchois—made some promiscuity inevitable. But the boy whose endearments were couched in familiar patois and who talked of going back home when he had made his way in the world and of settling down with a local girl, and who used these facts to clinch his arguments in seducing his compatriot, was a real danger to the lonely country girl

---

[1] Lottin, 'Naissances illégitimes', p. 306. At Lille 21–30 per cent were *dentellières*, 15–22 per cent spinners and doublers, 7–11 per cent *tricoteuses*, 7–10 per cent *couturières*, 11–16 per cent *servantes*, and the rest casual workers. At Vannes 60 per cent were *domestiques* and the rest workers in the garment trades and spinners; at Périgueux 85 per cent of 115 cases were those of *servantes*. (A.D. Dordogne B 1889–96, etc.)

[2] Lottin, 'Naissances illégitimes', pp. 319–21; on this as a continuing motive for recruitment, F. Buchalet, 'La Recherche de la paternité à Toulouse en 1792 et les volontaires nationaux', *Revue des Pyrénées*, xxiii (1911), 353 ff.

[3] Dreyer-Roos, *La Population strasbourgeoise*, pp. 188–9.

because his interest was in fact much more short-term and, once pregnant, her hopes of returning home receded.[1]

However, the unmarried father has never been a social problem, and our concern is with the mother and child. The mother, at least theoretically, had one of two options available to her: to fend for the child herself or to unload it on to charity. Keeping the child and looking after it directly herself was out of the question unless her earnings were gained in her own home and were sufficient to maintain a shelter. *Dentellières* and other textile workers occasionally managed to support their illegitimate children and are found on the lists of *bureaux de charité* as worthy of an occasional hand-out or parcel of worn clothing.[2] Usually, however, fending for an infant meant putting it into a baby farm against a small payment. Sometimes, perhaps, the father helped with the few *livres* necessary to pay a midwife to make the requisite arrangements:

pour entendre Marie Louise Tenon que Maître Robert m'a déclaré être sortie de la ville et que quant à son enfant il est chargé de le mettre à nourrice et qu'il en répond . . . l'accoucheur Guffroy a fait transporter son enfant par une femme sitost qu'il fut baptisé sans qu'elle sache ce qu'il est devenu.[3]

This did not demand an immense capital sum; a few *livres*, 5 or 10, would rid one of one's child completely, as many *sous* would pay for it on a weekly basis. Why were rates so low? Because the child was not expected to survive. For the mother it was a way of killing the child vicariously, without incurring the direct imputation of infanticide; for the woman who ran the baby farm it was a sordid means of making a living in a harsh world. These at any rate were the conclusions reached by Tronjolly, *procureur du roi au présidial de Rennes*, one of the few who looked closely at the practices of the poor *vis-à-vis* their children, not from the comfortable distance of an armchair, a salon, or the office of the *Comité de Mendicité*, but from visiting *garnis*, talking to women

---

[1] Dreyer-Roos, *La Population strasbourgeoise*, p. 188, and Cobb, *The Police and the People*, pp. 237–9.

[2] They appear to have had fairly sympathetic treatment in this respect: A.D. Calvados, C 955, Bureau de charité de Bayeux; A.D. Indre-et-Loire H 1909, Bureau des aumônes de Tours, 1773–4; A.D. Aude C 1151, Mendicité.

[3] A.M. Lille Registre 10781, 1er février 1755, cited Lottin, 'Naissances illégitimes', p. 318.

and parish priests, and consulting parish registers.[1] He noted, in particular, that in the parish of Saint-Helier of Rennes far more illegitimate children died than were born. Midwives, he said, would appear to deliver the newly born children

... à des femmes qui n'ont point de lait et qui sont dans la coupable habitude de se charger, sans doute à forfait, de plusieurs enfants à la fois qui périssent presque aussitôt. ... La preuve d'un monopole aussi barbare résulte du grand nombre des bâtards inhumés depuis cinq ans et peu de temps après leur naissance dans la paroisse de St Helier de cette ville. J'ai vérifié très scrupuleusement les registres de cette paroisse; j'y ai vu que depuis le 6 mars 1776, jusqu'à ce jour, il n'y avait été baptisé que 12 enfants naturels, que 100 y ont été inhumés. ... Presque tous ces enfants sont morts dans les premiers jours ou premières semaines de leur naissance: il n'en est que 5 qui aient vécu deux mois, trois qui aient existé trois mois, cinq quatre mois, deux cinq mois, un seul a été jusqu'à six mois.

34 de ces enfants sont décédés chez la femme d'un jardinier appelé Dujardin: il lui en mourut 17 en 1778, 10 en 1779, 3 en 1780. 12 sont morts chez Marie Naturas, femme Bizette; en 1777 il lui en mourut quatre dont trois le même jour et le quatrième deux jours après. En 1780 il en périt huit en dix mois chez la Perruchon: elle en fit enterrer deux dans le même jour. En 1776 il en mourut quatre chez la Rouaulx. Il en est décédé aussi huit chez la Durval-Joubert, quatre chez la Decaen, trois chez la Macé ...[2]

Further inquiry revealed that the children had been born in the neighbouring parish of Saint-Jean and had been passed on to these professional murderesses by eight *matrones*, fifty-four of them by one woman alone. Did their mothers realize what they were doing in consigning them to women who had no breast milk to feed them? Why were they not taken to the *hôpitaux des enfants trouvés*? The answer to the first question is, perhaps; but what option was there? To the second, that entry into a foundling hospital for the illegitimate child of known parentage was not automatic. The mother had first to demonstrate that both she and the father were destitute and that the state of destitution entailed physical debility not unemployment; if she could not do this then she had to make a payment of 70–80 *livres* to the

---

[1] Tronjolly's efforts are found in A.N. H[1] 618, États de Bretagne, A.D. Ille-et-Vilaine C 249, and A.M. Rennes 325. He also published several brochures. See below, pp. 339–40.   [2] A.M. Rennes 325.

foundling hospital before entry was allowed the child. A girl on her own simply could not provide such a sum. There were those who could not provide a few *sous* for a baby farm or even pay a rent that enabled them to give birth to their infants indoors and so lay in ditches or gardens.

La femme du nommé Joseph Chavetier ... estant venue avertir qu'une fille s'estoit accouchée sur la campagne et avait fait baptiser son enfant à la madeleine hors de la ville est rentrée ensuite sur le soir dans la ville l'enfant sans maillot sans rien que soit de manière que par charité l'un lui avait donné une pièce, l'autre une autre pour couvrir le dit enfant.[1]

Then the penniless girl had gone off carrying her bundle. She could, of course, attempt to abandon it anonymously, but the whole structure of the edict of Henri II was designed to make this difficult. In registering her pregnancy and the birth of the child she had given the authorities a guide to the child's provenance; if she failed to register the event and was caught out, then the penalties could entail a heavy fine; but some hospital authorities were more assiduous in checking up than others. In Artois and Flanders, in Rennes and Tours, the search for the parents of an abandoned child included a perusal of parish registers and a check that any recently born illegitimate children were still with their mothers; but the Auvergne was constantly criticized by the central government for its laxity in this respect; whilst Bourges and Rouen and Lyons, to cite three examples only, thought the exercise a futile one, since it was only possible to check urban registers, and even the suspicion, recorded at both Bourges and Rouen, that the country women who turned up volunteering to wet-nurse children were likely to be their mothers, does not appear to have been followed up by close investigation.[2] Montpellier nurtured the conviction that Cévenol mothers made the long journey into Montpellier, where they were unknown, to abandon their children and then conveniently present themselves as wet-nurses.[3] A great deal of the thoroughness, or the lack of it, in investigating the origins of the abandoned child depended

---

[1] Lottin, 'Naissances illégitimes', p. 318.

[2] A.D. Cher, Hôtel Dieu de Bourges, Registre d'entrée des enfants trouvés, 1737–67. When the nuns suspected the wet-nurse they wrote in the register 'il me paraît que cet enfant était fils de la nourrice'. At Rouen, in 1753 it was suspected that twenty-seven of the *enfants trouvés* were in fact being wet-nursed by their mothers.   [3] A.D. Hérault C 581, Enfants trouvés, 1761.

upon who was likely to have to support it, the hospital or the state.

In short, no doubt the illegitimate child whose mother had jettisoned it and wandered into the unknown had an important place among the *enfants trouvés*, but was it the predominant one?[1]

ii. *The Unwanted Legitimate Child*

That marriage and procreation were for any couple the origin of economic difficulties has been the concern of the first part of this volume. For any poor family the mere existence of children spelt economic disaster because of the period of four years at least when they were too young to earn their keep and when their income from begging was far from adequate. Parents were prepared to make sacrifices; as the *subdélégué* of Pontivy wrote in 1774: 'Je connais des pères chargés d'enfants qui pour procurer du pain de seigle à leur famille ne mangent que du pain de son, d'où proviennent ces fièvres malignes et putrides qui ont emporté beaucoup de monde et qui ont régné jusqu'à présent.'[2] But there came a time when sacrifices alone would not suffice, when it became glaringly apparent that the very existence of children— and it needed no more than two or three—reduced the entire family unit to a state of utter destitution. The problem of how to prevent an extra mouth from jeopardizing an already strained budget obviously presented itself to the working man and his wife, especially in the chronic inflationary period of the post-1770s. How could the family confront such a crisis without endangering the relationship between parent and child? What were the attitudes of parents to children, born and unborn, under such circumstances?

One must, of course, admit at the outset the limitations of one's knowledge of what went on between husband and wife in the poorest households. Inevitably most of the clandestine practices of back streets go unrecorded. Attempts to comment on the degree of contraceptive knowledge and sexual practices have had to lean heavily upon occasional references, in highly oblique terms, of isolated individuals. The curé of Athis, so often cited,

---

[1] F. Lebrun, 'Naissances illégitimes et abandons d'enfants en Anjou au XVIIIᵉ siècle', *A.E.S.C.* (1972), pp. 1183–9, feels that since parish registers do not display an increase in illegitimacy rates to match the increase in abandonments the evidence is sufficient to show the children were not illegitimate. This, however, presumes them baptized. [2] A.D. Ille-et-Vilaine C 1424, Pontivy, 1774.

complained to his bishop of 'cette fraude qui s'oppose à la population', practised, he claimed, in towns.[1] The curé of Bort, near
Billom, during the food shortage of 1740 claimed that his hungry
parishioners, living on grass and roots, 'assouvissent leurs
passions', taking care not to increase the number of their children.[2]
But he referred specifically to a crisis period and, indeed, shortage
of food was such that it alone may well have prevented conception. On the other hand, in times of intense hardship, marriage
rates fell, since couples refrained from taking the step until better
conditions returned. These characteristics, however, describe the
practices of periods of crisis rather than a situation wherein
difficulties could not be expected to be of short duration. As a
more generally significant tendency, demographic historians have
noticed lengthening intervals between births following upon the
advent of the second child, which may reflect positive attempts
at family limitation; nevertheless, the average woman could
expect a further couple of children.[3] In considering the practices
of the poor one must, in fact, recognize one thing above all
others. The poor were risk takers. They had hazarded marriage,
they would hazard procreation. One has constantly to contend,
in any consideration of the poor of the *ancien régime*, with a certain
built-in fatalism, an inner resilience to a lengthy consideration of
what the future might bring. It did not need a highly developed
intelligence, for example, to appreciate that old age and total
destitution were synonymous, but what could one do about it?
Saving was impossible out of one's meagre earnings and one
might not, in any case, live to reach old age. Confronted with
disease, the same spirit was manifest, sick and well shared the
same bed and the same utensils—not through ignorance, but
because there was no readily apparent alternative. Everything, in
fact, that is known about the psychology of the poor suggests
that they had to be presented with a problem personally before
they actually thought about how to cope with it. Allied to this
was the almost visceral appreciation that nature might in any
case provide its own check to the over-large family. Philippe
Ariès, working largely on literary sources, has noted the lack of
sentimentality in the treatment of the *baby*, as opposed to the

---

[1] A.D. Calvados H. Suppl. 1308, Letter of 2 Dec. 1774.
[2] A.D. Puy-de-Dôme C 897, Bort, 1740.
[3] J. Dupâquier, 'Sur la population française aux XVIIᵉ et XVIIIᵉ siècles', p. 73.

child, in quite elevated social circles because of the high infant-mortality rate. If this was true of the babies of the rich, how much more so of those of the poor? A mother suffering from mal-nutrition often found it impossible to feed her child, and when her milk dried up the infant was supplied with a rag dipped in water, neither of which was necessarily clean, and in any case the expedient would not keep it long alive. Or the working mother put her children out to wet-nurse with relatives in the country against a small consideration, while she carried on her employ full time.[1] The baby was not allowed to assume priority. Why should it, or, more pertinently, how could it? In parts of Brittany impoverished mothers did not even bother to toilet train their weaker children whose life span was hardly likely to merit the trouble.[2]

The struggling mother of a family who found herself with an unwanted pregnancy on her hands could, in most towns and villages, find some midwife or crone to terminate a pregnancy, but the woman who did this and had recourse to large doses of alcohol, sulphurous purgatives, and the rusty handle of a kitchen ladle was almost certainly endangering her life.[3] There were easier methods of disposing of an infant that were not dangerous and could be used if the need arose; they entailed no planning but an on-the-spot decision after the birth—but perhaps before any official baptism—of whether one could or could not afford to keep the child. The simplest and most obvious was just to abandon the baby; to leave it on the steps of the nearest *hôpital*

[1] This was probably numerically the greatest 'wet-nurse' traffic, in spite of the attention given to the practices of wealthy women.

[2] J. L. Bagot, *Observations médicales* (1790); some of these are incorporated into H. Sée, *La Santé publique dans le diocèse de Saint-Brieuc à la fin de l'ancien régime d'après les observations médicales de J. L. Bagot* (1922).

[3] There is in Rennes a remarkable collection on such practices: A.D. Ille-et-Vilaine C 2530, États de Bretagne, Letter of Professeur du Bois, e.g. 'Il se commet parmi les matrones un abus non seulement contraire à l'humanité et à la religion, mais même nuisible à la patrie; elles ont la témerité de donner des remèdes violens aux femmes et aux filles grosses (de détruire leurs enfants) par ces remèdes elles font périr la mère ou la font avorter. Si elles la font avorter, elles publient hautement qu'elles ont procuré la sortie d'un crapaud et le public ignorant y apporte la plus grande crédulité . . .', etc. The midwife or her less skilled counterpart, the *matrone* (a village crone), was widely mistrusted by curé and authorities (B.N. Fonds Joly de Fleury 1215, Enquête sur les sages-femmes, 1728-9). Occasionally the abortionist's victim appears in a hospital register: A.D. Hérault, Hôpital Général Reg. 11 E.8, Jeanne Francoise de Millau (Rouergue) 's'est fait saigner deux fois et une fois elle a été manquée . . .'. On the issue in Strasbourg the bibliography in Dreyer-Roos, *La Population strasbourgeoise*, p. 191, is excellent.

général or *hôtel Dieu*, in the porches of churches or public buildings, or even in the market-place. This, with increasing frequency, was what was happening throughout most of France.

The strong upward movement of numbers of *enfants trouvés* roughly coincides with the onset in each province of long-term deteriorating economic conditions. In the Auvergne it begins in the late 1730s,[1] in Brittany and Normandy by the 1750s and 1760s. The problem in Burgundy would seem to have been relatively insignificant until the 1780s; indeed, in an inquiry carried out in the 1770s only Auxerre, Dijon, and Bourg-en-Bresse admitted to the existence of *enfants trouvés* at all or of any provisions to assist them, though Belley and Seyssel thought that children were sometimes dispatched to Lyons, and Semur-en-Auxois stated that any foundlings were sent to Paris.[2] In Languedoc alone was the problem of no considerable significance by 1789, and even here the Mediterranean littoral, with a history of relatively infrequent abandonment, contrasts with the hinterland where, for example, in the city of Toulouse the reverse was the case.[3] The phenomenon was commonest of all in the *pays de grande culture*. Chartres, Troyes, Sens, Soissons have peculiarly high rates of abandonment but so, on the other hand, do northeastern France and the Breton hinterland.

The close relationship between the numbers of children thus abandoned and local conditions is perhaps the best pointer to suggesting the foundling to be the legitimate offspring of the poor, jettisoned because his family was under stress. The *Comité de Mendicité* was convinced that at least half of those abandoned should be so considered;[4] some *subdélégués* in the 1780s thought

---

[1] A.D. Puy-de-Dôme C 1323-4. By 1739 the numbers of *enfants trouvés* demanded 63,939 *livres* and it was claimed the numbers of children had tripled over the decade.

[2] A.D. Côte-d'Or C 379, Enfants trouvés, 1776. This vague statement contrasts with L 1209, État des enfants trouvés, 1790, which claims 155 children actually at the *hôpital* and 1,000 *en nourrice*.

[3] A.D. Hérault C 581, Enfants trouvés, 1788. Castres, Carcassonne, and Toulouse alone expressed concern at the problem. Regional diversities are stressed in A. Molinier, 'Enfants trouvés, enfants abandonnés et enfants illégitimes en Languedoc au XVIIIᵉ siècle', *Hommage à Marcel Reinhard* (Paris, 1973).

[4] Bloch, *L'Assistance et l'État*, p. 99; L. Lallemand, *Un Chapitre de l'histoire des enfants trouvés. La Maison de couche à Paris* (Paris, 1885), p. 37, estimates on rather dubious grounds that they formed a seventh, and Montlinot, *Observations sur les enfants trouvés* (Paris, 1790), estimates the same to be true of the *généralité* of Soissons. All were dealing in pure conjecture, or offering those of *known* legitimate parentage, which was quite another matter.

even more.[1] All were of course speculating on what seemed probable. But this evidence is surely reinforced by positive evidence that the abandoned child was a baby, not a grown child abandoned because of temporary hardship and likely to be reclaimed at a future date. Up to three-quarters of them were about a month old, and the decision to abandon them had obviously been made while the mother was suckling the child. Historically, in times of local crisis such as harvest disaster or epidemics, as in the 1690s, mid 1720s, 1740s, any young child up to the age of 7 or 8 might find itself thus left, often bearing pathetic messages promising to return for it when crisis passed:

Messeirs et dames qui avez inspection sur les pauvres enfants je vous supplie très humblement d'avoir la charité de recevoir mes deux enfants que j'ai mis à votre porte ... deux filles dont l'aînée s'appelle Louise âgée de trois ans et la cadette Jeanne âgée de douze mois, mais elle tette encore. . . . Je les laisseray le moins que je pourray et aussi vous aurez la charité de conserver le billet afin que lorsque je pouray les reprendre je puisse vous les redemander.[2]

The closing decades of the *ancien régime*, however, were characterized not by the sudden abandonment of grown children but by that of the young baby rarely more than a few months old.

The average age of the infant shows that there must have existed some complicity amongst the poor on the question of abandonment. A child who had been alive a month must have been known to neighbours and relatives, and his sudden disappearance cannot fail to have been noted. On the other hand, the *hospices* could not count on informers coming forward to indicate the infant's provenance. Nor did the baby any longer carry a distinguishing mark, a ribbon or coloured rag pinned to his clothing, or a letter revealing his origins and making future identification easy. Children with any information or piece of identification attached to them made up less than a handful in institutions numbering their *enfants trouvés* in hundreds by the

---

[1] For example, those of the Auvergne, A.D. Puy-de-Dôme C 1323: 'il y en a la plus grande partie de légitimes . . .' (letter of Orry, 1 Dec. 1738); C 1324: 'Les administrateurs sont d'avis que le plus grand nombre de ces enfants sont des enfants légitimes.'

[2] This case is cited by R. Gascon and Claude Latta, 'Une Crise urbaine au XVIIe siècle. La Crise de 1693–4 à Lyon: quelques aspects démographiques et sociaux', *Cahiers d'histoire*, viii (1963), 395. Usually messages were more succinct.

end of the *ancien régime*.[1] Those in distress were clearly ridding themselves once and for all of the burden. What were their chances of survival?

The abandoned child had received some, though scant, recognition in the provisions for the help of the poor that emerged from the work of Saint Vincent de Paul. However, the assumption widely held among the more affluent sectors of society that the *enfant trouvé* was probably illegitimate was crucial in determining the amount of help afforded him. The child posed seventeenth-century society with a moral problem. If one helped him was one condoning immorality and so making easier the path of vice? The lack of resolve with which this uneasy question could be answered withheld from the foundlings even the slight benefits of the philanthropic efforts of the seventeenth century. The dying rich, anxious to purchase maximum relief from purgatory, opted for a morally sure form of donation, to the sick or aged or the obviously deserving, rather than one whose merit was more open to debate and hence less sure of having the right effect on the balance of the final judgement. It is significant that even Saint Vincent de Paul regarded them unquestioningly as the product of sin, though he believed them worthy of compassion. He is, moreover, said to have worked long hours to persuade Louise de Marillac that foundlings were the children of God and, as such, worthy of human pity. That the foundress of the Sisters of Charity should herself have recoiled before something she had learned to regard as a product of sin and illicit pleasure, is indicative of the general distaste felt for these children. As late as 1768 M. de Cairac, *ancien président du tiers état*, sent to the États de Bretagne a letter of protest against the proposal to establish a foundling hospital. 'Un hôpital', he declared, 'n'est pas fait pour les chiens', and the *enfants trouvés* could be regarded as of no greater consequence.[2] This is no isolated example; the *hôpital général* of Redon in 1777 asked the *intendant* in Rennes, 'Comment pourrait-elle étendre sa bienfaisance sur les malheureux fruits de la débauche?'[3] And although most stopped short at such an un-

---

[1] Moreover, they ceased to carry the specks of salt which denoted baptism. A.D. Puy-de-Dôme C 1332, Letter from the *intendant* to Orry, Dec. 1742.

[2] A.N. H[1] 371, États de Bretagne, 1768.

[3] A.D. Ille-et-Vilaine C 1270, Hôpital de Redon, 1777.

varnished rejoinder, many could even point to conditions laid down in their act of foundation which precluded them on moral grounds from making any provision for the foundling. This was particularly true of the late medieval foundations. The *lettres patentes* of Charles VII given to the *hôpital du Saint Esprit* in Paris in 1445 are in this respect utterly typical, excluding the abandoned child because

Si on en recevait, il y en aurait une si grande quantité, parce que moult de gens s'abandonneraient et feraient moins de difficultés de eux abandonner à pécher, quand ils verraient que tels enfants bâtards seraient nourris davantage et qu'ils n'en auraient pas la charge première ni sollicitude.[1]

Alongside the repugnance felt for the abandoned child and the institutional barriers erected against him, however, existed the reality of the child. He was there, and a Christian society which regarded infanticide as sacrilegious could not leave him to die— not, that is, without making some token gesture, however minimal, to save him. Such provision as existed for the child received some formalization in the 1690s as a result of the harsh economic conditions which led to a rapid growth in the numbers not only of newly born abandoned but of grown children, some as old as 10 or 12, as well. A harassed government hastily enacted provisions which received several modifications to correspond with provincial custom. The *hôtel Dieu* or, where such an institution did not exist and an *hôpital général* did, the *hôpital général* was to serve as reception and distribution centre for the children. They were to be dispatched as soon as possible to wet-nurses and to remain in the country until the age of 7, when the *hôpitaux généraux* would take them in and teach them how to earn a living. The *seigneur haut justicier* of the parish in which the child was abandoned was to finance the child, except in Brittany and Flanders, and to some extent Provence, where the parish or the *assemblée générale des habitants* was to find the means. Usually in the *pays d'élections* the monarch was *seigneur haut justicier* and so was responsible for the children, but there were innumerable exceptions to this rule. Almost immediately the government admitted that many *hôtels Dieu* could not cope even with a handful of

[1] Reproduced in Bloch and Tuetey, *Procès-verbaux*, p. 589.

children; it sought to prevent *hôtels Dieu* from being overwhelmed by an influx of children by authorizing, under such circumstances, the sending of children to the Paris foundling hospital—the only institution of its kind in France, indeed, apart from the Netherlands, in Europe.[1] These provisions, enacted in the 1690s, were intended to cope with a situation regarded as abnormal and indeed transitory, which, in fact, in the short term, it was. Society saw no reason radically to redress its attitude towards the foundlings once the abandonment of grown children had ceased, as it did when the crisis abated, nor to enact more elaborate measures to provide for their welfare. In the opening decades of the eighteenth century, with the isolated exception of 1708–9, the numbers of children abandoned in any one year were not such as to constitute a severe social problem or to demand a radical revision of existing provisions. Such as the provisions were, they would seem gradually to have secured greater formalization by 1730. The monarchy, in instances where the king was *seigneur haut justicier*, agreed upon a fixed annual *abonnement* for the children with the local *hôtels Dieu*, based upon what was regarded at the time of fixing the *abonnement* as a likely annual average of abandoned babies, and tried to forget about them.[2]

But their growing numbers made such attitudes increasingly difficult to maintain, for the most immediate outcome of the increase in foundling children was the strain placed upon the *hôtels Dieu* and the Paris hospital. In the areas where the monarchy paid a fixed sum, the 1740s were to see the beginning of a long argument between the government and the *hôtels Dieu*, the latter seeking some more adequate provision for the children, or, more pertinently, to curtail the increasing drain on their revenues, and indeed their space, made by the children. But the situation in the *pays d'États* was little different, even if the monarchy was less involved, and the *hôtels Dieu* had to contend instead with *assemblées générales des habitants* (as in Brittany), provincial estates or town councils (as in Flanders and parts of Languedoc), and to involve themselves in continual litigation with individual *seigneurs*

---

[1] On this institution see Bloch, *L'Assistance et l'État*, pp. 105–10.

[2] The monarchy acquitted its debts or *abonnement* theoretically out of the proceeds of the royal demesne; in practice, and this was to become increasingly true, by sanctioning the imposition of an extra levy (*marc extraordinaire*) on the *capitation*, *taille*, or *vingtième*. The levy was not flexible and if imposed on the *capitation* was deeply resented by the towns, which claimed the children came from the country.

haut justiciers in order to secure their due.[1] The *hospices* tried in vain to make abundantly clear that the children had no real claim on their funds and that to use the money of the foundation on the care of the children was to distrain it from the real purpose of the benefactor, which clearly they had no right to do—a moral point of particular strength in the light of the heavy premium placed by Catholic society on the intentions of the donor. Moreover, since customary law made a nominal provision for the foundlings, they could reasonably claim either the *seigneur haut justicier* or *l'assemblée générale des habitants* financially responsible, and that as long as they served as a *dépôt* for the children they had more than played their part. But between their claims and what they were obliged to do existed a major rift.

The children had their own form of insistency. The sick and aged could be turned away: an option could be exercised on whether the institution received them; but a helpless bundle removed that element of choice. The children were there and had to be noticed. Even if one did no more than open the door to them, push them into a draughty attic with others of their kind, and still their cries with a rag soaked in milk and water, fairly confident that their days were numbered, unless one had recourse to deliberate starvation and total neglect which ensured speedy death, the *enfants trouvés* might very rapidly swamp both the institution and its resources. This in varying degrees of acuity was happening throughout the country in both large and small institutions. Moreover, the cost of placing a child *en nourrice* grew with the inflationary trend from a general 2 *livres* 10 *sous* per month at the beginning of the century to 5 or 6 *livres* (in Rouen, 7) by the end of the *ancien régime*.[2]

The *hospices* were urban institutions whose income varied in proportion to the importance of the town in question and the generosity of individual benefactors, who were likely to be most numerous in a substantial city. But while the cities had the greatest resources, they also faced the greatest strains, since, on the one hand, they served as poles of attraction to the dispossessed, who crammed the cellars and attics of cheap lodging houses in

[1] A.D. Ille-et-Vilaine 1 F 2239, Fonds Hardouin, L'Hôpital des enfants trouvés à Rennes, 1773–93, p. 19; A.D. Hérault C 983, Enfants trouvés, Castres. See above, pp. 165, 323.

[2] A.D. Puy-de-Dôme C 1318, C 1349; A.D. Seine-Maritime C 1001; A.D. Ille-et-Vilaine 1 F 2239; A.N. H¹ 1321, Hôtel Dieu, Aix, Marseille, etc.

the hope of finding some sort of job and, on the other, they were often the dumping ground for the unwanted children of the countryside. There is little variation in individual histories: to take a random but well-documented example, Saint-Yves in Rennes, though intended exclusively for the sick, found itself the unwilling recipient during the years 1768–73 of 937 living children of whom 489 died before the age of 7.[1] They were picked up by the *maréchaussée* from the porches of churches, doorsteps, ditches, and the hospital gates in all seasons and in all weathers. A few came by legal methods, the recognized illegitimate children of mothers too poor to support them, but the bulk were of unknown parentage. Most were newly born, though about a third were over a month old, and the mother's decision to abandon the child had been taken while suckling it or had been forced upon her by the realization that she could not afford to keep it. Saint-Yves had no facilities for looking after the children; they were dispatched as soon as possible to wet-nurses, where they stayed until they reached the age of 5, but thereafter there were problems of accommodation. They could not be kept near the sick in the *hôpital* because of the risk of infection and so were installed in the attics of the building, where they were frozen with cold during the winter and stifled during the summer. At any one time 150 of them were huddled together in this fashion, sleeping three, four, or five together on a straw mattress, constantly a prey to epidemics which in some years wiped out 75–80 per cent of them. The hospital's funds were as limited as the accommodation it could offer the children, and the administrators constantly pressed the États de Bretagne and the bishop for some solution to the problem. In 1769 they scored a distinct success by obtaining *lettres patentes* for the raising of a special wing to lodge the children out of a gift of 12,000 *livres* made by the *bailli de* Resnon and backed by a promise by Madame Marie Françoise de la Bourdonnais that she would leave a legacy of some 32,000 *livres* which in *rentes* would provide something towards the upkeep of the children to add to the sum already spent by the *hôpital* Saint-Yves.[2] Problems were not at an end, for the news of a special establishment served to make it the dumping ground of children from all

---

[1] Some of this history is collected in M. Denieul, 'L'Hôpital Saint-Yves de Rennes' (Diplôme d'Études Supérieures, 1955), and A.D. Ille-et-Vilaine 1 F 2239.
[2] Denieul, 'L'Hôpital Saint-Yves de Rennes', p. 89.

over Brittany and the economic difficulties of the eighties brought the number of entries to new peaks. Faced with mounting debts, the administrators drew the attention of the *États* to the problem:

La progression des admissions des enfants à l'hôpital est passée en 13 ans d'un à quatre. Le dépense d'un enfant peut être évaluée à 66 livres par an pour la nourriture et les vêtements, les étoffes étant fabriquées à l'hôpital général. Les 645 (enfants trouvés) que nous entretenons nous occasionnent donc une dépense de 42,470 livres, pour y faire face nous n'avons que 29,325 livres. Il y a donc un déficit de 12,000 livres. Depuis 1729, la dépense a constamment surpassé de beaucoup la recette; nous n'avons jusqu'à présent couvert ce vuide qu'avec les secours que les autres hôpitaux ont donnés à cet établissement. Ils montent à 52,000 livres; mais ces ressources sont absolument épuisées et on ne peut exiger que nous consumions à l'entretien de cet hôpital des fonds qui ont une destination différente.[1]

They made a plea for an annual grant of 12,000 *livres*; they got in fact 3,000 and were forced to make drastic economies which can scarcely have contributed to the comfort of the children. The high mortality rates of the sixties fell, but still remained high— at about 66 per cent—and in spite of the new buildings, the care given to the children in residence was clearly inadequate. In 1782 the following accusation was made in Rennes against the widow Radiguel, *économe des enfants de l'hôpital*:

D'avoir laissé dans l'ordure, manquant des soins, d'aliments propres à leur subsistance, les enfants qui lui étaient confiés, de les avoir mis à coucher, 5, 6, 7, 8 et jusques 14 sains et malades et parmi lesquels il y

[1] A.N. H¹ 523, États de Bretagne, 1780. Entry rates were as follows:

Year	Bâtards	Légitimes*	Total	Morts	Vivants à la fin de l'année
1774	121	44	165	126	75
1776	125	47	172	132	78
1777	113	42	155	112	88
1778	102	40	142	104	102
1779	143	31	174	130	89
1780	175	28	203	168	97
1781 } 1782 }	374	157	531	323	235
1783	172	65	237	123	280
1784	161	63	224	111	310

* i.e. of *known* legitimate parentage. The term *bâtard* included both the illegitimate and the '*don't knows*'.

en avait de moribonds dans un même lit situé dans un endroit extrêmement humide.[1]

In addition, Tronjolly the *procureur du roi*, proceeded to accuse her of giving several children to one wet-nurse, who could not adequately feed more than a single child, for a reduced fee. But the hospital sprang to her defence and claimed she was coping as best she could on inadequate funds, and Tronjolly lost his case against the hospital administration.

Wherever one turns, the situation outlined at Rennes is broadly applicable. Thus the Auvergne was totally without specific institutionalized relief for the *enfants trouvés*, and *hôtels Dieu* with resources inadequate to fend even for the sick found themselves obliged to accommodate or cater in some way for the children abandoned to them. The expenses for the children should have been largely defrayed by the monarchy, since the king was *seigneur haut justicier*, but from the late 1730s the monarchy was attempting to curtail payments on the grounds that officials in the Auvergne did not sufficiently investigate the foundling children. Trudaine complained in 1737 to the *hôpital* of Clermont:

La dépense pour les enfants exposés [at Clermont] à été portée beaucoup plus haut que dans aucune autre ville du royaume. Le roi ne prend soin des enfants exposés qu'autant que l'on ne peut découvrir à qui ils doivent la naissance, mais quand ils scavent assez parler pour que l'on puisse savoir qui sont ceux qui jusque là ont pris soin de leur première éducation, les officiers de police doivent les faire remettre à ceux de leurs parents qui en doivent être chargés.[2]

Children, Trudaine complained, rather than babies, were being admitted, abandoned by parents who were sloughing off responsibility. He agreed to pay, but warned the *hôpital* that next time the monarchy would not be so generous. The reclaiming a year later of seventeen children by their parents gave the *contrôleur général*, Orry, ample scope for refusing the funds demanded by the *hôpital*: 'Cette réclamation prouve de plus que dans le nombre prodigieux d'enfants exposés à Clermont, il y en a la plus grande partie de légitimes, et qui ne sont exposés par leurs propres parents que pour se débarrasser de leur nourriture jusqu'à ce

---

[1] A.N. H[1] 618, États de Bretagne, and A.D. Ille-et-Vilaine C 249, Intendant à Calonne, 1er mars 1785. This lawsuit bankrupted Tronjolly.

[2] A.D. Puy-de-Dôme C 1322, Letter of Trudaine, 25 Dec. 1737.

qu'ils aient atteint l'âge de 7 ans.'[1] Given this information and the total inadequacy of the revenues of the royal domain to meet the demands made of it by the Auvergne, the *contrôleur général* suggested that a general tax in the form of an addition to the capitation should be imposed upon the *généralité*, two-thirds to be borne by the towns and the remaining third by the parishes. In a cogent rejoinder the *intendant* pointed out that the existence of the children was an indication of the poverty of the province (indeed, only in the Auvergne was it recognized at this early date that many foundlings were the product of poverty), that the towns produced less in the way of foundlings than the country, which deposited the children it could not support upon the towns, and that in any case the province could not meet the sum of 63,939 *livres*, 3 *sols*, 9 *deniers* demanded for the upkeep of the children.[2] The government again ceded but against a hard bargain: it was prepared to accord a fixed sum to the *hospices* for the upkeep of the *enfants trouvés* out of the revenues of the demesne and existing taxes; anything in excess of that sum must be met either by the *hospices* or by additional taxes upon the province. The measure in fact stimulated local officials to carry out a closer examination than ever before of the children abandoned by their parents. Indeed, it is from this point that parents in the Auvergne ceased to have the children that they intended to abandon baptized, lest a possible correlation be made between the parish registers and the assessed age of the foundling.

A sum fixed in the 1740s could not but be grossly inadequate by the 1770s. Riom claimed in 1778 that, against the government's *abonnement* of 4,000 *livres* fixed in 1743, must be set an annual expenditure of 9,000 *livres* and hence the *enfants trouvés* were dipping into funds which were legally the preserve of the sick.[3] Issoire made an identical claim with the cogent description of foundlings piled three to a bed, cripples sharing a *paillasse* between two or three, debts mounting to the extent of 29,000 *livres*, and no disposable property to sell.[4] The government refused to increase its donation, but sanctioned instead an obligatory addition to the *taille* that would raise an annual 27,000 *livres* to be

---

[1] Ibid. C 1323, Letter of Orry, 1 Dec. 1738.
[2] Ibid. C 1324, Correspondence, Sept.–Dec. 1739.
[3] Ibid. C 1342, Letter of M. de Bonnaire de Forges, 6 Feb. 1779.
[4] Ibid., État des revenus et dépenses de l'hôpital d'Issoire, 1769 à 1788.

divided amongst the *hôpitaux* of Clermont, Riom, and Issoire—a sum fixed more with regard to what the *intendant* estimated he could raise from the *généralité* than by reference to the needs of the institutions. Simultaneously, the monarchy sanctioned similar steps to be taken in the *généralités* of Limoges, Moulins, Tours, and Alençon, all of which complained of mounting debts and the steady encroachment of the foundlings on the patrimony of the sick.[1]

Evidently economy did not make for the most effective treatment of the foundling children. As at Rennes, the *hospices* of the Auvergne claimed an annual mortality rate of about 60 per cent, 50 per cent in a good year. Indeed, this would appear an average figure for foundling hospitals throughout France. Something depended upon the condition in which the children arrived at the *hôtels Dieu*, even more upon the rapidity with which wet-nurses could be found and the quality of those wet-nurses. The last point worried the administrators of the *hôpital* of Clermont considerably. Making a report on 1 January 1776, the administrators stated:

On a envoyé pendant ces 15 années 2,923 enfants en nourrice; il en est décédé 1,316 la première année de leur exposition, 295 la seconde et 100 la troisième; il en est sorti pendant ce temps 176 et il en reste au 1er janvier 1776, 358 à l'hôpital et 571 en nourrice. On a peine à trouver des nourrices au prix fixé qui est de 6 livres pour les 15 premiers mois et 4 livres ensuite, car la dernière classe des citoyens paie les mois de nourrice à raison de 7 livres; l'hôpital est obligé de placer les enfants au loin, chez des nourrices pauvres, où ils sont mal soignés et périssent souvent.[2]

Theoretically, any one wet-nurse could only have at any one time one child, but, as at Rennes, something had to be sacrificed in order that the institutions might obtain cut-price rates. Such nurses were in any case running considerable risks. A syphilitic infant could pass on the disease to a healthy woman, who soon contaminated her husband and any children she subsequently bore. Parish priests tried to dissuade their parishioners from taking in foundlings, but the pressures of poverty were too great. The *hôtels Dieu* were to find an extra expense in tending women who had contracted venereal disease as a result of taking in a

---

[1] A.D. Puy-de-Dôme C 1343, Letter of Necker, 4 Nov. 1779.   [2] Ibid. C 1340.

foundling. In Montpellier the promise so to do was actually written into the hospital statutes. Moreover, if the *seigneur haut justicier* could be prevailed upon to support foundlings, he was certainly not prepared to pay for treatment for syphilitic wet-nurses, and so once more the expenses had to be met by deflecting funds from the sick and aged for whom the *hôtels Dieu* were really intended.[1]

The government had grandiose notions that the children should be located in the healthy countryside, there to learn the work of the agricultural labourer until they reached their mid-teens; but against this ideal must be set the stark reality of lack of funds and the likely social strata from which wet-nurses were drawn. The policy of most towns which had both *hôtel Dieu* and *hôpital général* was to use the *hôtel Dieu* as a reception centre, from which the children were dispatched to wet-nurses, and to take them back at the age of 7 to send them to the *hôpital général*, where they would be employed in some form of industry or useful work until they were old enough to earn their own living.[2] Boys were usually taught some form of trade, girls some form of handicraft unless they were merely destined for domestic service. Camille Bloch stated that the girls of the *hospices*, trained for nothing, ended inevitably on the streets; a statement which may well have been founded in some piece of Enlightenment propaganda; if it is true, then it can perhaps be said that they were, unlike others of the social *niveau* from which they were drawn, preserved from this fate until their late teens.[3] The *hôtel Dieu* preferred to take the

---

[1] On the question of the syphilitic children, see Hufton, *Bayeux*, p. 95. A.D. Hérault C 5956, Recueil abrégé des règlements de l'hôpital général de Montpellier; Bloch and Tuetey, *Procès-verbaux*.

[2] Work was easier to find for girls than boys and sometimes the *enfants trouvés* simply helped the nuns in the running of the *hôpitaux*.

[3] It may arise from the following report by the *Comité de Mendicité* (Bloch and Tuetey, *Procès-verbaux*, pp. 590–1): 'Le travail des petites filles est un peu plus suivi et fait même partie du revenu de l'établissement, mais sorties de la maison, ces enfants n'en tournent pas mieux; elles sont ordinairement demandées pour être servantes, quelquefois pour être ouvrières. Leur éducation les rend si peu propres à la fatigue qu'elles sont promptement renvoyées des maisons où elles entrent et beaucoup d'elles sans ressources, sans état, après être restées quelque temps sans place et avoir abusé de leur liberté, sont admises encore à la maison de St Antoine et mêlées dangereusement avec les jeunes filles à qui leur expérience ne peut être d'aucun avantage.' At Montpellier the syndic of the *hôpital* Saint-Éloi considered 'La pluspart et presque toutes les filles de la maison qu'on met en service dans la ville se perdent par le peu de soin qu'on a d'elles' (A.D. Hérault, Hôpital général II E 10).

children from their foster parents and put them into the *hôpitaux généraux*, since they could do this more economically with the funds allotted by the monarchy. On the other hand, the swelling numbers of *enfants trouvés* filled up space in the *hôpitaux*, gradually edging out other types of poor. They were the only type of pauper whom these institutions simply could not turn away. Even the aged had to cede place to them and hence the numbers of aged accepted by the *hôpitaux* diminished almost in proportion to the growth in numbers of *enfants trouvés*.

There is little variation in the history of *hospices* confronted with the mounting problem of increased numbers of *enfants trouvés*, but to study the problem merely with relation to local *hospices* is to neglect an important aspect.

Apart from the *hospices* there existed in many towns and villages of northern, western, eastern, and central France, organized rackets for the disposal of newly born children: a traffic, in fact, in abandoned babies between the provinces and Paris, whose grim features were disclosed by the Sisters of Charity attached to the *hôpital général* in the capital. By law, before 1779, children could be sent to the foundling hospital in the capital and could not be turned away; moreover, the nuns were obliged to pay the carters who conveyed the children the costs of the journey. The expenses of the institution were partially defrayed by the monarchy; that is to say the monarchy paid a fixed *abonnement* to the institution.

The original plan had been largely designed to offset the chronic lack of resources to cater for the children in the provinces and to enable the monarch, as *seigneur haut justicier*, to centralize and, it was hoped, minimize his responsibilities. The scale, however, on which the provinces sought to discharges themselves of the burden of the children was to raise problems that led in 1779 to the abolition of the scheme. The nuns at the Paris *hôpital* presented the government with the following figures. They had received, they said, since the 1740s and even more strikingly since 1770, numbers of children which stretched their resources to such an extent that the institution must close. In 1680, 890 children already were more than sufficient to occupy the very restricted precincts of the institution until wet-nurses could be found for them. By 1740 they had, however, to cope with 5,302 children, by 1767, with 6,018, and in 1772, 10,634 children had to be lodged, nourished, and educated by the institution. The problem, the nuns argued, was not specifically the problem of a decadent city whose garrets sheltered *filles de joie* and maidservants from the provinces burying their shame in the big city but something far more serious.[1]

The children, they claimed, were sent to Paris from the provinces, and they offered the following instances for the year 177 alone. In the space of ten months they had been forced to accept at the *hôpital* in Paris:

156 children from		Normandy
167	,,	,, Burgundy
178	,,	,, Artois and Cambrésis
105	,,	,, Flanders and Hainault
344	,,	,, the Trois Évêchés
65	,,	,, Liège

They made references to isolated arrivals from Brittany and the Auvergne and stressed that they had no idea whatsoever of the numbers who set out. Moreover, the conditions of the children who arrived reflected not only the rigours of the journey, but the poverty of their provenance. Syphilis was rampant to such an extent that the *hôpital* had to think of means of coping not only with diseased babies but with institutionalizing the wet-nurses they contaminated.[2]

The nuns also submitted harrowing accounts of the conditions under which many of the children made their trip to the capital. The infants were bundled upright in groups of four or five in pannier baskets strapped to the backs of donkeys. Those who died on the journey were just thrown out *en route*. The nuns claimed that the carters who conveyed the children gave them wine to drink not milk—for convenience or to still their cries and make them sleep. They had no idea of the numbers who set out—though they affirmed that only the exception from Lorraine and Brittany arrived alive—and they declared that of those who survived the journey 90 per cent died within the first three days.

Under the promptings of the Paris nuns an inquiry was held

[1] The nuns' revelations clearly shook the central government; it immediately dispatched their claims to the *généralités* to ask for confirmation, for example, A.D. Calvados C 800; A.D. Ille-et-Vilaine C 1286, Enfants trouvés; A.D. Puy-de-Dôme C 1339, Lettres de M. Necker, 25 Oct. and 13 Dec. 1777.

[2] Bloch, *L'Assistance et l'État*, p. 105.

which revealed some disquieting factors; the *intendant* of Rennes wrote:

més subdélégués de Vitré et de Fougères et les administrateurs des hôpitaux de Rennes m'ont affirmé que l'on envoie très souvent des enfants à Paris de toute la Haute Bretagne et que presque tous ces enfants périssent en route de mort naturelle ou autrement. . . . Il y a des voituriers qu'on soupçonne de se charger habituellement de ces enfants, et qui pourraient peut être en être convaincus si on venait à des perquisitions exactes . . .[1]

The practice in Brittany was peculiarly highly developed; indeed, there was an organized chain of correspondents: mid-wives, intermediaries, carters with links in all the main towns, Fougères, Rennes, Vitré, Laval—the route to Paris—for picking up the unwanted children.

In Fougères a Madame Harel, for a sum of money which was not infrequently provided by the parish in which the child had been abandoned, undertook to organize the transportation of any baby to Laval, where another organizer took over.[2] The same correspondent received batches organized by a man in the rue Sainte-Melaine in Rennes, but carters were also prepared to negotiate *directly* with parents. If the carter had a batch paid for by the syndicate, he was not averse to pushing a few extra in for very little, if not for nothing. The more that reached Paris alive, the greater his profit, because he was paid by head at the other end. He possibly had papers for some of the children—the prac-tice was, after all, legal—and they could be applied indiscrimin-ately to whoever survived the journey. All the subdelegates agreed with the view advanced by the one of Antrain when he wrote: 'On envoie souvent des enfants à Paris par des voituriers qui s'en chargent publiquement . . . et on m'a assuré qu'on y faisait souvent passer des enfants légitimes de parents pauvres . . .'[3] All were convinced that both illegitimate and legitimate children were being disposed of in this way, but to what extent or in what proportions they refused to speculate. Indeed, perhaps the most disturbing feature of the dispatch of these children from Brittany and the Maine is the fact that, while large numbers were known to have been sent, only handfuls were known to arrive. Brittany

[1] A.D. Ille-et-Vilaine C 1286, Enquête de 1777 sur les enfants trouvés.
[2] Ibid., Fougères.   [3] Ibid., Antrain.

was not an area that posed problems for the Paris foundling hospital comparable with the problems posed by the dioceses of Metz, Toul, and Verdun, which would suggest that here the numbers of departures were yet higher.

In Normandy the *hospices* themselves sometimes organized such a traffic in order to retain a degree of solvency. This was the practice of the *hôtel Dieu* at Bayeux and at Caen;[1] the replies to the questionnaire sent to the *intendant* at Rouen in 1777 were similarly explicit, revealing at the same time the difficult situation in which the institutions found themselves.

Il n'y a dans la généralité de Rouen que trois hôpitaux qui reçoivent les enfants trouvés ou exposés, l'hôpital général de Rouen et ceux de Dieppe et du Havre, mais ces trois hôpitaux non plus que ceux de toutes les autres villes ne sont pas fondés pour recevoir les enfants. . . . Il n'y a dans la généralité aucun hôpital qui ait cette destination particulière. . . . Les revenus des hôpitaux de la généralité sont de beaucoup audessous de leurs charges et en général toutes ces maisons peuvent à peine se soutenir.

L'hôpital de Rouen fait chaque année pour les enfants trouvés en nourrice une dépense de plus de 30,000 livres, tant le nombre en est considérable. . . . L'administration s'est portée depuis plusieurs années à donner aux pauvres habitants de Rouen, 50, 60 et même 72 livres pour éviter la nécessité de recevoir ces enfants dans l'hôpital.

Il est certain que l'on transporte chaque année de tous les lieux de la généralité un grand nombre d'enfants à Paris, mais ces transports n'ont pas lieu publiquement mais par les voituriers appelés meneurs dont l'état est de conduire les nourrices à Paris. . . . Il y a quelques hôpitaux qui envoyent ouvertement à Paris les enfants exposés qui y sont apportés. Ce sont ceux d'Évreux, d'Eu des Criel et de Blangy.

Le Havre and Louviers were less explicit but confirmed the existence of the practice. The *subdélégué* of Pont-Audemer was the best informed:

Il y a de tous temps des voituriers appelés meneurs chez lesquels les sages femmes font remettre les enfants qu'elles ont reçus et dont elles tirent des certificats . . . lorsqu'ils ont cinq ou six ils les transportent dans une petite voiture avec des nourrices qui les allaitent en route jusqu'à Paris . . .

On assure que ces sortes de voyages se font tous les quinze jours seulement pour les enfants dont la naissance est clandestine. L'on

---

[1] Hufton, *Bayeux*, pp. 95–6.

présume aussi que le bailliage de Pont Audemer peut fournir 50 à 60 enfants qui se trouvent dans le cas ci-dessus tant des paroisses qui sont dans son ressort que des paroisses voisines qui pour des raisons secrètes viennent y déposer leur fruit.[1]

Networks of the kind revealed in Brittany and at Rouen have their counterpart throughout the whole zone of recruitment of the Paris foundling hospital. There was a highly developed one at Auxerre, conducted by a widow Darmet, *vivandière* by profession; another at Metz.[2] The *hôpital* at Aurillac conducted a traffic similar to the one at Bayeux and, alone amongst the institutions of the northern Massif, chose the Paris outlet as an answer to financial problems. Indeed, the abolition of the practice in 1779, when the Paris *hôpital* declared its utter incompetence to cope and the dispatching of children to the capital was made illegal, revealed the extent to which some institutions had leant upon this means of dealing with the issue. For Aurillac alone, the difference in expenditure was between 15,000 and 18,000 *livres* over a five-year period.[3]

The government evidently could not stop the practice without providing the financial means to replace the losses incurred by the *hospices*. It promised, tardily and inadequately, to subvent the provincial *hospices* by a sum to be raised out of an addition to be made to the *taille* or the *capitation*, but such additions could only be made by reference to the resources of the provinces (ironically smallest where the proportion of *enfants trouvés* was greatest) and were of course impossible to impose in any case in Brittany in the light of the resistance of the *États*. The foundling hospital in Paris, perhaps alone of the institutions which had anything to do with foundlings, profited from the government's measures. Some tried to continue sending the children into the capital but with scant success. From the 1770s the history of any institution concerned with *enfants trouvés* is to be written in terms of prolonged bargaining with a government which would never pay anything in advance and with wet-nurses crucially dependent upon their monthly payments. For the government, the 15 million *livres* it

[1] A.D. Seine-Maritime C 1001, Enquête sur les enfants trouvés 1777. Reply to Necker from the *intendant* at Rouen, 14 Dec. 1777.

[2] P. Richard, 'Les Enfants abandonnés à Auxerre de 1776 à 1796', *Bull. soc. des sci. hist. et nat. de l'Yonne*, xcix (Auxerre, 1961–2), 10.

[3] A.D. Puy-de-Dôme C 1349, Enfants trouvés, Aurillac.

spent annually on this sector of the poor represented its most considerable outlay; moreover, with its increasing numbers, the *enfant trouvé* loomed menacingly large, crushing any hopes governments might have of limiting expenditure.

Yet the inquiries of the 1770s mark an important watershed in the history of official attitudes towards the *enfant trouvé*—even if one cannot record any substantial improvement in the actual treatment meted out to him. He was recognized, as a result of the questions put to priests, subdelegates, and *intendants*, to be not the unhappy product of a shameful union but the wretched progeny of poverty. As such, he had a right to more compassionate treatment: his role in society demanded greater consideration; he could not with the same ease of conscience be put into a draughty attic and forgotten. Such a realization must in the long run operate to his advantage.

iii. *The Murdered Child*

Depuis longtemps dans la province de Bretagne, on a cherché les moyens pour prévenir une infinité de destructions d'enfants, dont les monitoires si souvent et inutilement publics, ne servent, le plus ordinairement, qu'à scandaliser, et la découverte de leurs petits cadavres dans les caves, conduits, jardins et même dans les rues qu'on peut présumer sans la grâce du baptême nous en découvrent et apprennent journellement la perte.[1]

So wrote the bishop of Vannes to the bishop of Rennes, touching upon the problem of infanticide, a problem known to exist and, indeed, no unusual phenomenon, but one which is even more of a mystery to the historian than is the *enfant trouvé*. Contemporaries were certainly concerned about the issue; they had every reason to be so. A drain opened in Rennes, in the course of rebuilding the city after the fire of 1721, revealed the skeletons of over eighty babies suppressed in the first hours of life.[2] Few villages, let alone towns, were unfamiliar with the little corpse, usually with the umbilical cord untied, still blood-streaked from the birth process, and dead from suffocation, found in ditches, cellars, and, most frequently, drains. Enlightenment opinion allied infanticide with the unmarried mother, her harsh

---

[1] A.D. Ille-et-Vilaine C 1286, Vannes, 1749.
[2] Ibid. C 154.

treatment, and the inadequacy of the foundling hospitals, observations which tally with the cases of infanticide brought before the courts. Recorded cases in any *présidial* court relating to this subject are indeed few: one or two a year in most places, rising to four in some of the larger Breton *présidiaux*—and this perhaps represents the highest figure for France since the province was certainly in the nineteenth century that *par excellence* of the murdered baby.[1] The few cases brought before the courts, however, are no indication of the real size of the problem: they represent the girls who were caught, not the ones who got away, and inquiries into babies' corpses found in the street were not actively pursued by the police but often left to the parish priest alone.[2] Lawsuits of this nature brought profit to no one. The penalty was death in Brittany and when a case did come before the courts it was quite clear from the start what the verdict would be. Elsewhere, in Périgord, in the Lyonnais, in the south, a fine was imposed.

The woman tried for infanticide was, it would appear, always unmarried. Usually she was a servant girl. This is perhaps significant, because the issue was largely brought to the attention of the authorities by the parish priest, to whom the girl's employer reported her. The priest in conjunction with the police and a surgeon, would descend on the girl and would usually find the baby's corpse, but, if not, were satisfied with physiological evidence, the placing of the uterus, the womb full of blood, and so on. Her fate was clear cut in Brittany: breaking on the wheel and hanging.

But were the children anonymously disposed of in urban drains *un produit de la honte ou de la misère*? Perhaps of both. The women brought before the court were unmarried, poor, and resourceless, and had been caught; perhaps more got away. The married woman admittedly might find herself with an unwanted child and, since she did not have to declare her pregnancy to a public official and her body was not under the scrutiny of a suspicious

---

[1] See review, 'The Peasantry who Missed out on the French Revolution', *T.L.S.*, 31 July 1970, p. 859. Students of the University of Rennes are currently engaged on statistical surveys of such crimes, which in the nineteenth century were so common as to merit a mere few weeks' imprisonment.

[2] The lack of concern with cases of infanticide again reflects the priorities of a judicial system wherein emphasis was upon monetary compensation. There was no real place in *présidial* justice for the woman who had murdered her child.

employer, her opportunities for escaping infanticide unnoticed were greater. On the other hand, why strangle or suffocate the child and run the risk of a penalty when starvation could see an end to the infant within a few days? Perhaps only a girl desirous of covering up her situation and retaining her employment would run the risks involved therein. But again one enters the realm of conjecture, and in the last analysis one can only say of the murdered baby that he had died without making a hole in the revenues of any *hospice des enfants trouvés*; that he did not develop into a ragged toddler who daily besought passers-by for alms, clutching at coat-tails and hanging about street corners ready to recite a litany of woes—the toddler whose life cycle has been the concern of this volume.

POSTSCRIPT

POSTSCRIPT

POSTSCRIPT

THEFT, vagrancy, extortion (*mendicité avec menaces*), prostitution, child abandonment, infanticide, the neglect of the aged, the exploitation of the crippled certainly represent the seamiest aspects of the problem of poverty, but they were an integral part of the struggle for self-preservation of the poorest sectors of the community, grim reminders of the depths to which human beings can be driven by deprivation. Clearly the ethical code of the poor was not that held by contemporary comfortable society. The poor had their own rules of conduct, their own standards—an alien set of values which, however hard the historian might try, are not easy to piece together.

How much can one know of the thinking of a set of people who were largely inarticulate? Something, if far from all, can be inferred from the manner in which they responded to hardship. Clearly the poor were people of limited ambitions. They hoped to make out, no more. They were content with survival and were psychologically fully equipped to cope with a measure of hardship, provided they could avoid the worst consequences of chronic debt and extreme deprivation. Occasional hunger was to be anticipated; individual, if not cumulative, crises could be surmounted. The bounce-back qualities of the kelly doll which characterized earlier generations of peasants in the aftermath of pestilence, the spirit that permitted a crop of marriages and remarriages, a spate of new-born babies to replace those lost or never conceived, and the urgent desire to eliminate the memory of the past did not entirely forsake their descendants once these more spectacular crises had passed. True, below the surface always hovered the real fear of food shortage for any family not producing enough to supply its needs. Communities and individuals alike lived on their nerves. Lefebvre's description of the subsistence peasant as a man who lived in fear of himself is a very apposite one: the fear of those with a very little of those who had nothing at all and the fear of falling below such standards as one enjoyed, low as they might be, were merely two kinds of fear endemic in both urban and rural societies. In times of dearth these fears multiplied and others were added, not least the fear of calculating outsiders intent upon removing grain from a community to push up prices and the fear of village for town and of small town for large town, each suspicious that someone was enjoying better conditions and lower prices. Such fears could, predictably, turn into a bread riot which began as a collective, invariably bloodless, and most often quite orderly, attempt to stop the transfer of grain or to ensure its sale at a price consonant with that current in other communities. Although riots were most common in towns and in those rural communities immediately adjacent to towns or situated along the arteries used for the transfer of grain from village to town, most communities probably had experience of one such *émeute* in the last decade of the *ancien régime*. These riots are remarkable for their non-violent character and their intrinsic respect for legal forms, and this in a society which lived with, and accepted, violence.[1] Moreover, movements aimed at the detention of supplies were not merely or predominantly the work of the irrevocably *indigent* but of those who in normal times could manage and who were fighting to stay on the right side of the line between poverty and destitution —those, in short, who had the most to fear from the rapid inflation of prices, for they had the most to lose.[2]

Alongside fear of the future, however, there existed, when hunger was not actually on the doorstep, a propensity for almost frenetic gaiety, an obsessive urge to make the most of every moment of leisure and of every occasion for celebrating. Family reunions for marriages (above all) but also deaths and births, *fête*-days, *pardons*, *kermesses*, public processions, and fairs—all were occasions to bedeck oneself in whatever finery one possessed (and it might be little more than a clean kerchief, a less ragged shirt, a precious pair of inherited stays, a scrap of lace pinned on a bodice, a *coiffe* fabricated in snatched time, a crucifix, or a

---

[1] One of the best local studies of these phenomena is H. Hours, 'Émeutes et émotions populaires dans les campagnes du Lyonnais au XVIIIᵉ siècle', *Cahiers d'histoire*, ix (1964), 137–40. There is an impressive bibliography of riots as a whole in L. Tilly, 'La Révolte frumentaire, forme de conflit politique en France', *A.E.S.C.* xxvii (1972), 732, but this does not comment on the form of the riot itself. The French Revolution saw an intensification of violence in these movements: R. Cobb, *Terreur et subsistances 1793–1795* (Paris, 1964), pp. 211–342, and R. B. Rose, 'Eighteenth Century Price Riots. The French Revolution and the Jacobin Maximum', *Internat. Rev. Soc. Hist.* iv (1959), 435, 438.

[2] Hufton, 'Women in Revolution 1789–1796', *Past and Present*, liii (1971), 94.

flower) and to sally forth in search of enjoyment, determined to find diversion.

At the root of many festivities was the family. Weddings, however humble, were accompanied by some measure of feasting. Families almost without means were prepared to contract debts they could ill afford to provide food and drink for the relatives of the bride and groom and to pay a musician a few *sous* for his services.[1] Baptisms had their own particular ritual: the offering of wine or some little luxury at a family gathering extended to include the *sages-femmes* of the village who had 'assisted' at the delivery and who hung bags of salt or *scapulaires* around the child's neck to ward off evil spirits and ensure that it flourished.

These were the big events in the social life of the family but there were other kinds of more every-day entertainment. The poor were great story-tellers. Every *manuel de folklore* is a monument to a tradition of tales recounted, often to a gathering of several families before one hearth—for that way one could economize on fuel. In this way stories of Celtic heroes and superstitions were handed on from generation to generation: tales of disasters, fires and flood and famine. There could be few in 1789 who had not heard the personal survival histories of their great-great-grandparents in 1708–9, embroidered as the years went by and new generations took up the tale. There were stories of bombardments and invasions, or of legendary figures such as Marion de Faouët and Fleur d'Épine. All this while people continued to work, knitting stockings, making lace, spinning, cracking nut kernels for oil, basket-weaving, shoe-mending, and so on.

The *joueur de la veille* could turn a few *liards* in any village or town street in the late evening when people who had worked all day either sat and watched and listened or, if young, danced. Not all those who participated could afford to pay but they might offer something—a drink, fruit, shelter for the night. So long as someone was prepared to offer something, the musician did not grumble; he too had limited ambitions. The same was true of travelling story-tellers, the *diseurs de bonnes aventures*, organ-grinders, fortune-tellers, those travelling showmen who towed a bear, a monkey, a performing dog, or even a marmot. These people were genuinely welcomed by communities anxious to be

[1] Poitrineau, *La Vie rurale*, p. 490.

entertained. To be poor was not necessarily to be totally illiterate, though here immense variations marked one part of the country from another.[1] The pedlars of the blue books of Troyes, chapbooks aimed at a lowly market, stuffed with tales of lechery, debauchery, or bravado and with the heroes of popular legend, defiers of authority, Mandrin and Cartouche, or with semi-pietistical themes of saints and sinners, miracles and holy men, did a business unsupported by a wealthy reading public.[2] This is not to suggest that the poor were regular purchasers of literature but that someone in some community, temporarily perhaps in possession of a few *liards*, might thus invest to cheer his companions, expecting them to do the same when they had something. Or the pedlar himself might read a tale aloud in exchange for shelter.

Those with most real leisure were the young. In towns, employees in industry and in *boutiques* and *ateliers* could count on having Sundays and *fête*-days off; servant girls could only be sure of the latter. In the country the *valet de ferme* or *domestique* again could count on Sundays and *fêtes*, the *servante* only on the latter. The self-employed man in town or country usually could not permit himself so much time off. Many did not even take Sunday off in summer when work needed doing in field or garden, and curés only expected full observance in winter. When one looks for the leisure activities of the masses in eighteenth-century France one is struck primarily by the greater opportunities of the young and the difference between a rural and an urban environment.

On her day off, the rural servant girl employed in the town met up with other girls of her native village and sallied forth on *la promenade*, a practice shared by town-bred girls in company with their friends from work or the streets where they lived.[3] *La*

[1] M. Vovelle, *La Chute de la monarchie 1787-1792* (Paris, 1972), p. 76, offers a literacy map distinguishing a literate north (70 per cent) from an illiterate south (20 per cent), but if the criterion for literacy is based upon the ability to sign one's name it does not tell very much.

[2] R. Mandron, *De la culture populaire en France aux XVIIᵉ et XVIIIᵉ siècles* (Paris, 1964), and A. Dupront, *Livre et société dans la France au XVIIIᵉ siècle* (Paris, 1965), t. ii, are two recent attempts to analyse the contents of popular literature. Eastern France and the west liked pietistical literature; the south had more profane tastes.

[3] What follows is based upon the *registres de déclarations de grossesse* (see above, p. 320 n. 2); J. Depauw, 'Amour illégitime et société à Nantes au XVIIIᵉ siècle', *A.E.S.C.* (1972), 1155-82, and J. Sole, 'Passion charnelle et société urbaine d'ancien régime', *Annales de la faculté des lettres et des sciences humaines de Nice*, nos. 9-10, (1969).

promenade was a ritual. It consisted of a set itinerary through some public *place* or avenue—one can perceive the attractions of the Peyrou in Montpellier, the square before the Parlement house in Rennes, the walk past the Parlement house and the Palais des ducs in Dijon, but in small towns like Bayeux or Dol-de-Bretagne girls contented themselves with a parade around the old ramparts, muddy as they undoubtedly were. The young knew their itineraries and architecture was of secondary importance. The young girl expected to be surveyed and accosted by young apprentices and *domestiques* likewise in search of pleasure. She expected to share girlish jokes and confidences, perhaps to be introduced to the brothers or cousins of her girl-friends, and in turn to their friends and associates. In this way a network of contacts was built into her otherwise totally restricted existence. From *la promenade* newly constituted groups might move towards *buvette* or *guingette*; the girl might have purchased for her a drink, a few sugared almonds, a *galette* or fruit. The occasion might be marked by a dance (*fête baladoire*, *vogue*, or *fête dansante*) or it might possibly terminate in love-making of varying degrees of intimacy in some appropriate alley or adjacent copse. Such occasions could end in disaster for the girl, as the *déclarations de grossesse* attest, but the same testimonies reveal the degree to which 'walking' figured in the leisure activities of young working people and the expectations attached to the practice. A young couple seen regularly together by friends and work associates at *promenades* and *fêtes* were assumed to have intentions of marriage, and a girl abused in these expectations and with an unwanted pregnancy on her hands could call upon her fellow *servantes* to give evidence against the young man by attesting the visual manifestations of keeping company. To anticipate marriage was probably the norm amongst servant girls, at least in the towns; certainly regional studies show (exception made for a more chaste south) anything up to a third of all first children to have been conceived out of wedlock. On the other hand, the relatively low illegitimacy rates outside the large cities suggest that generally there was a fairly stable relationship between couples before sexual intercourse occurred.

'Walking' clearly did not serve the same purpose in village life: the servant girl in the country on a day off visited her family and then proceeded to the *fête baladoire*. The actual company there was doubtless already known to her. She needed no introductions. The proximity of family and relatives may have forced her to greater restraint in her personal conduct. Certainly women figure less predominantly in what one knows of village leisure activities. This may, however, reflect the changing nature of the evidence, which shifts from the female-centred *déclaration de grossesse* to the police file and the private suits of the *présidiaux*.

No one in eighteenth-century France enjoyed greater leisure than the *valet de ferme* with his regular Sundays and *fête*-days off. He had a right to sixty or seventy days a year of holiday, in whole or in part. How did he fill them? He too doubtless pursued the girls; certainly he drank heavily. (On Sundays and *fêtes*, the *cabaretier* made his money.) But more strikingly, and to a far greater extent than in England where throughout the period the young enjoyed less leisure and where energies were channelled into truly vicious, unregulated village sports, the French farm labourer and apprentice indulged in gratuitous, meaningless violence which none the less conformed to a certain ritual.[1] Historians for their own particular reasons have tended to underestimate this aspect of popular life. Some because they are concerned to show the eighteenth century as more theft-prone but less violent than an earlier epoch—a thesis which cannot be proven because, even if the volume of thefts grows, that of acts of violence does not diminish and because eighteenth-century courts were not designed to cope with most acts of violence unless a private suit was lodged.[2] Some have shunned a close analysis of violence deeming

---

[1] This theme is emerging from all close studies of *ancien régime* criminality: Hours, 'Émeutes et émotions populaires', pp. 144–8; T. Le Goff and D. Sutherland, 'Crime and Counter-revolution in Brittany', a paper delivered to the French Historical Association in 1972, traces crime patterns over the period 1760–96 and accords ritualized violence between parishes an important place; similarly, N. Castan, 'La Criminalité à la fin de l'ancien régime dans les pays de Languedoc', *Bull. d'hist. écon. et soc.* (1969), p. 64; Iain Cameron's work in progress on the *maréchaussée* of the Auvergne and the Bordelais stresses the same phenomenon. Violence, on the other hand, has received little attention as a study *in itself*, as the bibliography of A. Abbiateci and F. Billaçois, *Crimes et criminalité en France 17e–18e siècles* (Paris, 1972), reveals. The observations in this section are based upon the criminal records enumerated above, pp. 245–6. On parish faction fights as a continuing element in nineteenth-century society see A. Van Gennep, *Manuel de folklore français contemporain* (Paris, 1943), t. i, pp. 201–22.

[2] See above, pp. 245–6 n. 1. Le Goff and Sutherland, however, are insistent: 'if we take all the crimes committed in the region of Vannes in the period 1760–64 for example, the largest single group are assaults, or threats of violence; if we count all the crimes against persons, then they amount to about two-thirds of all criminal

that in some way it detracts from the essential worthiness of those predestined to win the ultimate political crown. The bread riot is the only act of popular violence to have received attention and this may have been because it can be categorized as a class struggle, but such protests bear no relationship to the ingrained violence of the working classes.[1] During *rixes*, young agricultural workers of one village were prepared to spend their *fête*-days slanging those of a neighbouring one; they would beat them up, tearing their clothes, having set forth and walked five or ten miles with such aggression in mind. The *maréchaussée* of the Auvergne claimed it already had a full-time occupation in keeping the peace between such gangs at fairs, without the extra burden of beggars and vagrants.[2] Organized parochially, these 'faction fights' were at their most vicious at *fêtes baladoires* or on the days of the *tirage de la milice*. Usually they took the form of an elaborate ballet, a set pattern whose rules permitted the young to beat each other insensible until, at a crucial juncture, authority in the shape of the *maréchaussée*, *archers*, village elders, or the officials of the *milice* would intervene, single out someone whose cuts and bruises and state of inebriation allowed him to put up little resistance, and bear him off—at which point the faction fighters amalgamated in an attempt to liberate him. Sometimes this was a deliberate diversionary tactic on the part of the police to prevent the destruction of property and ensure that the fighting broke up. They were not intent upon prosecution. If the occasion was the *tirage de la milice* and the man in question was

acts . . .' The data for Périgueux (A.D. Dordogne B 322–821), which is *exclusive* of private suits where violence invariably predominates, offers the following pattern:

	Total	Simple theft	Theft with violence	Simple violence	Simple vagabondage
1710–28	52	16	9	25	
1729–38	36	12	6	14	
1739–48	57	19	11	15	
1749–58	45	13	7	14	
1759–68	94	28	20	15	12
1769–78	193	81	25	31	16
1779–88	180	49	13	47	15

Figures such as these demonstrate the relative steadiness of suits relating to acts of violence. Clearly crime statistics need very cautious handling.

[1] Hours, 'Émeutes et émotions populaires', pp. 137–8. On the theme of violence in the context of revolution, R. Cobb, *The Police and the People*, pp. 89–92. Such violence was not born with revolution; it merely took unexpected turns.

[2] I am indebted to Mr. Iain Cameron for this information.

not a *domestique*, he was a sure candidate for the *milice*. A typical example would be the exploits which took place at Échalas in the Lyonnais on 20 June 1762, on the occasion of the *fête baladoire* held in commemoration of St. Lazare. The *brigade* of the *maréchaussée* stationed at Saint-Andéol knew what to expect, as each year the young men of Saint-Romain-en-Gier and Échalas on one side and of Saint-Andéol on the other came to blows. After a day of drinking, the young men of the first village came out of one *cabaret* at seven in the evening 'munis d'environ vingt pots de terre remplis de vin, qu'ils ont apporté sur le pré dudit lieu; et, se tenant par la main, se sont mis à danser autour desdits pots, buvant per intervalle et rassemblant tous les garçons' of their parish. When their opponents finally turned out, conflict began; finally, as dusk fell, the *maréchaussée* made their swoop and carried off a young man who was duly prosecuted and fined.[1] Such sport could result in loss of life: a boy of Thurins was killed on 10 August 1782 when the *maréchaussée* tried to break up the fighting with gunshot; on 30 June 1752 at Milléry a boy of Mornand died as a result of battery from the brooms of gorse which the village boys of Milléry used as their habitual weapons during their *rixes*. Such affairs could end before the *bailliage* or *présidiaux* where the families of the deceased or mutilated sought compensation, but they were on difficult ground since it was not always easy to pick out who was liable and villagers rigorously refused to give evidence against their own. In most instances death or mutilation merely sharpened the desire for revenge on the next occasion.

Violence of this kind between parishes can be discerned almost everywhere from the records of the *maréchaussée* or the private suits of the *présidiaux*. Moreover, such official sources reveal only the tip of the iceberg, for only in isolated instances were the *maréchaussée* on hand (though they invariably knew where *fêtes* were to take place) or prepared to intervene against heavy odds. Parish boys sorted out their own vendettas, and a society tolerant of every kind of violence left them to get on with it.

Immigrant youths in the cities brought faction fights with them but on a very reduced scale. Usually the casual nature of their employ gave them little official leisure. The water-carrier, the porter, the carrier of sedan chairs, and the thousand and one

---

[1] A.D. Rhône B, Maréchaussée, cited by Hours, 'Émeutes et émotions populaires', p. 144.

fringe workers of the cities could not keep the *fêtes*. More important, the parish complicity of the faction fights between village
and village was not reproduced in the towns. Occasionally the
servants of one household might come to blows with those of
another, and the servants' Sunday sport of beating up the *archers
de la ville* has been mentioned. Generally, however, in towns,
violence amongst the young was less organized than in the
country. There were also more opportunities in the town to meet
and to walk, to ogle shops, street pedlars, girls, to choose the
site of one's *guingette*, and so on.[1] Clearly for the *valet* of the
villages violence was part of the ritual of holiday. Curés were
bitter critics of *vogues* and *fêtes baladoires*, even of *kermesses*, because
they gave leisure to those who did not know how to use it, drove
them into *cabarets*, and put liquor into their heads—liquor which
could only drive them to violence, make them reckless or, in the
case of a girl, rob her of her reason, strip her of her virtue, or
transform her into one of the bestial female harpies who stood by
a fight urging on the young men to greater deeds of folly.

The organized, tolerated violence of the young has no echo
amongst the older sections of society. Nevertheless, the poor had
ready recourse to violence—though perhaps less ready than a
study based solely on legal records would suggest—they had *la
tête plus près du bonnet* than any other element in society.

Families avenged infractions upon their property, such as the
wrongful pasturing of a cow, the inevitable straying of a scraggy
but voracious goat, or the misuse of ponds and streams, not by
litigation, in first instance, but by beatings and threats. Housewives came to public blows in streets or markets or at washing-
places. Stocking-knitters relieved the monotony of their employ
as they sat at the door of their shacks by pouring obscenities upon
women of dubious repute or upon those they personally disliked,
as they passed by. Shepherds on lonely mountainsides would
wile away the hours in violent quarrels with their handful of
companions, would beat up a lonely traveller, not only with
theft in mind, but because they had a genuine taste for violence.
The bishop of Le Puy, perhaps mortified that the keeper of the
feuille des bénéfices could do no better for him, and appalled at the

[1] Le Goff and Sutherland are careful to accentuate the difference between town
and country in this respect: 'Violence such as this [parish violence] was contained
within the rural community and indeed was part of its normal life.'

violence of his flock, said that his poorest parishioners, shepherds, agricultural labourers, were not *people* but *animals*.[1] Every opportunity for quarrel, any insult—particularly if proffered by an outsider—was, he said, a pretext for a fight in which every available male participated. Admittedly, he was writing of a society where the men were underemployed and dependent upon their wives' activities as lacemakers, but the record of violence is not dissimilar to that for Brittany, Languedoc, Rouergue, or Périgord. Every Sunday had its ration of drunken brawls amongst the farmers or workmen of any community for whom Sundays, winter Sundays in particular, were precious moments of leisure. Ideally the man, his wife, and children went together to mass and participated in communal worship, followed by village business in which the parish syndic read out correspondence from the *intendance* and drew attention to new legislation. Then villagers caught up on whatever news was to be had. The curé, however, throughout the eighteenth century was in some regions—the Auvergne, Lyonnais, Provence, Bas Languedoc, Rouergue, Flanders, and even parts of Brittany—in active competition with the *cabaretier* for the leisure hours of at least a minority of his male spiritual charges.[2] Attempts to clamp down on Sunday opening met with no response. The *maréchaussée* turned a blind eye, and the exhortations of bishops and archdeacons alike were apparently of little avail to a hard core. Gregarious drinking was for the adult male a more than acceptable alternative to mass-going, perhaps the more so because his wife and children did not join him. If this was true in parts of the country, it was doubly so in the towns. Here the immigrant sectors of the population, apart from the servants who followed their employers' example, did not seek out the churches; if seasonal migrants, they took care to return at Easter to make their annual obligatory profession of faith. Nowhere, except in the largest cities—and even there with important reservations, such as last rites for the dying—had any real severance been made between the poorest sectors of the population and the Catholic Church, but what remained was a Catholicism dependent upon the opportunities it afforded for

[1] A.D. Hérault C 2625.
[2] These generalizations might have wider application: M. Vovelle, *La Chute*, pp. 79–81, offers a cautious synopsis of the current state of research on religious observance.

sociability, a superstitious, contractual Christianity in which the parish priest needed to identify himself closely with his flock and tread a cautious path if he was to retain their sympathy and confidence. The strength of the Church in the countryside, however, was guaranteed by the fact that the Church was a vital expression of the two loyalties paramount in peasant psychology, that to family and that to parish. It hallowed family festivals, it offered the opportunities for parochial fraternizing.

One can give endless examples of family and parish loyalties, some of which have already found expression in this volume. These were the ties that determined seasonal and permanent migrations and opportunities for employ. Parishes wished to close their ranks against the outside beggar and were indifferent to atrocities committed against outsiders within the parish. The strong sense of family honour which drove the pregnant country girl into the town lest her family discover her shame or throw her out would be one. Another is the vendetta. Families could elevate the vendetta into a full-time leisure activity, as in the instance of the Cormats and the Le Pallud family of Grand Champ in Brittany who quarrelled over the leasing of a piece of land for over eight years before the Cormats took the matter to court, having been regularly ambushed after every fair over the entire period by the Palluds.[1] The vendetta emerges as one of the most conspicuous features of Languedocian lawsuits.[2] In a village near Mende a woman fled for sanctuary to the priest away from her husband who had been bitten by a dog with rabies, and with whom she had not in fact cohabited for some time. In the meantime, the villagers gathered together and formed a band to exterminate the mad husband. They beat him to death. The widow then sought to avenge herself on the murderers of her husband. The village expected her to do so but was not going to disclose who, in fact, his murderers were.[3] The spirit of the vendetta thus came into headlong conflict with parochial solidarity, and the latter ultimately prevailed for nothing could be proven without eyewitnesses. Even the Church could do little when it came into conflict with family or parochial interests.

A Breton priest of a village near Concarneau, allegedly one of

[1] A.D. Ille-et-Vilaine 1 B^n 3615.
[2] N. Castan, 'La Criminalité familiale dans le ressort du Parlement de Toulouse', in *Crimes et criminalité*, pp. 91–107.   [3] A.D. Haute-Garonne B 2187.

the most devout regions of France, struggled for nine weeks before admitting total defeat to collect information relating to the abandonment of a new-born baby. The infant was found at midday *in the centre of the village* and it was inconceivable to the priest that someone did not know something. He himself suspected a number of girls whom he duly visited and interrogated. Someone, given the place of exposition, must have seen someone trying to dispose of a bundle. He pulled out all the weapons in the ecclesiastical armoury, threatened excommunication to those who held their silence, but got nowhere. Like the *maréchaussée* trying to force villagers to give information against fellow parishioners, he was on too delicate ground.[1] In the diocese of Vienne in August 1742 the *notaire* of Saint-Romain-en-Gal (collector of the *centième denier*) was killed at Sainte-Colombe-les-Vienne. The mutilated body revealed a particularly brutal attack, and the bishop enjoined the priests of the villages surrounding the area where the crime had been committed to threaten with excommunication those who knew who was guilty but withheld evidence. The result was a physical attack, largely by the wives of *bateliers* and *vignerons*, on the curés themselves as they read out the indictment. Vestments were torn, a few holy vessels dented in the scuffles, and the discountenanced priests were forced to try to reason with the angry women. The women claimed excommunication would bring hail to destroy the crops indiscriminately; the priest rejoined that only the guilty need fear. The women persisted, and the formal threat was never read out. What the priests in question felt to be true was that the women knew something (there was a little circumstantial evidence to suggest that the crime was the work of *bateliers*), that perhaps their husbands were involved, but that they feared the threat of excommunication might bring forward some informer and that this was the reason for their extreme reaction.[2] As events turned out, no informer presented himself, and for good reason. He feared for his skin, feared reprisals from those very women who had attacked the priest. He knew village communities had elephantine memories, that the vendetta was the only justice they understood and were wholly committed to, and that some time, somewhere, vengeance would be perpetrated upon the informer.

[1] A.D. Finistère B 1327, Exposition d'enfant, 1775–6.
[2] A.D. Rhone B, Maréchaussée, Affaire Godebert.

Those who look closely at the eighteenth-century poor cannot but be struck by their aggressive independence and their desire to be left alone to live out their lives without intrusion from higher authority, police, government official, ecclesiastic. Fragmentary though the evidence may be, it is clear that they had evolved their own impenetrable codes based on narrow parochial interests and family loyalties, just as they had defined their own priorities and worked out as best they could their own means of existence, whether based upon seasonal movements, parochial charity, or the nefarious practices with which a large part of this study has been concerned. True, the movement from country to town could partially sever ties with family and parish, but even in the cities immigrants strove to perpetuate in their own ghettos the links with their homes and their kin. Above all, the poor had learned to expect very little from anyone. Nominally, in the interests of the community, priest and syndic, municipal council, *subdélégué*, and *intendant* made their appeals to their respective higher authorities to come to the aid of the destitute, but the outcome would not have any effect upon the material conditions of the lives of the poor.

My researches began with a question: how did people ostensibly without the means of support manage to survive and procreate in the conditions of the *ancien régime*? The answer is loud and clear. They made out under progressively difficult circumstances, and with progressively less chance of success, by their own efforts, devious, ugly, cruel, and dishonest as these might be. No economic 'take-off' delivered them; neither public philanthropy nor government policy made any real impact upon their situation. The price of their survival was often a rejection of the precepts of comfortable society. Transcending any system of ethics is the obligation to stay alive. It was to the observance of this sovereign imperative that the poor perforce gave their first loyalty and their abundant resourcefulness. Their very survival was a triumph of human ingenuity.

APPENDIX I

CHARITABLE RESOURCES

Diocese of Mendé[1]

(*a*) Parishes recording no resources:

Albaret-le-Comtal, Albaret-Sainte-Marie, Alleuc, Antrenas, Arcomie, Arzenc-d'Apcher, Arzenc-de-Randon, Aumont, Auroux, Auxillac, Le Bacon, Badaroux, Bagnols, Les-Balnies, Balsièges, Banassac, Belvezet, Les-Bessons, Blavignac, Les-Bondons, Le Born-Saint-Martin, Le Bousquet-de-la-Barthe, Brenoux, Le-Buisson, Canillac, La-Canourgue, Cassagnes, Castelbouc, Chadenet, Le-Chambon-Saint-Symphorien, Chastamer, Chastel-Nouvel, Chateauneuf-de-Randon, Chauchailles, Chaudeyrac, Chauliac, Le-Cheylar-d'Ance, Cocurès, Cubièrettes, Cultures, Esclanèdes, Estables-de-Randon, Estables-de-Rive-d'Olt, La-Fage-Saint-Julien, Fontanes, Fontans, Fournels-Montaleirac, Fraissinet-de-Fourques, Fraissinet-de-Lozère, Frutgères, Gabrias, La-Garde, 144 Guérin, Grandieu, Grèzes, Hures, Inox, Javols, Jullianges, La-Champ-de-Quintinhac, Marijoulet, Molezon, Montauroux-Laval, Montialoux-Saint-Bauzille, Montjézieu, Naussac, Noalhac, Palhers, La-Panouze, La-Parade, Paulhac, Pierrefiche, Le-Pin, Planchamp, Prades-du-Tarn, Prinsuéjols, Prunet-la-Salle Montvaillant, Prunières-et-Apcher, Puylaurens, Randon, Rocles, Le-Rozier, La-Rouvière, Saint-Alban, Saint-Amans, Saint-André de Lancize, Saint-Andréol de Clerguemort, Saint-Bonnet près de Chirac, Saint-Bonnet de Montauroux, Saint-Chély-d'Apcher (ville), Saint-Chély-d'Apcher (village), Saint-Chély-du-Tarn, Sainte-Colombe-du-Peyre, Saint-Étienne-du-Valdonnès, Saint-Frézal-d'Albuges, Saint-Frézal-de-Ventalon, Saint-Gal, Saint-Hilaire-de-Lavit, Saint-Jean-du-Bleymard, Saint-Jean-de-Gabriac, Saint-Julien-d'Arpaon, Saint-Julien-des-Points, Saint-Laurent-de-Muret, Saint-Laurent-de-Trèves, Saint-Laurent-de-Veyres, Saint-Léger-du-Malzieu, Saint-Martin-de-Boubeaux, Saint-Martin-de-Campcelade, Saint-Martin-de-Lansuscle, Saint-Michel-de-Dèze, Saint-Pierre-de-Nogaret, Saint-Pierre-de-Triquiers, Saint-Pierre-le-Vieux, Saint-Préjet-du-Tarn, Saint-Privat-de-Vallongue, Saint-Privat-du-Fau, Saint-Romain, Notre-Dame-de-Val-Francesque, Saint-Saturnin, Saint-Sauveur-de-Ginestoux, Saint-Sauveur-du-Peyre, Sainte-Colombe-de-Montauroux, Sainte-Croix-Vallée-Française, Sainte-Eulalie, Sainte-Hélène, Les Salses et Les Hermaux, Termes, Vebron, Verdezun, Le-Villard, La-Villedieu, Villefort.

[1] A.D. Hérault C 561–3. The results of the *enquête* of the seventies for this diocese are scattered throughout these *liasses*. Three *bureaux de charité* for which records remain were not recorded, nor was the *Miséricorde* of Mende.

(b) Parishes with *fondations, rentes,* or monastic charities:

	Annual income *in* livres	or	Annual income *in kind*
Altier	100		
Barjac	500		
Bedouès	39		7 cartes de seigle
			7 cartes de millet
Brion	49		
La-Capelle			12 cartes d'orge
Chanac	40		
La-Chaze	300–400		
Chirac	408[1]		
Cubières	20		7 septiers de seigle
			3 septiers d'orge
La-Farge-Montivernaux	250		48 septiers de seigle
Fau			10 septiers de blé
Grandvals			3 septiers de blé
Grisac	36		
Marchastel			15 septiers de seigle
Monastier	12		66 septiers de blé
Montrodat	24		
Nasbinals	300		100 septiers de seigle
Quézac			4 septiers de seigle
Recoules-d'Aubrac	20		16 septiers de blé
Le Recoux	12		
Ribenès			3 septiers de seigle
Saint-Denis	310		
Saint-George-de-Lévéjac			4 septiers de seigle
Saint-Germain-du-Teil	21		
Saint-Jean-la-Fouillouze	70		
Saint-Julian-du-Tournel			18 septiers de seigle
Saint-Léger-de-Peyre			10 septiers de seigle
			2 septiers d'orge
Sainte-Énimie	9		
Salelle			6 septiers de blé
Serverettes	800		
Servières	250		18 septiers de seigle

(c) Towns or villages with *hôpitaux, bureaux de charité,* or other institutionalized relief:

	Revenues of hôpital général	Revenues of hôtel Dieu	Revenues of bureau de charité
Barre			Unspecified for aged and sick
Chirac			c. 200 *livres* (fluctuating *quêtes*)
Le Collet			65 *livres*
Florac			c. 500 *livres*
Ispagnac			70 *livres* 2 *sous*
			5 septiers de seigle

[1] This was largely a controversial, irregularly paid, monastic hand-out.

Langogne		300 *livres*	
Malzieu		200 *livres*	
Marvejols		3,540 *livres*	
Mende	15,570 *livres*		1,400 *livres*[1]
Saint-Étienne-Vallée-			300–500 *livres*[2]
Française			(fluctuating *quêtes*)
Villefort	Small and		*c.* 500 *livres*
	unspecified		

Diocese of Clermont[3]

(*a*) Parishes recording no resources:

Aix-la-Fayette, Apchat, Aubusson, Augnat, Autrac, Avèze, Aydat, Baffie, Bagnols, Beaumont-lès-Randon, Beaulieu-près-port, Beauregard-l'Évêque, Bongheat, Bonneval, Boudes, Bousselargues, Brenat, Brousse, Bulhom, Celle-près-Fernoël, Chalus, le Chambon, Chaméane, Champagnac, Champagnat-le-Jeune, Chapelle-Geneste, Chapelle-sur-Usson, Charbonnières, Chastel-Marlat, Chastreix, Châteaugay, Cheylade, Clémensat, Colamine-le-Puy, Collanges, Compains, Comps, Coudes-Mont-Peyroux, Courgoul, Courtesseire, Crestes-sous-Besse, Cros, Dauzat-sur-Vodable, Domaize, Doranges, Dorat, Dore, Drignac, Drugeac, Égliseneuve-sur-Billom, Égliseneuve-près-Condat, Églisolles, Escouteux, Espinchal, Estandevil, Fernoël, Flat, Gimeaux-sur-Allier, Godivelle, Isserteaux, Job, Labessette, Laps, Laqueuille, Larodde, Lempty, Leyvaux, Lugarde, Luzillat, Malintrat, Malvières, Marat, Marchal, Mauzun, Medeyrolles, Menet, Messeix, La Meyrand, Molèdes, Mont-Dore, Montboissier, Montgreleix, Montredon, Montvianeix, Moussages, Murols, Nerondes, Neuville, Noalhat, La Nobre, Olby, Orléat et Pontastier, Parentignat, Paslières, Peschadoires, Pessat-Villeneuve, Puy-Saint-Gulmier, Riom-ès-Montagne, Roche-Charles, Rozentières, Sailhens, Saillans, Saint-Alyre, Saint-Éloy, Saint-Étienne-sur-Usson, Saint-Ferréol-des-Côtes, Saint-Flour, Saint-Gal, Saint-Genès-Champespe, Saint-Gervais-sous-Meymont, Saint-Germain-sous-Usson, Saint-Gervase, Saint-Hippolyte-près-Riom, Saint-Ignat, Saint-Jean-d'Aubrigoux, Saint-Jean-d'Heurs, Saint-Jean-Glaine, Saint-Jean-en-Val, Saint-Jean-les-Monges, Saint-Julien-Puy-Lavèze, Saint-Julien-sur-Aydat, Saint-Just-de-Baffie, Saint-Martin, Saint-Martin-des-Olmes, Saint-Pardoux-la-Tour, Saint-Rémy-près-Salers, Saint-Rémy-près-Thiers, Saint-Saturnin, Saint-Sauves, Saint-Sauveur, Saint-Victor-près-Besse, Saint-Vincent, Sainte-Mandine, Saulzet-le-froid, Saurier, Sauvat, Savennes, Ségur, Sermentizon, Sugères, Sulfiniac, Tauves, Ternat, Teyssonière, Tinlhat, Torsiac, La-Tourgoyon, Tourniac, Trémoville-Marchal, Trézioux, Le Valbeleix, Le Vernet-Sainte-Marguerite, Vernines, Verrières, Vertolaye, Vialle, Le Vigean, Vitrac.

---

[1] See Appendix II. Reference is here to the revenues in the 1770s; in 1790 they were reckoned greater by 2,000 *livres*, largely because of the rise in value of *rentes* in kind.

[2] See Appendix III.

[3] A.D. Puy-de-Dôme C 927–34.

(*b*) Villages with *fondations*, *rentes*, or monastic charities[1]

	Annual income in livres	Annual income in kind
Cébezat	30	
Ronzières	10	24–5 septiers de blé

(*c*) Villages claiming *fondations* which had lapsed:

Dallet: 'Il y avait autrefois une frairie du St Esprit qui jouissait d'environ 20 livres de revenu; elle a été réunie à la fabrique par M. l'Évêque' (C 929).

Montaigut-le-Blanc-sur-Champeix: A distribution by the priory made on Maundy Thursday of 3 *septiers de blé* and 4 *cartons de fèves* was no longer paid.

(*d*) Towns or villages with *hôpitaux*, *bureaux de charité*, or other institutionalized relief:

	Number of beds[2]		Revenues
	Hôpital général	Hôtel Dieu[3]	Bureau de charité or Confrérie
Ambert	41		
Ardes		6	
Auzon		4	
Besse		11	
Billom	40		
Blesle		3	
Brioude		30	Unspecified
Cébezat			10 septiers de froment
Chomelis		10	
Clermont-Ferrand	394		
Coupière		6	
Issoire	28		
Lezoux		18	
Maringues	10–20		
Montaigut		4	
Noalhat			Unspecified
Riom	135		460 *livres*
Saint-Nectaire			No regular income
Thiers	100		

[1] The paucity of these in Auvergne is striking and may be attributed to (1) a poor clergy, (2) the relative meanness of those who had something to bequeath and the lack of tradition in this region of making such legacies or bequests.

[2] Information on the *hôpitaux* of the Auvergne is very scanty and dispersed (C 940–1063). The town replies to the *enquête* of the seventies are missing, and the area did not reply to the questionnaire of the *Comité de Mendicité*, which was forced to guess at its resources. There are plenty of estimates but they apply to varying periods and hence it seemed more realistic to deal in numbers of beds, which on the whole did not fluctuate. Generally in the Auvergne, the *hôpitaux généraux* also tended the sick and received *enfants trouvés*.

[3] These look for the most part so small that they can only have been a room in a cottage for the chronically sick tended by a nun or even a visiting nun.

(e) Towns or villages with *hôpitaux* which were closed in 1724 because they were too small (their revenues were absorbed by the larger):

Arlanc, La-Chaise-Dieu, Chaudesaignes, Langeac, Murat, Salet.

Diocese of Montpellier[1]

(a) Parishes recording no resources:

Aleyrac, Assas, Beaulieu, Boisseran, Brissac, Buzignargues, Campagne, Caillarguet, Cazevielle, Château-de-Londres, Clapiers, Combaillaux, Cournonsec, Frouzet, Garrigues, Grabels, Guzargues, Jacou, Juvignac, Lattes, Lauret, Les-Mattelles, Montel, Montferrier, Mujolan, Puéchabon, Rouët, Saint-Brès, Saint-Christol, Saint-Clément-de-Rivière, Saint-Félix, Saint-Hilaire-de-Beauvoir, Saint-Jean-de-Cornies, Saint-Jean-de-Coudes, Saint-Jean-de-Védas, Saint-Paul-de-Valmalle, Saint-Senel, Saint-Vincent, Sainte-Colombe, Saussan, Teiran, Treviers, Le-Triadou, Vacquières, Vailhauquès, Villetelle, Viols-en-Laval, Viols-Le-Fort.

(b) Parishes with *fondations*, *rentes*, or monastic charities:

	Annual income in livres	Annual income in kind
Argelliers	25	
La Boissière	25	
Castelnau and Le Crès	40	
Castries	Unspecified	
Le Causse-de-la-Selle	43	
Cournonterral	50	
Fabrègues	40	
	40 (from a regular *quête*)	
Galargues	50	
Lunel-Viel	230	
Montaud	9	
Mudaison	20	
Murviel	2	
Pégarolles	10	
Prades	12	
Restinclières	90	
Saint-Drézery	45	
	130[2]	
Saint-Geniès	5	
Saint-Georges	18	
Saint-Martin-de-Londres		6 septiers de méteil
Saint-Nazaire	20	
Sainte-Croix	20	
Saturargues	15	9 septiers de méteil
Saussines	26	
Vendargues	25	
La Vérune	30	
Vic	50	

[1] A.D. Hérault C 5957, Assistance publique, 1774.

[2] The two separate figures refer to two distinct *fondations* used for different purposes.

(*c*) Villages claiming *fondations* which had lapsed:

Villeneuve: 'Rien depuis la réunion de tous les hôpitaux à l'hôpital général qui fut en 1684.'

(*d*) Towns or villages with *hôpitaux*, *bureaux de charité*, or other institutionalized relief:

	Revenue of hôpital général *in* livres	Revenues of hôtels Dieu *in* livres	Revenues of bureau de charité
Agonès*			284 *livres* and unspecified income on a small field
Aniane*			220 *livres*
Baillargues			36 *livres*
Candillargues			60 *livres*
Cazilhac*			18 *livres*
Frontignan*			120 *livres*
Gigean*			177 *livres*
Lansargues*			No regular revenues
Lunel	1,098		150 *livres*
Mauguio*			95 *livres*
Montarnaud*			40 *livres*
Montbazin*			160 *livres*
Montpellier	*c.* 33,000	*c.* 22,000	Unspecified and dependent upon *quêtes* Small *mont de piété*
Perols*			30 *livres*
Pignan			600 *livres*
Poussan*			1,500 *livres* 26 septiers de méteil
La-Roque		65	
Saint-Bauzille-de-Montaud			32 *livres*
Saint-Bauzille-de-Putois*			143 *livres* 60 *livres, quêtes*
Saint-Gély-du-Fesc			30 *livres*
Saint-Jean-de-Buèges			10 *livres*
Saint-Just			200 *livres*
Soubeiras			No regular revenues
Sussargues			32 *livres*

* An asterisk indicates *bureaux* founded by Pradel in 1689–90.

Diocese of Rennes[1]

(*a*) Parishes recording no resources:

Acigné, Andouillé, Arbrissel, Aubigné, Bais, Betton, Billé, Boistrudan, La Bosse, La Bouexière, Bourg-des-Comptes, Bréal-sous-Vitré, Brie, Brielles,

[1] A.D. Ille-et-Vilaine C 1293–4, Mendicité, 1774–5, and Guillotin de Corson, *Pouillé historique de l'Évêché de Rennes* (1882), t. iii: *Les Hôpitaux et autres établissements d'assistance publique.*

Broons-sur-Vilaine, Cesson, Chancé, Chanteloup, La Chapelle-des-Fougeretz, Chartres, Chateaubourg, Chatillon-sur-Seiche, Chaumeré, Chelun, Chevaigné, Chienné, Coësmes, Corps-nuds, La Couyère, Domagné, Ercé-en-Lamée, Étrelles, Feins, Forges, L'Hermitage, Javené, Lalleu, Livré, Luitré, Mecé, La Mézière, Moigné, Montautour, Montreuil-des-Landes, Montreuil-le-Gast, Montreuil-sous-Pérouse, Montreuil-sur-Ille, Mordelles, Mouazé, Noyal-sur-Vilaine, Pacé, Pancé, Parcé, Parthenay, Le Pertre, Princé, Saint-Aubin-d'Aubigné, Saint-Aubin-du-Pavail, Saint-Didier, Saint-Christophe-des-Bois, Saint-Erblon, Saint-Helier-de-Rennes (campagne), Saint-Laurent-de-Rennes (campagne), Saint-Martin-de-Rennes (campagne), Saint-Médard-sur-Ille, Saint-Hervé, Saint-Sulpice des Landes, Saint-Sulpice-la-Forêt, Saint-Colombe, Saulnières, Le Sel, La Selle Guerchaise, Taillis, Thorigné, Trans, La Vallette, Vendel, Veneffles, Vignoc, Villerot.

(b) Parishes with *fondations*, *rentes*, or monastic charities:

	Annual income in livres	Annual income in kind
Amanlis	30	
Argentré	270	
Availles	200	
Balazé	10	
Bourgbarré	75	
Brecé	450	
Bruz	200	
Champeaux	1,000	
La-Chapelle-d'Erbrée		4 boisseaux de seigle
Chateaugiron		30 boisseaux de froment
		30 boisseaux de seigle
Chavagne	63	
Cintré	12	
Combourtillé	40	
Cornillé	200	
	40	
Domalain		64 boisseaux de blé
		32 boisseaux de blé
Domloup	400–500 from regular *aumône*	
Dompierre du Chemin	120	
Drouges	20	
Eancé	57	
Erbrée	190	
Essé	391	
Fercé	36	
Gennes	168	
La-Guerche	18	
	144	
	21	
	20	
Guipel		38 boisseaux de blé
Izé	1,204	
Janzé	50	
	20	

	Annual income in livres	*Annual income in kind*
Laillé	33	
	80	
Louvigné-de-Bais	Unspecified, for use of chronic sick	
Marcillé-Robert	60	
Marpiré	15	
Martigné-Ferchaud	300	
Melesse	20	
Messac	Rente sur 10,000 livres	
Mézières	240	
Mondevert	100	
Montgermont	40	
Moulins	8	
Moussé	18	
Moutiers	Unspecified	
Nouvoitou	65	
	Rente sur 600 livres	
Noyal-sur-Bruz	50	
Noyal-sur-Seiche	50	
Orgerès	361	
Ossé	374	
Pléchatel	24	
Pocé	80	
Poligné	100	
Ranné	Unspecified	
Rennes: parish		
Saint-Aubin	310	
Saint-Étienne	162	
Saint-Helier	91	
Saint-Jean	51	
Saint-Martin	30	
	unspecified	Bread distribution by Chapter
Retiers	144	
Le-Rheu	100	
Saint-Armel	180	
	600	
Saint-Aubin-des-Landes	139	
Saint-Germain-du-Pinel		56 boisseaux de seigle
Saint-Germain-sur-Ille	24	
Saint-Gilles	101	
	127	
Saint-Grégoire	200	
Saint-Jacques-de-la-Londe	Unspecified *rente*	
Saint-Jean-sur-la-Vilaine	41	
Saint Malo	22	
	120	
Sens		A bread distribution to 13 poor on Maundy Thursday
Servon	10	
Le-Theil	7	

	Annual income in livres	*Annual income in kind*
Thourie	50	
	84	
Torcé	130	
	220	
Vergéal	60	
Vern	400–600	
Visseiche	10	
Vitré	Sunday distribution of 18 *sous* to 18 poor	

(*c*) Parishes claiming *fondations* which had lapsed:

Guipel: 'Cette aumône (7½ boisseaux de blé noir) n'est plus distribuée depuis que la chapellerie est devenue la propriété de la seigneurie.'

(*d*) Towns or villages with *hôpitaux*, *bureaux de charité*, or other institutionalized relief:

	Revenues of hôpital général *in* livres	*Revenues of* hôtel Dieu *in* livres	*Revenues of* bureau de charité *in* livres
Availles		Sufficient for 12 sick	
Bain			600 (with *quêtes*)
Balazé			350
Bruz			200
Chantepie	*c.* 500		
Châtillon en Vendelais			Unspecified
Fercé			*Capital* of 12,500 *livres*
La Guerche	2,200[1]		254
Hennebont			Unspecified and not of permanence
Marcillé Robert			Small and unspecified[1]
Martigné Ferchaud			300
Piré			272
Rennes	*c.* 34,610	*c.* 50,000	*c.* 40,000
Tresboeuf			100
Vezin		Small and unspecified	
Vitré	Unspecified	3,000	2,000

Généralité of Rouen 1774–5[2]

(*a*) Parishes recording no resources:

Alges, Ambleville, Amécourt, Ancourt, Ancourteville-sur-Héricourt, Ancretteville, Andé, Angeville, Argueil, Aulage, Autels par Claire, Authieux, Authieux sous Bouchy, Avesnes, Bailleul, Baillolet, Bardouville, Basincourt, Bazomesnil, Beaubec, Beaumont-Beuzemouchel, Beaumont-le-

---

[1] For sick or crippled and for teaching of poor children.
[2] A.D. Seine-Maritime C 995 and G 841–6.

Hareng, Beaussault, Bertreville Saint-Ouen, Berville, Berville-en-Roumois, Beuvreville, Bezancourt, Biennais, Bierville, Biville-la-Rivière, Blacqueville, Bocasse, Boisemont-en-Vexin, Boisgautier, Bondeville, Boos, Bornambuc, Bosc-Asselin, Bosc-Béranger, Bosc-Bordel, Bosc-Édeline, Bosc-Geffroy, Bosherville, Bosc-le-Hard, Bosc-Roger, Bosville, Bouelles, Bouquelon, Bourville, Bractuit, Brandiancourt, Brémontier-Merval, Bretteville, Brique-dalle, Buchy, Buglise, Calleville, Capvalle, Catillon, Caumont, Cauville-sur-Mer, Cerlangue, Chapelle-Saint-Ouen, Civierre, Cléon, Collemarre, Com-painville, Cordelleville, Corny, Cottévraud, Cramesnil, Crespeville, Crevon, Criquetot-sur-Longueville, Criquetot-sur-Ouville, Croisy-la-Haye, Cuy-Saint-Fiacre, Dampierre, Dampierre-en-Bray, Dancourt, Doudeville, Dou-ville-sur-Andelle, Douxménil, Écotigny, Elbeuf-en-Bray, Elbeuf-sur-An-delle, Englesqueville-la-bras-longue, Englesqueville-l'Esneval, Épinay, Équiqueville, Ernemont-en-Bray, Escalles-sur-Buchy, Étampes, Farceaux, La Feuillie, Flipon, Folleterre, Fontaine, Fosse, Fréauville, Fresle, Fresnay, Fresquienne, Froment, Fry, Gamache, Gisancourt, Gommerville, Gouy, Grainville-sur-Fleury, Grigneuseville, Gros-Thiel, Guerny, Guitry, Har-court, Hermeville, Hérouchelles, Hodanc-en-Bray, Hodenc, Houppeville, Hoquetot, Houssaye Béranger, Hugleville-en-Caux, Icqueboeuf, Igoville, Illoy, Imare, Infreville, Isneauville, Lamberville, Launay-en-Caux, Leuqueu, Lizors, Loeuilly, Longuerne, Manneville-la-Goupil, Manoir-sur-Seine, Maromme, Mathonville, Maucomble, Manquenchy, Meinières, Ménerval, Ménesqueville, Mésanqueville, Mesnil-David, Mesnil-Durdent, Mesnil-Lieubray, Mesnil-Mauger, Mesnoual, Montagny-en-Bray, Mont-aux-Malades, Mont Cauvaire, Montebourg, Montmain, Montreuil-en-Caux, Mortemer, Nesle-en-Bray, Neuville, Neuville-Chant d'Oisel, Nolléval, Notre-Dame-de-Bonsecours-lès-Rouen, Noyers, Nullemont, Omerville, Orgeville, Orménil, Osmoy, Ouville-l'Abbaye, Parfondeval, Perduville, Petiville, Pierre, Pierrefiques, Pierrepont, Pitres, Pommeraye, Saint-Nicolas-du-Pont-Saint-Pierre, Pont-Saint-Pierre, Potérie, Préaux, Prée, Provemont, Puisneval, Quevreville-la-Millon, Quevreville-la-Potérie, Quincampoix, Rebets, Ricarville, Ricarville-près-Foulle, Rogerville, Romilly, Roncherolles-en-Bray, Ronchois, Roquette, Roumare, Rouvray, Ry, Saint-Aignan-sur-Ry, Saint-André sur Cailly, Saint-Arnoult, Saint-Arnoult-près-Caudebec, Saint-Aubin-de-Cretot, Saint-Aubin-de-Gournay, Saint-Aubin-Jouxte-Boulenc, Saint-Aubin-sur-Cailly, Saint-Barthélémy, Saint-Clair, Saint-Crespin, Saint-Martin-du-Bec, Serqueux, Valmartin.

(b) Parishes with *fondations*, *rentes*, or monastic charities:

	Annual income in livres	Annual income in kind
Aincourt	50	
Ambourville	4	
Aménucourt	50	
Anneville-sur-Seine	256	
Arthies	30	Rent on 15 *arpents* of
	36	plough land
	70	
Autisle	50	

	Annual income in livres	Annual income in kind
Anzouville	24	
	12*	
Bailly en Rivière	150	
Banthélu		Rent on 2½ *arpents* of plough land
Bec	6,000	Soup distributed 3 times a week
Bellengreville	8	
Belley	25	
Bennecourt	200	
Boisguilbert	100	
Bolbec (St Michel)	579	
Bouille	5	
Bourgthéroulde	72	
Bouttencourt	28	
Buhy	87	
Castenay	10	
Chaumont-en-Vexin	30	
Chauvincourt	100	
Chérances	70	
Clerre	100	
Contremoulins	345	
Coudray	36	
Criqueboeuf	599	
Criquetot sur Ouville	2	
Croixmare	96	
Cuverville-en-Caux	14	
Dangu	25	
	100	
Derchigny	15	
Doudeville-en-Caux	40	
Énencourt-Léage		3 septiers de méteil
Fécamp	50	
	15,000	
La-Ferté and St Sanson	76	
La-Feuillie	39	
Fontaine-en-Bray	3	
Frêne-l'Archévêque	57	
Freneuse	200	
	80	
Fresnes-l'Eguillon		3 mines de blé
Gaillefontaine	329	
Gommecourt	150	
Gonfreville l'Orcher	600	
Gonneville	10	
Grainville-sur-Ry		15 boisseaux de blé
		15 boisseaux de seigle
Guernes	100	
Guiry	94	
	80	

* Two separate *fondations* for different purposes.

	Annual income in livres	Annual income in kind
Hadancourt	5	
	50	
Harcanville	500	
Harcourt	46	
Hattenville	18 *pistoles*	
Hautot-le-Valois	23	
	10	
Hauville-en-Roumois	9	
Hebecourt	125	
Heugleville	9	12 loaves on Maundy Thursday
Heuqueville	*Rente* on 2 acres of land	
Hodenc	100	
Hodenger	100	
Intraville	6	
Jamméncourt	30	
Labosse	223	
Levaumain	102	
Lieuville	300	
Limais	200	
Lintot	50	
Mandétour	200	
	245	
	222	
Mélamare	10	
	20	
	55	
Moison	120	
Mons	44	
Montherland	43	
Montreuil-sur-Epte	50	
	65	
Monville	165	
Mousseaux	90	
Neufchâtel-Saint-Jacques	85	
Neuville-Ferrières	50	
Nointot	1 *écu*	
Notre-Dame-de-Varengeville	22	
	5	
Noyers	150	
Nucourt	100	
Raffetot	78	
Ricarville-près-Foulle	12	
Richemont	10	
Rocheguyon	248	
Rolleboise	40	
Saint-Antoine-la-Forêt	3	
Saint-Cyr-en-Arthies	80	
Saint-Léger	300	
Saint-Riquier	130	
Saint-Seure	10	

Annual income in livres

Saint-Valéry-en-Caux	645
Sasseville	150

(c) Parishes claiming *fondations* or *rentes* which had lapsed:

Saint-Ectot-sur-les-Baons: 50 *livres* from Saint-Wandrille.

(d) Towns or villages with *hôpitaux*, *bureaux de charité*, or other institutionalized relief:

	Revenues of hôpital général *in* livres	Revenues of hôtel Dieu *in* livres	Revenues of bureau de charité *in* livres
Aumale	2,001[1]	2,147[2]	
Blangy		2,793[3]	
Bully		Small[2]	
Caudebec en Caux		2,025[3]	
Criel sur Mer	3,250		
Dieppe	17,400[1]		
Elbeuf		2,995[2]	
Eu	4,839	3,885[2]	1,704
Fécamp		4,508[3] 80 boisseaux de blé	
Gaillefontaine		210[2]	
Gisors		7,500[3]	900
Gournay	1,622	3,003[3]	450 100
Grainville-la-Teinturière	5,983		
Harfleur	800[5]		96
Le Havre	50,444[4]		1,575
Honfleur	8,668[4]		500
Lillebonne		1,300[6]	
Magny-en-Vexin		3,640[2]	1,490 20 septiers de blé
Neufchâtel		4,606[2]	
Pavilly		Unspecified but small	
Rouen	341,270	(a) Unspecified (b) 113[7] (c) Unspecified[8]	

[1] For orphan children alone.
[2] For sick alone.
[3] For sick and orphaned.
[4] This figure is a joint one for both *hôpital général* and *hôtel Dieu*.
[5] The actual *hôtel Dieu* was so impoverished that it could no longer hospitalize the sick and dying and merely provided them with food on a fortnightly basis.
[6] For orphan girls.
[7] For *pauvres passants*.
[8] For aged women.

APPENDIX II

SPECIMEN *HÔPITAL* ACCOUNTS[1]

i. Hôpital général *of Mende, 1790*[2]

Money Income	Livres	Sous	Deniers
Rentes on Capital Investment			
on the Province of Languedoc	4,290	18	0
on the Diocese of Mende	4,675	14	8
on the Clergy of France	120		
on the Government	347		
Rentes foncières	1,780		
Rentes des biens fonds	1,454		
Rentes in kind			
Wheat 11 *septiers* at 20 *livres*	220		
Rye 75 *septiers* at 15 *livres*	2,625		
Barley 8 *septiers* at 13 *livres*	104		
Oats 8 *septiers* at 10 *livres*	80		
Rentes en censives			
Wheat 11 *septiers* at 20 *livres*	220		
Rye 75 *septiers* at 15 *livres*	1,125		
Barley 20 *septiers* at 13 *livres*	260		
Oats 14 *septiers* at 10 *livres*	140		
	17,441	12	8

Expenditure	Livres	Sous	Deniers
For *taille* in those parishes where property held	878		
To *seigneurs* as indemnity for mortmain	279	18	6
Payment of 8 *cens* to various *seigneurs*			
Wheat 1 *septier* 6 *cartes* at 20 *livres*	35		
Rye 20 *septiers* at 15 *livres*	300		
Oats 14 *septiers* at 10 *livres*	140		
Small *Cens*	25		
Payment of *rentes viagères*	1,769		
Fondations	787		
For the maintenance of 5 nuns	250		
Doctor's honorarium	50		
Surgeon's wages	100		
Syndic and 2 priests	440		
Gardener and *servante*	200		
Drugs and medicaments	300		
Upkeep of properties	1,200		
	6,853	18	6

Leaving 10,587 *livres* 14 *sous* 2 *deniers* for the maintenance of 257 people, of whom 163 live in the institution (which has 120 beds) and the rest are children *en nourrice* and orphan girls who help in the running of the house.

[*Footnotes on p.* 384

ii. Hôpital général *of Rennes, 1760*[3]

Revenus certains et casuels	Livres	Sous	Deniers
Métairies	592		
Rentes	4,553		
Octroi sur les boissons	10,807	19	6
Teintures funèbres	2,406	19	2
Viande de carême	3,407	8	
Reception d'officiers	447	7	2
Sergenteries	2,258	6	1
Moulins	3,102	10	4
Travaux Brocherie	1,371	16	2
Broderie	189	7	10
Dentelles	1,032	9	6
Aumônes	1,031	0	2
Convois funèbres	314	16	10
Billets d'enterrements	392	6	3
Cros publics	43	7	4
Confiscations	134	10	
Vente de cidre	81	18	1
Vente de jardinage	167	8	4
Vente de beurre	175	11	
Cour de Rennes	1,500		
Aumônes des États	600		
	34,610	1	9

This sum was applied directly to the upkeep of 700 internees. The house from the 1720s was accumulating debts of up to 6,000 *livres* per year.

iii. Hôpital général *of Aix, 1780*[4]

Revenus	Livres	Sous	Deniers
Rentes sur les États de Provence	1,884		
sur la communauté de la ville d'Aix, le clergé de France, etc.	1,776	16	3
sur les créanciers divers	1,229	11	3
78048.16.0. Capitaux sur divers corps et particuliers formant la succession de Mlle de Velaux qui doit demeurer distincte et séparée	2,768	0	6
Pensions sur divers particuliers	776	9	
	8,434	17	0
Divers effets de l'hôpital	1,002	10	
Aumônes fixes	1,048		
Revenus casuels	6,600		
Rentes sur les Cinq Grosses Fermes de 4000 sur laquelle est à déduire celle de 850 départie à la maison hospitalière du refuge de la ville d'Aix portant reste pour l'hôpital de la charité	3,150		
	20,235[5]	7	0

In this year the difference between expenditure and receipts was 833 *livres* 13 *sols*.

[*Footnotes on p. 384*

iv. Hôpital général *of Clermont*, 1750[6]

Revenus	*Livres*
Rentes foncières, des domaines, etc.	19,900
Casuels (quêtes, etc.)	3,000
Travail des pauvres dans la manufacture	10,500
Fonds versés par le domaine pour les enfants trouvés	17,000
Subvention pour les fous et filles de mauvaise vie	2,400
	52,800

Dépenses	
Nourriture de 500 pauvres	23,735
Officiers	4,355
Enfants trouvés[7]	24,000
Charges foncières	4,500
Rentes constituées	2,000
Rentes viagères	14,570
	73,160

[1] The examples given are not exceptional in any way. Two relate to large cities, two to small ones. They are intended to illustrate the range of sources of income.

[2] A.D. Lozère, Lx Assistance.

[3] A.D. Ille-et-Vilaine, Fonds Hardouin, Tableau des revenus et charges des hôpitaux de Rennes. This is a good example of an *hôpital* heavily dependent on minor privileges rather than land.   [4] A.N. H¹ 1311.

[5] In 1764 financial crisis had led to the sale of *hôpital* property; hence the almost total dependence upon *rentes*.

[6] A. Hosp. de Clermont-Ferrand, Hôpital général III B 8.

[7] The heavy expenditure on the *enfants trouvés* had been taken over by the monarchy by the 1770s; even so, the finances of this establishment were indeed precarious and the heavy payment of *rentes viagères* an indication of its predicament.

APPENDIX III

BUREAUX DE CHARITÉ[1]

i. *Saint-Étienne-Vallée-Française*[2]

Revenues (largely from *quêtes*)

	livres	sous	deniers
1769–70	1,526	18	
1770–1	270	12	3
1771–2	626	17	0
1773–4	557		
1775–80	1,207	15	6

Expenditure 1788

Baillé à Antoine Plagnée pour une journée de quête 20 sols et à Pierre des Bourgades pour une autre journée de quêtes 20 sols et tout ce 6 janvier	2	0	0
à Antoine Chauvet pour une journée de quêtes ce dit jour 6 janvier	1	0	0
au nommé Pierredon pour avoir aidé à faire la quête ce 8 janvier 1788	1	10	0
à un pauvre pour son mois d'aumône échu ce 10 janvier[3]	3	0	0
au nommé François pour deux journées qu'il a employées à faire la quête ce 13 dudit mois	2	0	0
au nommé Courland pour conduire la nommée Teroude de Lairis à Mende pour faire son cours d'accouchement cedit jour	8	0	0
au nommé Ponsard pour une journée de quête ce 17 janvier	1	0	0
à un pauvre cedit jour	1	4	0
au nommé Frion pour une journée de quête	1	0	0
à Marguerite Hugon pour avoir fourni à divers pauvres dans les besoins pressans	7	11	0
à Coustelesse pour un mois de nourriture de l'enfant d'un homme pauvre ce 30 janvier	6	0	0
à Antoine Lapeire pour une journée et demi de quêtes	1	10	0
à une pauvre femme ce 8 février	1	0	0
à un pauvre ce 9 dudit mois	1	4	0

[1] Whilst it is relatively common to find global figures relative to the funds distributed by *bureaux de charité*, it is rare to find details of how they were distributed, because the registers kept by the *bureaux* were often private property. Exceptions are the following and such spasmodic instances as are published, for example, in Hufton, *Bayeux*, pp. 288–97, Robin, *Semur en Auxois*, pp. 221–3.

[2] A.D. Lozère GG 12.

[3] This man, a total cripple, received a regular, monthly sum. He appears to have been the only such recipient.

à un pauvre pour son mois d'aumône échu ce 10 février	3	o	o
à une pauvre veuve ce 9 mars	3	o	o
à un pauvre pour son mois d'aumône échu ce 10 mars	3	o	o
à Marguerite Hugon qui a fourni à trois différents pauvres par ordre de MM les Directeurs, ce 5 avril	3	o	o
à la même pour fournitures faites à une pauvre veuve cedit jour 5 avril	3	o	o
à une pauvre pour son mois d'aumône échu ce 10 avril	3	o	o
J'ai payé au fermier de Veuve Deleuze de la Jarnune 12 sols pour la nourriture de l'enfant d'un homme pauvre ce 3 mai		12	o
à un pauvre pour son mois d'aumône échu le 10 mai	3	o	o
à Marguerite Hugon pour fournitures qu'elle a fait à 3 pauvres ce 15 mai	3	o	o
à la même pour autres fournitures à une autre femme cedit jour	3	o	o
au nommé Deshours, mâçon qui a raccommodé la maison d'un pauvre homme ce 17 mai	15	o	o
à une pauvre veuve ce 9 juin	2	8	o
à un pauvre pour son mois d'aumône échu ce 10 juin	3	o	o
à une femme vieille et veuve ce 21 juin	1	4	o
à Marguerite Hugon qui a fourni par ordre des directeurs à une famille honteuse, pain ce 3 juillet	3	o	o
à la même pour fournitures avancées à un pauvre homme cedit jour 3 juillet	3	o	o
à un pauvre pour les mois d'aumônes échu le 10 juillet	3	o	o
à Marguerite Hugon pour fournitures qu'elle a faites en pain à un homme pauvre et infirme ce 15 juillet	3	o	o
à la même qui a fourni à 2 femmes pauvres cedit jour	2	2	o
aux pauvres malades ce 6 août à un pauvre pour son mois d'aumône échu le 10 août	3	o	o
à un homme vieux et infirme ce 14 août	1	4	o
à M. Hugon pour pain ou autre choses qu'elle a fourni à divers pauvres ce 20 août	8	19	o
à une pauvre et vieille femme le 2 septembre	1	10	o
à une pauvre veuve le 6 septembre	2	8	o
à un pauvre pour son mois d'aumône échu ce 10 septembre	3	o	o
à Marguerite Hugon qui a fourni à une pauvre famille ce 24 septembre	3	o	o
à la même qui a fourni aux différents pauvres ce 29 septembre	5	3	o
à un pauvre vieux ce 30 septembre	1	o	o
à une pauvre veuve ce 6 octobre	1	10	o
à un vieux pauvre ce 7 octobre	1	10	o
à un pauvre pour son mois d'aumône ce 10 octobre	3	o	o
à une pauvre veuve ce 21 octobre	1	4	o
à une pauvre veuve et vieille ce 31 octobre	1	4	o
à un vieux pauvre le 8 novembre		12	o
à un pauvre pour son mois d'aumône le 11 novembre	3	o	o
à un homme pauvre ayant famille nombreuse le 30 novembre	1	4	o
à une pauvre veuve ce 9 décembre	1	4	o
à un pauvre malade ce 9 décembre	3	o	o
à un pauvre pour son mois d'aumône ce 10 décembre	3	o	o
à une pauvre veuve ce 31 décembre	1	4	o

ii. *Florac*[1]

The revenues of this *bureau* were totally unpredictable and consisted of two *quêtes*: one in kind, made in June, and one in money, usually converted into materials such as bedcovers. Distribution was *annual*.

Distribution de la quête du blé. 17 cartes de seigle ou orge distribués à deux boisseaux par personne le 3 juin 1734.

	Boisseaux
Famille Tresille	4
Montel	4
Daudenc	10
Neuve	10
Enfants de Vession	6
?	8
Maussion	4
Cordier	4
Soussière	8
Tourdez	6
Fille Brager et enfants	8
Jean Fleurs	4
Chabret	4
Livret	4
Veuve Michel	6
Salomon Brouplasse	4
Isaac	10
Veuve Barnat	4
Veuve Chausal	4
Veuve Dauderie	4
Enfants de Fresle	4
Bragne	4
Biscou	4
Belgisque	4
Veuve Coustand	4
Jassin vieux	4
Veuve Afflatel	4
Enfants Mynères	4
Chaligre	4
Bouderot	4
Vineste	4
Fille Argival	4
Laviala	
Veuve?	4
Laguey Lequier	10
Veuve Charbonne	4
Fille Bials	4
Montels	
Louraget	4
Veuve de Campran	4
Veuve de Rongnets	4
Bajet	4

[1] A.D. Lozère H 445. The register is in poor condition.

| Bondez | 4 |
| Jean Mosslet | 4 |

Salsièges

Veuve Sals	4
François le Blanc	4
Enfants Nirois	4
Les enfants d'un pauvre honteux	4

EARLY ARRESTS OF VAGRANTS
FOLLOWING THE LEGISLATION OF 1764

i. *État des mendians et vagabonds qui ont été renfermés dans les dépôts établis dans le royaume et de ceux qui ont été mis en liberté, engagés au service, morts et évadés pendant l'année 1773 et précédentes*[1]

Généralités	Entrés au dépôt	Prisonniers Élargis avec passe-ports	Prisonniers Élargis sans passe-ports	Prisonniers Réclamés avec soumis-sion	Prisonniers Réclamés sans soumis-sion	Total des ren-fermés mis en liberté	Engagés au service	Prisonniers Morts aux dépôts ou aux hôpi-taux	Évadés des dépôts	Total des enfans sortis des dépôts	Restans au dépôt dernier décem-bre 1773
Aix	2.025	788	196	76	11	1.071	10	373	416	1.870	155
Alençon	423	5	207	1	..	213	..	82	58	353	69
Amiens	760	..	526	71	..	597	1	70	14	682	78
Auch	67	..	4	..	..	4	..	..	..	4	63
Bayonne	777	12	117	121	37	287	1	151	62	501	276
Besançon	3.377	6	1.305	594	21	1.926	2	844	339	3.011	266
Bordeaux	3.563	250	1.338	133	165	1.886	..	768	374	3.028	535
Bourges	872	3	256	34	22	315	1	379	42	737	135
Caen	971	45	312	56	2	415	5	237	89	746	225
Châlons	1.599	1	651	288	95	1.035	11	298	86	1.430	169
Clermont	628	..	372	24	18	414	..	68	112	594	34
Dijon	2.130	13	1.048	572	129	1.762	3	818	135	2.718	412
Dombes	..	..	..	..	..	..	..	..	..	..	..
Grenoble	3.920	51	1.574	512	155	2.292	8	1.129	188	3.617	303
La Rochelle	1.617	..	473	190	97	760	21	409	184	1.374	243
Lille	1.567	..	1.084	191	..	1.275	2	126	20	1.423	144
Limoges	1.082	4	548	79	146	777	2	103	83	965	117
Lyon	1.993	..	680	429	86	1.195	6	289	194	1.684	309
Metz	2.062	..	1.370	101	44	1.515	4	231	79	1.829	233
Montauban	1.572	..	756	114	36	906	..	175	258	1.339	233
Montpellier	3.488	14	1.679	..	..	1.693	..	426	894	3.013	475
Moulins	1.122	19	429	40	64	552	..	307	123	982	140
Nancy	1.584	..	674	122	28	824	..	255	204	1.283	301
Orléans	3.630	1	1.176	270	328	1.775	76	1.131	167	3.149	481
Paris	18.523	2	11.877	15	1	11.895	88	3.158	1.963	17.104	1.419
Perpignan	401	24	103	69	52	248	3	43	66	360	41
Poitiers	825	18	270	27	34	349	12	126	197	684	139
Rennes	2.892	6	550	226	134	916	4	893	592	2.417	475
Rouen	1.413	..	538	115	46	699	12	228	177	1.116	297
Soissons	2.108	..	1.276	228	64	1.568	5	178	132	1.883	225
Strasbourg	1.370	..	512	267	5	784	2	189	183	1.158	212
Tours	1.946	50	925	147	83	1.205	7	358	131	1.701	245
Valenciennes	695	..	350	173	1	524	..	67	38	629	66
Totaux	71.760	1.314	33.003	5.243	1.899	41.459	298	13.899	7.489	63.145	8.615

[1] B.N. Fonds français, 8129, fol. 334, État des mendians.

ii. *Résultat de l'exécution de la déclaration du 3 août 1764 dans toutes les généralités du Royaume pendant l'année 1773 et les précédentes*[1]

| Généralités | Nombre de gens arrêtés | Prisonniers condamnés au renfermement | | Condamnés aux galères | Prisonniers | | | Restans à juger au dernier décembre 1773 |
		Par jugement	Par ordonnance		Évadés	Relâchés	Morts	
Aix	2.631	5	1.927	18	67	546	13	55
Alençon	427	8	296	5	4	94	2	18
Amiens	1.165	34	707	7	3	393	7	14
Auch	..	..	..	..	..	..	..	..
Bayonne	874	1	769	1	3	95	..	5
Besançon	2.849	8	2.348	9	3	467	6	8
Bordeaux	4.313	89	3.691	73	13	314	22	111
Bourges	1.208	32	812	44	4	264	17	35
Caen	1.099	11	801	5	16	247	15	4
Châlons	2.151	70	1.462	21	16	532	13	37
Clermont	550	3	480	9	1	45	6	6
Dijon	4.067	121	2.857	163	15	784	21	106
Dombes	290	..	252	9	..	28	1	..
Grenoble	4.504	14	3.748	29	31	631	16	35
La Rochelle	1.470	1	1.265	4	..	191	1	8
Lille	1.261	9	1.147	3	3	95	1	3
Limoges	833	..	800	..	..	30	..	3
Lyon	1.868	31	1.501	35	3	277	19	2
Metz	960	12	820	4	..	117	2	5
Montauban	545	..	464	2	9	70	..	..
Montpellier	4.113	30	3.434	17	29	563	2	38
Moulins	1.298	58	973	31	2	212	15	7
Nancy	1.306	2	944	1	4	319	7	29
Orléans	4.687	184	3.142	176	12	1.057	35	81
Paris	10.227	138	8.182	91	29	1.560	36	191
Perpignan	373	..	344	1	1	27	..	..
Poitiers	1.023	12	710	16	41	222	4	18
Rennes	2.547	5	2.180	3	8	334	13	4
Rouen	1.491	70	1.010	83	..	274	7	47
Soissons	1.880	91	1.470	59	7	239	3	11
Strasbourg	1.594	7	1.013	7	7	541	9	10
Tours	2.386	119	1.798	38	5	305	63	58
Valenciennes	471	5	447	4	..	10	..	5
Ville de Paris	5.544	..	5.032	..	1	79	..	432
Totaux	72.025	1.170	56.839	968	335	10.961	366	1.386

[1] B.N. Fonds français, 8129, fol. 335.

BIBLIOGRAPHY[1]

1. *Manuscript*

THE majority of the documents used for this study are to be found in the Series C, G, H, and L of various *archives départementales*. Principally, they were:

(i) Aveyron

2 L 98–105	Assistance etc. District d'Aubin
3 L 156–62	Assistance etc. District de Millau
4 L 85	Assistance etc. District de Mur-de-Barrez
5 L 234–46	Assistance etc. District de Rodez
6 L 279–81	Assistance etc. District de Saint-Affrique
7 L 136–7	Assistance etc. District de Saint-Geniez
8 L 174–81	Assistance etc. District de Sauveterre
9 L 199–208	Assistance etc. District de Sévérac
10 L 101–2	Assistance etc. District de Villefranche

(ii) Côte-d'Or

C 373–9	États généraux de tous les établissements, fondations, revenus et charités. Bourgogne
387	Dépôts de mendicité
3356–92	Mendicité, assistance, établissements charitables
L 1200	Hôpitaux, œuvres de bienfaisance et fondations charitables 1790
1209–13	Assistance publique par district, 1790

(iii) Hérault

C 141–4	États des filles et femmes de mauvaise vie arrêtées et renfermées dans la maison du Refuge et dans le dépôt de mendicité de Montpellier, 1787–9
550	Hôpitaux
559–60	Mendicité
561–3	Mendicité, 1721–75. États envoyés à l'intendant par ses subdélégués, faisant connaître les dénominations des établissements de charité, etc.
574–80	Dépôts de mendicité: Toulouse, Montpellier, Le Puy
581	Enfants trouvés, 1761–1785

[1] This bibliography is exclusive of the material on migrations, criminality, and smuggling to which reference is made in the leading footnote to the relevant chapter.

582–6	Mendicité. Ouvrages du dépôt de mendicité
588	Dépôt de Montpellier
5955	Mendicité, 1764–90
5956	Hôpital général de Montpellier, 1734–8
5957	États particuliers de tous les établissements, fondations et revenus de charité dans le diocèse de Montpellier
6556–7	Diocèse du Puy

(iv) Ille-et-Vilaine

C 1267–85	Hôpitaux et fonds de secours
1293	Mendicité. États des fondations, revenus et aumônes publiques qui ont lieu dans l'étendue des sub-délégations
1294	Mendicité, enquête de 1774–5
1295	Dépôts de mendicité
1300–8	Depôt de Rennes
1309	Dépôt de Quimper
1310	Dépôt de Vannes
1311	Dépôt de Nantes
1745	Secours destinés aux pauvres, 1785–6
1746	État des paroisses de la subdélégation de Montauban, 1785–6
1747	Liste des paroisses de la subdélégation de Rennes qui ont le plus besoin de secours, 1786
1748	Paroisses les plus pauvres de la subdélégation de Vannes
2647, 2660, 3177, 3184, 3796, 3804, 3840, 4937	Mendicité
L 1102–58	Assistance publique, 1790. Secours aux indigents. Listes des indigents par paroisses, etc.
1 F 2235–46	Fonds Hardouin [A large, miscellaneous manuscript collection relating to poverty, charity, and medical practice]

(v) Indre-et-Loire

H 827	Sœurs grises dites de la Charité de Tours
829	Dames de l'Union Chrétienne de Tours
899	Hôtel Dieu de Tours
900–7	Hôpital général de la Charité de Tours
908	Hospice des enfants trouvés de la Madeleine, à Tours
909–10	Bureau des aumônes de Tours

(vi) Lozère

C 62	Extrait abrégé des procès-verbaux de la capitation des communautés du diocèse de Mende

E 1000, 1049	Bureau de charité de Villefort
G 1834	Rôles du blé distribués aux pauvres de la paroisse. Les Bondons
1999	Rôle de la distribution d'une somme de 30 livres aux vraiment pauvres. Sainte-Colombe 1770
2088	État des revenus de l'évêché, chapitres, etc., du diocèse de Mende 1761
3106	1696–1706 Comptabilité de l'évêché; aumônes distribuées aux pauvres des paroisses de la mense épiscopale
3199	Succession de Monseigneur de Piencourt
3132	Comptabilité de l'évêché
GG 12	Bureau de charité Saint-Étienne-Vallée-Française
H 445	Bureau de charité de Florac
468–97	Hôpital de Mende. Testaments et donations
645–52	Lièvre des rentes et revenus de l'hôpital, 1759–91
658–61	Revenus et charges
820–914	Comptabilité. Hôpital de Mende
938–41	Secours aux familles honteuses, 1700–92
942	Rôle des pauvres de la ville de Mende et de diverses paroisses, 1681–1729
962–9	Enfants trouvés
1084	Œuvre de la Miséricorde
J 760	Fonds Volpellier. Bureau de charité de Chirac

(vii) Puy-de-Dôme

C 897–939	Assistance publique
940–1063	Hôpitaux
1044–1310	Dépôts de mendicité
1314–16	Femmes de mauvaise vie
1317–54	Enfants trouvés
1355–79	Épidémies

Archives Hospitalières

Hôtel Dieu	Clermont
1 B 80–100	Testaments et donations
1 E 10–108	Finances

(viii) Seine-Maritime

C 882–7	Ateliers de charité
995–7	Hôpitaux
1009–37	Dépôts de mendicité
2168	Mémoire sur les pauvres du Havre et d'Ingouville, 1788
2210	Commission intermédiaire. Mendicité
2211–12	États des pauvres et des secours par paroisses, 1788
G 841–6	États des pauvres, 1774
L 2648	Mendicité

Archives Nationales

M 672	Hôpitaux 1762
F⁴ 1026	États de distributions des fonds de la mendicité et du vagabondage, 1788–90
F¹⁵ 228²	Hospices, fondations, 1697–1792 Puy-de-Dôme
F¹⁵ 3560	Ateliers de filatures pour les pauvres, 1774–91
F¹⁶ 936	Dépenses de la mendicité, Languedoc and Roussillon, 1788–9
H¹ 340, 371, 373, 418, 556, 611	Mendicité en Bretagne
H¹ 892, 910, 912, 921, 927, 939	Mendicité en Languedoc

Bibliothèque Nationale

Fonds Joly de Fleury

1250	Miscellaneous *lettres patentes* of *hôpitaux*
1251 fols. 297–339	Enfants trouvés
1308 fols. 2–90	Filles et enfants de mauvaise vie

Fonds français

8129 fols. 334–5	Dépôts de mendicité
8130	Divers projets et mémoires sur la mendicité

Archives Communales

Rodez. Bourg et Cité

GG 1	Association de charité pour l'extinction de la mendicité
GG 2	L'Évêque propose l'établissement de l'Association de charité
GG 3	Enfants trouvés
FF 1–2	Femmes de mauvaise vie
Cité	
C 196, C 359	Ateliers de charité
CC 338, CC 346	Bureaux de charité

2. Printed

Archives Parlementaires:

t. XXIV, p. 445, *Rapport de la Rochefoucauld Liancourt au nom du Comité de Mendicité sur les dépenses des enfants trouvés, des dépôts de mendicité et des hôpitaux pour l'année 1791.*

t. XXII, p. 337, *Rapport fait au nom du Comité de Mendicité, des visites faites dans les divers hôpitaux de Paris 1790.*

t. XVIII, p. 435, *Quatrième rapport du Comité de Mendicité. Secours à donner à la classe indigente dans les différents âges et dans les différentes circonstances de la vie.*

t. XXII, p. 597, *Sixième rapport du Comité de Mendicité sur la répression de la mendicité, 1791.*

Bloch, C., and Tuetey, A., *Procès-verbaux et rapports du Comité de Mendicité de la Constituante (1790–91)* (Paris, 1911).

Dessuslamarre, P. de, *La Mendicité en 1789* (Marseilles, 1789).

Dralet, M., *Description des Pyrénées* (Paris, 1813).

Guilhamon, H. (ed.), *Journal des voyages en Haute Guienne de J. F. Henry de Richeprey* (Rodez, 1952).

La Mare, N., *Traité de la Police* (Paris, 1705–38), 4 vols.

Lempereur, *L'État du diocèse de Rodez en 1771* (Rodez, 1906).

Montlinot, M., *Discours . . . sur . . . quels sont les moyens de détruire la mendicité dans la ville de Soissons* (Lille, 1779).

—— *État actuel du dépôt de Soissons précédé d'un essai sur la mendicité* (Soissons, 1789).

—— *Observations sur les enfants trouvés de la généralité de Soissons* (Paris, 1790).

Ogée, D., *Dictionnaire historique et géographique de la province de Bretagne* (Nantes, 1778).

Sarramon, A. (ed.), *Les Paroisses du diocèse de Comminges en 1786* (Paris, 1968).

SECONDARY SOURCES

General works on social and economic conditions

Adher, J., 'Le Diocèse de Rieux au XVIIIᵉ siècle', *Annales du Midi*, xvii (1905), 490–510, and xxi (1909), 29–508 and 433–73.

Appolis, E., *Le Diocèse civil de Lodève* (Albi, 1951).

Azémar, T., 'Le XVIIIᵉ siècle à Massat', *Revue de Gascogne* (1933), pp. 322–37 and 435–500.

Baehrel, R., *Une Croissance: la Basse Provence rurale* (Paris, 1961).

Ballainvilliers, B. de, *État de l'Auvergne en 1765* (Clermont-Ferrand, 1846).

Bernard, R. J., 'L'Alimentation paysanne en Gévaudan au XVIIIᵉ siècle', *A.E.S.C.* xxiv (1969), 1449–67.

Bouloiseau, M., 'Aspects sociaux de la crise cotonnière dans les campagnes rouennaises en 1788–9', *Actes du 82ᵉ congrès des sociétés savantes* (Caen-Rouen, 1956).

Braudel, F., and Labrousse, C. E. (eds.), *Histoire économique et sociale de la France*, tome II: *Des derniers temps de l'âge seigneurial aux préludes de l'âge industriel (1660–1789)* (Paris, 1970).

Brunet, R., *Les Campagnes toulousaines. Étude géographique* (Toulouse, 1965).

Brutails, A., 'Notes sur l'économie rurale du Roussillon à la fin de l'ancien régime', *Mémoires de la société agricole, scientifique, et littéraire des Pyrénées Orientales*, xxx (1889).

Carrier, A., 'Notes sur la condition des travailleurs de la terre dans la région de Millau aux XVIIᵉ et XVIIIᵉ siècles', *A.H.R.F.* xvi (1939).

Chamboux, M., *Répartition de la propriété foncière et de l'exploitation dans la Creuse* (Paris, 1955).

Charbonneau, R., *Tourouve-au-Perche aux XVIIᵉ et XVIIIᵉ siècles. Études de démographie historique* (Paris, 1970).

Chauton, C., 'Les Baux ruraux, en Albret et en Chalosse [Lot et Garonne et

Landes] aux XVIIe et XVIIIe siècles', *Bull. soc. Bordelaise*, lxxxvii (1963), 161–83.

Chevalier, M., *La Vie humaine dans les Pyrénées ariégeoises* (Paris, 1956).

Chomel, V., 'Le Dauphiné sous l'ancien régime', *Cahiers d'histoire*, viii (1963), 303.

Colomès, A., *Les Ouvriers de textile dans la Champagne Troyenne, 1730–52* (Paris, 1943).

Coppolani, J., *Toulouse. Étude de géographie urbaine* (Toulouse, 1954).

Corgne, E., *Les Revendications des paysans de la sénéchaussée de Ploërmel, d'après les cahiers de doléances de 1789* (Rennes, 1938).

—— *Essai sur les classes sociales et la vie économique de Pontivy à la veille de la Révolution* (Besançon, 1942).

Couturier, M., *Recherches sur les structures sociales de Châteaudun, 1525–1789* (Paris, 1969).

Dardel, P., *Les Manufactures de toiles peintes et de serges imprimées à Rouen et à Bolbec aux XVIIe et XVIIIe siècles* (Rouen, 1940).

—— 'Crises et faillites à Rouen et dans la Haute Normandie', *R.H.E.S.* xxvii (1948–9).

De Hergne, J., *Le Bas Poitou à la veille de la Révolution* (Paris, 1963).

Deribier de Cheissac, *Description statistique du département de la Haute-Loire* (Le Puy, 1824).

Deribier du Chatelet, M., *Dictionnaire statistique du département du Cantal* (Aurillac, 1824).

Dollinger, P. (ed.), *Histoire de l'Alsace* (Toulouse, 1970).

Dubreuil, L., 'La condition des métiers à Évreux en 1789', *R.H.E.S.* ix (1921), 10–49.

—— 'Le Paysan breton au XVIIIe siècle', ibid. xii (1924), 478–92.

Du Chatellier, *De quelques modes de la propriété en Bretagne* (Paris, 1861).

Dugrand, R., *Villes et campagnes en Bas Languedoc* (Paris, 1963).

Dupuy, A., 'L'Agriculture et les classes agricoles en Bretagne au XVIIIe siècle', *Annales de Bretagne*, vi (1891), 3.

Dutil, L., *L'État économique du Languedoc, 1750–89* (Paris, 1911).

Enjalbert, H., 'Économie rurale du Rouergue à la veille de la Révolution', *Annales du Midi*, lxvii (1955), 170–5.

Esquer, H., *La Haute Auvergne à la fin de l'ancien régime* (Paris, 1911).

Foursans-Bourdette (Marie Pierrette), *Économie et finances en Béarn au XVIIIe siècle* (Bordeaux, 1963).

Ganiage, J., *Trois villages de l'Île de France au XVIIIe siècle; étude démographique* (Paris, 1963).

Garden, M., *Lyon et les Lyonnais au XVIIIe siècle* (Paris, 1970).

Gaultier, R., *Pourquoi les Bretons servent. La Dure Existence des paysans et des paysannes. Un Siècle d'indigence* (Paris, 1950), 2 vols.

Gille, B., 'Note sur la population de Clermont au XVIIIe siècle', *Revue d'Auvergne*, lxxxiii (1969), 123–4.

Girard, P., and Piole, C., 'Aperçus de la démographie de Sotteville-lès-Rouen vers la fin du XVIIe siècle', *Population*, xiv (1959).

Gobin, L., *Essai sur la géographie de l'Auvergne (Puy-de-Dôme, Cantal, Brioude)* (Paris, 1896).

Godechot, J., 'L'Histoire sociale et économique de Toulouse au XVIIIe siècle', *Annales du Midi*, lxxviii (1966), 363–74.

—— and Moncassin, S., 'Structures et relations sociales à Toulouse, 1749–1785', *A.H.R.F.* xxxvii (1965), 129–69.

Goubert, J. P., 'Le Phénomène épidémique en Bretagne à la fin du XVIIIe siècle (1770–87)', *A.E.S.C.* xxiv (1969), 1562–88.

Goubert, P., *Beauvais et le Beauvaisis de 1600 à 1750* (Paris, 1960).

—— 'Dans le sillage de Henri Sée. L'Histoire économique et sociale des Pays de l'Ouest (Bretagne, Maine, Anjou) du XVIe au XVIIIe siècles', *Annales de Bretagne*, lxxi (1961), 315–18.

—— 'Recherches d'histoire rurale dans la France de l'Ouest XVIIe–XVIIIe siècles', *Bull. soc. d'hist. mod.*, 13e série, no. 2 (1965), pp. 2–9.

Juillard, E., *La Vie rurale dans la plaine de Basse Alsace* (Strasbourg, 1953).

Kaplow, J., *Elbeuf during the Revolutionary Period* (Baltimore, 1964).

Lachiver, M., *La Population de Meulan du XVIIe au XIXe siècles (1660–1870)* (Paris, 1970).

Latouche, R., *La Vie en Bas Quercy du XIVe au XVIIIe siècles* (Toulouse, 1922).

Lefebvre, G., *Les Paysans du Nord pendant la Révolution française* (Bari, 1959).

—— *Études orléanaises* (Paris, 1962), 2 vols.

—— *Cherbourg à la fin de l'ancien régime* (Caen, 1965).

Lefebvre-Teillard, A., *La Population de Dôle au XVIIIe siècle* (Paris, 1969).

Lefort, A., 'Salaires et revenus dans la généralité de Rouen au XVIIIe siècle', *Bull. soc. d'émulation Seine-Inférieure* (1886), p. 219.

Le Goff, T., 'Vannes in the Eighteenth Century' (Ph.D. thesis, London, 1969).

Léon, P., *La Naissance de la grande industrie en Dauphiné, fin du XVIIIe siècle–1869* (Paris, 1954).

—— *Structures économiques et problèmes sociaux du monde rural dans la France du Sud-Est* (Paris, 1966).

Le Parquier, E., 'Les Communautés d'arts et métiers de Rouen au XVIIIe siècle', *Bull. soc. d'émulation Seine-Inférieure* (1930), pp. 113–36.

—— 'La Corporation des fabricants de bas et bonneterie au métier de Rouen au XVIIIe siècle', ibid., pp. 137–65.

Le Roy Ladurie, E., *Les Paysans de Languedoc* (Paris, 1966).

Letaconnoux, J., *Les Subsistances et le commerce des grains en Bretagne au XVIIIe siècle* (Rennes, 1909).

Martin, G., *Le Tissage du ruban à domicile dans les campagnes du Velay* (Le Puy, 1913).

Masson, P., *La Provence au XVIIIe siècle* (Paris, 1936).

Mège, F., *Charges et contributions des habitants de l'Auvergne à la fin de l'ancien régime* (Clermont-Ferrand, 1898).

Merle, L., *La Métairie et l'évolution agraire dans la Gâtine Poitevine de la fin du Moyen Âge à la Révolution* (Paris, 1958).

Morineau, M., 'Y a-t-il eu une révolution agricole en France au XVIIIe siècle?', *R.H.* 237 (1967), 299–326.

—— *Les Faux-Semblants d'un démarrage économique: agriculture et démographie en France au XVIIIe siècle* (Paris, 1971).

Muheim, H., 'Une Source exceptionnelle. Le Recensement de la population lyonnaise en 1709. Les Domestiques dans la société', *Actes du 89e congrès des sociétés savantes* (Paris, 1965), pp. 207–17.

Nicolai, A., 'La Population en Guyenne au XVIIIᵉ siècle, 1700–1800', *Bull. du comité des travaux historiques et scientifiques* (1906), pp. 40–88.

—— *La Population de Bordeaux au XVIIIᵉ siècle* (Bordeaux, 1909).

Péré, A., 'Démographie de Germ-de-Louron (Hautes-Pyrénées) de 1692 à 1840', *Saint-Gaudens et la Comminges et Revue Comminges*, lxxvi (1963), 184–96.

Poitrineau, A., 'Propriété et société en Haute Auvergne à la fin du régime de Louis XV. Le Cas de Vic', *Cahiers d'histoire*, vi (1961), 425.

—— *La Vie rurale en Basse Auvergne au XVIIIᵉ siècle* (Paris, 1965).

Rascol, P., *Les Paysans de l'Albigeois à la fin de l'ancien régime* (Aurillac, 1961).

Richard, J. M., *La Vie privée dans une ville de l'Ouest aux XVIIᵉ et XVIIIᵉ siècles, Laval* (Paris, 1933).

Rives, J., 'L'Évolution démographique de Toulouse au XVIIIᵉ siècle', *Bull. d'hist. écon. et soc.* (1968–9), pp. 85–146.

Robin, R., *La Société française en 1789: Semur-en-Auxois* (Paris, 1970).

Roupnel, G., *Les Populations de la ville et de la campagne dijonnaises au XVIIᵉ siècle* (Paris, 1922).

Rousset, J., 'Médecine et histoire: essai de pathologie urbaine. Les Causes de morbidité et de mortalité à Lyon aux XVIIᵉ et XVIIIᵉ siècles', *Cahiers d'histoire*, viii (1963), 71–105.

—— 'Les Épidémies à Lyon aux XVIIIᵉ et XIXᵉ siècles et les mesures de prévention médicale qui leur furent opposées', *Actes du 89e congrès des sociétés savantes* (Paris, 1965), pp. 145–88.

Saint-Jacob, P. de, *Les Paysans de la Bourgogne du Nord au dernier siècle de l'ancien régime* (Paris, 1960).

Sée, H., *Les Classes rurales en Bretagne du XVIᵉ siècle à la Révolution* (Paris, (1906).

—— 'Remarques sur le caractère de l'industrie rurale en France et les causes de son extension au XVIIIᵉ siècle', *R.H.* (1923).

Soboul, A., *Les Campagnes montpelliéraines à la fin de l'ancien régime* (Paris, 1958).

Sol, E., *La Vie économique et sociale en Quercy aux XVIᵉ et XVIIᵉ siècles* (Paris, 1950).

Thomas-Lacroix, P., 'La Vie économique et sociale à Ploërmel avant la Révolution', *Mém. soc. arch. hist. Bret.* xliv (1964), 149–62.

Tomas, F., 'Problèmes de démographie historique: le Forez au XVIIIᵉ siècle', *Cahiers d'histoire*, xii (1968), 382–99.

Toutain, J.-C., *Le Produit de l'agriculture française de 1700 à 1958*, Cahiers de l'I.S.E.A. (série A.F.), 1–2 (1961), 2 vols.

Trenard, L., 'La Crise sociale lyonnaise à la veille de la Révolution', *R.H.M.C.* ii (1955), 5–45.

Vacher, L., 'La Mortalité au XVIIIᵉ siècle', *Actes du 8e Congrès international d'hygiène et de démographie*, vii (1896), 18–32.

Valmary, P., *Familles paysannes au XVIIIᵉ siècle en Bas Quercy: étude démographique* (Paris, 1965).

Vidal, M. J. J., 'Étude démographique et sociale de la paroisse Saint-Pierre de Montpellier au XVIIIᵉ siècle' (Diplôme d'Études supérieures, Montpellier, 1963).

Vivier, R., 'La Sologne à la veille de la Révolution', *R.H.E.S.* ii (1923).

Vovelle, M., 'Structure et répartition de la fortune mobilière d'un ensemble urbain. Chartres de la fin de l'ancien régime à la Restauration', *R.H.E.S.* xxxvi (1958), 385–98.

—— 'Formes de dépendance d'un milieu urbain. Chartres à l'égard du monde rural, de la fin de l'ancien régime à la Restauration', *Actes du 93ᵉ congrès des sociétés savantes* (Aix–Marseille, 1958), pp. 483–512.

Wolff, P. (ed.), *Histoire du Languedoc* (Toulouse, 1967).

Works relating to the problem of poverty and to assistance

Adher, J., *Recueil de documents sur l'assistance publique dans le district de Toulouse de 1789 à 1800* (Toulouse, 1918).

Affre, H., *Lettres sur l'histoire de Rodez* (1874), pp. 299, 312 (*Hôpitaux*), pp. 313–20 (*Léproseries ou maladreries*), pp. 335–8 (*Charités*).

Anon., 'Introduction à l'histoire des établissements de charité de Poitiers', *Mém. de la société des antiquaires de l'Ouest*, xxxvii (1873), 28.

Aubert, L., *Les Hôpitaux de Langres. Essai historique des origines à la Révolution* (Dijon, 1913).

Aubry, P., 'La Chaudrière des pauvres à Lorient en 1762', *Bull. soc. d'émulation des Côtes-du-Nord*, xxxi (1927), 24–6.

Aymard, A., 'Notice sur les anciennes maisons hospitalières, dites aumônes ou charités, dans la ville du Puy', *Ann. soc. d'agric., sci., arts et comm. du Puy*, xix (1854), 306–16.

Barrau, H. de, *Statistique historique des hôpitaux et autres établissements de bienfaisance dans le département de l'Aveyron* (Rodez, 1838).

Batault, H., *Notice sur les Dames de la Miséricorde de Chalon-sur-Saône* (Chalon, 1878).

—— *Notice sur les hôpitaux de Chalon-sur-Saône avant 1789* (Chalon, 1884).

Beaurepaire, C., *Recherches sur la répression de la mendicité dans l'ancienne généralité de Rouen* (1887).

Benoiston de Chateauneuf, *Considérations sur les enfants trouvés dans les principaux états de l'Europe* (Paris, 1824).

Béral, P., *Histoire de l'Hôpital de la Charité de Montpellier* (Montpellier, 1899).

Bézard, Y., *L'Assistance à Versailles sous l'ancien régime et pendant la Révolution* (Versailles, 1924).

Bloch, C., *L'Assistance et l'État en France à la veille de la Révolution* (Paris, 1908).

Boceret, E. de, 'Les Établissements religieux et hospitaliers de Guérand', *Rev. hist. de l'Ouest*, xii (1900), 42–76.

Boissonade, P., *L'Assemblée provinciale du Poitou et la question de la mendicité 1787–90* (Paris, 1904).

Bolotte, Dr, *Les Hôpitaux et l'assistance en Bourgogne* (Dijon, 1968).

Borel, E., *Les Associations protestantes et religieuses et charitables de France* (Paris, 1884).

Bouchet, A., 'Parallèle entre l'Hôtel Dieu de Paris et celui de Lyon vers 1750', *Cahiers lyonnais d'histoire de la médecine*, iii (1966), 3–27.

Bouchet, Michel, *L'Assistance publique pendant la Révolution* (Paris, 1908).

Boudard, R., 'Sur l'hôpital de Bourganeuf au XVIIIᵉ siècle', *Mém. soc. sci. nat. arch. Creuse*, xxix (1944–6).

Bouvier, H., 'Histoire de l'assistance publique dans le département de l'Yonne', *Bull. soc. des sci. de l'Yonne*, liii–lv (1899–1901), 291–5.

Braquehay, A., *Histoire des établissements hospitaliers de Montreuil-sur-Mer* (Amiens, 1882).

Brièle, L., *Collection de documents pour servir à l'histoire des hôpitaux de Paris* (Paris, 1870).

Buchalet, F., *L'Assistance publique à Toulouse au dix-huitième siècle* (Toulouse, 1904).

Charmasse, A., *Notice sur les anciens hôpitaux d'Autun* (Autun, 1868).

—— *L'Institution charitable de l'aumône de St Léger à Autun* (Autun, 1890).

Chaudron, E., *L'Assistance publique à Troyes à la fin de l'ancien régime* (Paris, 1923).

Chevalier, A., *L'Hôtel Dieu de Paris et les sœurs augustines* (Paris, 1901).

Chôtard, H., 'La Mendicité en Auvergne au XVIIIᵉ siècle', *Revue d'Auvergne*, xv (1898).

Coiffier, J., *L'Assistance publique dans la généralité de Riom au XVIIIᵉ siècle* (Paris, 1905).

Combes de Patris, *Une Disette en Rouergue sous l'ancien régime* (Rodez, 1915).

Coste, P., 'Les Détenus de Saint-Lazare au XVIIᵉ et XVIIIᵉ siècles', *Revue des questions historiques* (1926), p. 30.

—— *Saint Vincent de Paul: Correspondance* (Paris, 1930).

—— *Les Filles de Charité* (Paris, 1933).

—— *Le Grand Saint du Grand Siècle: Monsieur Vincent* (Paris, 1933).

Costecalde, L., 'Notice sur l'hôpital de la ville de Mende et l'œuvre de la Miséricorde', *Mém. soc. d'agriculture, industrie, sciences et arts du département de la Lozère* (1915), pp. 333–78.

Cros-Mayre Vieille, G., *L'Assistance publique et privée en Languedoc* (Montpellier, 1914).

Croze, A., 'L'Hôtel Dieu de Beaune', *Rev. hosp. France* (1943).

—— 'L'Hôtel Dieu de Lyon', ibid. (1945).

—— and Colly, M., *Histoire de l'Hôpital de la Charité* (Lyons, 1934).

Delabarre, E., 'L'Hôtel Dieu de Rouen', *Bull. soc. amis monuments rouennais* (1924–5), pp. 117–43.

Delessart, F., 'L'Assistance aux indigents en Bourgogne pendant l'hiver de 1709', *Mém. acad. sci. arts et belles lettres de Dijon*, cxv (1965), 221–30.

Deschamps, Marie-Odile, 'Le Dépôt de mendicité de Rouen 1768–1820' (Diplôme d'Études Supérieures, Caen, 1965).

—— *Résumé. Bull. soc. fr. d'hist. des hôpitaux*, xix (1968), 24–5.

Dottin, G., 'Les Comptes des bureaux de bienfaisance de Rennes (1682–XVIIIᵉ siècle)', *Annales de Bretagne*, xxxiii (1918), 89–93.

Dubois, E., *Histoire des hospices de Bourg* (Bourg, 1932).

Dubuc, A., 'Enquête sur les pauvres dans la Haute Normandie en 1775',

Bull. soc. études locales de la Seine-Inférieure, xxvii (1935), 13–81; xxviii (1936), 14–60.

Dupoux, A., 'Sur les pas de Monsieur Vincent', *Revue de l'assistance publique* (1958).

Durand, R., 'L'Hôtel Dieu de Tréguier avant la Révolution', *Bull. soc. d'émulation des Côtes-du-Nord*, lvi (1913), 61.

Ebrard, Dr E., *Misère et charité dans une petite ville de France de 1560 à 1862. Essai historique et statistique sur les établissements et institutions de bienfaisance de la ville de Bourg* (Paris–Bourg, 1866).

Etchepare, M., *L'Hôpital de la Charité de Marseille* (Aix, 1962).

Fargues, P., *Les Hospices d'Angers* (Angers, 1933).

Faty, 'Le Rentier de l'aumône de Quimper', *Bull. soc. arch. du Finistère*, viii (1881), 96–9.

—— 'Les Hôpitaux de Quimper avant la Révolution', ibid. x (1883), 307–495.

—— 'La Police de la ville de Quimper au XVIIIe siècle', ibid. xi (1884–5), 212–32.

Fave, A., 'La Misère et les miséreux au pays de Léon', *Bull. arch. de l'association bretonne*, xxiv (1905), 276–88.

Fayard, E., *Histoire administrative de l'œuvre des enfants trouvés abandonnés et orphelins de Lyon* (Lyons, 1859).

Fleury, G., *La Mendicité à l'assemblée générale de la généralité de Tours* (Paris, 1904).

Font-Réaulx, J. de, 'L'Hôpital de Saint-Vallier' (Dauphiné), *Bull. soc. arch. Drôme*, lxv (1936), 318–28.

Fortin, M., *La Charité et l'assistance publique à Montbéliard sous l'ancien régime* (Strasbourg, 1933).

Fosseyeux, M., *L'Hôtel Dieu de Paris au dix-septième et au dix-huitième siècles* (Paris, 1912).

Fourcassié, J., 'Une Industrie pyrénéenne défunte: la mendicité', *Ann. de la féderation Pyrénéenne de l'économie montagnarde* (1940–1), pp. 63–4.

Gillet, *L'Hôpital de la Charité à Paris* (Paris, 1900).

Grasset, E., *Les Hôpitaux de Riom* (Clermont-Ferrand, 1900).

Guillotin de Corson (Abbé), 'L'Assistance publique avant 1789 dans le territoire de l'archidiocèse de Rennes', *Semaine religieuse de Rennes* (1880), pp. 820–3; ibid. (1881), pp. 49–53.

Gutton, J. P., 'A l'aube du XVIIe siècle. Idées nouvelles sur les pauvres', *Cahiers d'histoire*, x (1965), 87–97.

—— 'Les Mendiants dans la société parisienne au début du XVIIIe siècle', ibid., xiii (1968), 131–41.

—— *La Société et les pauvres; l'exemple de la généralité de Lyon, 1534–1789* (Paris, 1971).

Hamon, L., 'De l'hospice Saint-Méen', *Progrès de Rennes*, iii, v, vii (sept. 1850).

Hardouin, P., 'La Marmite des pauvres et la fondation des Sœurs de la Charité à Rennes', *Bull. mém. soc. arch. et hist. Ille-et-Vilaine*, lxx (1956), 41–77.

Harouel, J. L., *Les Ateliers de charité dans la province de Haute-Guyenne* (Paris, 1969).

Heruot, 'La Médecine et les médecins à l'hôpital général de Saint-Malo, 1679–1901', *Ann. soc. hist. et arch. de l'arrondissement de Saint-Malo* (1900), pp. 27–46.

Hours, H., 'Émeutes et émotions populaires dans les campagnes du Lyonnais au XVIIIe siècle', *Cahiers d'histoire*, ix (1964), 137 ff.

Hubert-Valleroux, P., *La Charité avant et depuis 1789 dans les campagnes de France* (Paris, 1890).

Joret, C., *Le Père Guévarre et les bureaux de charité au XVIIe siècle* (Toulouse, 1889).

Jourdan, F., *Histoire de l'hôpital d'Avranches depuis son origine jusqu'à nos jours* (Avranches, 1904).

Labrosse, H., 'La Police de la commune de Rouen sous l'ancien régime', *Rev. hist. de droit français*, xii (1933), p. 735.

Le Cacheux, P., *Essai historique sur l'Hôtel Dieu de Coutances, l'hôpital général et les Augustines hospitalières depuis l'origine à la Révolution* (Paris, 1895).

Lecoq, M., *L'Assistance par le travail en France* (Paris, 1906).

Leflaive, A., *L'Hôtel Dieu de Beaune et les hospitalières* (Paris, 1959).

Le Grand, L., 'Comment composer l'histoire d'un établissement hospitalier. Sources et méthode', *Revue d'histoire de l'Église de France*, xvi (1930), 161–93.

Le Mené, Abbé, 'L'Hôpital Saint-Nicolas de Vannes', *Bull. soc. pol. du Morbihan* (1896), p. 93.

—— *L'Hôpital général de Vannes* (Vannes, 1900).

Le Parquier, E., 'Une Enquête sur le paupérisme et la crise industrielle dans la région rouennaise en 1788', *Bull. soc. d'émulation de la Seine-Inférieure* (1935), p. 131.

Liris, R., 'Mendicité et vagabondage en Basse Auvergne à la fin du XVIIIe siècle', *Revue d'Auvergne*, lxxix (1965), 65–78.

Maître, L., *Rapport historique sur les hospices civils de Rennes* (Rennes, 1858).

—— *L'Assistance publique dans la Loire-Inférieure avant 1789* (Nantes, 1879).

Michel, P. A., *Monographie de l'Hôtel Dieu et de l'église Saint-Sauveur de Saint-Malo* (St. Malo, 1873).

Monceau, U., *L'Hôtel Dieu de Beaune* (Paris, 1927).

Mourlot, F., *La Question de la mendicité en Normandie à la fin de l'ancien régime* (Paris, 1903).

Murtin, M. C., 'Les Abandons d'enfants à Bourg et dans le département de l'Ain à la fin du XVIIIe siècle et dans la première moitié du XIXe siècle', *Cahiers d'histoire*, x (1965), 135–66, 233–47.

Panel, G., *Documents concernant les pauvres de Rouen* (Paris, 1917), 3 vols.

Parinet, E., 'Enfants trouvés à Bourganeuf à la veille de la Révolution', *Mém. soc. sci. nat. arch. Creuse*, xxxi (1950–3), 241–4.

Paturier, L., *L'Assistance à Paris sous l'ancien régime et pendant la Révolution* (Paris, 1897).

Paultre, C., *De la répression de la mendicité et du vagabondage en France sous l'ancien régime* (Paris, 1906).

Peghoux, A., *Recherches sur les hôpitaux de Clermont-Ferrand* (Clermont, 1845).

Pelleport-Bureté, P. de, 'Essai sur l'organisation charitable des paroisses de Paris', *La Réforme sociale* (1875).

Pergot, A. B., *Les Origines des hôpitaux en Périgord* (Périgueux, 1882).

Perrot, J. C., 'Notes sur l'utilisation des dossiers de la lieutenance de police pour l'étude de la vie urbaine et des structures sociales (à propos de Caen au XVIIIᵉ siècle)', *Actes du 82e congrès des sociétés savantes* (Bordeaux, 1957).

Pocquet du Haut Jusset, M., *La Vie temporelle des communautés de femmes à Rennes au XVIIᵉ et au XVIIIᵉ siècles* (Paris, 1916).

Querau-Lamerie, E., *Notes sur les bureaux de charité de Laval (1683–1803)* (Laval, 1904).

Quétin, M., 'L'Hôpital d'Aurillac de 1649 à la Révolution', *Revue Haute Auvergne*, xxxix (1965), 425–40.

Quignon, G. H., *L'Assistance dans l'ancienne France. La Confrérie de la Trinité ou des enfants bleus de Beauvais (1562 à 1792)* (Paris, 1904).

Rambaud, A., *La Chambre d'abondance de la ville de Lyon (1643–1777)* (Lyons, 1911).

Rambaud, P., *L'Assistance publique à Poitiers jusqu'à l'an V* (Paris, 1912).

Ratouis, P., *Études historiques sur l'Hôtel Dieu et les anciens établissements charitables de la ville de Saumur* (Saumur, 1868).

Rénouard, X., *L'Assistance publique à Lille de 1527 à l'an VIII* (Paris, 1912).

Richard, P., 'Les Enfants abandonnés à Auxerre de 1776 à 1796', *Bull. soc. des sci. hist. et nat. de l'Yonne*, xcix (1961–2), 5–15.

Saint-Jacob, P., 'L'Hôpital de Mervans', *Mém. soc. hist. arch. de Chalon-sur-Saône*, xxxv (1958–9), 50–7.

Saint-Martin, P. de, *La Mendicité à Besançon principalement au XVIIIᵉ siècle* (Besançon, 1910).

Sée, H., 'La Population et la vie économique de Rennes vers le milieu du XVIIIᵉ siècle d'après les rôles de la capitation', *Mém. soc. d'hist. de Bretagne*, iv (1923), 89–96.

—— 'La Santé publique dans le diocèse de Saint-Brieuc, d'après les observations médicinales de Bagot', *Comité des travaux historiques. Section d'histoire moderne et contemporaine*, viii (1924).

—— 'Remarques sur la misère, la mendicité et l'assistance en Bretagne à la fin de l'ancien régime', *Mém. soc. d'hist. de Bretagne*, vi (1925), 105–32.

—— 'Statistique des pauvres de Rennes vers la fin de l'ancien régime d'après les rôles de la capitation', *Annales de Bretagne*, xli (1934), 474–7.

Simard, *Saint Vincent de Paul et ses œuvres* (Paris, 1894).

Soucaille, A., 'Notice sur l'hôpital général de Béziers', *Bull. de la soc. arch. de Béziers*, xii (1883–4), 246.

Valran, G., *Misère et charité en Provence au XVIIIᵉ siècle* (Paris, 1899), 2 vols.

Vexliard, A., 'La Disparition du vagabondage comme fléau social universel', *Revue de l'Institut de Sociologie*, i (1963), 53–79.

INDEX

Abortion, 331

Actes d'avancement de succession, 113

Agde, 303; immigration, 92, 96, 101

Aged, in *dépôts de mendicité*, 242

Agenais, emigration, 94, 99

Agricultural conditions, 37; see also *Pays de petite culture*

Alais, 303; immigration, 96

Aix-en-Provence, child abandonment, *319*; *dépôt de mendicité*, 235; *filles repenties*, 309, 310; *hôpital général*, 383

Alençon, 202; *dépôt de mendicité*, 235, 240; foundlings, 342; vagrancy, 207

Alps, emigration, 80, 83

Alsace, diet, 44; emigration, 94; epidemics, 63; slump in viticulture, 16; smuggling, 296

Ambert, 110–11

Amiens, industry, 17, 41–2

Anan, curé of, cited, 60

Ancenis, 289, 290

Andalusia, French immigration, 87, 88

Anjou, child abandonment, *329*

Annonay, 302, 304

Antrain, 346

Anzy-le-Duc, 174

Aquitaine, immigration, 72, 78

Archers, 102

Ardes, migrations, 82–3

Army, and prostitution, 311, 313; and salt smuggling, 294

Arnal, Jeanne, 253

Artisse, Jeanne, 315

Artois, child abandonment, 328, 345; smuggling, 296

Aspet, 86

Assemblée générale des habitants, and foundlings, 335, 336

Atelier de charité, 182–93

Athis, curé of, cited, 11, 117, 123, 329–30

Aumônes générales, 163

Aurillac, 172–3, 178–9; baby traffic, 348

Autun, 165; charitable resources, 174

Auvergnats, 240, 264

Auvergne, 15, 16, 118; *actes d'avancement de succession*, 113; agricultural wages, 42; *ateliers de charité*, 191–2; begging, 109, 112, 126; *bureaux de charité*, 172–

3; charity, 114; child abandonment, 319, 328, 332, 340–1, 342; debts of poor, 60; *dépôts de mendicité*, 234; diet, 44–5; disease, 48, 64–5; drunkenness, 115, 364; edict of 1724, 156–7; emigration, 72, 73, 80–91, 93, 96, 98, 99, 101, 105–6, 120; government assistance, 177–80; *hôpitaux*, 150; housing, 49; vagrancy, 124, 224; *see also* Basse-Auvergne, Haute-Auvergne

Auxerre, 165, 168; child abandonment, 332, 348; drunkenness, 115

Auxois, immigration, 105

Avallon, 138

Averdy, de l', 160; and the *dépôts*, 226, 232

Aveu, 228–9

Avranches, 193

Bailliage justice, 264

Bain, 163

Baiotats, 274, 278

Balazé, 163

Bandes, 243, 266–83; smuggling, 300–5; see also *Vol avec attroupement*

Bande de Forez, 243, 268, 270, 271, 274, 275, 277, 281–2, 283

Bande d'Orgères, 221, *267*, 270, 283

Bande Hulin, 221, 243, 268, 270, 274–6, 277–81

Barcelona, immigration, 88

Basse-Auvergne, policing, 222–3; salt smuggling, 292–4

Bateliers, 121

Bayeux, *ateliers de charité*, 190, 193; *bureau de charité*, 116; child abandonment, 347; *hôpital général*, 146, 149, *153*, 157; immigration, 28; *manufacture des pauvres*, 168–9

Bawdy houses, 315–16

Bayonne, smuggling, 296

Béarn, emigration, 87, 89, 94, 99

Beauce, 240; agricultural labour, 34; the *bandes*, 266, 267, 274–81, 282–3; begging, 118, 126, 206; charity, 114; seasonal work, 120

Beaumont (Auvergne), epidemic, 65

Beaune, 165

Beauport, Abbey, 135
Bec, 125, 134, 137
Begging, 107–27, 195–216; and the law, 219–44; and urban immigrants, 101–3
Belley, 332
Benoît, Pierre Antoine, 241
Berger, Joseph, 255
Berry, criminality, 251
Besançon, *bureau de charité*, 57, 169–70
Besse, migrations, 82, 173
Béziers, immigration, 92, 96
Bishops, and *bureaux de charité*, 169–71; and the *dépôts de mendicité*, 234–5, 243; and the *hôpitaux*, 142, 144, 147, *153, 154*
Biville-la-Rivière, 200
Blesle, 179–80
Bloch, Camille, 343; *L'Assistance et l'État en France à la veille de la Révolution*, 4
Bonnecombe, handouts, 125, 136, 137
Bonneterre, 21, 109
Bonnichon, Marie Jeanne, 278
Bordeaux, child abandonment, *319*; crime, 254, 256, 258; *filles repenties*, 309; immigration, 28, 29, *69*, 72, 80, 86, 94, 96, 99, 104, 124; prostitution, 307, 311, 316
Bornambuc, 194, 201
Bort, curé of, cited, 123, 317, 330
Bourbon-Lancy, 173
Bourbonnais, salt smuggling, 293
Bourg, 165
Bourg-en-Bresse, 138, 332
Bourg-et-Nolay, 170
Bourg-Saint-Andéol, 303
Bourges, child abandonment, *319*, 328; *dépôt de mendicité*, 232, 233, 235, 240, 275; immigration, 93, 100
Boussard, François, 283
Bousselargues, 199
Bread riots, 356
Bresse, diet, 44; economic conditions, 15; emigration, 94; labour migrations, 28, 34; tuberculosis in, 67
Brest, begging, 102
Bridat, François, 243, *267*, 268
Brie, 221, 267; begging, 118; immigration, 105
Brioude, 173, 178–9; begging, 102; emigration, 82
Brittany, abortion, 331; *actes d'avancement de succession*, 113; begging, 114, 118, 126, 205; child abandonment,

332, 335–40, 346; criminality, 251, 254, 264, 265, 267, 268, 271–3; debts of poor, 61–2; *dépôts de mendicité*, 231, 240; diet, 44, 47–8; drunkenness, 115, 364; ecclesiastical handouts, 134–5; economic conditions, 15, 16, 21, 30; epidemics, 63–5; hemp spinning, 40; housing, 49, 50; illegitimacy, 324; infanticide, 349–50; informal relief, *197*; *hôpitaux*, 146, 153, *154*; lack of *ateliers de charité*, 186; migrations, 95; policing, 221; prostitution, 307, 317; salt smuggling, 288–92; vagrancy, 120, 207, 243; vendetta in, 365; village *fonds*, 138; *see also* États de Bretagne
Brive, 166
Brousse, 199
Bruz, 163
Bugey, economic conditions, 15; emigration, 94; labour migrations, 28, 34; tuberculosis, 67
Buisson, Antoine, 241
Burand, Jean, 241
Bureaux de charité, 55–7, 97, 116, 138, 159–73, 385–8
Burgundy, agricultural wages, 42; *ateliers de charité*, 186; *aumônes générales*, 165, 170; *bandes*, 267; child abandonment, 332, 345; *confréries*, 162; criminality, 251, 264; diet, 44; emigration, 105; epidemics, 63; *hôpitaux*, 153; monastic handouts, 134; smuggling, 296, 299; *see also* États de Bourgogne

Cabaretier, and smuggling, 302
Caen, 193; child abandonment, 347; *dépôt de mendicité*, 234, 235, 239, 240; immigration, 28
Cahors, 168
Cambrésis, child abandonment, 345; smuggling, 296
Caplongue, 198
Carcassonne, wages, 42
Castel, Étienne, 255
Castillon, emigration, 85–6
Catalonia, French immigration, 88; smuggling, 297, 298
Catholic historiography, and poverty, 4
Caussade, 172
Cerdagne, smuggling, 298–9; stocking industry, 39–40

Cévennes, economic conditions, 15; emigration, 98
Châlons, immigration, 96
Chalon-sur-Saône, 165
Champagne, 267; *ateliers de charité*, 189, 192; slump in viticulture, 16; smuggling, 296
Champion de Cicé, 235
Champlitte, 206
Charity, formal, 131 ff.; voluntary, 194–216; *see also* Monastic handouts
Chartres, 221; child abandonment, 332; immigration, 93, 96
Chasse gueux, 102
Châteaubriant, 289
Châtillon-en-Vendelais, 163
Chaumette, Anne, 275
Chaurand, Père, 143, 163
Chaussy, Marie, 315
Chavagnac, *seigneur* of Blesle, 179–80
Chavaniac, 297
Cherbourg, immigration, 28
Child abandonment, 318–51
Children, begging practices, 108–11, 213; crime, 268–9; in *dépôts de mendicité*, 241–2; as salt-smugglers, 287–8, 291
Chirac, 136, 163, 165
Choiseul Gouffier, Duchesse de, 168
Cival, handouts, 134
Clergy, and charity, 199–200; *see also* Bishops
Clermont, begging, 102, 106, 203, 210–11; child abandonment, 340, 342; *dépôts de mendicité*, 232; government assistance, 177–8; *hôpital*, 146, 153, 384; prostitution, 306
— diocese of, 21, 135, 163, 166; charitable resources, 371–3; informal relief, 197, 198; village *fonds*, 138
Clermont de Lodève, work force, 27, 30, 34
Clisson, 289
Collanges, 198
Colombier-le-Jeune, 302
Colson, Abbé, 297
Combraille, emigration, 81–2
Comité de Mendicité, 2, 4, 6–7, 19, 22–3, 108, 111, 112, 127, 143, 154, 159, 173–6, 193, 194; and child abandonment, 318, 332
Comminges, 20–1, 240; debts of poor, 60; drunkenness, 115; emigration, 80,

86–7, 89, 94, 96–7, 99, 103; vagrancy, 124
Commingeois, and crime, 256, 257
Compagnie des Indes, decline, 122
Compostella, pilgrims' route, 87
Comtat Venaissin, smuggling, 296, 299
Condé, 168
Condom, *hôpital général*, 153
Confréries, 162
Corlay, 245
Corvée, 185
Coubisou, 198–9
Counter-Reformation, and charity, 131–3
Couserans, emigration, 89, 94, 98
Crépon, 125
Crime, begging and vagrancy, 219–44; *see also* Theft
Curé, and *cabaretier*, 364
Cussy, Jacques, 280, 282

Dames de la Charité, 161–2
Dames de la Miséricorde, of Montpellier, 303
Dangers et Compagnie, 233
Dangles, Elizabeth, 312
Dardilly, 206
Darnetal, *ateliers de charité*, 193
Dauphiné, economic conditions, 15; epidemics, 66; emigration, 72, 94, 98; smuggling, 296, 300–5
Daverst, Marie, 263
Debt, and the poor, 54–62
Déclarations de grossesse, 30–1, 312
Delair, 279
Delair, Guillaume, 211
Dépôts de Mendicité, 227–44; and prostitution, 308–9, 316
Deserters, and smuggling, 301
Diet, 44–8
Digne, *dépôt de mendicité*, 235
Dijon, *aumône générale*, 165; Bon Pasteur, 309; child abandonment, 319, 332; *hôpital*, 153; immigration, 94; prostitution, 311; shoemakers, 97
— diocese of, 21–2, 138; informal relief, 200; monastic handouts, 134
Dimiers, 274, 281
Dinan, 322
Disease, 62–8
Divorce, 123
Dôle, *hôpital général*, 152
Dol de Bretagne, 171, 289; diocese, 135

Domestic service, 26–33, 118–19; conditions, 51; and crime, 254, 258; provincial monopolies, 95–6, 101; unemployment, 105; *see also* Servant girls, *Valets de ferme*, *Vol domestique*
Doré, 199
Doullens, 168
Dourdat, 292
Dowry, importance, 28–32
Drunkenness, 114–15, 360, 364
Duchamp, Jacques, 302
Dunod, Père, 143, 163
Dupas de la Pastèle, Jacques, 170
Dupuis, Marie, 283
Durenque, 198

Ecclesiastical handouts, 132–7
Échalas, 362
Écoles de filature, 167
Edict, of 1724, implementation, 155–7, 225; of 1749, and *hôpital* property, 158; of 1767, 223–4
Elbeuf, *ateliers de charité*, 193; wages, 42
Élie, Thomas, 203
Elne, 294–5
Emblavès, *bureau de charité*, 116
Enfants trouvés, *see* Child abandonment
Enlightenment, 194–5; attitudes to poverty, 3
Entre-Deux-Mers, emigration, 94
Epidemics, *see* Disease
Épiniac, 171
Errance, 124–5
Espalion, 166
États de Bourgogne, 170
États de Bretagne, 180–1, 186; and *dépôts de mendicité*, 235, 243; and foundlings, 334
États de Languedoc, 180; and *dépôts de mendicité*, 233
États de Provence, 180
Eu, 162

Fairs, and crime, 265
Falaise, *246*; prostitution, 307, 316–17
Families, deserted by father, 122–3
Family economy, 25–43, 106–7
Favre, Abbé, *Jean l'an pré*, 211–12
Faux-Saunage, *see* Salt smuggling
Fécamp, 125; handouts, 134, 137
Female labour, 26–32, 38–41, 92; *see also* Women

Fercé, 163
Ferme, and smuggling, 285–305
Ferney, 168
Filles de la Sagesse, 148
Filles publiques, *see* Prostitution
Filles repenties, 309–10
Flanders, begging, 126, 207; conflict between *curé* and *cabaretier*, 364; emigration, 94; foundlings, 328, 336, 345; illegitimacy, 324; smuggling, 292, 296
Flavin, 108
Flax combers, migrations, 82
Flechère, Marie, 206
Florac, 163, 165, 387
Foix, Pays de, begging, 110
Folleterre, 200
Fonds, village, 137–9
Fontevrault, 125, 137
Forez, diet, 44; emigration, 81, 94, 98; labour migrations, 28, 34; smuggling, 292, 302–3; tuberculosis, 67; *see also* Bande de Forez
Fougères, 289, 346
Franche-Comté, slump in viticulture, 16; smuggling, 296, 299
François de Sales, Saint, cited, 131
Franqueville, slump, 18

Gabelle, *see* Salt smuggling
Galleys, 226, 227, 252
Gamache, 200
Garbet, 110
Garnier, Antoine, 303
Gascony, 118; slump in viticulture, 16
Gautier, François, 243
Geneva, smuggling, 299–300
Gennes, 290, 294
Gévaudan, *actes d'avancement de succession*, 113; begging, 126; charity, 114; diet, 44; economic conditions, 15; emigration, 72, 79–80, 96, 98, 120; female labour migrations, 21; *hôpitaux*, 146; housing, 49, 62–3; smuggling, 296; vagrancy, 124
Gex, Pays de, smuggling, 296, 299
Gillioc, 302
Gournay, 162
Gouy, slump, 18
Gray, 119; *présidial*, 229
Grimal, Joseph, 263
Grizettes, *see* Prostitution
Gros Theil, epidemic, 66, 201

Guer, 181
Guévarre, Père, 143, 163
Guyenne, arrest of vagrants, 224; see also Haute-Guyenne

Hainaut, and the dépôts de mendicité, 231; foundlings, 345; smuggling, 296
Haute-Auvergne, smuggling, 297
Haute-Guyenne, ateliers de charité, 187, 190-1
Heilly, 168
Hemp spinning, see Brittany
Hennebont, 164
Henrion de Bussy, 111, 195, 235-8, 260
Hercé, Urbain de, 171
Hervilly, Marquis d', 168
Highway robbery, 250, 254
Hôpital du Saint Nom de Jésus, 140-2
Hôpital général, 131, 139-59; child abandonment, 319; foundlings, 335, 342-3; legislation of 1724, 219-20
Hôtels Dieu, 144; and foundlings, 335-7, 342-4
Housing, 48-50
Huet, Jean, 205
Hugloville-en-Caux, 196
Hugon, Abbé, 168-9
Hulin, Charles, see Bande Hulin

Île de France, agricultural labour, 34; arrest of vagrants, 224; emigration, 94, 96
Illegitimacy, 320-9; see also Déclarations de grossesse
Industry, 16-17, 40; edict of 1762, 41
Infanticide, 321-2, 349-51
Issoire, 178; foundlings, 341-2

Jacob, Catherine, 312
Janson, Anne Rosalie, 278-9
Jesuits, 143, 161
Jofre, 297
Jolicoeur, Catherine, 314
Julliard, Antoine, 241
Jumièges, 125, 134
Jura, economic conditions, 15
Justice, and the poor, 246-83; and prostitution, 306-7

La Besse, 47
La Bourbonne, 274
Labour migrations, 27, 34
La-Capelle-Farcel, 47, 198

Lace industry, and colportage, 121; see also Le Puy and Velay
Lacemakers, dowries, 32
La Chaise-Dieu, 125, 198
La Grave, 153, 159, 240, 309
La Guerche, 163, 181, 289
Laguiolle, 21
Lanchelles, 168
Langres, arrest of vagrants, 224; begging, 204; criminality, 254, 255, 257; immigration, 94; prostitution, 307, 313
Languedoc, agricultural labour, 34; begging, 118, 126; charity, 114; child abandonment, 332; conflict between curé and cabaretier, 364; criminality, 246, 251, 261-2, 267, 268; dépôts de mendicité, 231, 232, 233, 234; diet, 45; epidemics, 51, 66; housing, 50; hôpitaux, 153; illegitimacy, 324; immigration, 72, 79-80, 105, 120, 229; industry, 27, 30, 36, 38, 53, 105; smuggling, 298, 302-3; vagrancy, 124, 126; vendettas, 365; viticulture, 15, 61
Languengar, 273
Lanson, 21
La-Roche-Derrien, 273
La Rue brothers, 274
Lauragais, emigration, 28, 94, 96, 104
Lauzerte, 172
Laval, 291; hôpital, 152
Law, John, impact of schemes on hôpitaux, 153, 156
Lefebvre, Marie, 316
Legislation, begging and vagrancy, 219-44; illegitimacy, 321-3; see also Edict
Le Havre, 162-3; baby traffic to Paris, 347; child abandonment, 319; immigration, 96
Lelarge, Léonard, 297
Le moins imposé, see Taille
Lempdes, emigration, 81
Le Noir, 228, 260
Le-Pont-de-Beauvoisir, 301
Léproseries, 144
Le Puy, 363-4; bishop of, cited, 304
— diocese of, informal relief, 197; lace industry, 39
Les Bondons, 3, 113, 116, 197
Les Échelles, 301
Le Trosne, 287
Levalet, François, 229

Lezoux, 173
Liège, foundlings, 345
Lille, illegitimacy, 321, 325–6; immigration, 104, 105; industry, 41–2; prostitution, 311
Limoges, 98-9, 184, 342; diocese of, 163, 166
Limousin, *ateliers de charité*, 187; charity, 114; economic conditions, 15; emigration, 72, 89, 93, 94, 96, 103
Livestock, value to poor, 53–4
Livradois, emigration, 81
Lodève, smallpox, 63; wages, 42; work force, 27, 34
Loire, river traffic, 121
Loire valley, epidemics, 66
Lorient, 122; immigration, 96; tobacco smuggling, 297
Lorraine, diet, 44; drunkenness, 115; emigration, 94
Louise de Marillac, Saint, and foundlings, 334; and the *hôpitaux*, 140–1
Louviers, baby traffic to Paris, 347; wages, 42
Louvigné-de-Bais, 163
Lunel, 165
Lunel-Viel, 138
Lyons, begging, 118; *bureau de charité*, 55, 57; child abandonment, 123, 318–19, 328; conflict between *curé* and *cabaretier*, 364; crime, 254, 256, 258, 268; debts of poor, 56, 57; *dépôt de mendicité*, 240; edict of 1724, 156, 225; *filles repenties*, 309, 310; housing, 51; immigration, 72, 92, 94, 95–6, 99, 101; mastership, 36; prostitution, 307, 311, 312, 313, 316; silk industry, 17, 27–8, 30, 31, 34, 121–2; tuberculosis, 67
Lyonnais, agricultural labour, 34; begging, 118, 206; charity, 114; policing, 221; smuggling, 302–3

Mâcon, 165
Maine, salt smuggling, 289–92
Maison-Sainte-Pélagie, 309
Maladreries, 144
Malaria, 66
Malechecq, Jean, 245
Malherbe, Jean, 203
Maliche, Anne, 312
Mandrin, 286–7, 300, 303
Manie, Rimberge et Compagnie, 233
Manufactures des pauvres, 167–70

Marche, economic conditions, 15; emigration, 72, 93, 94, 111
Maréchaussée, reform, 156–7; *see also* Police
Mariac, 302
Marion de Faouët, 271–3, 357
Marmites des pauvres, 161–2
Marseilles, begging, 103, 212, 214; child abandonment, *319*; *filles repenties*, 309; *hôpital*, 146; immigration, 28, 72, 95, 96, 99, 101; prostitution, 311
Martel, 172
Martinets, 274
Mas d'Azil, 86
Masons, migrations, 82–3
Massat, 86, 110
Maundy Thursday, bread distributions, 138
Mauriac, policing, 222
Mazars, Anne, 314
Mazel, Marguerite, 253
Meaux, 221
Mecé, curé of, cited, 37
Mende, arrest of vagrants, 224; begging, 204; *bouillon des pauvres*, 162; *bureau de charité*, 165, 166; criminality, 251, 253, 254, 255, 262–3; *hôpital général*, 146, 151, *153*, 154, 380; *lanifice*, 169; prostitution, 307, 314–15; smallpox, 63; woollen industry, 36
— diocese of, 21; *bureaux de charité*, 163, 164, 165; charitable resources, 369–70; ecclesiastical handouts, 135–6; informal relief, 197; village *fonds*, 138
Merchants, of Nîmes and Lyons, and smuggling, 300
Mercier, 256, and almsgiving, 136
Métayage, 37
Métayers, debts, 60–1
Metz, divorce, 123
Mezonnac, 302
Michon, Jeanne, 115
Migrations, 69–106; *see also* Labour migrations
Miliary fever, 63, 66
Millau, 204; immigration, 28
Milléry, 362
Miniard, Nicolas, 242
Molières, 172
Monastic handouts, 125, 132–7
Monastier, 136
Mondidier, 168
Montaigut, 173

Montaigut-en-Combrailles, 296
Montaigut-le-Blanc-sur-Champeix, 135
Montauban, 172
Montlinot, Abbé, 275
Montousse, 21
Montpellier, begging, 102, 203, 211–12;
    child abandonment, 328, 343; crime,
    256; dépôt de mendicité, 238, 240; hôpital,
    146, 153; immigration, 28, 92, 95, 96,
    101; prostitution, 311, 312, 316;
    smuggling, 303
— diocese of, 21–2; bureaux de charité,
    164; charitable resources, 373–4; in-
    formal relief, 200; village fonds, 138
Monts Dores, emigration, 81
Morlaix, hôpital général, 145
Mortain, 193
Morvan, emigration, 105
Moulins, 98, 342; bureau de charité, 170;
    dépôt de mendicité, 240, 275; immigra-
    tion, 93; Ordinance of, 322–3
Mur-de-Barrèz, emigration, 87
Murder, 273

Nantes, 181; child abandonment, 319;
    filles repenties, 309
Necker, and ateliers de charité, 183–93;
    and bureaux de charité, 160; and the
    hôpitaux, 159; and the problem of
    poverty, 19
Noblesse, and the ateliers de charité, 188–
    90; and charity, 114, 196–7
Noë, Marianne, 315
Normandy, actes d'avancement de succes-
    sion, 113; arrest of vagrants, 224;
    ateliers de charité, 192; begging, 205;
    charity, 114; child abandonment, 332,
    345; criminality, 264, 269; dépôts de
    mendicité, 240; emigration, 94, 95–6,
    105; epidemics, 63, 64; hôpitaux, 153;
    illegitimacy, 324; manufactures des
    pauvres, 167, 168; poverty in, 21

O'Flanegan, Mademoiselle, 184
Old age, problems of, 111–13
Olive-oil industry, seasonal demands,
    77–8
Orleans, 168; begging, 103, 118, 209;
    immigration, 92, 93, 96

Paca family, 274
Pamiers, miliary fever at, 63
Papegault, 146

Paray-le-Monial, 174
Pariou, Guillaume, 251
Paris, begging, 102–3, 105, 118; child
    abandonment, 318, 336, 344–6; crim-
    inality, 246, 254, 255, 256, 260–1,
    268; edict of 1724, 156–7, 225; filles
    repenties, 309; Hôpital du Saint Esprit,
    335; immigration, 28, 29, 92, 94, 95,
    96, 99, 101; prostitution, 311
Parlement, and the corvée, 185; and the
    hôpitaux, 158–9; and Mandrin, 286–7;
    and monastic handouts, 136–7
Passports, 229
Paulines of Tréguier, 148
Pauvre Honteux, 214–15
Pays d'élections, and dépôts de mendicité,
    235, 237
Pays d'États, and ateliers de charité, 186;
    and dépôts de mendicité, 231, 237; and
    foundlings, 336; and government
    assistance, 177, 180
Pays de grande culture, and the bandes, 267
Pays de petite culture, 15, 19, 37; ateliers
    de charité, 184–93; bureaux de charité,
    172–3; emigration, 93; labour migra-
    tions, 73
Péaule, 200
Pedlars, 80–1, 83, 86, 88–9, 111, 120–1,
    123, 254, 259–60, 263, 264; and
    smuggling, 302–3
Pégorier, Pierre, 263
Périgord, charity, 114; criminality, 251;
    emigration, 94, 96, 99; policing, 221
Périgueux, arrest of vagrants, 224; illegi-
    timacy, 325; immigration, 100
Pertre, 290
Picardy, charity, 114; emigration, 94;
    salt smuggling, 292
Pickpocketing, 257
Pique, la, 83–4
Planchon, Marguerite, 314
Plélan, 181
Pleudihen, 171
Podevin, Marie-Madeleine, 202
Poitiers, hôpital général, 152
Poitou, epidemics, 64; smuggling, 296
Police, 220–4, 226–8, 253, 304; and
    begging, 102–3; and the bandes, 226,
    280–3; and rixes, 361–2
Ponchon family, 274
Pont-Audemer, 347–8
Pont-de-l'Arche, prostitution, 307
Pontivy, 329

Pont-Saint-Esprit, 303
Population growth, 14–15
Potato, introduction of, 44–5
Pradel, bishop of Montpellier, 164
Prévôtés, jurisdiction, 224–5, 246–66
Price rise, 16
Prostitution, 150, 306–17; see also *Vénériennes*
Provence, conflict between curé and *cabaretier*, 364; *dépôts de mendicité*, 234, 235; epidemics, 66; *filles repenties*, 309; foundlings, 335; *hôpitaux*, 153, *154*; immigration, 72, 85; pestilence, 156
Pseudonyms, 280–2
Pyrenees, begging, 110; charity, 114; economic conditions, 15; diet, 44; emigration, 71, 72, *73*, 74–9, 85–6, 89, 90, 94

Quercy, 118; begging, 126; *bureaux de charité*, 172; smuggling, 296
Question, 273
Quézac, 136
Quimper, begging, 206; child abandonment, *319*; diocese, 135; *filles repenties*, 309; *hôpital*, 154

Redon, 334; wages, 12–13
Renard, Marie, 312
Renaud, Léonard, 316
Rennes, baby traffic to Paris, 346; begging, 210; *bureau de charité*, 171; child abandonment, 123, *319*, 328, 338–40; *dépôt de mendicité*, 232, 234; *filles repenties*, 309; *hôpital*, 153, *154*, 180; illegitimacy, 327; immigration, 97, 100; infanticide, 349; *marmite des pauvres*, 162, 166
— diocese of, *bureaux de charité*, 163, 164; charitable resources, 374–7; ecclesiastical handouts, 134–5; village *fonds*, 138
Rentes viagères, 153
Rents, of houses, 51–2
Restif de la Bretonne, *Le Paysan et la paysanne pervertie*, 215, 257
Revendeuse, 259, 260–1
Rhône, and smuggling, 302–5
Rice, in diet of poor, 45
Richeprey, 111
Riom, 201; begging, 102, 106, *213*; child abandonment, 341–2; *dépôt de mendicité*, 232, 235–9, 240; government assistance, 178; immigration, 97

Rixes, 360–2
Rochefoucauld Liancourt, Duc de, 167–8
Rocher, François, 302
Rodez, arrest of vagrants, 224; begging, 204; *dépôt de mendicité*, 232, 233, 235, 243; *filles repenties*, 310; *hôpital*, 154; prostitution, 314, 315
— diocese of, 21, 108–9, 138; *bureaux de charité*, 163; informal relief, 197, 198; insufficiency of harvests, 46–7; monastic handouts, 136
Romanet, Madame de, 168
Rouen, *ateliers de charité*, 193; baby traffic to Paris, 347; bankruptcies, 30; begging, 110, 120; *bouillon des pauvres*, 162; child abandonment, *319*, 328, 337; *dépôt de mendicité*, 234, 235, 240; edict of 1724, 225; *hôpital*, 149, 150–1, 153, 154, 158–9; immigration, 92, 96, 100, 104, 105; industry, 17, 41–2; *manufacture des pauvres*, 169; wages, 42
— diocese of, 21; charitable resources, 377–81; ecclesiastical handouts, 134; informal relief, 200–1; *marmites*, 162; village *fonds*, 138
Rouergue, begging, 126; conflict between *curé* and *cabaretier*, 364; criminality, 251; diet, 44; drunkenness, 115; economic conditions, 15, 40; emigration, 27, 34, 72, 79–80, 87, 89, 90, 92, 96, 98, 111, 120; slump in Languedoc wine industry, 61; smuggling, 296; vagrancy, 124, 207
Rouler, 261–2, 267
Rousseau, François, 203
Roussel, Jean-Baptiste, 262
Roussillon, immigration, 72; smuggling, 296–7, 298–9
Route des abbayes, 125
Roye, 168

Sacrilege, see *Vol d'église*
Sailhan, 284
Saillagouse, 86
Saint-Affrique, cotton spinning, 40
Saint-Agrève, 301–2
Saint-Andéol, 362
Saint-Brieuc, begging, 102; *bureau d'aumônes*, 171; diocese, 204; *hôpital*, 151, *154*, 157
Saint-Didier, 292, 294
Saint-Drézery, 138

Sainte-Colombe, 205
Sainte-Colombe-les-Vienne, 366
Sainte-Eulalie-Vanosc, 302
Saint-Étienne-de-Saint-Geoirs, 301
Saint-Étienne-Vallée-Française, 164, 170, 385–6
Saint-Félicien, 302
Saint-Flour, 178; diocese of, 197
Saint-Gaudens, 86
Saint-Geniès, 136
Saint-Genix-d'Aoste, 301
Saint-Ignat, 199
Saint-Igny-des-Vers, 222
Saint-Jean-d'Ollières, 18, 82, 84, 85
Saint-Jean-la-Fouillouze, 136
Saint-Jean-Roure, 302
Saint-Laurent-d'Ott, 109
Saint-Malo, diocese, 135
Saint-Martin-de-Boscherville, 125, 134
Saint-Martin des Ollières, emigration, 82
Saint-Martin-de-Valamas, 301
Saint-Michel-de-Sommaire, 203
Saint-Pol-de-Léon, 102, 107; diocese of, 135
Saint-Romain-en-Gal, 366
Saint-Romain-en-Gier, 362
Saint-Seine-l'Abbaye, 125
Saint-Wandrille, 125, 134
Salelles, 136
Salt smuggling, 285–96
Savoyard, emigrations, 80, 93–4, 96, 98, 99, 101, 119, 120
Seasonal migrations, 229, 304–5; and begging, 240; and crime, 261–2
Sedan, wages, 42
Seigneur, and illegitimacy, 323
Seigneur haut justicier, 335–6
Seigneurial justice, 246
Seine Valley, epidemics, 66
Sélestat, case of infanticide, 54
Semur-en-Auxois, 332
Sens, child abandonment, 332
Serre brothers, 241
Servant girls, and infanticide, 350; leisure and courtship, 358–60; and prostitution, 311–13, 316
Seyssel, 332
Shoemakers, 97
Silk industry, see Lyons
Singles, emigration, 82
Sisters of Charity, 140, 148–9, 161–2
Sisters of Providence, 148

Sisters of Saint Thomas de Villeneuve, 148
Smallpox, 63
Smuggling, 284–305
Sociability, 356–8
Sœurs Chrétiennes de Nevers, 148
Sœurs Hospitalières de Saint Alexis de Limoges, 148
Sœurs Hospitalières de Saint Joseph du Puy, 148, 154
Soissons, child abandonment, 332; dépôt de mendicité, 235, 239
Spain, French immigration, 86–90, 106, 111
Sterne, L., Sentimental Journey, 214–15
Stocking industry, see Cerdagne
Strasbourg, abortion, 331; child abandonment, 123; epidemics, 63; filles repenties, 309; housing, 51; illegitimacy, 321; immigration, 92, 94, 96, 99, 104; prostitution, 311
Syphilis, 310; and foundlings, 342

Taille, 184–5
Tarif, 263
Tauves, emigration, 82
Terray, and the dépôts de mendicité, 238
Testaments, of working classes, 52–3
Testet, 47
Tetrelle, widow, 116
Teyssonière, 199
Theft, 45–83
Thiers, 110–11, 178–9
Tobacco smuggling, 296–305
Torture, 249; see also Question
Toulon, immigration, 96
Toulouse, begging, 103, 104, 110, 124; child abandonment, 332; crime, 246, 254, 256, 257, 258, 262, 268
— diocese, 21; divorce, 123; edict of 1724, 156; filles repenties, 309; illegitimacy, 325; immigration, 28, 29, 86, 92, 94, 96, 99; prostitution, 307–8, 311, 313, 315, 316; see also La Grave
Tournus, 165
Tours, ateliers de charité, 189–90; begging, 118, 195; bureau de charité, 57, 170; child abandonment, 328, 342; dépôt de mendicité, 232, 235
Towns, and begging, 208–16
Tréguier, 102, 135, 247
Tresbœuf, 163
Tridentine Councils, and charity, 131

Trois Évêchés, foundlings, 345
Tronjolly, 210, 326–7, 340
Troyes, *ateliers de charité*, 190, 192;
    begging, 120; *bureau de charité*, 57, 167;
    child abandonment, 332; *hôpital*, 146;
    immigration, 100, 104, 105; industry,
    17, 41–2; labour force, *27*; prostitu-
    tion, 311; shoemakers, 97
Trudaine, 340
Tuberculosis, 66
Tulle, diocese of, informal relief, 197;
    hôpital, 152
Turgot, and *ateliers de charité*, 183–4; and
    bureaux de charité, 160; and *dépôts de
    mendicité*, 243–4; and the *hôpitaux*, 158;
    and poverty, 19
Typhus, 64–6

Urban immigration, 92–106; and crime,
    256–7, 261; and prostitution, 311

Vabres, diocese of, informal relief, 197
Vagabondage, 124–7, 389–91
Vagrancy, 117–27; and labour migra-
    tions, 71; and the law, 219–44
Valets de ferme, economic circumstances,
    33–4; violence, *rixes*, etc., 360–1
Valois, immigration, 105
Vannes, child abandonment, *319*; crime,
    260; *dépôt de mendicité*, 232, 233, 239–
    40, 241–3; *filles repenties*, 309; illegi-
    timacy, 325; prostitution, 308, 316;
    tobacco smuggling, 297
— diocese of, ecclesiastical handouts, 135
Velay, Pays de, begging, 126; crime,
    254; diet, 45; domestic service, 118;
    economic conditions, 15; lace in-
    dustry, 38–9; smuggling, 300–5
Vendetta, 365
Vénériennes, 238, 312
Vernols, 297
Vesoul, 224
Vialarels, 47
Vialaret, Antoinette, 315
Vidal, Jeanne and Marguerite, 314
Vidal, Joseph, 262–3
Vienne, 366
Vigier, François, 242
Village *fonds*, see *Fonds*

Villarceaux, handouts, 134
Villefort, 163, 165
Villebourbon, 172
Villefranche-de-Rouergue, prostitution,
    307
Villeneuve, abbey,
Vincent de Paul, Saint, 158; and *bureaux
    de charité*, 161–2; and child abandon-
    ment, 319, 334; and the *hôpital général*,
    139–41
Violence, 360–1
Viticulture, difficulties, 16
Vitré, 166–7, 289, 290, 341; *bureau de
    charité*, 55–6; *hôpital*, 146; *marmite*,
    131, 162
Vivarais, diet, 45–6; economic condi-
    tions, 15; smuggling, 296, 301–5
Vivet, Jean, 277
Vocabulary of Poverty, 18–20, 117, 119,
    124, 195, 216, 228; see also *Pauvre
    Honteux*
Voiron, condition of weavers, 35
Vol avec attroupement, 253, 282; see also
    Bandes
Vol d'église, 251
Vol domestique, 250
Voltaire, 168

Wages, 12–13, 107; agricultural, 42;
    and *ateliers de charité*, 191; begging, 110,
    116; in cotton industry, 41–2; and diet,
    46; female, 26–7, 38, 40; industrial,
    42–3; in lace industry, 39; of police,
    223; of *valet de ferme*, 33–4
Widows, 115–16
Wine Industry, seasonal demands, 77
Women, in the *bandes*, 275, 278–9; in
    begging economy, 114–15, 213; and
    crime, 252–3; in *dépôts de mendicité*,
    236; as salt smugglers, 287, 295; see
    also Domestic Service, Prostitution,
    Servant girls, Wages
Woodcutters, migrations, 81–2
Woollen Industry, *see* Languedoc
Wouwermann, de, 311

Yellow Fever, 66
Young, Arthur, 299

Balais Balais

I. Edme Bouchardon, *Études prises dans le bas peuple ou les cris de Paris,*
Balais, Balais

Cotterets.

II. Bouchardon, *Cotterets*

Montagnarde

III. Bouchardon, *Montagnarde*

De la belle Fayance

IV. Bouchardon, *De la belle Fayance*

Vieux Maçon

Boucharden in.
A Paris chés Joullain.

V. Bouchardon, *Vieux Maçon*

Peaux de Lapin.

Bouchardon *in.*   A Paris Chez Joullain.

VI. Bouchardon, *Peaux de Lapin*

VII. Bouchardon, *Gagne petit Auvergnat*

HV 4094 .H84 1974

Hu

Th

eighteenth-c

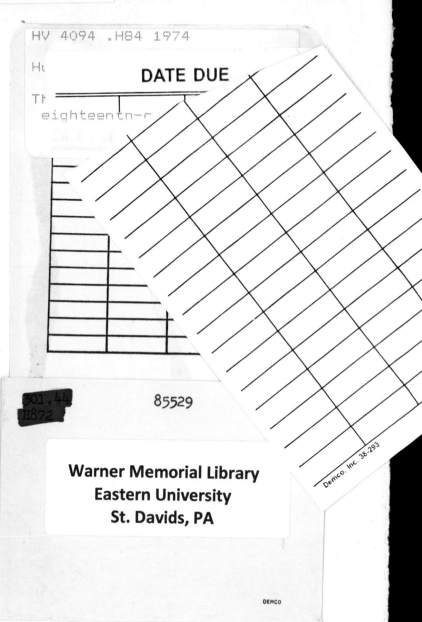

DATE DUE

Demco, Inc. 38-293

DEMCO